CAVIAR AND ASHES

MARCI SHORE

Caviar and Ashes

A WARSAW GENERATION'S LIFE AND DEATH
IN MARXISM, 1918–1968

YALE UNIVERSITY PRESS   NEW HAVEN & LONDON

Published with assistance from the Koret Foundation.

Printed in the United States of America.

The Library of Congress has cataloged the hardcover edition as follows:
Shore, Marci.
Caviar and ashes : a Warsaw generation's life and death in Marxism, 1918–1968 /
Marci Shore.
p. cm.
Includes bibliographical references and index.
ISBN 0-300-11092-8 (alk. paper)
1. Communism—Poland—History—20th century.   2. Poland—Intellectual life—
1918–1945.   3. Poland—Intellectual life—1945–1989.   I. Title.
HX315.7.A6S45 2006
320.53′23′09438—dc22
2005014528

ISBN 978-0-300-14328-7 (pbk. : alk. paper)

A catalogue record for this book is available from the British Library.

10 9 8 7 6 5 4 3 2 1

For my friends, the women who kept me company

CONTENTS

ACKNOWLEDGMENTS

IN THE COURSE OF researching and writing *Caviar and Ashes* I have incurred a tremendous number of debts, and I am very happy to be able to acknowledge some of them here. I owe the most to my unceasingly generous advisor Norman Naimark and the other members of my dissertation committee at Stanford—Hans Ulrich (Sepp) Gumbrecht, Amir Weiner, and Steven Zipperstein. They believed in this project from the very beginning, and I am enormously grateful for their ideas, critiques and support. I cannot imagine that anyone has ever had a better experience as a graduate student. I owe more than I can express here to Norman for teaching me to love the archives and for keeping me grounded, with unfailing honesty and saintly patience, when my ideas wandered; and to Sepp for sharing his beautiful, inspiring imagination, for loving this project as much as I have—and for wanting to hear more about the caviar at Bruno Jasieński's Moscow dinner party. The first draft of this book was written as a dissertation at Stanford during the 2000–2001 academic year. My warmest thanks to Amelia Glaser, who shared her home in Napa Valley with me and read everything; to Meredeth Rouse and Daniel Shore who (besides being the only tourists in Warsaw the previous January) helped edit the entire text and suggested a "Cast of Characters"; and to Alexander Zeyliger who, among many other things, helped me decipher the handwriting in Władysław Broniewski's NKVD files and shared his love and intuition for Russian literature and the Russian language.

This book was made possible by the opening of the archives that followed the collapse of communism in Eastern Europe and the Soviet Union. It was made possible as well by what were undoubtedly difficult decisions on the part of this book's protagonists and their heirs to preserve (and make accessible) personal correspondence. Researching *Caviar and Ashes* took me to seventeen archives in five countries. That these trips were successful owes much to archivists, friends, and colleagues. I am especially indebted to Sławomir Kędzierski and Regina Kaźmierczak of the Władysław Broniewski Museum in Warsaw, who were always generous with their time and their knowledge. Sławomir Kędzierski also answered countless, intricate questions via email. My thanks as well to Grzegorz Sołtysiak, who provided me with much material from his archive in Warsaw; Padraic Kenney, who introduced me to Grzegorz; Ksenia Zadorozhnaia, who took me to the Mayakovsky Archive in Moscow and was a constant source of support in Russia; Gennady Pasecznik, who was so helpful at Adolf Berman's archive in Tel Aviv (and made hundreds of pages of photocopies for me); Jerzy Tomaszewski, who was a warm and generous advisor in Warsaw; Jan Gross, who pointed me towards the Central Committee of Polish Jews Collection at the Jewish Historical Institute; Iwona Butz, who facilitated my access to everything at the Jewish Historical Institute; Eleanora Syzdek, who pointed me toward Kiev; Serhy Yekelchyk, who put in a good word for me at the archives in Kiev; and the American Councils for International Education staff in Washington and Moscow, who arranged my trips to Russia and Ukraine.

I have been fortunate as well to have had so many colleagues and interlocutors. Lara Heimert, my first editor at Yale, effectively reminded me that the absence of both conscience and integrity is not exclusive to fanatical believers in historical determinism. Molly Egland took good care of the manuscript. Gavin Lewis was a remarkably attentive and talented copyeditor. Jessie Hunnicutt managed the production of this book with unwavering enthusiasm. Henry Dasko, Jan Gross, Tony Judt, Antony Polonsky, Yuri Slezkine, Timothy Snyder, and Michael Steinlauf read and commented on the whole manuscript at various stages; Brian Porter, Luisa Passerini, Janet Rabinowitch, and Gabriella Safran read and commented on chapters. Asia Bartczak, Kacper Bartczak, Ewa Domańska, Małgorzata

Fidelis, Anna Frajlich, and Alexander Zeyliger offered suggestions about translation in specific instances. Iwona Butz and Joanna Swat helped me to decipher Władysław Broniewski's and Aleksander Wat's handwriting, respectively. Władysław Bartoszewski, Emanuel Berman, Marek Edelman, Władysław Krajewski, Mr. and Mrs. Aleksander Masiewicki, Teresa Torańska, Lucyna Tychowa, Ewa Wasilewska, Ryszarda Zachariasz, and the late Czesław Miłosz, Irena Olecka, and Chaim Finkelstein spoke with me about the protagonists of this book whom they had known. Aleksander Masiewicki allowed me to use his letters to Adolf Berman. Ewa Zawistowska provided me with copies of Wanda Wasilewska's letters to her grandmother, Janina Broniewska, and shared with me much from her own life in a fascinating correspondence about her grandparents. Exposing one's own life to the scrutiny (and implicit voyeurism) of a historian is rarely a painless choice, and I remain enormously grateful for their openness and generosity.

I owe thanks as well to many other people, including Hanna Markowicz and Wacław Przemysław Turek for teaching me Polish, and teaching me well; Gertrud Pacheco and Margaret Tompkins at Stanford for supportively easing various logistical crises; Luisa Passerini and her research group "Europe and Love" in Essen for being such interesting company; Joshua Safran for hosting me in New Haven; Tony Judt for recommending a lighter introduction; Piotr Sommer for discussing Wat's correspondence with Miłosz—and for loving Mayakovsky; Henry Dasko for being so enthusiastic; Gail Glickman for sharing her love of languages and literature for over three decades; Henning Ritter at the *Frankfurter Allgemeine Zeitung* for asking me to write without footnotes; the young taxi driver in Kiev for spending (and enjoying) an afternoon at Wasilewska and Korneichuk's dacha in Pliuto; Ina and Jonatan Markovitch and their children for keeping me company in Kiev; the late (and much-missed) H. Gordon Skilling and the Czech seminar in Toronto for creating a wonderful intellectual space; Jacek Leociak for many conversations in Warsaw; David Holloway and Barton Bernstein for believing in my scholarly potential before there was any good reason to do so; Eva Kalivodová, for introducing me to the (very intricate) world of Slavic grammar—and of translation; Brian Porter for rescuing my panel in Tampere, Finland, and giving such an exciting, entirely impromptu discussant's paper; Nicholas Basila for saving me during my various and sundry computer crises; Chad Martin for putting together my desk in California; Bradley Abrams for a decade's worth of conversations about Eastern Europe; Mikołaj Kunicki for giving me a copy of *Lucyfer Unemployed* as a present; Hiroaki Kuromiya for having faith both in this manuscript and in the complexity of the human psyche; my adopted nephews Moshe Chaim Bookstein and Max Patyk-Finkel for being my little buddies in Warsaw and Stanford, respectively; Robert Shore for asking what existentialism means; Dariusz Stola for asking why I felt so close to these angst-laden poets; Jan Gross for being so supportive, and most of all for introducing me to Stephanie; Stephanie Steiker for loving this project—and for more than I could ever thank her; Agata Jagiełło for coming to our Hannah Arendt seminar in Warsaw in 1997 and for speaking to me in Polish; Kasia Chamera for keeping me sane during the Polish winter (and checking the Polish diacritical marks in my notes); Ross Forman for moral support; Ian Bremmer for insisting that I write novels; Lida Havriljukova for telling me that I have a Russian soul; Konstanty Gebert for telling me he felt responsible for communism as a person on the left, but not as a Jew; the late Chaim Finkelstein and his wife Jadwiga for the vegetarianism analogy; The Russian School at Middlebury (and my teachers Todd Armstrong, Yulia Morozova, and Lyudmila Parts) for being amazing; and Lyudmila Parts for explaining to me that the world is divided into two kinds of people: those who have read *The Brothers Karamazov* and those who have not.

A thank you as well to all my friends and colleagues at Stanford, Columbia, and Indiana Universities. At Indiana University the History Department benefits from the friendliest staff I have ever encountered, and the Slavicists benefit from excellent library resources cultivated by Murlin Croucher. In Bloomington I have also been extremely fortunate to find myself amidst three extradepartmental bodies: the Russian and East European Institute, the Polish Studies Center, and the Jewish Studies Program. The opportunity to be a part of all three and to surround myself with colleagues with such rich knowledge of both Slavic and Jewish studies has been a unique one for which I am grateful. I share, moreover, with Maria Bucur a vibrant group of graduate students.

I also want to acknowledge all those who generously supported the research for this project over the past six years: the Institute of International Education Fulbright Program, the Center for Russian and East European Studies at Stanford, the International Research and Exchanges Board, the

Fulbright-Hays Program, the Mellon Foundation, the Taube Center for Jewish Studies at Stanford, the Harriman Institute at Columbia University, the American Council for International Education, the Russian and East European Institute at Indiana University, the Borns Jewish Studies Program at Indiana University, and the Kulturwissenschaftliches Institut in Essen, where I wrote the final two chapters. The History Department at Indiana University gave me leave in fall 2004; and the Institut für die Wissenschaften vom Menschen, an extremely congenial place to work, was my host in Vienna during the final stages of preparing this manuscript. The responsibility for what I say in the pages that follow is, of course, my own.

A final note: In transliterating from Cyrillic I have followed a modified version of the Library of Congress system, with the exception of instances in which other transliterations have become conventional, and when citing English-language sources that have already adopted a transliterated version of a given name. All translations of sources cited in Polish and Russian are my own—as are all inadequacies. And a final thank-you: to Timothy Snyder—for asking (and subsequently not asking) about the Berman brothers.

Bund   *Der Algemeyner Yidisher Arbeter Bund in Lite, Poyln, un Rusland* (The General Union of Jewish Workers in Lithuania, Poland, and Russia)

KPP   *Komunistyczna Partia Polski* (Communist Party of Poland)

NKVD   *Narodnyi Komissariat Vnutrennikh Del* (People's Commissariat for Internal Affairs)

PPS   *Polska Partia Socjalistyczna* (Polish Socialist Party)

PZPR   *Polska Zjednoczona Partia Robotnicza* (United Polish Workers' Party)

ADOLF BERMAN (1906–1978)—younger brother of Jakub Berman; a teacher and writer, trained as a social psychologist; one of the leaders of the Marxist Zionist party Poalei Zion Left; active in the Jewish resistance and in Żegota during the war; emigrated to Israel in 1950 and became a member of the Israeli Knesset. Died of cancer in Tel Aviv in 1978.

JAKUB BERMAN (1901–1984)—older brother of Adolf Berman; a liaison of the Communist Party of Poland with the intelligentsia during the interwar years; one of a triumvirate of postwar Stalinist dictators in Poland; oversaw cultural affairs and the security apparatus during the Stalinist years; expelled from the Party in 1957. Died in Warsaw in 1984.

MARIAN BOGATKO (1906–1940)—a bricklayer by trade who became Wanda Wasilewska's second husband; active in the Polish Socialist Party during the interwar years. Killed by the NKVD in Lvov in 1940.

JERZY BOREJSZA (1905–1952)—brother of the Stalinist security officer Jacek Różański; enchanted first with Zionism and later with Spanish anarchism before becoming a communist; a leading figure in cultural affairs during and immediately after the war. Died prematurely in 1952 shortly after his fall from the Party's grace.

MIECZYSŁAW BRAUN (1902–1942)—a poet from Łódź associated with the poetic avant-garde in the 1920s; friend of Władysław Broniewski; flirted with Marxism in the interwar years. Died in the Warsaw ghetto in 1942.

JANINA BRONIEWSKA (1904–1981)—author of children's literature as well as three volumes of memoirs and two wartime notebooks; a journalist in the Soviet Union during the war and a Party activist in the postwar years; the first wife of the poet Władysław Broniewski and the closest friend of Wanda Wasilewska. Died in 1981.

WŁADYSŁAW BRONIEWSKI (1897–1962)—a poet who fought against the Soviets in Piłsudski's army during the Polish-Bolshevik War; flirted with the futurists in the 1920s, yet remained more a lyrical poet than an avant-garde poet; a revolutionary poet by the mid- to late 1920s; imprisoned in the Soviet Union 1940–1941; spent the latter part of the war in Jerusalem after leaving the Soviet Union with the Anders army. Died of throat cancer in Warsaw in 1962.

WŁADYSŁAW DASZEWSKI (1902–1971)—a communist-sympathizing artist and scenic designer who frequented Café Ziemiańska during the interwar years and had many friends among the poets; most likely the provocateur in the arrests of Władysław Broniewski, Aleksander Wat, Anatol Stern, and Tadeusz Peiper in Lvov in January 1940. Died in 1971.

ISAAC DEUTSCHER (1907–1967)—born in a Galician shtetl; a Zionist in his youth before becoming a Polish communist; expelled from the KPP in 1932 for belonging to the Trotskyite opposition; emigrated to England at the outbreak of World War II where he became a biographer of Trotsky. Died in Rome in 1967.

MIECZYSŁAW GRYDZEWSKI (1894–1970)—friend and editor of the Skamander poets; editor of the liberal cultural weekly *Wiadomości Literackie* during the interwar years; emigrated to London when the Second World War broke out and never returned to Poland. Died in England in 1970.

JAN HEMPEL (1887–1937)—older communist activist in the cultural realm who joined the KPP after much ideological searching; editor of *Nowa*

Kultura in the 1920s; imprisoned with the editorial board of *Miesięcznik Literacki* in 1931; emigrated to the Soviet Union. Executed in Stalin's purges in 1937.

JAROSŁAW IWASZKIEWICZ (1894–1980)—one of the Skamander poets who made his debut in 1918 at Pod Pikadorem; close to the Piłsudski government in the interwar years; remained in Warsaw during the war and together with his wife was active in hiding Jews in and around their estate in Stawisko; served as president of the Writers' Union after the war. Died in 1980.

BRUNO JASIEŃSKI (1901–1938)—a futurist poet from Cracow who wore a wide tie and a monocle in the 1920s; co-author with Anatol Stern of one of the first books of Marxist revolutionary poetry in Poland titled *The Earth to the Left;* in 1925 left Poland for Paris, where he wrote the novel *I Burn Paris;* emigrated to the Soviet Union after being deported from France in 1929; arrested in 1937. Executed in 1938 in the Stalinist purges.

LEON KRUCZKOWSKI (1900–1962)—began his professional life as a chemist before becoming a writer; by 1936 an important figure at the communist-front Congress of Cultural Workers in Lwów; called into the army as a reserve officer in September 1939 and soon captured by the Germans; spent over five years as a prisoner of war; leading figure in the cultural realm during the Stalinist years. Died in 1962 in Warsaw.

IRENA KRZYWICKA (1899–1994)—daughter of Bundist parents and daughter-in-law of the famous Marxist sociologist Ludwik Krzywicki; writer, journalist and for many years the lover of the literary critic Tadeusz Boy-Żeleński (1874–1941); close friend of the Skamander poets; feminist and advocate of birth control and women's sexual liberation; one of the first to write openly about homosexuality in interwar Poland; author of the memoir *Wyznania gorszycielki* (Confessions of a Scandalous Woman). Died in France in 1994.

ALFRED LAMPE (1900–1943)—a young Zionist before becoming a Polish communist; member of the KPP Central Committee who spent much time in prison in interwar Poland; close to Wanda Wasilewska during

World War II, when he played a leading role in the creation of the Union of Polish Patriots. Died in Moscow in 1943.

JAN LECHOŃ (1899–1956)—Skamander poet; broke with his old friend Julian Tuwim in New York during World War II due to Tuwim's support for the Soviet Union. Committed suicide in New York in 1956.

MICHAŁ MIRSKI (1905–c. 1990)—a member of the KPP in the 1920s and 1930s; active "on the Jewish street" and in the cultural sphere; editor of both Polish and Yiddish postwar communist publications; left Poland in the wake of the "anti-Zionist" campaign of 1968. Died in Denmark.

TADEUSZ PEIPER (1891–1969)—poet and literary theorist; born in Cracow and spent the years of World War I in Spain; leading theoretician of the Cracow Avant-Garde; founder in the 1920s of the constructivist journal *Zwrotnica;* arrested and imprisoned in Lvov in 1940; returned to Warsaw after the war and spent his last years in isolation. Died in 1969.

JULIAN PRZYBOŚ (1901–1970)—born into a peasant family and studied at Jagiellionian University in Cracow; poet of the Cracow Avant-Garde; leading figure in the literary sphere in the immediate postwar years; became embroiled in polemics about poetry and socialist realism. Died in Warsaw in 1970.

ANTONI SŁONIMSKI (1895–1976)—Skamander poet and author of a famous weekly column in *Wiadomości Literackie* during the interwar years; spent the Second World War in England; returned to Warsaw in 1951 and lent his support to the new communist regime; leading dissident figure in the last decade of his life. Died in Warsaw in 1976.

STANISŁAW RYSZARD STANDE (1897–1937)—poet and Party activist; one of the first to join the KPP after its creation; second husband of Adolf Warski's daughter Zofia Warska between 1927 and 1935; co-author with Władysław Broniewski and Witold Wandurski of one of the first volumes of Polish proletarian poetry titled *Three Salvos;* left Poland for the Soviet Union in 1931. Executed in Moscow in 1937.

ANDRZEJ STAWAR (Edward Janus) (1900–1961)—Marxist literary critic who took an anti-Stalinist line in the 1930s; close friend of Aleksander Wat; spent the war years in Hungary; his work was banned in communist Poland before his rehabilitation in 1955. Died in France in 1961.

ANATOL STERN (1899–1968)—a futurist poet and co-author of various futurist manifestos together with Aleksander Wat in the early 1920s; translator of Vladimir Mayakovsky into Polish; co-author with Bruno Jasieński of one of the first books of Marxist revolutionary poetry in Poland titled *The Earth to the Left;* later a screenwriter; arrested in Lvov in January 1940; returned to Poland after spending the war in the Soviet Union and Palestine. Died in Warsaw in 1968.

JULIAN STRYJKOWSKI (1905–1996)—born in a Jewish shtetl outside Lwów/Lemberg in Austrian Galicia; a Zionist in his youth; became a Polish communist after his expulsion from his Zionist youth group; worked as a proofreader of Polish-language Stalinist publications in the Soviet Union during the war; became a novelist in the postwar years; returned his Party card in 1967 in the wake of the Kołakowski affair. Died in 1996.

JULIAN TUWIM (1894–1953)—luminary Skamander poet originally from Łódź; politically unengaged during the interwar years; fled Warsaw in September 1939 and spent the war years first in Paris, then in Rio de Janeiro, and finally in New York; returned to Poland in 1946 and lent his wholehearted support to the new communist regime. Died in Warsaw in 1953.

WITOLD WANDURSKI (1891–1934)—graphomaniac and manic-depressive poet who was among Mayakovsky's first Polish translators; directed a workers' theater in Łódź in the 1920s; co-author with Władysław Broniewski and Stanisław Ryszard Stande of one of the first volumes of Polish proletarian poetry titled *Three Salvos;* left Poland for Kiev following a stay in Polish prison; directed a Polish theater in Kiev. Executed in the Soviet Union as a Polish nationalist in 1934.

WANDA WASILEWSKA (1905–1964)—daughter of independent Poland's first foreign minister, Leon Wasilewski; Polish Socialist Party activist and novelist from Cracow; became the Polish Left's personal connection to Stalin during the war; remained in Kiev after the war with her third husband, the Ukrainian communist playwright Oleksandr Korneichuk. Died in Kiev in 1964.

ALEKSANDER WAT (1900–1967)—a futurist poet in the early 1920s; became a Marxist by the late 1920s; editor of the legendary Marxist newspaper *Miesięcznik Literacki,* 1929–1931; imprisoned in the Soviet Union during the war; returned to Poland in 1946; spent the latter part of the 1950s and 1960s abroad in western Europe. Committed suicide in Paris in 1967.

OLA WATOWA (1904–1991)—Aleksander Wat's wife from 1927 until his death in 1967; deported to Soviet Kazakhstan during the war; author of the memoir *Wszystko co najważniejsze* (Everything That Is Most Important). Died in France in 1991.

ADAM WAŻYK (1905–1982)—nicknamed *Ważyk brzydki twarzyk* ("Ważyk with the ugly little face"); an "independent" avant-garde poet aligned neither with the futurists nor with the Cracow Avant-Garde; Poland's first translator of the French futurist Guillaume Apollinaire; one of the postwar dictators of cultural policy and "terroreticians" of socialist realism in the Stalinist era; author of "A Poem for Adults," which in 1955 inaugurated de-Stalinization in the literary sphere, the so-called Thaw. Died in Warsaw in 1982.

JÓZEF WITTLIN (1896–1976)—poet and prose writer associated with expressionism in his early years; a Jew who converted to Catholicism; spent his youth in Lwów/Lemberg and his university years in Vienna; lived in Łódź from 1921 to 1927 before coming to Warsaw; close to the Skamander poets and to Aleksander Wat; left Poland for France in 1939 and emigrated to the United States in 1941. Died in New York in 1976.

Introduction

But for us the joy came from the fundamental collapse, that there
was now room for everything, that everything was doable.

—*Aleksander Wat*

IT WAS EARLY WINTER in Berlin, thirty-six years after Nietzsche had
declared that God was dead. Now in 1918, Rosa Luxemburg wrote to Adolf
Warski, for the past three decades her fellow ideologue of internationalist Marxism in the Polish lands. She told him that their current position
of supporting Bolshevism while rejecting Lenin's call for "national self-
determination" was "enthusiasm coupled with a critical spirit." And what
more could they desire? Like her comrade, she was uncomfortable with
Bolshevik terror, but assured Warski that it was aimed only against internal
enemies supported by European capitalists. All of this could—and with
full certainty would—be resolved when the European revolution came.
She added reassuringly: "And this is coming!"[1]

Rosa Luxemburg introduced Adolf Warski to the woman who would
become his wife. The marriage produced a daughter, Zofia Warska. As Luxemburg wrote to Warski of the coming European revolution, the man who
would one day be his son-in-law was studying philosophy and philology at
the university in Cracow.[2] Zofia Warska and her second husband Stanisław
Ryszard Stande belonged to a generation of Polish literary intellectuals
born at the turn of the century—into a Poland that had not yet come into
being but was rather only imagined in the minds of its patriots. These
young people grew up at the margins of three great empires—Habsburg,
German, and Russian, creations of centuries past. Those born in Warsaw

inhabited the western reaches of the tsarist empire; they grew up amid various languages and cultures: Polish and Russian, and often Yiddish, German, and French. Those among the Polish intelligentsia who were "of Jewish origin" were first- or second-generation assimilated Jews, Polish patriots and cosmopolitans, their families often split apart by differing responses to a modernity that had arrived somewhat later in Europe's east. Aleksander Wat's father was a Kabbalist whose spoken language was Yiddish, but who read Nietzsche in German and Tolstoy in Russian; as a child Wat saw Jews as antisemites did: "in gabardines, dirty, merchants, money."[3] Julian Tuwim, growing up in an assimilated Jewish family in Łódź, felt a similar aversion to those "uniformed men in beards and their Hebraic-German garble and their traditional mutilation of Polish speech."[4] Jews were—in the eyes of the assimilated—regressive characters of a dying, separatist, undesirable world. And so among these young intellectuals even the Jews—inspired by Romantic and modernist Polish literature—grew up Polish, at a time when a Polish state did not yet exist, had not for over a century.[5]

Patriots of a bygone Poland had never resigned themselves to statelessness. For them the nineteenth century was an age of insurrections and of inculcating in their children the words of the national hymn: "Poland has not yet perished, as long as we still live." Polish politics continued in the Polish state's absence, a politics preoccupied, as throughout nineteenth-century Europe, with nation and class. Rosa Luxemburg's Social Democratic Party denied the possibility—or desirability—of future Polish independence in favor of international revolution, a legacy of self-annihilation that would linger long afterwards. On this point she argued with Lenin. More influential on the Left was the Polish Socialist Party (PPS), a blend of socialism and patriotism created by, among others, Józef Piłsudski. Piłsudski's vision of a reborn Poland was a multiethnic federalist one, united by a civic Polish patriotism. By the turn of the century Piłsudski's rival for the nation's heart was Roman Dmowski, leader of the National Democratic Party, and theorist of a more willful "national egoism," of a nationalism growing increasingly xenophobic and antisemitic, of a patriotism "virtually defined by hate."[6]

Stanisław Ryszard Stande and Zofia Warska were young children when the 1905 Revolution reached Warsaw. In the center of the city, on Theater Square, Stande's mother was killed during demonstrations, and

Stande suffered an injury that would disfigure his face for the rest of his life.[7] Antoni Słonimski watched the charging of the tsarist cavalry, the Cossacks on horseback, the massacre on the Square. He fled with his brother to their home on Niecała Street, where their physician father was already treating the wounded.[8] At a safe distance, in the courtyard of his building, the five-year-old Aleksander Wat led his own "children's division"; they waved a red flag and sang revolutionary songs. When his wounded brother returned home later that day, it was the first time the boy saw blood.[9] A decade later, those children born at the fin de siècle, too young to fight, watched one Europe destroy itself and another come into being during the First World War. The war was a radical break in time, the end of empires, of the partitions of Poland, of the old world. Warsaw was liberated from the Russian Empire, as was Cracow from the Austro-Hungarian Empire, and Poznań from Germany. In the midst of this came the Bolshevik Revolution, although what it was, no one yet knew. The occupying German army departed from Warsaw, Piłsudski arrived in the city a hero, and an independent Polish state came into being. It was a state too ethnically diverse to embody Dmowski's concept of nationhood—with only two-thirds ethnic Poles, and the remainder Ukrainians, Jews, Belarusians, Germans. In the capital city of Warsaw, Polish Jews were one-third of the city's population. A fairly cosmopolitan small empire, yet insufficiently satisfying—or secure from the Bolshevik threat—for Piłsudski.[10] At once he fell into a mutually expansionist war against the Soviets in the east, a war determining Bolshevism's western boundaries, and a war in which many of those too young to fight in the First World War now participated. Most often they did so themselves not knowing what the new Soviet state meant, fighting more for love of Piłsudski and of Poland than for hatred of the Bolsheviks.

While some did suffer physical battle wounds, it was a war that seems to have left astoundingly few scars on the young intellectuals, who afterwards had little to do with the military.[11] Theirs was a particular generation, the last to be educated in Russian or German under the partitioning empires and the first to come of age in the universities of independent Poland. Following the Polish-Bolshevik War, they returned, for the most part, to Warsaw, to a Poland in which the patriotic burden of poets had been lifted, replaced by a license for more daring exploration, a license for transgression. The young poet Jan Lechoń captured a certain temporal ethos when he wrote: "And in the spring let me see spring, not Poland."[12] There was something else present as well: a sense that the First World War had altered notions of possibility in Europe, engendering utopianism, nihilism, and catastrophism all at once. Everything was now possible, a dizzying endlessness of possibilities. It was a time when the boundaries between Marxism in theory and communism in practice were not clear, when both meant revolution, and revolution meant consummation, an escape from nothingness. Crusty apparatchiks—balding or otherwise—had not yet appeared, nor had anyone glimpsed ominous specters of show trials; for many young Polish literati of the 1920s, communism was cosmopolitan, avant-garde, sexy.

For this generation of Varsovian intellectuals born at the fin de siècle, life was unbearably heavy. They moved about in entangled circles with shifting boundaries, connected to one another by not more than one or two degrees of separation. They were quintessential cosmopolitans, polyglots who felt at home in Moscow, Paris, and Berlin—yet who at once felt inextricably bound to Poland, who believed in their role as "the conscience of the nation," who very much felt that Warsaw belonged to them. They suffered (sometimes advantageously, sometimes painfully) from a certain pathological narcissism. They sat in their café called Ziemiańska and believed, with absolute sincerity, that the world turned on what they said there. Often they fell into bouts of despair and self-hatred, and—not despite, but rather precisely because of their narcissism—they embodied the observation that intellectuals comprise the only class that loves to hate itself.[13]

The story that follows is theirs. The young avant-garde of the early 1920s became the radical Marxists of the late 1920s. They abandoned dadaism and futurism and ceased their games with words, having come to the conclusion that such carnivalesque possibilities were merely bourgeois decadence. Rather, they decided, there was in fact such a thing as a person's "actual condition" in society, and the true calling of a writer was to enlighten people—most especially workers—as to this actual condition. I begin with their coming of age after the First World War and continue through the Second World War, the Stalinist era, the Thaw of the post-Stalin years, and finally the "anti-Zionist" campaign of March 1968, exploring why and how these intellectuals came to embrace Marxism at different moments and what those choices meant. My periodization transcends conventional historiographical boundaries delimiting the interwar years, the Second World War, and the Stalinist era—a categorization that implicitly conceptualizes the Second World War as a moment of absolute discontinuity. I want to escape the tendency to examine the war in isolation, as if these were years that existed outside of time. For those about whom I write, the war was both a temporal rupture and a maturation period. Polish history has been written primarily through the prism of politics; I have attempted to move away from politics per se, in favor of a history of ideology and aesthetics whose focal point is the act of opting for—and often ultimately out of—Marxism. This book is a cultural and intellectual history, a biography of a milieu, and a post–Cold War exploration of Marxism as a belief system. That said, this was a century, and a part of Europe, where a space to be unengaged, to be "outside of" politics, effectively dissolved; and in this sense a political subtext is ever present. The story of these individuals and their relationships is a story of a journey from the cafés to the corridors of power, a story of faith and betrayal.

These cosmopolitan intellectuals, many of them "non-Jewish Jews," in their friend Isaac Deutscher's words, very much felt themselves to be Poles; their Jewish identity was fluid and often subtle.[14] Several of them—Adam Ważyk, Julian Stryjkowski, Jakub Berman—came from families divided between communism and Zionism, between Polishness and Jewishness. Jakub Berman rose to become one of a triumvirate of Stalinist leaders in postwar Poland, and dictator in the realm of culture; Adolf Berman became a Marxist Zionist leader and a member of the Israeli Knesset. During the interwar years each of three Berman brothers, as well as their two sisters, made distinctive ideological choices, choices that brought them together as activists of the Left and members of the avant-garde intelligentsia, and choices that later placed them on opposite sides at a moment when the world was being reinvented. In the pages that follow I say little about Polish-Jewish relations, or the "Jewish question" in Poland per se, yet in a sense the whole book is about that.[15]

Intertwined with a shift away from politics as such is a reading of the past in which the loci of power are complex, constantly in flux.[16] Much of the archival material I use consists of personal correspondence—and I have tried to preserve a natural polyphony, a mosaic of individual voices, public as well as private, with attention to their points of intersection and departure.[17] A motif of entanglement lurks throughout. These were people whose lives were intertwined with one another's, and while a larger "public," political narrative plays itself out on one plane, the people I write about play out their own "private," personal relationships on another. In this connection among my greatest intellectual debts is that to Hayden White. In writing this book I have—I hope—remained sensitive to White's observation that in necessarily narrativizing history, historians have been biased in favor of order and coherence, that we have "always already" tended to edit out the chaos and disorder that is the more natural condition of any moment in the past. In writing a story that already to some extent possesses a narrative trope—that of "The God That Failed": conversion, disillusionment, repentance—I have tried to elude the imposition of typologies or teleological narratives in favor of respecting, and revealing, the nuances and idiosyncrasies of the past.[18] To Hans Ulrich Gumbrecht I am grateful for the notion of the *quereinschießendes Detail,* a detail, perhaps "excessive," that hits obliquely. In the course of researching this book I came, I believe, to know the subjects of my manuscript well, even intimately—yet even so, each time I went into the archives I would discover another occasion when they did not act the way I would "logically" expect them to act based on the "objective" (to use that "monstrous distinction," as Aleksander Wat once said) circumstances in which they found themselves. People betrayed people who saved them, and forgave people who betrayed them. The tensions implicit in structuring a narrative of many different life trajectories connected by a peculiarly persuasive ideology without imposing artificial narrative coherence emerge on the pages to come. Yet perhaps in the end this book's central contribution to our understanding of Marxism lies in this, in the exploration of Marxism as a lived experience, its messiness and the failure of typologies. Rather than delineate a paradigm, I have tried to understand what it meant to live Marxism as a European, an East European, a Jewish intellectual in the twentieth century.

The foundational work on the engagement of European intellectuals in politics is the French philosopher Julien Benda's *The Treason of the Intellectuals,* prefaced with the comment that "our age is the age of intellectual organization of political hatreds."[19] In Benda's reading, the involvement of intellectuals in politics was ipso facto a betrayal of their vocation. This is certainly the moral of *Past Imperfect,* Tony Judt's history of a conversation

among French intellectuals, led by Jean-Paul Sartre and Simone de Beau-
voir, who rose to ascendancy in the postwar years and came to support
communism, including the Stalinist regimes. Judt's writing sparkles, yet
his tone is moralistic and self-righteous. The book "is not a history of
French intellectuals; it is, rather an essay on intellectual irresponsibility,
a study of the moral condition of the intelligentsia in postwar France."[20]
The author reaches the normative conclusion that perhaps in the future
intellectuals should make the moral choice not to be engaged.

While I depart from Judt in choosing not to draw such conclusions
(this is, to me, not the point of the story I am telling), and in my greater
empathy for those about whom I write, I share with him certain ideas
about twentieth-century European intellectuals who came to be engaged
with Marxism. Judt begins by describing intellectuals as a "self-abnegating"
class. Never has this been more pronounced than among Marxist intellectuals, caught in their role as vanguardists often a priori implicated by their
bourgeois origins, acutely cognizant of belonging to a class destined for
eradication by History. Sartre, as Judt points out, harbored a famous sense
of worthlessness; and Judt posits the thesis that communism's insistence
on intellectuals' accepting the authority of others was part of its appeal.[21]
I draw also to some extent upon the Existentialist categories that Judt describes in relation to Sartre and his friends, in particular the predominant
notions of *engagement* and "choice," and the problem of responsibility in
an absurd world. I agree with Judt that a temporally specific idea existed
that the world was divided into communists and anticommunists, and
there was no space to occupy in between. This relates as well to what Judt
notes as Sartre's contribution to the idea of "revolution"—that is, revolution as a categorical, existential imperative.

I make every attempt, writing now against most of the existing literature, to avoid being either hagiographic or demonizing. I depart as well
from Czesław Miłosz's classic work *The Captive Mind*, written just after his
defection from Stalinist Poland in 1951. For Miłosz even the most fanatical
belief is not absolute; from an Islamic tradition he borrows the explanatory
notion of "ketman," a kind of splitting of the self, and from the Polish
novelist Stanisław Ignacy Witkiewicz (Witkacy) he borrows the allegory
of the Murti-Bing pills, an intersection of psychological opportunism and
belief. The real-life inspirations for the communist writers Miłosz calls
Alpha, Beta, Gamma and Delta, some of whom appear in later chapters,

are a generation younger than the protagonists of this book.[22] The subjects of Miłosz's case studies came to communism after the war, through their experiences in the war, when communism was already Stalinism, and Stalinism was coming to power in Poland. In contrast, the generation I write about came to Marxism for the most part in the 1920s, at a moment when no one was entirely sure what communism in power meant, a moment before Stalinism, before socialist realism, before Marxism meant the imposition of Soviet power in Poland. Their Marxism was a much more multivalent and contestatory one. This excuses nothing, of course, but it does demand that Polish Marxism be taken seriously as an authentic, indigenous current, influential in Polish intellectual life long before Soviet occupation. There was little space for far-left opportunism at that moment: on the contrary, the Marxist intellectuals born at the turn of the century suffered persecution in interwar Poland. Perhaps they suffered for their own narcissism, but that, after all, is a separate issue.[23]

The backdrop for this story is that of Marxism as an ideology of modernity, a modernity that encapsulates a shift in conceptions of time from cyclical to linear and a consciousness of the present as an ephemeral moment on the path towards the future. In this respect, to draw upon a favorite term of the futurists, I see no possibility for dismissing Marxism in its historical context as passé. The enormity of the experiment in the European twentieth century remains in some ways to be understood—not because Marxism should be reinvoked in the contemporary political sphere, but rather because understanding Marxism and its seductive force is so critical to understanding European (and not only European) modernity. Jacques Derrida suggests as much in his beautiful, poetic essay *Specters of Marx*, a self-described "hauntology" on the need to (re)claim the inheritance of the multiple, heterogeneous *spirits* of Marx. He reminds us that Marx's specter haunting Europe is a specter *to come,* and prophesies that the spirit of Marxism, its ghost—the whole ontology of Marxism, Hegelianism, progress, teleology—will continue to haunt us forever.[24]

At the end of his life, the poet Aleksander Wat asked, "Why was our group so much destroyed by history and communism? Why did communism destroy the lives of those people, and why did the people who joined the communists in the mid-thirties make such careers for themselves?"[25] In existentialist terms, the decisive moment for these fin de siècle–born intellectuals was the moment of making a choice, the act of opting for Marxism; and guilt is the true motif of Wat's extraordinary, angst-laden memoirs. What, then, did it mean to make the world anew at a moment when the world seemed poised at the crossroads of catastrophe and utopia? Certainly this was a time when there was a sense of the force of History, yet given that, where was the realm of fate and determinism and where was the realm of choice and contingency? I have tried in my own reading of the past to assume absolute contingency—the "momentum of History" being something the people I write about believed in, but I as their historian reject. In particular, I have tried to resist all impulses to filter the interwar years through the Second World War, to allow, rather, the moments at which other outcomes were possible to reveal themselves. Yet here, with respect to the challenge of dispensing with teleology, I am sympathetic to Michel Foucault's compelling passage on the difficulty of evading the clever, and potentially sinister, Hegel: "But to truly escape Hegel involves an exact appreciation of the price we have to pay to detach ourselves from him. It assumes that we are aware of the extent to which Hegel, insidiously perhaps, is close to us; it implies a knowledge, in that which permits us to think against Hegel, of that which remains Hegelian. We have to determine the extent to which our anti-Hegelianism is possibly one of his tricks directed against us, at the end of which he stands, motionless, waiting for us."[26] I have tried throughout to pay my respects to Hegel by illuminating both the tension between subjectivity and telos within modernity, and the Marxist phenomenon in which individuals become agents in the destruction of their own agency. At once, however, I see the history of these Marxist intellectuals most fundamentally as a story about making choices—and a story of a moment when the space for being "unengaged" dissolved and there was an existential imperative to make a choice. For these intellectuals, the paradox of choosing Marxism was the way in which they came to take a creative role in the conscious liquidation of their own subjectivity, abdicated in deference to History. Questions of guilt and responsibility aside, the narrative topos of this generation is one of idealism and disillusionment, and their story is a tragic one.

CHAPTER ONE

Once upon a Time,
in a Café Called Ziemiańska

There is not a gray hair in my soul,
no senile tenderness in me!
Having thundered the world with the might of my voice,
I—beautiful, twenty-two years old
go.

—*Vladimir Mayakovsky*

IN THE ELEGANT CAPITAL city of Warsaw, the editor Mieczysław Grydzewski would bring his two dachshunds to a café called Ziemiańska.[1] In
the summer the café on Mazowiecka Street opened its garden, yet the
place of honor remained a table poised on a platform protruding from
the stairway. In these years following the First World War, a small group
of poets would gather at Ziemiańska. Their Warsaw was a city of cafés
and cabarets, of droshkies pulled by horses through cobblestone streets.
Often they fell into depressions, overcome with nihilism, with the premonition that the world would soon end. Even so, these were lively times
at Ziemiańska. The beautiful Ola Watowa, who might have become an
actress, loved their café life: "At Ziemiańska our friends, people we knew
sat around every table, passing from one to another. The atmosphere was
lively, amusing, people were witty. There were some venomous jokes as
well: instances of ridicule, like . . . 'Ważyk with the ugly little face' [*Ważyk
brzydki twarzyk*]. Painters, writers, poets. Słonimski was incomparable in
his sharp wit. . . . Impassioned discussions would break out constantly,
everywhere. . . . On rare occasions the wonderful Witkacy would appear.
In the summer Stefan Żeromski—beautiful, imposing—would sit in the
garden at Ziemiańska. . . . I would mix chocolate into my coffee."[2]

The table on the platform belonged to the young poets of the journal
Skamander—Julian Tuwim, Antoni Słonimski, Jan Lechoń, Kazimierz

Wierzyński, Jarosław Iwaszkiewicz, and their friend and editor Mieczysław Grydzewski. They "believed deeply in the present."[3] Their luminary was the bibliophile Tuwim, with his unearthly ear for sounds and penchant for Esperanto.[4] Tuwim, the son of a quiet bank clerk, was a Jewish boy from Łódź who attended a Russian school and resolved to become a Polish poet. His sister thought him to be a panacea for all ills and believed him to be surrounded by a magical aura. Tuwim suffered from agoraphobia; at times he appeared restless and fretful. He suffered from something else as well: there was a large birthmark on his face, about which he was terribly self-conscious. Those around him, though, saw something else. The Russian novelist Ilya Ehrenburg was struck by Tuwim's beauty; Jarosław Iwaszkiewicz by his sparkling eyes.[5] The young Iwaszkiewicz had come from Ukraine; he became the host of the legendary Stawisko, an estate where he lived with his beloved wife Anna—and often with his male lovers as well. Iwaszkiewicz was gentle; his letters home during his days in the military were delicate and loving. "My dear Mama!" he wrote home from the army, "Yesterday I tramped around Ostrowa all afternoon with Chwat [Wat], a neofuturist in the machine-gun company here."[6] After Antoni Słonimski fell from a horse in 1919, he was bedridden in his mother's home for weeks. Iwaszkiewicz would come to visit him, and would cringe at Słonimski's harshness towards his mother.[7] Słonimski's acerbic edge was also his most distinguishing character trait, so much a part of his brilliance as an essayist—which made his youthful, unrequited love for a married woman the more poignant.[8]

Also frequenting Ziemiańska were the futurists. Tadeusz Peiper, an avantgardist from Cracow just a few years older than the others, returned from a trip to Spain to find that a younger generation, without so much as a glance requesting permission, had seated themselves around the table of literary life. Peiper began to make out their faces: Bruno Jasieński, Anatol Stern, Aleksander Wat.[9] The avant-garde included as well "independent poets"—Władysław Broniewski, Adam Ważyk, Stanisław Ryszard Stande, Mieczysław Braun, and Witold Wandurski—although the latter two resided in Łódź and came to Ziemiańska only when they found themselves in Warsaw. In January 1922 Broniewski lamented in his diary that he had been reading the Skamander poets and saw that his own poems were only wretched imitations.[10] Stanisław Ryszard Stande was thin, with an oblong, pale face and a wry grimace, a face that would take on a mocking expression when he smiled. Jan Lechoń interpreted Stande's expression as revealing disgust—or at the least distaste—for his Skamander friends, yet this was perhaps unjust: that grimace was the physical result of an accident. During the 1905 Revolution, as an eight-year-old child, Stande was trampled by horses.[11] In 1919 he became the first of the poets to join the Communist Party of Poland (KPP).[12]

Irena Krzywicka, the free-spirited daughter-in-law of the great Marxist sociologist Ludwik Krzywicki, was present at the café Pod Pikadorem where the Skamander poets made their debut in November 1918. A young, shy student, she came to the café with her aunt and uncle, who were taken aback by the young poets who had departed so radically from their predecessors. Krzywicka herself felt differently. "I devoured those young people, whose every poem seemed a revelation of the new poetry," she wrote, "with my eyes, my ears, my entire soul."[13] She was sensitive to the aesthetics of physicality: "Iwaszkiewicz was enormous, slender, with a rare beauty and dreamy, slanting eyes, a thick, sensual mouth, an idle grace; Słonimski had the wise face of a typical intellectual, with a powerful gaze from behind his glasses and narrow, joking lips; Lechoń was ugly, thin, with a prominent nose, all crooked with sharp angles, but unlike anyone else; Wierzyński—the most banal and the most handsome in the common sense of that word; well and finally he, Tuwim, with a dark birthmark on his cheek, with raven-dark hair and burning eyes and a strongly bent nose, a typical southerner with an explosive temperament."[14] Irena Krzywicka noticed that conversations with Tuwim tended to take on a fantastical character. She knew Antoni Słonimski's verses by heart, and watched the beautiful married woman who was Słonimski's inspiration.[15] Krzywicka liked Aleksander Wat very much, but was never able to acknowledge him as a literary master. She was skeptical of futurism, and felt neither inclined nor competent to "write without sense." The skepticism was mutual, and Krzywicka was criticized for being a *"passéiste"*—a criticism to which she in part attributed her own literary paralysis. And so she remained "only a fan of constructivism," not a participant.[16]

Yet it was Wat who was intellectually the most sophisticated. He read prolifically in all the languages around him—Polish, Russian, French, German—with the exception of Yiddish, the only language his father spoke well. His childhood reading included Nietzsche, Kierkegaard, and Darwin, and when he was only just on the verge of adolescence he had

FIGURE 1   Café Ziemiańska. Caricature by Jotes, 1930; courtesy of Muzeum Literatury imienia Adama Mickiewicza.

already become a Darwinist—who would insist to his Catholic nanny that God did not exist and humans were descended from apes.[17] When in school he became friends with Anatol Stern, Stern gave Wat the name Buddha-Zarathustra, and together they experienced the negation of all possibilities.[18] Adam Ważyk was not alone in believing that the young Wat actually harbored religious longings, of which he was terribly ashamed.[19]

In January 1919, at the age of eighteen, in a feverish, manic, "trance-like" state Wat composed the long prose poem *JA z jednej strony a JA z*

drugiej strony mego mopsożelaznego piecyka (I from One Side and I from
the Other Side of My Cast-Iron Stove). Some five years earlier, the Italian
futurist Filippo Tommaso Marinetti had liberated words from syntax.[20] Wat
had not yet discarded syntax, but he did stretch syntax to its threshold,
to that liminal space beyond which meaning in its conventional sense
was no longer possible. Hovering at this threshold, Wat now told a story
of rotting and decay, of the degeneration of civilization. The esoteric sophistication and density of the language betrayed a knowledge of foreign
languages, the Bible, European literature, and Greek myths astounding
for an eighteen-year-old—a self-education that devastatingly pointed to
catastrophism and nothingness. He wrote of eternal nights; of the horror
of encountering at midnight one's own sallow image; of the nightingales
that sang him to death; of his faces, which he changed with each zenith
of the sun. Wat's web of images and allusions played with an inversion
that might have been carnivalesque were they not so dark, so macabre.
Sleepy castrates moaned in the corners of a grotesque arcade; children
emerged from graves to suck his fingers; and "God with a swollen hydrous
body trembles from çold and loneliness." "At midnight," the young Wat
wrote, "it is always necessary to place your head under the dazzling, yes!
dazzling knife of the guillotine." The piece was saturated with a deep
sense of moral degeneration, of the collapse of civilization, of the "ac-
cursed *principium individuationis*" that paralyzed him. Nothing redemp-
tive remained, there was no salvation, and the blasphemy throughout the
poem suggested less heresy than it did nihilism. Sexuality had become
licentious and grotesque: "I leave for your meeting, where trembling in
tears and without sensation you will surrender, *you* will surrender, he (she)
will surrender, we will surrender, all of you will surrender, they (they the
women) will surrender." Images materialized in his feverish mind: Anda-
lusian witches clapping castanets danced with a long dark thin musical
Jew in the heavens of the inhabitants of the Kirghiz steppes. The knight
Death approached with rattling gold taps, the knight Hell just behind
him. They kissed the narrator's fragrant hands. Palimpsests moved gray
sheets of lice and in the corner of a closet a louse was crunched under
the large fingernail of a mad god. Wat's friends appeared as well, as did
the smile of the woman Antoni Słonimski loved. To the Skamander poets
Wat devoted the following passage:

Sage's Slit: to Ant. Słonimski.

Stagnation of steam marbles. Polymorphism and
  polychromism of your skull bewitched you.

Signboards will spit and growl: Old scoundrel.

To Julian Tuwim.

In the polar glowing spaces let love be weakness, which you
  want to eradicate. *naa NN aaa Na Naaa.*

To Jar. Iwaszkiewicz.[21]

In the last stanza Wat returned to himself, tormented by his own narcissism, and wrote that it was he himself who was burning in the "inquisitorial interior" of his cast-iron stove. This was "too much" for Irena Krzywicka, but not for the older, magnificent Witkacy, who loved *Cast-Iron Stove* and forced his whole court in Zakopane to read it. Later Bruno Schulz told Wat that it was *Cast-Iron Stove* that had inspired him to begin writing.[22]

Wat had spent his youth absorbing books he found in his parents' home and imagining a bleak future for himself as a drunk in the gutter, a *clochard,* or a hermit philosopher living in extreme poverty.[23] His life played itself out somewhat differently. In the spring of 1923, around the time of his twenty-third birthday, Anatol Stern and Jarosław Iwaszkiewicz came with Wat to an end-of-the-year ball at Warsaw's drama school; it was there that Wat met Ola Lew, a first-year drama student. Irena Krzywicka pointed out that while Wat was "very ugly," Ola Lew was beautiful. Shortly after that ball, Wat saw Krzywicka on the corner of Nowogrodzka and Krucza streets and called to her, "Have you seen what good fortune has come to me? Such a beautiful girl—and she wanted me."[24]

Ola Lew was the greatest stroke of good fortune in Aleksander Wat's life. Her parents, however, were not sympathetic; because she brought home a futurist and not a doctor or a lawyer, they refused her a dowry.[25] Undaunted, she left her parents' home and entered Wat's world of colorful personalities. She met Anatol Stern, the only person Wat's tolerant father ever threw out of their home, and Bruno Jasieński, whose memory for poetry was extraordinary.[26] Hovering about their circles as well was Adam Ważyk "with the ugly little face," the first in Poland to translate the French futurist Guillaume Apollinaire. This independent avant-garde poet came upon the stage with a dazzling first book, *Semafory* (Semaphores), given a glittering review in Mieczysław Grydzewski's *Wiadomości Literackie* (Literary News).[27] Ważyk's brother Saul kept their Jewish surname Wagman and wrote poems as well—Zionist poems.[28]

POLISH FUTURISM

The Polish futurists enjoyed far less popularity among the reading public than did the Skamander poets. This was largely of their own doing, the result of their efforts to transgress all boundaries of propriety. Polish futurism as a semicoherent endeavor materialized in 1918, when Bruno Jasieński and two other poets organized a futurist club in Cracow. Jasieński himself had only arrived there recently, after graduating from a Polish secondary school in Moscow in the spring of 1918.[29] Of all of them, it was Jasieński who had been closest to the Russian Revolution. He was also the most elegant, and the most pointed cultivator of dandyism, with his top hat and gaunt figure cloaked in black. To some he seemed very self-controlled, closed unto himself, as though he had inside him some obsessive thought that he chose not to share with anyone.[30] Such a demeanor could be off-putting, but also seductive; it did not escape Jarosław Iwaszkiewicz that "schoolgirls went crazy when they saw him."[31] Jasieński drew the attention of his male classmates as well: "I would see him almost every day in front of the main building, with a monocle on his eye: his huge tie suggested the Romantic era, bygone nineteenth-century elegance, and this almost theatrical accessory seemed all the more flagrant on a writer who, in all other respects, had broken with the past and with tradition."[32]

The following year, in 1919, the Cracow futurists' Warsaw counterparts Aleksander Wat and Anatol Stern made their debut with a poetry reading titled "A subtropical evening organized by White Negroes." The number of Polish futurists was small, but not without interlocutors, including Witkacy and the avant-garde theater director Leon Schiller, as well as Cracow avantgardists Julian Przyboś and Tadeusz Peiper. It was Peiper who proclaimed the slogan of "the metropolis, the masses, the machine." Wat's circle, whose own attitude towards civilization was far more ambivalent, exalted in the revelation of the materiality of language and the liberation of language from representation. For Wat it was this freeing of words that was most essential: "You see, that slogan, the idea of words being liberated, that words were things and you could do whatever you liked with them,

FIGURE 2 Bruno Jasieński. Portrait by Witkacy, 1923; courtesy of Muzeum Literatury imienia Adama Mickiewicza.

that was an enormous revolution in literature; that was a revolution like, let's say, Nietzsche's 'God is dead.'"[33] While Wat credited Marinetti with imbuing him with the idea that words could be liberated, Anatol Stern credited his mother. It was she who taught him to have faith in words, a faith that now set him "ablaze like a live torch!"[34]

The futurists embarked on various creative experiments with language, playing with typefaces, neologisms, and phonetics. Wat's *namopaniki*, like the Russian futurists' *za-um* poems, were aesthetic exercises based purely on sounds with a deliberate disregard for semantic meaning. *GGA*, the "first Polish almanac of futurist poetry," began:

**the great rainbow monkey named Dionysus took his last breath
long ago.**
we are throwing away his rotten legacy we declare

I. CIVILIZATION, CULTURE
WITH ITS JUSTICE—TO THE TRASH HEAP.[35]

Having dispatched civilization to the trash heap, the manifesto announced
the abolition of history, posterity, and tradition, and the destruction of
the cities. Wat and Stern also articulated a program for futurist poetry.
They declared their belief in the self-referentiality of language—that is,
language was to be reified, words were no longer to be signifiers representing things, but rather to be things themselves.

> poetry. we are allowing rhyme and rhythm to remain as they
> are primary and fertile. **the destruction of rules constraining
> creativity the virtue of awkwardness.** freedom of grammati-
> cal form, spelling and punctuation, independently of the
> creator. mickiewicz is limited. **słowacki is incomprehensible
> mumbling.**
>   WORDS have their own weight, sound, color, their own
> design. THEY TAKE UP ROOM IN SPACE. here are the deciding
> values of a word. the shortest words (sound) and the longest
> words (a book). the meaning of a word is a subordinate matter
> and is not dependent upon the concept ascribed to it it is
> necessary to treat words like phonetic material USED NOT
> ONOMATOPOEICALLY.[36]

The manifesto went on to state: "we glorify reason and therefore also reject
logic, that limitation and cowardice of the mind. nonsense is wonderful
because of its untranslatable contents which set off our creative breadth
and power."[37] In declaring their intention to "destroy civilization," including all the mechanisms of "airplanes, trams, inventions, telephones," the
Polish futurists departed from the cult of technology that was integral to
Italian futurism. Their ecstatic reification of words more closely resembled
the Russian futurists Aleksei Kruchenykh and Velimir Khlebnikov's theory
of "the word as such." Stern and Wat's deliberately offensive rejection of

the revered nineteenth-century Polish poets Adam Mickiewicz and Juliusz Słowacki mirrored the Russian futurists' order in their 1912 manifesto "A Slap in the Face of Public Taste" to "throw Pushkin, Dostoevsky, Tolstoy et al. from the steamboat of modernity."[38]

GGA was emblematic of a predilection for programmatic manifestos that characterized the avant-garde throughout Europe. Wat and Stern intended to be shocking, and the early futurist evenings could be characterized by carnivalesque scandal. On one occasion the futurists crashed a Zionist meeting and recited caricatured antisemitic speeches.[39] Iwaszkiewicz described the futurists at the time he was serving in Piłsudski's army during the Polish-Bolshevik War:

> In Ostrowa I also met Aleksander Wat, whom I had already known from Warsaw, who served in a machine gun company and with whom I now spent long hours in conversation about literature. He seemed to be a sensible person, although his previous Warsaw appearances did not at all possess the quality of sensibleness: with his friend Anatol Stern he had created a literary group of "neo-futurists" and the performances of that group distinguished themselves by improbable extravagance. On one serene Sunday, for example, Stern brought Wat in a wheelbarrow from the Belweder Palace to Castle Square. Stern appeared naked to recite their poetry, with only a fig leaf which was supposed to be burned at the conclusion of their program, etc.[40]

With the exception of a call for liberation from "*passéisme*," the futurists' programs tended to lack theoretical coherence, vacillating instead between a fetish for the future and a call for a primitive, Adamite paradise. Stern later admitted that such contradictions could present problems for the uninitiated: "Something that could certainly lead to conceptual confusion on the part of the unprepared reader was the fusion of anticivilized moments with the apotheosizing of contemporary technology. Of course this was the result of the complicated synthesis on which was founded, on one hand, the aspiration of the 'primitivists to salvage original, primitive sensitivity and to smother all kinds of diseased and decadent manifestations in the psyche of the urban-dweller—and yet on the other hand an apotheosis of civilization, not so much contemporary as that which was only supposed to be approaching. From that resulted a host of understand-able antinomies."[41]

Like most avant-garde endeavors, Polish futurism did not enjoy lon-gevity; unlike Skamander, the futurists never did succeed in establishing a stable publication. In 1921, Stern founded the journal *Nowa Sztuka* (New Art) in collaboration with Jarosław Iwaszkiewicz and Tadeusz Peiper; it was an ambitious project that included avant-garde literature and happen-ings throughout Europe. Peiper, who had given his translations of Spanish poetry to the less radical editor Grydzewski, later took them back and gave them to Stern for *Nowa Sztuka* instead. If he was going to participate in a group endeavor, then he wanted it to be with the most innovative group.[42] The Polish futurists had no doubt that they were this, and notwithstanding their provocative behavior, they took themselves very seriously. In July 1921 they sent a letter to the Russian futurist Vladimir Mayakovsky, which be-gan "the Polish futurists, establishing relations with futurists of all coun-tries, send fraternal greetings to the Russian futurists." The letter solicited contributions from Mayakovsky, Vasilii Kamensky, David Burliuk, and Velimir Khlebnikov for the "first large international journal-newspaper devoted to futurist poetry from all over the world in all languages." The letter was signed by Bruno Jasieński, Aleksander Wat, and Anatol Stern "in the name of the Polish futurists"—that is, themselves.[43]

Nowa Sztuka was short-lived. Iwaszkiewicz declined to work on the following issue "due to certain disagreements" and the second issue of February 1922 was also the last.[44] The next collaborative venture came in the form of Peiper's journal *Zwrotnica* (The Switch), which declared itself to contain "art of the present." The first issue, which appeared in May 1922, was largely Peiper's own creation, a reflection of "the metropolis, the masses, the machine."[45] Peiper aspired "to inflame in our man a love for newness, which he himself has created. . . . I desire to awaken in him faith in the miraculous epoch in which he lives, and distaste for the dead epochs that live in him."[46] Disparagement of the past was very much part of the cultural zeitgeist—a trend that in turn soon embraced futurism itself. In October 1923, in the sixth issue of *Zwrotnica*, Peiper presented an extensive criticism of Polish futurism. Even more significant was Bruno Jasieński's recantation. Jasieński began by describing futurism as a "cer-tain form of collective consciousness," and insisted that in order to speak of it, it was first necessary to "overcome" it in oneself. He went on to tell

FIGURE 3 Bruno Jasieński, c. 1924. Photo by F. Zwierz-chowski; courtesy of Muzeum Literatury imienia Adama Mickiewicza.

the story of the "falling ill" of Warsaw, and of his acquaintance with Wat and Stern. Jasieński announced futurism's closure and commented on the sources of the futurists' guilt:

> The whole of our guilt lies in the fact that there was a certain
> moment of collective consciousness, common to all of us,
> which we seized upon, which we declined to repudiate,
> which we endeavored to grasp in certain new artistic forms.
> Only when those forms are created will it be possible to
> speak about the overcoming of that exact moment. By passing
> over it in silence we fail to move forward by even an inch,

moreover—we exclude the possibility of any kind of forward movement. This is, consequently, the source of many very amusing reversals. The present situation, for example, presents itself to be entirely the opposite of what the public judges it to be. I am no longer a futurist, whereas all of you are futurists. This appears to be a paradox, yet so it is.[47]

This issue of *Zwrotnica* did not go unnoticed by futurism's critics. An article in *Wiadomości Literackie* called the issue of *Zwrotnica* a "liquidation of futurism."[48]

SKAMANDER

Despite Polish futurism's dadaistic self-referentiality, Wat and the other futurists were always engaged in many conversations; these began, perhaps, with the young Skamander poets, who themselves carried out an implicit dialogue with the older writers of Young Poland. The birth of Skamander as a literary entity coincided precisely with the regaining of Polish independence and Warsaw's reemergence as a European capital city. On 29 November 1918, the young poets Jan Lechoń, Julian Tuwim, and Antoni Słonimski premiered at the Warsaw café Pod Pikadorem ("Under the Pikador"). The advertisement for their first appearance read:

> Countrymen!
> Workers, soldiers, children, old people, people, women, intellectuals, and dramatic writers! On Friday November 29th at 9 in the evening opens: The First Warsaw Café of Poets "POD PICADOREM," Nowy Świat Nr. 57. The conscience of young artistic Warsaw! The General Headquarters of the Army of the Salvation of Poland from all of the homeland's contemporary literature. Daily tournament of poets, musicians and painters.[49]

On that day Jarosław Iwaszkiewicz was summoned by acquaintances from the aristocratic home where he worked as a tutor; two young poets—Julian Tuwim and Antoni Słonimski—wished to see him. When Iwaszkiewicz arrived at Nowy Świat number 57, the café was still being painted. On the program for that evening, below the name "Pikador," was the slogan "Poetry, to the streets!" Iwaszkiewicz took the slogan seriously. "It seemed to me—as it undoubtedly did to my contemporaries as well—that reading a few verses of poetry between one cup of coffee and the next was poetry's getting out to the street."[50] A year later, in January 1920, the original Pod Pikadorem poets, now with Iwaszkiewicz and Kazimierz Wierzyński, began their own periodical. In the first issue of *Skamander* they offered a self-introduction: "We want to be poets of the present and this is our faith and our whole 'program.' We are not tempted by sermonizing, we do not want to convert anybody, but we want to conquer, to enrapture, to influence the hearts of men, we want to be their laughing and their weeping. . . . We believe unshakably in the sanctity of a good rhyme, in the divine origin of rhythm, in revelation through images born in ecstasy and through shapes chiseled by work."[51] Anatol Stern was unimpressed; for the author of futurist manifestos, here was a "programmatic article" in which "one can find everything except a program."[52]

A program was unnecessary. The Skamander poets were a dazzling success, becoming at once the darlings of Polish readers.[53] Their poetry drew upon the spoken language and in this sense reflected the more general impulse of leftist intellectuals to liberate themselves from bourgeois elitism. The work of these young poets, though innovative, was not radical; in contradistinction to the "transsense" endeavors of the futurists, the Skamander group had not broken with representation. Adam Ważyk described Skamander as "the only formation in Europe of that time that, amidst the confusion of the postwar years, lit the lantern of the heart."[54] In essence Skamander played the paradoxical role of the traditional wing of the avant-garde. While the more radically experimental writers, often engaged in polemics with Skamander, were implicitly the Skamandrites' rivals, they were simultaneously bound to the Skamandrites by both literary collaboration and personal ties. The liberal newspaper *Wiadomości Literackie*, published from January 1924, served as a forum for the Skamandrites as well as the avantgardists. In an era of newly regained independence, the paper embraced cosmopolitanism, devoting much attention to literary and artistic developments abroad, particularly in Russia, France, Czechoslovakia, and Italy.[55]

Not all polemics among the poets were innocuous. Just before a 1921 futurist poetry reading organized with Witkacy in Zakopane, the Skamander poet Jan Lechoń appeared and began informing the local butchers that Jews had arrived in town with the intention of insulting the Virgin Mary. Presumably Lechoń understood the implications of his instigation, and the reading ended in violence.[56] Yet even incidents of this kind did not end relations between the avantgardists and the Skamander poets. In 1927 Tuwim was a witness at Wat's wedding, and this was after Wat and Stern had abused Tuwim in their booklet *Żydek-Literat* (The Jew-Boy of Letters), a parody of Polish antisemitism.[57] Tuwim had described himself in 1918 as "the first Polish futurist," although he never actually participated in the futurists' literary endeavors.[58] Nonetheless, there were natural affinities. Tuwim's response to an interviewer who, in 1926, asked what his passion in life was revealed that Tuwim's own creative impetus was close to Wat's: "The word, the word, and the word!" "A word is as real a thing as a tree. Words are truly alive." The interviewer then cited a fragment of one of Tuwim's verses: "I feed my famished body / with words like fruits."[59] Moreover, despite Tuwim's love for Pushkin—whom the Russian futurist Vladimir Mayakovsky wished to throw from the steamboat of modernity—Tuwim was among Mayakovsky's (and Marinetti's) first Polish translators.[60]

Wat looked upon Skamander with both admiration and condescension. The dazzling young poets failed to understand one thing: "A pleiad of talent one encounters once in a hundred years, an almost instantaneous mastery of poetic technique—moreover, in Poland, a revolutionary turn. One had to have been a witness to Pikador and to have been aware of the poetic constellation in Poland at that time in order to appreciate the dimensions of their revolution. But 'the peacock and the parrot of nations' had already long since been excluded from the conscious circulation of poetic language and ideas. And the revolution of the Skamandrites was pre-Rimbaudian, naïve—it failed to question itself. They were naïve—naïve and deaf and blind to the fact that the old world had collapsed irreversibly."[61]

UNFRIENDLY OBSERVERS

Attacks on futurism by those outside of the literary world revealed moments of solidarity between Skamander and the futurists. When Stern was arrested in December 1919 on charges of profanity, the Skamander poets came to his defense. Antoni Słonimski began a petition stating, "We, the undersigned, in the name of justice, claim as writers that the poem being spoken of does not contain profanity, and that only a certain awkwardness of form has brought about a painful misunderstanding."[62] Stefan Żeromski, the older novelist of the patriotic, neo-Romantic group known as Young Poland, was among the signatories. The petition was only partially successful: it was only two years later that the charges were dropped. Stern spent several months in prison.[63]

Nor was this the last attack from the government. In July 1922 a group of right-wing parliamentarians initiated a protest against the futurists' posters. The National Democrat Tadeusz Dymowski, a vocal advocate of liberating Poland from Jewish economic influence, led a campaign insisting on the enforcement of a 1917 law that permitted the display of posters in languages other than Polish only under the condition that a Polish translation be simultaneously provided. Futurist texts were in violation of this law, Dymowski argued: "The futurists have been organizing a whole host of evenings at various spas, as part of which they hang posters of the oddest content and in futurist language, which is the most horrible corruption of the Polish language. Because we are aware that there exists a law that permits the display of posters only in cases when a Polish-language text is simultaneously provided—as far as we are aware, futurist language has not been acknowledged as Polish—accordingly we regard that allowing such posters to be displayed is worthy of punishment."[64] Dymowski's campaign against the futurists failed in the Polish Sejm. On this occasion the Skamandrites again came to the futurists' defense, mocking Dymowski and his supporters by citing the linguistic and stylistic errors in Dymowski's and his allies' own texts. In response, Dymowski tore down the futurist posters by himself.[65]

Dymowski was not the only one unpleasantly predisposed towards the futurists. Aleksander Wat's aunt was similarly horrified, and prayed that God not punish her nephew for mutilating their beautiful Polish language.[66] A more painful attack was that by Stefan Żeromski. In his book *Snobizm i Postęp* (Snobbism and Progress), which appeared in December 1922, Żeromski condescendingly chastised the futurists for snobbery. "By the expression 'snob,'" Żeromski began, "one defines and characterizes a person who passionately practices pretentious dandyism and adheres to the canons of fashion with exaggeration and excessive solicitude." It was mimicry, however, which was the decisive marker of snobbism: "Blind imitation—this is the most essential, the fundamental characteristic of snobbism." Żeromski accepted "the most modern artistic currents" elsewhere in Europe, but disparaged their Polish counterparts: "These trends are in essence new pages of Italian, French and Russian literature. In

Poland, however, they are 'cigarette butts,' alien, colorless, unreadable, material evidence of snobbism."[67]

Żeromski's attack was taken seriously, not least by the young aspiring poet Władysław Broniewski, who wrote in his diary on New Year's Eve of 1922: "Żeromski's book enlightened me as to the other side of the coin—a critical light on my literary enthusiasm. New poetry and snobbism."[68] Wat later concurred: they were under the influence of foreign poetry, of Russian futurism. Jasieński had been in Russia in 1917, he had seen the Revolution. Moreover, he had an unusual memory for poetry; Vladimir Mayakovsky was forever in his mind. And not only Jasieński, but all of them—Tuwim, Jasieński, Przyboś, Słonimski, Stern, Wat, and Ważyk—would come to be among the breathtaking Russian futurist's Polish translators. So, too, would Władysław Broniewski.

THE SEARCHINGS OF A YOUNG POET

As a young man Władysław Broniewski wore the gray uniform of the Polish Legions, decorated with a sky-blue ribbon *Virtuti Militari*.[69] His room in his mother's apartment on Danilowiczowska Street in Warsaw emanated the ambience of the Polish nobility: Persian rugs, crossed swords, ancestral daggers—and an upright piano.[70] He came of age as a soldier in Marshal Józef Piłsudski's Legions fighting for Polish independence—and as the author of a diary that he described upon its October 1918 inception as an "intellectual garbage bin."[71] Irena Krzywicka was happy that the shy soldier with literary ambitions did not "succumb" to futurist fashion. When Broniewski read his poems aloud, even "the most zealous of the futurists would fall silent at their irresistible beauty and strength of expression."[72] Of all the clientele at Ziemiańska, it was Broniewski who most embodied Cezary Baryka of Stefan Żeromski's novel *Przedwiośnie* (The Spring to Come), the romantic youth who, following youthful mistakes, self-absorption and decadence, found his way to the Revolution. Broniewski was moreover most heir to the legacy of nineteenth-century Polish patriotism and Polish literature, with his lyricism and romanticism. He himself was not unaware of this—moreover, he was not unaware of himself as a "pure Slav" amidst a literary scene that included so many assimilated Polish Jews.

Alongside his shyness and self-doubt, Broniewski harbored a certain arrogance. At the age of twenty, in October 1918, he commented in his

FIGURE 4 Władysław Broniewski in his Legionnaire uniform with his grandmother Jadwiga Lubowidzka, 1921. Courtesy of Muzeum Władysława Broniewskiego.

diary that "a woman who is not pretty should be sensible, otherwise she is intolerable."[73] In fact Broniewski's entanglements with women would absorb much of his energies in the next few years. More important, perhaps, was his changing attitude towards the army. By October 1918, he no longer wished to return to "those murderous, empty, thoughtless days,

idiotic and banal conversations with idiotic friends, the abominable vegetation of the barracks. The desire to pose as a national hero has left me
long ago—and there remains only a tough, inflexible obligation—to which
I submit despite everything."[74] The following month he wrote critically
in his diary: "Today's meeting irritated me. What cattle they are! Hurrah-
patriotism combined with primitive antisemitism."[75]

It was not an easy path from decorated Legionnaire to avant-garde
poet, and Broniewski was plagued by ideological uncertainties. On the
same day of that unpleasant meeting Broniewski wrote of how, despite
his respect for the Left, he was not yet able to embrace its program. In
spring 1919 he began to read—and increasingly respect—"that Trotsky
who is so despised in our country." He admired Trotsky's quickness, his
flexibility of thought, yet concluded that the ideas themselves remained
too orthodox, too canonical to justify the sacrifice of his individualism. In
his diary Broniewski wrote: "I am beginning to understand how average
and below-average communists imagine the social equality of the future.
These people are similar in their psyche to some sectarians or Jesuits:
often, in their naïve conceptualization, they fail to realize how far they
are departing from Papa Marx *et consortes*." At the same time he dreamt of
"some kind of fantastical romance with a demonic woman"—set against
the backdrop of war.[76] He longed for an entanglement of love and war,
and despaired of boredom, his "life's tragedy." He felt unconnected, as if
he had departed so far from all defined realms that he no longer had any
place. By January 1921 he had clarified what he needed, again in the language of nineteenth-century Polish literature: "to find an idea that would
rejuvenate me, that would force me to treat my own life as a backdrop,
that would propel me towards sacrifices, towards battle. As it was seven or
eight years ago. . . . To find a creative power for myself, that would allow
me to become 'immortal in the effects of my own action.'"[77]

Later that year Broniewski encountered the avant-garde; he met Aleksander Wat, "one of the extreme futurists."[78] By the end of 1921 he found
himself under the futurists' influence. No longer was their work opaque
to him, and Broniewski resolved to follow in their path.[79] This was not to
be easy. Broniewski wrote to Bronisław Sylwin Kencbok, a friend from
his days in Piłsudski's Legions, that he was suffering from depression
and was unable to write: "So, my dear one—insofar as it turns out that
my literary pseudo-talent is not a fiction of arrogance and graphomania,

then perhaps there will come a time, after a couple of years, when those who know me will be able to say: 'Ah, I, too, know a futurist'—in a similar way as they would speak of their aunt who is a black woman. Either way, my literary 'to be or not to be' remains my heaviest and very uncertain dilemma."[80]

Broniewski experienced the classic symptoms of a self-doubting intellectual: depression, literary paralysis, self-hatred. In February 1922 he told Kencbok that he was undergoing a period of the most intense abomination of himself. That spring he explained that he simply felt things more intensely than others did. Moreover he was engaged in a battle against himself, not so much to embrace new values as to cast off the old. He had begun to read Nietzsche. Late that summer, in a letter dated 26 August 1922, he wrote to Kencbok: "In fact, however, society is divided into those who truly want reform and such people who, while making a few declarations, endeavor to maintain the old state of things. . . . The others are divided into two fundamental groups: those who want change at the cost of violent change—of battles *per fas et nefas* as a principle: the end justifies the means—and those who want to achieve those same goals via a legal, bloodless path, yet who do truly aspire to those goals. To this last group Piłsudski belongs.—My dear one. Life has ordered me to reflect upon whether that last path is the right one. . . . Until now I've taken the position of bloodless battle, but whether I'll maintain that position, whether life will allow me to—I don't know."[81]

The letters oscillated between fits of self-doubt and moments of supercilious arrogance. Broniewski's self-doubt was not without its own melodrama. On 24 November 1922 he wrote: "What do I—with all my weaknesses, my quasi-culture, quasi-talents, without willpower, without decided aspirations in a single direction, placing a question mark *above everything*—whatever in the world do I have to say to people? Perhaps to put a question mark over my own obituary?" He went on to compare himself to a weathervane—to function he must have air—let that air be love, passion, a noble idea, insanity, something other than nothingness. In this letter to Kencbok, Broniewski despaired that all he had done in his life had been the result of chance, contingency, external impulses. He craved change, innovation, action.[82] With these feelings, Broniewski drew closer to Wat's circle; in December 1922 he described his relations with them: "At 'Mała Ziemiańska' I've been meeting with a small group of writers from *Nowa Sztuka:* Stern, Wat, Braun, Brucz. All Yids. People of much intelligence and erudition. . . . I have benefited much from that—above all because I've become acquainted with the new Russian poetry. . . . Mayakovsky, the most important of them all, has revealed to me completely new worlds."[83]

By March 1923, under the influence of Mayakovsky, Broniewski had undergone a change—a new enthusiasm had healed his former despair, and he rejoiced in his newfound faith in the constancy of his ideas. He compared his former "individualism," his "egocentrism," to an old car: yes, he had been very attached to the old automobile, but it had broken down and was in a state of disrepair, useless and dysfunctional. He had finally accepted the necessity for separation. Now, he wrote, "I feel united with the whole world of people who—in one way or another—are moving forward. To where? But the point here is not the destination, but rather the path itself. The fight for a better, more beautiful life."[84]

Later that spring Broniewski's letters returned to literary matters. His new friend Mieczysław Braun from Łódź pointed out that Broniewski's poems were "lacking in what we call heart." Furthermore, Broniewski was reading Bruno Jasieński's poetry, and judged that Jasieński's recent poem "Pieśń o głodzie" (A Song about Hunger) would have seemed impressive—had Broniewski not already read Mayakovsky and so seen in Jasieński's work only imitation. Jasieński, they all saw, was a victim of his own uncanny memory for poetry. Broniewski was reminded of *Snobbism and Progress,* and the charge of imitation.[85]

By winter Broniewski had fallen into another depression, and he experienced another period of Hamletesque self-questioning. In November 1923 he wrote to Kencbok that he did not yet know how to live. By the following spring, he had clarified the problem: "It is necessary to believe in something, to love something, to be a fanatic about something."[86] He longed for simplicity, and simplicity was not what he was finding at Café Ziemiańska. Now Broniewski became very critical about the futurists whose ideas had been so revelatory to him the year before. In the same letter to Kencbok, he went on to say:

> I'm fed up with those Jewish literati from "Ziemiańska,"
> with whom I've had a lot to do lately (with the exception of
> Braun, whom I value and who is not in Warsaw). After closer

acquaintance, I've become convinced that these people have psyches very distant from my own. Here are the characteristic traits of their intellect: flashiness, quick development, false depth, and quick exhaustion. We Slavs have an intellect that's heavier, less imaginative and ethereal, but also heavier qualitatively and with a deeper, farther-flowing current. A fundamental relationship to truth in life, in creative work, in everything separates us from them. They are masters of outcry, of a noisy-gloomy passion entangled in itself, of boasting. A Slav always questions: in the name of what? to where? for what goal?— Yet they respond to those questions superficially or not at all.

Yet Broniewski cautioned Kencbok against assuming that his wariness of the Jewish literati implied that he had "turned to the right": "On the contrary," Broniewski wrote, "I'm intensely aware of the abyss that divides the past from the future, which is manifested in the example of the new creative work in Russia and the pitifully boring literary mustiness in Poland. I stand powerfully and deeply in new, revolutionary art. And I treat it seriously."[87]

Mieczysław Braun also encouraged Broniewski to stay away from Ziemiańska. In October 1923 Braun admitted to Broniewski in a letter that he had "dropped by that terrible city [Warsaw] only for a few hours and returned all the more quickly":[88]

Every, even the shortest, stay in Warsaw teaches me a lot and confirms me in my terribly unfortunate awareness that "surgunt indocti et rapiunt coelos!" Cloaca maxima of literature (literally as per Verlaine's sense of "literature," and not poetry) —Ziemiańska breathes poison on me with its badly disguised distaste and ill will—the cause of which is probably not difficult to ascertain.

I'm not speaking about true poets, to whom I'm connected by a more than heartfelt friendship, but rather about those whitened sepulchers, those insipid mediocrities, heads without talent, for whom everything is easy, who have an answer for everything, who sniff out and go after "catchy words" and "sayings," not knowing that it's necessary to mature into every poem, to reach the poem by hard, internal labor, who, finally, in the fact of the matter are equally as distant from poetry as they are from ethics.

I'm certain you understand me, Władzio. I have much faith in you and I can feel in you a poet—that is why I'm writing this to you, however well you know this yourself. I want to *warn* you against that awful atmosphere of literati and their bad literature, because I know that it's difficult not to suffocate in their fumes. I'm begging you in the most passionate manner, insofar as you have a self-preservation instinct as a poet, distance yourself from all of them. Don't go to Ziemiańska at all. Keep away.

CHAPTER TWO

Love and Revolution

Poetry is not a private matter.

—*Mieczysław Braun*

MIECZYSŁAW BRAUN CONCLUDED HIS May 1923 letter to Władysław Broniewski with the words: "Down with the decaying bourgeoisie! and down with the dull proletariat! Long live pure poetry!"[1] Yet the notion of the proletariat's dullness was quickly becoming unpopular. Bruno Jasieński, a year after his 1923 recantation of futurism, published a collection of poetry together with Anatol Stern titled *Ziemia na lewo* (The Earth to the Left). The cover, a collage by the young constructivist Mieczysław Szczuka, was a bizarre juxtaposition of photographs, including portraits of Stern and Jasieński, and in this sense was still very much within a futurist aesthetic.[2] In their introduction, in which they identified themselves as "former futurists," the authors revealed that much of their wrath against *passéisme* had shifted to bourgeois-ism:

> Poets, choose. The little salon of bourgeois culture sent by
> exotic, crumpled cushions of sentiment—or the naked street
> convulsing with birth pains. But even the historians of bour-
> geois culture themselves voice its decline. We are sensitive.
> And we mercifully desire to hurry its death, so as to raise a
> new foundation in a completely clean place. We hate the bour-
> geoisie—not only that which today obstructs our world with
> a shabby banknote—but the bourgeoisie as an abstraction,

its view of the world and everything that belongs to it.
We desire a new Poland—not a new store.

The Earth to the Left is the first volume of poetry in Poland
dedicated to the man of the masses, that hidden hero of
history.[3]

The publication of The Earth to the Left coincided with the collaboration of Wat, Stern, Broniewski and Jasieński with the Marxist journal
Nowa Kultura (New Culture). The editor of that endeavor, Jan Hempel,
was a committed Party member who had come to communism via theoso-
phy, anarcho-syndicalism, the PPS, and an unsuccessful search for God.[4]
Hempel's magazine had debuted a few months earlier, in July 1923, with
this programmatic introduction:

> "New Culture" is not an empty sound or a pretty-sounding
> phrase. The workers' movement, in its desire to realize the
> enormous act of its social and economic liberation, must create
> new cultural values. . . . Today it is still difficult to define the
> day of the victory and wonderful rise of a truly new civilization,
> created by the collective efforts of the boundless popular
> masses, so long kept in darkness, steeped in ignorance, given
> over as prey to prejudices and superstitions. . . . What of the
> fact that the building of the new cultural world meets with so
> many difficulties? What of the fact that one establishment after
> another falls under blows? What of the fact that in Cyprian
> Norwid's expression—against a few thoughts so many threat-
> ening forces and weapons are mobilized? We believe that the
> seed has not fallen on stony ground, that it will sprout in abun-
> dance and astound the world with its fruits. We believe that
> the longing for new shores and the gathered will of the multi-
> tudes are precisely that wind that turns the cards of history.[5]

It was through Władysław Broniewski that the futurists became involved
with Nowa Kultura, an alliance Wat named "that Ark of the Covenant."[6]
Broniewski had met Hempel, Stanisław Ryszard Stande, and Witold Wandurski in 1922, through the People's University, an organization of leftist
intellectuals who wished to bring socialist culture to the masses.[7] By then
Stande was already a Party member. His poetry, and that of Mieczysław

FIGURE 5 Cover of *The Earth to the Left*. Designed by Mieczysław Szczuka; reproduction by Biblioteka Narodowa.

Braun, appeared in *Nowa Kultura* in August and September 1923, before official collaboration commenced; and Witold Wandurski contributed a long article on the Workers' Theater in Łódź as early as August 1923.[8] The article was as pointed a revelation of Wandurski's graphomania as it was of his subject position vis-à-vis the proletariat. On one hand Wandurski acknowledged the theatrical collective's artistic gaps and weaknesses; on the other hand he glorified these gaps and weaknesses as evidence of proletarian authenticity.[9] His unconscious condescension towards "the workers" was even more striking in his next article. There he announced that the current intellectual level and aesthetic taste of workers left much to be desired. Yet Wandurski was not despondent, for this would inevitably change. Such was historical necessity.[10] This article was followed several issues later by Wandurski's poem "Do panów poetów" (To Messrs. Poets) in which he attacked café life and "independent creative work" with a Biblical reference: "Oh, independent hypocrisy! Freedoms of Onan! / How does it fail to disgust you, poets, this verbal masturbation?"[11]

In January 1924, formal collaboration with *Nowa Kultura* commenced. The magazine now took on a different appearance. Hempel was still writing many of the articles, but there were new voices as well. Appearing in the first issue of 1924 was Aleksander Wat's short story "Prowokator" (Agent Provocateur), a tale of forty-year-old Grzegorz, a former revolutionary and veteran of prison and hunger strikes, and now a professional provocateur informing on his former comrades, full of nostalgia for his Catholic childhood, longing for God's love, and searching for his true identity:

> Everything exists in dual form: good and evil, truth and false-
> hood, light and dusk, the policeman and the revolutionary.
> For how can there exist a higher perfection, a higher degree
> of existence than the connection of these two in one person,
> than their synthesis, than their unity, than a provocateur!
>   God—he thought further in an enraptured burst of passion
> —is the omnipotent creator of everything, and so falsehood
> as well as truth, evil as well as good. Evil, towards the greater
> victory of good, since the greater is the strength of evil,
> the greater the triumph of good. How then should I name
> the highest essence, if not a provocateur! how then should
> I name the whole world, if not an enormous provocation![12]

Grzegorz the provocateur fantasized about the end of the world. He envisioned an unending row of electric chairs, a policeman standing in front of each, a revolutionary sitting in each, and Grzegorz the provocateur himself, raised on the highest platform, preparing to ring a bell. When he did, each policeman pressed a button, and in each chair a revolutionary perished. Following this fantasy, Grzegorz became ecstatic over a plan to entice the whole of the revolutionary proletariat into committing terrorist acts so as to turn them all over to the police at the appropriate moment. He lured more and more revolutionaries into the world of terrorism, but the moment was still not right. Too late, he was awakened during the night by a banging at the door and was arrested. The verdict was execution. As he was being shot he imagined that the barrels of the rifles were aimed not at himself, but rather at the "highest provocateur, whose name is not uttered in vain."[13] Wat's story was neither futurist nor proletarian, but rather a metaphysical, absurdist parable about guilt, existential dilemmas, and making choices.

The following two issues included Wat's poem "Policjant" (The Police-man) and Stern's poem "Karnawały" (Carnivals), neither of which could be described as proletarian poetry, as well as translations of Apollinaire and Mayakovsky.[14] Several weeks later *Nowa Kultura* published a review of Stern and Jasieński's collection *The Earth to the Left;* and this more or less marked the end of the former futurists' presence in *Nowa Kultura*.[15] Jasieński was largely silent. He had been overcome by a creative crisis, a conviction that it was no longer possible to write as before.[16] While Jasieński was seeking out the classics of Marxism, something in the way of an epilogue to the futurists' contributions to Hempel's journal came in March 1924 with Mieczysław Braun's short piece titled "My Personal Opinion about Poetry." Here Braun insisted on the "independent creativ-ity" that Wandurski had just been mocking:

> I write about everything I must write about. Nothing limits
> my freedom: neither aesthetics, nor style nor proclivity. I am
> guided only by internal compulsion. . . . A poet is a parliamen-
> tary representative of human society, the difference in the
> metaphor being that society did not choose him. . . . In poetry
> there are no more important or less important themes. For
> instance, war or revolution can mean as much as the crowing
> of a rooster in the courtyard. . . . In society's battles the poet
> must stand on the side of the laboring branch of humanity.
> He himself works hard. He waits so many years for each word!
>   And the world is large: two words do not capture it.[17]

Hempel was displeased with Braun's declaration. Two issues later there appeared an article titled "Literary Misunderstandings," proclaiming the failure of the collaborative experiment, and attacking Braun in particu-lar for his bourgeois "programlessness" and absence of ideology vis-à-vis poetry. The verdict was the following:

Unfortunately it very quickly became evident that these pieces of writing were artistically incomprehensible to our readers. Not for the reason that they might be overly intelligent, rather simply for the reason that they are ideologically alien to the workers' movement. . . . A personal discussion with these poets, conducted because of their works, only manifested our differences still more powerfully. We spoke as if in different languages. They were entirely unable to understand what our point was and why we were not pleased with their work—thematically revolutionary, condemning war, religion and courts of justice. They judged that we were demanding that they write versified political slogans, they reproached us with a desire for dictatorship over poets and appealed to freedom of inspiration.

We, however, must only demand that a poet who wants to write for the working class live by the workers' ideals, think workers' thoughts, love and hate not only that which, but also in such a way as the worker loves and hates. Then nothing (except—of course—the Press Department of the police) will limit his inspiration.[18]

Hempel, obedient to the Party, severed ties with the futurists; and Broniewski was replaced by Hempel's comrade, the KPP member Witold Kolski.[19]

Braun had been skeptical about the alliance between Hempel and the poets from the outset. In December 1923 he wrote to Broniewski inquiring whether, in the end, they had all decided to cast in their lot with *Nowa Kultura*.[20] In January Braun wrote that, thanks to Wandurski, he had read in *Nowa Kultura* a wonderful story by Wat. Braun had not been "disillusioned," he wrote to Broniewski, by the results of Broniewski's plans for an artistic takeover of that venture; yet at the same time he expressed his doubts that ultimately such an alliance could succeed, and insisted to Broniewski that "they"—those who are "foreign to our aspirations"—had not given the poets a free space to work. "Do you plan to continue to busy yourself with the 'smuggling' of poetry?" Braun asked.[21] And when Broniewski's experiment did reveal itself to be extremely short-lived, Braun did not fail to say "I told you so." A month later, he reminded Broniewski that he had warned everyone against such collaboration. In any case, he was glad it was now over. With respect to Hempel and his KPP comrades, Braun wrote of their "complete lack of respect for intellectual work, and a blatant disregard for poetic creation. Our marriage, as you say, was a *mésalliance* on both sides."[22]

Not everyone had been ill-disposed towards this collaborative project. In 1924 from Łódź, Witold Wandurski had begun a prolific correspondence with Broniewski. Unlike Braun, Wandurski had been a great enthusiast for Broniewski's collaboration with *Nowa Kultura*. He wrote to Broniewski in January 1924: "each issue of *Nowa Kultura* that reaches me brings me true joy."[23] It was another case of fiery enchantment and quick disillusionment. By May 1924, Wandurski lamented the pervasiveness of pseudo-Marxists from "pseudo-new culture" and had forgotten his previous enthusiasm:

> What you're saying does not astonish me at all . . . yet we've all known about this for a long time. We had only deluded ourselves that we would be successful at changing something for the better. . . . In short, and practically stated—what remains for us is "splendid isolation." . . . I've become disillusioned with the people from *Nowa Kultura* not only in a literary-artistic sense, but also politically. There can be no talk of the revolutionariness of those bookish know-it-alls: they're cool-headed theoreticians who—en route to intellectual ardor—accepted the program of the communists. Yet intellectually not only are they not Bolshevized, but they also fear any kind of truly revolutionary catastrophe . . . like the devil fears holy water. . . . None of them want to understand that revolution is a painful tragedy, a glorious fire, in which you must burn yourself, descend into savagery, into barbarism—in order to discover in yourself the simple joy of life. . . . All of it of course—and first and foremost the rabbinical confinement of intellectual (I'm no longer saying—aesthetic) horizons pushed me away from those people and from communism. Presently I've become very much interested in theoretical anarchism (as organically I've always been an anarchist)—a synthesis of cooperative communalism with individualism.[24]

In 1924 the former futurists also contributed to Stefan Kordian Gacki's new *Almanach Nowej Sztuki* (Almanac of New Art), which continued into 1925 and survived for four issues. Yet by that time Polish futurism was well past its half-life. Even as the futurists participated in *Almanach Nowej Sztuki,* it was a time when, according to Wat, "our group of futurists and dadaists got fed up with futurism, that is, when we came to the conclusion that things couldn't go on like that."[25] Thus, following their disengagement from *Nowa Kultura,* did the futurists set out upon different paths. Braun rebelled against both proletarian poetry and the avant-garde, telling Broniewski in January 1925 that he was now writing in a classical style: "Today I'm at a new stage. Nothing connects me to the so-called new art. I'm reaching out to other places for 'models.' I'm writing classically. I don't care at all about the gains of futurism, Russian poetry is alien to me; Mayakovsky, Esenin, Apollinaire fell somewhere into a void and utterly disappeared for me."[26] Wat wrote a collection of short stories titled *Bezrobotny Lucyfer* (Lucifer Unemployed), which he dedicated to Ola Lew as a wedding gift. The stories were parabolic, anti-utopian and nihilist—departing from futurist phonetic experiments and dadaistic self-referentiality, but also betraying no traces of ideological engagement. Rather Wat portrayed a historical moment in which all previously understood values and notions of order had suddenly been subjected to radical contingency, a radical contingency demanding a radical antidote.

In Wat's story "Żyd wieczny tułacz" (The Eternally Wandering Jew), Nathan, an orphaned Talmudic student from the shtetl Zebrzydowo, traveled through all of Europe to America in search of his benefactor, the rich Baron Gould. The story was framed by the refrain, "there is always mud in Zebrzydowo," and set during a moment when Europe stood poised at the edge of an abyss: "cannibalistic, impoverished, mystical, sadistic, prostituted."[27] In New York, now as Baron Gould's secretary, Nathan conceived of the ideal social world as one that reconciled communism and Catholicism. He insisted that the Jews must convert to Catholicism *en masse;* and the yeshiva student himself became Pope. The story ended hundreds of years later, when the last antisemites came upon Zebrzydowo. There they converted to Judaism and restored the ancient Hebraic traditions. The circular structure of "The Eternally Wandering Jew" read against all Hegelian narratives of History. Ultimately there was no telos—and no exit.

LOVE LETTERS

It was around this time that Władysław Broniewski made the acquaintance of Janina Kunig in Kalisz, having arrived in her hometown "already surrounded with the halo of being 'our poet.'" Janina Kunig and her friends "were embarrassed by the popularity preceding him and above all by his age, for he was twenty-six. A Legionnaire, a reserve captain, impossibly mature."[28] In a soft voice, he commanded his young audience to listen—and he read them his revolutionary poem "Pionierom" (To the Pioneers), ending with the stanzas:

> So what if they're stomping? So what if they're strong?
> So what that their rifle butts have crushed faces?
> Towards the wall—head first. Heart leaping.
> Bastille Day—victorious—marches on.
>
> Let them pound your chest—it will not break.
> Close your mouth, though inside is blood . . .
> There will be brighter, more beautiful days,
> there will be joy and there will be song.[29]

When Broniewski had finished reading there was a long silence. The young Janina Kunig felt that "any word after that poem could only be a banality."[30]

Afterwards Broniewski sent Janina Kunig flowers and a postcard from a hotel. Through Broniewski she met Stande and Wandurski, who seemed to her even more adult than Broniewski. Their courtship grew more serious, and there followed a period of deliberately not seeing one another as a final test of their feelings. In the absence of visits, there were letters—filled with the language and characters of Stefan Żeromski's novels. The letters, opening with a plethora of versions of diminutives of her name, drew upon aristocratic, antiquated Polish. Broniewski's first letter to Janina, dated 24 July 1925, began "To My Gracious and Revered Young Lady!" He had been thinking of her entirely too often.[31] Two days later: "I'm writing to you on a Saturday night. I cannot sleep, I'm pacing about the apartment, lying down on various pieces of furniture, and constantly, constantly thinking of you." He had recently reread all of her letters, he told her: "I experienced them again, I recalled how I had read them with anger and regret, how I was grieved in an irrational and childish way,

and again how they awakened in me an insane joy, likewise not terribly justified and childish. Ah, I will not philosophize any longer on that
theme! I know only one thing: I want to be with you—yet this devout wish
clarifies nothing. Perhaps in general I'm hovering on the border of some
kind of monstrously amusing arrogance."[32]

In February 1926 Broniewski responded to Janina's apparent comment that their deliberate separation was purposeless. He vowed not to
give up her love, not to be satisfied with only her friendship. And yet—for
his own self-respect, he insisted—he wanted to remain pure. He relished
the drama of self-restraint, of ostensible selflessness, and wished for nothing banal, ordinary, vulgar to taint their romanticism. Beneath it all, as
this letter disclosed, lurked his reluctance to be married: "I wish you
happiness, regardless of what kind of fate awaits me as part of that. You've
rightly observed that something hostile is coming into being between us
against the background of the fact that internally, I have not agreed to all
that today plays the greatest role in your happiness—yet neither you nor
I can do otherwise. And rightly: Your feelings, in which I believe, are honest and strong, yet you should protect them even against the thought of
someone else, even against yourself. You should cultivate them in yourself,
enlarge and ennoble them."[33]

Janina Kunig responded to his lavish romanticism with some guilt,
writing in March 1926: "I have something to say to you: namely, why do
you spoil me so? I look at these flowers and think, how have I deserved
this? More bad than good has come to you from me and it makes me feel
terribly stupid, as usual, when I accept something undeserved. I have
the impression that I'm exploiting your feelings for me in a distasteful
way."[34]

Broniewski's letters reflected a remarkable constancy of feeling during that first year of their epistolary courtship. By August he had decided
to marry Janina. That month he received a glowing letter from Irena Krzywicka, full of praise for his decision. Krzywicka added that, despite her
frequent solo travels about the world, she valued her marriage tremendously and regarded life as a couple as a beautiful thing.[35] In September
1926 Broniewski wrote: "Jaśka! So you truly love me? You write of that
with such joy and . . . I feel the truth of your words! Listen to me, I am
going insane with joy. I don't know how to tell you, I don't know how to
write to you how much this means to me. Your love is for me the condition

of everything . . . for it I'm prepared to do anything, to exert the greatest efforts, to make sacrifices, even to commit crimes, if that were necessary for you. Only now do I feel that I am alive, that I can do something, that I want to live and that life makes me so happy. Everything in me is awakening as in spring."[36]

Yet something had happened during their separation: a woman in Cracow was pregnant with Broniewski's child. Now Broniewski's tone, once so lofty and refined, became harsh, almost crude: "With K . . . it's quite strange. After my arrival I found several letters, which I answered very explicitly in a negative sense, although I didn't yet write about you. As soon as I had sent that letter, I received yet another one by express, which distinguished itself by two kinds of threats: first, that she will harm herself, and secondly, that she will not liquidate you-know-what. This letter I haven't answered . . . The most amusing thing is that in this last letter she called me a seducer—a great exaggeration, who really seduced whom here?" Broniewski went on to write of other topics; he seemed confident of Janina Kunig's support. He ended by reminding her: "Forgive me in advance, if I repeat too often that I love you like a lunatic and in no way can I live without you."[37]

Janina Kunig was tolerant (or perhaps, rather, forgiving) of this development. The following day Broniewski wrote to her: "Demand from me what you want, even the worst lunacy, so that I would know I am nothing to you, so that I would hear from you that incomprehensible, wonderful word: I love. Look, it's never been this way with me! There's something unheard of in my present feelings for you—it's greater than love, it's some kind of union, fused into one person, it seems to me that I think and feel through you. I'm writing this to you, you exasperating girl, so that you'll know of your 'importance' to me and do with that what you wish, even if it were to be to defend yourself against me."[38] Despite his decision, Broniewski's hesitancy to marry lingered, even as he reassured the object of his affection that there was no reason for her to be concerned with the fate of the woman in Cracow.

> Jasiek, you write that I should marry you as soon as possible, because you fear some kind of change. I'm not worried about changes: with me it's out of the question, and I have so much faith in you, perhaps even more than you deserve (a wealth of

experiences). I believe you that you love me, finally, with serious, enduring emotion, and if that faith deceives me, then let
happen what will. . . . Don't think about Cracow, Jasiula. Nothing can any longer happen there that would change us. There
remains only regret, and it's best to forget that. These matters
grate on me a bit: that woman continually threatens that she
won't go to Poronin. Yesterday I wrote her a thick letter (after
a four-day silence), in which I conducted an analysis of the
entire relationship. In conclusion I demanded categorically that
she liquidate the known projects, threatening that if she does
not I don't want to hear anything about her and I'll take the
child, though by force. . . . One way or another, these matters
haven't the slightest influence on me. They only irritate me.
I'm feeling a bit unwell.[39]

In November, a friend of Janina Kunig wrote to Broniewski, urging
him to marry Janina as soon as possible.[40] Broniewski's grandmother,
Jadwiga Lubowidzka, was not pleased by this prospect: Janina Kunig was
not a Catholic and the wedding would not take place in a Catholic church.[41]
She wrote an inflamed letter to her grandson. She had been aware that
he was no longer a practicing Catholic, "but that you would forget—at
such an important moment, a decisive one for the future of your entire
life, my beloved Władzio, that I cannot comprehend. I know that your
mother is also opposed, and does the sacred memory of your father and
grandfather mean nothing to you?"[42] Jadwiga Lubowidzka's wishes were
ignored. In December 1926 Broniewski and Janina Kunig were married;
on 27 December 1926 he wrote his first letter to her as her husband.[43] Soon
afterwards, he brought his young wife to Warsaw, where Irena Krzywicka
befriended her. It was, from the beginning, a difficult marriage.[44]

A PROLIFIC MANIA

The mid-1920s were a time of many changes for Broniewski: his marriage,
his debut as a proletarian poet, and his increasingly close friendship with
Witold Wandurski. After being arrested by the Bolshevik Cheka in Ukraine
in 1920, Wandurski had made his way back to Poland in 1921.[45] Following
his return to Łódź he composed a beautiful album of photographs, poetry,
and prose for his young daughter. He showed it to Irena Krzywicka, who

was touched by the fatherly love and the artistic sophistication.[46] To Broniewski, however, Wandurski spoke not of his little girl but of revolution. In July 1924 Wandurski wrote to Broniewski suggesting that they should have "drunk to their brotherhood" long ago and begun addressing each other by first name. He enclosed a poem he had dedicated to Broniewski and inquired as to the latest developments at the "literary-artistic market at Ziemiańska."[47] Wandurski's letters were long, manic, eager for replies. On 12 February 1925 he wrote, "You're as silent as a yogi. What's happened to you?"[48] Broniewski now answered quickly, and several days later, on 17 February 1925, Wandurski responded to Broniewski's resumed state of depression with a discussion of "joy," the new key word in this post-futurist-proto-Marxist era of these writers' lives:

> There is no joy in you—regardless of your great reserve of
> masculine strength, which others lack. Of course, joy cannot
> be dispensed by a prescription; one arrives there organically.
> . . . I'm already on the path. Joy gives me the conviction that
> I'm disposed with my entire being towards life, towards every-
> thing that matures, that fights for its right to existence, that is
> healthy, manly . . . (I'm now a decided atheist. It happened
> somehow suddenly and unexpectedly—and gave me a feeling
> of extraordinary joy and freedom.) I'm living wonderfully—
> not so much in material terms, perhaps, as in the sense of a
> physical frame of mind. I know that I'm maturing. I know that
> I'm a true futurist-constructivist: that means: all the force of
> my decision is directed towards the future—and the present
> is only a joyful ladder towards the approaching future.[49]

By April 1925 Wandurski was preparing his play "Śmierć na gruszy" (Death on a Pear-Tree) for the Workers' Theater in Łódź, and was rumored to be a "dangerous communist."[50] Little pleased him more, and in his letters he referred to police informers with ill-concealed pride. The attention was uplifting. "Prove to them that you're not a camel," Wandurski wrote to Broniewski in Russian, in reference to the impossibility of convincing the Polish police that he was innocent of revolutionary activity. "I'm writing this to you so that you'll be careful. The gentlemen-policemen weren't pleased by your last letter, they even wanted to take it with them, but—since they were tired—they somehow forgot about it and I destroyed it." He concluded with an allusion to Broniewski's poem "To the Pioneers": "Just a little bit more, a little more, and 'there will be brighter and more beautiful days, there will be joy and there will be song.'"[51]

Yet even as Wandurski was embracing his new reputation as a danger to the state, he remained unable to embrace fully the revolution in Russia. In a June 1925 interview, Wandurski discussed plans for a new play about "the problem of contemporary culture and the tragic quality of revolution." He was, alas, convinced that even if he should complete the work as he wanted to, neither in Poland nor in Russia would theaters want to perform it—in the former case out of consideration for "order and public safety," in the latter case due to its "very critical relationship towards revolution."[52] At the same time, Wandurski was working towards revolution on his own terms. While consumed with his role in the Workers' Theater, Wandurski also found time to co-author a collection of revolutionary poetry together with Władysław Broniewski and Stanisław Ryszard Stande. *Trzy Salwy* (Three Salvos) appeared in 1925. The poets wrote in their introduction: "We are not writing about ourselves. We are workers of the word. We must express that which other people of the workbench cannot express. In the proletariat's merciless battle with the bourgeoisie we stand decidedly on the left side of the barricade. Anger, faith in victory, and joy—the joy of battle—command us to write. Let our words fall like salvos on the downtown streets, let them thunder with an echo in factory districts. We are fighting for a new social order. Battle is the highest content of our creative work."[53]

Broniewski's grandmother was little pleased. She was, in fact, happy with very little about her grandson's life since he had left the army. In 1925 she wrote to him from his hometown of Płock: "And now, my Władzio, as for your poetic creations—after having read them, I wept bitterly. I spilled many tears during your time at war (I am writing of this for the first time), but those were tears of concern about your life and safety—these tears are entirely different and very painful. I know that you have little faith, but that you would blaspheme against sanctities, that you would be capable of this—that I never expected. It's true that people in Płock told me that you were "very progressive," but I had understood that differently."[54] Others were more admiring, and Broniewski began to receive letters from the aspiring proletarian poet Stanisław Wygodzki in the gloomy town of Będzin.[55] The correspondence began in late 1925, during Wygodzki's early

FIGURE 6 The authors of *Three Salvos*. Left to right: Stanisław Ryszard Stande, Władysław Broniewski, Witold Wandurski. Courtesy of Muzeum Władysława Broniewskiego.

imprisonment for communism. He addressed Broniewski formally, in the third person, and enclosed his poems written in prison for Broniewski's evaluation.[56] By his next letter, Wygodzki was addressing Broniewski in the communist and socialist style of the second person plural.[57] The letters continued steadily throughout 1926, as Wygodzki was released from prison and then imprisoned again. He fell into depressions, alternating between expressions of enormous gratitude and desperate pleas for responses —which were often slow in coming.

Stanisław Wygodzki was not alone in experiencing difficult periods. By November 1925 both Wandurski and Broniewski had lapsed again into depressions. "You're depressed?" Wandurski wrote, "So am I."[58] At the same time, Wandurski had become very popular, and wrote a week later, "If you only knew what pilgrimages have reached me every day since the publication of *Three Salvos*. How many shoemakers, lathe-hands, weavers, electricians."[59] Of course, they liked the introduction the best. Stande was—Wandurski emphasized—too difficult for them to understand, "not Polish enough." *Three Salvos* was being passed around at labor union meetings; who—asked Wandurski—among the Skamander poets could say the same?[60] Wandurski continued to oscillate between self-congratulatory rapture and intense depression. In January 1926 Wandurski learned of the young Russian poet Sergei Esenin's suicide, and his mood descended once again. "He couldn't accept a sober Marxist relationship to reality," Wandurski wrote. Esenin, he told Broniewski, had been too much of a romantic, never a real communist. The letter was full of pity. Wandurski insisted that Broniewski write about "the poor fellow" in the next issue of *Wiadomości Literackie*, and reminded him that of all the Russian poets, it was Esenin who was closest to Broniewski, no one had translated him so well as Broniewski. "I feel depressed myself, as after the loss of a close friend," Wandurski wrote.[61]

A few weeks later came an epiphany. On 22 January 1926, in a long letter to Broniewski from Łódź, Wandurski exclaimed that he had searched through his "spiritual baggage" and found that something was not right with him. He spent too much time with pen and paper, and true knowledge and maturity would come only in praxis, in engagement. Now he had found revelation and catharsis.

> Simply put, I'm lacking knowledge and maturity of thought.
> Both the first and the second are available for acquisition.
> But they're to be acquired in *active work*, in battle—not in lazy
> contemplation, in the closet of one's own room, at one's desk.
> At least for those with natures such as mine—aggressive,
> agitated—this is the only path.
>   You speak about some kind of "danger," about the fact
> that conforming to people of Hempel's type can very quickly
> destroy me inside—I've considered that—and I've come to
> the conclusion that this is only self-deception.—First and fore-
> most, I'm conforming not to "people," but to the cause, I'm
> actively entering the workers' movement. . . . My obligation—
> *and aspiration*—like yours, and Staszek's [Stande]—is to make
> that movement *powerful and valuable*. And that is only possible
> when a person of our type (that means a stagnated and stub-
> born "individualist") wholly and without reservations conforms
> to the *general* line, to general discipline, when he becomes

thoroughly acquainted with the program and work method,
when he becomes active in the general movement—and only
then does he have the right to be in the opposition, naturally,
an opposition of a tactical nature, relatively, substantially. *Such
an opposition can be creative.* Our present "intellectually independent" position is only masked intellectual opportunism,
lack of decisiveness, distaste for discipline, avoidance of effort,
appeasement. . . . Yes, appeasement!. . . . But negation alone
will not get you far. Two roads lead from negation of the actual
state of things: the road towards the past and the road towards
the future, to Catholicism and to communism. Our entire
"freedom," our "independence" lies in "freedom of choice,"
nothing more. It's necessary, finally, to choose one of the
extremes—and to oscillate around that extreme. Everything
else—is self-hypocrisy, remnants of romantic-literary supersti-
tions, the rebellion of a "poetic individualist." . . . I want *content.* I want *life.* Knowledge. Joy—joy! direct joy! With what
pleasure I've returned now to the bed of the river that I swam
when I was 17–19! . . . I'm *learning.* I want to be a true *futurist.*
. . . You write: where are the new aesthetics, law, ethics?—
Where—In our head—and in our activity. *We* have to create
them—through direct contact with the workers' movement.
As ordinary soldiers of class war. . . . As of several days ago
I am now formally the secretary of the Leather Workers' Union
and the Construction Workers' Union—two of the "reddest."
And I feel wonderful.[62]

Wandurski concluded with an attack on *Wiadomości Literackie,* among
others on Stern and Grydzewski (whom Wandurski sarcastically called
"arch-Polish" and referred to by his former name Grycendler): "The kikes
are now outright cynically causing problems and playing sanctimonious
hypocrites."[63]

Thought, feeling, knowledge came in action, Wandurski now knew.
He reminisced nostalgically about 1917, the year of the Revolution, the
most beautiful time of his life, the moment that brought him to writing.
He had come to the conclusion that he could not exist outside the Revolution. He was ready to fight—and reminded Broniewski that when the

moment had come, Broniewski had not pondered for long but rather had taken his gun and gone to join the Legions. Wandurski had never been in the army, thus far he had been "a slouch." But no more. As for his friend's reservations about "dialectical materialism," they were exaggerated. Historical materialism was only a method. After all, did Kantians or Hegelians abdicate their freedom of thought? The entire realm of emotions remained open. Wandurski was certain that once Broniewski became more closely acquainted with the dialectical method, he would come to appreciate this for himself.

A month later, on 17 February 1926, Witold Wandurski was arrested. This time he was released on the same day, and seemed not in the slightest bad humor about the arrest. He was terribly busy, and his work had put him in an elevated mood. "Today I no longer feel alone," he wrote on 19 February 1926, "My connection with the proletariat is becoming more powerful, more heartfelt with each passing day. . . . Today I know what I want. I know how to speak and what to say." As for the literary scene at Ziemiańska, he had become still more dismissive. It was all "awful stuffiness and stench." Worse—and now he switched to Russian—"in general it's an empty place, the hole in the bagel." This did not surprise Wandurski. After all, "life is only on the *left* side."[64] Before long Wandurski began to notice undercover police informers following him—and he took great pleasure in unmasking them. Upon spotting them, he would call out "Something stinks!" and hold his nose.[65] Wandurski was full of plans in that spring of 1926. He was confident that he could produce authentically proletarian art, poetry, literature, theater. He had written a play for the Workers' Theater and he was convinced that it was truly proletarian, truly Polish, not an imitation. Furthermore, he had a wonderful group of workers at the Workers' Theater. Of twenty-three members in the collective, he reported happily to Broniewski, only three or four were Jews![66]

In May 1926, Marshal Józef Piłsudski came to power in a coup and Poland became an effective dictatorship, albeit initially a relatively benign one. Julian Tuwim and his friends were among Piłsudski's supporters. Piłsudski had been a patron of literature in the early days of Polish independence, and Antoni Słonimski remembered fondly the Piłsudski of the Pod Pikadorem era. This was the Piłsudski who agreed to let the young poets perform their satirical cabaret at the government's Belweder Palace, the

Piłsudski who canceled cabinet meetings so that the poets could use that room as their performance space. This was the Piłsudski who was not insulted by the satire that did not spare him as the object of its jokes, and who afterwards fed the young cabaret poets pastries.[67] In May 1926, the Communist Party of Poland, under Adolf Warski's leadership and in accordance with current Comintern policy, made the decision to endorse Piłsudski's coup. Many of Wandurski's workers then facilitated the coup's success by means of a transit strike.[68]

Yet in his letters to Broniewski, Wandurski appeared too self-absorbed to pay Piłsudski's coup much attention. By that summer he had still more plans, for a Club of Proletarian Cultural Workers, for an almanac, for a nationwide social-artistic organization that would be part of the international workers' movement.[69] An era of "unengaged" artistic experimentation had drawn to a close. In summer of 1926, Anatol Stern declared that poetry had become an anachronism.[70] In the very last issue of 1926, *Wiadomości Literackie* published a retrospective of the café Pod Pikadorem, with reminiscences by the Skamander poets. Antoni Słonimski even set aside his usual sarcasm and wrote nostalgically of autumn 1918 when Warsaw emerged as the capital of newly independent Poland, and when "the words 'freedom,' 'independence,' 'Poland,' 'communism,' and 'revolution' did not contain a shadow of the gray quotidian or even disillusionment or discouragement—we were full of enthusiasm, strength and hope. On the evening when Pikador first opened the entire elite of contemporary Warsaw was gathered there."[71] It had been a time when the young Skamander poets held the country in their hands, when the young avant-garde was overwhelmed by the simultaneous sense of the ending of the old world and the endlessness of present possibilities. This lasted only for a moment. In December 1926 Julian Tuwim felt acutely the change in atmosphere:[72] "Futurism! New art! How tiresome they are today and how new and attractive it all was then!"

CHAPTER THREE

A Visit from Mayakovsky

For the first impression that he made was precisely this:
an impression of enormity.

—*Anatol Stern on Mayakovsky*

IN 1928, WITOLD WANDURSKI at last found himself in prison. There
he felt liberated from all previous anxieties and depressions. Time passed
quickly; he had never felt better. In April he wrote to Broniewski: "I've made
many valuable observations here, I've acquired much experience—and in
general I've enriched my psychological capital. Presently I am convinced
that for a proletarian writer a stay in prison—just like a stay in a hospital
or work in the labor unions—is simply essential, practically imperative."[1]
Prison had given Wandurski new confidence, and he spoke to Broniewski
now with a sense of heightened status:

> It is precisely now—and precisely from here—that I could take
> the floor in the polemic over proletarian poetry. The prisoners
> are—in spite of the opinion of various Hulkas—intensely
> and particularly interested in that issue—and the percentage
> of workers in our prison is around 70 percent. . . . The three
> of us, our work has been subjected to harsh and material
> criticism.—Recently there occurred an interesting incident.
> I'm in a cell with two workers. I'm teaching them. During a
> geography lesson I read them an ancient Egyptian prayer to
> the Nile, which evoked sincere admiration and several obser-
> vations so cogent, that I was amazed at my student's (a weaver

from Pabianice) vigilance towards beauty. They relate to me
in a straightforward manner, warm and very friendly. We laugh
a lot, we poke fun at one other—but we also converse seriously.
In general the mood is wonderful, manly and sober.[2]

Wandurski was not Broniewski's only epistolary contact with the world
behind prison walls. Stanisław Wygodzki, the aspiring poet from Będzin,
had also found himself incarcerated once again and was not in such good
spirits. For Wygodzki prison was all too familiar; it was uninteresting and
gray; the cell was crowded; conditions for creative work were abysmal.[3]
Broniewski was slow to reply, and by February 1927 Wygodzki was pleading for some word from the poet, and in particular an assessment of his
poems. The uncertainty, especially in this vulnerable situation, was destroying Wygodzki, paralyzing him.[4] In April Wygodzki wrote that he had
been delaying writing this next letter, waiting until he had some stronger,
better work to enclose, work that would reveal his soul to the more senior
poet. "I remain under your influence," he informed Broniewski, "and I
have no scruples about that, as I regard you as an artist of the new ideological school, despite the fact that [stylistically] you're a Skamandrite."[5] On
May Day Wygodzki and his comrades in prison had recited Broniewski's
poetry. "If we were to be released at this moment," Wygodzki told him,
"sixty agitators would carry news throughout the Basin of the existence of
proletarian, revolutionary, powerful, joyous poetry."[6] Now Broniewski did
respond with a postcard; and Wygodzki was very grateful, he had feared
that the older poet had forgotten about him.[7] Yet afterwards Broniewski
was silent again for a time, willing to answer Wygodzki only after his release from prison in late 1927.[8] Wygodzki was angry and hurt, yet his tone
remained deferential. By January 1928 all seemed to have been forgiven,
and Wygodzki asked Broniewski for permission to translate some of his
poems into Yiddish.[9] That year Wygodzki made his own contribution to
literary polemics with an article in *Wiadomości Literackie* about the tasks
presently facing Polish poetry.[10] Anatol Stern was displeased. In Stern's
opinion, Wygodzki was himself not terribly well read, and had ignored,
among other works, Jasieński's and Stern's own *The Earth to the Left*, mis-
dating Polish proletarian poetry from the appearance of *Three Salvos*.[11]

Broniewski himself continued to suffer from insecurity, despite the
legendary aura he was acquiring. Once, after Broniewski had given a

poetry reading for some leftist students, one of them asked the poet what he had been doing years earlier when he had fought for Piłsudski against the Bolsheviks. Another student shouted at the first to be quiet, but a third agreed that Broniewski should account for his actions. "And is it not enough," Broniewski answered his audience, "that I am with you now?" Broniewski's student admirers felt then the painful loneliness of the poet they adored.[12] Yet Broniewski was about to become less alone in the world than ever before. In November 1929, Janina Broniewska gave birth to their daughter, Anka. It was a transformative moment for Broniewski, who now embraced fatherhood from its first moments. Of Anka's birth Janina Broniewska wrote, "And here most likely began the greatest, most important love in Władek's life. Love at first sight, his most faithful and most enduring love—for Anka."[13]

COLLABORATIVE VENTURES

The failed *Nowa Kultura* was not the last attempt at collaboration between the avant-garde and the Polish Communist Party. When the next project came into being, the dynamics of collaboration were quite different. By this time the literary critic Andrzej Stawar, surrounded "by the myth of the worker-autodidact," had joined Broniewski, Stande, and Wat. Stawar was rare among the now fellow-traveling writers in the depth of his knowledge about Marxism and in having begun his intellectual life as a communist.[14] The journal, named *Dźwignia* (The Lever), was an alliance between writers leaning towards Marxism and constructivists in the visual arts, in particular the husband and wife Mieczysław Szczuka and Teresa Żarnowerówna, who conceived of the journal as a vehicle for propagating revolution through art. *Dźwignia*, whose first issue appeared in March 1927, did not on the surface look so different from *Nowa Kultura;* yet now control had shifted: the Party member Jan Hempel was only a contributor, while the influence of Stawar and the fellow-traveling poets was most pronounced. Wat became involved through Stawar.[15] *Dźwignia's* programmatic statement of March 1927 defined its purpose:

> The task of *Dźwignia* is to gather those cultural workers
> (writers, artists, etc.) who base themselves on the aspirations
> of the contemporary proletariat. There are considerably more
> such people in Poland today than it might seem, but they are

scattered and isolated. Our publication is intended to connect them, to focus their efforts. It is intended as well to orient the reader amidst the chaos of bourgeois culture's present decay and to point the way to the creation of new values.

We are fully aware of the preparatory character of our work, as well as of the meager possibilities for realizing our activities in the framework of the present order of things. We are working for the future with the complete feeling that the future belongs to us and that at some point, in conditions of complete freedom, we will conduct our work incomparably more broadly and more efficaciously.[16]

Dźwignia published poems by Stande and Jasieński, as well as translations of Vladimir Mayakovsky. There were long-winded and self-righteous pieces by Wandurski, including an article on the Workers' Theater in Łódź. Wandurski also published an attack on the Russian novelist Ilya Ehrenburg (who that year visited Tuwim in Warsaw) enclosing his "revolutionary-ness" sarcastically in quotation marks. In his article on Ehrenburg, Wandurski coined the term *erenburszczyzna*—that is, literature characterized by "perverse necrophilia, the quasi-philosophy of Smerdiakov from *The Brothers Karamazov,* bourgeois vindictiveness." Wandurski drew attention to Ehrenburg's origins as the son of a Jewish merchant.[17]

Andrzej Stawar's voice was most prominent. He, the one who was not a poet himself, was the star, the most sophisticated writer. A literary critic, Stawar passed judgment on his friends. He wrote that of the three authors of *Three Salvos,* Broniewski "undoubtedly demonstrated the greatest lyrical force and the least consistent social feeling."[18] Stawar believed that in the postwar era, prose had fallen incomparably far behind poetry, a crisis revealing the primitive nature of literary culture in Poland. Stawar's understanding of dialectical materialism was his own; and he made no pretenses either of ingratiating himself with the Party or of speaking to the working class from which he himself had emerged.[19] In another article Stawar analyzed "ostentatiously and proudly emphasized Westernness" as a bourgeois slogan, a bourgeois construct allowing for the use of East versus West as a naïve opposition of two worlds: black and white, evil versus good: "The Westernness of Poland, Poland's belonging to the West, constitutes one of the favorite motifs of ideological reflections by representatives of the Polish bourgeois intelligentsia," he wrote.[20] This came at a moment when *Wiadomości Literackie,* while not alienating itself from Russia, was embracing a European cosmopolitanism and even beginning to publish occasional issues in French under the title *La Pologne Littéraire.*

Survival was difficult for *Dźwignia;* and Janina Broniewska felt the criticism from the Left most painfully. In her reading, some of this leftist criticism came from neophytes, and some from Marxists who attacked Broniewski and his friends for a lack of orthodoxy. Stawar pointed to the opening line of Broniewski's "To the Pioneers"—"If your heart in your chest is too heavy / open your chest, tear out your heart"—with the criticism that a real worker did not have to tear out his heart, even symbolically.[21] Moreover, there was repression from the state. In April 1927, Broniewski wrote to his wife, "I don't know why or what for, but today the police came to Hipoteczna Street looking for me. I'm supposing from this that a search awaits me, and who knows if not arrest. I don't have reason to worry about all that, but everything is possible before the first of May."[22]

It was around this time that someone ran into Café Ziemiańska, distraught by the unanticipated news that Adam Ważyk, who had kept his distance from *Dźwignia,* had been arrested during the night. Janina Broniewska was shocked: "Pugnacious Adam Ważyk, the poet, the chess player, a great chum, but at that time still quite far from being engaged in the cause and distant from circles compromising enough to result in police repression. What sort of story was this?" She was the one sent to go for help, as a reward for which she was given a pastry from Ziemiańska. She ran to Julian Tuwim, who had friends in the government: "My God, Juleczek! Why Ważyk? Have they gone mad?. . . . as I love God, he's no 'żydokomuna' [Judeo-Bolshevik]!" She asked Tuwim to call the commissioner at City Hall, and Tuwim answered her: "'Must I? He's the last person I feel like talking to just now . . . But what I wouldn't do for you, my little witch!'" So off rushed Tuwim to intervene; Janina Broniewska repaid him with a kiss on the forehead. When Tuwim put down the telephone, he was rather disgusted: the commissioner had ordered his officers to search all the cells, and Ważyk was nowhere to be found. When the avant-garde poet finally returned from prison a few days later, it emerged that the commissioner had indeed searched for him as promised, but the search had initially proven fruitless because everyone had forgotten that "Ważyk" was only a literary pseudonym. Later Janina Broniewska was uncertain as to whether her efforts merited that pastry, but she never regretted the kiss. It was, she believed, well deserved for the many times that Tuwim would come forward to help their friends.[23]

Julian Tuwim was not the only one who felt affectionately towards Władysław Broniewski's young wife. Janina Broniewska only once, in her words, "offset the losses" of her husband's infidelities, and it happened in the second year of her marriage. One night, when she pulled herself away from a gathering that had gone on past midnight, Andrzej Stawar decided to escort her home. "We were standing for a while by the gate," she told, "and suddenly my caretaker smacks me awkwardly on the cheek and confesses to me a love of many years. The scene was so little romantic, the confession so schoolboyish, that I burst out laughing. And then in the glow of the lantern around the house number on the gate, I saw something so evil in Jędrzej's [Stawar's] eyes, that fury seized me as well."[24] Despite such emotion she rejected him. Stawar was angry; in his mind, she *had* given him some hope. The very principled Janina Broniewska demanded that Stawar tell his friend, her husband, who was so trusting towards him—and so Stawar did. Upon hearing Stawar's confession, Broniewski was more sympathetic than angry; he returned home and asked his wife to "grant amnesty" to his poor friend.[25]

Larger events were occurring around them. Piłsudski was no longer very much of a socialist; and Polish communists soon regretted having assisted the Marshal's coup. On 1 May 1928, less than two years after encouraging the transit strike on Piłsudski's behalf, the veteran communist leader Adolf Warski—whose daughter Zofia Warska had married Stanisław Ryszard Stande the year before—appeared in Theater Square, at the head of an enormous demonstration against Piłsudski's dictatorship. Among the crowd of demonstrators were Piłsudski's former allies. The Marshal was taken aback; his militia shot into the crowd. Isaac Deutscher watched as hundreds were wounded, and Warski held up his white-gray head to address the crowd.[26] On the same day Broniewski wrote to his wife: "I'm writing this letter under the impression of the bloody massacre in which I found myself today on Theater Square. I was there when the militia . . . shot into the crowd."[27]

MAYAKOVSKY COMES TO WARSAW

In *The Spring to Come,* Stefan Żeromski had envisioned just such a clash between the authorities of the young Polish state and the revolutionaries who felt betrayed by it. As a generation, it was, perhaps, the young intellectuals' identification with Żeromski's coming of age novel and their love for the Russian futurist turned revolutionary poet that set them apart. It was a love that consumed them with particular intensity. For these poets, the Revolution spoke in the words neither of Marx nor of Lenin, but of Vladimir Mayakovsky. Witold Wandurski met Mayakovsky in Moscow in 1920. In autumn of 1921, when Wandurski, dressed in rags, made his way back to Poland from the east, he brought with him a pair of old socks, a single shirt, and several volumes of Russian poetry—Nikolai Aseev, Velimir Khlebnikov, Sergei Esenin, and Vladimir Mayakovsky. Soon after his return to Poland, Wandurski met with his old classmate from Łódź, Julian Tuwim. Tuwim "greedily threw himself upon" the books of Russian poetry, lamenting that in Poland, "we all live in such a boring, colorless way."[28]

"It was the first new Russian book that I'd held in my hands in five years," Tuwim wrote. "I can compare the poetic jolt that I experienced, reading Mayakovsky for the first time, only with the unremembered impact of the voice and sight of the sky torn apart by lightening. A setting in motion, upheaval, thunderbolts, flames—everything new, without precedent, wonderful, terrifying, revolutionary. Verse—revolution, rhythm—revolution, illustration—revolution. The feeling that in poetry something of an enormous dimension, in the sense of an artistic turning point, had taken place."[29] The following day Tuwim brought Wandurski to Café Ziemiańska, where they introduced Antoni Słonimski to Mayakovsky's work. Soon a chorus of Ziemiańska's clientele was reciting Mayakovsky's poetry; "even the waiters," Wandurski wrote, "were running among the tables in time to Mayakovsky's 'March,' as if someone were spurring them on—'Left.'"[30]

In April 1927, Mayakovsky came to Warsaw. He spent little more than a day in the Polish capital; he was on his way to Paris. Broniewski, Żarnowerówna, and Stawar were among the few who met Mayakovsky that evening.[31] Immediately afterwards Broniewski wrote to his wife: "Yesterday I was at the Krzywickis. . . . We'd been drinking quite a lot and in all likelihood would have stayed there longer had Teresa [Żarnowerówna] not found out by telephone that Mayakovsky had come and they were waiting for us. . . . [He was] large, with coarse features, and a voice low and deep and so strong that when he speaks loudly the upright piano jingles, he plays the cynic but one can sense some kind of shyness in him."[32] Wandurski had the impression that Broniewski did not like Mayakovsky.[33] Broniewski's feelings were conflicted, as he wrote to his wife: "So it is, that I prefer the Mayakovsky of seven years ago to that of today. He read a lot of things written recently; an exaggeratedly disgusted relationship to everything that he sees on this old globe, a parody of 'poetic-ness.' It seems to me that I don't have a defined relationship to this writer, I must reflect upon this more deeply. But the old poems that he recited: 'Left March' and 'Our March'—acquire a completely new content in the author's recitation. Imagine a live, talking locomotive."[34] The following month, in May 1927, the Russian poet returned to Warsaw for ten days on his way home from Paris. Wandurski, Wat, and Stawar awaited Mayakovsky's train.[35] Police informers looked on. Then Anatol Stern arrived late, breathless. Wandurski watched as from the railway car there emerged a "tall, broadshouldered man with a smooth face, as if chiseled in stone and with deep, double wrinkles between wise, penetrating eyes."[36] Stern described the Russian poet as "gigantic, filling out space with himself."[37] The Polish poets introduced Mayakovsky to *Dźwignia;* it seemed to Wandurski that Mayakovsky was pleased, seeing the Polish journal as akin to the Russian revolutionary literary group Lef. And in fact Mayakovsky wrote of *Dźwignia* that it was "closest to us."[38]

The Soviet embassy held a banquet in honor of their revolutionary poet. Ola Watowa was seated next to Mayakovsky; for the first time in her life she drank too much and was unable to get up from the table. Mayakovsky gallantly lifted her, together with the chair.[39] "When the doors of the embassy hosting him closed behind him," Stern wrote, "the impression of something gigantic remained with us."[40] This feeling was shared by all of them. Wandurski was "shaken, nearly deafened by the power and unusual strength beating from that man."[41] A second banquet in Mayakovsky's honor was organized by *Dźwignia* at Café Astoria; Ważyk, Stern, Słonimski, Tuwim, and Grydzewski were also invited. Stande was absent; he had traveled to the Soviet Union for the tenth anniversary of the Revolution.[42] Mayakovsky arrived wearing the same gray English wool suit that he had been wearing when he had gotten off the train; and it did not escape Wandurski's attention that whereas the writers associated with *Dźwignia* were also dressed casually, their less radical counterparts arrived in dinner jackets.[43] With respect to these less radical counterparts, Mayakovsky found Słonimski to be "calm, self-satisfied." Of Słonimski's fellow Skamander poet Mayakovsky observed: "Tuwim, obviously very talented, restless, fearful of being misunderstood, once wrote and perhaps now, too, wishes to write authentic works of battle, but is clearly thoroughly reined in by official Polish tastes."[44]

On another evening Ola and Aleksander Wat hosted a party for the visiting poet. At a certain moment, Mayakovsky stood up from the table, put his leg on the chair and, holding a pickle, began to recite the poem that had so captivated Café Ziemiańska:

> Chest forward with might!
> Let banners be raised to sky's height!
> Who starts to march with the right?
> Left!
> Left!
> Left![45]

Mayakovsky recited the lines in such a strong voice that the window-panes shook and the doors of the cabinet fell open. With "such a voice," Janina Broniewska wrote, "it would be possible to fill a great stadium, a hall of a factory!"[46] Yet she saw something else as well; she saw that "this giant had something boyish in himself. 'A live and talking locomotive,' as Władek concisely described him after his first meeting. Disgust for all kinds of 'poetic-ness'? And if that were self-defense against shyness and lyricism?"[47] She went to help Ola Watowa wash the glasses, and from the kitchen she watched Mayakovsky's eyes follow Aleksander Wat's beautiful wife: "How much enchantment in those eyes, how much lyricism, despite what that energetically delineated mouth talks about so thunderously:—Constructivism? Yes. That's expediency! And only expediency! The usefulness of an object defines its form. Behold, even that cup of yours. . . . What are those little patterns, those gildings, those flowers for?—Mayakovsky argues, turning around the delicate little cup in his large, powerful hands. And his eyes once again in pursuit of someone who was virtually the quintessence of fragility, gilding, ornamentation, a pure mimosa crossed with ivy, fulfilling the role of hostess at the most revolutionary of revolutionary literary gatherings."[48] Ola Watowa, too, sensed the thunderous poet's paradoxical delicacy. It seemed to her that "at once in that figure of a giant there was something very gentle, disarming, something that at moments seemed like weakness."[49] Her husband felt it, too: "a gentleness that smacked a little of cosmic melancholy."[50]

Mayakovsky's voice ensorceled all of the Polish poets. For Wat it was unmistakable: "that wasn't a man, that wasn't a poet; that was an empire, the coming world empire."[51] The Polish poets felt a respect that was closer to reverence, and which contained enormous affection. They gave Mayakovsky copies of their own books, inscribed them with dedications:

- Władysław Broniewski, "To Vladimir Mayakovsky, the poet of the revolution 17 May 1927"[52]
- Bruno Jasieński, "with comradely greetings France 23 VI 1927"[53]
- Anatol Stern, "To Vladimir Mayakovsky, my first teacher—with love and gratitude 14 V 27"[54]
- Aleksander Wat, "To the greatest of poets of contemporary times, Vladimir Mayakovsky, with comradely greetings 12 V 27"[55]
- Adam Ważyk, "To Mr. Vladimir Mayakovsky with respect 14 V 1927"[56]

Mayakovsky returned to Moscow with the books he had been given in Poland. There, in his journal, he noted the new acquaintances he had made: Stawar, Wandurski, Broniewski, Słonimski, Tuwim, Stern, and Wat. Of Wat he wrote, "a born futurist."[57] Of Warsaw he noted: "Some Poles call Warsaw a small Paris. In any event, it's a very small Paris. . . . Other Poles say that Warsaw is Moscow. This is simply a mistake."[58]

Aleksander Wat and his wife saw Mayakovsky again two years later, in 1929; and it was during this second visit that the two poets grew close.[59] Mayakovsky no longer wanted to talk about politics, about anything Soviet, about the dissolution of Lef or about attacks by the Russian Association of Proletarian Writers. He seemed to Wat to have grown melancholic, and he spent most of his time in the Soviet embassy playing billiards, drinking, and talking obsessively about Aleksandr Blok, Sergei Esenin, and Viktor Shklovsky.[60] He was pathologically clean; he washed his hands constantly. Ola Watowa accompanied him on shopping trips when he bought enormous quantities of scissors and razors and other objects—which he then gave away to his friends when he returned to Moscow. She knew that something was wrong. "He was dying in front of our eyes," she wrote.

One day she arranged to meet Mayakovsky at the Soviet embassy, so that he could continue his shopping. He seemed nervous, as if frightened. He was waiting for a telephone connection to Paris: "At last the telephone. The conversation took place in the adjacent room. Mayakovsky returned completely transformed. One felt as if he had been struck, that something irrevocable had happened. He was speaking with a woman whom at that time he loved very much. She was a 'White' Russian and lived in Paris. He had been trying to persuade her, perhaps pleading with her, to leave Paris and go with him to Moscow. And just then, while I was present, he received the final rejection."[61] In October 1928, Mayakovsky had fallen in love with the Russian émigré Tatiana Yakovleva in Paris. The following year Mayakovsky once more traveled west from Moscow, attempting to make his way to Paris to see her again.[62] His hopes were disappointed. In October 1929, upon hearing that Mayakovsky had either been denied a visa to France or had been warned strongly against applying for one, Yakovleva accepted another man's marriage proposal.[63]

Wat wrote that Mayakovsky's 1927 visit "galvanized" the Polish poets.[64] No other single figure was ever so beloved by them. No one else embodied so beautifully the convergence between the avant-garde and the Revolution. For Wat, Mayakovsky became "a gangplank that conveniently led from the avant-garde position, formal innovation, to communist, revolutionary writing."[65] After Mayakovsky's visit, Broniewski described how Russian revolutionary poetry had been the greatest influence on his work. "To Mayakovsky," he wrote, "I owe my final break with symbolic rubbish and a relationship to the word as to an instrument of battle."[66] Just days after Mayakovsky had left Warsaw, Stern published an article about him in *Wiadomości Literackie*. "Mayakovsky had in himself, in contrast to his comrades," Stern wrote, "that internal imperative of self-limitation, by which, as Goethe said, one can recognize a master."[67] Yet Mayakovsky's visit to Warsaw was more than the visit of a master; for the Polish poets it was something more intimate. He was their greatest love affair, the nexus point through which they fell in love with the aesthetics of the Revolution. Wat said of his and Ola Watowa's relationship with the Russian futurist: "We simply fell in love with him as a poet. The image of him—with all that strength and size and a certain great inner tenderness. Tenderness—he was very tender."[68]

A POLISH POET MOVES TO PARIS

Bruno Jasieński was not in Warsaw when Mayakovsky arrived. He had already met the Russian futurist, in Paris. In 1925 Jasieński and his wife Klara Arem had left Poland. In March 1928 Jasieński wrote to Broniewski from Paris, angry at Stern for having signed Jasieński's name to an open letter concerning "proletarian art."[69] The attestation of his break with Stern was the beginning of Jasieński's correspondence with Broniewski. Since his departure Jasieński had drifted away from the Polish literary world; now he asked Broniewski to send him a more detailed account of leftist literary ventures, adding that he would be very willing to support *Dźwignia* with his "modest person." Given their common ideological platform, and the "thinness of ranks," they should, Jasieński believed, maintain "the tightest solidarity."[70] He added, "With respect to my old 'comrades-in-arms' from around *Nowa Sztuka,* we've broken up in directions too varied and today speak languages too different for there to remain anything from the platform (even purely artistic) that once united us, apart from memories. In their examples, I see how very demoralizing the atmosphere at home that you have to breathe today must be."[71]

In Paris Bruno Jasieński and his wife lived in poverty. The Polish writer Stanisław Brucz, who had been among those at the futurists' table at Ziemiańska in the early 1920s, saw Jasieński shortly after his arrival in Paris: "In December 1925 I found Jasieński in the least expected neighborhood: in lower Montmartre, in the impasse Poissonière, on a back street crushed into a block of tenement houses at the intersection of boulevards Rochechouart and Barbès. And so in a workers' district, noisy and crowded, full of cheap bazaars, shoddy market stalls, bistros, mechanical workshops sprawling the whole width of the sidewalks and resounding with racket from morning to night."[72] Aleksander Wat visited Jasieński in May 1926 in the same neighborhood, yet Wat found it beautiful, "very typically Parisian," and "very petty bourgeois." By then Jasieński had undergone a transformation; little remained of the "arch-snob" "prowling about and surrounded by young women."[73] He had grown much calmer. Brucz found Jasieński focused on his work, his day carefully divided: work on his long poem *Słowo o Jakubie Szeli* (A Word about Jakub Szela) in the morning; paid work for newspapers in the afternoon; correspondence and study in the evenings.

In Paris Jasieński surprised me with his homebound lifestyle.
And not only with that. The Jasieński I had remembered from
Warsaw was full of anxiety. He, always so restrained, so embarrassed every time a conversation concerned his intimate affairs,
often he could not hide his heightened nervous sensitivity,
some kind of internal irritation, a neurasthenic tendency
towards sudden jumps from spasmodic boredom to explosions
of cold irritation. Of course one could have explained this
by the pressure of the Warsaw literary atmosphere, financial
problems, quasi-homelessness, the necessity of spending the
greater part of the days and nights in cafés and bars, briefly
stated—by the gypsy-like chaos of his life, which in truth he
very much disliked. Here the evenness of his temperament
and his serenity astounded me.[74]

When Jasieński had finished *Jakub Szela,* it made its way to Poland in a
covert edition, a pocket-size pamphlet printed on a hand hectograph that
circulated among progressive student circles with the note "after reading,
pass along to someone else."[75] The students were enthusiastic. Julian Tuwim was less so. "It's difficult for me to believe in artificial sincerity / basted
in a sauce distinctly snobbish," he wrote in a poem about *Jakub Szela.*[76]

While the text circulated in Poland, Jasieński remained in Paris. He
was in full agreement with his visitors concerning the salutary effects
of his absence from his own country. In November 1926 he wrote to his
Warsaw friends:

> This trip abroad in general has done me well. I felt it right
> away, from the first moments. . . . Quite obviously I had been
> lacking some necessary distance and had felt that I wouldn't
> manage to do anything. My departure to Paris and months of
> 'separation' from Poland have cured me of that forced inactivity
> and have enabled me in the course of a few winter months to
> execute without difficulty a plan I'd harbored for a long time,
> not having found the right 'approach' to it. . . . In the course
> of the long years spent there, I took Poland so much into my-
> self that at the moment I feel no 'nostalgia' for my homeland.
> Perhaps it will come with time at some point. . . . When I deter-

mine that I have nothing more to learn from the French—
I'll gladly move on to another place. Traveling is a disease that
has always consumed me and consumes me and from which
I will certainly die.[77]

To Stefan Priacel, a French journalist and onetime secretary of the
left-wing periodical *Monde,* it seemed that integration into Parisian life did
not come easily to the Polish poet who wore a monocle and spoke of himself as a communist. Priacel sensed Jasieński's insecurity in the French
environment; he rarely left his home and rarely frequented the literary
cafés, harboring a distaste for both the Polish émigré intelligentsia and
the French, who—Priacel judged—he in turn understood poorly. "Frankly
speaking," Priacel wrote, "one sensed in him the poorly masked despair
of a man who has the constant awareness of his alienness and struggles
against the difficulties piling up around him."[78] Making connections in the
French literary world was complicated; and Jasieński's French was weak.
He was aided by an enthusiastic recommendation from Tomasz Dąbal, a
Polish communist and former parliamentary deputy, which brought some
assistance from the communist-sympathizing author Henri Barbusse.[79]

Though Jasieński had dabbled in proletarian poetry while still in Poland, it was in Paris, while living in poverty, that his explicit identification
with communism began—and the novel *Palę Paryż* (I Burn Paris) came
into being.[80] Wat saw Jasieński's indignation upon seeing the French writer
Paul Morand's novel *Je brûle Moscou* in a bookstore window. As Jasieński
understood it, the title meant "I Burn Moscow," although Wat saw the linguistic misunderstanding: the verb *brûler* could also mean "to pass through
a place quickly."[81] It was not only the title that upset Jasieński, though.
Morand's novel included the characters Vasilissa and Ben, a couple who
lived with the communist poet Mordecai Goldvasser, who was terrified
of contamination and obsessed with cleanliness—an unflattering satire
of Mayakovsky and his close friends, the revolutionary intellectuals Lilia
and Osip Brik. Jasieński was enraged.[82]

His rage was a creative one. *I Burn Paris* depicted a deathly plague
transmitted through contaminated water in the French capital. When the
bourgeois city was destroyed it was the prisoners, whose water supply
drew from a different source, who were spared. *I Burn Paris* was not a

socialist realist novel; its fantastical plot reveals the experimental nature of Marxist literature in the 1920s.[83] Another Polish writer in Paris began to see Jasieński at the Café du Dôme in Montparnasse. At times Jasieński would come with his wife and they would all sit together; at times he would come with Ilya Ehrenburg, conspicuous for his "enormous black crop of hair and strange-colored greenish clothing."[84] By then the French edition of *I Burn Paris* was appearing in excerpts in *L'Humanité;* the Polish writer, who was following the novel, found it weak. *I Burn Paris* seemed less weak and more threatening to the French government, however, and in 1929 Jasieński was forced to leave France—despite efforts by Barbusse to organize protests against his expulsion.[85] From Paris Jasieński went to Leningrad.

MIESIĘCZNIK LITERACKI

Shortly after the publication of *Lucifer Unemployed*, Aleksander Wat's active engagement with the Left began. In 1928, for the tenth anniversary of Poland's regained independence, Wat, together with the scenic designer Władysław Daszewski and theater director Leon Schiller, was invited to put together a Poznań theatrical production titled *Polityka społeczna* (Social Policy). Wat considered Schiller "a fine specimen of the salon communist." Daszewski had been born into the *déclassé* nobility; he was sexy and charming and occasionally vicious. Both were among those Marxist cultural figures who embodied a certain irony of Piłsudski's Poland: they were radicals who were nevertheless close to the regime. As Aleksander Wat recalled, "[Schiller] was on very friendly terms with the minister of internal affairs and was close with Beck and Pieracki. But that's Poland. And when left-wing writers came from the West, from Germany or France, like Priacel, Barbusse's secretary, they couldn't get over our sitting in the Café Ziemiańska with the colonels, with Wieniawa-Długoszowski."[86] Wat considered the play he produced with Schiller and Daszewski to be "pure communist theater," a montage based on authentic material dealing with labor, working conditions, and (violations of) social legislation. Wat was paid well, and used the money to seek out European contacts for the next venture in revolutionary literature; he and Daszewski, together with their wives, set out abroad. Their trip included Berlin, where Stande and his wife Zofia Warska, on the KPP's instructions, had also gone.[87] There in Berlin in 1928 Wat saw "decadence, a Babylon of debauchery." In Paris,

FIGURE 7 Jan Lechoń, Julian Tuwim, and Antoni Słonimski (left to right) sitting at their table at Café Ziemiańska with Colonel Bolesław Wieniawa-Długoszowski. Caricature by Władysław Daszewski. From *Wiadomości Literackie* 36 (1928); reproduction by Muzeum Literatury imienia Adama Mickiewicza.

Wat, Brucz, and Jasieński went out together on the Rue Blondel, in the red light district. The street of naked women and brothels was one of Jasieński's favorite places to visit, but they would go only for a beer.[88] On the banks of the Seine, the Polish poet Józef Wittlin told Wat that Wat would end up a Catholic.[89]

Wat was reluctant to join the Communist Party. The KPP was illegal in Poland, and the rejection was mutual: for the KPP, the Polish state was the "ugly bastard of the Versailles Treaty."[90] Despite such mutually hostile sentiments, there were communist members of parliament. Stawar approached Wat with the proposition that the Party nominate him for election to the parliament, but that would have involved joining the Party, and Wat demurred; he feared infecting the Party with his intellectualism.[91] Now precisely because of his non-Party status, Wat became the ideal candidate to found and edit the (tenuously legal) Marxist literary periodical *Miesięcznik Literacki* (The Literary Monthly), a successor to the failed *Nowa Kultura* and *Dźwignia*.[92] His editorial board included Hempel, Broniewski, Daszewski, Stawar, and Stande. Ola Watowa was the secretary; Władysław Daszewski designed the cover for the second issue.[93] Isaac Deutscher, who had been writing for the Jewish (and Zionist-sympathizing) paper *Nasz Przegląd*, had joined the KPP in early 1927, at the age of nineteen, and now began to work on *Miesięcznik Literacki*.[94]

Adam Ważyk's participation was minimal.[95] Anatol Stern was not part of the project at all; he was writing screenplays and producing films, and according to Wat was deteriorating into a life of drinking and decadence.[96] This was perhaps the case, but along with decadence came dabblings in Catholicism. In a "Confession" that prefaced his 1927 poetry collection *Bieg do Bieguna* (A Run to the Pole), Stern admitted that while he had once been "the most extreme adherent of Marxism," he had become disillusioned with the vulgar materialism of the proponents of a proletarian dictatorship. In his desire to respect what was emotional and spiritual in humanity, Stern had arrived at the doors of the Church. Presently he was convinced that Marx's teachings in no way opposed religious spirituality, that rather these two sources of wisdom constituted one another's "mutual fulfillment," "without which the battle for the happiness of humanity would have no foundations."[97] This was the theme of the collection's title poem, which concluded "Like a diamond, tossed into clear water, / so would I like to dissolve and disappear in Christ. / AMEN."[98]

Wat had cut himself off from all spiritual seductions, and stood now firmly on the side of the materialists. The strategy of selecting a non-Party member as editor was initially successful; and for a time following its debut in December 1929 *Miesięcznik Literacki* did manage, despite persecution, to maintain a nominally legal existence. Hempel played the role of transmitter of the Party's wishes. To Wat, the older communist was both saintly and cowardly. He was "a man of great goodness," who ran back and forth between Wat and the Party, always in fear that the Party leaders might be unhappy with Wat's editorial decisions.[99] The Party sent other liaisons as well, including a well-educated Party member Wat's own age named Jakub Berman.[100]

The journal's premiere was awaited in the Warsaw cafés; Café Ziemiańska anticipated something extraordinary.[101] When it did appear, *Miesięcznik Literacki*'s first issue was the project of a small editorial circle; it included a fragment of Broniewski's play *Proletarjat* (The Proletariat); Wat's critique of Remarque and German pacifist literature; an article about Mayakovsky's friend, the Russian literary theorist Viktor Shklovsky; and a harsh review of Jasieński's *I Burn Paris*.[102] The reviewer began with the Revelation of Saint John describing the fall of Rome; he went on to comment that at the time of the Apocalypse the oppressed masses were incapable of independent battle. Rather, in the Apocalypse a judgment was handed down upon a depraved world in which only the chosen few were saved. This New Testament prophecy was, in the reviewer's opinion, the dominant allegory of *I Burn Paris*—Paris became a new Babylon, a city of debauchery, a Sodom in which all inhabitants were condemned to death. Just as Christians had substituted Christians for Jews as the chosen people, so had Jasieński appropriated Christian mysticism and substituted the communist nation as the chosen one. According to the reviewer, the model of the Apocalypse was radically inappropriate; the proletariat was a class that would self-consciously rise up against its oppressors, not a chosen few who would be saved by a metaphysical miracle. The verdict: Jasieński had failed to understand scientific determinism, had failed to grasp that Marxism was based on materialism as opposed to metaphysics, that in proletarian ideology "there is nothing mysterious, nothing mystical, nothing religious."[103] In short, while Jasieński may have intended to create communist literature, he had failed miserably. It was a time, however, when the *Miesięcznik Literacki* editors themselves were unsure precisely what communist literature meant.

CHAPTER FOUR

A Funeral for Futurism

The futurization of Polish life failed definitively.

—*Aleksander Wat*

SOME AT CAFÉ ZIEMIAŃSKA, having anticipated something extraordinary, were now disappointed by *Miesięcznik Literacki*. In his weekly column in *Wiadomości Literackie,* Antoni Słonimski attacked the very first issue. By no means generously predisposed towards Wat and his editorial staff, Słonimski accused them of naïveté, primitivism and a lack of connection to real life: "The publication presents itself quite poorly. The meagerness results not only from the lack of literary force and the staleness of the material, but above all from the narrow-mindedness of its naïve class conceptualizations of complicated matters of human creativity. Polish 'Marxist criticism,' like, after all, other positions of our intellectual life, presents itself quite dismally. One must admit that 'proletarian chatter' for the time being breaks all records for boredom and primitivism. In the space of the entire issue of *Miesięcznik Literacki* the reader fails to come across the minutest trace of organic life."[1] Słonimski added that *Miesięcznik Literacki*'s editorial staff lacked any coherent conception of proletarian literature. He advised them, with his usual sarcasm, to "go off to the side and come to some agreement as to what is proletarian and what isn't. Then come talk to us." In connection with this Słonimski mocked the journal's fetishization of the word "bourgeois": "The word 'bourgeois' is used with the greatest satisfaction by *Miesięcznik*'s staff. The word is not only supposed to define a writer's class membership, but also bears a hue of disgust. 'Bourgeois' literature, 'bourgeois' poetry, 'bourgeois' pacifism, and 'bourgeois' theater. . . . We now know that there is a 'bourgeois' view on electron theory and the proletarian truth about electrons." Słonimski concluded, "Everything together is very childish and naïve, and most importantly—entirely unnecessary. Glancing at *Miesięcznik* one feels like asking 'From whom is this child?' as the children of Israel say."[2]

While it was not Słonimski's first attack against the radical Left in his weekly columns, the feuilleton took *Miesięcznik Literacki*'s editor by surprise. In the months prior to the journal's premiere, Wat's relations with Słonimski had been good.[3] Now Słonimski's December 1929 feuilleton began a polemic between *Miesięcznik Literacki* and *Wiadomości Literackie;* Wat and his editorial staff answered Słonimski in the second issue. They pointed out that Słonimski had once written of literary criticism as serving the purpose of an advertisement. Now Słonimski, they said, had applied this commercial theory to *Miesięcznik Literacki,* composing an anti-advertisement. *Miesięcznik Literacki* drew an analogy with an undertone of antisemitism: "Mr. Feinkind stands in front of his shop and calls out: 'Don't go to my competitor, he has stale merchandise: buy only at my shop.' Ultimately Mr. Feinkind is Mr. Feinkind, shouting in such a way is his right—but with respect to literary affairs it's customary to do this more delicately than Mr. Słonimski has done. And yet he's failed to secure any objective. Mr. Feinkind stands in front of his shop and with a dramatic air points at his competitor and asks: 'From whom is this child? Who will buy that, who will read it?'"[4]

In reply Słonimski compared *Miesięcznik Literacki*'s low intellectual level to that of Christian literature, exacerbating the hostility between poets who several months earlier had been friends: "I have in front of me the new issue of that monthly. I've already written about the first issue, and the offensive words with which I was answered have not changed my gently derisive relationship towards that refuge of all those who have experienced disappointment and proven themselves to be failures. And yet it was possible to expect that despite all *Miesięcznik*'s dullness it would have at least made attempts to apply Russian methods to the conditions and demands of a different terrain. This expectation was unmet. Those materialist-literati did not fall upon the idea of taking changed conditions into consideration, and with lazy mental inertia transposed ready-made models of Russian criticism onto Polish ground." Słonimski did not shy from ad hominem attacks:

> The editor of *Miesięcznik,* Mr. Wat, to whose person I intend to devote a few words, did not pass through a revolutionary period. It's sufficient to look at the confession of his youth, located in issue number two of his publication, to remind oneself of all the buffoonery, humbugs and instances of making a fool of himself—by which he attempted to arrive at literature. It happened during those times when the poets of the old group 'Skamander' were creating new values, the by-products of which the majority of 'proletarian' poets are still feeding on today. Mr. Wat passed very quickly from fashionable futurism to the later more fashionable neo-Catholicism in order to finally, in his search for orthodoxy, take shelter in the camp of bourgeois-snobs-turning-communist. The path of Mr. Wat's deterioration is similar to the stories of present-day Jewish chauvinists. Despite a few good stories [Wat] is a lazy writer without a following and without significance; it thus should not surprise us too much that he so easily passes from Catholicism to Marxism in search of a comfortable situation through which to recoup his losses.[5]

The notion of "snob" popularized by Stefan Żeromski in 1922 had endured. It was now paired with the "bourgeois," and Wat responded with an article about Słonimski and his friends as "men of fashion," salon writers, and salon snobs. He referred to Słonimski as "our snob" and invoked the rather eccentric-sounding verbal noun *usnobizowanie*—that is, the process of becoming a snob.[6] Yet another, equally belittling piece in *Miesięcznik Literacki* was titled "The *shmoncesman* [Jewish cabaret humorist] abroad: What Mr. Słonimski saw in London." A mini–photo essay, the piece consisted of pictures of destitution, homelessness, and violently beaten workers in London, with such captions as: "The unemployed, not finding space in the overfilled shelters, sleep under bridges, under factory walls. In the working districts of London this kind of picture belongs to a normal series of 'street landscapes' relished by 'adventurous tourists.'"[7] On the same page, *Miesięcznik Literacki* quoted from Słonimski's recent essay in *Wiadomości Literackie* about his trip to London: "'I saw as well communist May Day parades. It's similar to the Saturday crowd at Ziemiańska. There are mostly semitic-type women and very elegantly dressed men. The unemployed, of whom London cannot in any way rid itself, predominate.'"[8]

So the attacks went on. In a column that same month, July 1930, Słonimski derided "the little crowd of our pious Marxists" whose entire activity was limited to proclaiming their connection to the proletariat—to the exclusion of producing actual literary work.[9] It was a criticism that found resonance on the Left as well. Three months later, a communist from the town of Rzeszów wrote to Broniewski: "In following the development of *Miesięcznik Literacki* and glancing through the most varied publishing catalogues, I come to the same conclusion as does that smelly Jew Słonimski. I consider your productivity to be equal to zero plus very little, which very much saddens us, the gray masses. We are doing everything in our power to have you among us, but what of that when you're elusive . . . not a book, not a poem, not a play, not a theater, so where are you? With us, with them, or perhaps you don't exist?"[10] Neither was this the only internal criticism. When Broniewski's poetry appeared in *Miesięcznik Literacki,* his closest friends attacked him for "doleful sentiments" and "exuberant individualism." It was a time of painful criticism from those "on the same side of the barricade," and more than once Janina Broniewska saw her husband return home unhappy from *Miesięcznik Literacki*'s editorial board meetings.[11]

New dynamics were emerging among the old friends from Café Ziemiańska. In 1929 Julian Tuwim, long a supporter of Piłsudski, composed "Do prostego człowieka" (To the Simple Man), a poem widely read as expressing a deep disillusionment with Piłsudski's Poland. For Tuwim the poem was radically *engagé*, albeit less in the direction of communism or even Marxism more broadly understood than of pacifism. In it Tuwim called to "the simple man" to be aware that his patriotic sentiments were being exploited for the material gain of the ruling classes. The poem concluded:

> Throw your machine gun onto the pavement.
> The oil is theirs, the blood is yours.
> And from capital to capital

Cry out, guarding your toil:
"Gentlemen of the nobility, you do not fool us."[12]

The attacks came from all sides. Right-wing critics demanded that Tuwim be led to the gallows, and the Left considered the poem a typical bourgeois expression of pacifist sentiment.[13] Tuwim's friends described his lack of comprehension at the controversy: the older poet Leopold Staff tried to speak to Tuwim about the poem, only to hear that Tuwim was thinking exclusively about poetic assonance.[14] Once Tuwim had been made to understand the political implications, however, he published a qualification: the poem was meant to express only humanitarianism and in no way advocated the disarmament of Poland; it would be an absurdity to extrapolate from the poem that he did not honor heroism in defense of his country's independence. He accepted the blame for any misunderstandings.[15]

Earlier, in 1928, Tuwim had given an interview to a PPS periodical about the relationship between literature and the working class. His views were vague. He likened literature and socialism to "two enormous rivers each flowing along its own channel," and spoke abstractly of how the working class was neither homogeneous nor monolithic, about how it was engaged in a relationship of osmosis with the bourgeois world. He reminisced about his childhood in the factory city of Łódź: as a young boy he had seen the bloody 1905 Revolution, and while growing up he had seen the workers' poverty and exhaustion. He felt connected to workers by an awareness of their suffering, but insisted that this was not an awareness to be expressed "programmatically." While Tuwim was not nearly so harsh as Słonimski, he, too, criticized the "bourgeois snobbery" among the "young, so-called proletarian poets."[16] A short note that Tuwim wrote to Broniewski in February 1931, gently taunting Broniewski's very serious sense of engagement, was revealing of the complicated personal dynamics: "Wołodia! I dreamt that you were a Spanish general and were suppressing the revolution. What does that mean?"[17]

RECANTATIONS OF FUTURISMS PAST
In the second issue of *Miesięcznik Literacki*, which appeared in January 1930, Wat initiated an attack against his own futurist past. He reflected upon his own history, beginning with the judgment that boredom and

aversion were the midwives of Polish futurism. He told the story of the birth of Polish futurism, the movement's Italian and Russian origins, its battles against *passéisme,* and its own decadent and anarchist character. Wat wrote of inaugurating Polish futurism together with Anatol Stern in late 1918, just as Skamander came into being. The Skamander poets declared themselves the heirs to the great Romantic tradition that the futurists derided.

The Skamander poets, in Wat's reading, aspired to attain and succeeded in attaining the status of official poets, largely by declaring a cult of "programlessness" and a slogan of "life as such," and by desiring above all to protect their own youth from the winds of revolution. He regretted now the cooperation with Skamander and the way in which the Polish futurists "to a certain extent conformed to Skamander as the latter's subordinate left-wing." A political subtext, Wat implied, had been present from the beginning, despite the self-declared anarchism and decadence of futurist activities.[18]

Now Wat saw that while the futurists had aspired to a "progressive revolution of forms of expression," they had instead engendered only anarchization. There was no place in bourgeois art for a battle against *passéisme;* yet the futurists' own battle against *passéisme,* which should have led to social revolution in Poland as in Russia, led them instead towards anarchism and decadence: "For the social stratum from which the Polish futurists originated, it was a time of panic and fear of revolution, and at once a time of hedonism, debauchery, speculation, self-enrichment not on the basis of production but on the basis of inflationary exploitation. Polish futurism only exaggerated these frames of mind. Its dynamic was not civilizing—just the opposite: it was decadent, anarchistic." The futurists were ensconced in a paradox: "those who saw their own right of existence in the contemporizing of poetry, in the vindication of the present day, were especially isolated from their own concrete domestic contemporaneity. We were building ourselves into an imagined contemporaneity, formed from programmatically distorted, predominantly imported components." Yet the situation was not and could not remain static. On the contrary, it was *inflacja* that most marked the futurist era—a term meaning literally "inflation" (and perhaps inspired by the hyperinflation of the early 1920s) but more abstractly encompassing a sense of relentless intensification in an effort to sustain liminality. "Inflation," Wat wrote, "was at that time a form of seeing things. . . . The right of identity ceased to obtain. A thing ceased to be itself. The day after tomorrow it would no longer be what it had been the day before. Inflation tore apart the identity of a thing with itself." Moreover, the growing revolutionary tide could not fail to affect the futurists as well, and more specifically, "the worker had begun to make even the futurist poets aware of his existence."[19]

It was in 1921, around the time of *Nowa Sztuka*, in Wat's retrospective reading, that the divisions between avant-garde poetry and *passéiste* poetry—that is, between the futurists and Skamander—began to deepen. This was a time of formal inventiveness and a search for new slogans, definitions, names, a time of "inflation of programs." In contrast, "programlessness" and a "fetish for talent and inspiration" characterized Skamander, as did notions that "we ourselves are the greatest innovation" and "we want to be banal, we won't betray our hearts for novelty." Here Wat indicted the Skamandrites in their role as court poets, for they were implicitly collaborating with the enemy that was the state. Their "programophobia," Wat explained in a line of argumentation increasingly proto-Stalinist in form, masked their reactionary nature: "Skamander's programophobia resulted naturally from its traditionalism. A program is unnecessary and even harmful to a traditionalist group in a certain period of its evolution for it would unnecessarily reveal its reactionary physiognomy."[20]

Conversely, Wat wrote that Polish futurism, in spite of its errors, did contain progressive and proletarian elements. He cited Żeromski's *Snobbism and Progress* as representative of the central attack on futurism—that is, "later and so imported, and hence foreign, artificial, snobbish"—and insisted that Polish futurism was not merely an imitation, that it necessarily differed from its Italian and Russian predecessors due to the influence of Poland's socioeconomic conditions. Here Wat was, in a sense, at cross-purposes with himself. The article was a self-criticism of his futurist past, which at once noted futurism's contribution and presented a teleological path from decadence to communism. By returning again and again to the futurists' lack of popularity, Wat betrayed a lingering sense of outsiderness, a resentment of social rejection—despite his self-conscious engagement in transgressing social norms. Futurism had indeed begun with a petty bourgeois character, yet it had matured and progressed, and the result was not entirely negative: "I claimed that futurism in its first, primitive period had a petty bourgeois physiognomy. . . . In connection with that I wrote about the anti-civilizing and reactionary nature of the first period of futurism, which ultimately did not exclude the presence in futurism of revolutionary embryos."[21]

Wat also wrote critically of *Zwrotnica,* accusing Tadeusz Peiper of "urbanism," "aestheticism," and identification with the legacy of nineteenth-century Polish positivism, which called for "productive, organic work" on behalf of the nation. According to Wat, *Zwrotnica*'s "aestheticizing character" revealed itself most plainly in the issue devoted to futurism when Peiper expressed his opposition to futurism's "extraliterary activities." Here Wat quoted Peiper: "'The way in which (the futurists) related art to life acknowledged the supremacy of real-life activity over artistic creation and permitted artistic reforms only because they were part of general, real-life reforms. This is a false, unartistic mode of relating. Art needs life the way a traveler needs a walking stick. But the final goal must be exclusively artistic. The cause must be art and only art.'" Now the editor of a communist journal, Wat followed his critique of *Zwrotnica* to its logical conclusion: together with urbanism, positivism, and aestheticism, *Zwrotnica* was guilty of "grand capitalist tendencies." Here Wat concluded self-righteously that instances of cooperation notwithstanding, the relationship of "proper" futurists to *Zwrotnica* was always one of distaste.[22]

Wat also revisited the futurists' engagement with Jan Hempel's *Nowa Kultura.* It was at this point that they had begun to move unsteadily towards radicalization, an impulse Wat attributed not only to deeper social causes, but also to rejection by the official literary establishment. He cited Jasieński's "A Song about Hunger" as a manifestation of the futurists' leftist evolution, although he was critical of Jasieński's and Stern's *The Earth to the Left* as failing to embody revolutionary ideology. Here Wat offered a self-criticism of the futurists' collective failure to understand historical materialism, while at the same time criticizing Marxists for failing to appreciate futurism's innovations: "On one side extreme individualism and a lack of familiarity with the elementary bases of Marxism. On the other side a lack of understanding of the progressive formal values that futurism had brought to literature produced a discouraging effect."[23] The time following the 1924 break with *Nowa Kultura* was one of further vacillations manifesting themselves in *Almanach Nowej Sztuki,* which Wat credited with a high intellectual standard. The collaborators came together on the common platform of formalism, yet in the end formalism threatened them with a void and they failed to formulate a coherent program. It was political and ideological divergence that was the true cause of *Almanach Nowej Sztuki*'s short life, Wat wrote, as well as of the impossibility of building a front of New Art.

Wat's narrative of Polish futurism was not devoid of a certain nostalgia. His memoir was self-critical, yet restrained; he remained, as he had been in his futurist years, defensive vis-à-vis Skamander. His conclusions were laden with ambivalence; his condemnation of his futurist past was juxtaposed with an insistence on futurism's progressive intentions—however misguidedly they might have been expressed—as well as an assertion of the value of futurism's aesthetic innovations. While noting that the "objective" results of futurism had not yet been sufficiently ascertained, he ventured to conclude that futurism added much color to Polish literary life, serving as a laboratory of new forms as well as a point of departure for Polish proletarian poetry. Polish futurism, Wat concluded, was the revelation of the dark side of contemporary Polish society, "the crooked mirror in which Caliban looked at himself with a grimace of abomination."[24]

These memoirs of futurism met with at least one protest. In *Miesięcznik Literacki* Tadeusz Peiper criticized Wat's description of *Zwrotnica* and contested Wat's portrayal of Peiper's positions. In his letter, Peiper denied having ever used the word "urbanism," pointing out that not everyone who wrote about the city was an urbanist, just as not everyone who wrote about the future was a futurist. He further accused Wat of distorting his words by drawing upon incomplete citations. *Zwrotnica* had never called for a return to positivism; neither had Peiper opposed only futurism's extraliterary ventures, but rather the entire system futurism implicitly embraced—while at once recognizing futurism's importance within the rubric of New Art. Moreover, Peiper insisted on his own socialist beliefs and protested Wat's portrayal of *Zwrotnica* as a capitalist project. As a socialist, Peiper had gathered together diverse talents precisely because he wished for Poland to be as creative as possible on the day of the proletariat's victory. His own socialism he defined as an aspiration, not allied with any particular party or party program, towards abolishing social classes through the socializing of the means of production. Various people of different beliefs collaborated on *Zwrotnica*, Peiper corrected. Moreover, the editor himself—that is, Peiper—was and remained a socialist.[25]

In his reply, Wat conceded nothing. He defended his description of Peiper's journal as aestheticist and quoted Peiper (in what could be a self-critical attack against his own literary coming of age as well): "'Because we love words: just as you, Madame, love cameos and you, Sir, I beg you, love old coins as well as new ones.'" While acknowledging the possibility of Peiper's own socialist beliefs, Wat maintained that *Zwrotnica* did possess "objectively" dominant grand capitalist tendencies—a phrase that betrayed the influence of an emerging Stalinist idiom.[26]

THE DEATH OF MAYAKOVSKY

Miesięcznik Literacki was not only about sharp polemics over Marxist literary criticism and bourgeois pacifism. Nothing about the Revolution in Russia was as close to Wat and his friends, or as personal, as Mayakovsky, and the journal's harsh tone softened when Mayakovsky took his own life on the morning of 14 April 1930. The first detail that reached Janina Broniewska and Władysław Broniewski in Warsaw was the phrase from Mayakovsky's suicide note, "liubovnaia lodka razbilas' o byt" (the love boat crashed against the everyday). The news fell upon Janina Broniewska as something incomprehensible; but Ola Watowa and her husband had felt a certain premonition.[27] Wat dedicated the May issue of *Miesięcznik Literacki* to his Russian friend who had led him to the Revolution. Broniewski, Stande, and others contributed as well, but it was Wat who wrote the eulogy, which began below a photograph of the beautiful Mayakovsky lying in his coffin, his head wreathed in flowers.

What Wat wrote was devoted to Mayakovsky's life rather than his death; Wat said almost nothing about the suicide. He wrote of the Russian poet's development in a tone obligingly critical in light of the suicide, but also warm. He revisited the origins of Mayakovsky's futurism in nihilism and cited Mayakovsky's own understanding of his coming into futurism: "He bore the pathos of a socialist convinced of the necessity of the destruction of the obsolete." In the beginning, Mayakovsky's pathos was that of "an outcast intellectual, an anarchist, almost a nihilist ('I erect above everything that has been made nihil'), brought to socialism by hatred towards and rebellion against the existing state of things." In Wat's reading, it was just this rebellious quality of Russian futurism that was the essence of its departure from its Italian counterpart. Wat described Mayakovsky's poetry as a laboratory of innovation and Mayakovsky himself as a contemporary Pushkin, and a poet of the street who revolutionized Russian poetic language through the language of the masses.

There was a touching personal description of Mayakovsky's "heroic sublimity" and the moving experience of hearing him read his own poetry: "There is nothing that can be compared to the suggestiveness of his voice, thundering—not metaphorically." Wat credited Mayakovsky with having foreseen the Revolution and with having had the strength to temper his own individualistic tendencies: "He learned to discipline his own anarchistic egotism, he accepted revolution not only as a realization of aspirations, but also as a fundamental revolution in his creativity. From a poet-rebel he became a poet of a revolution . . . from a negator 'blowing up bourgeois society from within,' he became a participant in battle, a creator of positive values." Mayakovsky's art was a struggle to rebuild the world, and Wat cited Mayakovsky himself describing the critical shift in notions of literature from representation to transformation: "'We came not to photograph the world, but to fight for the future with literary tools, to rebuild the world.'" That Mayakovsky succeeded in transcending his own "anarchistic hyperindividualism" and becoming a poet of revolutionary collectivity Wat saw as perhaps the poet's greatest achievement—and here Wat's writing was so poignant, and as engaged as if he were speaking of himself as well: "For Mayakovsky the path towards revolution was not a given, but rather a struggle, and in the end he was not able to resolve all of his internal contradictions." He continued to be plagued by "a lack of agreement between the register of his voice and the topic. That great poet of enormous strength to shape and influence, perfectly in agreement with the tempo of revolution, with the dynamics and effects of the fight of the masses, had a voice too highly tuned and too little differentiated for the tasks which the social reality of the reconstruction period presented."[28] Several of Mayakovsky's poems followed Wat's eulogy, as did poems in memoriam by Stande and Broniewski. "Glory to him who has fallen," wrote Broniewski, "Let us go on."[29]

Mayakovsky's death effected a temporary peace between *Miesięcznik Literacki* and *Wiadomości Literackie,* the former futurists and Skamander, the more radical and less radical writers. In response to Mayakovsky's "Levyi Marsh" (Left March), Słonimski had once written a "Kontrmarsz" (Countermarch), replacing Mayakovsky's refrain "Left! Left! Left!" with "Up! Up! Up!" and describing his own army as marching neither to the right nor to the left, but rather upwards, "as smoke and lava spurt to-wards the sky." When in Warsaw Mayakovsky had thanked Słonimski for Słonimski's Polish translation of "Left March," Słonimski had asked him, "And for the response as well?" Mayakovsky answered: "For 'Up' let the powers that be in Poland thank you."[30] Now, however, even the acerbic Słonimski published an affectionate poem to the dead Russian poet, concluding with the words:

> Yet when the great meteor no longer shines,
> When it burns out, when it buries itself in the earth,
> We who, alien and distant, are revolving still
> Send you greetings with lights in the mist.[31]

THE END OF *MIESIĘCZNIK LITERACKI*

In his earlier polemic with Wat, Słonimski was not entirely correct in his accusation of simplistic importing of Russian models: the discourse embodied by *Miesięcznik Literacki,* despite the ever-present dialogue with Soviet literature, was a Polish one. The Soviet Union was a model, but not a master; and Stalin was absent from the monthly's pages. The language of criticism was not yet codified or formulaic; there was still a search for an appropriate idiom. Wat and his friends were much closer to Leninism than to the nascent Stalinism that was developing in the east; they believed that a revolutionary vanguard was needed to bring class consciousness to the masses—and in so doing to nudge History along. It was a time of these intellectuals' genuine effort to find a proletarian literature that would express the exigencies of the class struggle and to find a voice, a language, and an aesthetic with which to write for and about the workers in Poland. No one was certain in what such a literature would consist, or precisely what form it would take.

The culmination of the monthly's attempt to find a proletarian voice and to engage the workers themselves came in Wat's campaign for report-age. In a series of articles, Wat described the evolution from bourgeois to proletarian literature as a move from fiction to fact. He struggled to develop a theory of a communist literary genre, and argued for reportage as the most rational and efficacious literary form.[32] In connection with this, Wat confronted the problem of *Miesięcznik Literacki*'s insufficient accessi-bility to the working masses. Writers must work harder at expressing themselves more directly. Yet at once Wat was defensive: Marxist culture was not about easy lessons. While readers complained about difficult language, "*sometimes* a complete resignation from certain difficulties in expression would be equivalent to a resignation from thought."[33] Here Wat was critical of the workers: until recently their submissions of poetry and prose had been impossible to publish due to weak artistic merit or expression of false ideology. Yet recently the journal had launched a reportage contest, and the results had been remarkably positive—that is, while the workers had not succeeded in writing poetry or fiction, they had succeeded in writing reportage.[34] Wat's call for reportage was closely tied to an implicit progression towards the end of strictly literary literature, and in this way his campaign was self-negating. He himself published neither fiction nor poetry during this time; he believed that there would be no literature as such in a happy communist society. Literature was irrational; and the future had to be built scientifically.[35]

Marxist literary criticism was to be part of this scientific development, and it became the focus of polemics on the pages of *Miesięcznik Literacki*. Apart from examples of proletarian poetry, *Miesięcznik Literacki* published very little in the way of literature, and the journal's content focused rather on discussions of what a true proletarian genre—and true Marxist literary criticism—should be. Andrzej Stawar and Stanisław Ryszard Stande were central figures in this debate. Stawar made the most significant contribution with a series of articles about the development of literary criticism as a genre, the role of the Marxist critic, and the difference between Marxist and bourgeois critics. He contended that the critic's role expanded as the reading masses enlarged. Ultimately literary criticism should serve to facilitate a change in the "mass reader's" "relationship to the whole shape of literary matters—a relationship after all created under the influence of a hostile class ideology."[36] Stande, a poet himself, contributed his own "Talmudic polemic on the subject of the Marxist critic."[37] He was didactic: Marxism was a philosophy, not merely a political doctrine; and Marxist criticism could contribute to the development of class consciousness among the proletariat. Ultimately, however, the proletariat must liberate itself.[38]

Thus in the end, while the journal did publish examples of reportage and autobiography written by actual workers, its pages were dominated by intellectual discussions of Marxist criticism that were internal to the

editorial staff. *Miesięcznik Literacki*'s relations with authentic workers remained tenuous at best, and the workers in its pages often seemed to be
more icons than comrades. This did not go unnoticed. The communist
intelligentsia criticized the monthly's editorial board for publishing overly
intellectual articles and using too many foreign words. In October 1930,
a communist in the Polish provinces wrote to Broniewski: "When are [all
of] you finally going to speak to us in our language, for us?"[39] For these
and other reasons, the KPP also had reservations about *Miesięcznik Literacki*. The Party wanted a less blatantly communist publication, which
could win the support of uncommitted intellectuals with leftist sympathies. It was Wat, Broniewski, and Stawar who had no tolerance for the
uncommitted.[40]

Despite this criticism, *Miesięcznik Literacki* was received with reverence, even (and perhaps especially) by those unable to grasp the intrica-
cies of the debates over Marxist literary criticism. While attacked by his
old friend Słonimski and criticized by the Party he believed in, Wat was
received warmly by the many workers who came to visit him. In general,
they did not complain: "They'd say, yes, it's difficult; you have to take some
trouble and keep on reading, but that's how you learn."[41] The periodical fell
into the hands of a young worker, who remained grateful for his initiation
into the Marxism of intellectuals: "I will not say that at that time my age
and my general level allowed for complete understanding of the content of
that literary publication, intended for readers with an education different
from my own. Yet thanks to *Miesięcznik Literacki* I became acquainted with
the proletarian poems of the poet Władysław Broniewski. . . . At the same
time the book reviews taught me to look critically at everything that presented itself to be read and everything that was happening around me."[42]
In this way, *Miesięcznik Literacki* exerted an unusual influence. Perhaps
for this reason, the monthly attracted unfavorable attention from the state.
Two issues were confiscated, and Wat was forced to move from city to city,
from Warsaw to Cracow, Poznań, and Lwów, in an attempt to evade the
censors. He never had any doubts that it would all end in prison.[43]

INITIATIONS IN PRISON

And so it did. In September 1931 *Miesięcznik Literacki* held an editorial
board meeting at Ola Watowa's parents' apartment in Warsaw. Janina
Broniewska was in another room, visiting with Ola and her newborn

FIGURE 8 Aleksander Wat and Ola Watowa with their infant son, Andrzej.
Reproduction by the Beinecke Rare Book and Manuscript Library, Yale University.

son Andrzej. The delivery had been difficult; Ola Watowa remained ill,
and Broniewska began to help her with the infant. As Broniewski's wife
undressed the baby to change his diaper, she was startled to see that the
revolutionary couple—apparently, despite everything, loyal to the Jewish
tradition of their parents—had had their child circumcised. It was the first

time she had seen this done to a baby, and it saddened her. Ola Watowa, embarrassed, tried to explain: it had been on the doctor's advice.[44]

Then the doorbell rang. Some ten policemen carrying revolvers came into the apartment, led by the assistant commissioner. In the living room where the editorial staff was meeting, stacks of manuscripts lay on the table. Wat sensed the assistant commissioner's disappointment when he discovered it was only editorial material, not actual Party documents.[45] The search went on for several hours. Before being led away, Broniewski managed to whisper to his wife: "If you can manage in time, clean up a bit at home."[46] Searches of the editorial staff's individual apartments followed. Janina Broniewska rushed home to check for potentially incriminating materials before the police arrived. She glanced at her husband's desk and contemplated the book dedicated to him by Mayakovsky, which had by then rested there for several years. How many times had the police already read Mayakovsky's dedication during their searches? She left the book in its place. Yet this time the police did take the book that meant so much to Broniewski, since it served as evidence of "personal contact" with Russian communists.[47] The police escorted Wat back to his own apartment; and Wat worried that materials there relating to a protest he had organized against new prison regulations would incriminate him. What they found instead when they reached his apartment, however, was his maid in bed with "some guy . . . very good-looking."

> A dress coat and dress shirt were hanging on the chair. It turned out that he was a footman from the Italian fascist embassy, a Pole, her sister's fiancé apparently. He was in despair of losing his job. The plainclothesman wanted to take him in along with me. He explained that he worked in the embassy, but the plainclothesman didn't believe him. Finally, we all started laughing because the situation was laughable. The plainclothesman called the embassy to find out if he worked there and then handed him the receiver. He took it and explained that he had dropped by an apartment and the communist who lived there was being arrested. And clearly the people on the other end asked him, "Who is this guy?" to which he answered, "How should I know who the guy is?" That I found irritating. He sleeps with my maid in my

marriage bed and, to top it off, speaks like that of me. And so
I said to the plainclothesman in jest, "You know, maybe we
should be brought in together." But of course they let him go.[48]

They did not let the editorial board of *Miesięcznik Literacki* go. That night
the police arrested Aleksander Wat, Władysław Broniewski, Andrzej Stawar, and Jan Hempel, together with a KPP member who had been at-
tending the meeting as a Party representative and Wat's twenty-year-old
brother-in-law, a medical student who was uninvolved in the project.[49]

Ola Watowa and Janina Broniewska, in consultation with each other, began their visits to lawyers. Broniewska paid a visit to Stawar's mother
as well, who received her warmly, although they had never met.[50] Ola
Watowa went to see an attorney. "Now, please tell me," he asked her,
"which would you prefer: that your husband sit in prison or that he cheat
on you?" Revolutionary proclivities aside, with respect to her marriage
she remained a traditionalist. "Let him sit in prison," she answered without hesitation.[51] She went as well to the Skamander poets—Tuwim, Słonimski, and Wierzyński—who attempted to use their influence on behalf of
the imprisoned revolutionary writers.[52] Tuwim made a date to meet with
Janina Broniewska "ostentatiously" at Café Ziemiańska; he helped her put
together food packages and take them to the prison.[53] Moreover, Słonimski
now behaved generously, publishing a public response, the pretext for
which was a letter from a reader of *Wiadomości Literackie*. The reader had
inquired if, given what he had heard about the arrested staff of *Miesięcznik
Literacki*'s having been maneuvering large sums of money, the journal
would continue to exist and if so, might they be accepting new people.
Słonimski concluded his response: "I don't know in what kind of world
you were born, but in any case your birth was unnecessary. I burned your
letter, since it was a curiosity of madness, greediness, stupidity, and moral
misery. I don't want to keep such distastefulness in my home."[54]

For those on the editorial staff, the prison experience was a significant
one. In the initial period following their arrest, all six of their group were
in Security, in basement cell number 13, where Tuwim's friend Colonel
Wieniawa-Długoszowski sent them two large bags of food and vodka from
Hirschfeld's delicatessen.[55] Wat learned quickly that, while he did not
behave in too cowardly a way, he did not have the endurance for prison.

What he did possess was an "inborn sense of fatalism." Daily food packages came from his family, always with a letter from Ola tucked inside the head of the herring. Prison was difficult for Stawar as well, who became closed into himself and fatalistic about their possible sentences. Hempel, older and a Party member, fared better.

Jan Hempel emerged as the wise father figure in the cell. The KPP was in turmoil during this time; Hempel had been living in constant anxiety about what the Party leadership would say, whether the Party line would suddenly change. Now in prison his anxiety dissipated, he knew how to act, he grew calm. He reconciled conflicts in the cell and taught the others how to behave in prison.[56] Communist discipline came easily to him. On one occasion the communists in prison had concluded a hunger strike and the commune leader was sent from cell to cell to inform the other communists that the hunger strike was over. Hempel, however, was reluctant to credit such informal notification and demanded to be sent something in writing.[57] His faith was the most unproblematic; it stabilized and contented him. Awakened at night by painful stomach ulcers, he would tell his companions that at that very moment, in the new Soviet town of Magnitogorsk, socialism was being built. Both Wat and Broniewski were struck by this "quiet passion."[58] Broniewski wrote a poem about sitting with Hempel in cell number 13 and counting the hours when Hempel groaned, awakened, sat up and told him, "You know in Magnitogorsk / today two great furnaces are being fired."[59]

Shortly after arriving in prison, Broniewski asked his wife to send food that could be easily shared, underwear, a cup and spoon, cologne, shaving supplies, *Wiadomości Literackie*, a Russian dictionary, and everything by Pasternak.[60] To Wat, Broniewski appeared somewhat crazed, pacing in circles around the cell like "an animal, a caged lion," unable to reconcile himself to the enclosure, conjuring up fantastical escape plans.[61] Wat accused Broniewski of behaving like a "horrible egoist," and yet noted that "there was something attractive about him. *Indomitable*, totally undaunted, he was constantly pacing the cell, marching around, smoking one cigarette after another."[62] It seems that it was Broniewski's narcissism that saved him. Even in prison, he was always a poet. Suffering from insomnia, he would not let the others sleep either. He would toss and turn, leap out of bed, grab one of his friends by the hand, and begin to recite poetry—sometimes his own, sometimes Polish Romantic poetry of the previous century. Wat was resentful; he wanted to sleep. But he admired his friend: Broniewski was a poet "in the good sense of the word, who absolutely refused to descend from that *mode d'exister* that is the poet: poetry in any circumstance."[63]

Wat and Broniewski were not together for very long. The *Miesięcznik Literacki* prisoners were moved upstairs to Centralniak, Warsaw's central prison, where they now found themselves in separate cells with real workers, real communists. The KPP members were experienced at spending long periods of time in prison; they used the time to rest from their work on the street, and to solidify their Marxist education. Polish prisons served as universities for communists, who were extremely organized and disciplined about their time there. Wat was struck by their phenomenal memory for quotations and statistics, and speculated that some of them must have had Talmudic education in their childhood.[64] The communists maintained a rigid schedule of lessons, discussions, and lectures. They knew that *Miesięcznik Literacki* had joined them in prison, and from the larger-than-life revolutionary writers they harbored various expectations. Communist discipline, however, did not come easily for Broniewski and Wat, both fellow travelers unused to Party rules of behavior. Broniewski was neither very interested in the lessons nor eager to take part in them. He was busy translating Gogol. Young workers in the cell could not understand why Broniewski, an intellectual, would not want to participate; a delegate had to raise the matter with him twice.[65] Wat was willing to give lectures as requested, but this, too, was not without its problems. The prisoners had books, including one by Bukharin. Wat was unimpressed by the Bolshevik theoretician and struck by his overly simplified philosophy. When Wat began to polemicize condescendingly against the text, the workers sensed that something was wrong, and Wat's role as a lecturer was quickly put to an end.[66] On another occasion, Wat upset the commune leader by refusing to share his food packages according to the commune's mandates—that is, he said he would share, but at his own discretion, and not that of the commune. The commune leader appealed to Broniewski to use his influence on his friend, and Broniewski obligingly smuggled a letter to Wat chastising him and accusing him of being "a communist for 1,200 złotys a month."[67]

Despite these tensions, prison was a positive experience. While Wat and Broniewski were reluctant to submit to commune discipline, they were full of affection for the workers. The workers, Wat noticed, "did not reciprocate that affection, though on the whole relations were good."[68] Broniewski had a talent for making contact with people, and impressed others with his ability to forge a relationship with a young semiliterate worker. He found a common language with the prison guard as well, and would sit on a table in the corridor, reciting his poetry to the aging guard with a big belly who sat and listened with tears in his eyes. The singing of poetry set to a melody was a popular prison ritual among communists, and Broniewski sang to his fellow communist cellmates his 1929 poem "Bezrobotny" (Unemployed). "Unemployed" became a favorite, and Broniewski became a legend as a poet who captured the prison experience for communists.[69]

In the communist tradition prison was a rite of passage. Before this moment, Wat had been plagued with insecurity, with guilt for not having been imbued with the true spirit of the moment, for carrying within himself the legacy of poetry, of bourgeois decadence. It was only in prison that he was given an opportunity to become worthy; he saw his imprisonment as a coming of age, a potential liberation from his fear of contaminating the cause with his intellectualism:[70] "But this was also a certain baptism, a knighting. . . . I consoled myself that I would come out of it not as a broken, flabby intellectual but as a manly, courageous revolutionary." Spirits were high and the revolutionary writers "found prison so interesting that there really was no time to think about ourselves. Those were lively days."

CHAPTER FIVE

Entanglements, Terror, and the Fine Art of Confession

Bruno Schulz would come to visit us . . . Andrzej, a small child at that time, having remained with us for a little while, gazed with curiosity at our guest and suddenly left for the bathroom. He returned after a while with a fairly large piece of wood and, having approached me, said: "Mommy, beat me!" . . . And this because, in connection with that wonderful writer's drawings, he was regarded in Warsaw as a masochist . . . Was it some kind of magnetic fluids? Telepathy? or perhaps—simply—the whimsical act of a child?

—*Ola Watowa*

MIESIĘCZNIK LITERACKI WAS NO more. Janina Broniewska called the editorial offices of *Wiadomości Literackie* to tell them her husband was in prison and would not be coming to work. The director at the office took the news graciously, proposing that Janina Broniewska fill her husband's position in the interim. She accepted, although not without some nervousness. Her new boss was supportive, promising not to be overly demanding in Broniewski's "momentary," as they called it, absence.[1] The situation was indeed temporary. Jan Hempel was the first to be released. He was seriously ill when *Miesięcznik Literacki*'s editorial board was arrested, and after negotiations through an attorney was released on the condition that he leave Poland. The Party gave its assent, and Hempel departed Warsaw's central prison for Moscow.[2] This communist rite of passage had concluded for the others within some two months' time. On 8 November 1931, Broniewski's grandmother wrote to him from Płock. She had been overjoyed to find his letter, after having given up all hope that he would leave the "sanatorium." She hoped her grandson had learned his lesson and would henceforth be more careful in his activities and his choice of company. Perhaps now he would, at long last, find his way to God.[3] The experience did elicit a certain faith in Janina Broniewska: from this period of her life she took "the ability to insert proofreader's marks and a faith in friends who appear and prove loyal in times of real crisis."[4]

Wat returned from prison to find his favorite sister, Ewa Chwat, in the hospital; she died the following day. His maid went to work for Tadeusz Boy-Żeleński, the famous literary critic a quarter-century older than Wat who was Irena Krzywicka's lover.[5] *Miesięcznik Literacki* no longer existed, and Wat began to search for work. Who would employ him with the label *żydokomuna* (Judeo-Bolshevism) attached to him? In the end, Wat was introduced to Jan Gebethner, the owner of a publishing house, and Gebethner hired Wat as editor of the literary division. Wat raised the publishing house from the ground—making only one mistake: he rejected Witold Gombrowicz's manuscript *Ferdydurke,* which subsequently became a literary sensation. Gombrowicz came to Café Ziemiańska, and Wat did not like him.[6] Gebethner became Wat's friend and defender against right-wing, National Democratic attacks.[7] Wat's life resumed. He saw Witkacy again, they went drinking. Witkacy stared at Wat, uncomprehending. How could a person stand eight weeks in prison? Later when Wat visited Witkacy in Zakopane, the older writer "kept grabbing his head and saying, 'Aleksander, how could you stand it? Eight weeks!' We talked about a hundred different things, but he kept interrupting: 'How can a person stand eight weeks in prison?'"[8]

Wat had no certainty that this was the conclusion of his prison experience. Following his release in autumn 1931, Wat was subject to frequent searches, particularly before workers' holidays such as May Day. At times the police officers conducting the searches would appear to be scrutinizing Wat's books with genuine interest. One policeman in particular stayed in Wat's mind, as "a former half-intellectual"; he was impressed with the selection of books and asked questions about the authors. He behaved so well that Ola Watowa invited him to sit down with a book over a cup of tea. Other times the tone was less pleasant, and books would fly onto the floor. Once Stawar happened to be visiting, and at a certain moment fixed himself in one spot on the floor and stood there for a long time. Ola Watowa became annoyed that he was getting in the way of the men conducting the search, and told him to sit down somewhere. Afterwards he berated her for that, as he had been standing on an illegal publication.[9]

In 1933 the police found illegal publications in Adam Ważyk's apartment. He was arrested and detained for three weeks under suspicion of cooperation with a communist organization. Then he was released.[10] Broniewski and his wife were also subjected to more frequent searches.

One day in December 1932 Janina Broniewska was at home when, among the police functionaries conducting the search, there appeared for the first time a female officer "in heavy make-up, red nail polish and bleached curls."[11] This time she and her husband were both taken to prison. Janina Broniewska was released the following morning, and Broniewski not more than a day later. This was, though, the beginning of the end of her career as a schoolteacher, even though she refused to submit her resignation. She went to Kalisz to visit her mother and contemplate a new profession. "And what now?" she asked, "Begin life all over again? How, where?"[12] Yet she did begin anew, finding her second career as a children's author.

THE ROAD EAST

While Wat and Broniewski endured police searches and threats of arrest, some of their friends had escaped from what they spoke of as fascist Poland, heading east into the depths of the Soviet Union. *Miesięcznik Literacki* had strengthened contacts with the USSR, and now Wat and the others were frequently invited to receptions at the Soviet embassy in Warsaw, where no one spoke about politics and "everyone threw themselves greedily and unceremoniously upon the caviar."[13] The gatherings were "of enormous importance because to us those were people from 'over there,'" Wat wrote, "Russia, a gigantic country, savage, neglected for hundreds of years, where a new life for humanity was to be built, where humanity would be organized on ideal foundations."[14]

Notwithstanding his enthusiasm for prison stays in the company of authentic workers, Witold Wandurski, once released on bail in 1928, had crossed the Polish border illegally. He traveled to Berlin, Gdańsk, and Moscow before settling in Kiev, in Soviet Ukraine, where he directed an amateur Polish workers' theater.[15] In an introduction to a Russian edition of Broniewski's poetry, Wandurski described his now faraway friend as a "revolutionary lyricist." Yet the introduction was neither uncritical nor devoid of a certain condescension. Wandurski reflected back upon Broniewski's past in Piłsudski's Legions and traced Broniewski's journey from Polish patriotism to socialist patriotism—a trajectory Wandurski described as "typical for the better representatives of the central European intelligentsia from bourgeois backgrounds who have become fellow travelers of proletarian literature." Moreover, Broniewski's evolution remained incomplete, imperfect: "Broniewski did not fully embrace the ideology of the revolutionary proletariat. He did not possess the philosophy of dialectical materialism. In the poet the idealist-romantic struggles with the materialist-revolutionary."[16]

Wandurski was not alone in heading east. As a result of *I Burn Paris*, in May 1929 Bruno Jasieński was arrested in France and escorted to the German border. He stayed in Berlin for several days before sailing on to Leningrad, where he arrived on 21 May. His reception upon disembarking was grandiose: a delegation of writers awaited him at the train station. At the Arch of Triumph a crowd of several hundred had gathered to greet the Polish revolutionary who had been deported from bourgeois France.[17] Among the crowd was the Hungarian writer Antal Hidas, the husband of the Hungarian communist leader Béla Kun's daughter Agnes. Hidas watched Jasieński step off the train carrying a small suitcase, pursued by a policeman, moved and confused by the delegation awaiting him. A voice from the crowd announced: "the Soviet constitution guarantees to every revolutionary persecuted in his own homeland or in another country the right of asylum."[18] A Russian literary newspaper wrote of the arrival of "Bruno Jasieński—the most dangerous enemy of the bourgeoisie and the most faithful friend, the most devoted fighter of the working class."[19] It was one of many such articles. Attracting the most attention was the laudatory piece by M. Zhivov, the Russian translator of both Jasieński's poetry and Żeromski's *The Spring to Come*. Zhivov used Jasieński's biography to expose the suffering and persecution to which revolutionary writers were subjected in the "'highly civilized' countries of the West." Zhivov presented the twenty-nine-year-old Jasieński as a proletarian writer engaged in the struggle against fascism in literature, the victim of bourgeois literary critics beginning with Żeromski, the victim as well of the police in his own country, where he was denied opportunities to publish and eventually forced to emigrate to a life of poverty and suffering in Paris. While idealizing Jasieński's biography and praising his work, Zhivov also acknowledged—echoing Wat's self-criticism of Polish futurism—that "in Jasieński's conclusions one sometimes feels anarchistic tendencies." He was confident, though, that a stay in the Soviet Union and collaboration with Soviet proletarian writers would help Jasieński to cast off this tendency.[20]

Not everyone appreciated Jasieński's enthusiastic welcome. On 7 June 1929, Stanisław Ryszard Stande composed a letter, addressed to Jasieński but sent to the KPP section of the Comintern, protesting Zhivov's portrayal of Jasieński's persecution in Poland and his leading role in Polish proletarian literature. Stande affixed, moreover, the signatures of Jan Hempel, Witold Wandurski, Władysław Broniewski, and Andrzej Stawar. Jasieński replied in a thirteen-page typed letter to the KPP section of the Comintern, which did not neglect to counterattack his Polish comrades. He denied the charge of "self-advertisement." He attached a statement by Jan Hempel in which Hempel denied that he had authorized Stande to use his name, as well as a statement by Zhivov to the effect that any inadvertent distortions in his article were his own error and responsibility, not those of Jasieński—who had in any case arrived only on the day that the article was published and had not been involved in its composition.[21] Jasieński continued, in a lengthy account of his publishing history in Poland, to defend Zhivov's statement: it was true that the doors of publishing houses in Poland had been largely closed to him. It was only with the assistance of Comrade Barbusse in France that he had been able to find a French publisher for *I Burn Paris*.[22]

The second half of Jasieński's response acquired a more insidious character. If Wandurski had at times been condescending, Jasieński was vicious. He denied having falsified the history of Polish proletarian culture in the interest of self-promotion. His poetry readings had been organized under the slogan of a battle against bourgeois culture. This was true despite the fact that this battle was "an impotent battle, due to insufficiently taking into account political battle and being cut off from the daily revolutionary battle of the working masses." Jasieński's and Stern's work may have been anarchistic, but it was an expression of protest against religion, against bourgeois art and culture; here Jasieński admitted that Stern was indeed presently a "panegyrist of Piłsudski and a neo-Catholic," but reminded them that at that time Stern had been "a lampooner of the bourgeoisie and an antireligious poet." Moreover, back then Stande had been appearing publicly with mystical and religious poets like Józef Wittlin and Comrade Broniewski was appearing with the "loyally-submissive-to-Belweder and aestheticizing group Skamander." Jasieński did not stop there. He returned to Stande's original letter, quoting the sentence directed at himself: "You know well, that a whole series of people *from the first years of independence—not only those signed below* . . . were creating the foundations of proletarian culture in Poland, they went with the live word to the labor unions, to the factories, to the mines and to other reservoirs of proletarian masses."

Stande's claim was the point of departure for Jasieński's counterattack:

Who among the comrades who signed the letter was creating the foundations of proletarian culture and went with the live word to unions and mines "from the first years of indepen- dence"? Passing over Comrade Hempel, whose signature, after all, was affixed to the letter without his consent and knowledge, and who perhaps with the greatest justification could sign un- der that sentence, even Comrade Stande, being a Party mem- ber from the first years of independence, in those first years in the realm of superstructure cannot boast that he was creating the foundations of proletarian culture. His poetic appearances from those times in one front with the mystics Wittlin and Stur cannot in any way be regarded as foundations of proletarian culture. Comrade Stande joined his literary activity to a certain extent to the class movement only considerably later. Comrade Broniewski in the first years of independence was a Legion- naire and a Piłsudskiite and as a writer was not yet present. Until the time of my departure from Poland, that is, until 1925, he was taking his first literary steps under the wings of the loyally-submissive-to-Belweder group Skamander, publishing in their publications and appearing at their literary evenings. His first romantic lyrical poetry, published by the bourgeois publishing house Czarski, likewise cannot in any way qualify as "foundations of proletarian culture." In this period, when all of bourgeois criticism, beginning with Żeromski, ending with the last literary hack, qualified my literary activity (too flatteringly after all) as Bolshevism in literature, when the police, possessing, apparently, a better sense of smell than you, dear Comrades, broke up my poetry readings (Warsaw, Nowy Sącz), banned me from public appearances (Lwów), removed me via administrative means from some districts (Nowy Sącz), claiming in their order that my (literary!) activity on the terrain of the given district was "undesirable in the interest of the Polish Republic," at that same time the co-author of your letter

and alleged creator of proletarian culture "from the first years
of independence," Comrade Broniewski, was welcomed by
bourgeois criticism (Pannenkowa) almost enthusiastically
as a talented new pupil of the aestheticizing Skamander, he
was even for a certain time the editor of the Belweder-court
Wiadomości Literackie (standing in for Grydzewski). Others
may, but Comrade Broniewski should not be signing himself
under the number of those "before whom the doors of publishing houses were essentially closed." He took the first steps
of his creative work under the protective wings of favorable
bourgeois criticism, he had at his disposal the bourgeois publishers of the Skamandrites, at a time when none of us could
even dream about a publisher for poetic works.

Whoever else of those comrades signing the letter "were
creating the foundations of proletarian culture from the first
years of independence"? Was Comrade Wandurski, who not
long before my departure from Poland in the same *Wiadomości
Literackie,* in an interview given to the editors, announced
to everyone his critical attitude to the October Revolution,
attesting that his most recent play could never be performed
in the USSR because the censors there would not permit it,
standing in the pose of a martyr, "the spirit of the eternal
revolutionary," persecuted on both one side of the barricade
and the other?[23] . . .

For this reason your sentence directed at me claiming that
"at that time" I was not among you is amusing in its pompous-
ness. Likewise at that time, in the first years of independence,
neither were you, Comrade Broniewski, nor you, Comrade
Wandurski, nor you, Comrade Stawar, not in the mines, not
in the factories, nor in the communist party. Your connection
with the revolutionary movement at that time was just as
indirect as mine.[24]

Jasieński was relentless. He reminded his critics that even while his
early work might have borne the character of anarchistic rebellion, he
had always stood for unconditional affirmation of the October Revolution.
Moreover, as far as he was concerned, during his entire time in Poland

no groups of proletarian writers as such even existed—*Three Salvos* appeared only in November 1925, three months after his departure. In the meantime Broniewski and Stawar were attacking him in *Dźwignia* and in the bourgeois *Wiadomości Literackie*, claiming that in his long poem about a rebellious peasant hero, *A Word about Jakub Szela*, Jasieński was apotheosizing Szela, who was in fact an agent of the Austrian imperial authorities.[25] Despite this, Jasieński continued, when years earlier Anatol Stern had criticized the authors of *Three Salvos*, Jasieński had stood in full solidarity with Broniewski, Wandurski, and Stande. That current articles in the Soviet press overlooked the latters' contribution to Polish proletarian literature in favor of aggrandizing Jasieński's own role was not Jasieński's fault. If, of course, he were to write his own article for the Soviet press he would never "usurp" for himself a monopoly and would rather place his own name clearly together with theirs—despite his hesitations regarding some of their work. This was, after all, not a time to quarrel over small differences when in Poland there were so few in their camp at all. Rather than bickering over who was first, Jasieński suggested, they might all benefit from submitting their literary work to harsh Bolshevik criticism in the interest of "in the fire of discussion ridding ourselves of rudiments alien to the ideology and psyche of the proletariat, which we inherited from the class we all came from, and which often manifest themselves in an improper, un-Bolshevik approach to matters."[26]

Perhaps Wandurski, Stawar, and Broniewski had agreed to have their names signed under Stande's letter, perhaps they had not. In either case, Jasieński's reply was potentially devastating, at a moment when accusations among communists were not taken lightly. In the Soviet Union, the purges had already begun. Across the border in Poland, it was true that Stern continued to struggle to negotiate his Marxism, his Catholicism, and his Polish patriotism. His lengthy 1934 poem "Piłsudski" portrayed his efforts to reconcile his feelings about the poverty and suffering he saw in Poland with both his nostalgia for the romantic tradition of the socialist patriots and his awareness that this era had passed. So it was that little remained of Piłsudski the socialist. In spring of 1930 Piłsudski arrested some hundred oppositional parliamentary deputies and imprisoned them in a camp in Brześć; the November 1930 elections were fraudulent. In "Piłsudski" Stern wrote of being told by Cezary Baryka, the young protagonist of *The Spring to Come*, that communism could be created now just as it could at another time; to win independence for a second time, however, would be much harder. "I want to fight only in liberated Poland," Stern wrote. Yet in the last stanza he returned to both *The Earth to the Left* and Mayakovsky's "Left March":

> Enough already.
> The past of your dreams returns.
> Our hand will not quiver like a leaf
> the hand that raised the lever of Polish freedom.—
> To the left, leader of Poland!
> If you want to go together with the Poland of labor—
> to the left!![27]

CREATING POLISH SOVIET CULTURE

Stanisław Ryszard Stande had in truth been among the very first in Polish literary circles to devote his work to the communist movement. He had joined the Communist Party of Poland just after the First World War; his own prison initiation came a full decade before the arrest of *Miesięcznik Literacki*'s editorial board.[28] By September 1931, when his friends were arrested, Stande was no longer in Warsaw. In 1931 he and his second wife Zofia Warska moved to Moscow, where they lived with Warska's father, the legendary Polish communist leader Adolf Warski.[29] Initially Stande did not envision his stay as permanent; in late 1932, he wrote to Broniewski that his poor health had delayed his return to Poland.[30] Whatever his original intentions, Stande, like Jasieński, came to play an active role in Soviet cultural politics, participating in the poetry section of the Soviet Writers' Union, traveling to literary gatherings in areas of Soviet Ukraine and Belarus with large Polish populations, publishing poetry and Polish translations of Russian literature, and devoting much time to work in the International Association of Revolutionary Writers.[31] Among Stande's projects was the Polish-language monthly *Kultura Mas* (The Culture of the Masses).

Kultura Mas had actually come into being some two years before Stande's arrival under the supervision of Bruno Jasieński. Upon his arrival in Moscow, Jasieński had immediately joined the Russian Association of Proletarian Writers and acquired a Russian wife, the obese journalist Anna Berziń, even as his first wife, Klara Arem, was en route with their infant son to join him in Russia. In June 1929, Jasieński, as the editor of *Kultura Mas,* disseminated a call for Polish writers in the Soviet Union to contribute to the magazine; he called as well for criticism of the first issue's "insufficiencies."[32] In addition to Jasieński, Hempel and Wandurski were among the paper's main contributors. That the venture was jeopardized by a scarcity of suitable authors emerged from Jasieński's letter of June 1929 to Broniewski and Stawar in Warsaw, pleading with them to send him material.[33] Jasieński inaugurated the paper with a daring article about linguistic revolution, a tendentious call for self-criticism among Poles in the Soviet Union who were corrupting Polish with Russicisms. Poles active in the Soviet Union must not lose their connection either with the working masses in "fascist Poland" or with the Polish peasant masses in the Soviet Union, Jasieński argued. He insisted that the task of the moment was the "weeding out" of Soviet Polish; the replacing of Russian socialist expressions with Polish ones; and the vigorous enforcement of the entire process. *Kultura Mas,* Jasieński promised, would do its part.[34]

From Kiev, Wandurski donated his own prolific thoughts regarding the creation of Polish proletarian culture. A 1929 issue included his characteristically long-winded article "Let's Make a Polish Revolutionary Film." After all, according to Wandurski, Polish filmmakers possessed splendid, firsthand material in the Polish proletariat, "presently striding in the first ranks of the revolutionary avant-garde of the capitalist West." He cautioned potential revolutionary filmmakers to avoid "literature" in the cinema, as such was "the road to kitsch." Most importantly, films should be optimistic and include a "revolutionary 'happy ending,'" a phrase Wandurski invoked in English. He returned to the language of joy and optimism that had colored his letters to Broniewski several years earlier, and suggested a film about the International Organization for Aid to Revolutionaries that would bear the title "Let's Have the Courage to Look Joyfully!"[35] A second article by Wandurski, published in early 1930, told of his new Polish theater, barely five months old, founded from the old Teatr-Studium in Kiev. Given that this old theater was "allegedly artistic but in essence snobbish and anti-Soviet," everything had to be built anew, an enormous task, but one for which he was prepared, having drawn upon the examples of the Ukrainian and Jewish theaters. "A Soviet Polish theater possessing the strength to battle for cultural revolution—this we do not yet have," Wandurski wrote, "But we will. Whatever conditions may be, this must be a revolutionary theater, worker-peasant, proletarian in content, Polish in form (language, style, culture, emotions)."[36]

In a 1931 essay for *Kultura Mas* about Polish proletarian literature, Stande revisited the Polish literary scene of the 1920s, presenting an alternative narrative to the one by Zhivov that had so angered him. In the early years of independence, he began, both the intelligentsia and a certain segment of the working class had been ensorceled by illusions about newly independent Poland—illusions Stande perceived as purposefully cultivated by Piłsudski's Polish Socialist Party so as to strengthen the bourgeois state. In Stande's telling of the story, prior to 1925 it was not possible to speak of any proletarian cultural movement, but only of individual activists. Stande emphasized the role of Hempel; he wrote of *Three Salvos, Dźwignia,* and the graphic artist Mieczysław Szczuka, who had died tragically in the Tatra mountains during *Dźwignia's* short life. Stawar, in Stande's reading, came into his own as a Marxist critic in *Dźwignia,* and Stanisław Wygodzki, among others, began his poetic career there. Moreover, Stande wrote, "finally the excellent prose writer Aleksander Wat crossed over to our group from the petty bourgeois camp." Much of the second half of the article was devoted to the recently deceased *Miesięcznik Literacki,* which represented a new epoch in Marxist literary thought. While, Stande wrote, "a 'higher force' in the form of fascist censorship did not permit us to develop that discussion further in the direction of deepening self-criticism," this should not diminish the accomplishments of *Miesięcznik Literacki:* its reportage competition, its battle against fascism, its development of ties with Ukrainian and Jewish proletarian writers. Unlike Jasieński, Stande remained openly attached to his pre-Soviet life. "While submitting our errors and insufficiencies to self-criticism," he concluded, "it is nonetheless necessary to emphasize the enormous achievements that this period brought."[37]

The emphasis on culture socialist in content and Polish in form bore dangers. By the beginning of the decade, Stalin had consolidated his power in the Soviet Union, and Jan Hempel's 1933 self-criticism on behalf of the paper was saturated with conspicuously Stalinist language. Hempel cited Stalin from the Sixteenth Party Congress to the effect that the entry into socialism had not meant that national languages were dying out and merging into one common language, but rather just the opposite: national languages and cultures were further evolving. Moreover, the theory that posited the melting together of all nations into one great Russian nation was a chauvinist, anti-Leninist theory. Hempel went on to criticize *Kultura Mas* for not having succeeded in gathering around itself a group of writers and activists who would ignite battle on the Polish cultural front. What exactly this Polish cultural front would consist of was a delicate question; and Hempel considered the paper's earlier declaration that the development of Polish socialist culture in the Soviet Union would be possible only with the victory of the Revolution in fascist Poland as an opportunist error. Although this erroneous view had been recanted and its leading representatives had publicly acknowledged their error, Hempel made clear this should not be understood to mean that these views had been fully overcome.[38]

The Soviet *korenizatsiia* campaign to "indigenize" communist culture coexisted uneasily with accusations of bourgeois nationalism. Even for the most disciplined communists, the shifting Party line was difficult to follow; and *korenizatsiia* proved to be a double-edged sword. By late 1930, Bruno Jasieński, under pressure, had signed a self-criticism confessing to "nationalist deviation." Now he gave up the editorship of *Kultura Mas* to become more and more a Russian writer and cultural figure. Wandurski, too, was accused of "nationalist opportunist" inclinations. Unlike Jasieński, however, Wandurski refused to sign a "declaration of repentance," until threats of expulsion from the Communist Party and other repressions forced him to relent.[39] By late 1932 Wandurski could apparently no longer endure Soviet life. When Władysław Daszewski traveled to the Soviet Union as an official representative of Polish scenography, Wandurski went to see him in Moscow, desperate to find a way back to Poland. Daszewski put Wandurski in contact with the military attaché at the Polish embassy.[40]

MANNEQUINS AND TADZHIK EAGLES

Jasieński's resignation from the editorship of *Kultura Mas* was symbolic of his break with the Polish world and immersion into the Soviet one. Sovietization, even writing in Russian, came easily to him. In 1930, Jasieński played a leading role at the World Congress of Revolutionary Writers in Kharkov as the accuser of Henri Barbusse, the editor of the French paper *Monde,* who had been his patron and protector in Paris.[41] In May 1931, now two years after his arrival in Russia, Jasieński published an autobiographical essay, revisiting his childhood, not neglecting to confess to his "petty bourgeois origins," and describing his father, a provincial doctor who lived his entire life twenty-five miles from the nearest railway station and offered free care to impoverished peasants. Jasieński had entered university in Cracow in 1918, "that wonderful year when independent Poland burst forth from the ruins of the Habsburg and Hohenzollern monarchies, blown up by the dynamite of the October Revolution."[42]

Jasieński traced his literary trajectory from his rebellious youth to his communist commitment. His first works, which appeared in 1919–1920, still bore traces of "formal searchings," as a result of the "intentional vulgarity" of his treatment of the sacred and untouchable ideals of independence, national culture, religion, and the cult of war. He added, however, that the following year he condemned these same works in poetic self-criticism. He considered his 1922 "A Poem about Hunger" to be the first meaningful work in postwar Polish literature hailing the social revolution. It was while translating articles by Lenin that he had become acquainted with the theory and practice of class war. In retrospect, he saw the years 1924–1928 as a time of internal creative crisis, a time when he believed that writing in the old way was erroneous, but when he did not yet know how to write in a new way. *Jakub Szela* was his first step on the path to proletarian literature. Thereafter, his need for engagement in battle led him to abandon poetry for prose, the result of which was *I Burn Paris*. Here in the Soviet Union he had recently written *Bal manekenov* (*The Mannequins' Ball*), "a grotesque play about contemporary social democracy in the West." He had been moved to write it, he explained to his readers, "by the lack of cheerful plays in our revolutionary repertoire that would allow the proletarian viewer to spend two hours engaged in healthy laughter at his enemies."[43]

That same year, 1931, *The Mannequin's Ball* appeared in Russian. The play was set in Paris, and began in a fashion house during the mannequins' ball. A tango played in the background; mannequins whirled about the stage and discussed rapidly changing fashions. "There's a rumor flat-chested figures won't be in vogue next year. Women with well-developed busts are coming back into fashion again. If that's true, then we'll all be tossed on the scrap heap next year," said a female mannequin.[44] They spoke disparagingly of their human counterparts: "I don't believe there's anything to be learned from humans. I've seen more than enough of all those dandies who frequent our workshops. They're all only worthless copies made in our image! I feel like bursting out laughing when I look at those twisted monstrosities. . . . I simply can't understand why our clothes should be given to them. No matter what you do, on them everything will always look ghastly."[45]

The mannequins' festivities were interrupted by the intrusion of Ribandel, a bourgeois socialist leader on his way to a party thrown by an auto manufacturer. Ribandel had wandered into the mannequins' ball by accident, having followed a female mannequin there, unaware that she was not a woman. The appearance of the uninvited guest was not pleasing to the mannequins, who decided that Ribandel's head should be cut off. They did so with a pair of scissors, and afterwards drew lots for the head. The happy winner donned the human head and proceeded to the auto manufacturer's ball in Ribandel's place while Ribandel, headless, wandered away in blind pursuit of his severed head. It was in the mannequin-impostor's encounter with Ribandel's world that Jasieński's exposé of bourgeois society emerged. Although Ribandel carried all the correct cards—he was a member of the League for the Protection of Human and Civil Rights, the French Socialist Party, and so forth—he was nevertheless inextricably wedded to the decadent bourgeois world. The play concluded when the headless Ribandel had finally found his way to the ball. His impostor rushed towards him: "Please, here's your head! Take it. Take it quickly! I've had enough of it! I was tempted for nothing! When I won the head, I was happy. I thought I'd found a treasure. To hell with your head! Now I know what you need it for! We made the right decision to cut off that bad apple's head. But what's the use? Can we cut off all your heads? There aren't enough scissors. And it's really not our business. Others are coming who can do a better job than we could."[46]

The Mannequins' Ball was communist theater woven from futurist and absurdist elements, at a moment when the Party had begun to dictate the proper form of communist literature. On 21 September 1933 the play had its world premiere in Prague, but it was never performed in the Soviet Union during Jasieński's lifetime. It was seen by Soviet critics as too fantastical and too little realist, despite a generous introduction by Anatolii Lunacharsky, one of the main theoreticians of socialist realism, who wrote:

"Once you have accepted the mirror of the fantastic held up by the author, you will grasp how curiously, originally, delectably and sarcastically it reflects the 'bourgeois-socialist' world."[47]

Jasieński defended his play, even while engaged in recanting other ideological stances he had recently embraced. In a June 1932 letter to the executive Comintern committee on the restructuring of the International Association of Revolutionary Writers, Jasieński offered a lengthy confession of his earlier errors. Having recanted two years earlier his right-wing nationalist deviation, now he regretted not having fought harder against left-wing deviations and specifically not having cooperated sufficiently with the "broad masses of the petty bourgeois intelligentsia." "I regard as one of the most serious errors committed by the leadership of the International Association of Revolutionary Writers and by myself personally," he wrote, "the breaking of ties with significant groups of writers and artists friendly towards the socialist enterprise." He regretted as well having been so quick to place Barbusse in the "social-fascist" camp. Nonetheless he tried to justify himself: at the time when he wrote the resolution against Barbusse, Barbusse's magazine *Monde* was publishing articles "reviling the French Communist Party as a party of prevaricators and schemers and *Monde*'s political line was almost entirely in accord with that of French social fascism." He admitted responsibility for his error. "As the only communist from the leadership of the International Association of Revolutionary Writers," he wrote, "I participated in the French revolutionary movement and should have demonstrated much more farsightedness in this matter; furthermore, I should have taken under consideration the amplitude of the oscillations of French petty bourgeois fellow travelers who, departing 'to the right,' can suddenly turn 'to the left.'" Much of the rest of this lengthy letter was devoted to accusation. The object was Stande and his "opposition group" in the International Association of Revolutionary Writers, who had leveled "unfounded, undocumented reproaches" against Jasieński during his stay in Tadzhikistan.[48]

Jasieński did not shy from taking the offensive in Soviet literary politics. He found socialist realism too constricting and insufficiently inventive. At the All-Union Congress of Writers in September 1934, in an implicit defense of *The Mannequins' Ball,* he counterattacked Soviet writers for their stylistic and aesthetic conservatism, for the reticence of their imaginations: "I accuse our literature of being too timid, too empirical in following on the heels of reality. . . . I raise my voice in a toast: to bold invention, erected on the material of living reality, but not afraid to step across into tomorrow, full of the unexpected."[49] Jasieński argued for the expansion of Engelsian realism—the typical individual in typical circumstances—and accused Soviet writers of having limited themselves too much to stereotypical circumstances, the result of which had been schematism and ossification. This is why, Jasieński related, "our worker, after reading another book about new building, impatiently asks, 'This is the new book? But I've already read it!'"[50] The following year, at the Congress of Soviet Writers in Minsk, Jasieński was still fighting to salvage elements of his futurist past: "I accuse our literature of a lack of courage in making use of artistic fantasy," he declared, arguing that, by following reality too empirically, in fear of being accused of creating fiction, Soviet writers impoverished their reality. In April 1935 he spoke at the Writers' Union in praise of Mayakovsky, whose influence on writers "emerging from a petty bourgeois milieu" was so enormous in "reactionary Poland" and whose books were "explosive material for us." In an article in a Russian literary newspaper, Jasieński wrote: "Almost all of the revolutionary Polish poets 'went crazy' over Mayakovsky." He added, "And not only the revolutionary ones."[51]

Bruno Jasieński's own daily life was not devoid of fantastical elements. While on vacation with his second wife Anna Berziń in the Caucasus, he encountered some boys who were playing with eagle nestlings. Afraid that the boys would exhaust the little birds, Jasieński bought the eagles from them. He originally thought he would take them to Moscow and give them to the zoo, but then he grew attached to them. Mayakovsky's onetime lover Lilia Brik was astounded to find Jasieński calmly sharing his work space with the birds, wholly undisturbed by their constant squalling.[52] When the Polish writer Zygmunt Nowakowski returned from a visit to Moscow, he told Jarosław Iwaszkiewicz that when he had had dinner with Jasieński, a chained eagle had joined them in the dining room.[53] That evening took place in December 1933. Nowakowski was invited to a dinner party with the gaunt Jasieński and his wife, "a fat, ugly, monstrously neglected Russian woman." She did not take part in the conversation, she was busy in the kitchen. Any personal animosity notwithstanding, Stanisław Ryszard Stande was there as well. "The party was wonderful," Nowakowski wrote, recalling the lavishness with some suspicion:

The table was actually straining from the dishes, the silver, and the crystal. Glasses with the monogram of the last Russian emperor caught my attention. Caviar, beluga or sterlet, and other specialties. There was no need to freeze the alcohol, a ringing frost penetrated the room. Frost and filth. The host was dressed in a way impoverished beyond any expression, although he must have put on his best clothes. He looked like someone who was afraid of something. His eyes flew around in all directions, his hand shook when he poured the drinks. We could see our breath when we spoke. I glanced in the direction of the stove. A spider's web enveloped the iron doors. Jasieński, a character and an eccentric, was undoubtedly talented. . . . He had written *I Burn Paris,* a spoof not without force and fantasy. Our conversation faltered. My hands were stiff, and at a certain moment I was overcome by the desire to say to my host: "Comrade Jasieński, you're burning Paris, but why are you not burning anything in the stove?" I didn't say it, because I had come to feel sorry for the poor man. The dishes, the food, and the liquor were of an eminently elegant, and even theatrical, nature. Apparently it was important to someone, some agents, that Polish writers be convinced of how a writer in the Soviet Union lives. Hence the caviar and the crystal. I couldn't help feeling that as soon as we left, someone would appear who would immediately take away all that remained of the food and drink, who would pack up the dishes and silver, and poverty and hunger would reside in the apartment as they had before.[54]

Jasieński resented that his Polishness had apparently been forgotten in Poland.[55] Yet after his resignation from the editorship of *Kultura Mas* and his confession to nationalist deviation, Jasieński did become, increasingly, a Russian writer and a Soviet cultural figure. He became, moreover, immersed in frequently vicious Soviet literary politics. In Moscow, the Hungarian writer Antal Hidas grew close to Jasieński, whom he described as a multilingual internationalist, a very thin man married to an obese enthusiast. Together, Jasieński and Hidas became involved in a conflict with the newspaper *Pravda* under Lev Mekhlis's editorship. The conflict originated in the question put to participants at the 1930 Writers'

Congress in Kharkov: What is your opinion about war preparations? Hidas and Jasieński decided to give the responses to *Pravda*. The paper's editors rejected the material; and Hidas and Jasieński proceeded to write a letter to Stalin with accusations against the editorial board. Mekhlis pleaded with them to withdraw the letter, but they refused. Mekhlis was very persuasive and Hidas would have relented had his friend not been unwavering. This time the two writers were victorious; Stalin took their side and the responses appeared not only in *Pravda,* but also in *Izvestiia*. Hidas told of how Jasieński, having become "the hero of the day," berated his friend for having had doubts. "As they say," Hidas concluded his story, "we became fashionable." Soon the two men were invited to speak everywhere from universities to factories and military bases.[56]

Jasieński also became engaged in the Sovietization of Tadzhikistan, Tomasz Dąbal's having involved him in the project of a Central Asian musical theater troupe during his Paris days. Jasieński made his first trip to Tadzhikistan in 1930; various trips followed during the next several years.[57] In a June 1931 article he spoke of the International Association of Revolutionary Writers' decision to send writers to Tadzhikistan to write about the blooming of proletarian culture.[58] In January 1935 Jasieński made a speech at the Tadzhikistan Party Congress framed by the motif that the Russian proletariat had rescued Tadzhikistan from the soldier's boot of British imperialism. Jasieński characterized Soviet rule in Tadzhikistan as salvation from national annihilation, and argued that Soviet power had given far more to Tadzhikistan than the republic had given the Soviet Union in return. What Tadzhikistan owed the Soviet Union, moreover, was quite specific: cotton. The speech ended on an agitator's note far removed from the sphere of culture: the people of Tadzhikistan owed it to the Soviet Union to work harder, to resist bourgeois thoughts, to grow cotton for the Union.[59] In 1936 Jasieński seems to have been dispatched to Tadzhikistan as an agitator for higher cotton production. Late that year he gave a speech to students from Tadzhikistan studying in Moscow praising the Tadzhik *kolkhozniki* for having been the first in the Union to fulfill the cotton plan for the second time. They were victorious, Jasieński emphasized, because they had promised the great socialist homeland that they would be, and because it was impermissible to deceive the homeland that surrounded the Tadzhik nation with such maternal love and care. "I am proud," Jasieński told the students, "to wear the symbol of this wonderful republic on my lapel. I am proud to have sung the praises of the wonderful Tadzhik nation and its innumerable possibilities at a time when all of our country still knew so little about the new socialist Tadzhikistan in the process of being born. But I am prouder still that all of my writings pale before the living reality of today's Tadzhikistan."[60]

LIFE AFTER *MIESIĘCZNIK LITERACKI*

Following Wat's release from prison, a communist acquaintance told him that Stande would be traveling west from Moscow and wanted to meet him in Berlin. Wat was told to go to Upper Silesia, to a place not far from the German border where a certain miner would be waiting for him. Wat was to cross the border in a worker's clothing. In the end, Ola Watowa dissuaded him from making the trip, fearing it would be too dangerous so soon after his release from prison. It may also have been that the prospect of the trip was insufficiently compelling; Wat saw Stande in part as "a poser, a dandy of communism." It was Stawar who counted most for Wat intellectually. Moreover, in the years following his imprisonment, Wat began to have doubts about communism. During *Miesięcznik Literacki*'s existence, Stalin had not existed in Wat's mind, yet now, in the early 1930s, the specter of Stalinism was palpable. Nevertheless, Wat remained in close contact with the Party. He even acquired a personal Party instructor, the protégé of Irena Krzywicka's father-in-law, the famous Marxist sociologist Ludwik Krzywicki. Wat's tutor was Jakub Berman.[61]

In the 1930s, Jakub Berman was charged with working with Wat to fill the void in the Marxist literary press following the liquidation of *Miesięcznik Literacki*. The legendary monthly conspicuously lacked a successor. In April 1933 Tadeusz Peiper tried to organize socialist writers, but his effort failed to result in anything significant.[62] The literary vacuum was apparent. In a 1935 letter, a socialist from Wilno wrote to Broniewski lamenting the "impasse" of the proletarian poets: "It is high time for the old team of *Dźwignia* and *Miesięcznik* to set to work . . . we want you to jump on Wat, Stawar, and possibly others, such as, for example, Wasilewska. . . . We have in mind in particular the old and tested avant-garde of *Miesięcznik, Dźwignia,* for you are the ones responsible for the decline of our literary criticism and creative production and the obligation to 'catch up and overtake' weighs on you."[63] Nineteen thirty-five saw the official Comintern decision to embrace a broad, left-wing alliance against the growing threat of Nazism. During the first two years of the Popular Front there were numerous attempts to start up a new magazine. Berman instructed Wat as to "how far we can go in terms of concessions." At moments, plans for collaboration with the less radical left-wing activists came close to being realized, then faltered on the question of the Soviet Union. Jakub Berman explained to Wat that the Party was in favor of a noncommunist, wide-ranging, tolerant publication—with one exception: there would be "no provocations vis-à-vis the Soviet Union." And Wat agreed. Whatever ominous news might be arriving from Poland's eastern neighbor, the homeland of the proletariat had to survive.[64]

Negotiations between the KPP and the PPS over establishing a Popular Front publication continued, despite the PPS's ambivalence regarding cooperation with the communists. At a certain moment in 1936 talks broke down as a result of the appearance of the newspaper *Oblicze Dnia* (The Face of the Day), edited by Wanda Wasilewska and named after her novel about strikes in Cracow, a novel that had already acquired an almost cult-like status on the Left. Wasilewska, still formally a PPS activist, was by 1936 already known as a "crypto-communist"; and Wat sensed that the PPS felt betrayed by the fact that the communists were publishing a paper without them, and moreover under the cover of a supposed PPS activist.[65] Janina Broniewska made her journalistic debut in *Oblicze Dnia* with an article based on her discussions with recently released political prisoners about the changing political climate in Poland. They were optimistic; they felt that they were no longer alone.[66] Neither Broniewska nor Wasilewska had joined the KPP, but both were moving closer to the Soviet Union.

THE SPECTER OF TROTSKYISM

Even the most radical Left was far from monolithic. While Wat was being guided by Jakub Berman, two of the former contributors to *Miesięcznik Literacki* had made different choices. Isaac Deutscher, close to Yiddish circles as well, had always comprised a category unto himself. He used to stay with the journalist Bernard Singer and his wife, who would host parties where they served vodka and herring on newspaper and the women sat on the laps of men who were not their husbands. At one such evening Wat watched in rage as Deutscher pulled Ola Watowa onto his lap. Wat whisked his wife away; and Deutscher called him "a petty bourgeois harboring foolish prejudices."[67]

Wat's attendance at such gatherings was an ephemeral phenomenon. The question of Leon Trotsky had been a problem for the KPP for most of the 1920s, and now Deutscher was one of the first of their crowd to defect, to become openly anti-Stalinist, a supporter of Trotsky. Wat's relationship with Deutscher came to an end one day when Deutscher appeared at Wat's apartment, asking to borrow some books by Lenin. Wat had acquired the books during the time of *Miesięcznik Literacki;* he had been given them for free, they were gifts sent from Russia. He said no to Deutscher: How could he give him books he had received as gifts from Russians to use against them? Deutscher was enraged and called Wat a petty bourgeois. Wat ordered him out of the apartment. After that they saw each other once after Wat had spent a night in prison; Deutscher had also been in prison and at seven in the morning, they met in the office of the investigating magistrate. "Of course," Wat said, "we talked with each other as if nothing had ever happened."[68]

Andrzej Stawar, too, rejected Stalinism. He began to publish a paper named *Pod Prąd* (Upstream) for which he wrote several exhaustive, academic treatises on topics such as Bonapartism and fascism, Soviet bureaucracy, and Leon Trotsky. *Pod Prąd* was the venture of a tiny group of anti-Stalinists; Stawar solicited Wat's participation, but Wat was reluctant. "I didn't want to do anything against the Soviet Union," he explained, "I regarded Stalin as terrible, someone doing horrible things, but that was the only proletarian state! Stalin would pass, but the homeland of the proletariat would remain. And, well, one could not aid the enemies."[69] Yet Wat had doubts, and so he provided some vague assistance, reading over articles, making some suggestions, but he would not write for *Pod Prąd*.

In 1932 Isaac Deutscher was expelled from the KPP for his role in forming the Trotskyite opposition.[70] When the show trials of Old Bolsheviks began in Moscow in 1936, Deutscher was among those unpersuaded by their confessions. In August, just after the death sentences of Lenin's comrades Lev Kamenev and Grigorii Zinoviev, Deutscher published under a pseudonym "The Moscow Trial," a pamphlet denouncing the trial as falsity and absurdity.[71] Deutscher was not directly involved with *Pod Prąd* since the magazine was somewhat critical of Trotsky as well as Stalin, although he did join Stawar in a subsequent 1937 publication titled *Nurt* (Current).[72] *Pod Prąd* was sold openly, and not confiscated; nonetheless the costs for Stawar were high. In the Party he was boycotted, excommunicated. His closest friends refused to greet him. Stawar had been Wat's teacher in Marxism, and it was known that the two remained close; people suspected Wat of writing under a pseudonym for *Pod Prąd*.[73] Nor was Wat Stawar's only pupil. Janina Broniewska recalled her master in Marxism's betrayal with bitterness: "And one day a true wall arose among those closest to us. Our most principled sectarian, our mentor, the one guarding Władek from all 'Żeromszczyznas,' undergoes an evolution. He converts—like a woman of loose morals falling into religiosity in her old age—to Trotskyism." Janina Broniewska and Wanda Wasilewska viewed this defection as particularly insidious, as anything written against the Soviet line could be easily exploited by the Polish government, moving ever more to the right in the 1930s, in particular after Piłsudski's death in 1935. They even suspected that the government had been intentionally smuggling *Pod Prąd* into the communist-filled prisons as anti-Soviet propaganda. Broniewska's own relationship with the Marxist literary critic who had once upon a time confessed his love to her ended sadly. One day in her Warsaw neighborhood of Żoliborz she unexpectedly ran into Stawar on her way home from Wasilewska's apartment:

> Spontaneously or out of old habit we greeted one another, warmly even. But I could not maintain that instinctual intimacy for long and I asked him brusquely:
> "What's with your recent preoccupation with water?"
> "And why?" he scowled.
> "*Pod Prąd, Nurt*. But grist for whose mill here in our country? In this system and under this regime?" I naïvely asked so seasoned an erudite and politician. . . . And so I parted with my old political and personal friend for good. In the park in Żoliborz there grew up between us a symbolic barricade.[74]

Aleksander Wat remained in contact with the Party leadership until 1936, although relations had grown cooler. That year Jerzy Borejsza approached him. Borejsza had joined the KPP in 1929, having passed through a socialist Zionist phase and later a fascination with Spanish anarchism, before returning to Poland from a stay in France enchanted with communism.[75] Now he invited both Wat and Stawar to a meeting.[76] Among the others invited was Borejsza's brother, Jacek Różański, a KPP member who had spent his student years in the socialist organization *Życie* (Life) together with Jakub Berman.[77] At the meeting Władysław Daszewski and Jerzy Borejsza announced the project of creating a Popular Front–inspired Democratic Club. In the end, however, Wat and Stawar decided not to participate. As Wat later learned, the Party regarded him as a sympathizer, a fellow traveler, "not one of us, but decent, progressive." Wat only voiced his doubts and criticisms in private conversations; he put nothing against the Party in writing. In 1935 Wat even co-authored a Popular Front call to writers, whose other signatories included Władysław Broniewski, Wanda Wasilewska, Leon Kruczkowski, Jerzy Putrament, and Adam Ważyk.[78] Yet the following year Wat did not even receive an invitation to the 1936 Congress of Cultural Workers in Lwów.[79]

SŁONIMSKI PAYS A VISIT TO RUSSIA WITH TWO FRIENDS

The Skamander poet Antoni Słonimski's relations with old friends on the Left suffered as well after his trip to the Soviet Union in 1932. The book Słonimski published in excerpts in *Wiadomości Literackie* upon his return was among his best. Structured in short episodes in the spirit of his feuilletons, *Moja podróż do Rosji* (My Trip to Russia) was written with Słonimski's characteristic sharp edge. The story began on the train heading east, where Słonimski was accompanied by his (imaginary) friends, The Enthusiast and The Skeptic. Sometimes his friends argued, sometimes one conceded, sometimes one or the other stayed behind in the hotel room. The author was self-reflective in his conversations with them; he embarked on the trip with the awareness that he carried with him the enormous baggage of all the information about Russia he had absorbed in Poland. Had he been deceived by bourgeois propaganda? By Soviet propaganda? By both? Słonimski asked himself sincerely, "Am I going to the country of Red terror, or to the state of living socialism, of which we have all dreamt since childhood?"[80]

When Słonimski reached the Soviet border, he was joined by a (real) interpreter, a superfluous one as he spoke Russian, but one who had been ordered not to leave his side nonetheless. So did the threesome become a foursome. In his attempt to extricate himself from this very nice woman, he learned how the government took pains to prevent tourists from seeing anything unpleasant. Słonimski's entire trip became a struggle to see "what life is actually like," to peer behind the curtains.

Słonimski's perspicacity, his ability to see contradictions, ambiguities, nuances, tormented him now. "For long days," he wrote, "I was persecuted in Moscow by the memory of those eyes that I saw in the Museum of the Revolution in the photograph from the times of famine in 1922. They were the eyes of a peasant man and woman condemned to be shot for the crime of cannibalism. Those eyes had an expression of complete calm and well-being." He could not believe the claims of Soviet writers that they worked in freedom. "When I would speak with writers," he related, "they would always answer me that self-criticism does exist in the Soviet Union, that self-criticism is alive and vigilant; or they would answer that they had complete confidence in the government's policies and didn't feel any need to fight. Unfortunately, I can't believe that." Just beneath the surface of Słonimski's skepticism about true conditions for Soviet writers was the specter of Mayakovsky's suicide two years earlier. "I remember," Słonimski wrote, "how in Warsaw at a party for Mayakovsky, Boy[-Żeleński] had a drink with the enormous Mayakovsky. Boy winked at him, and Mayakovsky smiled. Mayakovsky didn't know any language besides Russian, and Boy knows all languages with the exception of Russian, and so they could either rub noses and slap one another on the shoulders, or smile. This has its own meaning, even if the world does not attach sufficient weight to the smiles of poets."[81]

Though Słonimski never parted with his skepticism, it was in this book that he revealed most poignantly how much he would have liked to believe, how much his heart was with socialism. He wished for the great experiment to succeed, and yet he saw that the two eggs fed to all schoolchildren each day were imaginary and suspected that the emperor could be naked. He noted the ubiquitousness of naïve self-praise, yet was touched by the ubiquity of faith in socialism. As he rode the train back to Poland, he reflected upon what he would say, aware of the responsibility that each word he would write about the Soviet Union carried. He was—so uncharacteristically—uncertain about expressing his opinion. "What will I answer to the simple question: how is it in Russia?" he asked, "No, I can't answer that question. I don't have the courage to judge." His two comrades, The Skeptic and The Enthusiast, sat beside him as the train rolled towards Warsaw and conversed among themselves: "In the imbalance of today's world—the Enthusiast says—the existence of the Soviet Union is the only hope for all the injured and exploited. . . . That's valid—answers the Skeptic—but is there not being born in the world a new fear of impassioned class fanaticism? Bolshevism has provoked hatred."[82]

My Trip to Russia ended with Słonimski's arrival at the Warsaw train station. As he waited for a taxicab, he told the porter that he had just returned from Russia, and the porter asked him how it was there:

> In this quiet, discrete question there is much confidence,
> that particular confidence that people from the proletariat have
> in relation to Party comrades. I admit that this atmosphere of
> community appeals to me, I feel like telling him something
> that would bring us still closer together, something that he
> wants to hear from me. I know, I'm certain, that if I were to
> say to him: "It's good there, comrade," he would carry my suit-
> case lightly and quickly into the taxi and would smile farewell.
> Finally I say:
> "It's difficult to say in a few words. Both bad and good."
> Now I know what the porter carrying my suitcase thinks of me.
> He thinks of me as an enemy. There are no intermediary posi-
> tions. Whoever is not with us is against us. With a feeling of
> choking loneliness I ride through the city.[83]

The painful implications of his answer were not only imagined. In an August 1932 letter to his sister in Poland, Jan Hempel wrote from Moscow: "Supposedly, Słonimski has been writing some kind of monstrous lies in Wiadomości Literackie."[84] Słonimski's life in Warsaw was not the same afterwards. Two years later, in 1934, he wrote, "Since the time of My Trip to Russia I've been on the blacklist of Soviet officials. Every so often they invite all the literati and feed them caviar and as punishment I have to stay home."[85]

POLISH CHIVALRY AND REVOLUTIONARY RUSSIA

Władysław Broniewski was contemplating his own trip to Russia. The impulse was as much personal as ideological. Notwithstanding his marriage, the romantic poet had long been surrounded by "candidates for the role of muse." The previous year, after Janina Broniewska's teaching career had been abruptly ended by her brief stay in prison, she had gone to Kalisz to visit her mother and contemplate a new career. When she returned,

FIGURE 9 Władysław Broniewski, Jarosław Iwaszkiewicz, and Antoni Słonimski (left to right). From a 1933 postcard series; courtesy of Muzeum Władysława Broniewskiego and Muzeum Literatury imienia Adama Mickiewicza.

there were rumors floating about that her husband had been seen with "a certain girl . . . supposedly a student."[86] In the end Broniewski told his wife himself, in a letter asking for her patience while he sorted out his feelings. He expressed no such confusion, however, to his new, young love, Irena Hellman, to whom he sent a letter on *Wiadomości Literackie* stationery in March 1933:

> Beloved and naughty Irenka! Summon some courage and
> come here. In truth I cannot say "Don't be afraid, I won't eat
> you" (this is precisely what I feel like doing!), but following
> your arrival I can promise you nothing other than happiness.
> Yours and mine. . . . And so do not think, in particular do
> not philosophize during the nights, do not forbid yourself
> anything—youth, beauty, love—this is the highest philosophy.
> When you come, we will go on walks together from early
> morning, somewhere around the Vistula, because it's from
> this direction that spring comes. We will speak only about silly
> things, and so about our lives, about love and death, about
> how the grass grows, from where the wind blows and why
> I have fallen in love with you like a schoolboy from the 6th
> grade. . . . I'm simply drunk—on you and on spring. Your
> W.(ariat) [crazy one][87]

Janina Broniewska, the liberated woman, put no obstacles in the way of the new couple's being together. Instead she returned to Kalisz, to her mother, who comforted her that being unemployed, homeless, alone was only a passing crisis. When Janina Broniewska reappeared in Warsaw, she refused to humiliate herself by clinging to her husband. One day she received an unexpected visit from Irena Hellman's mother. The bourgeois Jewish merchant's widow was appalled by her daughter's romance with a "goy," and moreover a Bolshevik in her opinion, and sought out Janina Broniewska as her natural ally. Yet far from embracing this alliance, Broniewska assured the mother that she had nothing against her husband's relationship with Irena Hellman and on the contrary thought that, to the extent it was serious, it should be made official.[88]

If Janina Broniewska made all attempts to avoid what she considered scenes reminiscent of romantic melodrama, Broniewski's inclinations took him in the opposite direction. In November 1933, Irena Hellman's brother, at the behest of his mother, challenged Broniewski to a duel. Broniewski's young lover herself appeared rather unaffected by this. She wrote to Broniewski in a light, joking tone, her Polish interspersed with Russian, that she had fallen in love with a charming general, and he with her. He came for tea and went for walks with her. When she told him that she was a student of law, he responded: "Of course, of course, law by all means, but personally I wish for you that you marry as soon as possible." She was prepared to take offense. "Is sexual longing the dominant expression on my face?," she asked. But the general added: "For you see, of any hundred women only one is a true woman—the rest are the female sex, but you are just such a woman." She was coquettish in her writing. Yet a moment of scholarly seriousness came when she spoke of Słonimski's columns in *Wiadomości Literackie,* and about how, upon reading them, she saw that he wrote of the Soviet Union exactly what she felt as well. She was pleased and grateful that there was at least one more "impartial person" who thought as she did, "as her boy, it seems, is of another opinion." Yet this reasoned sobriety took on an almost perverse implication as she wrote just as lightly of the upcoming duel: "Is that affair with my brother worrying you so? My dear little son, on that subject, unfortunately, I can advise nothing, but it is not worth becoming worried and anxious over. I know you're living with the feeling that something unpleasant lies in wait for you, but after all, it will pass, you only have to struggle through this one week. To be sure, what idiocy this is! I've been continually tense because of this, particularly now it's eminently irritating to me—moreover, I tremble for you, at the thought that he might do you some kind of injury."[89] In the end this regression to nineteenth-century drama did come to pass. The duel took place on 16 November 1933, ending with minor wounds to both participants.[90]

Broniewski's affair with Irena Hellman proved to be temporary. His infatuation passed, and this became only the first of Janina Broniewska's various wanderings, separations from and reconciliations with her prodigal husband. Through it all, she proved herself to be the stronger one in her unconventional marriage. The effects on her own life were not exclusively adverse, and the following year she began to come into her own as a writer and an activist. On 7 March 1934 she made her literary debut in a children's magazine, signing her first published story with her maiden name. The choice was "self-evident." She wanted that beginning to belong to herself alone; she did not want to be in the shadow of a famous poet. Her assertion of independence was facilitated by Broniewski's decision to escape from Warsaw for a time in the direction of the Soviet Union. In his absence, Janina Broniewska was once again engaged as his replacement at *Wiadomości Literackie*.[91]

When Broniewski returned to Warsaw in May 1934, he bore gifts of folk art for his wife and daughter.[92] He also published a long article in *Wiadomości Literackie* about the Ukrainian segment of his trip, beginning with reflections on his last visit to Ukraine—fourteen years earlier as a soldier in the Polish Army, fighting against the Bolsheviks. He had offered a cigarette to a Bolshevik prisoner of war. The boy took the cigarette and inquired as to when he was going to be shot. Broniewski was surprised: prisoners of war were not shot, and why was he asking?

> "Right after I was captured I said that I was a communist and they should shoot me. They brought me here. So let's end this right away."
> "Calm down"—I repeat—"we don't shoot prisoners of war. You'll go to a prisoner of war camp and sit there until the end of the war, and that's all."
> The young prisoner's attitude is one of undisguised distrust.
> "Where are you from?" I ask.
> "From Kharkov."
> "An intellectual?"

"No, a worker."

Of course he's lying. He looks like he's in the seventh grade.

"And what's going on in Kharkov?"

"Well, we're building."

"What are you building?"

"Everything. A new life. Socialism."

"Well and how's it going?"

"It's going well. But it must be admitted that now you've done us quite a sound injury."[93]

Broniewski offered him another cigarette. Now, fourteen years later, the former soldier in Piłsudski's Legions revisited the land where life was "socialist in content and Ukrainian in form." Just two years earlier several million peasants had starved to death during the famine in Ukraine. Now Broniewski mentioned the famine only in passing, attributing it to the kulaks' battle against the Soviet authorities, believing it was the rich peasants who had decided to starve their neighbors. If he did see hunger in Ukraine in March 1934, he did not write of it. Instead he wrote of the young poets and translators eager for news from the West; of factories where one-quarter of the workers were girls; of banners praising workers who exceeded their quotas. He read his poetry aloud, and his listeners were touched that a foreign poet had feelings similar to their own about the accomplishments of socialism in places like Dnieprostroi and Magnitogorsk. In Soviet Ukraine, in the people's certainty, their faith, he had found something magical. As in his love letters of almost a decade earlier, Broniewski remained a romantic. Wat, though, was disconcerted by news of the famine, and felt a more ominous side of his friend's enthusiasm for Soviet Ukraine: "When he came back, I asked him about various things, including the famine in the Ukraine and collectivization, mentioning that the press had reported that five million peasants had lost their lives. And he said, 'Yes, that's right; it's being talked about a lot.' . . . And so I said to Władzio—I remember this exactly; there are moments in life you don't forget—'So, is that the truth?' He whisked his hand disparagingly, dismissing the subject; what did those five million *muzhiks* mean to him. He didn't say it, but that gesture!"[94] Adam Ważyk insisted this was impossible, that Broniewski could not have had so little regard for the lives of five million peasants, that Wat had misinterpreted his gesture.[95]

Broniewski had also traveled to Moscow. Stande was away from the city at the time of Broniewski's arrival, but promised that his wife and friends there would arrange everything for him.[96] Jasieński sent a letter from Tadzhikistan; bad feelings over Stande's letter to the Comintern seem to have passed. If Broniewski had indeed knowingly signed his name to that letter, all had now been seemingly forgiven, and Jasieński's letter was warm. Now that both poets had found themselves in the socialist home-land, Jasieński switched to the informal mode of address. He had a request: when Broniewski returned to Warsaw, would he stop into Jasieński's pub-lisher there and check on Jasieński's manuscript *Człowiek zmienia skórę* (A Man Changes His Skin)?[97] During Broniewski's stay in Russia Jan Hempel wrote to his sister: "We have here now Broniewski, who has been very well received by Russian writers. He traveled to Ukraine and saw Dnieprostroi, the great coal mine, afterwards he traveled to the Caucasus to Tiflis and admired the wonderful blossoming of Georgian national culture. At the moment he's visiting Moscow factories—the great automobile factory, textile factories, enormous chemical plants. . . . Broniewski is undoubtedly the most gifted of the revolutionary poets in Poland—it's only a pity that as a person he's very weak."[98] Hempel felt ambivalently towards the poet who had been his companion in cell number 13, and who had secured for him the collaboration of the avant-garde ten years earlier. Another letter to his sister, written in August 1934 when Broniewski had already returned to Poland, revealed both Hempel's romanticization of Soviet reality and his critical feelings towards Broniewski:

> You who are there in the old world cannot even conceive of the
> fullness of the life we live here in every, absolutely every realm
> . . . I recall the arguments of various bourgeois smart alecs who
> contended that under socialism stagnancy and routine would
> reign. In reality a whole new world is unfolding before us,
> a world of joyous (joyous because necessarily victorious, even
> while difficult) battle, a world built anew with our hands, with
> millions of hands and minds directed by a common will, con-
> sciousness, deliberately cultivating a new life. For the first time
> in human history man has begun to consciously create his
> own history. . . . People coming here from capitalist countries
> often see only the external accomplishments: the enormous

factories, the new agriculture, new cities arising in the wilder-
ness. Yet how seldom do they see the birth of the new man who
is creating it all. This new man grows here with every step—
new, young, he looks daringly into the future, perfectly aware
of his own strengths and aspirations, deeply and powerfully
conscious of the fact that he is building the whole of the new
world with his own hands. For example Broniewski, who
was here a few months ago, did not see, did not perceive that.
He saw only external things, things it is impossible not to
see, which even the biggest bourgeois dullard could not miss.

Amidst his enthusiasm, Hempel admitted one qualification: "Of course,
as I've written to you more than once—there are darker sides of this battle
as well. Like every great battle, this one is mortally difficult, it demands
sacrifices, great sacrifices that can seem to some who are shortsighted to
cloud the horizon."[99]

THE FIRST TO GO

Broniewski's trip to the Soviet Union took place in the period just following Stalin's consolidation of power, as purges of "enemies of the people"
gained momentum, especially in Soviet Ukraine. Following his declaration
of repentance for nationalist-opportunist errors, Witold Wandurski was
arrested on 11 September 1933, some six months before Broniewski arrived.
Wandurski's subsequent testimony for the Soviet security apparatus was
an extensive, fabricated confession of his Polish national sentiments and
his engagement with Piłsudski's "fascist" Polish Military Organization.
The ritual of elaborate, self-flagellating confession was already in place;
Wandurski repeated himself over and over again. The testimony—a joint
creation by Wandurski and his interrogators—was damning to Tomasz
Dąbal, Bruno Jasieński, Władysław Broniewski, and even Wandurski's
schoolmate, Julian Tuwim.[100]

In the interrogation chamber, Wandurski recounted his biography as
a story of the struggle between his nationalist inclinations and his communist sympathies. The story went like this: throughout his student years
he had been exposed time and time again to Polish nationalist circles. His
first contact with Piłsudski's Polish Military Organization had come in
1915; two years later in Moscow, he was pulled into a publication founded

by a professor who gathered around himself counterrevolutionary elements. After Wandurski was arrested unexpectedly in August 1920 by the Kharkov Cheka, he spent five weeks in a camp where he lived among Poles in an atmosphere of extreme nationalism. He was eager to return to Poland, to see Poland in its new independence. Encountering Polish soldiers upon crossing the border, he was filled with national pride. The first year of Wandurski's stay in Poland was one of the confused searchings of a disillusioned Piłsudskiite. In 1922 he became friends with the former Legion captain Broniewski, who told him of his earlier work for the Polish Military Organization and his participation in the Polish-Bolshevik War on the side of Polish forces occupying Ukraine. Broniewski continually tried to dissuade his new friend from joining the Communist Party; Wandurski's parents and younger brother did the same, they called him a traitor to his homeland. Wandurski vacillated; even as he read Marx, Engels, and Lenin, his communist convictions were being shaped by a Party member who had once belonged to the Polish Military Organization, a Party member in whose psyche remained much of his previous patriotism. Wandurski's own sentiments and convictions inclined him towards social revolution, but within the framework of Polish independence. It was with these predispositions that he joined the KPP in 1923. Afterwards he remained conflicted; he oscillated between his ties to the proletariat and to Polish nationalism; he was constantly under the influence of Polish fascists and petty bourgeois writers such as Julian Tuwim and Leon Schiller. When Wandurski was periodically arrested for communist activity, the counterintelligence officers who arrested him would try to persuade him to break with communism. He would meet with a member of the KPP Central Committee in Gdańsk, who praised Piłsudski and all connected with Polishness and noble descent. This comrade criticized Wandurski's literary work, calling it "kacapski" (a pejorative slang for "Russian") and advised Wandurski to pay less attention to Soviet literature, to learn more from Żeromski. When the invitation to the Soviet Union came from Tomasz Dąbal, this comrade from Gdańsk and others encouraged Wandurski to accept; he could exploit his position there to strengthen Polishness in the Soviet Union.

Wandurski continued: leaving Poland had not been easy, he had felt the loss of something very close to him. Once in the Soviet Union, he became possessed by impulses of national self-defense against Soviet proletarian culture, impulses encouraged by Dąbal and Jasieński, impulses on behalf of Polish fascism of the Belweder school, impulses aimed towards realizing Poland's imperial aspirations towards Ukraine. In the external appearance of his Polish theater in Kiev he declined to cultivate a Soviet style in favor of a bourgeois one. He avoided plays with Soviet themes, citing as an excuse the political immaturity of his actors. He popularized, albeit in the form of caricature, the figure of "Granddad Piłsudski." In directing the theater, all of his efforts aimed to spread the idea of Polish nationalism, to facilitate Polish expansion in Ukraine. Under the influence of Dąbal and Jasieński, his work in the theater took on a more tangible shape, it endeavored to spread ideas of Polish nationalism and bourgeois-aristocratic influences among the Polish population in Ukraine. Accused of nationalist deviation, Wandurski was removed from his position in the theater in Kiev. In late September 1931 he moved to Moscow, where, the following year, in November 1932, the Polish painter Władysław Daszewski told him that the Polish military attaché wanted to meet with him. Wandurski agreed; they met in Daszewski's Moscow hotel room. The Polish colonel reminded him that they had been high school students together in Łódź. He wanted to tell him about the Polish Military Organization's work in Kiev, he wanted to know if Wandurski would continue his work on behalf of the Polish Military Organization, on behalf of Polish nationalism.[101]

On the basis of his fabricated confession, Wandurski was sentenced to death on 9 March 1934, while Broniewski was visiting Ukraine. On 1 June 1934 Wandurski was shot, just after Broniewski had returned to Warsaw.[102] Wandurski's friends had learned earlier that his Polish theater in Kiev had come under attack for "nationalist opportunism."[103] Now news of his arrest reached Warsaw.[104] Broniewski, it seems, was largely silent for a time. Then one evening in autumn of 1934, at an expensive Warsaw restaurant named Adria, he and Mieczysław Grydzewski were sitting with Jasieński's Polish publisher when an unfavorably predisposed poet-satirist approached their table. The inebriated satirist began to taunt Broniewski about Wandurski's arrest. A scene broke out; Broniewski ordered the uninvited guest to leave the table. The now-public scandal did not conclude there in Adria. The satirist published a poem-lampoon titled "Do poety-komunisty" (To the Poet-Communist), referring to Wandurski's imprisonment and including the refrain "and what do you have to say about that,

Mr. Broniewski." On 21 November 1934 Broniewski responded with his own poem "Prztyczek 'smalonemu dubkowi'" (A Jab at the Bullshitter), a crude satire of a conversation with his antagonist.[105]

A FRIENDSHIP BETWEEN WOMEN

When Broniewski set off for his Soviet adventure, Janina Broniewska stayed in Warsaw and threw her energy into her new career at the publications section of the Polish Teachers' Union. It was there in 1934 that she met Wanda Wasilewska, already a prominent activist in the left wing of the Polish Socialist Party and the author of *The Face of the Day*. This novel was for Broniewska "a book we finished in one sitting. . . . A revolutionary book of those times, written from the workers' center itself, in an empathic language, a language as authentic as life itself."[106] Wasilewska herself had already attracted much attention. While still in her twenties, she was active in organizing women for socialist causes. In 1932 she wrote to her mother of her experience speaking in Cracow: "In truth it seemed to me that my hair was rising on my head, that I must be in flames. It was something simply extraordinary—I experienced a moment of such happiness, such as one must feel when in ecstasy—The hall gave me an unprecedented ovation . . . I felt simply, physically, as if something were emanating from me—like fire. It was strange, but wonderful."[107]

Before she was a socialist activist chain-smoking and drinking endless cups of black coffee, Wanda Wasilewska was a child enamored of the countryside and of little Antek, her first proletarian playmate who mesmerized the five-year-old Wanda with his charisma.[108] She was, from her adolescence, a woman of great passions—for Poland, for social justice, and above all for a man named Janek who was her first love. In the diary she kept as a teenager she exalted in masochistic fantasies of lying at his feet and licking off the dust that clung to his boots, of feeling his spurs digging into her flesh until she bled.[109] "Because I believe in you," she wrote in her diary, speaking to Janek, "And for me you are the highest essence, you are my master, my ruler. If you were to so order, I would fulfill anything. Even the worst humiliations, injuries, I would bear with a smile if you so much as wanted that."[110]

Wanda Wasilewska was the daughter of Leon Wasilewski, independent Poland's first minister of foreign affairs and one of Józef Piłsudski's closest friends in the PPS. The first of May was a holiday for her family from her earliest childhood.[111] As a child in Cracow she was ensconced in political circles insisting on both Polish socialism and Polish independence, and hating Russia in any and all of its political incarnations. She was close to her father—by her own account, as well of those of her sister, she was his favorite among his three daughters. When abandoned by her first love in 1921, while still a teenager, it was to her father whom she cried:

> Janek, despite his solemn promises, has not appeared at all, I
> don't even know what to think. And I'm terribly sad. . . . Daddy,
> do you know that now it occurs to me, it's a terribly bad thing
> you're not with us. In fact it's as if you didn't exist at all. . . .
> And sometimes I feel like going to say something to my adored
> Daddy—and he isn't here. For you don't even really know me.
> And I think that it can't be that way. I'm growing up and going
> out into the world and you'll always be something so terribly
> far away. As if, if you were here, perhaps I would be different
> as well. I'm going to waste and nothing will become of me.
> In truth I'd like to die. Please don't be angry at me for writing
> such foolish things, but I feel so terrible that I really don't
> know where to begin.[112]

While Wanda Wasilewska's self-effacing romance with Janek was long, their engagement was short. In May of 1923 she wrote in her diary that 'the royal prince has gone,' and that a chapter in her life had ended.[113] Before long she married another man and gave birth to a daughter; soon afterwards her young husband died. A short time after his death, she met the bricklayer Marian Bogatko, an "authentic worker" with whom her courtship began during a kayaking trip on the Vistula river. Wasilewska was a weak swimmer, and after their kayak overturned, Bogatko, quite romantically and heroically, saved her from drowning.[114] At the age of fifteen, Wanda Wasilewska had written in her diary that she judged being a man's lover to be "more noble" than being his wife.[115] It was a view she now returned to, and soon Bogatko (for whom, she confided to her mother, she felt much more than she ever had for anyone before) had become her lover and partner—as well as her secretary. In 1933 she sent a long letter to her mother, justifying her decision to continue living with Bogatko without a wedding and insisting that she rejoiced in the absence of formalities. How good that there had been no marriage. "For once, finally," Wasilewska

wrote to her mother, "I'm a person and not someone else's appendage
... even though Marian and I share the same values [of equality], on my
side there would be the minus that I am a woman, and as a result would
always be the other one, and not myself."[116] Wanda Wasilewska and Marian
Bogatko married only in 1936, and then only to secure a spousal visa for
Bogatko so that they could travel together to the Soviet Union. They paid a
visit to a Calvinist parish in the town of Leszno. The pastor was displeased
by their attitude: "When the pastor requested some kind of declaration
of religious affiliation, and we were very much in a hurry, he grew angry
and in the end, exasperated, asked: I don't understand what your point is
here—a wedding or the documentation? I answered: The documentation,
exclusively. Then he gave up on everything, we had mortally offended
him, but he did issue us the marriage certificate, and limited the whole
ceremony to some abbreviated rituals."[117]

When Janina Broniewska wrote of the day she met the extraordinary
Wanda Wasilewska, she began with Wasilewska's clothing. It was late autumn as "one small, purely feminine detail indicated": Wanda Wasilewska
was wearing a blue wool dress, buttoned tightly under her neck, with
a Scottish-style checkered collar. They spoke little that first day, or for
the next few days. Wasilewska seemed as if inaccessible. As time passed
Janina Broniewska learned it was only Wasilewska's shyness that made
her sometimes seem arrogant, and then began a friendship that quickly
grew in intensity. Soon they could not endure a single day without each
other.[118] The two women would walk through Warsaw's northern district
of Żoliborz incarnating themselves as "various feminine types," drawing
their models from conversations overheard on the streets, on buses and
trams. Sometimes Marian Bogatko would accompany them, and would be
at once a bit proud and a bit irritated when passersby would recognize his
wife and whisper: "Look, look, there's Wasilewska! Oooh, sweet." Sometimes a crowd of enthusiasts would follow her, and Bogatko would begin
to mock them—and at once to mock Wasilewska: "yes, yes, sweetness herself! Their *tsadik* in a skirt. Jasia, next time we're going out by ourselves.
Let her collect her laurels on her own." And Broniewska would come to
her defense: "It's tough, Marianek. Jealousy is devouring me as well, but
what can we do, but be the courtiers of our 'sweet' queen."[119]

There were risks as well as accolades. Julian Tuwim once said to the
two women: "How I envy both of you. You're not afraid, whereas I'm

mortally afraid."[120] Yet it was not quite true that these women had no fear. During Wasilewska's interrogations in the 1930s, Janina Broniewska would wait for her, drinking black coffee in a neighboring café for hours, "barely alive with anxiety," waiting to see if her friend would return, or if she would find her in prison.[121] When the telephone rang there would always follow the question: to take a toothbrush or not? Take it, just in case, Broniewska would say. And sometimes Wasilewska would and sometimes she would not. On other occasions the game went further: "Do you have money for a droshky?" Wasilewska was asked. This was a standard question put to those arrested: Could they pay to take a cab to prison? "'I don't want a droshky,'" she answered, "'I want to walk through the city under the policeman's bayonet. Let there be a whole scene.'"[122]

Wasilewska never did spend any time in prison.[123] She remained, moreover, close to her father: "My relationship to him was not a hundred percent, but rather a thousand percent positive. When he died I was already an adult, and my comrades, communists—whose relationship to him was quite well defined—came to me with bouquets for 'Wanda's father.' They knew what the death of my father meant to me."[124] Yet she did not cry at his funeral. On the day of Leon Wasilewski's death in December 1936, Marian Bogatko called Janina Broniewska to tell her the news, to tell her they would be there soon. When they arrived Wasilewska sat down on the couch, Janina Broniewska passed her an ashtray, matches, cigarettes, and watched her light the first one. Broniewska and Bogatko waited in vain for a "normal reaction, tears, despair manifested—be it even in a way most typical of a woman."[125]

The death of Leon Wasilewski was Wanda Wasilewska's tragedy, yet at once her liberation, for she would not make an open political break with him during his lifetime. His death allowed for her unabashed radicalism. In autumn 1937 Wasilewska and Broniewska led a sit-down strike in the Polish Teachers' Union. Tension with the government had been mounting, particularly within the publications department of the Teachers' Union, threatened with searches and purging of its socialist-sympathizing staff. It was Bogatko who first voiced the idea, in response to his wife's question that morning: "and what happens if it turns out that the curator is in the building?" Bogatko answered "almost nonchalantly," "in that case you'll have to enact a sit-down strike." When that evening the two women called their husbands to say that they would not be coming home, as they were busy occupying the building, "it was only with difficulty that Marian controlled the note of satisfaction in his voice." Władysław Broniewski, too, was enthusiastic—and refused when requested by a colleague, a Polish writer supportive of the government, to try to persuade his wife to come home. Moreover, from her husband, Janina Broniewska learned that the strike was "even being discussed 'on the upper level' at Café Ziemiańska." Its patrons and waiters sent pastries to the Teachers' Union building.[126]

Wanda Wasilewska had shattered her ties to the Polish government. Leaving domestic life and care of the children to their husbands, she and Janina Broniewska shared a mattress in their office during days and nights of little sleep.[127] On the very first day, the KPP activist Szymon Natanson came to Wasilewska. She consulted with him, but would not accept any open assistance from the KPP. She did not want to provide the Polish government with a pretext for declaring the strike illegal.[128] The Polish prime minister, infuriated, called the women "two rabid broads." While they considered this a self-evident compliment, they "refrained from falling into megalomania."[129] The revolutionary career of the "two rabid broads" was only beginning. They were prohibited from returning to work, told that because of their convictions they could not be editors of a publication for children.[130] Moreover, there was the problematic matter of Broniewska's communist-sympathizing husband. Before long, the women decided on a hunger strike to protest their exclusion from the Teachers' Union.[131] Not long afterwards, they traveled to Wilno to testify at the trial of Henryk Drzewicki and Stefan Jędrychowski, two young communist activists. It was the first time Broniewska had met Jędrychowski in person, "but without a moment's thought I added him to the list of very close friends." The women were confident that History would vindicate them. After they had returned to their hotel, Wasilewska said to Broniewska apropos of the sentences the young men received, "Four years, who knows who by then will be the accused and who the judges?"[132]

THE CONGRESS OF CULTURAL WORKERS

In May 1936, Janina Broniewska sent her husband and her best friend off to Lwów for the Congress of Cultural Workers. The communist-driven gathering of intellectuals was a celebration of the Popular Front, coming at a time when the KPP exerted much influence among the Polish intelligentsia.[133] Broniewska herself stayed in Warsaw with her daughter Anka and impatiently awaited Broniewski's report.[134] When the 16 and 17 May congress had concluded, not only his wife, but also all of Warsaw received Władysław Broniewski's report in *Wiadomości Literackie*. Topics of discussion at the congress had included fascism, prison camps, anti-semitic attacks, the burning of books, and the relationship of fascism to culture. When Broniewski read his poem "Zagłębie Dąbrowskie" (The Dąbrowski Basin), in response to the poem's concluding line, "are you ready?," the whole hall resounded with "we are ready!"[135]

As Broniewski then described it, writers, artists, and cultural activists, Poles, Jews, and Ukrainians all gathered "in an atmosphere of sincere brotherhood and solidarity."[136] In multiethnic Lwów, the congress pro-claimed the Left's desire that the cultural needs of all Poland's nationali-ties be met.[137] Among those receptive to this call was Julian Stryjkowski, trilingual in Hebrew, Yiddish, and Polish, who had spent most of his life in an east Galician Jewish shtetl—devout, enclosed, impoverished. He had been a young, impassioned Zionist, before he was cast out of the Zionist youth organization *Shomer* by boys who did not like him.[138] Now he embraced Marxism, and listened to Wasilewska greet the congress with the words: "'I bring greetings to Ukrainian Lwów in the name of War-saw.'"[139] Wanda Wasilewska's expressed sympathy for ethnic minorities in the Polish state was sincere. She was also in close contact with Jewish Marxist movements; and among her interlocutors in these Popular Front years were Jakub Berman's Marxist Zionist brother Adolf Berman, the communist Michał Mirski active on "the Jewish street," and the Bundist leaders Wiktor Alter and Henryk Erlich.[140] Now Wasilewska was the queen of all the nationalities at the Congress. It was a time when communists in Poland were speaking of a Western Belarus with a capital in Wilno, and a Western Ukraine with a capital in Lwów—to be attached to the neighbor-ing Soviet republics.[141]

Nationality was subordinate to class at the congress, however. "Wasi-lewska, speaking about proletarian literature, emphasized its conscious 'tendentiousness,'" Broniewski wrote, "It is literature in the service of an idea, in the service of working-class interests, obliged to vigilance, the will of battle, faith in victory."[142] Afterwards Wasilewska wrote of those two days as an ecstatic experience of mass hysteria. When she moved towards the podium, the whole hall, several hundred people, rose and shouted "Long

Live Wasilewska." In a letter to her mother, she wondered whether she would ever be able to live up to their expectations:

> Lwów was something so wonderful, that I don't know if I will experience two such days ever again. Days of mass hysteria, elation, brotherhood, some kind of complete ecstasy. All of Lwów was set in motion—the whole city took part in all kinds of ceremonies and festivities. It's a good thing I don't suffer from megalomania, because it would have gone to my head. They went crazy over everyone, but with me they overdid it in a way that surpassed all boundaries. In the first place I was welcomed very enthusiastically at the congress, the proceedings of which lasted until Saturday evening. But afterwards it was even worse. At the authors' evening everyone was received in such a way as in general occurs nowhere. But when I came up to the podium, the entire hall, several hundred people, stood up, and for a good ten minutes shrieked, stamped their feet, applauded and cried out: long live Wasilewska. It was the same at the ceremony, the same on the streets, in front of the theater. . . . The League's speech was on Wednesday, and I was given an ovation ten times as boisterous as the first time, when you were there. It's beginning to become problematic. Marian had to cause a scene on the street with a crowd of Jewish girls who were running after me so as to touch my coat like a rabbi's gabardine.[143]

Aleksander Wat was not the only one not to receive an invitation to this ecstatic gathering. Antoni Słonimski did not receive one either, and wrote the following month in *Wiadomości Literackie* that he had learned of the congress from Broniewski's article. Himself rejected, Słonimski was not predisposed to be generous. "The average reader," he wrote, "might seriously think that some kind of literary elite gathered in Lwów. In reality, apart from a few communist-leaning writers, there was no one from among the more serious representatives of literature." Why, for instance, had Julian Tuwim and Tadeusz Boy-Żeleński—and himself—not been invited? Słonimski asked.

> I must admit that this lack of confidence is mutual. Independent or leftist writers were not invited for the same reasons that

Ukrainian socialists were not, because it was made clear to them that at the congress it would be impermissible to speak against the dictatorship in the Soviet Union. How can I have confidence in a congress whose chief concern was supposed to be the matter of freedom of speech and conscience as well as the battle against terror and oppression, when that very congress began by not allowing socialists to speak, apparently in fear of offending Comrade Maksim Gorky. It's therefore possible in the local theater building in Lwów, with the permission of the Polish authorities, to protest against "concentration camps" and "brutal political terror" [in Poland], but it's not permissible even to mention that in the Soviet Union there are also "concentration camps" and "brutal political terror." If one of the fundamental principles of culture is supposed to be tolerance and freedom, then the Lwów congress was a quite miserable and unfortunate parody.[144]

THE SPECTER OF FASCISM

Despite the spirit of the Lwów congress and the warm relations at Wanda Wasilewska's gatherings, it was a time when for Polish Jews of the Left, and for "Poles of Jewish origin," a dual Polish-Jewish identity was becoming increasingly uneasy. As the promising 1920s became the depressed 1930s, the influence of right-wing National Democratic ideology increased. By the time of Piłsudski's death in 1935, little remained in the regime he had set in place of his former socialist, federalist, multiethnic vision. The Poland of the late 1930s saw a *numerus clausus* and ghetto benches at the universities, campaigns for economic boycotts against Jews, and increasing right-wing violence.[145]

On the twin subjects of antisemitism at home and the specter of fascism from the West, no one was more perceptive than Antoni Słonimski, the son of a secular Jewish father and a deeply religious Catholic mother. For Słonimski, the legacy of his father was the value of secular enlightenment.[146] He wrote with an uncharacteristic warmth and admiration of his grandfather, his father's father who had escaped from the ghetto, an autodidact who became a Renaissance man. For Słonimski, his grandfather's biography vindicated his own cosmopolitanism. "I don't know if my grandfather was a good Jew or a bad Jew," Słonimski wrote of him, "but he was a magnificent person."[147] In 1923, Słonimski had returned from the Middle East to write a poem about an elderly Polish Jew he had met by the Jaffa gates during his travels in Palestine. The old man longed only to return to Warsaw.[148]

Słonimski was a liberal who very much felt himself to be a Pole, a Varsovian, a cosmopolitan. The unassimilated Polish Jews of the interwar years had few critics outside the right-wing camp harsher than he. In a vicious 1924 article Słonimski began: "One of the cardinal and most characteristic traits of Jews is their disregard for the most sacred conquests of the human spirit. Jews show a lack of regard for everything: they mutilate the language they speak, they disregard the purity of speech, body and heart, yet at the same time they inexplicably overvalue the significance of money." Jews, in Słonimski's observation, scorned physical labor; they were a nation producing nothing, engaging instead in trade, playing the role of intermediaries.[149] It was one of Słonimski's sharpest attacks on the Jewish community in Poland, but far from the only one. In a 1934 column he praised a journalist's reportage about the Polish Jewish community; the journalist had written of the barbarity of the Jewish ghetto and the need for Jewish self-criticism.[150] "Precisely now," Słonimski wrote, "is an excellent time for Jews to seek out some of the causes of antisemitism, in order to modify somewhat their relationship to the world." Why, Słonimski asked, did the Jewish intelligentsia not fight against the backwardness, the obscurantism of Hasidism? He proposed that Jews "initiate their own, proper antisemitic action," refuting the anticipated counterargument:

> But in this respect—as I've already mentioned—there is the argument that now is not the time. When then, will that time finally come?—thanks to the Jewish God it's already lasted a couple of thousand years. The English, the French, other nations have attentively reined in their nation's mistakes, some nations have had revolutions, others have had great satirists and iconoclasts. But the Jews could not, it was not time for the reason that at a given moment the Assyrians didn't like them, the Egyptians or the Spanish were angry at them . . . and so still greater courage in self-criticism is necessary, it's necessary for the Jewish intelligentsia to fight to raise young Jews as residents of Europe and for the Zionists in their new homeland

to wean themselves from the cheder, from the Talmud and the rabbis, which is an older and more dangerous enemy to them than Hitler.[151]

Słonimski was also one of the fiercest opponents of right-wing anti-semitism, and his indictment of the obscurantism of Jewish tradition did not at all imply a disregard for the danger of Nazism. Adolf Hitler's victory in the 1933 German elections was the focus of many of Słonimski's weekly columns for the remainder of the decade. In 1933 he wrote that the Polish National Democrats' "love for Hitler is very touching." The same year he took fascist stupidity as one of his pet themes: "We often hear such an opinion about Hitler: 'But he must be a wise person, if he came to power' or: 'There must be something in his program, if people are listening to it.' Nonsense, nothing of the sort. Let us tell ourselves once and for all, that an ordinary fool, a completely ordinary idiot can be a dictator." He went a step further: if there existed among his readers' acquaintances such an idiot, they were cautioned to keep in mind that he could become their future ruler, and they should thus be careful to "treat him appropriately—of course, appropriately badly."[152]

Few were spared in Słonimski's feuilletons, and Słonimski was not at all uncritical of what he saw as demagoguery of the Left. In a column following the 1934 Seventeenth Congress of the Communist Party of the Soviet Union, Słonimski sketched the ominous implications of the absence of discussion following Stalin's speech. What did it mean that after Stalin spoke the only response was "Long live the great Stalin!"?[153] Słonimski was moreover a skeptic about the cultural level of the so-called masses and a traditionalist with respect to literature. "I must with sadness assert," he wrote in 1934, "that I am a pessimist as to the understanding and feeling of poetry by even the most class-conscious proletariat."[154] The proletariat was no more immune from Słonimski's criticism than was his own circle. Both the former and the latter included not a small number of "snobs and graphomaniacs" in Słonimski's opinion.[155] This stance naturally made him unpopular more than once among his own friends. Janina Broniewska was unforgiving; her husband was more generous. When in 1935, during a conversation with Wanda Wasilewska and Marian Bogatko, Broniewska recalled Słonimski's column about the terror in Russia, she was interrupted by her husband. "The good-natured Władek" told her to calm down, that yes, Słonimski had said some stupid things in his column, but that had been several years earlier. Bogatko remained skeptical that Słonimski had undergone any kind of evolution.[156] Moreover, despite the vicious ad hominem attacks of the *Miesięcznik Literacki* period, Słonimski and Wat did not remain permanently estranged. Hostility passed, and friendship resumed.[157]

As Hitler consolidated power in Germany, Słonimski relaxed his indictment of Jewish obscurantism in the face of increasingly virulent antisemitism. In a 1936 column Słonimski mocked the right-wing Polish publicist Stanisław Piasecki: "Mr. Piasecki claims that Jews invented communism. If one considers the fact that Jews invented capitalism as well, it could seem that in relation to us their accounts are all squared. We could likewise add that Jews also invented Christianity, but let's not complicate Mr. Piasecki's ideological situation, which is already so complicated as it is."[158] The mocking of absurdity became a favorite motif of Słonimski's columns. After the Italian futurist-turned-fascist Marinetti announced that "war is beautiful, because harmonious force blends with goodness," Słonimski wrote: "If that is too little for you, consider this argument by the Italian fascist: 'War is beautiful, in as much as rifle shots, cannonade, pauses of silence, and the scents and odors of putrefaction symphonize with one another.' Imagine that someone you knew were to say: 'I'm glad that your child is ill, because a child's illness is beautiful, since the scent of medications harmonizes with the scent of cyclamen and alpine shots.' What would you say in response? Likely, that he's a lunatic and given that, he can kiss yours. But that would be a mistake. Don't let the lunatics kiss you, because today the lunatics are biting."[159] It was not Słonimski's only such acerbic analogy. "It would be much more convenient if Jews were not people but coffee," he wrote the same year, "There's too much coffee, so coffee is thrown into the sea. There are too many Jews, so throw the Jews into the sea. The Jews would thus increase in value, and every country's ambition would be to possess the greatest quantity of Jews." "Those searching for primitive solutions," Słonimski acknowledged, "suffer in a very particular way when it comes to *Wiadomości Literackie*. They desire, they dream that *Wiadomości Literackie* would be Bolshevik, so that it would be possible to catch the editor during the night taking money from Stalin by the gate. They want the publication that's uncomfortable for them to be Jewish, to publish poor writing and bad poems. How pleasant that would be!"[160]

Słonimski was still inclined to downplay the seriousness of the anti-semitic threat. In 1936 he wrote of having met an old Polish Jew in America who asked him if the Jews in Poland were suffering very much. In response Słonimski explained to him that the situation was really not so terrible. In his view the "Jewish-Polish conflict" was "primitive and stupid," and the Jews themselves were "lacking in self-preservation instinct" and "unable to speak, walk, to live together in a human way." What then would be the solution? In a bad marriage, Słonimski pointed out, when the couple cannot go their separate ways, they have to try to organize their lives in the most tolerable way possible. "My comparison is a bit grotesque, but the Jewish minority in Poland is a bit like the Jewish wife, whose husband, when he gets plastered, pummels her in the head." Of course a man should not beat his wife, Słonimski acknowledged, but it was the case that in such a bad marriage it was generally best that a husband and wife, simply through mutual avoidance, see each other as little as possible. Even so, he considered the ghetto benches at the university in Lwów to constitute a great injury to students of Jewish origin who felt themselves to be Poles. He supported the Polish students who responded by sitting together with the Jews—leaving the "National Democrat hooligans" to sit separately.[161] In 1937 he proposed a more concrete solution for making a bad marriage tolerable. The Jewish question in Poland could most democratically be solved, in Słonimski's most programmatic assertion, by "making it possible for some Jews to be Jews in Palestine and others to be Poles in Poland."[162]

By the late 1930s it was the fascists who were most often the objects of Słonimski's ridicule and disgust. In 1937 he posed to his readers the question: "If such an enormous majority of the nation is Judaized and communized and the rest is composed of Masons, Germans, and Ukrainians, then where are the real Poles?"[163] The subject of another column that year was how often one heard today "Are you a Pole? A quarter-Pole? Can you prove your Polishness?"[164] In autumn 1938, Słonimski discussed an essay published in a Wilno paper in which someone had thought up a wonderful way to distinguish a Jew from a non-Jew: one need only ask the person whose identity was in question his opinion about Hitler—for

Jews were filled with hatred towards Hitler. While an Aryan might also not like Hitler, the Wilno author explained, the Aryan possessed a certain objectivity on the subject; he was able to acknowledge Hitler's intellectual merits. "A very good method," Słonimski commented, "and perhaps that same method could be applied in case there is any doubt as to whether one is speaking with an idiot or not."[165]

By the time of *Kristallnacht* in November 1938, Słonimski had relented in his criticism and stood in solidarity with Jews, imperfect as they might be. He wrote of the burning of synagogues in Germany, and of how so many German Jews were loyal and patriotic German citizens. "After the Moscow trials it might have seemed that the imaginations of cruel people could not manage to come up with anything more," he wrote, "but it's turned out that Bolsheviks, just like Nazis, constantly require new thrills of cruelty, and their imagination in that direction is inexhaustible."[166] In one of Słonimski's last columns for *Wiadomości Literackie,* he wrote of the elegant Warsaw café named Swann after Marcel Proust's protagonist, where there had recently appeared the sign on the coatroom "Aryan premises." Jews were no longer allowed in Swann; the café was among the first in the city to introduce an Aryan code. Now he wrote of the irony that Proust himself was not an "Aryan" and his character Swann was a Jew! The "crazy aesthetes" who opened the café and named it after a Proustian hero obviously had not read Proust, Słonimski concluded. If they had they might have noticed the absurdity that Swann himself could not have gone into Swann for a cup of tea.[167]

JEWISHNESS AND ITS DISCONTENTS

In 1937 Słonimski devoted one of his columns to right-wing protests against the use of Tuwim's poetry in Polish schools, on the grounds that a Jew should not be teaching Polish children.[168] Like Słonimski, Tuwim felt a profound ambivalence about his Jewish origins. In a 1935 interview with Broniewski's former lover Irena Hellman, Tuwim described the milieu in which he was raised as "tolerant and progressive"; there were no so-called Jewish traditions in his home, he had grown up "free and unconstrained."[169] The verses he wrote while still in secondary school, however, allude to the fact that even this "unconstrained" upbringing did not free him from insecurities about his identity, that he was haunted by his origins from the very beginning of his literary career. In a lamenting poem dedicated to "Witold W." (most likely Wandurski), Tuwim told his Aryan friend at once of his mythologized genealogy as a Jew, and of his love for Poland. "There flows in me semitic blood / Hot blood, passionate blood," he wrote. Yet the passion contained in that blood was a passion for Poland: "Oh Aria! how I love you! / Oh sun-Poland! My land!"[170] A second poem, "Tragedia" (Tragedy), drew like the first on juxtapositions of archaic and modern language and described the conflict between his Jewishness and his love for Christian Poland as the narrator's greatest tragedy. A repetitive duality and a sense of the yoking of contradictions emerged in the perfect masculine rhymes.

> My greatest tragedy—that I am a Jew,
> And have come to love the Aryans' Christ-like soul!
> That at times by some inner gesture something bursts
> And recalls the ancient heritage of the Race
>
> That at times with a sudden, primal reflex something
> Rebels in my blood, wildly, unconsciously
> And semitic blood battles with an other Spirit,
> In the gales of future ages, in the enormity of thought!
>
> And then I am proud—I, an aristocrat,
> Son of the oldest people—of the embryo of messianism!
> And I am shamed, that I am the blood brother
> of a vile, enslaved nation of cowards with no home![171]

Later, in his 1918 poetry collection, Tuwim wrote of Jews as "tragic, nervous people" "who do not know what homeland means."[172] In a 1924 interview Tuwim described how, despite the fact that "the Jewish question lies in my blood," from the time of his childhood, "subconsciously I attached myself with my entire soul to Polishness." As in his school days, however, the "Jewish problem" remained a source of melancholy, "a tragedy, in which I myself am among the nameless actors."[173] Most often in interviews he only reluctantly agreed to speak about his Jewishness. Once, in 1927, he expressed the opinion that Skamander had only hurt relations between Poles and Jews: "Culturally and emotionally I regard myself as a Pole, yet I realize that there exist fundamental differences between myself and my friends who are Aryans. The embryos of that

FIGURE 10 Julian Tuwim with his dog, 1930. Courtesy of Muzeum Literatury imienia Adama Mickiewicza.

difference lie in blood—I feel them in my temperament, which is more organic than the Polish temperament. I am a semite and I've never denied that. . . . I do not believe in assimilation, it is not possible. It's difficult to foresee how relations will take shape. I don't belong to those who are excessively optimistic. I've suffered much myself as a result of my Jewishness. I consider that I and my friends of Jewish origin from Skamander have only inflamed 'Polish-Jewish relations.'"[174]

By the mid-1930s, Zionism seemed to Tuwim to be the only solution—but not for himself. Nor did he wish to discuss this; he wanted to talk about poetry.[175] In a 1935 interview for the Zionist-leaning newspaper *Nasz Przegląd,* Tuwim offended the interviewer with his criticism of the Polish Jewish community. Why, the interviewer asked, in such a difficult time for Jews, was Tuwim criticizing them? Tuwim's answer was strikingly reminiscent of Słonimski's: since there had never been a time in human history when the Jews had not been persecuted, such logic would dictate there would never be a time when criticism was permissible.[176] Towards the traditional Jewish community of his hometown of Łódź, Tuwim felt more repulsion than kinship: "Terribly many black Jewish 'uniforms.' Those who wore them used a hideous, rattling speech, again half German. . . . It is high time, gentlemen, to cut off those long overcoats and side curls, but also to learn respect for the language of the nation among whom you live. The black Hasidic rabble has remained in my memory from the Łódź of times past like a nightmare."[177] When questioned about his reaction to right-wing denials of his Polishness, Tuwim answered that his Polishness was "my private affair, deeply and fundamentally resolved in my conscience."[178]

Mieczysław Braun, Broniewski's old friend from Łódź, reacted differently to the climate of rising antisemitism. After 1926, his poetry was forced to compete for time with his new career as a lawyer; throughout the late 1920s his ties to Warsaw literary life grew weaker. In 1929 he ceased contributing to *Wiadomości Literackie,* although he maintained contact with the PPS and its paper *Robotnik* (The Worker), where his poems continued to appear until 1931. Braun drifted away, but did not entirely disappear, from the world of letters. Like Tuwim, he was a devotee of Esperanto, a language in which he saw hope for the end of national antagonisms.[179] Yet he departed from the paths taken by those like Tuwim and Słonimski in his public embrace of a dual Polish-Jewish identity. In a 1929 article in

Nasz Przegląd, Braun lamented the inaccessibility of Yiddish literature for Polish readers and pleaded for more translations into Polish. In literature, "the universally human realm of art," Braun saw hope for an "ark of the covenant" between nations, who, while longtime neighbors, "barely know each other by name."[180] Yet Braun felt himself to be a Polish poet, even as the antisemitism of the mid-to-late 1930s cast the identity of "Poles of Jewish origin" into question. For a writer, Braun argued, language was identity, and a Jew—like himself—writing in Polish was a Polish writer.[181]

It was the late 1930s when Aleksander Wat's seven-year-old son Andrzej learned what the word "Jew" meant. One day the boy returned from a walk with his nanny and quite cheerily reported, "You know, Mommy, they're breaking the shopkeeper's windows." The shopkeeper was a poor Jewish woman who sold candy and flavored soda water. When Ola Watowa asked why he was so happy about this, the boy answered, "Because Jews are terrible, they're ugly and they're dirty." It was to be his first lesson in his own Jewishness. Wat began the conversation like this:

> "Is mommy ugly?"
> "No, she's pretty."
> "Is mommy dirty?"
> "No, she's not dirty."
> And in the end: "Do you love mommy?"
> He answered: "Yes, very much."
> "Well, you should know that your mommy is a Jew. And
> so, do you love your mother?" My little Andrzej reflected upon
> that, hesitated a moment, and said: "I would love her even
> more if she weren't a Jew."[182]

One day Ola Watowa ran into Jarosław Iwaszkiewicz on the street. He was disappointed because Irena Krzywicka—his close friend, and a Jew herself—had recommended to him a wonderful bookbinder on Świętokrzyska Street, but Iwaszkiewicz could not become his customer because the bookbinder was a Jew. There was a slogan current at the time: "each to his own with his own affairs."[183] Iwaszkiewicz, though, was much more complicated than this. At Ziemiańska he would gibe at Grydzewski, "You Jew-boy!"[184] Yet he was very close to Grydzewski, as he was to Słonimski and Tuwim. In 1933, Tuwim began a multilingual letter to Iwaszkiewicz, who was in Copenhagen at the time:

Oh you *Goy*, you good, handsome youth!

But is he really a "goy"? Without any, even if far removed, admixture of that Jewish blood which has poisoned our old Aryan, Nordic world for us?

Forgive the fact that I'm beginning this letter with such a doubt, but you have no idea how sensitive I've become on this point. On dit, que le Pape même . . . Horreur! Enfin . . . si son Maître et Chef . . . Mais laissons! [They say that even the pope . . . Horror! In the end . . . if his Lord and Boss . . . But let's leave that!][185]

It was a time when all of the writers were somehow engaged with the Jewish question in Poland. In response to a 1937 *Wiadomości Literackie* questionnaire about antisemitism, the ostracized Andrzej Stawar distinguished between sporadically arising distaste towards Jews and programmatic "militant antisemitism." The latter he saw, in Marxist terms, as a relatively recent construct of fascism, a reactionary myth prophesying that the nation's economic problems could be transformed into a national renaissance through the battle against Jews. In his Marxist reading, Polish antisemitism aimed to deflect attention from the workers' movement and to weaken class consciousness.[186] Wanda Wasilewska composed an equally long response to the questionnaire. Like Stawar, she saw antisemitism through the lens of class conflict. She harbored as well a conviction of the natural goodness of the masses. In search of evidence for such a conviction, she set out on a journey to discover whether antisemitism existed in Poland—that is, antisemitism that was "real, essential, flowing from the depths and embracing the broad masses." Notwithstanding her near-drowning incident of several years earlier, now she and Bogatko embarked on a kayak trip through the eastern Polish provinces, stopping in villages and seeking out antisemitism. What they found were Polish, Jewish, and Belarusian children playing happily together. Moreover, Wasilewska claimed a visit to the countryside served to debunk the stereotype of the Jew as petty merchant: outside of the cities she found Jews engaged in hard, manual, productive labor. There was, of course, some antisemitism—a Jewish boy who took them to a place where they could stay for the night would like to go to high school in a nearby town, but recognized that this was impossible because he was a Jew. In his own village, though, among his neighbors, he did not feel his otherness. For Wasilewska, here was the truth of Polish antisemitism: everything was harmonious "on the ground," in the countryside, where relations were authentic; antisemitism was a foreign import from the oppressing class. It was the rich who exploited them whom the peasants truly resented.[187]

Janina Broniewska was just as principled, albeit less romantic; like Stawar, she saw antisemitism as right-wing propaganda aimed at diverting attention from the true problem of class. For her antisemitism was a weapon of "those on the other side of the red barricade"; and she wrote resentfully of hearing "Don't buy from the Jews" throughout the 1930s, as if Jewish competition were responsible for the intensifying economic crisis.[188] She and Wasilewska resolved to take their daughters, Anka and Ewa, on vacation to Medem, a Jewish sanatorium, so as to immerse the girls in a completely Jewish—and socialist—atmosphere among the children of Bundists. On her deathbed Broniewski's Catholic mother put some money in her daughter-in-law's hand, saying "Take this, Jasieńka, take it, it's for Anka for that strange, but perhaps good, vacation."[189]

THE TERROR

An atmosphere of hostility and suspicion was intensifying to the east as well. Despite Witold Wandurski's damning 1933 testimony, the NKVD came for Bruno Jasieński only four years later. After Tomasz Dąbal and two other Polish acquaintances in the Soviet Union were arrested in 1937, Jasieński wrote a series of letters berating himself for "insufficient vigilance." On 5 February 1937 he wrote to the Soviet Writers' Union that he had just learned of the arrests and considered it his obligation as a Party member to present a complete history of his relations with the accused. He elaborated:

> Shortly after my arrival in the Soviet Union in one of the
> articles (about language) I committed an error. I wrote that
> the language used by the Polish population in the Soviet Union
> is quite impoverished, and that our Soviet Polish press and
> Soviet Polish literature should be drawing from the repository
> of language spoken by the worker and peasant masses in
> Poland. On this basis I advanced the false conclusion that it
> is not possible to build Polish (in form) socialist culture in the

Soviet Union without organic ties to the life of the revolutionary masses in Poland. Having become aware of my error, I retracted everything in the press. I should have already at that time reflected upon why Dąbal, who seemed to be an old and tested comrade, did not point out that error to me at once, and also committed it himself.[190]

It had been a difficult, but well-learned lesson in vigilance, Jasieński concluded.[191]

When in April 1937 there followed an article in *Pravda* denouncing him for his ties to supposed spies and traitors, Jasieński wrote to Stalin a pleading, yet arrogant self-defense, in which he attributed the accusations against him to his accusers' desire to "avoid self-criticism." The letter began:

> It would go against my conscience to take up your time with personal matters. Yet the Party rightly demands from us, Soviet writers, the creation (especially for the occasion of the twentieth anniversary of October) of politically timely—and artistically solid—literary works. Since the time of the publication of my last novel, *A Man Changes His Skin,* three years ago, I have been working on my next book directed at the enemies of the people—the Trotskyites and their master, German fascism. In this work two worlds will stand in opposition to one another —the world of communism and the world of fascism. Against this background I am attempting to portray the conspiratorial methods of the Gestapo and their agents in our country, Trotskyite traitors. . . .
>
> Neither the Writers' Union nor anyone else has helped me in my work. I would only wish, however, that they would not hinder me. Unfortunately, one of the comrades entrusted with literary matters, Comrade P[avel] Iudin, conceives of his task entirely differently. In the 23 April issue of *Pravda* in the article "Why It Was Necessary to Liquidate RAPP," Comrade Iudin equated me with the Trotskyite [Leopold] Averbakh, an enemy of the people, putting forth strange reproaches shameful to me as a communist.[192]

Jasieński questioned Iudin's motivation and inquired provocatively about who stood to benefit from the accusations against him:

> To whom would it be important to increase the camp of Trotsky-ite traitors at the cost of entirely untainted communist writers who have never been politically connected with Trotskyite ban-dits, who have never shown any deviations from the Party's general line? Comrade Iudin's unfounded reproach can have only one result—desistance from creative work. Now I will be forced to put the novel aside and occupy myself with searching for published evidence of the fact that I have never belonged to the Averbakh group, I will have to dig through old maga-zines, recall conversations of five years ago with individual comrades, give reports and explanations at dozens of meetings. You yourself understand that in such conditions it is impos-sible to continue work on the novel. In connection with that I will not succeed in completing, before the twentieth anniver-sary, my work designed to mobilize the people to battle against their enemies and their enemies' helpers.[193]

Despite his certainty of tone, very shortly after sending this letter Jasieński reconsidered his situation. In a second letter to Stalin dated just three days later, he recanted both his self-defense and his attack on Iudin. He had learned the art of self-criticism well. Now he told Stalin that "having thought through the entire history of my acquaintance with Averbakh once more, I have come to the conclusion that the criticism is rightful and deserved." He realized only now that he had been an in-strument in the maneuvers of Trotskyites: "You have taught us to have the courage to confess fully to our errors, but I am ashamed to confess to them before you.[194] I will do all that I possibly can to help our party eradicate from the literary milieu the decaying roots of *averbakhovshchina*. I am convinced that the injury done to literature by being at the time a tool in Averbakh's schemings is less than the advantages I can give to the Party by working as a writer. I believe that the Party will not repudi-ate me for the delayed, but sincere, worthy-of-a-Bolshevik confession of literary-political errors."[195] Jasieński now faced an even more serious ac-cusation. To Stalin he wrote, "Unfortunately, in the article in *Pravda* there was presented another, terrible political reproach—of a connection with the spy Dąbal."[196] Now Jasieński pleaded for Stalin's support: "I turn to you now, as the proposal to expel me from the ranks of the Party is being considered. All of my work as a writer has been work in the service of the Party. My last novel, about which I wrote to you, was directed precisely at enemies of the people—Trotskyites and their Berlin masters. I have withdrawn the novel from print. I am not able to publish it, being thus accused. You understand the full horror of the situation in which I find myself. Only you can avert such a great punishment, disproportionate to my offenses. Help! All of my life, all of my literary talent I will devote even more powerfully, more decidedly to the battle against the enemies of the people and to the Party!"[197] The same day Jasieński wrote to the editor of *Pravda* that the "harsh criticism" was truthful and legitimate; that he was "submitting an exhaustive and frank criticism" of his errors; and that he would like to publish a self-criticism in *Pravda* acknowledging the justness of the criticism against him and telling of the lessons he had drawn from that criticism.[198]

A few days later, on 2 May 1937, Jasieński wrote to Nikolai Yezhov, head of the NKVD, asking that his alleged connections with the spies Wandurski, Averbakh, Dąbal, and others be investigated as quickly as possible. With respect to Wandurski, Jasieński wrote, "it was widely known in literary circles that this individual led a fierce battle against me."[199] Jasieński's situation was ever more bleak, particularly after the arrest of his former wife Klara Arem. He had had no contact with her for seven years, but he understood well that her arrest would be counted towards his guilt. In his next paragraph, Jasieński set out the central line of what was simultaneously his self-defense and his self-criticism: "An enormous offense towards the Party was the fact that I did not demonstrate sufficient vigilance vis-à-vis camouflaged traitors, and I maintained friendly contacts with unmasked traitors, the likes of T[omasz] Dąbal. . . . Yet all of that does not give anyone the right to place me in one camp with Polish spies."[200]

This was only the beginning of Jasieński's letter-writing campaign. On 3 May he wrote to the Soviet Writers' Union, acknowledging news of his former wife's arrest; he had been notified by a neighbor who had asked that he take care of his son in Klara Arem's absence. This time Jasieński distanced himself from Arem even more emphatically: "In the course of the past seven years I have not maintained any contacts with

K. H. Arem-Jasieńska, and I was forced to break off any acquaintance with her due to the scandal that she dealt to me after the divorce. K. H. Arem-Jasieńska has married on several occasions since that time (for example she was living with some German, an actor) and involved herself in circles entirely unknown to me. My connection to her was limited to sending alimony for the support of the child, my presently eight-year-old son, on whose upbringing I did not even have any influence as the result of the hostile inclinations of his mother."[201] In the same letter he described his relations with Wandurski, which, he now claimed, had never been very close: "In Poland I did not know W[itold] Wandurski, member of the Communist Party of Poland, who was revealed to be a provocateur and spy. I met him only once at the premiere of his play in Cracow in 1923 or 1924. About Wandurski's 'communist convictions' I knew nothing at the time; I regarded him simply as one of the formally leftist Polish writers. Our acquaintance was completely incidental. . . . I met Wandurski for the second time in 1929 in Berlin, where I spent a week after my first deportation from France. Wandurski was there as a member of the KPP, who, with the Party's agreement, had escaped from prison across the border before his trial."[202] He had never liked Wandurski, Jasieński insisted. If their relations had been cordial it was only because Jasieński had understood him to be a devoted member of the Party and a literary colleague and felt it his obligation to have proper relations with him. Wandurski, however, had not reciprocated the gesture and had even "unleashed an active campaign" against Jasieński in the International Association of Revolutionary Writers. Moreover, while living in Jasieński's apartment during Jasieński's stay in Tadzhikistan, Wandurski had signed over Jasieński's food stamps to himself. Jasieński now returned to the subject of Stanisław Ryszard Stande's 1929 letter of protest against Jasieński's "self-advertisement." Now, though, Jasieński omitted Stande's name entirely, placing the blame instead on Hempel, Wandurski, and Broniewski—despite Jasieński's warm correspondence with Broniewski, and despite Hempel's having denied signing Stande's letter: "After my arrival in the Soviet Union, when in many articles the Soviet press presented me as a leading Polish revolutionary poet, W. Wandurski, J. Wiślak [Hempel] (later arrested by the NKVD), and W. Broniewski (who today has transformed himself into a leftist-bourgeois writer still living in Poland) turned to the Polish section of the Executive Committee of the Communist International, and if I remember correctly, to the editorial board of *Izvestiia,* with a protest against the undeserved praise I received as a Polish proletarian writer."[203]

Jasieński's firm tone in this letter notwithstanding, both he and his wife Anna Berziń knew that his situation was growing ever more dire. In May 1937, Berziń wrote two desperate letters to Stalin, pleading with Stalin to see that Jasieński's case be properly investigated so that the truth of his innocence could be revealed. Berziń was a journalist, yet the style of her pleas was less sophisticated and more obviously desperate than that of her husband. She began: "Comrade Stalin! You speak often, and more than others, about respect for living people. And so neither the writer Bruno Jasieński nor I—his wife, nor anyone from our family is an immortal. We are all alive, we want to live and work."[204] On 31 July 1937 Jasieński was arrested.

During interrogations on 15 September Jasieński signed a long and self-flagellating confession of Polish nationalism and conspiratorial activity on behalf of the Polish Military Organization, which in reality had not existed since the end of the Polish-Soviet War:

QUESTION: Towards what goal would it be helpful for five Polish spies to bring an honest revolutionary worker into the Party? It is known to the investigators that at the moment when you entered the All-Union Communist [Bolshevik] Party, you were a member of the Polish Military Organization!

ANSWER: When I emigrated from Poland in 1925, I did not break all my contacts with the petty bourgeoisie world from which I came. . . . I had not overcome Polish nationalist influences.

QUESTION: And what more?

ANSWER: Doubtlessly for these reasons Dąbal, whom I met in person in 1929, pulled me into work in the Polish Military Organization. . . .

QUESTION: On what concretely was your activity as a Polish Military Organization member based?

ANSWER: From the moment of my nomination as editor of the Polish magazine *Kultura Mas,* together with the Polish Military Organization member Dąbal, I began to propagate in the pages of that paper Polish nationalist ideas, in particular the damaging and counter-revolutionary idea about the impossibility of building a Polish socialist culture in the Soviet Union in the absence of ties with the ethnographically Polish masses. I similarly developed these ideas on the pages of the Kievan *Proletariacka Prawda* [Proletarian Truth], in articles devoted to the Polish proletarian theater, in which I praised the Polish theater of the provocateur Wandurski. I conducted these activities in the years 1929–1930 directly under the leadership of Dąbal, who, as editor of the central Polish newspaper *Trybuna Radziecka*, supported and popularized nationalist ideas.[205]

Several days later Jasieński recanted his testimony. In a letter to Yezhov dated 21 September 1937, he said, "Having been broken morally and physically after uninterrupted 'standing treatment,' in a flood of despair I signed my name to testimony dictated to me in which I confessed to crimes that I never committed. I hoped for this price to buy myself death, since life deprived of the state's confidence is unthinkable for me. . . . If you are convinced of my guilt (I am unable to offer proof of my innocence)—shoot me. This method, although I do not deserve it, will be an entirely legal form of the Soviet state's self-defense against enemies. I ask for this unrepiningly. Do not allow me to suffer further. This is my only and final request. I truly have no more strength left."[206] On 2 October 1937, Jasieński wrote a similar letter to the NKVD. He accused himself of a lack of vigilance, and stated that he should be punished harshly for this. Yet he insisted he was innocent of the other crimes attributed to him, particularly that of belonging to the Polish Military Organization. He repeated what he had written to Yezhov: "Having been broken morally and physically (two days of uninterrupted 'standing treatment'), in a moment of despair I confessed to crimes I did not commit. I hoped that for this price I would buy myself a speedier shooting, as I cannot and I will not live with the undeserved stamp of spy and enemy of the people."[207] Jasieński wrote at least one more letter to a Soviet magistrate, in which he stated again that under torture he had signed his name to false confessions. He emphasized that he made no accusations about improper interrogation techniques, as he regarded these techniques as just given the enormity of the suspected crimes; once again, he expressed his willingness to be shot.[208]

In January 1938, from his prison cell, Bruno Jasieński composed his last literary work. It was an autobiographical testimony. He wrote of his youth, of Mayakovsky: "Being under the strong influence of the ideas of the October Revolution, absorbed predominantly through the prism of the first years of Russian Soviet literature after the revolution (above all Maya-kovsky), I expressed in my poems rebellion against the bourgeois state, against bourgeois religion, bourgeois morality, bourgeois art, while not yet knowing exactly with what I intended to oppose them. . . . It was not a coincidence that my favorite poet was the pre-Revolution Mayakovsky, his poems of the first years of the Revolution, reflecting the total destructive and purifying force of October."[209] Jasieński wrote of his Polish years, his Parisian years, and the past decade in the Soviet Union. He had last seen Jan Hempel on the street in 1936; Hempel complained to him then of miserable material conditions and asked him for a recommendation to a Soviet magazine where he wanted to publish some articles about Polish literature. Jasieński never gave the recommendation. He wrote of Stande's now former wife, Zofia Kubalska (Warska), who had once been his transla-tor and more recently had taken an active part in his expulsion from the Party.[210] In conclusion he revealed his present feelings: "It was only the NKVD authorities who opened my eyes, and helped me to understand my guilt, to perceive the full depth of the muck in which I was wading about like a blind man. I am grateful to the NKVD authorities for the fact that, thanks to the methods applied to me, they helped me to regain my sight and are helping to wash away all of the filth that has clung to me since I came into contact with the criminal gang of spies and villains."[211]

So was Wandurski only the first of many. His demise in 1934 seems to have given rise to only limited forebodings in the intervening years. On 6 December 1936, Jan Hempel wrote to his sister in Poland, "We have lived to see the realization of what humanity's best minds have been dreaming of for a thousand years. I couldn't not share with you that great joy pulsating through all of us."[212] On 19 January 1937 Hempel was ar-rested. He subsequently shared the fate of other KPP activists. The arrest and execution of the man who was a grandfatherly figure to his younger comrades in Polish prison was symbolic of the impending fate of Polish communists. The same year they came for Stande as well—as they did for his now former wife Zofia Warska, her first husband, and her father Adolf Warski, Rosa Luxemburg's longtime comrade. The NKVD informed Zofia Warska's teenage son from her first marriage that his family had been sentenced to the gulag without the right of correspondence.[213] When the Moscow show trials began, the KPP leadership in Poland expressed solidarity with the death sentences. In the course of 1937 almost the entire

Politburo of the Central Committee of the KPP was arrested by the NKVD. Alfred Lampe was among the only survivors of the Party leadership; he was in Polish prison at the time.[214] For Polish communists in the 1930s, Polish prison was often the safest place to be. Jakub Berman's name appeared on a Comintern list of suspected spies and provocateurs, but Berman kept his distance from the Soviet Union and in this way survived as well.[215] In 1938, the Comintern, with Stalin's permission, dissolved the Communist Party of Poland on charges that it had been infiltrated with spies and provocateurs. Stanisław Ryszard Stande was arrested and shot around the same time that Jasieński was writing of him in prison.[216] Jasieński's first wife Klara Arem was shot on 19 January 1938. Their son was turned over to a Soviet children's home.[217] Jasieński's second wife Anna Berziń was arrested in 1938 and sent to the gulag. As for the young futurist poet of long ago, "by nature an *enfant terrible*," strolling around Warsaw and Cracow in his elegant clothes, with a monocle in his right eye and a cane with a silver handle in his hand, he was executed in a Stalinist prison on 17 September 1938.[218]

PARTING

In Warsaw life continued. Władysław Broniewski finally drove his wife away. "This time," Janina Broniewska wrote, "it was essentially three strikes and you're out. I didn't appear at Ziemiańska, for the first time my indignation had not yet abated."[219] She moved with her daughter Anka into an apartment in a two-story house in Żoliborz. Before long, Wanda Wasilewska and Marian Bogatko took to playing matchmakers, presenting Janina Broniewska with their communist friend Romuald Gadomski. After so many partings and reconciliations, in late spring of 1938 Broniewski received a letter from his wife's lawyer informing him that she had applied for a separation.[220] Broniewski, too, was engaged in another romance by that time, with the widowed actress Maria Zarębińska, who had a young daughter close to Anka's age. Zarębińska was devoted to Broniewski, but terrified of his growing attachment to alcohol.[221] In the meantime, Gadomski moved into Janina Broniewska's apartment; only then did she tell Broniewski of her new relationship. He was quiet on the other end of the telephone. Later Broniewska learned from Maria Zarębińska how he had responded. "What's happened to you?" his new love asked when he put down the receiver, "why are you so shaken?"

"Do you know what Jaśka did to me? She informed me that
she has a husband! And he's a wonderful person!"

"For a moment now I wasn't able to catch my breath,"
Marysia told me. "Then with difficulty I got hold of myself
and finally I asked very sweetly: Władeczku, and to whom
are you telling this?' It didn't register immediately. Male logic,
isn't it?"[222]

The story did not end there. When Janina Broniewska's landlord began
to search for a tenant for the downstairs apartment, she invited her ex-
husband and his new wife and stepdaughter to move into the house in
Żoliborz. When Zarębińska worried that her Catholic father would not
be happy with the arrangement, particularly since Broniewski had never
obtained an official divorce, Janina Broniewska offered to talk to him. She
found the elderly man to be "charming and full of gallantry," despite his
awareness that she was also living in sin, and with a man who had spent
five years in prison for illegal communist activity. Janina Broniewska was
persuasive; Zarębińska's father accepted the unconventional household.[223]
Soon the two couples and their children were living under one roof, and
the two women became close friends.

AS NEWS REACHED WARSAW

Antoni Słonimski was among the first to grasp the grotesqueness of the
show trials. In 1936 he wrote of the Moscow trial against the Trotskyites as
one of the most terrifying events of their times: "History does not know a
case where sixteen old and hardened revolutionary activists demanded the
death sentence for themselves and spit mud at their many years of activity.
The words that one of the most famous communist leaders, Kamenev,
declared, are not words from this world: 'The sentence such as will befall
me will not be an expression of cruelty but evidence that everything has
its boundaries, even Soviet generosity. For that reason I hold in contempt
all cries about the cruelty of the sentence executed on me.'"[224] Słonimski
reminded his readers of the Inquisition, when under torture the accused
would admit to sexual relations with the devil. Six months later he wrote
of the protocols of the Moscow trials as the script of a play whose author
obviously did not fear criticism about the scenario's verisimilitude.[225]

On April Fools' Day of 1937, Słonimski signed his name to his most daring satire yet. "Stalin, Emperor of the Proletariat" was a full-page fictitious reportage in *Wiadomości Literackie,* decorated with large photographs, of Stalin's coronation as "emperor of the proletariat, king of the bourgeoisie, and the grand prince of technical experts and the intelligentsia."[226] Słonimski's criticism only sharpened as the trials continued:

> No one fools Stalin. They killed Kirov. It was known that these
> were right-wing elements, White Guardists, the sons of former
> tsarist officials, professors, and decaying intellectuals. Eighty
> such "former people" were sentenced to death. But the wise
> Stalin discovered right after the executions that it was the
> Trotskyites who did it. Stalin would have certainly absolved
> them from guilt, but they themselves at all the trials confessed
> to the crimes and pleaded for a death sentence. Stalin is not
> only wise, he is also good. He refuses nothing to Soviet citi-
> zens, even death. One of them, in the courtroom, suddenly
> began to deny [the charges]. They took him back to the cell,
> and by the next day he confessed to everything. They didn't do
> anything to him. They only told him not to worry Stalin.

The essay concluded with a "P.S. For gentlemen-idiots and editors of some publications: The sentence 'Stalin is not only wise but also good' is used ironically. It is to be understood in the contrary sense."[227]

Others in Warsaw were less outspoken, yet no less disconcerted. Władysław Broniewski experienced the purges, and in particular the death of his friends, painfully. He turned more and more to vodka. Aleksander Wat, too, could not accept the accusations.[228] In later years he dedicated a few lines in a poem to Jasieński's death, in a stanza reminiscent of their shared futurist past with its oddly juxtaposed, somewhat nonsensical verb tenses:

> Like on the Blondel, for two francs, arrogant Bruno
> he clasped the glass, bangs his horse-like head,
> downs the drink, sets it down, "ah, gud beer," he smacked his
>   lips, he is falling down, he will die in the tortures
> of the gulag in the far, oh so far away, North. Poor woodcutter.
>   Let us say
> a bedtime prayer for him.[229]

As the thirties drew to a close, the literati continued to gather. Wat and his wife Ola continued to keep an open house, full of guests and alcohol.[230] But he was haunted by "an absolute premonition that Ola, Andrzej, and I would die horrible deaths, that Poland would go under."

CHAPTER SIX

Autumn in Soviet Galicia

A poet of the revolution
should perish in the Soviet slammer?
History, why this is tactlessness,
one of us is behaving like a child!

—*Władysław Broniewski, "A Conversation with History"*

ALEKSANDER WAT WAS NOT alone in his foreboding of catastrophe. The 1930s had seen the emergence in Wilno of a circle of young catastrophist poets drawn to metaphysics and flirting with Marxism, among whom were Jerzy Putrament, Stefan Jędrychowski, and Czesław Miłosz. In their poems they expressed a sense of impending disaster on a cosmic scale. Then came the catastrophe itself. On 23 August 1939, the Popular Front vaporized: Vyacheslav Molotov and Joachim von Ribbentrop signed the Nazi-Soviet nonaggression treaty. Shortly afterwards, Wat saw Władysław Daszewski at Café Ziemiańska. Daszewski had spent much of the previous few years in Lwów, working at a theater there. Yet he had remained close to his Warsaw friends. He wrote letters to Broniewski, asking him to send greetings to "the beautiful and the ugly sex with whom we're acquainted and especially with whom we are more intimate."[1] Daszewski was also close to the Skamander poets, and now Wat was struck by his schadenfreude in anticipating his friends' reactions to the imminent Nazi attack. The scenic designer was rubbing his hands together. "They'll shit their pants, you'll see. Słonimski, Tuwim—they'll shit their pants in fear," he told Wat.[2]

This was among Wat's last visits to Café Ziemiańska. Daszewski's malicious prediction foreshadowed the end of Skamander—and the end of the era when a Polish poet could write "And in the spring, let me see spring—not Poland." Now everyone waited for the fall. It came on 1 September 1939. As the first German bombs fell on Warsaw, Wanda Wasilewska and Janina Broniewska appeared at the door of the Military Scientific-Educational Institute; they wanted to offer their services to the anti-German cause. They found open doors and an empty building, save for stacks of paper strewn about on the floor along with index card files of all those who had volunteered to assist with anti-Nazi propaganda.[3] Shortly afterwards, the two women fled Warsaw, heading east. Władysław Broniewski, too, set out in this direction. Despite his very respectable military record, the poet, now in his early forties and moreover known as a communist, was not mobilized. Undeterred, he volunteered, and on 7 September set out on a bicycle in search of his regiment. After he had traversed the route from Warsaw through Lublin and Tarnopol to Lwów, he checked into a hotel and, wearing his military uniform, awaited his assignment.[4] He had come too late. On 12 September Broniewski found his regiment; five days later the Red Army invaded eastern Poland. The Polish military was taken by surprise; the order was given not to resist.

Wanda Wasilewska and Marian Bogatko left Warsaw in September; together with the Bundist leader Wiktor Alter, they soon found themselves in the Volhynian town of Kowel.[5] In late September, the Ukrainian communist playwright Oleksandr Korneichuk broadcast a radio appeal in the name of the new Soviet authorities, calling to Lwów Polish writers and artists whom the war had tossed to the east, promising them material assistance and favorable working conditions. Among those he invited by name were Wanda Wasilewska, Władysław Broniewski, and Julian Tuwim.[6] Wasilewska learned of the invitation from a *politruk*, a Soviet political officer, who found her in Kowel. The officer instructed her to present herself to Korneichuk or Nikita Sergeevich Khrushchev. She had, at the time, absolutely no idea who Khrushchev and Korneichuk were, but was too embarrassed to ask the *politruk*. Compliantly she departed by train for Lwów.[7]

During the first days of the Luftwaffe's bombing of Warsaw, Wat continued to go to work at Gebethner's publishing house—where the Gestapo soon came looking for him as one of the members of the Polish intelligentsia to be shot. Ola Watowa and their young son Andrzej hid in the basement during the hours Wat spent at work. On the sixth day of the war, they fled Warsaw in two cars with Wat's sister and brother-in-law.[8] Somewhere in the eastern borderlands of Poland the two cars lost one another. Wat traveled on to the Volhynian provincial capital of Łuck, in search of his family. It was there that Wat had his first experience of the Soviets occupying eastern Poland. Łuck was full of the stench of boots and birch tar, of sweaty feet and cheap tobacco, and to Wat the Russians resembled oriental barbarians, "Asia at its most Asian."[9] He did not flee Łuck immediately though, instead wandering amongst the cafés, handing out hundreds of cards saying that Aleksander Wat was searching for his wife and son. In this way they finally found one another in Lwów, where Watowa was staying first with the Lwów writer and PPS activist Halina Górska and later with the poet Józef Wittlin's mother.[10]

A COSMOPOLITAN CITY

It was a time when many among the Polish intelligentsia were arriving in Lwów, a cultural center of more than 300,000 people, a cosmopolitan city with a mixed population of Poles, Ukrainians, and Jews. Like Warsaw, Lwów had been bombed by German aircraft on 1 September; eleven days later the Germans began a direct assault on the city.

Within another week the Red Army had arrived, the Germans ceded the area to their Soviet allies, and by the time Wat was reunited with his family there, Polish Lwów was rapidly becoming Soviet Lvov. Russian writers arrived as war correspondents, including Viktor Shklovsky, who was full of appreciation for the city's baroque architecture. Shklovsky knew of Wat from Mayakovsky, and was very warm to him, although reluctant to speak about politics. Wat met Shklovsky's fellow war correspondents as well. All of them were looking for Wanda Wasilewska. Apparently Stalin had insisted that she be found.[11] The eagerly awaited Wasilewska arrived before long, the most exalted among thousands of refugees fleeing into a city that had become a chaotic juxtaposition of anarchy and Soviet totalitarianism. Ola Watowa experienced the Sovietization of the city as a regression into ancient times, an "incursion of the barbarians."[12] Wat's friend Adolf Rudnicki, the younger Polish-Jewish prose writer, saw the city as an "eastern bazaar" filled with refugees in grotesque clothing, combinations of peasant sheepskin furs and urban raincoats. It was a place where "even the most thick-skinned felt how difficult it was to live without one's mother."[13] Wat, too, experienced newly Soviet Lvov as a city ensconced in fear. Moreover, it was a city whose beauty had now been drained from it, and Wat mourned its prewar incarnation, which had had "none of the grayness of Warsaw." To Wat interwar Lwów had always been a colorful, exotic, European city.[14]

For the friends of the late Witold Wandurski, Bruno Jasieński, and Stanisław Stande, the avant-garde poets who had become fellow travelers, it was in this cosmopolitan European city that they had their first real encounter with communism in power. Very quickly they discovered that it bore little resemblance to the Marxism of Café Ziemiańska. And they were all scared to death. Julian Stryjkowski titled his autobiographical novel of this time and place *Wielki Strach* (Great Fear). The story began with Artur, a young Jewish intellectual, a devoted communist and a former political prisoner, who found his way to Lvov in the early months of the war. He soon encountered Leon, his cousin Rachela's ex-husband. Leon the opportunist greeted Artur the naïve believer warmly, and chastised Artur for addressing him formally: "You're calling me 'mister'? Who the hell today says 'mister'? After all I've always been a [communist] sympathizer, don't you remember, my dear?" After their meeting Artur reflected:

> He's the son of a rich merchant. A Zionist activist. A sympathizer? Perhaps. How is it connected? Among the Jewish intelligentsia anything is possible. Even if it's abnormal. The whole nation is abnormal. Abnormal conditions. Flowing borders. Not on earth, but rather somewhere in the air. Like with Sholem Aleichem: *luftmensch, luftgesheft.* He was also once a *shomer.* In high school he wore a gray shirt with a scout badge on the sleeve. The best of the communist youth, the best of the Komsomol came from the ranks of *shomer.* First he read Herzl's *Old-New Land,* Max Nordau's *Paradoxes.* And then Bukharin. On one side Zionism, on the other materialism. For a long time he resisted. Bukharin prevailed. This was before [Bukharin] was unmasked as an imperialist spy.[15]

Artur's reflections on Leon recalled his own biography, and he began to feel increasingly guilty: he was himself not more than one degree of separation removed from Zionism. He had failed to reveal everything in his own Party autobiography: his older brother had gone to Palestine as a Zionist, a kibbutznik. His mother was in Palestine as well. Artur fell asleep that night having resolved that the next day he would confess "like a Bolshevik . . . to petty bourgeois remnants, to nationalist sentiments." Yet the next day he hesitated—and in the end made no such confession.[16]

Stryjkowski's naïve Artur saw newly Soviet Lvov as a place of chaos and inversions. Nonetheless his faith remained intact, he believed there must be good reasons, solid explanations for the violence and the terror. "A face made insane with fear," Stryjkowski wrote, "How is it possible? In the center of the city there is a hunt for a man. Red Army soldiers for a Red Army soldier. A Polish soldier never fled from his own patrol. A Polish patrol never shot at their own soldier. In capitalist Poland. There must be terrible reasons to have to flee from your own."[17] Wat saw Lvov as a kind of hedonistic, anarchic inferno. The red light district became the center of black-market trade in hard currency, gold, and diamonds.[18]

And there was antisemitism. Stryjkowski's Artur was scandalized by antisemitic jokes and suggestions by Ukrainian communists that Russia would turn over German comrades of Jewish origin to Hitler. When Artur was handed a Polish pamphlet titled "Death to żydokomuna!" he destroyed it. Later, when a Soviet acquaintance explained to Artur that he was a Jew, not a Pole, Artur responded:

> "I'm both one and the other."
> "How is that possible? Half and half?"
> "Both one and the other."
> "Funny. Here each person holds onto his own nationality.
> A Ukrainian is a Ukrainian, a Tatar a Tatar."[19]

Stryjkowski's Artur was not alone among those yet to understand the role nationality would play during this war. Not long after the deluge of refugees hit Lvov, the flood reversed itself: mass registrations to return to the German-occupied zone began. Wasilewska was astonished to see even Jews applying en masse for repatriation to German-occupied Polish lands.[20] Wat's younger brother was among those Polish Jews who made the decision to return to Warsaw. Wat himself remained in Lvov and attempted to assimilate the new reality. He felt there was no going back. "For me," he told, "those years between the wars had been a stage set, with dummies made of plywood and cardboard."[21]

The Nazi-Soviet nonaggression treaty still obtained; once it had invaded eastern Poland, the Soviet Union did not consider itself to be at war.

It was Poland alone that was decimated and occupied. The Soviet Union declared the purpose of its presence in the eastern territories to be that of assisting the Belarusians and Ukrainians oppressed by Polish rule, and held that Poland would never rise again. Local Soviet authorities pressured Polish communists to recant their critical position towards the Molotov-Ribbentrop agreement. At the Polish-language communist newspaper *Czerwony Sztandar* (Red Banner), Soviet authorities requested that the newspaper's staff members come forth with self-criticism of their initially unfavorable position towards the pact.[22] Nikita Khrushchev, First Secretary of the Ukrainian Communist Party, arrived to oversee a Soviet-style election campaign culminating in October elections to the new People's Assembly of Western Ukraine. Among the successful candidates was Halina Górska, who had befriended Wat and his family; Wat described her as "a sentimental socialist, a pure soul, terribly elegiac; everything pained her, every act of injustice in the world."[23] Once in existence, the assembly promptly asked that "Western Ukraine" be incorporated into the Soviet Union. The assembly's meeting was held in the Grand Theater; and from the gallery Wat watched as Halina Górska abstained from voting.

THE WRITERS FALL INTO LINE

Soviet authorities quickly set about the institutionalization of culture in a city overflowing with refugees. One of those charged with organizational duties was the young Polish writer from Lvov, Aleksander Dan, a friend of Józef Wittlin, and rumored to be connected to the NKVD.[24] Dan took a special interest in Wat. He adored Ola Watowa and Andrzej and was full of friendship for his colleague. It was from Dan that Wat learned that the Ukrainian dramatist Oleksandr Korneichuk had been entrusted with organizing literary life in the city. Dan further assured Wat that he understood the precariousness of his position as a "fellow traveler" whose relations with the Party had cooled, and that they should go together to see Korneichuk at the Hotel George. "We waited for a long time in front of his room, his suite," Wat described, "then out came two very good-looking, ample-bottomed girls, and a little while later he invited us in. He was wearing silk pajamas, acquired in Lwów of course, and a lot of cologne. He had the charm of a waiter."[25] Korneichuk struck Wat as possessing the kind of beauty alluring to homosexuals, "masculine, but at once servile, sweet-scented."[26] They spoke little that day. Korneichuk told Wat that he had heard about him and would be glad if Wat would join the board of the Writers' Union.

From room 31 of the Hotel George Korneichuk ruled over cultural life in Lvov. There were two lists on his desk: communists and noncommunists, respectively, with whom he intended to initiate cooperation. The second list included Wanda Wasilewska and Tadeusz Boy-Żeleński. Very soon, still in early autumn, there was a meeting called of the literary Left. Wat was elected to chair the meeting; he listened as Korneichuk told them: "'You don't trust us, I know that, and I don't require any trust from you in advance. Have a good look at us. We have time; take a year or two. If you like it, wonderful; if not, tough. It's up to you. But meanwhile, we'll give you conditions in which you can live, work, and observe us in action. We won't put any pressure on any of you; we won't use any propaganda on you. You'll judge for yourselves. You should take your time. Why rush? There shouldn't be any rush.'"[27] By late October, the Writers' Union of Polish, Ukrainian, and Jewish writers was operating with an organizational board including Aleksander Dan, Halina Górska, Boy-Żeleński, Broniewski, and Wat.[28]

The Writers' Club was located on the first floor of a palace, once the property of Count Bielski. The count still lived upstairs with his beautiful wife, whose lovers were rumored to have perished in duels over her hand.[29] Bielski's palace was both a haven and a trap for Wat and his colleagues. The NKVD did much recruiting there; the Stalinist security apparatus was ubiquitous in the Writers' Union, as elsewhere in Lvov.[30] Broniewski kept away from the Writers' Club, saying he preferred not to see his old friends and colleagues in that place.[31] One day Boy-Żeleński and Wat were taken aside there and told to sign a resolution expressing satisfaction at the incorporation of Western Ukraine into the Soviet Union. Both grew pale; they were made to understand that the consequences would be harsh if they declined. Boy-Żeleński turned to Wat, asking him what they should do, but Wat was at a loss as well. They were granted a fifteen-minute grace period to make their decision. In the end, both Wat and Boy signed their names.[32]

The Writers' Union was not the only Polish cultural institution reconfigured by the new Soviet regime. A Polish Theater was established in autumn 1939 with Broniewski as literary supervisor and Daszewski as scenic designer. The Ossolineum, which was a library, museum, and scholarly publishing house founded in the nineteenth century, was reincarnated under Jerzy Borejsza's supervision; Tadeusz Peiper and the once avant-garde poet Julian Przyboś found positions for themselves there.[33] Relations were tense between Wasilewska and Borejsza, who—Jerzy Putrament noticed—was perpetually unkempt: "His clothing always covered with dandruff, unshaven, with a cigarette dangling from his lower lip. His hair in disarray. His hand in his pocket."[34] Wat had met the former catastrophist poet Putrament several years earlier, in the mid-1930s, when Putrament had traveled to Warsaw from Wilno with the idea of beginning a Warsaw-Wilno publication. Now in Lvov they began to see each other more often.

INSIDE *CZERWONY SZTANDAR*

When Julian Stryjkowski's protagonist Artur put his mother on a boat to Palestine, he waited until the last moment to tell her that she was going alone, that he would stay in Poland. After the Nazi invasion, when in Lvov Artur encountered Leon the onetime Zionist, now opportunist-sympathizer, Leon quickly asked him where he was working. When Artur answered nowhere, Leon offered him a job at the newspaper *Czerwony Sztandar,* where Leon was administrative director. The editorial offices of the newly formed Polish-language Soviet newspaper became the setting for much of the rest of the novel and its themes of naïveté, terror, and antisemitism. *Czerwony Sztandar* was Stalinist in both form and content. Gone was the wild, experimental Marxism of the 1920s, the proletarian poetry of *Dźwignia,* the "Talmudic polemics" of *Miesięcznik Literacki. Czerwony Sztandar* drew upon a codified Stalinist idiom and underscored that Poland's fall was irrevocable.[35] A declaration of the Polish writers' support for the incorporation of Western Ukraine into Soviet Ukraine was published in November 1939. It was signed by Jerzy Borejsza, Władysław Broniewski, Tadeusz Boy-Żeleński, Aleksander Dan, Halina Górska, Aleksander Wat, and Adam Ważyk, among others. Broniewski was ill at the time, but someone else had signed his name.[36]

Czerwony Sztandar's staff included Adam Ważyk and Julian Stryjkowski. At the urging of Aleksander Dan, who insisted it would be the safest place for him, Wat accepted a position at *Czerwony Sztandar* as well; he shared an office with Ważyk.[37] The atmosphere in the editorial offices was macabre. Anyone could denounce anyone at any time; anyone could become his co-worker's executioner. In the proofreading room Wat was overcome with a terror-laden obsession that he would overlook errors—in particular the fatal error of misspelling "Stalin" as "Sralin" ("Shitlin"). Stryjkowski shared this obsession—and in the end was fired for a proof-reading error, albeit a less deadly one: he inadvertently reduced the anniversary of the founding of the Red Army by one year. For an error involving Stalin's name, Stryjkowski could have been shot.[38] Everything was treated with deathly seriousness. Wat was largely silent, sitting hunched over with his coat around his shoulders as if he were perpetually cold. "At moments he would smile sadly," Stryjkowski wrote, "and then he would look at you with eyes full of cruel knowledge."[39]

For Ola Watowa as for all of them, Lvov was a place of great fear. She was certain that most of those working at the paper did not believe in communism. Perhaps, she thought, Ważyk and a few others remained believers, but they were the exceptions; the others hoped that employment there would save them from persecution.[40] Stryjkowski arrived at the newspaper's offices barefoot, hungry, homeless. He wanted to survive. Yet it was not only desperation, but also communist faith that brought him to *Czerwony Sztandar.*[41] Ważyk, who nine years earlier had kept his distance from *Miesięcznik Literacki,* now was full of faith. He concluded his poem "Do inteligenta uchodźcy" (To the Intellectual-Refugee) with the ecstatic line "The past will fall off you and what remains will be the primitive form of the new man!"[42] In a New Year's article Ważyk wrote in *Czerwony Sztandar:* "We welcome the year 1940 as the beginning of a new epoch for us, as incentive and training for free and happy work. . . . Our fortune-telling: the irrefutable certainty, based on Marxist knowledge, that we are champions of an idea coming to embrace the entire world."[43]

Aleksander Wat was disgusted with himself. He wrote no poetry about Stalin, but he lied. He was terrified for his family, and he pretended he had regained his faith in communism. Awaiting arrest, he in the meantime "told lies, in cafés, conversations, union meetings, saying that I was a communist 100 percent, that now I understood everything, that Stalin was a wise man."[44] Among these acts of dissimulation was a panegyrical article about the new Soviet woman, liberated from her oppression by the Bolshevik Revolution: "Daughters of urban and provincial poverty, today delegates to the Supreme Soviet, directors of factories, pilots, engineers—leading representatives of the millions of fully valued, equally enfranchised Soviet women. Among them are women who grew up in the gloom and destitution of the tsarist times, treated like dirt by their parents, husbands, employers, women whom October made conscious, educated, made equal in rights with men, inspired with the revolutionary will to build and brought forth in the first ranks of the daily battle for socialism."[45] Wat also joined in the condemnation of prewar Poland: "Autumn 1939 was the last autumn of autocratic Poland, oppressing classes and nations. This autumn not only leftist, but all respectable writers fled from the shame and infamy of their country, becoming 'refugees in socialism,' as the poet S. Kirsanov said."[46] This oppressive Poland Wat contrasted with a glowing portrait of Soviet Lvov, where "the observer is struck by the mental state of those who frequent the cafés—joyful greetings, sparkling eyes, an unrestrained tone." He wrote of the "militant and often noble" tradition of Polish leftist literature, a literature that had developed in adverse conditions and despite the ceaseless persecution of Marxist periodicals. He told of his attempts to extend the life of *Miesięcznik Literacki* by preparing an issue in Warsaw, registering it in Lwów, printing it in Poznań, and sending it back to Warsaw. He spoke as well of Broniewski, Wasilewska, and Górska, of Przyboś and Stern, the "former futurist and translator of Mayakovsky." Perhaps it was in retaliation for Ważyk's faith that Wat mentioned Ważyk critically, as the author of "one of the most beautiful collections of Polish 'pure poetry'" who more recently had been composing prose that was "somewhat obscure" and "far removed from life."[47] This may well have been an article that the editors "touched up"—a few sentences excised, a few adjectives added, a few words changed. Nonetheless, Wat felt ashamed. "Poland was undergoing a tragedy," he later said, "and there I was taking the grand tone."[48]

At least once Wat engaged in formal self-criticism. It was during a purge of *Czerwony Sztandar*'s staff. A group of two or three arrived at the editorial offices, one of them "a good-looking redhead but a forbidding girl."[49] Aleksander Dan was left untouched; the others remained, as ever, under suspicion. Everyone was seated in a certain room; each was required to tell his life story. "I played it like an actor, knowing that I was playing for my life and Ola's," Wat described. He performed "inner surgery": "I played it like an actor, splitting myself in two. . . . Like a guillotine." And then he spoke: yes, he had said in the past that there was terror in the Soviet Union, that everyone lived in fear, but now that he was among

Soviet people himself, now that he spoke with them every day, he saw how wrong he been. How could anyone even imagine that there was terror here, when the city was full of lively, spontaneous, fearless people? Afterwards he went home to Ola, bathed in sweat. Apparently the inner surgery had been efficacious. "'Yes, yes,'" one of the communists on the editorial board said to him, "'your self-criticism was convincing, but you left out one thing you shouldn't have—your friendship with Stawar.'"[50] In this way Wat knew that in the cafés and in the Writers' Union his friendship with Andrzej Stawar was still being discussed. Notwithstanding his performance, Wat's position was not secure. By January of 1940, his coworkers in the editorial offices were afraid to speak to him. There were signs he would be arrested, that Broniewski would be, too. Wat learned quickly that in the Soviet Union these things could be sensed in advance because "a void forms around a person."[51]

THE POET WHO MOURNED TOO MUCH FOR WARSAW

Władysław Broniewski, against the wishes of *Czerwony Sztandar*'s editors, declined to join the newspaper's staff. Such a decision made him still more vulnerable. "Our beloved Władeczek is a great revolutionary poet," some said, "but why doesn't he want to work with us in our proletarian publication?"[52] Broniewski, the most deeply attached to the legacy of nineteenth-century Polish patriotism, experienced the fall of Poland the most painfully. He drank—and wrote poetry. And for a time he was honored by the new authorities. Wat wrote of him as the "favorite of the working masses, the bard of the Polish people's battle and suffering, and at once a subtle, innovative lyrical poet."[53] Dan, too, published a laudatory article. "In [Broniewski's] poetry," Dan wrote, "we see the Polish reality that, until recently, we experienced in all of its sordidness and baseness: abuse by the counterintelligence service, mass murders in the city and in the village, cruel oppression of the Ukrainian and Jewish masses, the suppression of any kind of instinct for political independence. Broniewski's poetry hastened with words of encouragement to every place where the man of labor suffered and fought."[54]

That autumn Broniewski wrote to M. Zhivov, now his own Russian translator, "We are all suffering very much from the destruction and cruel fate of Poland. We hope that within a short time the conditions of international politics will change in such a way that we will return to Red

Warsaw."[55] Zhivov was not alone in his eagerness to see Broniewski's latest work. *Czerwony Sztandar* also requested new poems from Broniewski; he gave them "Żolnierz polski" (The Polish Soldier), written in September 1939 and beginning with the line that had already become well known in the cafés: "With his head lowered, slowly / goes the soldier from German bondage."[56] The Soviet Union was still allied with Nazi Germany, and *Czerwony Sztandar* rejected "The Polish Soldier."[57] Witold Kolski, who had worked with Broniewski and Hempel on *Nowa Kultura* in the 1920s and was now one of *Czerwony Sztandar*'s editors, reproached Broniewski for his "independent position" during the time of *Dźwignia* and *Miesięcznik Literacki* and attacked him for what he was now writing—and what he was now not writing.[58] But Broniewski, unable to adjust to the new reality, would not be silenced. There floated about Lvov a second poem, "Syn podbitego narodu" (Son of a Conquered Nation):

> Son of a conquered nation, son of an independent verse,
> Of what, how can I sing, when my home lies in debris,
>   in ruins?
> September as the tank rolled through my fatherland's breast,
> And my hand defenseless, defenseless my fatherland.
>
> I will return to that land, I want to save her, to deliver her
> From there I want to set the world's heart aflame by the fire
>   of a poem
> I want socialism to grow with the concrete from Warsaw's
>   ruins,
> I want St. Mary's bugle-call to rustle with the red banner.
>
> Beautiful, proud Warsaw, glory to your ruins,
> I want to count, and to kiss your suffering bricks.
> Give me your hand, Belarus, give me your hand, Ukraine,
> Give me your hammer and sickle, independent, for the road.[59]

Now Broniewski wandered the streets of Lvov, dazed and enraged, drinking vodka and reciting his poetry on every possible occasion.[60] He stubbornly refused to accept the incompatibility of his communist sympathies and his Polish patriotism. In the background an atmosphere of terror continued unabated. But Broniewski was not predisposed—or not able—to hide his doubts; he had never been known for his diplomatic grace. Moreover,

Wat told, he "was still raving on about a Soviet Poland and singing songs like 'Moskva moya, Moskva moya' (Moscow, my Moscow). He had all that inside him at the same time, meaning that his emotional experiences were in a frenzy before he intellectualized them: a patriot, Poland, Poland's defeat, the Soviets, their friendship with the Germans, not being allowed to read anti-German patriotic poems."[61]

Broniewski had heard nothing from his family. Then the Soviet authorities intervened with their allies, the Nazis, to allow Wanda Wasilewska's family to leave German-occupied Poland and reunite with her in Lvov. Permission was granted for five people, but Wasilewska's mother refused to leave, and Franciszek Bogatko, Wasilewska's brother-in-law, likewise declined. There were now extra spaces on the pass, and Broniewski's wife Marysia Zarębińska and her daughter Majka were invited to accompany Wasilewska's daughter Ewa to Lvov.[62] In this way Broniewski was reunited with his wife and stepdaughter, and at a holiday celebration Majka was to recite her stepfather's children's poem "Lotniczka" (The Girl-Pilot). The verse, however, was rejected by the censors for its patriotism, particularly that implicit in the last stanza:

> I'll dare to fly over mountains and sea,
> for a moment above Żoliborz to be,
> There I want to see our little place,
> of which today remains but a trace,
> There I want to see my own city,
> always most dear, though no longer so pretty.

The censors demanded that Majka leave out this last passage. Broniewski insisted that she recite either the whole piece or nothing at all. Majka was loyal to her stepfather: she appeared on stage, and stood in silence.[63]

THE SCENE OF THE CRIME

Broniewski ignored warnings; he continued, as he always had, to recite his poems, which circulated by word of mouth, and easily found their way into anticommunist hands. His friends, including Soviet communists, were concerned about him. This was so, as Wasilewska understood, because of "his psychological makeup, his relationship to alcohol, the irresponsibility of some of his declarations, which we didn't take seriously, but if someone

wanted to take them seriously, literally, it could bring unpleasant consequences." There were omens his position was precarious, and it seemed
to some who knew him that Broniewski "signed his own sentence."[64]
There was talk of trying to take him away from Lvov to Moscow as soon as
possible, as Wasilewska and others believed that "in Moscow everything
would be okay, but in Lvov some kind of misfortune could result."[65]

Some kind of misfortune did result. It happened January of 1940,
when autumn had passed and it was already winter in Lvov. Wat remained
unusual among his friends in his lack of taste for vodka. He did not often
go to bars, but now in Lvov he went out every so often with Daszewski.
They had been very close during the period of *Miesięcznik Literacki*. Now
Daszewski was director of the Polish Theater and Wat told him openly
that he wanted to extricate himself from *Czerwony Sztandar* and asked
Daszewski to find him a job at the theater. This never came to pass. Instead, one evening in Lvov, when Ważyk was visiting with Wat and his
family, Daszewski appeared at the doorstep. He seemed to Ola Watowa
to be very excited, and said that he had spoken to the militia chief about
arranging for his wife to cross the border from the German zone to Lvov.
He regretted that they had not spent more time together thus far, and told
them it was finally time to get together and talk, that he was planning a
party at a restaurant and intended to invite all of their Warsaw friends. Wat
protested: they did not go out at night. Daszewski insisted. It had already
been arranged, he told them.[66]

On the evening of the party the featured author at the Writers' Union
was the young poet Leon Pasternak, who as a boy had worshipped Broniewski and dreamt of being invited to join the Skamandrites' table on the
platform at Café Ziemiańska. Now he was an adult, a poet in his own
right, and the room of the poetry reading was filled to capacity. People
stood in the hallway because all the seats were taken. Among those in the
corridor waiting for the reading to conclude were Ola Watowa, Marysia
Zarębińska, and Stern's wife, Alicja Sternowa. Daszewski found them
there and reminded them about his party, inviting them to go in his car,
saying their husbands would follow. At that moment Tadeusz Peiper appeared. Daszewski was pleased to see him, and told Peiper he had heard
that Peiper had written a play before the war, which Daszewski was now
interested in producing in Lvov. Peiper, excited, wanted to run home at
once to retrieve the manuscript, but Daszewski restrained him, and invited

him to the restaurant, saying they would talk there. Downstairs a black limousine with a chauffeur awaited them. Ola Watowa was astonished by the car; she asked Daszewski where he had acquired it. He told her his friends had lent it to him, and she should get in. She did.

The atmosphere in Lvov was not conducive to parties, and Wat remained unenthusiastic about Daszewski's invitation. He persuaded Ważyk to join him, although Ważyk had been likewise reluctant: it seemed to him Daszewski had not really invited him. They prepared to leave. Then Aleksander Dan, pale, found Wat and grabbed him. He begged Wat not to go. But it was too late. Ola was already at the restaurant waiting for him, and it was their thirteenth anniversary. Outside the winter sun was bright. Snow was falling; it melted quickly onto the streets of Lvov. There was a warm, gusty wind drying the sidewalks; early spring was in the air. On the second floor of an abandoned apartment, the restaurant was spread through an enormous three or four rooms, and Daszewski had arranged for a large table in a private room. Ola Watowa sat down next to Marysia Zarębińska, and Zarębińska next to Daszewski, who played the host, moving about and asking his guests what they desired, ordering vodka and hors-d'oeuvres. When Watowa reminded him that no one had very much money, he quieted her, telling her not to worry. Broniewski had not been at the poetry reading; and when he appeared at the restaurant, he was greeted with applause. He had already been drinking.

Ola Watowa began to drink as well. She was petite and it required little alcohol to lift her mood. Broniewski began to make jokes, and her apprehensions about the evening dissipated. She turned to Daszewski, "You know, you were right, it's nice to be here."[67] Then the doors to the private room opened and an unfamiliar couple walked in. The man was tall and bald and seemed to Ola Watowa "unearthly" and "gorilla-like." His expression struck Wat as caustic. The bald man's date was an attractive blonde actress from the Polish Theater with a promiscuous reputation. She was heavily made up and wore long black gloves and a black hat with a large brim. Ola Watowa, in her mind, named her Marlene Dietrich. The couple walked silently to a small table in the corner and sat down. Daszewski stood up, approached them, exchanged a few words, and then returned to his own table. This was a well-known Soviet art historian who wanted to become acquainted with Polish writers, he told his friends. Everyone agreed.

The couple sat down at one end of the table, a door covered by a curtain behind them. It was impossible to hear very well over all the talking. Ola Watowa listened as a Polish poet active in the peasant movement attempted to begin a conversation with the actress, whom he seemed already to know. Wat supposed that there must have been some kind of unfriendly exchange between Broniewski and the Soviet art historian, because a moment later Wat saw Broniewski clenching his teeth and the peasant movement activist leaning in front of the Russian man and saying something to the actress. Leon Pasternak noticed that Broniewski had become enraged; Broniewski stood up and made a gesture with his hand, as if to shield the actress from attack. At that moment, the peasant poet got a fist in his face from the art historian, who revealed himself to be quite strong, whisking away the tablecloth and sending bottles, plates, and food flying off the table. The yanking away of the tablecloth served as a signal; now several NKVD officers flew into the room and hurled themselves at Daszewski's guests. Pasternak looked on as one of them, a "drunken giant, grabbed onto the arm of the chair, swerved to the back, and thrust himself onto Władek. . . . The squeal of women, screams, on some faces blood. Above me a table leg whistled, the tops of the tables were flying, bottles under legs, pieces of glass. Everyone in everything."[68] Broniewski and Peiper struggled with their attackers on the floor. Wat was hit in the jaw; one of his teeth came loose and blood poured from his face. He fell over.

In minutes the entirety of the private room was demolished. There were broken windows and broken glasses, the smell of spilled alcohol. Ola Watowa crawled to her husband under the flying bottles; she poured water on him and pulled him out into the larger room, where she sat him down, half-conscious, at a table; she wet a napkin and wiped his face. Pasternak and his wife soon found Wat in the next room with a handkerchief in his mouth, and brought him a glass of water. Wat's hands were shaking, there were tears in his eyes. He showed Pasternak his teeth, which were loose in his gums. Pasternak's wife took a handkerchief from her purse, wet it with water, and told him to put it on his lips. At a certain moment the doors to the private room opened and Daszewski came out. It was time to get out of there, he told Ważyk. Ola Watowa ran to Daszewski and asked him what was happening. He did not say a word. The cloakroom clerk was ready with his coat and hat; Daszewski took them silently and opened the doors leading to the stairway. Ola Watowa hung onto him, calling out to him. Daszewski remained silent. He ran down the stairs and she followed. On the stairs two rows of NKVD officers stood with bayonets in their rifles. They let Daszewski pass, but pushed her back into the restaurant. She ran then to Ważyk, who was already wearing his coat, preparing to leave, and told him that Wat was not well and needed help. Ważyk gave his coat back to the cloakroom attendant and went to Wat.

In the foyer a crowd of people pushed its way towards the exit. The NKVD began to check documents, allowing some people to leave, detaining others. Pasternak went to retrieve his coat from the cloakroom attendant; he argued for Wat's as well. He tried to convince the attendant he would bring her the ticket in a little while—and then gave her a big tip. When Pasternak returned from the cloakroom, he found only the waiters sweeping up, and his wife, who told him that Wat had been called into the other room by an officer. They fled, leaving Wat's coat on a chair.

Outside gas lanterns colored the snow blue. Ola Watowa, Marysia Zarębińska, and Tadeusz Peiper's girlfriend were among the women who waited on the sidewalk. Walking in knee-deep snow, Pasternak and his wife found a good observation point by a narrow gate; there they watched the customers as they left the restaurant. And then no one was coming out any longer. After some time had passed the black limousine that had taken the women to the restaurant approached, and Wat, Peiper, Stern, and Broniewski were led outside. Soon afterwards the black car departed, now with those arrested as its passengers, to Zamarstynów prison.[69]

A CALL FOR VIGILANCE

Ważyk believed that Daszewski was innocent, that he must not have understood the consequences of his invitation.[70] Nevertheless, the die was cast, and Ważyk was among those who abandoned Ola Watowa and would cross the street when they saw her. It was a time of great fear for all of them, and no one came to visit her. She went to see Aleksander Dan, who looked at her in terror and turned her away. One evening the prose writer Adolf Rudnicki did appear, unannounced, leaving without a word after a few minutes, and she could feel how much courage this took. She was visited as well by a former classmate, who once upon a time had fallen in love with her at a school performance. His was an unrequited love, "an amusing youthful love with tears." When the classmate, now married, found out what had happened, he came to Watowa to tell her in parting that she was the only woman he had ever really loved. One day another man came to her as well, a stranger who approached her on the street and whispered to her to go to the nearest gate. There he said that he knew about the arrests, and that she had been left alone with a child and no means of support. He asked her to accept a thousand rubles from him, which she would doubtlessly repay when Wat was released from prison, and refused to leave until she had taken the money. He was someone who had once played in the orchestra at the Warsaw cabaret Qui pro Quo, where he had known Wat.[71]

Soon after the arrests, the editorial secretary at *Czerwony Sztandar* pushed towards Stryjkowski's fictional alter ego Artur the issue of the newspaper with a feuilleton by Konarski. "Among others," Artur said, "Broniewski had been arrested. In fact almost the entire feuilleton by the former member of the Central Committee was devoted to him. The great proletarian poet revealed to be a masked traitor, a double agent, an officer of Piłsudski." In a conversation with one of his co-workers at the newspaper, Artur confessed he never would have believed that those arrested were traitors. In response he was told that the enemy masked himself. It grew quiet around the empty chair of the arrested poet.[72]

Stryjkowski's Konarski was Witold Kolski, an editor at *Czerwony Sztandar*, a KPP activist and former political prisoner in interwar Poland. Kolski's article "Crush the Nationalist Reptiles!" appeared in *Czerwony Sztandar* three days after Wat, Broniewski, Peiper, and Stern were taken to Lvov's Zamarstynów prison. It was the time of the "intensification of the class struggle" and the call for heightened vigilance and ceaseless unmasking of "servants of capital," "Trotskyite-Bukharinite agents of counterrevolution," and "nationalist instigators." Kolski wrote of the arrests of a "group of depraved persons" who had been passing as "revolutionary writers." Their moral depravity and drunken orgies had been the backdrop against which they had conducted their counterrevolutionary activities:

> The entire past of these people points to the fact that they did not come to Soviet soil in order to, together with workers, peasants and the intelligentsia, honestly and earnestly work for the communist cause. . . . Not for this reason did Broniewski come here, the Legionnaire captain, the officer of the Second Depart-

ment (military counterintelligence) from the times of the
war of White Poland against the Soviet republic, an inveterate
alcoholic. . . . Not for this reason did Stern come here, who
in gentlemen's Poland began his career with the counter-
revolutionary Jasieński in a literary group spreading the rot
of decaying bourgeois culture—and ended it as the writer
of hurrah-nationalist Polish films in honor of Piłsudski. Not
for this reason did Wat come here, who conducted Trotskyite
agitation in Warsaw, nor Pajper [sic], pursuing to the end
degenerate, anti-people's literary activity.[73]

In a conversation with his cousin Rachela, the voice of morality and
clear-sightedness with whom Artur, at this point in Stryjkowski's novel,
was now having a romantic relationship, Artur noted that the Soviet powers had not hesitated to arrest the revolutionary poet Broniewski. Their
conversation continued:

> "Konarski called the scene by its name in his feuilleton."
> "That's slander. Do you prefer slander to lying?" Rachela sat
> down and hugged her arms around her knees.
> "Was Broniewski not Piłsudski's officer?"
> "You've gone crazy!"
> "Those are facts!"
> "And all of his poetry doesn't count?"
> "What counts is his political past, and it's not possible to
> completely liberate yourself from that. Unfortunately!"
> "What kind of past? What's wrong with the fact that he was
> in the Legions? After all I heard that even Wanda Wasilewska
> was angry about Konarski's article."[74]

Wanda Wasilewska was indeed angry. She learned of the arrests at six
o'clock the following morning. Shortly afterwards she left Lvov for a trip
east, believing there had been some kind of drunken scene but not knowing exactly who had been arrested, and believing it all to have been a misunderstanding that would clear itself up within twenty-four hours. The story
about the arrests having been the result of a drunken brawl was spread
for a long time, despite the fact that witnesses unambiguously described
to Wasilewska that the "scene was entirely provoked, from beginning to

end." She learned "concretely" that some people had been brought to the restaurant on purpose, so as to be arrested.[75] She was upset further, upon returning to Lvov, to discover that Jerzy Putrament and two of his Polish colleagues were collecting signatures for a petition condemning those arrested. Ważyk was terrified, but he refused to sign.[76]

Wasilewska tried to calm Marysia Zarębińska and Ola Watowa, reassuring them that it had undoubtedly been a mistake and their husbands would be released. She promised to do everything possible. And she did. The process drew out indefinitely, beginning with interventions with local authorities and continuing in Kiev and Moscow. She spoke to Stalin, who called Beria and asked him to investigate the matter. She spoke then to Beria for a long time; it was their first conversation. He told her that his "apparatus" was searching for Broniewski, but that his name did not appear in the Soviet prison registry; since he could not be found, it was not possible to release him. He promised Wasilewska they would continue to search.[77]

WANDA WASILEWSKA, MAN OF STATE

Now, after the arrests, Wasilewska took over Broniewski's job as literary supervisor of the Polish Theater.[78] She remained no less passionate a believer in the Soviet system, and Wat was among those who had no doubt her passion was authentic. "As for me," he wrote, "I saw Wasilewska; I spoke with her. The air was full of lies; many of the old communists were lying, but I am absolutely certain that she was sincere."[79] Wasilewska came to occupy an exceptional place in Lvov; this was the moment of her extraordinary rise to power. She had never been a member of the KPP; all through the interwar years she had remained a PPS activist. Now this made her all the more worthy of the Soviets' trust: the previous year Stalin had dissolved the Communist Party of Poland, and Soviet functionaries were often suspicious of former KPP members.[80] Stryjkowski saw that within Wasilewska, the daughter of a liberal socialist, there remained "very many authentically humanitarian remnants." She and Wat had never been close, but Wat respected the fact that in the Soviet Union, amidst fear and terror, she "behaved very decently" and maintained "firm moral principles and Kinderstube."[81] She did what she could to help her friends and colleagues, and it was a time when she could do very much. From Stryjkowski's point of view, "[h]er signature meant nearly as much as did Stalin's."[82] On one occasion, as a train filled with Poles about to be deported into the Soviet interior was departing, Wasilewska ran onto the railway platform and pulled Boy-Żeleński, the literary historian and essayist Jan Kott, and two Polish painters off the train.[83] She promised to do all she could for the two Bundist leaders Wiktor Alter and Henryk Erlich, her former comrades from the Popular Front years, upon their arrests in 1939, and in the next few months was at least successful in learning and relaying the news that they remained alive.[84]

Wasilewska's position during this period was inseparable from the personal relationship she developed with Stalin. Rumors circulated that they were lovers. Her novels had been published in Moscow before the war, and Stalin was favorably predisposed towards her before they had even met. When Wasilewska was responsive to Korneichuk's summons by radio and, once in Lvov, revealed herself—despite her PPS past—to be very clearly on "their" side, she was immediately taken under special Soviet care. It was early winter of 1939–1940 when Wasilewska met Stalin for the first time. She had gone to Moscow with her former KPP liaison Szymon Natanson and inquired as to how one went about making an appointment with Stalin. She was told to put her request in writing. Wasilewska was from Cracow; unlike her Warsaw friends, she had not been educated in Russian. It thus fell to Natanson to write the letter, saying that Wasilewska was requesting a personal meeting as "she had many matters to see to on the terrain of Western Ukraine." Wasilewska signed it. Afterwards she received a phone call informing her that Stalin had received her letter and would see her; he wanted to know how long she would be staying in Moscow. She waited. Then, on the day she was set to depart to Lvov, the same person telephoned with the message that Stalin had asked to see her and a car was on its way. Wasilewska brought her luggage with her.[85] Upon seeing Wasilewska in person, Stalin offered her tea and cigarettes and remarked how much she looked like her father—adding, "Your father worked against us, and you are with us, with the communists. Dialectics."[86] He inquired about her impressions regarding the mood among Poles. A war with Germany would come sooner or later, he told her.[87]

In March 1940 her position was heightened further by her election to the Supreme Soviet of the Soviet Union. These spring elections saw Wasilewska again drawing upon the oratorical talent that had made her so valuable in PPS circles before the war. In a meeting with voters at the end of the same month, Wasilewska expressed how moved she was to be part of the Soviet Union:

> Just six months ago the Red Army was a legend and a dream for me. Just six months ago it was something far away, unreachable.
>
> And now I'm standing among them. I'm speaking to them. I'm listening to their words—words about the Soviet Union, about the international brotherhood of the Soviet nations.
>
> And it's difficult for me to speak. And I feel stupid because tears are falling from my eyes, because my voice is stuck in my throat. They—the soldiers of the Red Army—are the ones who are to vote for me. Smiling youthful faces, comrades, young comrades, who have grown up under the red banner, for you cannot understand what it is for me, for a person hunted and persecuted, a person who for years has observed the most appalling aspects of the dismal life of slaves, to stand here among you, and for you to express words of confidence to me, for you to smile warmly at me, to squeeze my hand—you, to whom I owe freedom and life and a homeland, your homeland and mine, the homeland of the worldwide proletariat.[88]

A VERY BRIEF STAY IN LVOV

Marian Bogatko did not experience newly Soviet Lvov with the same euphoria as his wife. Unlike Wasilewska, Bogatko had doubts. He was indiscreet in his comments about Nazi Germany, which at this time was treated with official respect as a Soviet ally. People saw him as withdrawing, as reluctant to cooperate with her, as a potential obstacle in her work.[89] After he and Wasilewska returned from their travels to Moscow and Kiev, Bogatko pointed out to his wife that she saw only what was shown to her, whereas he saw the workers' poverty, their despair, and their hopelessness. He saw apartments it would be difficult to define as habitable for humans, he saw people without food, without clothing, without shoes. Wasilewska grew enraged; she refused to allow such conversations in her home.[90] But the former bricklayer felt, as Ola Watowa understood him, that as a proletarian in a proletarian state—that is, in a country that theoretically belonged to him—he could say everything he was thinking.[91]

Wat and Broniewski were friendly with Bogatko, whom Wat described as "a fantastic athlete, a truly handsome young man, always game for anything. He was intelligent, quick, with a sense of humor, strong, cheerful." He believed that Wasilewska loved Bogatko very much. One afternoon, after Bogatko and Wasilewska had returned from Kiev, there was a mass rally in Lvov. Wasilewska was speaking about her recent trip; and Wat went with Broniewski and Bogatko:

> It was the usual bombast—happy life, everything is rosy, all the clichés that were ever used in the press. But she spoke with real passion, fire. A tough, dry, big-boned woman, with a broad, flat face, large powerful eyes; her gestures were passionate.
>
> Afterwards Bogatko said to me and Broniewski, "Let's go to a bar." And so he dragged us to a bar; he drank like mad. And just imagine, in a bar full of Soviet officers, Bogatko started telling us all sorts of other things right after that meeting, his voice booming, "Remember when you go to Kiev, as soon as you get to Kiev, when you take your first step off the train, grab onto your bags with one hand and your cap with the other, or they'll snatch it right off your head."[92]

Wat and Broniewski trembled from fear—but laughed at the same time.[93] Bogatko later complained of being followed by intelligence agents, and confided to someone that he had plans of returning to German-occupied Warsaw, even if he had to go alone.[94]

Bogatko never did return to Warsaw. One day in April 1940 "unknown perpetrators" rang the doorbell of the villa where Bogatko lived with Wasilewska and her daughter Ewa. He opened the door. The visitors shot him. Another resident of the villa heard the perpetrators telephone their superior afterwards to say that the order had been carried out.[95] Bogatko, wounded, was taken to the hospital, where a Polish friend, a doctor, was not allowed to see him. Within a short time he was dead.[96] Some believed that Bogatko had died from a bullet intended for Wasilewska; the official account attributed the assassination to Ukrainian nationalists. When Wat learned of Bogatko's death from a Ukrainian prisoner who joined their cell, he had no doubt it was the work of the NKVD. He believed it to be a message sent to Wasilewska "so that she would have no illusions. *Point de rêveries.*"[97]

Nikita Khrushchev had been assured, even before he met her, that Wasilewska would understand the Soviet position and would be on their side; and he was very intrigued as to who she could be. When Wasilewska finally did appear in Lvov, it was in a short sheepskin coat and ordinary shoes, looking "like a simple woman, although she had come from noble Polish stock." She never betrayed the slightest shame for her PPS past or for her father, and Khrushchev became an admirer of Wasilewska, and in particular of her honesty and directness. "I heard myself," he wrote, "how she said very unpleasant things straight to Stalin's face. Despite that he listened to her, and afterwards invited her many times for official and unofficial conversations, for social lunches and dinners. Wasilewska had such character!"[98] Given his fondness for her, Khrushchev was very disturbed to learn that "their Chekists" had killed her husband:

> It was an accidental killing, as they admitted to me honestly.
> Yet I was shaken. Wanda Lvovna's husband belonged to the
> PPS, he had working-class roots, although he was less active
> than she was. Immediately the question emerged: How will
> this matter be reflected in Wasilewska's relationship to us?
> Will she not think that we did away with her husband for some
> kind of political reasons? Different things can come into one's
> head in the aftermath of such a tragedy. I told my Ukrainians,
> Korneichuk and Bazhan: explain to Wanda Lvovna honestly
> how it happened, don't hide anything. . . .
>
> We told Wanda Lvovna the whole truth and asked for her
> understanding. Wasilewska believed that there had been no
> premeditation in this case and she continued to work actively,
> and to be well disposed towards us.[99]

Wanda Wasilewska did continue to be well disposed towards Khrushchev and the new Soviet order. Not only did she forgive Soviet authorities for the "accidental" murder of her husband, but she also seemed to recover from the trauma in good time. Before long she took Oleksandr Korneichuk as her lover, and later her husband. Marriage to a man who was a Ukrainian playwright and Soviet dignitary brought her still deeper into the Soviet life she now embraced. *Czerwony Sztandar* published an account of Wasilewska's speech given several months later, in September 1940 when she had already become a delegate to the Supreme Soviet: "In the most simple words Wasilewska speaks of the great happiness our Red Army has brought us, of the happiness of stepping onto the open road leading upwards, towards the sun. In powerful, masculine words, she challenges her listeners to now, after a year of freedom in work has passed, perform an honest accounting of their own consciousness and ascertain if they have always worked and are working with such passion and dedication as the epochal significance of our day demands."[100]

The tall, thin woman with dark circles under glistening eyes became a man of state.[101] She continued to smoke endless cigarettes and took energetically to the role of representing the Poles to Stalin. "He told me," she later recalled, "—this sentence I remember perfectly: everyone must understand that sooner or later we will go to battle with the Nazis and then the Polish cadres can play a large role."[102] This was during her second meeting with Stalin, when they had a long conversation about "everything possible," including the status of Polish communists from the now-dissolved KPP and interventions in the matter of Poles who had been arrested. With respect to the partyless Polish communists, Wasilewska found a partner in Alfred Lampe, a high-ranking KPP member who had spent much of the interwar years in Polish prison. She met him for the first time only in Lvov, in 1940, when he came to her and said it was necessary to raise the issue of the former KPP members. He hoped to gather the dispersed Polish communists and rebuild the party, or in some way reinstate them as communists. The result was a letter to Stalin co-authored by Lampe and Wasilewska in her Lvov apartment. In the letter they said nothing about a separate Polish party, but rather inquired about the possibility of accepting Polish communists into the All-Russian Communist Party. It was not Stalin, but Khrushchev who replied, with an invitation to breakfast at his apartment. There he told her that Comrade Stalin had received her letter and regarded it as just that Polish comrades should be accepted into the All-Russian Communist Party.[103]

Wasilewska, in her newfound role as man of state, did not neglect her work in the cultural sphere. On 17 September 1940, Jerzy Borejsza, Tadeusz Boy-Żeleński, Aleksander Dan, Halina Górska, Julian Przyboś, Jerzy Putrament, Adolf Rudnicki, Wanda Wasilewska, and Adam Ważyk were among the Polish writers who joined the Union of Soviet Writers of Ukraine as a symbolic gesture on the first anniversary of the Soviet takeover of the eastern borderlands.[104] Some six months later, in March

1941, a new Polish newspaper, *Nowe Widnokręgi* (New Horizons) made its debut in Lvov. By now the intensive Ukrainization campaign had begun to wane, and Soviet cultural policy towards the Poles had softened.[105] The result was a literary and journalistic endeavor that differed significantly from *Czerwony Sztandar,* and a statement by the editorial board appearing in the first issue bore much less of a Stalinist tone: "We who live in the Soviet Union are guardians of that which is best and most wonderful in the Polish nation.—Our publication is to serve Polish culture, its preservation and evolution."[106] Wasilewska, Boy-Żeleński, Przyboś, Rudnicki, Janina Broniewska, and Szymon Natanson were among the paper's editors and contributors.[107] Bruno Schulz received a special letter inviting him to work with *Nowe Widnokręgi*. He responded with confusion, "But what can I possibly write for them? I'm more and more persuaded of how far I am from actually existing life and how little I'm oriented in the spirit of the times. Somehow everyone has found a place for themselves, but I've remained stranded. It comes from a lack of flexibility, from a certain uncompromising attitude, which I do not laud." In the end, Schulz did send *Nowe Widnokręgi* a story about the hideous little son of a shoemaker, but it was rejected. Supposedly one of the members of the editorial staff told Schulz, "we don't need Prousts."[108]

Nowe Widnokręgi published much poetry. It was decided that a new Polish translation of Mayakovsky's "Left March" was needed since the revolutionary poem had originally been translated by the "decadent bourgeois liberal Słonimski." It fell to Ważyk to undertake the new version.[109] Ważyk's own poem "Biografia" (Biography) was a response to the success of Wasilewska's and Lampe's appeal to Stalin. It spoke about the verification processes now taking place for former KPP members applying for membership in the All-Russian Communist Party. Ważyk, who had never belonged to the KPP, rendered empathetically the tragedy of the partyless Polish communists who yes, had committed errors and were guilty of insufficient vigilance, but who had paid their dues in Polish prison, suffering for the Revolution, and who remained sincere and desired more than anything to redeem themselves:

> He pushed aside the prison wall, but how to bear
> the burden, still weighing on his heart,

> that he failed to see betrayal in time, that he had
> the dignity of Ludwik, but not the vigilance of Feliks?[110]

Ludwik Waryński was a pioneer of Polish socialism; Feliks Dzierżyński was the founder of the NKVD's predecessor, the Cheka.

A CONVERSATION WITH HISTORY

"When I heard the key grind in the lock," Wat told, "I knew that this was the last grind of the lock, Judgment Day."[111] In his cell Wat fell asleep and dreamt of being surrounded, about to be arrested. He awoke in a sweat to find himself already in prison. The nightmare of waiting was over. The black limousine that had carried him away from the restaurant on the snowy January evening of Daszewski's party had delivered him to Zamarstynów prison in Lvov, where he now found himself, together with twenty-seven companions, in an eleven-and-a-half-square-meter cell. He hoped that Wasilewska would manage to free them. There was also the possibility that a war between the Soviet Union and Germany would come; at night the prisoners listened for the tanks. In the meantime, Wat began the process of socialization into his cell. Unlike in Warsaw's Centralniak, in Zamarstynów there was no inspiring solidarity among communists imprisoned by an anticommunist regime. Those in Wat's cell—communists and anticommunists alike—had been imprisoned by the workers' state. One day a one-armed, right-wing activist, a former student thug, arrived in their prison cell. As in Centralniak, here, too, Wat had the status of an intellectual and was called upon to give lectures. On this day he was lecturing about Russian poetry, about Mayakovsky. The right-wing prisoner grew suspicious; he accused Wat of being a provocateur. Wat was enraged and tried to strike him, but the man defended himself with his single, terribly strong arm.[112]

In prison Wat was tormented: an old and close friend had betrayed him, delivered him into the hands of the NKVD. Something else tormented him as well: he would never see Ola again, and he had not said goodbye to her.[113] Now he descended into a period of obsessive guilt and self-reproach, fixating on one memory from his childhood that caused him the most anguish: on one bright summer evening, he had jeered at a young student of Talmud. As he mocked the boy with peyes and a yarmulka, he saw through the window the boy's mother, lying in bed, dying. It was unforgivable. Now Wat began a period of intensive contemplation of the kind of religious faith he had mocked as an adolescent. Unlike the communists who were his prison companions in Warsaw, many of his cellmates in Zamarstynów were traditional, religious people, Roman Catholics and Ukrainian Greek Catholics. In their prison cell, they sang prayers and hymns to the Virgin Mary. Wat was moved by the Ukrainians' faith, which seemed to him "beautiful, pure, without obscurantism." Yet this community of believers excluded Wat, and his alienation tormented him. He envied them their faith, but found within himself no belief in God's existence—apart from the sense that he had been rejected by God for failing to believe in His existence. His only faith was in this rejection.[114]

In addition to prayer, the empty hours in the cell were filled with the killing of copious lice, who behaved most manically after the prisoners had gone to the baths, perhaps out of anger for having been disturbed. The prisoners crushed the lice "at first with disgust and then later out of habit and with pleasure, great pleasure. It almost became a delight, like vodka, alcohol." The culture of lice-killing fostered a certain technical proficiency. The prisoners began to participate in contests to see who could kill the most lice. Tallies were kept with great accuracy; the prisoners would write the day's date and the number of lice killed on the wall of their cell. From time to time the number would surpass four hundred. The most attentive of the lice killers was a young man, a Ukrainian peasant with a beautiful voice, one of the ugliest people Wat had ever seen, who resembled "a gnome, an earth spirit. He was small, with a nose that was long and lumpish at the same time. One eye was higher than the other; one looked to the right, one to the left; one was large and the other small. His mouth was distinctly crooked, but only one half of it. An extremely pointed jaw, which looked like a beard." The gnome-like peasant was a passionate animal lover whose love for animals failed to preclude killing them. On the contrary, his own lice were insufficient for him, and he begged the other prisoners to let him kill their lice as well. His interactions with the lice became quite sophisticated. Wat, suffering from insomnia, often heard the peasant playing a game of interrogation with his lice during the night: "'Confess! What assignment did the Gestapo give you?' He retraced the entire course of his own interrogation with the lice. He was in no hurry to kill them."[115]

For Ola Watowa and Marysia Zarębińska lice acquired great sentimental value. Shortly after the arrests, they managed to learn that Wat and
Broniewski were being held at Zamarstynów. They received permission to
send food and a change of underwear, and after waiting for a long time at
the prison gates, their turn came; they delivered their packages and picked
up their husbands' dirty undergarments. At home Ola Watowa unpacked
the bundle and saw lice and blood stains on the shirt hems: "Lice, which
persecuted him, yet at once lived together with him, so very recently had
been with him, had nourished themselves on his blood. . . . And Marysia
Zarębińska calls me and says: 'Ola, I found lice in Władek's shirt!' And I
said: 'Me too, me too!' Our joy. . . . We were both moved." In the bundle of
dirty clothes Watowa found socks as well, with pieces of *watolina* (padding)
inside. She read the "watolina" as a code, and her imagination began to
play: "socks, so legs. Legs walk. Watolina. Wat goes to Olina (this is what
he called me, he was Ol, and I—Olina). And so he was probably telling
me that he would return before long. Wat will return to Olina."[116] The
watolina inside Wat's socks, however, told a very different story.

Not long after the arrests, perhaps still in January, when the prisoners
from the next hall were walking to the latrine, Wat heard Broniewski's
voice. He stood by the door of his cell and whispered, "Władek, have you
heard anything about my family?" The answer came: they would talk
tomorrow. The following day, on his way back to his cell from the latrine,
Broniewski whispered to Wat that he had left a note for him by one of
the toilet handles. There Wat found it, pasted to the toilet with a piece of
bread. Written in the note was the prison alphabet. Wat went back to his
cell, and Broniewski began tapping on the wall. Wat was a novice, but
one of his cellmates, a young mathematician, mastered the code quickly.
And so Wat and Broniewski chatted through the wall, the mathematician
serving as Wat's interpreter. Naturally Broniewski, like Wat, had heard
nothing of Wat's family, but he did have some thoughts about their case.
Later that day when the guard visited their cell, another cellmate—an impassioned communist convinced that his arrest was the sole exception to
an otherwise perfectly rational system—told the guard that two prisoners
had been engaging in illegal conversations with someone in the next cell.
Confronted with the accusation, the young mathematician panicked. It
was not he, but Wat who was guilty, he told the guard. Wat confessed: he

had heard Broniewski's voice through the wall and had hoped for news of his family.[117]

A day later, Wat was brought to the punishment cell, a small cubicle with a glassless window where he nearly froze to death. He tore material from his coat—*watolina*—to pad his socks. For five days and five nights Wat walked around his cell in circles, so as not to freeze. Broniewski was in the adjoining punishment cell, and Wat was in awe of his friend's endurance: "Władzio was incredibly brave, enormously strong, a young eagle. But that wasn't the only reason I admired him. I walked about my cell in circles, intellectual style. But Broniewski—and I envied him this—marched like a soldier, beating time, and singing all those Legion songs. He sang the whole time; he sang for five days and nights. . . . And so I felt like a miserable weakling. Broniewski had shown me how to retain human dignity, strength, and fighting spirit. . . . back then, compared to Władzio Broniewski, a full person, I felt like a worm. I never saw anyone bear himself better, with more dignity, than Broniewski did then."[118] The admiration was hardly mutual. Through the wall Broniewski told Wat that he had nothing but contempt for him for confessing. Broniewski had confessed to nothing.[119] It was a moment when he rose to the occasion; he refused to be broken. Moreover, as in Centralniak, in Soviet prison, too, Broniewski did not cease to be a poet. To his daughter Anka he wrote a letter from prison in verse, telling her

> On traces of exiles I step
> and must carry the burden of poetry
> to that far bank of my years.[120]

The romantic poet composed as well a bitterly sarcastic poem about the vagaries of History, now conceived as a capricious woman, amused by baboonery, smiling half jeeringly.[121]

INTERROGATIONS

"In prison interrogation," Wat attested, Broniewski "conducted himself wonderfully, uncompromisingly, defiantly."[122] During his February 1940 interrogation in Lvov, the former Legionnaire behaved with remarkable composure. He answered questions about his past in Piłsudski's Legions in detail, matter-of-factly. He responded matter-of-factly as well when questioned about his correspondence in Lvov: he had received one letter from Wanda Wasilewska and two from his wife Marysia Zarębińska, which had reached him via Janina Broniewska in Białystok. He gave truthful answers in Russian. When asked how and when his wife had come from Warsaw to Lvov, he told his interrogator that on 12 December 1939 she had come on a pass acquired by Wanda Wasilewska's family from the German authorities in Warsaw. When accused of having made declarations against the Soviet Union and the Red Army, Broniewski denied the accusation with a monotone repetitiveness that mimicked the phrasing of his interrogator's question:

QUESTION: The investigation is aware that while in Lvov, you grouped around yourself nationalistically inclined and reactionary Polish writers for the purpose of struggling for the restoration of the Polish state. The investigation insists that you give truthful statements in response to this question.

ANSWER: That is not true. I did not group around myself nationalist writers, and rather I revolved around communist-inclined writers and I did not conduct any work harmful to Soviet power.

QUESTION: With which writers living in Lvov did you engage in anti-Soviet conversations?

ANSWER: I never engaged in anti-Soviet conversations with writers in Lvov.

QUESTION: From which persons did you hear statements of dissatisfaction in relation to Soviet power?

ANSWER: I don't remember.

QUESTION: Say when and in conversations with which persons you stated your dissatisfaction about the fact that your work was not being published in the Soviet press here in Lvov.

ANSWER: I don't remember.[123]

The NKVD interrogators collected testimony from others against him. A Polish illustrator who had joined Jerzy Putrament in collecting signatures for the petition condemning the arrested poets gave the following statement to the NKVD:

After the Red Army had come to Lvov in October 1939 Broniewski wrote a poem titled "The Polish Soldier" in which

he expressed sadness and regret that Poland no longer existed
as an independent state, that there were no longer soldiers
with eagles, that Polish soldiers sat and cried while looking
at other, foreign soldiers. Broniewski's poem "The Polish
Soldier" is saturated with Polish national patriotism and constitutes the logical continuation of his social patriotic poem
"Bagnet na broń" [Fix Bayonets]. Broniewski recited his poem
"The Polish Soldier" in a circle of Polish writers where I was
present as well. My wife, Wanda Wasilewska, Halina Górska
know about this poem. I know from having heard that Broniewski's poem "The Polish Soldier" was broadcast by French
radio from the city of Toulouse.

When questioned what he knew about "Paitser" [sic—Peiper] the illustrator answered: "Tadeusz Peiper brought futurism into Polish literature. I
know Tadeusz Peiper very little personally, but I am acquainted with his
writing. In an artistic book written by him—the novel *Mam 22 lata* [I Am
Twenty-two] he, Peiper, introduces heroes who break with socialism and
cross over to the camp of riflemen and legions."[124]

Broniewski was interrogated primarily as a Polish nationalist and reactionary. Wat was interrogated simultaneously as a Trotskyite, a Zionist,
a Catholic, and a Polish nationalist.[125] Among those who testified against
Wat was Jerzy Borejsza, and Wat attributed this in part to Borejsza's resentment of the fact that someone like Wat, already for several years a
renegade, had been on the board of the Writers' Union in Lvov. Wat's
interrogator read him Borejsza's deposition. Borejsza had testified that
Wat, in Lvov, had "forbidden" him to speak badly of their Polish literary
colleagues in front of the Soviets. "Of course," Wat explained, "that was
nonsense. I couldn't forbid him to do anything, but I had a conversation
with him, that means I said to him normally that what's café bickering
in Warsaw could become a hatchet here in Lvov."[126] Much more damning was Borejsza's testimony regarding *Miesięcznik Literacki:* he told the
NKVD that Wat had founded and edited the paper with Hempel, Stande,
Jasieński, and Wandurski, all later unmasked as Polish spies and executed
in the Soviet Union. While this one sentence alone was sufficient for
him to have been executed, Wat's investigators failed to pick up on it.

Wat speculated that his connections with these Polish communists who had already been purged in the Soviet Union must have been too grave a matter for his lower-level NKVD interrogator.[127]

Yet if there was a taboo on the subject in Wat's case, it did not obtain in Broniewski's. The specter of Jan Hempel emerged in Broniewski's interrogations; and Broniewski delicately alluded to his older friend's death through a shift in verb tense. This part of the interrogation began with a discussion of *Nowa Kultura*:

ANSWER: In the first place, Jan Hempel served as editor of that journal. Hempel, in my opinion, received orders from the KPP; moreover, taking part in the journal was Witold Kolski (Cukier), who also revealed himself to be a member of the KPP. In the second place, we published articles that were, in their content, in favor of the communist order. Moreover, in 1924, as a journal undesired by the Polish government, after many confiscations during publishing, it was banned.

QUESTION: How was it known to you that Jan Hempel and Witold Kolski were communists?

ANSWER: I personally had quite close comradely relations with them; and they themselves spoke to me about their membership in the Communist Party.

QUESTION: Where are Jan Hempel and Witold Kolski presently?

ANSWER: In 1932 Jan Hempel went to the Soviet Union and was in Moscow; Witold Kolski is in Lvov and works in the editorial offices of *Czerwony Sztandar*.

QUESTION: What did you do following your work on the editorial staff of the journal *Nowa Kultura*?

ANSWER: At the end of 1924, I went to work as secretary of the editorial staff of the journal *Wiadomości Literackie*, where I worked until 1937. At the same time I was engaged in translations of Russian literature into Polish; and I also wrote poems and articles in journals. I began to engage in poetic creation seriously in 1924, and already in January 1925 the first volume of my poems, *Wiatraki* [Windmills], was published, in which my socialist radicalism was already then laid out.

QUESTION: Be more precise, what kind exactly?

ANSWER: Bourgeois critics praised my poems, but immediately they defined them as a "Bolshevik danger." In 1925 I became acquainted with the poets Stanisław Stande and Witold Wandurski, and by 1926 the three of us published a collection of revolutionary poems under the title *Three Salvos*. In the same year I published a new volume of my own poems, *Dymy nad miastem* [Smokestacks over the City]. Beginning in 1926, until 1931, I directed a workers' theater in Warsaw, which put on agitational-propagandistic plays in the halls of left-wing labor unions. In 1929 I wrote the poem "Komuna Paryska" [The Paris Commune] and published it with illustrations by the artist Władysław Daszewski; the book was confiscated by Polish censors.[128]

During his interrogations, Broniewski was shown depositions against him by Jerzy Borejsza, Jerzy Putrament, and the latter's two fellow signature collectors.[129] Broniewski was questioned, too, about his imprisonment in connection with *Miesięcznik Literacki:*

ANSWER: Apparently they found out that I did not belong to the Communist Party and they released me. I think that with respect to the others as well they did not manage to prove their guilt.

QUESTION: After being released, what did you occupy yourself with?

ANSWER: After being released, I continued to write poems, and in 1933 I published a new volume of poems, *Troska i pieśń* [Care and Song], from which the Polish censor expunged part of the poems as undesirable for the ruling circles of Poland. In 1934 I resolved to travel to the USSR, after which, in summer of 1934, I published essays about my excursion through the Soviet Union in the journal *Wiadomości Literackie.*

QUESTION: What was the purpose of your trip to the USSR?

ANSWER: To become acquainted with socialist construction and Soviet writers in the USSR.

QUESTION: Who arranged the trip to the Soviet Union for you?

ANSWER: Wishing to go to the USSR, I personally turned to the Soviet embassy in Warsaw, to Antonov Ovseenko, who knew me personally and obtained permission. In addition, I turned to the editor of the journal *Wiadomości Literackie,* Mieczysław Grydzewski, who helped me obtain permission from the Polish authorities for a trip to the USSR.[130]

Unlike Wat, Broniewski, and Peiper, Anatol Stern was freed after three months.[131] Wat guessed that Stern was pardoned for his "moral disintegration," but Ważyk disagreed. Stern himself believed that among those things that saved him was that he had published Mayakovsky in Polish. Moreover, Stern had had no contact with the now-dissolved KPP; he had not been involved with *Miesięcznik Literacki*. He was also the author of a great number of interwar Polish screenplays, and in those films there was nothing anti-Soviet. Ważyk believed that Stern's release was a tactical move as well—that is, to show the literary milieu in Lvov that not everyone who was arrested would be found guilty.[132] None of them really knew.

THE STEPPES OF CENTRAL ASIA

While in prison, Wat began to engage in a parapsychological ritual: he would visit his wife and son during the night. This venture into shamanism grew increasingly potent, part of a bargain he imagined having made: he could go home to them each night if he would return to prison in the morning. Every night he would walk through the streets of Lvov, stopping at 9 Nabielak Street where the concierge would open the gate for him. He walked up the dark stairway and entered the apartment where Ola and Andrzej were waiting. He would sit at the round table, drinking tea with Ola on one knee and Andrzej on the other. He came to feel that he had a doppelgänger, that one of him truly was present with them during the night. Then one day in the spring he failed to reach them. It was 9 April. In his mind he entered the building, then the apartment, and found there a void.[133]

Four days later, on the night of 13 April 1940, Ola Watowa and Andrzej Wat joined over 300,000 Polish citizens who were deported into the Soviet interior.[134] She did not hear the NKVD officers when they entered the room; her first moment of recognition came when she saw five of them pointing bayonets at herself and Andrzej. One of them ordered her to collect her things. She was indifferent and did not care to pack, but one of the officers urged her to take everything, saying her husband would be waiting for her where she was going. She and Andrzej were pushed into a cattle car among some sixty other people, on a train that sat motionless for three days before it departed. During that time Tadeusz Peiper's girlfriend made her way to Ola Watowa's wagon, bringing sugar, a half-liter jug, and a pillow, and begging the NKVD officers to allow her to go with them, in fear that Watowa would not manage on her own. Peiper's girlfriend was refused, and the train departed. The others trapped in the cattle car began to whisper that Watowa's husband was the editor of *Miesięcznik Literacki,* that Watowa was being sent with them as an informer. She protested and pleaded: it was not true, she was not an informer, her husband was in prison. The other Poles were not persuaded, and they hated her.[135]

After a very long trip the mother and son found themselves in the steppes of Kazakhstan, near a remote settlement called Ivanovka, where they nearly died of starvation. All of the deportees were forced to perform hard labor; in the winter many among them froze to death and were buried under the snow. Watowa was attacked and nearly raped. She and Andrzej lived among other Polish deportees who were initially hostile to them; the exception was Wanda Wasilewska's friend Stefania Skwarzyńska, who became Watowa's friend as well as her teacher in Catholicism. It was Skwarzyńska who persuaded the other Poles that Watowa was not an informer, that she was telling the truth about her husband's being in prison, that she was a victim just as they were. She taught Watowa prayers, and wanted to baptize her in the river. Watowa was not ready for the baptism, though, and in any case did not feel the need for formalities. Yet she did feel something akin to faith; she was touched by the beauty of the steppe, and despite the horrific conditions she held onto a delicate, aesthetic appreciation for that beauty. For the first time in her life she became a religious believer. Then, after three months, Wasilewska intervened and Skwarzyńska was sent back to Lvov. Ola Watowa and Andrzej were left alone.[136]

Letters did travel back and forth, and Ola Watowa corresponded with Marysia Zarębińska, who sent news that Wat had been taken to Kiev on 9 August, that he was healthy, serene, and worried only about his wife and son.[137] Sending packages was prohibited, but Wasilewska arranged for Watowa to receive a quilt that Halina Górska had bought for her. In the end this gift from the two women saved her. On behalf of herself and the Polish deportees, who now trusted her, Watowa wrote to Wasilewska of the conditions in Ivanovka. Wasilewska answered quickly: she was requesting that a commission be sent from Moscow. The commission arrived; its members were given meat, grain and other gifts—and sent away at once to the nearest train station. Watowa wrote as well to Ilya Ehrenburg, whose Polish translator Wat had been. In reply Ehrenburg sent her three hundred rubles and a telegram: "I talked to Wanda Wasilewska. We will do everything necessary and possible to alleviate your fate."[138] In December 1940, upon her return to Lvov, Skwarzyńska wrote to Watowa, reminding her of their conversations and the prayers they had said together. Skwarzyńska was convinced that they would meet again, as they had not yet said all, "in God's name," that they needed to say to each other: "My very dear—you do not depart from my thoughts; I constantly see your pale face bent over me in farewell. . . . I am especially present with my soul as you freeze. Where will the strength come from to endure it? And yet *I believe,* I believe most deeply that you will endure and that from the most secret garners of His mercies God will give you some strength—that you will manage."[139] And, unlike many of their companions in the cattle car, she did.

A BED FROM GENERAL ANDERS AND THE DEVIL IN SARATOV
There was truth in the news from Marysia Zarębińska. Wat had been taken from Zamarstynów, not to Kiev but to Moscow. During the journey northeast, he was held briefly in various prisons; he did not know where he was going, if he was to confront the ghosts of people like Jan Hempel, Adolf Warski, Stanisław Ryszard Stande. His last investigator had said to him, "'I didn't know you were such a big fish.'" Eventually Wat found himself in the very center of Moscow, very close to Red Square, in the infamous Lubianka prison, where in the prison latrines "you could read the plain human truth about Stalin's Russia—there and only there."[140] In Lubianka, Wat inherited his bed from General Władysław Anders, his sister the actress Seweryna Broniszówna's onetime fiancé. On this bed Wat wrote letters inquiring about his family to Stalin—who never answered them. Broniewski had been taken to Lubianka as well; he and Wat did not see each other, but Wat surmised that if he had been taken there, then Broniewski likely had been as well. Tadeusz Peiper, too, was in Lubianka.[141]

Gone now were the religious feelings Wat had experienced in Zamarstynów. Lubianka was an intellectuals' prison, and Wat embarked on an intense period of study and reflection. In addition to rooms devoted to torture, there was a library, and Wat returned to literature: letters by Tolstoy, Saint Augustine, and Machiavelli; the first volume of Proust's *Remembrance of Things Past.*[142] Broniewski, too, read over three hundred books in Lubianka. He was most distressed by the lack of cigarettes; he had no money for the prison canteen and was forced to rely upon the generosity

of his cellmates. This was of no help during the first two months following his arrival in Lubianka on 22 May 1940, when he was in an isolation
cell.[143] Wat had been spared Broniewski's attachment to cigarettes and
alcohol; rather what he came to part with in Lubianka was his lingering
attachment to avant-gardism in literature. The impetus to this farewell
was Evgeny Dunayevsky, one of Wat's first cellmates, who had a deep
interest in etymology:

> The result of spending many months with a man who tracks
> down the roots and history of each word, who re-creates a
> certain historical and anthropological reality in the roots and
> history of each word, was, at least for me, the sudden falling
> away of the essence of avant-gardism—it began to fall away
> from me once and for all—all of what Marinetti had unleashed
> with his slogan "The liberated word": nihilism, linguistic mate-
> rialism, the word as an object with which you can do as you
> please. For me that's a basic distinction in poetics—in even
> more than poetics, for what distinguishes the worldview of the
> avant-garde writer and poet from the traditional or classical
> view is precisely the concept of the word as a material thing.
> Living close by Dunayevsky, I was pulled into his game, a won-
> derful game for killing time. But that game also caused a re-
> gression into feeling the biological connections of words on a
> higher level, not a mineral, biological, or even archetypal level
> but in connection to history, to the incredibly alive tissues of
> human destiny, the destinies of generations, the destinies of
> nations. And the responsibility for every word, to use every
> word properly. And then, intuitively—for I realized all this only
> later on—I had an intuitive sense both of the responsibility
> and of that which is perhaps the only thing that distinguishes
> a poet from the others who speak the language: the poet's task,
> or mission, or instinct to rediscover not the meaning of each
> word but only the weight of each word.[144]

Wat's interrogators in Lubianka, in their attempt to infiltrate the Polish leftist psyche, were extremely interested in Polish literature, and in
particular in Stefan Żeromski. Wat obligingly offered them his analysis
of *The Spring to Come*, which he "could see was very much to their taste."

Now Wat and his interrogator began to have the sorts of conversations Wat had once had in Café Ziemiańska. Wat had grown up in the cafés, he loved to talk about literature, and his hostility towards his interrogator melted. Then one day the interrogator with literary interests brought Wat a copy of *Nowe Widnokręgi*. For Wat it was a wrenching moment, he became consumed with a feeling of alienation, with the feeling that all of his friends were having a party without him. It was winter then in Moscow, but Wat pictured them—Ważyk, Rudnicki, Boy-Żeleński—sitting in summer cafés, debating, writing, chatting. Only Wat had been cast out.[145]

High culture sifted through the otherwise impenetrable walls of Lubianka. On Easter Sunday of 1941 the prisoners took their daily walk on the roof, and Wat could hear Bach's *Saint Matthew Passion* playing on a radio. Around that same time Wat acquired a new cellmate, Misha Taitz. Taitz was the former deputy director of the Marx-Engels Institute and had a phenomenal memory for quotations from Marx. Like Wat, Taitz knew the Russian poet Semën Kirsanov. Wat and Taitz became close friends, and now Taitz, notwithstanding having become an anarchist in prison, replaced Stawar as Wat's teacher of Marxism. Unlike Wat, Taitz was tortured in prison; he would return from these sessions with torture marks on his legs and buttocks, and spoke of how coming back to the cell after torture was like returning to a warm womb. Twice Taitz had signed a confession stating that he had been a spy for the Gestapo. And twice he had later recanted. And so Wat would talk with his interrogator about Polish literature and with his cellmate about Marxism.[146]

It was now 1941 and summer in Moscow. One day in June, Wat and Taitz returned to their cell to find that the windows had been painted over in blue. The Germans had broken the nonaggression pact with the Soviets. Operation Barbarossa had begun. Wat and Taitz waited. One day the guard shouted at them to get their things. The doors to all the cells were opened; prisoners streamed out into the corridors and down the stairs, making way for the NKVD officers to pass through the crowd. Wat saw the officers carrying as many files as they could hold, files marked never to be destroyed. The day became still more remarkable when, among thousands of people, Wat suddenly saw Broniewski—and then Tadeusz Peiper—on the stairs. Wat managed to reach Broniewski, and that evening they were locked together in a tiny cubicle, where they spent the night gasping for breath—and talking. Broniewski had not forgiven Wat for confessing to tapping messages in Zamarstynów, and Wat abandoned hopes of trying to explain. Still, it was a warm reunion; the two men embraced. Then Broniewski raised the issue of the more recent interrogations, Wat's testimony, his depositions. He was not very pleased with Wat's behavior under questioning: Wat had confessed he had had "anti-Soviet conversations" with Broniewski in Warsaw. Wat defended himself: all of their colleagues had testified to that. The interrogators had insisted that he name names, and it was impossible not to mention Broniewski, everyone knew how much time they spent together. How could Wat claim they had never spoken about the Soviet Union? But Wat had been prepared: when his interrogator asked him what Broniewski had said during these conversations, Wat replied that Broniewski had taken a view opposite to his own. Broniewski, resentful, was unpersuaded by Wat's explanation. His own interrogator had read him Wat's deposition, and it had said only that Wat had expressed anti-Soviet opinions, not that Broniewski had opposed them. Unlike Wat, Broniewski when interrogated had denied everything. Now Wat "felt denigrated, lowly, contrite in the face of [Broniewski's] heroism, his—how to put it—manliness."[147] That night in their airless cubicle Wat and Broniewski spoke about how Poland would look in the future. They envisioned a Poland with social justice for the working class, but without Bolshevism. Broniewski was no longer a communist, and Wat sensed that Broniewski no longer knew who he was.[148]

The next day they were taken south to Saratov, a warm and sunny provincial town. As they pulled in to their destination, Wat and Broniewski found Peiper in the column of prisoners. Nearby was the Bundist Henryk Erlich, whom Wat and Broniewski both knew from Warsaw. Erlich was pale and weak and could barely stand; Wat and Broniewski held him up as they walked. When Peiper reached them he exclaimed that he had wonderful news: he had seen Ola Watowa among the women prisoners! Wat was skeptical; by then Peiper frequently perceived things that were not there. Nonetheless, Wat began to work his way through the crowd, asking if Ola Watowa were there—but received no answer. At a certain moment one of the prisoners began cursing Stalin in a loud voice, and the whisper came from the crowd: "That's old Steklov." Nakhamkes Steklov was a hero of the Bolshevik Revolution, the longtime editor of *Izvestiia*, a friend of Lenin—and a friend of Stalin right up until the moment of his arrest. He was tall and very thin, and Wat was struck by his dignity, by the humanity of his face, by his gentlemanly demeanor.[149]

Unlike in Lubianka, in Saratov the cells were large, holding some hundred prisoners. Wat, Broniewski, Erlich, and Peiper stayed together; and it did not take long before an intellectual club formed in the cell. Peiper by this time suffered from extreme paranoia and immediately told Wat that in Cracow, Gestapo agents disguised as university students had rented the apartment opposite his and had followed his every movement from their window. In contrast to Peiper, the Bundist Erlich was calm and "objective"; he accepted his fate. Soon he was taken away. Also taking part in the discussions were another Bundist, a microbiologist, an officer, and a few other Russians. So there was "a fine club" with "interesting, pleasant conversation. . . . The time passed pleasantly."[150] Moreover, Wat was no longer alienated from faith. The faith of the Ukrainians he had so envied in Zamarstynów became his own only in Saratov. There Wat had a vision of the devil, a vision with "flourishes of vulgar laughter that kept approaching, then receding far away for a long time, a very long time." He insisted that he saw the devil there, that he saw the devil vividly—and felt God's presence in history somewhat more vaguely. He became a Christian.[151]

In Saratov, Wat fell so ill that he was finally sent to the hospital, where he met the famous Steklov who had been cursing Stalin. In the hospital Wat asked Steklov the question that had been haunting him since the Moscow show trials: Why did the Old Bolsheviks confess? Did they fear torture? Steklov answered him: What was torture, after all, for them, the heroes of the Revolution? They were all up to their elbows in blood—all of them, without exception. From the very beginning. Torture was unnecessary, they all saw before them the long lists of their own crimes and debasements. To confess to this or that no longer had any meaning. Wat shuddered. The nurses came and their conversation ended. As they took Steklov away, he shouted to Wat from the doorway,[152] "'When you return to Poland, tell people how old Steklov died!'"

CHAPTER SEVEN

Into the Abyss

Not only history, but the whole world, all of human life is divided
into before the war and after the war.

—*Julian Stryjkowski*

IN AUGUST 1939 JAROSŁAW Iwaszkiewicz saw Julian Tuwim in the
resort town of Zakopane, where Tuwim enchanted Iwaszkiewicz's daughters. Iwaszkiewicz, too, was charmed to see Tuwim against the backdrop of
the mountains, in a setting "other than bourgeois." And suddenly Iwaszkiewicz, who had known Tuwim for some twenty years, was struck by the
whole "uncanniness of his person," by Tuwim's "radiant, striking marks
of greatness." This was someone, Iwaszkiewicz wrote a few days later,
"for whom there exists only one issue: poetry."[1]

Iwaszkiewicz had witnessed the very last moments when only poetry
mattered to Julian Tuwim. At the moment when Oleksandr Korneichuk
summoned Tuwim by radio, inviting him to Lvov, Tuwim was making his
way west. He, Słonimski, and their wives had left Warsaw on 5 September
and headed to the town of Kazimierz, on the other side of the Vistula
River, where Słonimski thought they could wait out the first phase of
the war. "Our reasoning," Słonimski described self-mockingly, "was very
simple. Because, as was known, German tanks were made of cardboard,
they wouldn't be able to cross the Vistula, and if they were to try, they'd
come unglued."[2] As they set out, Tuwim saw the first plumes of German
bombs above the Polish capital.[3] In Kazimierz, Słonimski's wife rented
a room, putting down a deposit of one hundred złotys. However, as the
supposition regarding the cardboard tanks quickly revealed itself to be less

than accurate, and the poets learned that Germans had already reached Puławy, they left Kazimierz right away, forfeiting their deposit. Here the Skamandrites parted ways, with the Tuwims finding a place in an automobile, and Słonimski, his wife, and Mieczysław Grydzewski continuing on in their rented wagon to the town of Krzemieniec. There they met Stanisław Baliński, a poet and friend, who was carrying with him a folder of Adam Mickiewicz's letters, as well as the family jewelry. In Krzemieniec Słonimski's wife rented another room, this time paying a fifty-złoty deposit. Within an hour they had already departed, again forfeiting the deposit.

At this time, the war still seemed to Słonimski to be from a story book; he and his wife did not believe it would go on for very long. Even as bombings pursued them from one town to the next, life in the provinces continued in its slow, calm rhythm. Then suddenly Słonimski watched as, "as in a film, everything sped up, began to whirl. . . . The horses who had broken away from the provincial carriages neighed plaintively . . . barbers in white coats were almost floating in the air like in a Chagall painting."[4] The friends continued on. When they approached the Romanian border the local mayor ordered them to turn back. Their party went on to Zaleszczyki, where Słonimski's wife did not even have time to lay down a deposit. Instead they crossed the Zaleszczyki Bridge over the Dniester River into Romania just a few hours before the Soviet armies arrived. Słonimski left Poland with the faith that the western Allies would defeat the Nazis quickly, and that he would return to Warsaw before long.[5]

Friends tried to persuade Tuwim to journey with them to Lwów. He demurred, in the end choosing a southeasterly route, listening to the planes flying above him. Then Tuwim, too, saw the image from a Chagall painting: "some kind of cataclysm, a hellish bang, the clear sight of falling bombshells, then roofs, doors, windows, shreds of some rather undefined objects or creations flying above us."[6] People they knew, the car, their minimal baggage, everything perished in that hell, and Tuwim and his wife Stefania were now alone, hitchhiking, feeling like beggars. They reached the Galician provincial capital of Stanisławów, where they found the mayor working day and night distributing border passes to refugees. They acquired passes, and on Tuwim's forty-fifth birthday crossed the Polish-Romanian border. In a restaurant on the Romanian side, two civilians unexpectedly approached him, saying, "Mr. Tuwim? Come with us!" The two men had already collected, as it turned out, both his passport and his wife. They put Tuwim in a car; they were Polish officers, they told him, with orders to get him out of that town. Despite antisemitic accusations that Tuwim was not a real Polish poet, the Polish government continued to consider him a national treasure. The officers dispatched Tuwim and his wife to Bucharest, to the care of the Polish ambassador. In late September, after traveling through Yugoslavia and Italy, the Tuwims crossed the French border.

The Tuwims were not alone in Paris. Słonimski, Lechoń, and Grydzewski had made their way there as well. Słonimski was among those who did not suspect what the war would bring—despite the warning of a taxi driver, a Russian monarchist émigré in Paris, who, upon hearing Tuwim and Słonimski speaking in Polish, advised them to buy a taxi now, as later it would be difficult.[7] Being among the first wartime emigrants, the Skamander poets became the recipients of charitable contributions and the centerpiece of social events. With Grydzewski once again as editor they regathered around Wiadomości Polskie (Polish News), published as a continuation of the prewar Wiadomości Literackie. They found a café for themselves in Paris, the Café de la Regence, and Słonimski observed that it was this stay in Paris that finally satisfied Jan Lechoń's "insatiable hunger for snobbery." Lechoń rented an apartment that Jean Cocteau had once decorated, and where the Rothschilds and Paul Valéry would drop by to socialize.[8] Also in Paris was Ilya Ehrenburg, who fell ill and kept to himself; many of those who were once his friends chose to avoid him in light of the Nazi-Soviet pact, as "friendship was friendship, but politics was politics." The exception was Tuwim, who embraced his Russian friend when they met.[9]

That winter Tuwim was thinking only of Poland. Paris was alien to him.[10] He was plagued with vacuity and "poetic impotence." In April 1940 from Paris he sent a letter to a Polish philosopher friend, describing the pain of being unable to write:

> And everything that the Great Idiot called humanity produces
> in the world, all of the iniquity, rapes, wars, clamor, politics,
> economic and social theories, etc., etc.,—everything has its
> cause in one thing: that they, that is, people, would like (and
> cannot) To Become Closer, subconsciously they feel the need
> to achieve the shortest (the most direct) path to happiness (the

final goal of every being), and they have an intuition, the cads, that poets somehow *can*—and for that reason they idolize them so and hate them at the same time. Creative work is in truth an overcoming of death; better: a process of overcoming. And that's no trivial source of satisfaction, my beloved Pan Bolesław! And so when it's not there—I come to resemble that criminal gang to whom it seems that in building various Chicagos and flying in airplanes, they're "pushing the world forward" (so-called "progress"). And the world and life are in their deepest essence—immovable. It is CONSTANCY. There are two possibilities for coexistence in the world: with a woman and with a deity. All others (states, nations, classes, races, and other similar inventions)—are no good.[11]

RIO DE JANEIRO, 1940–1941

Skamander's Parisian interlude was cut short. In June 1940 France fell to the Germans, and the Skamandrites fled. Lechoń was evacuated with the Polish embassy to Spain and Portugal, and from there to Brazil.[12] Tuwim went to Bordeaux, where he received a visa to Portugal. In Lisbon he met a Brazilian poet who, without waiting to be asked, escorted Tuwim to the consulate and arranged for his Brazilian visa. Upon finding himself on the other side of the Atlantic Ocean, in Rio de Janeiro, Tuwim was dazzled; he discovered there "the incarnation of childhood dreams of the tropical world."[13] Moreover, Polish culture managed to reconstitute itself in this alien tropical world, and the Polish émigré community organized poetry readings by Tuwim and Lechoń.[14] Yet it was in Brazil that Tuwim grew aware of how completely he was the "antithesis of cosmopolitanism." In the paradise of Rio de Janeiro he longed only for Poland: "How cruelly I am cut off outright from that which is dearest to me, from that which is my life, my blood, the essence of my creative work, of my self: from Poland! What are my further intentions? Will I go, perhaps, to the United States? Who can foresee what fate will bring? I know one thing: I must write! and I want to RETURN, TO RETURN AS QUICKLY AS POSSIBLE!"[15]

In September 1940, Tuwim wrote to Kazimierz Wierzyński, who had remained in Portugal for a longer time after the fall of France, describing Rio de Janeiro as "exclusively a beach-amusement and café-strolling place."

Lechoń frequented these cafés, consuming enormous quantities of ice cream and Brazilian pastries. Tuwim, in contrast, had lost his appetite. "The beauty of this city is so staggering that the scale is almost so great as to be indescribable. Once here a couple of weeks, when you've seen enough to be satiated—you feel like vomiting," he wrote to Wierzyński. Nothing happened in Rio de Janeiro. Tuwim spoke French to the Brazilians, and found them to be polite and good-natured, but not terribly interesting. He began to think more about New York, where he imagined life would be harsher and more difficult—which would be preferable to the lightness of Brazilian beaches, and the tropical atmosphere that was "alien and morose to our broken and sick hearts."[16]

There by the beaches Lechoń and Tuwim indulged in literary rivalry. After Lechoń surprised Tuwim with a new poem, Tuwim locked himself in his room, coming out only after he had written a few hundred verses of "Kwiaty polskie" (Polish Flowers).[17] The epic poem told of the pain of exile, of longing for Poland, and of a dream of Warsaw dogs "fulfilling canine duty" and wreaking vengeance on the Germans. "My lot," Tuwim wrote,

> was to receive
> a Polish home. This—is fatherland,
> And other countries are hotels.

Warsaw was a "heroic Troy," Cracow a "distant, holy Mecca."[18]

THE BELARUSIAN ROUTE, 1939–1941

When Władysław Broniewski and Romuald Gadomski, Janina Broniewska's past and present husbands, had set out for the front at the very beginning of the war, both had told her—as they left her alone with ten-year-old Anka and pregnant with Gadomski's child—that she was so capable, surely she would manage on her own.[19] She did. Moreover, despite the birth of her and Gadomski's child, Stanisław, Janina Broniewska declined to pursue a formal divorce from Broniewski. Principled and dogmatic, she was also a fiercely loyal woman. She explained her decision: "Carrying out such a simple, trivial formality would be worse than unfaithfulness in marriage. It would be a disavowal of everything that joined us throughout our lives. Solidarity, boundless confidence in the sincerity and earnestness of our shared convictions made it impossible to divorce a communist imprisoned in a Soviet prison."[20] Broniewski's imprisonment she attributed to his own naïveté in flagrantly manifesting his Polish patriotism at an inopportune moment. She blamed, moreover, not the Soviet Union but rather his Polish colleagues in Lvov who had betrayed Broniewski and acted as provocateurs in his arrest.[21]

Janina Broniewska, joined soon by Gadomski, spent the early stages of the war in Soviet-occupied Białystok, before moving east to Minsk. On 17 September 1940, she was among those who joined the Union of Soviet Writers of Belarus as a symbolic gesture on the anniversary of the Soviet occupation of eastern Poland.[22] Like "Western Ukraine," "Western Belarus" had been annexed to a Soviet republic. In Minsk Janina Broniewska directed the literary department of the Polish-language newspaper *Sztandar Wolności* (Banner of Freedom), and was now transformed from a fellow-traveling author of children's stories to a serious communist journalist.[23] In spring 1941 she began a correspondence with the elderly Feliks Kon, veteran of the nineteenth-century Polish Marxist party Proletariat. She addressed Kon with reverence, telling him that "for us, for Poles, you are precisely the most real embodiment of the tradition of the Polish revolutionary movement." She asked two things of him: an article about Proletariat, and an honest appraisal of *Sztandar Wolności*'s "insufficiencies and shortcomings."[24] When Kon wrote to her with words of praise for the newspaper, the editorial staff was ecstatic, but Broniewska answered with self-criticism: "Yet it is still not the newspaper that it should be, on this quite peculiar Polish terrain, where everyday life [*byt*]—that is to say, the system—has changed so fundamentally in the course of less than two full years, while consciousness has remained from ages past—which is to say, as it was shaped for years by capitalist Poland."[25]

Joining Janina Broniewska were Aleksander Wat's onetime KPP liaison, Jakub Berman, and Alfred Lampe. A member of the KPP Central Committee, Lampe, like Borejsza and Stryjkowski, had come to the Communist Party from the ranks of the young Zionists. He was a veteran of interwar Polish prison. When Polish authorities had tried to send him to the Soviet Union as part of a prisoner exchange in 1924, Lampe had refused, preferring to serve out his sentence in Poland so as "to contribute to the general awareness of citizens, and first and foremost of the working masses, that the state is a police regime."[26] It was a fortuitous preference: Polish prison was the safest place for a prominent Polish communist to be in the 1930s. When the Nazis attacked Poland, Lampe escaped from prison, where he was serving yet another term, and headed east. By this time the KPP no longer existed, the Terror of 1937–1938 had passed, and Stalin's purge of the Polish communists had begun to wane.

When in the summer of 1941 the German bombing of Minsk began, Jakub Berman had no way of communicating with Broniewska and Lampe, who were in another part of the city.[27] The three were separated; Broniewska and Lampe together fled together the burning city. Once again they headed east, towards the Soviet interior. Broniewska was full of admiration for her companion. During their journey from Minsk southeast through Russia, "one could see plainly how in the most difficult conditions Alfred was able to be a teacher, a tutor and friend of our commune, which was packed into a single common room at the time. How much buoyancy there is in that man worn out by imprisonments, how much warmth, how much goodness. Ordinary human goodness. And how much patience. Here, for us, Alfred Lampe is an ideological compass, the one who is able to think in terms of political perspectives far beyond the present, by no means easy, day."[28] In the end they traveled for ten days before settling on a state pig farm near the southern Russian city of Kuibyshev, just north of Kazakhstan. There Broniewska and her daughter worked the fields, with Anka suffering from malnutrition.[29] Jakub Berman arrived in the city of Ufa, southeast of Kuibyshev, where he became an instructor at the Comintern school, training activists who in 1942 would form a new party for Polish communists, the Polish Workers' Party.[30]

THE ROAD FROM LVOV, JUNE 1941 AND BEYOND

The 22 June 1941 German attack on the Soviet Union was for Wanda Wasilewska a perversely ecstatic moment; the end of Nazi-Soviet cooperation enabled her to reclaim her Polish patriotism. As soon as she learned that there was a war, she presented herself first thing in the morning at the regional Party committee and asked what she could do. They gave her a rifle. This startled her, yet she took well to her new role, and proceeded to move about Lvov with that rifle, wearing a border guard's cap that she found by chance. When the Germans took Lvov, Wasilewska went on to Kiev. There she was given a uniform, and she spent the two or three days immediately thereafter working to evacuate people who had fled Lvov further east. After three days, she, Oleksandr Korneichuk, and Mykola Bazhan formed their own group, working on propaganda and on preparing materials for illegal organizations remaining on the evacuated territories. Later she went to Saratov, where she found Stefan Jędrychowski, whose trial she and Janina Broniewska had attended in Wilno, and the literary translator and former KPP member Wiktor Grosz; they contributed to broadcasts for the Saratov radio station.[31]

This was the moment when Wanda Wasilewska came into her own. The PPS activist from Cracow who chain-smoked and drank endless cups of black coffee was now catapulted into a unique position; and the story of the Poles cast into the Soviet Union during the Second World War was largely a story of the extraordinary relationship Leon Wasilewski's daughter developed with Iosif Stalin. Now that Nazi Germany had invaded the Soviet Union she could fully express her hatred for the Germans; now she was free to devote all her talents to mobilizing people into battle against the fascist enemy. She immediately took advantage of the dramatic alteration in international politics to publish the poems Broniewski had been continually reciting in Lvov: "A Polish Soldier" and "Son of a Conquered Nation" appeared in *Nowe Widnokręgi* that summer.[32] She gave speeches full of a grandiloquent faith. She embraced the ideal of Slavic brotherhood and praised the Soviet Ukrainians, to whom she was infinitely grateful for having sheltered the Poles when the Germans attacked, for having made from "homeless refugees citizens with full and equal rights."[33] Her mastery of the language of propaganda was all the more potent for its passionate sincerity. At a radio meeting in Saratov on 27 November 1941, she spoke to her fellow countrymen in wartime exile: "Poles! That call resounds in our hearts with a loud echo. Liquidate all Germans, who have fallen upon Polish land in an armed invasion. Have no mercy on the wild beast drinking our blood, tormenting women and children, raping young girls, murdering the best sons of our Fatherland." She concluded with a rallying call affirming the new international alignments: "Long live the Soviet Union, Great Britain, and the United States of America! Long live nations fighting for freedom! Long live victory!"[34]

Jerzy Borejsza, director of the Ossolineum, was by chance in Kiev when the Germans attacked the Soviet Union. It was now too late to return; he remained in Kiev and enlisted in the Red Army.[35] Julian Stryjkowski, together with a group from *Czerwony Sztandar,* also fled Lvov in the direction of Kiev. On the road they met the red-haired communist who was the wife of Witold Kolski, the man who had written the scathing feuilleton against the arrested writers. Kolski's wife was returning to Lvov with her small child; she could go no farther, she told them. Stryjkowski pleaded with her not to go back and offered to carry the child, but she was determined. She insisted that something must have happened to her husband since he had not come for her, and was convinced that he would be looking for her in Lvov. She asked Stryjkowski, if he were to see Kolski first, to tell her husband where she had gone.[36]

In Kiev Stryjkowski did in fact find Kolski, who was one of the few Polish communists who had been honored with acceptance into the All-Russian Communist Party (Bolsheviks). When he had been in Kiev not more than a day, Stryjkowski encountered Wasilewska. He and an acquaintance were walking along the street when a car stopped, and through an open window Stryjkowski saw a familiar face: it was Jerzy Borejsza; Wasilewska was sitting next to him. The car stopped, Borejsza greeted them and said that things at the front were "not bad." He was headed to the cinema. The car drove off and turned down a side street, and Stryjkowski's companion suggested that Borejsza had only wanted to show them that he was in a car with Wanda Wasilewska.[37]

NEW YORK, MID-1941—MID-1942

Kazimierz Wierzyński did join Julian Tuwim and Jan Lechoń in Brazil, but their tropical interlude was brief. With the help of Wierzyński's goddaughter, a painter and sculptor now married to the American ambassador, they all obtained visas to the United States.[38] The Skamandrites' arrivals in New York coincided approximately with the Nazi attack on the Soviet Union and, in its wake, the resumption of diplomatic relations between the Soviet Union and the Polish government-in-exile in London. The Nazi-Soviet nonaggression pact was no more, and now from New York in late August 1941, Tuwim sent a telegram to Ilya Ehrenburg confirming his friendship, his love, and his faith.[39] Not all the Skamandrites shared Tuwim's feeling of solidarity with the Soviet Union. In September 1941, Tuwim wrote to his sister that he was avoiding Lechoń, as he was more generally avoiding the right-leaning branch of the Polish émigré community.[40] After their long years together in Poland, now in exile the poets saw their relations poisoned by politics. That November Tuwim wrote to his sister that with Lechoń and Wierzyński he now shared only old jokes; it was difficult for him to talk to his old friends about what was important to him now. More and more Tuwim gleaned the impression that they saw the Poland of the future as being ruled by a center-right "group of colonels"—as had been the case after Piłsudski's death, during the last half-decade before the war.[41] By the end of that winter, Tuwim saw his friends less and less and felt that they were avoiding him as well. "It's difficult," he wrote, "—I've placed my bets on an entirely different world than they have, I openly voice my battle for that world, exposing myself to the opinion of being a 'Bolshevik.'"[42] Until early 1942 the exiled Skamandrites nevertheless remained close, as they had a tacit mutual agreement not to speak of politics. On 22 May 1942, however, Tuwim and Lechoń spoke by phone about the death of Tadeusz Boy-Żeleński, who had been shot by the Nazis in Lvov the previous July. Following that conversation Tuwim wrote to his sister: "It was our first conversation on the topic of Russia and fascism! Our first! Several minutes long. And already we began to fight."[43] One week later Lechoń sent Tuwim a letter, severing all relations due to Tuwim's "blind love for the Bolsheviks."[44]

If Tuwim was hurt by the estrangement from his old friends, he said nothing of this. In June 1942 he wrote to Józef Wittlin, "I'm doing nothing, despairing over the loss of talent, reason, humor, youth, health, homeland, library, and the possibility of practicing alcoholism with impunity." He added, "Have you been seeing our friends the fascists? With regret I've found that I do not miss them."[45] He wrote similarly to his sister in July:

> For me the break with Leszek [Lechoń] was rather a relief,
> because I cannot stand insincere situations. Lately our entire
> friendship has resided in the connection of memories and in
> perpetual fooling around with jokes and anecdotes. A friend—
> that must be something deeper. In an essential friendship
> more deeply concealed chords must harmonize. And in me,
> after long years of suppression, there occurred a reeling storm
> of feelings, instincts, and momentum of a social, societal,
> universal nature—and that (finally! finally!) I became aware
> of the poverty-stricken, narrow categories of thought by which
> the milieu that I came from—and the subsequent milieu in
> which I grew up—operates, and so I haven't felt the absence
> of those people for even a moment.[46]

ALMA-ATA—MOSCOW—KUIBYSHEV, SUMMER 1941—
SPRING 1942

While Julian Tuwim, Jan Lechoń, and Kazimierz Wierzyński sat in Brazilian cafés, their friend Władysław Broniewski sat in Soviet prison. For Broniewski, it was the period of his imprisonment after Lubianka that he found most difficult; the heat and the vermin in Saratov were unbearable. Finally he was formally sentenced: to five years exile in Kazakhstan, where he was to work on a kolkhoz. On 24 July 1941 he was taken from Saratov to Alma-Ata. Two weeks later, there in the Kazakh capital he was released from prison; 562 days after Daszewski's ill-fated party he began his forced labor in exile.[47] That same day, 7 August, he wrote to Janina Broniewska in Moscow: "Jaśka! I have a feeling that you're in Moscow. A short while ago I got out of jail and I'm going to Semipalatinsk for five years of exile from the date of my arrest. I don't know anything about my family. Write, telegraph. . . . I'm healthy, in good spirits, bursting with energy. About my experiences, my impressions—another time. I thought about Anka constantly and as a rule every evening before falling asleep. I've sent a telegram to Wanda. Terribly ragged and bald. Kisses to everyone."[48]

The outbreak of the Nazi-Soviet war bore heavily on the fates of the imprisoned Polish poets, and the telegram he sent to Wanda Wasilewska that day was a fortunate one. The Soviet Union now joined the Allies. Broniewski's telegram arrived just after Polish Prime Minister Władysław Sikorski and the Soviet ambassador in London, Ivan Maiskii, had signed an agreement providing for the amnesty of Poles in the Soviet Union and the creation of a Polish army. On this occasion Wasilewska was called back from the front to Moscow, where the Soviet Central Committee asked her if there was anyone who, in her opinion, needed to be released right away, even before the official announcement. She immediately mentioned Broniewski. The next day she received a phone call notifying her that Soviet authorities were very worried because they had not been able to find Broniewski. "And with joy," Wasilewska related, "I dictated the address, because the morning of that same day I'd received a telegram from Władek: 'Telegraph what's [going on] with my family.'" The very same day Broniewski was freed.[49]

Broniewski quickly left Kazakhstan for Moscow; when he arrived on 20 August, Wasilewska was already gone.[50] The following day he wrote again to Janina Broniewska, whom he had by now located on the pig farm outside of Kuibyshev.

Beloved Jaśka!

They let me out of jail on the beautiful day of 7 August in
the beautiful city of Alma-Ata and from there, now no longer
as a prisoner, I went to Semipalatinsk to sit out the three and
a half years remaining for me in exile. I was there, but only
for three days and I hadn't even managed to get to the Novaia
shulba kolkhoz, when I was summoned by telegraph from
Moscow. I would guess that here the telegram I sent to Wasilewska on the 7th helped . . . and so since the evening of the
20th I've been in Moscow. But I'm writing here everything
beginning from the end. . . . Well so, speaking in the broadest
of terms, it was difficult, it can't even be compared with 1931,
absolute isolation, a very harsh regime, no favors. . . . I was
constantly thinking that somehow you would get me out, but it
turned out that the intervention of History was more effective.

Prison had been miserable, but now it was in the past and in retrospect
that whole period seemed to Broniewski "quite preposterous." At the conclusion of his interrogations, Broniewski related, he learned of the "fantastical wretched things" that Jerzy Borejsza and others had said about him
in their depositions for the NKVD. He could say much about all of this,
but that would come when they spoke in person. Leave the pigs to their
own fate, he told her, and come to Moscow. He sent kisses to his former
wife and her new husband, and wanted to know: did Anka now have a
little brother or a little sister?[51]

Four days later Broniewski sent another letter. He had been in Moscow for five days and still had no plan as to how to support himself; at
the moment he was under the "care" of the NKVD, who had given him
two thousand rubles as part of the amnesty agreement. The day before
he had met with General Władysław Anders, whose bed Aleksander Wat
had inherited at Lubianka, and who was now to lead the Polish army being organized as part of the Sikorski-Maiskii agreement. "The simplest
thing to do," he wrote, "would, of course, be to enlist in the army, but
I'm still vacillating and I don't know in what way I could most effectively
serve the common cause. As you've figured, I'm not an enthusiast of
Sikorski's camp, but there's no choice." He was also uncertain as to how
the Polish authorities would react to his offer to serve, given the Polish

government's unfavorable predisposition towards communism and his own communist past. Moreover, physically he was still weak and unable to walk very far; his hair was beginning to grow back, although there was still "nothing to comb."[52]

Broniewski did not vacillate for very long. That day he went to visit Ilya Ehrenburg. By the next day, Broniewski had come to a decision to enlist in the Anders army.[53] He was anxious to see his family, especially Anka. In yet another letter from Moscow to Janina Broniewska, he wrote that if coming to Moscow with the children was too difficult due to air raids, she should leave the children with a friend in Kuibyshev and come alone.[54] He wrote separately to Anka, in a letter full of patriotic concern for her Polish education:

> You know that every evening around ten, when I'd laid down
> to sleep, I thought about you, about Marysia and little Marysia
> [Marysia Zarębińska's daughter Majka] and about everyone
> close and dear to us and I fell asleep only when I had recalled
> to myself some shared experience, for example our trip in the
> Tatras two years ago, or the stay in Zakopane with the Marysias.
> Right now I don't feel like thinking or writing much about my
> imprisonment, when we see each other, there will be some-
> thing to tell. . . . My dear, for almost two years we haven't seen
> each other, you must have grown, developed. What have you
> read, what have you thought about? Write in detail. In prison
> I thought very often how good it would be if I had the chance
> to point you towards and explain to you some books by Żerom-
> ski, Prus, everything that connects us with our hearts to the
> land we've left by force, the land we so love and long for. Well,
> Anula, we'll be there most likely in a year.[55]

Broniewski, among all his friends, had proven the most resilient in prison. He left Saratov full of energy, eager to fight for Poland. He left Saratov in some way still a believer in socialism. On 27 August 1941 he volunteered for the Anders army, although he understood that an army of exiled Poles returning from Soviet labor camps would not be an auspicious place for a well-known communist poet. While waiting to receive a reply, Broniewski worked as a cultural attaché at the Polish embassy in Kuiby-

FIGURE 11 Władysław Broniewski with his daughter Anka in Kuibyshev, 1941. Courtesy of Muzeum Władysława Broniewskiego.

shev.[56] In October 1941 he received a Polish embassy summons to join Polish Army troops—but as a war correspondent, not as a soldier.[57] Afterwards he made his way back to Kuibyshev, where the streets were filled with exhausted Poles dressed in rags, returning from labor camps and not at all favorably disposed towards the Soviet Union or towards communism.[58] There he shared a mattress with Anatol Stern, who had made his way to Kuibyshev after his release from Soviet prison in September 1940. Stern enlisted in the Anders army, and began to work with the army's film crew.[59] Finally, in March 1942, Broniewski received a communication from the man who had almost become Aleksander Wat's brother-in-law, Władysław Anders, addressing him as a captain and summoning him to report for duty.[60] Becoming a soldier again was the fulfillment of a prison wish: that September of 1941 Broniewski had written a poem in which he told of hearing shots fired outside his Moscow prison cell, of wanting to steal a rifle, of wanting to fight.[61]

LONDON, SUMMER 1940–SUMMER 1942

After the fall of France to the Nazis, Mieczysław Grydzewski, Antoni Słonimski, and Słonimski's wife sailed across the Channel for the shores of England. There Słonimski encountered Polish activists from across the political spectrum, including Stanisław Grabski, who in his youth had been the editor of the paper *Robotnik* (The Worker) in Berlin, but who later had left the socialist camp and joined the National Democrats. In England, Słonimski asked Grabski why he had departed from socialism. The elderly professor, who was growing deaf, put his hand to his ear and asked, "from what?" "Why did you depart from socialism?" Słonimski repeated. "From socialism?" Grabski answered, "I don't remember." It was an answer, Słonimski believed, that "painted the mood in London quite well."[62]

Now far away in England, Słonimski read Broniewski's poem about hearing the shots fired outside as he sat in his Moscow prison cell. Słonimski, always invested in his ironic distance, was now moved to sentimentality. In a poem addressed to his friend, Słonimski wrote of how it would be Broniewski's poetry and Broniewski's rifle, his rebelliousness and his romanticism, which would raise the spirits of the weak ones—like Słonimski himself—who had fled. In exile Słonimski had found new sympathy for Broniewski's leftist faith, and wrote that Broniewski's voice would remain everywhere "where Poland will be, where socialism will be." It would be thanks to Broniewski and others like him that Poland would rise again "on the ruins of Warsaw, on the ashes of mourning." Słonimski, the iconoclast and liberal, now made a choice to align himself with socialism; from London he sent greetings to Broniewski's Moscow.[63]

The sardonic Słonimski had one great love, and it was for Warsaw. In London he published a collection of wartime poetry titled *Alarm*. The title poem, which enjoyed unusual popularity in Nazi-occupied Poland, Słonimski had written in Paris in autumn 1939; it ended with the words "I sound an alarm for the city of Warsaw. May it endure!"[64] In 1942 he composed a long poem titled "Popiół i Wiatr" (Ashes and Wind), mourning his ruined home. He wrote of the waiter who lazily shuffled about in an empty Café Ziemiańska, and of the impossibility of reconciling himself to the fact that in his city there remained only ashes, ruins, and the sound of the wind. Słonimski, the prodigal son, would not even be able to return and "bow [his] head before the former threshold of [his] home." In 1942,

Słonimski foresaw that Warsaw would be burnt to ashes before any of them would see their city again.[65]

Scattered across the globe, the Skamander poets learned that exile need not bring solidarity. The Polish emigration mirrored all of Europe in its Manichean divisions: Polish émigrés were split between the Right and the Left. Through the two decades of interwar Poland, the Skamander poets had willfully resisted the spiraling ideological polarization. Now the space for being unengaged truly no longer existed. So in London did Słonimski cast his lot with the Left, which did not go unnoticed. He was seated at the podium for a poetry reading at a Polish military encampment in Scotland when one soldier stood up and demanded that Antoni Słonimski be erased from the program for "insulting the national youth." This spurred a dozen cries of "away with him!"—after which there followed silence. Słonimski took the rejection well, even nostalgically. "I cannot say," he wrote, "that this scene caused me particular distress, it reminded me of my homeland, of the prewar years, and I even felt something like affection."[66]

Słonimski's relationship with Mieczysław Grydzewski and the circle around *Polskie Wiadomości* deteriorated. In September 1941 Grydzewski wrote to Tuwim of the newspaper's difficulties; its subsidy had been withdrawn and Grydzewski had been forced to raise the price. Yet Grydzewski was convinced that the paper would survive. After all, he reminded Tuwim, as Rabbi Ben Akiba had said, "it has all already been."[67] Grydzewski added that his relations with Słonimski were not good, their "Parisian differences" having deepened still further.[68] At the same time, not fully understanding Tuwim's increasing dogmatism, Grydzewski wrote to him, "My dear ones, how much I miss you and regret that you didn't come here; this pertains to Leszek [Lechoń] and Kazio [Wierzyński] as well."[69]

The feeling was not mutual. The tension between Grydzewski and Tuwim centered around the Soviet Union: Grydzewski was critical of Stalinism, while Tuwim placed his hopes for Poland's future on an alliance with the Soviets. "If there is such slavery, hunger, stench, cruelty, and the worst of everything there, then why and for what are they fighting so furiously?" Tuwim wrote to Grydzewski.[70] The editor thought otherwise. He did not agree with Tuwim, and now he was more forthright. "But you'll doubtlessly forgive me," he wrote in a January 1942 letter, "if—repaying frankness with frankness—I tell you in advance that your letter is saturated with the climate of *Merkuriusz* [a right-wing journal] *à rebours:* there you had 'żydokomuna,' here you have 'a fifth column.' For the 'anti-Russian sulking' in *Polskie Wiadomości* I take full responsibility."[71] Responding to Tuwim's refusal to publish in *Polskie Wiadomości*, Grydzewski stood behind his paper:

> As I learned later, your telegram regarding not publishing
> in *Polskie Wiadomości* was prompted by a change in opinion
> about the "National Democrats." ... I'm not speaking about
> aesthetic-opportunist considerations, but after all the endeks
> [National Democrats] are dying just as are others in the battle
> against the Germans, they're dying just like others on Polish
> battlefields. ... Does that truly have no meaning?
>
> I have to tell you that in a certain sense I admire the "vital-
> ity" of your reactions: you have the time and the temperament
> today to remember the endeks, ozon, to remember that Mac-
> kiewicz doesn't consider you a "Polish" poet, etc., to remember
> that there was antisemitism in Poland (in the end not so many
> wrongs were done to the Jews) and similar things.
>
> As far as *Polskie Wiadomości* is concerned ... it will always
> be accessible to people from all camps, without inspecting
> their party cards.[72]

Grydzewski must have been aware of Tuwim's openly critical attitude towards him and his émigré circle in London; he had heard that Słonimski had published in *Robotnik* (The Worker) some "damnations" about *Polskie Wiadomości* that Tuwim had expressed in a private letter.[73] Even so, the optimist Grydzewski nourished hopes that their differences would pass; perhaps he failed to recognize the depth of Tuwim's resentment.

Słonimski found himself isolated in London just as Tuwim did in New York, and for similar reasons. The common experience was not lost on either of them, and Tuwim clung to Słonimski from across the ocean. In July 1942, now a year since Nazi Germany had gone to war against the Soviet Union, Tuwim wrote in a long letter to his old friend from Pod Pikadorem and Café Ziemiańska: "Thank you, my dearest Toleczek—more beloved than at any other time in life—and in a certain sense the *only one*! Other friendships have utterly boiled to death in the kettle of war, while my feelings for you, attachment to our shared past, a similar—so I think—view of the future, attitude in the present—have grown and (forgive this little word) 'fortified' themselves. Believe me, that I, on American soil, am equally as alone as you are in London (as far as old friendships are concerned). Leszek [Lechoń], as you most likely know, has cut off relations with me. With Kazio [Wierzyński] I barely, barely maintain 'strained relations.'" Tuwim insisted to Słonimski, as he had to his sister, that he was not hurt by the loss of his old friends: "But do not judge that this solitude is painful to me. On the contrary: it gladdens me and rather solidifies the fact that finally, finally a distinct 'line of partition' has emerged. In the past you didn't want to believe that 'the barricade has only two sides.' Do you believe it now?—And after all, as compensation I have new friends, people I've met here: strong, noble, and uncompromising where the final goal of battle is concerned. . . . As far as Mietek [Grydzewski] and his co-workers go, that gang doesn't concern me at all."[74] As for Słonimski, he was either more vulnerable or more confessional than Tuwim. The alienation was painful for him and the loneliness he felt in London the most bitter he had ever experienced. He was plagued with the thought that he had left himself behind in Warsaw. In that city, he wrote, "remained my literary output, my reader, my significance, my sense of existence. . . . In Warsaw the streets and the cafés knew me, here I was an indistinguishable passerby, here I could garner only sympathy."[75]

KAZAKHSTAN, NOVEMBER 1941–JANUARY 1943

Unlike Władysław Broniewski, who was among the very first to be released in the amnesty, Aleksander Wat was freed only in November 1941. Just before his release, his hair was shaven one more time. He emerged from prison a skeleton, emaciated, his skull visible, his eyes seeming huge. Now he joined a new category of people in a country in which, as a Soviet maxim held at the time, there were only three categories: those who were in prison, those who are in prison, and those who will be in prison.[76] In the hospital someone had told him that his family had most likely been sent to Kazakhstan, and advised him to go to the NKVD in Alma-Ata and inquire about their whereabouts. At the Saratov railway station it appeared that "all of Russia was on the move." *Urks,* as the Soviets called orphaned child-thieves, wandered about the station waiting for an opportunity to steal, everyone lived on the floor, in one spot Wat saw a woman being raped. No one paid the scene any attention. He learned from another Pole there that Wasilewska and Ważyk were in Saratov making some speeches. They would have welcomed him—and potentially been a tremendous source of help in finding his family. But the thought of seeking them out did not even come into Wat's mind. He was headed for Kazakhstan.[77]

In the meantime, Ola Watowa and Andrzej had abandoned their barracks in Ivanovka after the amnesty and set out for nowhere, heading south. Eventually they found themselves on the state farm Antonovka, where they had hoped to find food, but where there were only cotton fields and more starving people. In Antonovka they lived in a room with a woman and her elderly mother, who maintained a strict domestic regime. Ola Watowa stole bits of bread and cabbage from the old woman to feed to Andrzej and in the evenings read Tolstoy to her by the oil lamp. Only once did the old woman show generosity, on the holiday of the pig slaughter, when she invited her tenants to join the family for a feast. Invited as well were two men, no longer sober when they arrived. At a certain moment in the festivities, with their host's encouragement, the men began to dance. As they drank more they began to "court" Watowa; she excused herself and went to bed, but the men followed and tried to join her there. Terrified, she jumped onto the floor, and the drunken men began to chase her around the room. The old woman looked on and laughed.[78]

At the enormously crowded Saratov railway station, a Polish Jew named Krakowski was aboard a freight train waiting to depart when the doors opened and a man was pulled into his wagon. The man's appearance "contrasted strikingly with the surrounding backdrop: he was wearing a fur coat with an otter-fur collar and . . . a bowler hat."[79] Wat was unable to support his own weight, he slid down onto the floor. Krakowski and his traveling companions adopted him. During the journey Wat told them the story of his imprisonment, he told them of his coexistence with lice, their habits and psychology. Then, at one of the railroad junctions, Wat decided to depart. Krakowski and his companions attempted to dissuade him; he was too weak to set out alone in search of his family. Wat was insistent. He got off the train.[80]

Wat found himself in the Kazakh town of Dzhambul, where he went to the baths, looked at himself in a cracked mirror, and cried. Doctors there examined him and told him that he had two weeks left to live. At that moment he was undisturbed by the news. Two weeks seemed a long time, and in any case he was focused only on reaching Alma-Ata and finding his family. By the time Wat arrived in the Kazakh capital, it was winter in Kazakhstan, and Wat was enchanted by the ice-covered poplar trees, which seemed to glisten with diamonds. A Polish delegation had already been established there, and Wat was introduced to its head, Kazimierz Więcek. The delegation sent him to a doctor, who, in contrast to the doctor in Dzhambul, told Wat that he could survive, but that he was suffering from a vitamin deficiency and needed food. Neither food nor housing was to be found easily. Wat spent his first day in Alma-Ata wandering the streets, searching for a place to sleep. In the end he reached the delegation hotel where many people were spending the night in the lobby and there was no place left to sit. He noticed a statue of Lenin with his arm outstretched, and curled up in a small hidden corner behind the revolutionary leader. At one point during the night Wat awoke; documents were being checked and as a former prisoner he had no right to be in the Kazakh capital. Wat remained unnoticed, however. Lenin had sheltered him. The following day he went to the NKVD where he approached a small window and inquired about the whereabouts of his family. Within ten minutes he received an answer: In September Ola Watowa and Andrzej Wat had arrived on a state farm in the Semipalatinsk province; later they had left to go farther south with the other Poles—but it was unknown to where. Now Wat wrote some two hundred postcards to all the Polish delegates in the former Soviet Union, seeking news of his family. He wrote to Wasilewska, as well as to Broniewski, who was at the Polish embassy in Kuibyshev. Broniewski replied that someone had seen Ola Watowa around Chimkent, that she had gone to see the delegate there, who had given her two hundred rubles. This was all Broniewski knew.[81]

Wat later remembered this period in the Soviet Union as one in which his sense of national identity grew stronger: he became more of a Jew and more of a Polish patriot. Yet this was also the time in his life when he was most closely integrated into Russian circles. This began with Mayakovsky's friend, the literary theorist Viktor Shklovsky, whom Wat had last seen in Lvov in the autumn of 1939. When Wat ran into Shklovsky in Alma-Ata, Shklovsky asked him no questions. Neither—it seemed to Wat—did Shklovsky want to hear anything, he was only glad to see Wat and said that his whole group of friends was there and Wat could join them. When Wat was wandering about the city, not strong enough to work on a kolkhoz and knowing he could be deported at any moment, Shklovsky found him again and hid him in his own hotel room. There Wat met Shklovsky's circle: the novelist and playwright Konstantin Paustovsky, the humorist Mikhail Zoshchenko and his young wife, the screenwriter Mikhail Shnaider, and the film director Sergei Eisenstein. Eisenstein appeared to Wat to be "a fantastic person in a demonic sort of way. His eyes. When he looked at you, you knew you were being photographed. But he did that with his soul; it wasn't just physical."[82]

Wat was the only Pole. Despite his history, so closely intertwined with Russian literature, Wat remained in some sense a foreigner within Shklovsky's circle. About Soviet communism Shklovsky said nothing. From Shklovsky and his friends Wat learned that "in polite society" one did not speak about socialist realism. Rather, they spoke of art, of film and literature, and of Wat's experiences in prison. They all knew, of course, what went on in Soviet camps and prisons, but they seemed to find Wat's way of relating the experience particularly interesting. Wat talked to them as well about his conversion to Christianity in Saratov prison, a story that captured Zoshchenko's attention. On one occasion Zoshchenko pushed Wat to define his faith more clearly, asking Wat if, at this very minute, he truly believed—in the divinity of Christ, the resurrection, the immortality of the soul. Wat was unable to answer.[83]

Around New Year's of 1942, Wat finally received an answer to one of the many letters and postcards he had sent from Alma-Ata. The reply was from a doctor, an embassy delegate, telling Wat to write to a certain woman in Kazakhstan. Ola Watowa had received no news of her husband. By this time she had sold her last possession—a worn-out pelisse—for a bit of flour, a piece of bread, and a small quantity of animal fat. It was January of 1942; she was sitting at a wooden table, reading Tolstoy to the old woman, when a sixteen-year-old boy appeared at the doorway. He did not come in, he only stood by the door, holding up an envelope. Watowa recognized her husband's handwriting; the boy asked what she would give him for the letter. She took all of the pieces of flatbread she had baked for dinner and gave them to him, and he left her with the letter written to his mother, the woman whom the doctor had suggested Wat contact. The letter was dated 18 January 1942; Wat wrote that he had been amnestied on 20 November 1941 and knew only that his family had been deported from Lvov in April 1940 and had moved south after the amnesty. He begged the woman to tell him everything possible, even if the worst had happened; he promised to repay the cost of telegrams and enclosed a return envelope, giving the address of the Polish delegation in Alma-Ata and signing "Aleksander Wat (Chwat), writer from Warsaw."[84]

Ola Watowa immediately sent a telegram. Receiving it extricated Wat from his numbness. He felt himself coming alive again. Alma-Ata was transformed: "I began to see colors, to hear, to smell, to see women, to smell women."[85] In his long response to his wife's first telegram he told her, "Only now can I look at women (to the devil with all you women) and children without sharp aversion."[86]

> I never knew how much I loved you and one of my worst
> sufferings was the fact that I couldn't tell you—our awful part-
> ing—my stupor at the time, that whole nightmare of our 13th
> anniversary! I know, I've guessed, what you've in fact experi-
> enced, and with fear I think about what kind of state I'll find
> both of you in—but the most important thing is that we'll be
> together, that the worst has passed. I will never forget that you
> were able to save yourself and our son—I cannot live without
> you both. I will be considerably better, wiser, more loving to
> both of you—I will not so foolishly ruin your life and mine. I
> suppose I've changed quite fundamentally—I've actually expe-
> rienced a strange period of some kind of second maturation,
> a second coming into being—but we'll speak much about that.

He told her about Mayakovsky's friend Viktor Shklovsky, and about how Mayakovsky's stories of Wat served him well in Alma-Ata with his Russian friends. He told her of how Shklovsky had taken him in despite the risk, how he had taken care of Wat like a child. Wat was desperate to see his family, he was also insecure. "I am not asking about anything," he wrote, "—nothing can diminish my love for both of you. Maybe you've stopped loving me?" He signed the letter "always, until the end of life regardless of anything, Yours Ol."[87]

She had not stopped loving him. On 24 January Ola Watowa wrote to her husband, "My Beloved, My Dearest, My Only One." She wrote more the following day: "How to find words to express to you what I feel at this moment. . . . Andrzej is healthy. I love him first of all for the reason that he is yours and for you, with all my strength, force of will, faith, and suffering I did everything that was in my power and beyond my power—so as to return him to you to love with that little part that he has as well from me. . . . I regret nothing, not a moment of suffering in the course of these two years, if only these years have not left any painful scar on you."[88] It was a quixotic hope. A week later, on 1 February 1942, she sent another letter, this time after having received his: "Ol. What to call you! My loved one, my dear one!—You are my Fate, my Destiny, my Life. I give thanks to Providence for that. I laughed and cried, reading your letter. That uncertainty, that perhaps my heart had changed, and yet you offer me all of yourself, all of yourself for the rest of our lives. Ol. I was perhaps never as much yours as in the course of these two years. You did not leave me for even a moment. You were pulling the oxen on the drag-rake with me, and when it seemed to me that I would fall—you and Andrzej called out that you needed me."[89] They discussed how to find one another. Traveling was difficult, and Wat concealed the fact that he did not have the strength to go very far. It was winter in central Asia and hundreds of miles divided them. Finally they reached a decision: Ola and Andrzej would go to Alma-Ata. They set out.

The journey from the south to the Kazakh capital was not an easy one. On a freezing winter night, assisted by sympathetic strangers who helped them to make the necessary bribes, the mother and son boarded an overcrowded train. The air was thick, in semiconsciousness they began to look for a place to sit, and Watowa tried to comfort her son, telling him that now everything would be okay, that they would see his father soon. When he heard her speaking in Polish, a man on the train turned to her, and in that moment she noticed the Polish uniforms of Polish soldiers. It was the Anders army. One of the soldiers pulled Andrzej onto his lap and told Watowa that they were saved, there was an army, Anders. The celebratory atmosphere in that overfilled wagon moved her to tears. The journey to Alma-Ata lasted two days and two nights, but they were joyous days, days of being fed and cared for by Polish soldiers, of singing patriotic songs.[90]

So in March 1942 did Ola Watowa finally reach Alma-Ata. There on the outskirts of the city, she came to a small wooden house, to a dirty room where the corpse of a small child dead of scarlet fever lay. She found an old man with a lit pipe and a woman with a handkerchief tied around her head standing by the stove. She asked about Aleksander Wat. Without a word, the old man nodded his head towards the right, and there in the middle of the second room Ola Watowa saw her husband, writing something. They were both much changed. When she had last seen him getting into the black limousine in front of the restaurant in Lvov he had been thirty-nine years old—young, strong, with dark hair and sparkling eyes. Now he had gone gray, and she saw standing before her a haggard old man. Under his unbuttoned shirt she saw a large black cross. Wat looked at his still young wife and saw a sixty-year-old woman, her skirt riddled with holes, she herself "completely ravaged."[91]

During the night they lay down and whispered to each other of their experiences of the past two years, with the faith that now that they had found each other, nothing bad could happen to them any longer. Wat sent a letter to Krakowski, the man who had adopted him on the train ride from Saratov to Dzhambul, saying that he had found his family, and that his wife had revealed herself to be a "courageous, capable, and truly wonderful woman."[92] Wat brought Ola to meet his Russian friends, the writers who had been evacuated from Moscow as the result of the approaching front and who now gave her a "very warm welcome, the kind only Russians can give."[93] Viktor Shklovsky brought her rice and took her and Andrzej, who had tuberculosis, to see a doctor. And so she joined their group, the Russian intellectuals she saw as "slaves, threatened with prison or the gulag at every moment."[94] It seemed to Wat that the Poles and Polish Jews now in the Soviet Union, however unintentionally, treated the Soviets as subhuman, as oriental, barbarian. Wat was very attached to his own Russian circle, a pocket of space where the otherwise predominant condescension and resentment between Poles and Russians ceased to obtain. Shklovsky and his friends were well educated in philology, and Wat found the level of their conversation to be much higher than that at the Skamandrites' table at Café Ziemiańska. Moreover, even in wartime Kazakhstan, they were quite stylish. It was Mayakovsky, dead for over a decade, who had inducted Wat into this circle, and a newspaper editor as well as a Georgian author writing about Mayakovsky attempted to persuade Wat to write down his reminiscences about his Russian futurist friend, offering to pay him well. Wat refused. He refused even to speak of Mayakovsky, he could not bear anything that had drawn him to communism in his youth.[95]

This period in Alma-Ata was a happy, but nonetheless unstable one. Wat had neither work nor permission to live in the city. Finally the Polish delegate Kazimierz Więcek told Wat that he would be able to employ him, but as a delegate in the distant town of Molotovobad. Wat agreed; and the family set out for the long journey. Yet when they arrived it quickly became apparent that things would turn out badly; moreover the doctor there told Wat that the altitude in Molotovobad was dangerous to his health. Wat sent a telegram to Więcek, saying that he and his family were returning to Alma-Ata. Wat wrote as well to Shklovsky, telling him of the beauty of the landscape in Molotovobad, and asking Shklovsky if he could find him work in Alma-Ata. Shklovsky promised to try, but was not very hopeful, especially since Wat, as a former prisoner, would not get official permission to remain in the Kazakh capital.[96]

On the train heading back to Alma-Ata, the family's luggage was stolen; they returned with nothing. When Wat went to the Polish delegation, he learned that a package had come for him, together with fifteen hundred rubles. Wat suspected that the delegation had also received instructions to employ him in Alma-Ata, because soon he began working there as a school inspector and interpreter. Gifts and supplies began to arrive from England and the United States. Wat found some used clothing among the gifts coming from abroad and took an elegant tan suit for himself and a winter coat for Ola. One day while Wat was working at the delegation, among the Poles who arrived emaciated and in rags there appeared the fervent communist prisoner at Zamarstynów who had informed the prison guard that Wat had been talking to Broniewski through the cell walls. Now he looked at Wat in terror. Wat told him to leave.[97]

This time of Wat's employment in the delegation and the arrival of gifts from abroad was a respite from wartime hunger and the threat of starvation. He, his wife and son lived with a wonderful Russian family in Alma-Ata, whose son was a year older than Andrzej. The two boys became close friends and avid readers, in particular of an old copy of *The Count of Monte Cristo* the family had in the house. The boys would retreat into separate rooms and write each other letters: "Dear Count," "Dear Marquis." Wat foresaw, however, that the reconciliation between the Soviet and the Polish governments was drawing to an end and feared what would follow. He wrote to Broniewski, asking him to try to find a place for Wat in the army: "Władek, get us in too, because we'll die here when the army leaves." Broniewski's reply was not promising: The atmosphere in the Anders army was not good. Wat would be unhappy there.[98]

THE MIDDLE EAST, SPRING 1942 AND BEYOND

When Broniewski had reported for service on 14 April 1942, he was assigned to the Sixth Infantry Division. He was happy to be fighting for Poland at last. The same week he wrote to his daughter, "I feel good in a uniform and in general as if I had rid myself of all worries with the exception of those about you and what will happen with you. I have beautiful cavalryman's pants, but so tight that they're pushing my stomach all the way into my throat. The tunic, on the contrary, is too big and bulges out in the front, as if I were pregnant."[99] Broniewski's initial enthusiasm proved ephemeral. Unlike during his days in Piłsudski's Legions, in the Anders army Broniewski was without close friends; moreover, the other Polish officers bore hostility towards him for his communist past and continued leftist views. On 17 May 1942, after just one month in the army, he wrote to his daughter that he was lonely, that he had failed to become close to the officers, and that he was doing much reading but no writing, as the days were taken up by military exercises and demonic heat and the evenings were without light. In late summer Broniewski was evacuated with the Anders army to the Middle East. Two days before his departure from the Soviet Union, on 17 August 1942, he wrote to Anka that this would be his last letter from his present location; he was setting off into the distant world. He begged her to remember her country and to read Polish literature. "Keep warm, my daughter!" he wrote, "Your mother won't let anything happen to you, and after the war we'll meet in Żoliborz. Remember everything I spoke to you about before my departure, love your country and your father. Read Polish books, look for them in used bookstores and try to speak pure, proper Polish."[100]

At a banquet in Iran, Broniewski recited a poem expressing his longing to return home to Warsaw; to hear the crickets chirping in Żoliborz; to see the Polish flag waving on the ruins of the castle.[101] In December 1942 Anders called Broniewski for a meeting and proposed that, given the hostility of various officers towards him, he accept a long-term military leave. Broniewski would go to Jerusalem to work at the Polish Information Center established there that year. He accepted, and traveled to Jerusalem via Baghdad, Damascus, and Haifa.[102] He had fared better than Janina

FIGURE 12 Władysław Broniewski at the editorial offices of the Polish newspaper *W Drodze* in Jerusalem, 1943. Courtesy of Muzeum Władysława Broniewskiego.

Broniewska's second husband. Soon after his own enlistment Romuald Gadomski was arrested—most likely as a Soviet agent or communist infiltrator—and sent to prison in Palestine. It was only with difficulty that Wasilewska managed to get him released.[103]

In Jerusalem Broniewski found more favorable company than he had among the army officers, and the following six months were prolific ones for him. On 30 May 1943 he wrote to Anka, telling her that his last months in the army had been unpleasant and full of insults, that he had been released on a two-year leave as of February and had reached Jerusalem twelve days later. His immediate future was unclear: an acquaintance in the Polish London government had promised to try to arrange for Broniewski to come to London, but it was unknown what would come of that. Another possibility would be to return to the army when the time came to go to the front; he had asked this of Anders, he did not want to miss the fighting. For the moment, however, Broniewski was happy in Jerusalem, writing well, giving readings, and publishing a new volume of poetry to come out simultaneously in Jerusalem and in London. Moreover, in Palestine he had met many Polish Jews he had once known in Warsaw; they had brought volumes of his poetry with them from Poland, and thus he had texts for his own poetry readings.[104]

As for Palestine itself, Broniewski was not enchanted by religious Jerusalem:

> Some kind of meddlesome market-stall atmosphere of all
> confessions, obtuse and purposeless fanaticism. Christ's grave
> is wholly uninteresting, only Via Dolorosa has a bit of charac-
> ter thanks to the fact that it's remained an alley where, like
> two thousand years ago, there reigns squalor, hubbub, and
> commerce, something like Miła Street at home. And this is
> precisely the authentic background of the tragedy from two
> thousand years ago, which our own time has surpassed a
> million times over. How many political prisoners do we have
> today who are crucified one way or another? My daughter,
> I don't believe much in progress. The Wailing Wall is a bunch
> of old stones, which at one time constituted the foundation
> stones of Solomon's Temple. Jews come there and sob in-
> tensively. Tedium.[105]

Nor was he very impressed with the more modern Tel Aviv, largely the work of Polish Jews, which he described to his daughter as "something like several Żoliborzes taken together, but shoddier and without character."[106] Broniewski's heart was with the kibbutzniks, the socialists, the idealists. He told Anka of his visit to a kibbutz, "a socialist agricultural collective, something like a kolkhoz." Socialism amidst capitalism did not seem "constructive" to him, yet he nonetheless felt sympathy and admiration for the kibbutzniks. About Zionism more broadly he remained uncertain. He told Anka: "Jews here speak in Hebrew and when one hears children speaking in that antiquated, dead language, children who don't know how to speak in any other language, one believes that they will grow up to be the future creators of culture and the Jewish state. After all, the devil knows, because there are twice as many Arabs here as Jews, and it's unclear how everything will turn out after the war."[107]

If Broniewski's time in Soviet incarceration had disillusioned him about communism in practice, his experience in the Anders army had repelled him from the anticommunists as well. In an interview published in Tel Aviv in 1943, Broniewski was asked if his time in prison had altered his leftist views. He answered unequivocally: "There is no prison that can induce a renunciation of ideals. It seems to me that I have not changed at all as far as my views are concerned. Given that I found myself there under lock and key, then something must have changed there. In liberated Poland I will continue to fight for the realization of social postulates, renouncing absolutely nothing. The preliminary condition, however, for changes in the Poland of the future is the battle for her liberation, for her independence. I am ready at any moment to devote my life to that."[108] In Jerusalem in 1943 Broniewski remained as he had been in Lvov in 1939: committed to both Polish patriotism and socialism, persuaded that the two could—and would—be reconciled.

KUIBYSHEV, 1942

After Broniewski's release from prison, he and Wasilewska made efforts to move Janina Broniewska from the pig farm where she had been working near Kuibyshev.[109] Wasilewska was concerned about all of her colleagues—even those she did not particularly like—and she was especially concerned about Janina Broniewska. She sent vitamins from the front.[110] Then in March 1942, Alfred Lampe surprised Broniewska with news that he and Wasilewska were reincarnating *Nowe Widnokręgi,* which had ceased publication in summer 1941. Now Lampe told Broniewska to come with him to Moscow to discuss the details with Wasilewska. Janina Broniewska, modestly, asked how she would be useful. She felt "only too well the whole distance between us despite our personal friendship. Alfred is our brain, our political-ideological teacher. A member of the Central Committee of the KPP." He reassured her, telling her not to talk nonsense, that he would feel better having her along. "With one smile," she wrote, "he silences my fuss. He has a very particular smile. With such a smile one can put a person back on his feet. Well, and so he did. We're off."[111]

It was cold in Moscow, although it was already April. Janina Broniewska walked with Wasilewska through the city as the sidewalks began to freeze over with ice. "I cling to Wanda," Broniewska wrote,

Now we walk along arm-in-arm in unison. We look like a very affectionate married couple. Wanda has her hair cut short, she

has a fur cap, a military trench coat and the badges of a colonel.
A very handsome and stately colonel. And suddenly we pause
on the icy Moscow sidewalk.

This dialogue follows:

ı: Why, just think, Dziuńka, why think . . .

WANDA: . . . if someone had told us so three years ago
in Warsaw . . .

ı: that you would be wearing the uniform of a Red Army
colonel . . .

WANDA: . . . that I would be walking with you with
this ladies' kerchief on my head along the streets of
Moscow . . .

BOTH OF US AT ONCE: . . . What life manages to think
up . . . [112]

Very quickly an editorial staff for the new *Nowe Widnokręgi* was gathered
in Kuibyshev. Wasilewska was the formal editor-in-chief and would fly in
from time to time from the front, while Lampe fulfilled the actual func-
tions of chief editor. Broniewska worked alongside Lampe; the whole
staff was squeezed into two small rooms and worked from early in the
morning until late at night.[113] Lampe quickly made contact with Jakub
Berman in Ufa.[114]

The first issue of the new *Nowe Widnokręgi* appeared in May 1942.[115]
The paper had been transformed. Now no longer a literary monthly directed at the intelligentsia, the Kuibyshev *Nowe Widnokręgi* was a biweekly
social-political newspaper intended more broadly for Poles living in the
Soviet Union. By this time Polish-Soviet diplomatic relations had resumed
and there was a Polish embassy in Kuibyshev; *Nowe Widnokręgi* needed
to strike a delicate balance between Polish patriotism and pro-Soviet par-
tisanship. The newspaper also served as a center for correspondence and
communication among Poles dispersed throughout the Soviet Union. The
editorial staff received large numbers of letters, and Stefan Jędrychowski
and Broniewska as a rule answered all of them, privately by post.[116]

The role Janina Broniewska now played far exceeded anything she had
done in interwar Poland. She adapted well. Like Wasilewska, Broniewska
wore her hair short during the war. One day in May 1942, during the first
weeks of the reconstituted *Nowe Widnokręgi*, she was looking at herself

in the mirror when her daughter Anka, unhappy with her mother's appearance, said, "Mom, you don't have to make yourself look older than you are. That hair—you're a veritable nun." Broniewska, however, was of the opinion that this "wartime elegance" would have to do and set off for the editorial offices.[117] No longer was Anka left home alone with her much younger brother Stanisław; her mother had acquired a third child as well: Wasilewska's daughter Ewa, whom Wasilewska had given her friend "as a wartime deposit" before setting off again to the front.[118] Broniewska, for her part, bore no resentment of her politically inferior position; on the contrary she subordinated herself to Wasilewska's instructions with enormous affection. There in Kuibyshev in 1942, Broniewska knew nothing about what was happening in Poland. She assumed there were comrades carrying out the antifascist war at home, but she did not know their names or even their pseudonyms. She understood that Wasilewska and Lampe must know, but willingly conformed to their implicit, internal discipline and never asked more questions than were appropriate. The women's closeness did not suffer. From the front Wasilewska sent letters, and Broniewska wrote of the friends' separation then: "And who knows, if once again in some kind of mystical way we didn't feel ourselves beside each other, as during those wanderings along Marszałkowska Street of long ago?"[119]

Wasilewska and her husband Korneichuk did come to Kuibyshev for a month during the summer of 1942. Stalin desired from the couple some literary works about the war, and both were obliging. There in Kuibyshev in July, Korneichuk wrote the play *Front* (The Front), and Wasilewska wrote the novel *Tęcza* (The Rainbow).[120] *The Rainbow*, despite its hurried composition, came to play a significant role as literary propaganda for the Soviet side. A film was quickly made and shown with great success both in the Soviet Union and abroad. After its premiere in New York, Wasilewska's old friend from Cracow, the economist Oskar Lange, sent telegrams of congratulations.[121] The novel was set in a Ukrainian village where the men had already gone off to fight, and the women and children were left alone to experience the brutality of the German occupation. It was a story of the solidarity, patriotism, and superhuman will of the peasants who refused to collaborate regardless of what was done to them. *The Rainbow* was not pure socialist realism; it relied more on a certain unadulterated sentimentality, facilitated by an omniscient narrator who delved into the

minds of not only the heroic peasants, but also the Germans and in particular the leading German officer's Russian whore-collaborator, Pussy.
The work was very much the imaginative embodiment of Wasilewska's
speeches, and a reflection of the purity of the Manichean universe she
inhabited. Yet it was in some sense a feminist story as well, portraying
the loyalty of the women and children to their men in battle, but above
all showing how the peasant women emerged as the greatest heroes, the
ones who were strongest and most self-sacrificing, who could endure and
survive the worst hells. In the end, it was these women and children who,
together with the returning Red Army and Soviet partisans, liberated the
village.[122] When *The Rainbow* won the Stalin Prize, Wasilewska donated
her prize money to fund a Soviet airplane. She asked that the airplane be
named "Warsaw." Stalin sent her a note, promising that her wish would
be granted.[123]

WARSAW UNDER GERMAN OCCUPATION

Jarosław Iwaszkiewicz's own instances of prewar antisemitism notwithstanding, during the war he devoted himself to hiding Jews in and around
his home in Stawisko, just outside of Warsaw. Iwaszkiewicz's wife Anna
secured false documents for those in hiding. She knew someone in the
community who "drank with the Germans." The Iwaszkiewiczes paid
him, he bought vodka, and the German officer stationed there stamped
the documents. Of Anna's wartime activities Iwaszkiewicz's daughter
said, "My mother was very courageous, although my father would say
that with women this isn't courage, but only a lack of imagination."[124] In
his own wartime journal, Iwaszkiewicz devoted much space to reminiscences. On 29 November 1943, he wrote in his diary on the anniversary
of Skamander's debut:

> Today twenty-five years have passed since the opening of
> Pikador! Tuwim, Wierzyński, Lechoń are in America, Słonim-
> ski in London, I am alone in this pitiable castle. What fates
> have awaited, persecuted, oppressed us during these twenty-
> five years. The beginning was a true revolution. 'Poetry, to the
> street!'—my friends called out. Not I, I was always cautious. . . .
> I'm curious if they, there, this evening, are remembering this
> anniversary? Are they reflecting upon it, did they remember?

How many things separated and separate us—but how many
connect us! That day long ago, 29 November 1918, joined us.
A far-away day—yet memorable, vivid, a day that still flows
with the blood in our veins. It was good, that beginning![125]

News of Iwaszkiewicz's friends was intermittent and scattered. Soon
after the January 1940 arrests of Wat, Broniewski, Peiper and Stern, the
story appeared in an underground song in Warsaw.[126] The news of the arrests was not the only thing to travel back to Warsaw from Lvov. Marysia
Zarębińska and her daughter Majka returned as well. It was not an auspicious decision: in 1943 Zarębińska was arrested by the Germans and sent
to Auschwitz.[127] Mieczysław Braun, Broniewski's old poet friend from
Łódź, had also fled to Lvov during the first months of the war, but returned
in January 1940 to the German zone, where his wife had remained, and
spent the early months of the occupation in Warsaw. In autumn 1940 the
Nazi authorities ordered all Jews in Warsaw to move to a segregated area
of the city. Irena Krzywicka made the decision not to go; Tadeusz Boy-
Żeleński's wife took her in until she had found another place to live in
hiding. In July 1941, Krzywicka was awakened by a man's footsteps. She
got out of bed, but no one was there. She felt a premonition then: her
lover had died. And in fact he had. The Nazis had arrested Boy-Żeleński
in Lvov and shot him.[128]

After the Germans ordered all Warsaw Jews into the ghetto, a friend
offered to hide Braun in his apartment in the Mokotów district, but Braun
declined. He and his wife both went to the Warsaw ghetto. With each passing day conditions in the ghetto grew worse. The streets were filled with
emaciated children begging for food and the corpses of those who had
starved to death. Braun worked in the post office and continued to write
poetry. He sent letters to friends on the other side of the wall, letters in
which he wrote about Polish literature, about Joseph Conrad, Adam Mickiewicz and Stefan Żeromski.[129] In early 1942, Braun fell ill with spotted
typhus. He died in the ghetto in the first days of February.[130]

In the Warsaw ghetto together with Braun were Jakub Berman's two
brothers, Mieczysław and Adolf, both Zionists. The outbreak of the Second
World War was the moment when Adolf, the youngest brother who had
once been part of Wasilewska's Popular Front gatherings, came into his
own. During the initial bombardment of Warsaw, he dragged children

out from under the fallen debris and found food and shelter for them. When the ghetto was formed, he organized housing, food kitchens and underground schools. The moment when the news reached the ghetto of the German attack on the Soviet Union was a magical one for Adolf Berman. Now the anguish of the Molotov-Ribbentrop pact had passed and he watched as orthodox Jews prayed for the Red Army to save them from the Nazi hell. When the dissolved KPP was reconstituted as the Polish Workers' Party in the Soviet Union, the Polish-Jewish communist Józef Lewartowski arrived in the Warsaw ghetto to organize left-wing activists there. Adolf Berman joined him at once.[131]

In January 1943, Mieczysław Berman was gassed in Treblinka, together with his wife.[132] He was not the first one in the Berman family to die in the gas chambers. His father, his sister Anna, who was a beautiful and quiet Germanist, Anna's husband, and their six-year-old daughter had gone with earlier transports.[133] By January 1943, Adolf Berman was no longer in the ghetto. In September 1942, he and his wife Basia had managed to cross to the so-called Aryan Side.[134] There they established contacts with the *Armia Ludowa* (People's Army), the Polish communist partisans, as well as with the *Armia Krajowa* (Home Army), the anti-Nazi Polish underground associated with the government-in-exile in London.[135] His liaison with the Home Army was the young Catholic activist Władysław Bartoszewski, recently returned from Auschwitz, where he had been imprisoned early in the war. Now the young Catholic patriot and the older Marxist Zionist joined together in the creation of the Żegota, the Home Army's Council for Aid to the Jews.[136]

Żegota had no contact with the Jewish Combat Organization that was preparing for an uprising in the Warsaw ghetto, as that was the responsibility of a different branch of the Home Army.[137] Adolf Berman, however, filled multiple roles and maintained contacts on behalf of the Jewish Combat Organization with the communist underground as well. He thereby placed himself in an ethically and logistically problematic position amidst two rival undergrounds, which at this moment were already on the verge of a civil war. The People's Army wanted a communist Poland; the Home Army feared that Soviet occupation could follow Nazi occupation. Adolf Berman could have been shot by the Home Army as a traitor. He never spoke of his communist connections to Bartoszewski, but the younger man suspected his involvement: "But I knew and it very much disturbed me, internally, that [Adolf] Berman most likely was working with the communists in the anti-Nazi underground. . . . Well, I explained it to myself by reasoning that the Jews were in such a desperate situation that they were looking for contacts absolutely everywhere possible. But I have to say that it bothered me. It was never said openly, but of course various things are known that are not spoken of openly."[138] Adolf Berman was bold and idealistic, perhaps naïve, unquestionably energetic and determined. He believed in the solidarity of those who were on the side of good. "He was a fool," said Marek Edelman, a Bundist commander of the Warsaw Ghetto Uprising. Edelman added: "You can't dance at two weddings at once."[139]

MOSCOW, 1943–1944

In January 1943, Wanda Wasilewska and Alfred Lampe sent a letter from Kuibyshev to Vyacheslav Molotov, the Soviet commissar for foreign affairs. Some kind of central organization to coordinate Polish affairs in the Soviet Union was necessary, they told him. The letter pointed to the anti-Soviet tendencies predominant among many Polish groupings and argued that, given the various institutions at the disposal of the "reactionary and anti-Soviet Polish emigration," a counterweight to these forces was needed in the form of an organized center of pro-Soviet, "progressive elements." Wasilewska and Lampe further noted that many Poles in the Soviet Union had experienced repression and were not favorably disposed towards the Soviet Union, and that even many Poles who had not undergone repression did not possess equal rights in the Soviet Union—they were not accepted into the army or for work in war industries—and were bitter towards the Soviet government. Given this, Lampe and Wasilewska argued, the need for a central coordinating body was all the greater.[140]

A few weeks later, in late January 1943, Wasilewska and Korneichuk were on their way from Saratov to Stalingrad when they were suddenly called back to Moscow. Wasilewska was unhappy about the summons. In November 1942 the Soviet army had gone on the counteroffensive in Stalingrad; by late January 1943 General Paulus, despite Hitler's orders, was preparing to surrender, and Wasilewska wanted to be with the Red Army at this moment of triumph. When the couple arrived in Moscow Korneichuk was told that Stalin was waiting to see him. When Korneichuk returned from that meeting, he told Wasilewska that Stalin had asked him whether she was "willing to go to all lengths to help us with the Polish question?" Korneichuk was surprised that Stalin would even feel he needed to ask. The answer was obvious: absolutely. Then Stalin told him that it would likely soon come to a "decisive conflict" between the Polish government in London and the Soviet Union, and in that situation Wasilewska "would be able to do very much." Conversations with Stalin and Molotov followed about establishing a new publication to be named *Wolna Polska* (Free Poland), which should not appear to be the initiative of only a few people, but rather such as to attract all of the Poles in the Soviet Union. Given this, it was necessary to create an organization behind the publication. Stalin suggested the name *Związek Patriotów Polskich* (Union of Polish Patriots). Wasilewska was dissatisfied. She explained to Stalin that the word "patriot" was quite compromised in Polish by its association with nationalism. But Stalin reassured her: every word could be imbued with new content. By this time, there were some Polish communists already in Moscow; a large group remained in Kuibyshev, and Wasilewska made the decision to move the whole editorial staff of *Nowe Widnokręgi* to Moscow so as to create a large editorial center there.[141]

So in March 1943 did Janina Broniewska pack her things and set off for Moscow.[142] There *Nowe Widnokręgi*'s editorial offices found a new home in a couple of old rooms near the square named after Feliks Dzierżyński. Initially there were two editorial offices and two editorial staffs, one for *Nowe Widnokręgi* and one for *Wolna Polska,* but given that the same people were writing for both papers, the distinction was less than clear.[143] By the time Broniewska arrived in Moscow, the first issue of *Wolna Polska* had already appeared, including a statement by the Union of Polish Patriots announcing its task of gathering all Poles on Soviet lands to fight for an independent, democratic Poland liberated from the Nazi yoke.[144] The international context was changing quickly. On 25 April 1943 the Soviet Union severed diplomatic relations with the Polish government in London. The pretext was the massacre in the Katyń forest of some 15,000 Polish officers, including Irena Krzywicka's husband. The Soviet Union insisted the massacre was the doing of the Germans; the Polish government suspected the Soviets.[145] Three days later, Wasilewska gave a radio broadcast announcing the break in diplomatic relations and declaring that General Sikorski's government-in-exile did not represent the Polish nation.[146] She maintained that the severing of diplomatic relations did not equal a change in the relationship of the Soviet government to Poles as a nation or to Poles in the Soviet Union. The question of whether or not they would return to Poland, she announced via radio, would not be decided by this or that passport or by this or that piece of paper, but rather by their attitude, their behavior, their participation in the battle against fascism. The reference was a particular one: there was a large group of Poles who, even under coercion, refused to accept Soviet passports.[147]

It was the time of Wanda Wasilewska's unparalleled power. Jerzy Borejsza arrived in Moscow in late June 1943 and joined *Wolna Polska*'s editorial staff only with great reluctance. He had come to Moscow as an officer in the Red Army, and was deeply offended to learn that now Wasilewska would be his superior and would decide in what capacity he was needed.[148] Stalin granted Wasilewska much freedom in decision-making, and not everyone was happy with her decisions. In April 1943, as the Nazis undertook the final liquidation of the Jewish quarter, the Jewish Combat Organization began an uprising in the Warsaw ghetto, aided by Wasilewska's old friend from Popular Front gatherings, Adolf Berman. While communist partisans in Warsaw supported the Jewish resistance, *Wolna Polska*'s priorities were elsewhere; the paper published nothing. An editor at *Wolna Polska,* however, broke down and told Julian Stryjkowski of the Jewish uprising. Stryjkowski was stunned: "As a communist I did not feel myself to be a Jew. A communist is not a Jew. The death from one day to the next of any nation would be a shock. But what happened in Warsaw returned my Jewishness to me."[149] Stryjkowski—unknown then as a writer—himself had joined the newspaper's small circle after making his way to Moscow. He slept in a collective hotel room for the editorial staff, where he met Tadeusz Peiper. Having been released from prison in the wake of the amnesty, Peiper was now writing for *Wolna Polska.*

Stryjkowski soon had the occasion himself to meet Wanda Wasilewska, "the great personality with a very complex psyche" towards whom he felt a respect tinged with awe.[150] The occasion was not an auspicious one. It was the evening of the All-Slav Congress in Moscow, and Stryjkowski was proofreading the next issue of *Wolna Polska*, which had to be ready early for the congress' opening. A Russian journalist had written a feuilleton for *Wolna Polska* under the pseudonym "The Observer," taking advantage of the fact that writing for the Polish newspaper—given the attempt to build a broad coalition of Poles dispersed throughout the Soviet Union—gave him more freedom of expression than he would have otherwise had in the

Soviet press. At this moment a significant battle was expected in a certain area. Until this time there had, however, been silence on this topic. "The Observer" took advantage of this silence in a feuilleton where, like a chess player, he foresaw the movements of the German and Soviet forces. The censor removed the article. Stryjkowski, however, who had been awake all night frantically trying to prepare the issue for the printer in time, failed to recall the censor's decision. A scandal resulted: all the delegates to the Congress had now read the text that was to have been censored. Now in terror Stryjkowski waited for the verdict. His superior, Wiktor Grosz, came to him then to say that Wasilewska would talk to him on Thursday, that he should only listen to her and say nothing.[151]

Thursday came. "Wanda Wasilewska," Julian Stryjkowski wrote, "in the uniform of a Soviet colonel, stood behind the desk, tensed, tall, slim, masculine, severe, with an oblong face and a long nose, and small eyes with black-rings from lack of sleep, and I on the other side of the desk small, pale, with a strong determination to be silent, to behave decently, with dignity." They stood opposite one another. A long moment passed.

Wiktor could not endure it and hid behind a curtain like Polonius in *Hamlet*.

Wanda lit a cigarette. Apparently she didn't know how to begin. It was one of the human moments in her life.

The mass orator began with difficulty. She was unnerved. She hesitated.

I waited calmly. I was in a better situation than Wanda Wasilewska, the second person after Stalin. I knew from Wiktor that I wasn't under any threat. With her beautiful alto voice, with which she seduced men and crowds at meetings, she called out:

"You idiot, don't be a fool. Get out of there!"

Wiktor, shamefaced, abandoned his hiding spot.

As a former teacher, Wanda Wasilewska took advantage of that intermezzo to assume a mentorial pose, deprived of Soviet pedagogical sweetness. For a moment there was a waft of Austro-Hungarian Cracow and the home of the foreign affairs minister, Wanda's father, the Piłsudczyk, the scholar Leon Wasilewski. I didn't take advantage of the moment to call out: Wanda, my friend, I, too, was a teacher like you, a Polonist like you, an Austrian subject like you. So much connects us! We were born in the same year!

"Are you, my comrade, aware of what you have done? Actually, what you did not do?" she corrected herself as if she were a pedagogue confessing to an error.

I looked at Wiktor. Should I say something or not?

Wiktor nodded his head.

"Yes," I confessed with the contrition of a grammar school pupil.

"And the potential threat to you?"

I didn't look at Wiktor and I was silent.

"It's better that you didn't know."

"How could he have known?" Wiktor unexpectedly intervened.

Wanda aimed a harsh look at him.

"I didn't ask you. But such a chatterbox as you could have told him."

"I myself didn't know," Wiktor defended himself. "If I had said it, it wouldn't have been anything bad, anything against the Party."

Wiktor's presence served me like a lightening rod. Wanda's anger was directed against him.

"You can . . ."—Wanda controlled her perturbation with difficulty—"please, don't waste time, write—go sit and write your own satirical feuilleton. The last one didn't make me terribly . . ."

Wiktor left.

Wanda lit a second cigarette. Now it was coming to me.

"So you, comrade, didn't understand the potential threat to you. . . . If what happened to you were to happen to a Soviet comrade . . . it would end differently, completely differently. . . . But our attitude to comrades is one of *li* . . ."

"*litością* [mercy]," I finished in spirit.

"*Li*beralism," Wanda Wasilewska finished her sentence.[152]

NEW YORK, 1943–1944

The courage Julian Tuwim had so admired in Wanda Wasilewska and Janina Broniewska became his only on the other side of the Atlantic. Now on the Upper West Side of Manhattan, Julian Tuwim became an *engagé* poet in a way he had never been in Poland. In March 1942, the Polish communist Bolesław Gebert invited him to a celebration in Detroit on the occasion of the tenth anniversary of the Polonia Association there. Tuwim and his wife refused to stay in a hotel; they wanted to stay with a real worker, and so accepted the hospitality of a proletarian immigrant from Warsaw who worked at an auto factory. There in Detroit Tuwim spoke of how moved he was to have forged a new union with the working class. "'I am a child from Łódź, from the great factory city of Łódź . . . and so in fact I was formed and I grew up in the atmosphere of the Polish proletariat,'" he told the Polish workers in Michigan. He told them as well that they would fight together against fascism for a new, better world, a world raised from the ruins by their own hands. When he had finished speaking, some twelve hundred people gave the poet in exile a standing ovation. Afterwards Tuwim told Gebert, "This was the first time in my life that I, a child from Łódź, spoke to workers and they understood me. They trust me and value my poetry. This is a great joy."[153]

In early 1943 the news reached Tuwim that the Polish Bundist leaders Henryk Erlich and Wiktor Alter had been put to death in Soviet Russia.[154] In March Grydzewski sent Tuwim a telegram from London: "I await your article or poem concerning Alter and Erlich."[155] Grydzewski waited in vain. Tuwim refused. In April 1943 he wrote to his sister in London, "Like you, I experienced and experience painfully the affair of Erlich and Alter (I don't believe that they're guilty—and I don't believe that they're not guilty; a lovely situation from the point of view of reason and conscience; but such times have come that one has to live with absurdities even of this kind)." He added that neither this affair nor others could shake his "deepest conviction, that only and exclusively on Russia, on agreement, on friendship with Russia . . . does our national future depend." Given this, he asked that she convey to Grydzewski that he would write neither a poem nor an article about the Bundists, and told her to remind his former editor of what the Polish Renaissance poet Jan Kochanowski had once written:

Niezłe czasem zamilczeć, co człowieka boli,
By nie znał nieprzyjaciel, że cię ma po woli.

At times it is not bad to be silent about what pains one
So that the enemy does not know that he has you in his
    power.[156]

As Tuwim became estranged from his old friends, he sought out new
ones "on the left side of the barricade." In a June 1944 letter to a Polish
socialist worker who had emigrated to the United States in 1902, Tuwim
revisited his own political history, reflecting on his youthful enchantment
with Piłsudski and the tragedy of Poland:

> The more I reflect upon the events and spirit of that period
> —of the period when Piłsudski, openly or covertly, dominated
> —the more I'm ensconced in wonder that we, contemporaries,
> allowed ourselves to be so dazed and asphyxiated by the "ro-
> mantic fluids" that Piłsudski radiated. I openly confess that I,
> too, for a long time belonged to the asphyxiated ones. Many
> reasons played into that, among others: an intoxication with
> independence, an emotional wading in various historical false-
> hoods taken in by my generation, the terrific ballast of poetry
> and "mysticism," which we, most unnecessarily, accepted from
> the nineteenth century, instead of freeing ourselves of it—that
> is, placing it where it belonged: in the sphere of artistic, literary
> jewels—we deluded ourselves and others that we were some
> kind of singularity in history, that we had some such "historical
> missions," "destinies," and similar bagatelles. It was as if
> Piłsudski were the embodiment of all these turbid and hollow
> (speaking as one does in Warsaw) "ideas."[157]

Tuwim drew nearer as well to the economist Oskar Lange, an old
friend of Wasilewska who was now an American citizen, and who, in
April 1944, paid a visit to their mutual friends in Moscow. Stalin had not
been in favor of the visit. Lange was an American suspiciously close to
American president Franklin Roosevelt, and Stalin did not trust him.
Wasilewska, however, did, and was insistent. In the end Stalin relented
—and acknowledged afterwards that Wasilewska had been right. When
Lange returned to the United States, he brought with him a letter for

Tuwim from Janina Broniewska.[158] Tuwim was very happy to receive it; his heart was very much with his old friends who were now in Moscow. After the Red Army's victory at Stalingrad in February 1943, the war had turned. Now it was the Soviet Union that was on the offensive, pushing the Germans back westwards. In late July 1944, as the Red Army approached Warsaw, Tuwim sent a telegram to Ehrenburg in awkward English: "Three years ago during the darkest hours of the heroic struggle of the soviet people I sent to You and to russian writers words full of faith in future victory over the teutonic barbarians stop Today in the bright hour of fulfillment when the indomitable Red Army approaches the very heart of Poland and brings the liberation of my people I share with You the immense joy when the right cause triumphs over the evil one stop."[159] In 1943 Polish Prime Minister Sikorski had died in an airplane crash in Gibraltar. Stanisław Mikołajczyk of the Polish Peasant Party succeeded him, and the following year planned a trip to Moscow in spite of the absence of diplomatic relations. In August 1944, Tuwim wrote to Oskar Lange that whatever the outcome of Mikołajczyk's trip to Moscow, the London government would soon cease to have a deciding voice. Tuwim was confident that rather it was Warsaw who would decide, "and so most likely our friends." At the same time, speculating about the future composition of the Polish government, he bemoaned the fact that Lange was an American citizen and so would be unable to hold any leading office in Poland. As for himself, he added, "In all likelihood I don't need to explain to you that personally I'm not considering any 'post' or 'office.' For four reasons: 1) I don't know how to; 2) I don't like to; 3) I can't; 4) I don't want to. Moreover: I will return to the homeland at the first opportunity—and to the highest office—the office of poet."[160]

In December 1944 Tuwim, clinging to those of his old friends who now found themselves on his side of the "red barricade," sent an emotional letter to Słonimski in London. Tuwim thought often of Słonimski and believed that alliances between the London government and rightwing Polish émigrés must have removed any remnants of illusions Słonimski might have had about "the socialism of London socialists and the democracy of National Democrats." As for Tuwim, he called these forces, in a satirical twist on the nineteenth-century Polish insurrectionary slogan "for your freedom and ours," those battling "for your fascism and ours."[161] For Tuwim the war years were a time of redefining his loyalties as well as his identity. In 1944 his open letter *My Żydzi polscy* (We, Polish Jews), addressed to "my Mother in Poland or her most beloved shadow," was published in Tel Aviv. The essay, written under the spell of the news of the Holocaust, began:

> And at once I hear the question "Where does the 'We' come from?" A question to a certain extent justified. It's posed to me by Jews, to whom I've always explained that I'm a Pole, and now it will be posed to me by Poles, for an illustrious majority of whom I am and will be a Jew. So here is an answer for the former and the latter.
>
> I am a Pole, because it so pleases me. This is strictly my private affair, of which I have no intention of rendering to anyone an account, or explicating, explaining or justifying. I do not divide Poles into "indigenous" and "nonindigenous," leaving that to indigenous and nonindigenous racists, to native and non-native Nazis. I divide Poles, like Jews, and like other nations, into the wise and the stupid, the honest people and the criminals, the intelligent and the obtuse, the interesting and the boring, the injurious and the injured, gentlemen and non-gentlemen, etc. . . .
>
> I could say that on the political level I divide Poles into antisemites and antifascists. Because fascism is always antisemitism. Antisemitism is the international language of fascists.[162]

For Tuwim writing from New York in the wake of the Holocaust, being a Pole was "neither an honor, nor a source of pride, nor or a privilege. It's the same with breathing. I've yet to meet anyone who is proud of the fact that he breathes."[163] Having titled his letter *We, Polish Jews,* Tuwim went on to list the reasons for his Polishness: because he was born, and grew up, and first fell in love in Poland, in Polish; because poetry came to him with Polish words; because when he died he wanted to be buried in Polish soil; because he took from Poles some of their national faults; because his hatred for Polish fascists was greater than his hatred for fascists of other nationalities.

He anticipated a response: "'Good. But if a Pole, then in that case why 'We, Jews?'" He answered: it had to do with blood.[164] No, he defended himself, this was not racism. The blood that made him a Jew was not the blood of genetic kinship that ran in his veins but rather the spilled blood of millions of innocent people. It was from this position that he now spoke to the Jews: "Accept me, Brothers, to that honorable brotherhood of Innocently Spilled Blood. To that community, to that church I want, beginning today, to belong."[165] He wrote of a Poland where the Star of David sewn on the armbands worn by Jews in the ghetto would become one of the highest distinctions, awarded to the bravest Polish soldiers. The murder of Polish Jewry had made Tuwim a Jew. "So with pride," he wrote to his mother, no longer living, "with mournful pride we will bear that rank, eclipsing all others—the rank of Polish Jew—we, who miraculously and arbitrarily have remained alive. With pride? Let us say rather: with contrite and biting shame. Because it fell to us for your suffering, for your glory." He revised, at the end, his original title: "And so perhaps not," he wrote, "'We, Polish Jews,' but rather 'We, Specters; we, Shadows of our murdered brothers, Polish Jews.'"[166] The great Polish poet Julian Tuwim, who in his youth had been repulsed by "black Hassidic rabble," had come to communism and to Jewishness together.

MOSCOW, JANUARY 1943–MAY 1944

The Union of Polish Patriots was largely Wasilewska's creation, the product of the unusual relationship she had developed with Stalin. She had a special telephone, a direct line to Stalin, and she was the Polish milieu's only personal contact with the Soviet leadership. Jakub Berman supposed that despite Wasilewska's "sense of mission," she must have been somewhat disconcerted by the fact that she, a former PPS activist, was taking the place of KPP members. She was at least aware that some Polish communists resented her for this reason. Jakub Berman was not among them; he was grateful she was able to do so much. In her own mind Wasilewska built her relationship with Stalin on the principle of partnership.[167] As to how Stalin perceived their relationship, and whether he genuinely liked Wasilewska, Jakub Berman reflected with some laughter: "Presumably he liked his daughter, but as to Wanda, it's hard to say. The familiarity that grew up between them required a lot of moral courage on Wanda's part, and she had that courage, perhaps to a greater extent than did KPP members, since she wasn't used to the extremely strict discipline that was deeply rooted in Polish communists, sometimes restricting their freedom of expression. But in my opinion Stalin's positive attitude towards Wanda flowed from his sense of realism; Stalin was very calculated in his actions, and he valued people who were useful and necessary to him."[168] Jakub Berman was chosen as secretary of the domestic section of the Union of Polish Patriots, and he grew very close to Wasilewska. When asked if he had been Wasilewska's lover, Jakub Berman answered obliquely, "Who knows, perhaps that was the case. That, however, is not the point."[169]

In Moscow, Janina Broniewska filled the role of "female butler" during long gatherings over much coffee with Lampe and others at Wasilewska's Moscow apartment.[170] In spring 1943, during one of these meetings, they discussed the possibility of forming a Polish army division to fight along-side the Red Army.[171] In April Wasilewska sent a respectful, albeit asser-tive letter to Stalin in which she insisted that "the time has come when the creation of a Polish army unit has become simply a necessity."[172] The decision came that same month. Jerzy Putrament and the others were at Wasilewska's apartment when the telephone rang. Wasilewska went into the next room, the others listened to her responses in Russian: "Yes, yes, yes . . . tomorrow at one. Yes, I understand. Well, yes, of course you understand what this means to me." When she returned to her guests she was changed. She told them there had been a decision. A moment of silence followed. Then Putrament stood up, went over to Wasilewska, and kissed her on the cheek. There was joy in the room. They would have their own army division.[173]

Thereafter things moved quickly. Only two weeks after the break in Polish-Soviet diplomatic relations Julian Stryjkowski was proofreading the announcement of the creation of the First Division of the Polish Army. The Union of Polish Patriots was ecstatic. Jerzy Putrament and Adam Ważyk "exchanged their pen for a rifle" and joined the Polish division.[174] Wasilewska quickly assumed the role of commander, giving orders to her best friend—which Janina Broniewska happily followed. Soon she was awakened in the middle of the night by the telephone. Wasilewska was calling: "Jasia? You'll make a sketch of the regulation military uniform by tomorrow. The Polish one. Exactly—" "I'll make the sketch. Yes, sir," Broniewska answered. Before long Wasilewska called again, asking her for two sketches of a military banner with the text "First Division in the Name of Tadeusz Kościuszko" on one side and the slogan "For Our Free-dom and Yours" on the other. Wasilewska ordered her friend to hurry.[175]

By the time the first congress of the Union of Polish Patriots was held in Moscow on 9–10 June 1943, the Polish army division was already in existence. Wasilewska and her colleagues summoned Poles dispersed throughout the Soviet Union, locating sympathizers by drawing on the files of letters written to *Nowe Widnokręgi*. The Union of Polish Patriots cast its net widely, turning as well to Poles who had never even been communist sympathizers. These included the Zionist leader Emil Sommerstein and the Polish Peasant Party delegate of the London government Andrzej Witos, who joined the Union of Polish Patriots after Wasilewska extracted him from a Soviet prison camp.[176] Notwithstanding her own dogmatism and uncompromising character, this Popular Front ethos was what Wasilewska did best.

The lack of news from the home front tormented her.[177] When Wasilewska opened the first congress by speaking of how the Germans were destroying "all that is Polish," she herself knew little of the Nazi occupation in Poland. She never believed that her loyalty to the Soviet Union could compromise her Polish patriotism. When she addressed the congress, she called on Poles in the Soviet Union to help the Polish homeland:

> At home a bloody battle is going on, and we're living as if on the margins of events. The homeland must have asked itself the question: What are the Poles in the Soviet Union doing for us? When will the Polish army appear on the eastern front? This state of affairs was the basis on which the Union of Polish Patriots was born. People were aware that it is not acceptable to stand on the sidelines when the nation is fighting for its existence. We also want to work and fight. It would be to our shame if we were to wait until other people brought us freedom. The Union of Polish Patriots has come into being to organize all Poles on Soviet territory. The Union turned to the Soviet government with the request to create a Polish armed force. The Soviet government has given its approval and is giving us all the means to create an army. The Union of Polish Patriots should work in such a way as to preserve the good name of Poland. We should develop Polish culture. We have Polish children, who should return home as Poles.[178]

Wasilewska emphasized the need for loyalty to the Soviet Union, Poland's greatest friend and defender. She told participants in the congress: "None of us—neither today nor in the future—may forget for a moment that the Soviet Union gave us the opportunity to participate in the armed battle against the German invasion and the possibility to preserve Polish culture, today being bloodily and mercilessly exterminated on Polish lands."[179] The gesture was not unappreciated. Stalin sent a telegram, thanking Wasilewska for relating to the Soviet government "so warmly and with friendship."[180]

It was actually Alfred Lampe, according to Stryjkowski, who was the "ideological brain of the Union of Polish Patriots" and who represented a more Polish line than Wasilewska's.[181] During the early months of the organization that was their mutual creation, Wasilewska's relationship with Alfred Lampe grew strained. Whatever their differences might have been, they reconciled in November 1943, and she told him then that her life had been much poorer as a result of his absence from it. They kissed and embraced, happy that their separation had ended.[182] But the reunion was short-lived. The following month, on 10 December 1943, the phone rang in Wasilewska's Moscow apartment. She heard that she was to come right away, that Lampe had died: "So I, like a crazy person, flew over there and when I got upstairs Lampe was lying dead on the bed with Różka [Lampe's wife] lying next to him, shouting in a wild voice: 'Summon Wanda, he has to live!' It seemed to her that if I were to come, it would revive him. When I appeared, he was without any doubt dead, but she grabbed me by the hand and shouted: 'He died, do something, he has to live!'"[183] Lampe was only forty-three years old. Two days before, Janina Broniewska had thought he only looked a bit paler than usual. For Broniewska, Lampe's tragedy was that of Moses: after having led the masses to the Promised Land, he was not permitted to enter himself. "At the moment," she wrote in the days following Lampe's death, "I can't think about, I can't even grasp with my imagination the whole brutal truth: that he, he—didn't live to see it. He didn't live to see what he fought for throughout his entire life."[184]

ILI, SOVIET KAZAKHSTAN, 1943–1944

In Alma-Ata just prior to the collapse of Polish-Soviet diplomatic relations, the situation of the Polish delegation grew ever more precarious. After the Anders army had evacuated the Soviet Union in spring and summer of 1942, delegates of the Polish London government were arrested. On the street Wat pretended not to recognize Viktor Shklovsky and his other Russian friends, so as not to place them at any greater risk. Then came the news of the victory at Stalingrad, a celebration for everyone, and a celebration of Stalin even for those who hated him. For Wat and his Russian friends it was a transcendent moment, "truly a period of love for Stalin." Shklovsky shed tears.[185] Whatever else Stalin had done, he had now dealt the Nazis a defeat. In February 1943, amidst this ecstasy, Wat and his family were forced to leave the Kazakh capital. They set out for the town of Ili, some fifty miles northeast of Alma-Ata.

In a workers' settlement overgrown with weeds, little huts made of manure and clay stood on dirt and sand. At the end of town, by the river, there was a small building that served as a library, club, and hospital. The town's inhabitants lived surrounded by cows, camels, and criminals; there was constant hunger. Women—exhausted, starving, dying—would come through Ili as they returned from the gulag. Ili was a Kazakh town, but had become a settlement for Polish refugees, almost all of whom were Jews. They were shtetl Jews—orthodox, religious. The women seemed to Ola Watowa to be stronger than the men.[186] Wat wore on a string around his neck a brown bakelite cross he had received from the Polish delegation. Nor did he hide the fact that he was a Jew, and he might have been persecuted as a heretic who had betrayed his people. The dynamics were otherwise; these were orthodox Jews harboring great Polish patriotism who wanted very much to return to Poland, and Wat, a representative of the Polish London government, was received very warmly there. He began to study shoemaking with a Jew from Radom, an old communist full of nostalgia for Poland, even with its antisemites.[187] In Ili Wat fell gravely ill with typhus and was put in the small hospital by the river. When it seemed to be the end he struggled to whisper to Ola, "promise that when you manage to get back to Poland, you'll take my ashes with you. I don't want to rest in this cursed land."[188]

Wat did not die in Ili. He recovered and left the tiny hospital. Then in March 1943 the news reached Ili that the NKVD was engaged in a campaign to force Poles to accept Soviet passports. Wat was skeptical about the Union of Polish Patriots; he suspected that both its formation and the passport campaign were part of a plan to turn Poles into Soviet serfs, and he began to organize the Poles—Polish Jews—in their settlement to resist.

The first meeting took place at the home of the shoemaker, the Jewish communist from Radom.[189] Wat, the assimilated cosmopolitan, the Polish communist turned Catholic, became for the first time in his life a leader among Polish Jews. He became their instructor in resistance; he incited them to rebel, and they listened to him. When summoned by the NKVD, they were to bring along a bag with those things that would be most essential in a camp. He taught them not to engage in any conversations that could only be used against them. When asked if they would accept the passport, they were to answer with a simple "no." When asked why, they were to say only, "because we're Polish citizens." When it was Wat's turn, his interrogator Colonel Omarkhadzhev, "a handsome Mongol," indicated that he knew who Wat was and alluded to his past as the editor of *Miesięcznik Literacki*. Then the colonel asked suddenly, "In as far as I'm not mistaken, you were a communist?" Wat answered: "A communist? . . . Perhaps. But that was so long ago that I don't remember at all."[190] He and the others went to prison, where Wat was threatened but not beaten. He was told that if he continued to refuse, he would be sent to a camp where he would die—and why did he not just accept the passport? It was, after all, his interrogators argued, only a piece of paper. Wat, who had once upon a time fallen in love with Mayakovsky, the author of a celebratory poem about his Soviet passport, refused. It was hot in the Kazakh prison cell, and Wat took off his shirt, revealing his cross. "I was the leader of those pious Jews in prison," Wat described himself, "me, a Jew with a cross around his neck."[191]

Then they came for Ola Watowa. She said goodbye to her eleven-year-old son and was taken to prison. "Well, so tell us," the NKVD officers asked, "why don't you want to accept a Soviet passport? Is it some kind of shame?" She answered them: "For a simple reason—I'm a Pole, a Polish citizen. And I'm certain that in an identical situation you would do the same thing. For none of you would accept Polish citizenship, it would be equivalent to a betrayal of your homeland." At that one of them shouted at her: "What a clever girl!" She was taken to a cell in a transit prison where criminals and prostitutes were held before being sent to the camps. The door to the cell closed behind her. Inside the other women prisoners forced her and the young Polish woman who was with her to strip naked. They took the clothes for themselves and began to beat the young woman. Ola Watowa watched and waited for her turn. Then they urinated on her and beat her as well. She heard the screams of the men being beaten in the other cells, they were calling out for help, and she recognized the voice of the old shoemaker from Radom.[192]

In this way the Polish Jews of Ili were broken. The next day the women submitted. One of the NKVD officers who had been particularly sympathetic to Ola Watowa now handed her the Soviet passport and said, "You see, citizen, I was right." And so the Poles left the Kazakh prison with Soviet passports, but not Wat. If he had been weak in prison earlier, he was no longer. This was his heroic moment. Upon returning to Ili, Ola Watowa learned that her husband was still in prison. She went to see Colonel Omarkhadzhev, who explained to her that a man as intelligent and educated as her husband, a poet, a writer, could be a professor at the university in Moscow and not living in poverty in Ili. Why was he resisting? Why was he inciting the others to resist? The colonel instructed her to impart reason to her husband: if he were only to accept the passport, everything would change right away. The family could go live an intelligentsia life in Moscow. Otherwise he would be sent to the gulag. Omarkhadzhev added that the Union of Polish Patriots, too, had given orders for Poles to accept the passports.[193]

In prison with his head shaven, Wat's ascetic appearance frightened the superstitious Kazakh gatekeepers. One of them wanted to know if he were a sorcerer and asked that he not cast spells on them, the gatekeepers, because they were not the guilty ones. When the guard turned the key in the lock behind him, Wat faced Valentin, the cell's leader. Valentin was large, strong, and beautiful. He looked at Wat as he prepared to beat him. At that moment, Wat suddenly asked this man if he believed in God. Valentin shouted back angrily: Why was he asking? And Wat answered: "'I know that you're supposed to beat me, to beat me as long as I don't take the Soviet passport. So, if you believe in God, I beg you, beat me so well and so effectively, that I don't suffer for too long, that it doesn't last for too long. Because I won't take the Soviet passport.'" In the cell the others waited for their leader's verdict. Then Valentin aggressively pushed the other prisoners out of his way and moved towards his place under the window. He made his announcement: no one was to touch this man. In the weeks and months that followed Wat grew close to Valentin, an experienced criminal who had managed to escape from other camps and prisons with great ingenuity—and great suffering. They told one another the stories of their lives, as well as stories from literature—Stendhal's *The Red and the Black,* O. Henry stories that Wat had translated in Poland. Valentin, whose specialty was holding up freight trains, had read Gorky, Tolstoy, and Dostoevsky. He and his fellow prisoners knew Pushkin's poems by heart, and at night they would sing Esenin's poem "Pis'mo materi" (Letter to my Mother)—in addition to simulating sounds of beatings so that nothing would be suspected.[194]

In the meantime, Colonel Omarkhadzhev had given Ola Watowa permission to visit her husband so as to persuade him to accept the Soviet passport. When she arrived she found Wat pale, with a shaven head and eyes that seemed larger. He embraced her and told her softly not to worry, that he was not being hurt there, that she should keep this a secret. He was thin, his complexion was gray, but he bore no signs of beatings or torture. He radiated, rather, calm, goodness, affection. She told him about her visit with Omarkhadzhev, about what he had offered and what he had threatened. And that was all. She made no pleas nor did she ask for a reply to Omarkhadzhev's offer. Wat felt at that moment that she had given him the greatest proof of her love—in not trying to persuade him, in leaving him the freedom of choice. Three months later, Wat was told he was being sent to a camp. He said goodbye to the other prisoners and to Valentin, giving him his family's address in Ili. Yet when he was taken from his cell, he was instead given back his original Polish documents and released. It was afternoon when Wat, with a long beard, appeared at his family's mud hut in Ili. His hair had grown back and was still more grayed, his complexion was sallow, but once again he seemed calm, happy. He had not accepted the Soviet passport. At the doorway of his home he held up the documents they had given him upon his release: on them was the stamp of the Polish government in London.[195] He did not know why or how he was released, if it were perhaps out of deference to the legend of *Miesięcznik Literacki,* or if one of his old friends in the Union of Polish Patriots—Wanda Wasilewska or Jakub Berman or Adam Ważyk—had saved him.[196]

One day some time after Wat's return from prison, Ola Watowa saw a "tall, broad-shouldered man with a powerful, well-proportioned head and a very expressive, almost beautiful, masculine face" standing at their doorway.[197] He was dressed elegantly in a dark suit and shiny black shoes. One arm, heavily bandaged, was in a sling. The man inquired calmly if

Aleksander Wat lived there—and in the next moment spotted Wat himself and shouted his name with joy. Wat was stunned. He jumped up, ran towards the man and kissed him on both cheeks, calling out to his wife that this was Valentin, Valentin! Upon hearing this she ran towards him as well, squeezing his hand with enormous gratitude, while young Andrzej looked upon the scene with fascination. Valentin told them that he had, of course, escaped from the prison and had gone to "his woman," who helped him prepare for further travels. To facilitate this he had stolen money—and a Bolshevik Party card—from an NKVD officer. Now Valentin casually pulled a huge clump of money from under his clothing and gave it to Ola Watowa, telling her to go to the market and buy anything she wanted for all of them.

They spent a miraculous, celebratory day together, the four of them. Valentin had a plan about heading to the front and turning himself over to German captivity, from where he would eventually make his way to Poland and begin a new life as an honest man—although, of course, he might have to do a bit of stealing there in the early stages, because how else would he get the money to open a restaurant and begin a clean life? They gave Valentin the address of Wat's sister, the actress Seweryna Broniszówna; they gave it to him without hesitation, knowing that Valentin had his own moral code. When the day drew to an end, they accompanied him to the train station. There Valentin listened for the train coming from a distance, glancing from time to time at Wat and his wife with a look of something approaching tenderness. They were all silent. Then at a certain moment, Valentin suddenly got up; without realizing what was happening, they watched him jump across the fence and towards the tracks. He stood then on the platform, and they watched as he drew signs of farewell in the sky with the flame of his lit cigarette. They looked on until his train disappeared into the horizon.[198]

THE EASTERN FRONT, 1943–1944

Stalin spoke well to Khrushchev of Wasilewska. Khrushchev became ever more her great admirer, and welcomed the news that the formation of the Polish army division had been entrusted to her.[199] Stefan Jędrychowski felt similarly. Wasilewska, he observed, possessed "an uncommon gift of eloquence" and a "powerful, broadly resonant but at once soft and pleasant-sounding voice"; her appeals to Poles in the Soviet Union and now in the Polish Army had "enormous persuasive force." She was a born leader.[200] Perhaps once she became a colonel in the Red Army she made a conscious effort, with her hair cropped short and a man's army uniform, to effect a masculine appearance. It was only in part effective. A Polish streetcar driver was among the soldiers in the Polish army division. Wasilewska was their superior, and they were to report to her, yet in fact a strange situation developed: the boys would melt before her gaze, take off their hats, and kiss her hand—in the best tradition of Polish gallantry. The former streetcar driver was terrified to see himself submit to the same impulse—and find himself kissing the hand of his superior officer.[201]

Wasilewska was tremendously invested in the Polish division; the Polish Army was above all her creation, her child. It was she who authored the soldiers' oath, an oath that included the promise of loyalty to the Red Army and the Soviet Union. She explained: "You can't forget that people came crying, they kissed the rifles. And from whom did they get them? From the Soviet Army."[202] In August 1943 she wrote to Stalin begging for permission to send the First Polish Division to the front on 1 September, the anniversary of the Nazi attack on Poland. The training period would not yet be quite over, yet the occasion was so important, so symbolic, as to justify any prematurity, she argued.[203] Stalin asked her: would they fight honorably? "It was a question," she later reported, "I answered with a thousand percent conviction: they would. And I said it in such a way that the question would not be repeated." Stalin granted his permission to send the Polish division to the front.[204] Despite her faith in the troops, Wasilewska regarded their commander, General Zygmunt Berling, with undisguised distrust. She even refused to attend a party Stalin was hosting because Berling would be there—a refusal that scandalized Molotov, who insisted that one simply did not decline an invitation from Stalin. Yet Wasilewska, on principle, did. The following day a Soviet daily newspaper attributed her absence to illness.[205] Jakub Berman found Wasilewska's extreme attitude towards Berling rather unnecessary, and called it "all a bit typical of a woman."[206]

Wasilewska was not alone in her family in her enthusiasm for the army. In June 1943, Wasilewska's daughter Ewa and Broniewska's daughter Anka, initially in secrecy from their mothers, volunteered for the Polish Division. Anka was thirteen years old, but claimed she was sixteen; Ewa was fourteen and a half but declared herself seventeen. The two mothers went to General Berling and told him that despite the girls' being under age, they were not to be pampered. Moreover, Berling was not to reveal that he was aware of the deception regarding their ages; they were to be treated just like everyone else in the army and made to feel serious. She and Wasilewska, Broniewska later swore, maintained complete neutrality with respect to their daughters' subterfuge, "even if only because our nerves couldn't take it. If we were to have dared to express the slightest doubt, those two little wasps would have stung us to pieces. And aren't there enough problems without that?" When Anka said goodbye to her mother she gave her a letter to send to her father, who was then in Jerusalem, telling her, "censor it as necessary!" The point was well taken. "I'll most certainly censor it," Broniewska wrote, "Not as a mother, but as the Military Department. . . . A letter going abroad. As if that were a mere trifle!" In her letter to her father Anka wrote: "We did 20 kilometers of marching during training. Regulation load—30 kilograms. But I prefer my hard soldier's lot to your oranges, lemons, and beauties of the South." Ewa Wasilewska was similarly delighted to be in the army, yet in the end their military careers were short-lived; Berling preferred not to bear responsibility for them. The girls came home in September; and Broniewska wrote: "our two soldiers, their birth certificates unmasked, have returned. They don't talk to us, they only hiss. . . . [Anka] doesn't talk to me and doesn't believe that I really did maintain a loyal neutrality in this matter."[207]

Like her daughter and her best friend, Janina Broniewska was enamored of the army, anxious to get to the front, and jealous of the war correspondents already there. Nor were the two women the only ones from literary circles who experienced this infatuation. The Union of Polish Patriots boasted several uniformed poets, including Adam Ważyk. Of the diminutive poet carrying a large weapon it was said at the time "there goes the rifle with his Ważyk." Broniewska commented more gently that Ważyk tended not to "distinguish himself as a particularly martial figure."[208] Be that as it may, he did find his way to martial poetry. His verse-turned-marching song abandoned all the obscurities of his old avantgardism for the mobilizing refrain "Set off, our First Corps!" "Tighten your belt / it's time to go," Ważyk told his fellow soldiers; they were heading west.[209]

As an instructor in the Military Department of the Union of Polish Patriots, Janina Broniewska soon had her opportunity to go to the front,

FIGURE 13 Janina Broniewska as a war correspondent, 1944. Courtesy of Muzeum Literatury imienia Adama Mickiewicza.

and she was ecstatic to be there. Early in her career as a war correspondent she cited, at once ironically and with pride, the Polish proverb "where the devil can't manage, he sends a woman."[210] Her time at the front was the time of her most fervent faith and unabashed exaltation. She experienced the joy that followed Stalingrad and an enchantment with the bravery of her comrades, Polish soldiers fighting alongside the Red Army. In February 1944 she recorded an episode from the brigade headquarters at the front: "The loader of the first section of the first battery of the artillery brigade, loading a heavy shell into the breech of the gun said simply, without particular grandiloquence: 'For Katyń!'"[211] She was enchanted as well with taking orders from Wasilewska, and wrote lovingly of how the soldiers at the front spoke of "our Wanda," who had made them soldiers and who would enable them to return to Poland. About this unusual absence of formality, Broniewska commented, "'Our Wanda'? In such a familiar manner? With no subordination? Without the appropriate titles? They're not needed, for certain they're not needed, especially as this ["our Wanda"] is perhaps the title of the highest rank, considering the emotional investment it contains."[212]

LUBLIN, 1944–1945

Stefan Jędrychowski, like Wasilewska, insisted that the Polish communists in the Soviet Union had always taken the position that they could not prepare ready-made solutions for liberated Poland, that they could only assist. Moreover, Jędrychowski and Lampe, before his death, worried that Wasilewska had taken too much upon herself, that the burden was too great for one person.[213] As soon as the news arrived of the existence in Poland of the communist-run *Krajowa Rada Narodowa* (Domestic National Council), the Union of Polish Patriots recognized it as Poland's rightful political representation and announced its readiness to subordinate itself accordingly.[214] On 22 July 1944, the Manifesto of the *Polski Komitet Wyzwolenia Narodowego* (Polish Committee of National Liberation), growing out of the Domestic National Council, officially called into existence the new communist-dominated provisional government in Lublin. Warsaw remained under German occupation.[215]

On 24 July 1944, Janina Broniewska was riding with an army chauffeur when they crossed the Molotov-Ribbentrop border for the first time. He looked at her and said, "Poland." "I nestle my face in his back," she wrote, "I blubber like any old woman. And I'm not at all ashamed. Not even a little. We kiss one other in turns. And do they have dry faces? No!" Four days later she visited Majdanek, the crematoria. "I look," she wrote in her notebook, "and I understand nothing. Nothing of this nightmare penetrates me. There is nothing human, nothing of man in that smoldering corpse." Her horror mobilized her: "No! No! No! We will not forgive! Nobody and nothing! . . . Hatred is invigorating and beautiful." Her faith in the revived Party, the avant-garde of the working class who would rebuild a new Poland, was complete. Upon seeing Majdanek she and a woman comrade spontaneously declared their faith in the iron laws of History. Together they recited from memory the words of the early Polish Marxist leader Ludwik Waryński from his 1886 declaration before a tsarist tribunal: "We do not stand above history. We submit to its laws. We look at the revolution to which we aspire as the result of the evolution of historical and social conditions . . ."[216]

It was around this time that Tuwim, from New York, sent a long letter to Janina Broniewska, who had once kissed him on the forehead for his help in extricating Ważyk from Polish prison. The letter was filled with longing and nostalgia, as well as much guilt that he had not shared their fate—and their battle—in the Soviet Union.

Beloved Janeczka!

. . . My dear! Where to begin? Likely from the fact that I'm anxious to be with you. More than once I've thought to myself that *from the beginning* I should have been with you and should have taken an active part in the realization of that "zavetnaia mechta" [dream of dreams] of my life that is Polish-Soviet friendship. It was necessary then, on 5 September 1939, to go to Pińsk, not to Kazimierz—then I would have doubtlessly shared with you all of the fortunes and adversities of flight and wanderings, perhaps I would have suffered more physically (which for an aging and not terribly strong fellow would be a difficult matter), but all those potential hardships and difficulties, even dangers, would have meant that I would have found myself there where my rightful place is: between Moscow and Warsaw, not along the Hudson River. . . . I know that the smoke from fires and the stench of corpses is now blowing from those parts, but there are aromas as well, such a freshness of old, beloved fields and of new times, which nothing in the world can replace. My flight from Warsaw and everything that followed from it was chance, surprise, the result of favorable or unfavorable coincidences. These carried me first to Paris, later to Portugal, next to Rio de Janeiro (miracle of miracles!), finally to New York. It might have just the same carried me to London (—thank you, dear God, that it didn't!—), to Calcutta, or to the African hamlet of Kidugale Njamba. But it *ought to have,* I repeat, thrown me to Russia.

Tuwim told of his isolation in New York, an isolation provoked by his "fanatical faith that it will not be Hitler who goes to Moscow but Stalin who goes to Berlin." He told Broniewska that all those who hated the Soviet Union had begun to look at him strangely; among Polish émigrés in the United States he had become a "traitor" and an "agent of Stalin." At the same time his ties with the working class were growing stronger. He told Broniewska that in autumn 1941 he had gone to Detroit and Chicago on the invitation of workers' unions. "I have to praise myself," he wrote, "I was received enthusiastically and I read my poems, I gave speeches. I began to publish my work in the publications of our friends, and I sent a telegram to *Polskie Wiadomości* in London that they should not dare to publish even a word of mine." And so the accusations that he was an agent of Moscow acquired still more force. He told her of the "historic" letter he had received from Jan Lechoń in spring 1942, cutting off relations with him, and of how Kazimierz Wierzyński had done the same. Yet he had found in New York a small group of people, gathered around Oskar Lange, who shared his views. Tuwim also discussed methods by which he and like-minded people in the United States might be able to help his friends in Moscow. He was full of energy and anxious to contribute to the cause, all the time acutely aware—and pained by the fact—that he was so far removed. "Dear friends!" he wrote in conclusion, "I'm writing this letter to Janka Broniewska, but it's for all of you—for you, who in Moscow and Lublin are raising Poland from the ruins and laying the groundwork for Her new life."[217]

Even as the communist government in Lublin was taking shape and Wasilewska was beginning to make trips into newly liberated Polish territory, she was becoming ever more Soviet. At a meeting in Lublin to establish a plan for agricultural reform, she encountered opposition from Andrzej Witos, the Peasant Party activist whom she had extracted from Soviet prison and brought to Moscow. Wasilewska wanted to reach a resolution quickly, and Witos was stalling for time. When they took a short break for lunch, someone said something about the weather, and Wasilewska turned to Witos, "I wonder how the weather is in the Autonomous Soviet Socialist Republic of Komi during this season?" Afterwards Witos sat in silence, interpreting the question as Wasilewska's suggestion that she could send him there again, back to the gulag, if need be. According to Wasilewska, it infuriated her that someone she had personally extracted and made into an activist was behaving in such a way—thus the need to remind him of his debt towards the leftist movement. Thenceforth the debates over agricultural reform resolved themselves quickly.[218]

As the war reached its end, Khrushchev, who had become good friends with Korneichuk and Wasilewska, turned to her and said, "'In a short time we won't be seeing each other so often.' 'Why?'—she was surprised. 'Because of your obligations. You'll certainly move to Warsaw and you'll come to Kiev more rarely.' 'No!'—she was a decisive person—'No, nooo! I won't go there.'" She told him she would move permanently to Warsaw only when Poland became a Soviet republic. Insofar as that did not happen, she had nothing to do there. Khrushchev, however, was unpersuaded, believing that the true explanation was her reluctance to leave Korneichuk.[219] With Stalin she had a similar conversation. They were at the Kremlin with various spicy foods on the table before them, including a small, green, very hot pepper—which Wasilewska particularly liked. At a certain moment Stalin turned to her:

> "Well so, maybe it's been enough of this Ukrainian citizenship?" He approached the table, poured a glass for me and for himself with the words: "Come, let's toast." And the glass shook in my hand. "Why is your hand shaking so?"
> "It seems to me that you understand perfectly why. In the first place, I have Soviet, not Ukrainian citizenship, and in the second place, are you of the opinion that I haven't deserved it?"

"What are you talking about? Do you want to become
a Soviet citizen?"

"That must be clear to you."

"That means that you want to be active on a worldwide
scale?"

"No. I want to be active on the scale of the Soviet Union."

"That means on a worldwide scale, and not only on a Polish
one. Well, so that's very good. In any case it's better for us."[220]

In May 1945, when a friendship agreement was signed in Moscow
between Poland and the Soviet Union, Wasilewska was present as a guest,
not as a participant, having decided to remain in the Soviet Union. When
a group photograph was taken, Wasilewska moved aside, considering that
she had no reason to figure there. Her time as a Polish leader had come
to an end. Stalin, however, thought otherwise. He asked: "And where is
Wanda? Maybe others can, but when there's talk of an agreement with
Poland, we can't do it without Wanda." So did Wasilewska appear in that
photograph, although she was no longer a Polish representative, but rather
a Soviet guest.[221]

WARSAW, AUGUST–OCTOBER 1944

On 1 August 1944 the Polish Home Army, under orders from the Polish
government in London, began the uprising in Warsaw for which they
had waited throughout the long years of the war. Much of the city had
not existed since the Warsaw Ghetto Uprising of spring 1943. Now as he
watched the rest of the capital go up in flames, Jarosław Iwaszkiewicz
wrote in his diary: "I didn't like the old Warsaw. But in the course of these
few years, when I've seen her so stubborn and so strong, I've come to love
her entirely differently and entirely anew." He paced his home without
strength, unable to do anything: "Everything is burning and perishing.
People are coming, constantly telling the same story in an infinitely terrifying and monotone way. And it's impossible to help them, one has to
only listen to those helpless, shapeless words, give them a hand, be glad
that they're here, that they're returning from there. . . . How many similar
to them will no longer ever come again."[222]

Stanisław Mikołajczyk, the prime minister of the Polish government in
London, knew that the Home Army was encountering unfriendly responses

from the Red Army, and that some Home Army soldiers had been arrested and even shot by the Soviets upon revealing themselves.[223] He came to Stalin anyway, because both Winston Churchill and Franklin Roosevelt wanted him to do so; the Soviet Union was, after all, their ally. Mikołajczyk appeared in Moscow in late July; when Stalin finally met with him on 3 August, he assured Mikołajczyk that a Soviet offensive on Warsaw was planned for three days later.[224] In Moscow, it was Mikołajczyk who told Wasilewska of the uprising. She was shocked. At the same moment, according to the Soviet government, there was no uprising, and when she asked Stalin, he told her he had received no news of anything like that. Mikołajczyk, on the contrary, was beaming when he told Wasilewska that in two or three days Warsaw would be liberated, in two or three days they would all be in Warsaw. Wasilewska felt otherwise; she was angry and distraught and told him that this was a monstrosity, that he had lost Warsaw.[225] Jakub Berman insisted that he and others in Moscow that August made repeated requests that help be sent to Warsaw, but to no avail.[226] Janina Broniewska, far away in Lublin in August 1944, wanted so much to be able to tell her friend in person that their Żoliborz was in flames. "Our city is burning," she wrote, "Our city, the most dear in the world. In a ring of Nazi encirclement. You can neither reach it nor save it. Who began this battle? Without armored units, without guns, without aircraft, without a plan of attack?"[227]

In the course of the two months of August and September 1944, Warsaw was reduced to ruins. The Red Army sat in Praga, just on the other side of the Vistula River, and did not come to the city's aid. After two months, the Home Army surrendered to the Germans, and the Germans set fire to what remained of the city. Warsaw, and with it Café Ziemiańska, was burned to ashes. In November Iwaszkiewicz wrote in his diary, "I cannot think about the fact that Warsaw is no more. Such an enormous chapter departing together with her, such a mass of experiences! Warsaw was not beautiful. And yet!"[228] Far away in the Middle East, Broniewski learned by radio of the uprising. He wrote a poem addressing his city in the vocative, calling her "Warsaw alive above the ruins," speaking to the city as to a lover: "I lost my home, those near and dear, / my love lies in the ruins there."[229]

On 17 January 1945, the Red Army crossed the Vistula River and took the emptied Polish capital. The Nazi occupation of Warsaw was over. In Lublin people cried on the streets and strangers embraced. Warsaw was liberated. The next day Janina Broniewska flew from Lublin to Warsaw. From the plane she could not even recognize the streets. There was nothing there. "Here is a burial ground," she wrote, "Here is Death. This isn't Marszałkowska, Wspólna, Nowogrodzka. This is the most horrible dream. Words have no place, no purpose." She returned to Lublin without having visited her old neighborhood in Żoliborz, having lost her desire to go there. She concluded the notebook she kept as a war correspondent: "Warsaw—the heart of our country. We will raise her from the dead, from the ruins, from bits and pieces. She will rise and be wonderful, more beautiful than she was—the city of our love, the city of our dreams."[230] Far away in Jerusalem, Broniewski had received news of Marysia Zarębińska's death in a Nazi concentration camp. In March 1945 he wrote to Anka of his pain, "This was the most heartfelt relationship in my erotic life, deeply trusting, giving me 'tranquility of heart.'"[231] In fact the news was false. Marysia Zarębińska had survived Auschwitz. Following her arrest in 1943, her extended family had given up her daughter Majka to an orphanage in the provinces. Now, after Warsaw's liberation by the Red Army, Janina Broniewska found the daughter of her former husband's second wife and brought Majka home to live with her and her own children.[232]

Wanda Wasilewska reached Warsaw a day later, when Janina Broniewska had already returned to Lublin. The day before a plane had come for Wasilewska in Kiev, taking her back to Lublin, from where she and Jakub Berman traveled to Praga; there they spent the night. It was only the next morning, on 19 January, that together they crossed the pontoon bridge into Warsaw. The city was still burning in some places; the first of the city's surviving inhabitants, expelled after the uprising, were just beginning to return. The pilgrimage to her old neighborhood was a difficult one, and at a certain moment she found herself unable to discern where she was in the city that no longer existed. In the end she reached Żoliborz on foot. She wrote of her impressions at the time: "Before me a broken city—Warsaw. Heaps of bricks, twisted iron rods, piles of stone, the remnants of walls barely standing. That Warsaw that fought in 1939, that fought in 1944, crushed, burned, torn, undaunted, unyielding, unbroken. People are already returning to the ruins. They don't cry. A smile brightens their faces.

They know—they will rebuild, raise up, revive, they will create just as they fought—with tenacity, endurance, clenched teeth, all the way until victory."[233] It was late at night when she and Jakub Berman returned to Praga, walking across the pontoon bridge.[234]

CHAPTER EIGHT

Stalinism amidst Warsaw's Ruins

The time of the aesthetes has passed.

—*Adam Ważyk*

IN MARCH 1945 JULIAN Tuwim told a Polish journalist in New York, "In May it will be five years since I've come to America. But for me it has been one long drawn-out day. I didn't live American life, I was sitting the whole time on the suitcase that I will now take back."[1] For the Warsaw literati, the Second World War had been a time of dispersion. Now they began to make their way home. Poland's ashes were seductive. The repatriants found communism in power, encroaching Stalinism, and socialist realism. For those who offered body and soul, poetry and prose to support the new regime, it was a time of unprecedented power over life and death. Janina Broniewska was among the first to return to Poland. She was soon joined in Lublin by Jakub Berman, Julian Przyboś, Jerzy Putrament, Jerzy Borejsza, and Adam Ważyk. Jakub Berman remained rather inconspicuous, ever the éminence grise, Wanda Wasilewska's closest advisor. Jakub's brother Adolf, arriving from the west rather than the east, a survivor of the Warsaw ghetto, became a representative to the Domestic National Council. Ważyk was among those who were uneasy about returning home. The nearer he came to his country, he wrote, the stranger he felt, the more he feared returning to a city of ruins and memories, to streets he had once loved.[2] He wrote of gazing at his native city through binoculars and recalling the years which were also your times,

people of not quite bad will

buried in my heart as if in a common grave.[3]

In late summer and autumn of 1944 a new Polish Writers' Union came into being in Lublin. At its August 1944 meeting, the union reinstated Wat's membership *in absentia*.[4] A new literary journal came into being as well; the first issue of *Odrodzenie* (Rebirth) included an obituary of Witkacy, who in September 1939 had fled Warsaw, heading east. Later that month, upon learning of the Red Army's invasion of eastern Poland, he committed suicide. Witkacy's was not the only obituary in this debut issue; *Odrodzenie* also included obituaries of Halina Górska, Mieczysław Braun, Bruno Schulz, and other writers killed by the Germans. Alongside the obituaries was an excerpt from Tuwim's "Polish Flowers," in which the narrator asks to be allowed to clean the ashes and ruins of his homeland, to raise his home from a cemetery.[5]

After the Nazi attack on the Soviet Union in June 1941, Władysław Daszewski had attempted to make his way east. After a few weeks, however, he returned to Lvov. The city was by then under German occupation, and he soon realized he could not remain. He went into hiding in the surrounding provinces until October 1941; then he managed to reach Warsaw, where there were signs the Gestapo was looking for him. After several days, Daszewski went to a small village. Making use of falsified documents, he spent the next three years of the occupation in a shelter for deportees. He worked with the intelligence of the Polish communist partisans, making drawings of Germany army positions.[6] Now in light of the creation of the Polish Committee of National Liberation, Daszewski reemerged from his incognito life in the provinces; he appeared in Lublin and put himself at the disposal of the pro-Soviet Polish government. In March 1945 he moved to Łódź. There he joined the newly formed Polish Workers' Party and became the scenic designer at the Polish Military Theater. The Stalinist years were creative ones for the man who had stage-managed the arrests of his closest friends.[7]

The postwar cultural "rebirthing" of Poland, vigorous and animated, took place against the background of an increasingly bloody Stalinist security apparatus, the *Bezpieka*. Between 1945 and the winter of 1947–1948 there was some space for leftist plurality, for the Popular Front ethos revived in the Union of Polish Patriots. It was a space, though, existing amidst terror and chaos. Jewish survivors returning from Nazi concentration camps were not infrequently greeted with violence by those (and not only by those) who had assumed ownership of their property, and the year 1946 saw a bloody pogrom in the city of Kielce.[8] Moreover, a civil war continued between communists and Home Army partisans; in the east Ukrainian nationalist partisans continued to fight as well. Stalinism proper triumphed in Poland in 1948 when the Polish Workers' Party absorbed the Polish Socialist Party to form the United Polish Workers' Party (PZPR). An era of Stalinist terror followed, including the persecution of Home Army figures, civilians associated with the Polish government in London, and communists. Stanisław Mikołajczyk was forced to flee the country. In June 1951 the proceedings were broadcast over the radio of the trial against the Home Army officer Stanisław Tatar and "his gang of conspirators and spies," in which the defendants' read scripted "confessions" to the effect that they had worked for Anglo-American imperialists. The Tatar trial defendants were not given death sentences, although death sentences were handed down in many lower-level trials.[9]

WŁADYSŁAW BRONIEWSKI'S AND ANATOL STERN'S HOMECOMING

Despite his popularity in Jerusalem, Władysław Broniewski was not eager to settle there permanently. Neither did the Middle Eastern heat cure him of his dependence on vodka.[10] His friends were concerned about him, including Polish friends who in June 1945 helped him to obtain a British visa. It was too late. By this time, he had decided to return to Poland. In August he wrote to them that he could not do otherwise, that further emigration would mean further separation from his wife and daughter, and further depression. Yet he was uneasy about the political situation in Poland, and wrote to his friends in England, "I am not enthusiastic about the situation at home, yet I expect that I'll be able to live, to contribute to the rebuilding in one way or another and to write. . . . After all, I observe [in Poland] the animated activity of the great majority of our writer friends."[11]

From New York Julian Tuwim wrote to Broniewski in Jerusalem.[12] In October 1945 Broniewski sent a reply from Tel Aviv, telling Tuwim that he was preparing to return to Poland. "You must be aware of my fate during this war?" Broniewski asked. He summarized: "So in January 1940, to my amazement, I was arrested in Lvov and for 19 months I sat in prison, mostly in Lubianka in Moscow. Afterwards for half a year I was at the embassy in Kuibyshev, where (that is, in Kuibyshev) Jaśka was, too, with Anna [Broniewski's daughter]. In the spring of 1942 I entered the army. With the army I went to Persia-Iran. I experienced various nasty things, given that the pack of counterintelligence hounds regarded me as an undesirable and dangerous foreign body, as a result of which I left the army and came to Jerusalem."[13] He was doing much writing, including a novel in verse titled *Bania z poezją* (A Balloon with Poetry), which was to be a kind of history of Poles in the war. He believed that only in Poland would he be able to write more and well. The most important thing, he told Tuwim, was that in July the news reached him that his wife Marysia Zarębińska had survived Auschwitz. He had already received two letters from her: she was now in Łódź with Anka and Majka, working as an actress in the theater there with great success. As for Janina Broniewska, Broniewski wrote that she was in Warsaw and had "dumped Gadomski, but I don't know for whom." Broniewski gave Tuwim Zarębińska's address and asked him to send a package to her.[14]

Tuwim shortly obliged. In November he wrote to Zarębińska of how he had learned from Broniewski of her miraculous survival. "How good it is that you're alive and will continue to be Władek's greatest happiness," Tuwim told her. He wrote further, "As soon as I learned that Władek was returning to the country, a huge stone fell from my heart. It was terrible when my former friends, poets, were publishing an Andersonian weekly in New York, they were waving Władek about like a little banner, using his name, reprinting his poems, etc. My blood boiled no less from the story of Władek's imprisonment. I don't know who those zealots are who issued that moronic order, but they must not have known themselves what they were doing. I am writing of that precisely in the name of my fervent friendship for the Soviet Union."[15] Tuwim also made "a sentimental request": Would she go to Kościuszko Avenue 27 and find out who lived on the first floor, in the apartment to the left from the front of the stairs? It had once been the home of his parents. "They used to sit on the balcony," he wrote, "and look out for their son, who from time to time would stop by Łódź . . .

for a couple of hours. For the son was very 'famous' and very busy in the capital, so he could never stay for long. Now I regret it."[16]

By February 1946, when Zarębińska wrote to thank Tuwim for the letter, the gloves, and the other gifts he had sent, Broniewski had joined her in Łódź. They had last seen each other in January 1940, when Broniewski had been taken away from Daszewski's party in a black limousine. Their reunion now after six years of separation was "the most beautiful happy ending," she told Tuwim. She wrote of the Łódź theater, of the popularity of the literary cabaret in the style of the Warsaw cabaret Tuwim had once written for—"in a word, people want to forget about the war." She herself was not feeling well; after her return from Auschwitz, she was afraid to be alone, "as if beside me on the bed there were constantly another corpse." In Auschwitz she had developed heart problems; now she was on vacation, resting. She promised that as soon as she returned to Łódź she would visit Tuwim's childhood home. Majka and Anka had already been there, they had wanted to see where the young Tuwim had written his first poems.[17] Broniewski scribbled his own note beneath Zarębińska's letter: "Roll up your pants and get yourself across that puddle of the Atlantic. You and your poems are very much missed here." He added that upon his own arrival in November he had been greeted with much pomp and circumstance. At his inaugural reading at the House of Workers' Culture young people waved flags and an orchestra played the national anthem and the Internationale.[18] As for their old city, "Warsaw looks terrible. You walk along those ruins and from time to time you sob."[19]

Broniewski had enjoyed tremendous popularity among Polish-Jewish émigrés in Palestine. Polish Jewry was not foreign to him, and among the most poignant acts of homage paid to the Jews who fought in the Warsaw ghetto was Broniewski's poem appearing in *Odrodzenie* in spring of 1945. "Żydom polskim" (To the Polish Jews) was dedicated to the memory of Szmul Zygielbojm, the Bundist representative to the Polish government-in-exile who had committed suicide in London during the Warsaw Ghetto Uprising. Zygielbojm's was a protest against the world's passivity. "I immerse my words in blood, and my heart in enormous tears, / a wandering Polish poet, for you, oh Polish Jews," Broniewski wrote. He sung the heroism of the ghetto fighters: "Sons of the Maccabees! you, too, know how to die, / to undertake without a shadow of hope, a battle begun in September."[20] Broniewski expressed the solidarity between Poles and Jews who fell in battle against the Nazis, who were united now by Auschwitz and Dachau, by blood spilled in the same war. He had come to feel part of the Polish-Jewish community in Palestine.

Broniewski had also grown close there to Tuwim's and Ważyk's friend, the Polish-Jewish journalist Paulina Appenszlak.[21] In her new homeland in Palestine, Appenszlak's heart remained in Poland, with Polish literature, and she could not bring herself to penetrate the wall of the Hebrew language—perhaps because it was too late, perhaps because it was not worth it. "I need to become conscious of the fact," she wrote to Broniewski in 1946, "that my world has perished, and that I perished together with it."[22] She was moved to hear from Broniewski following his return to Poland, especially as she understood that friends in Palestine were reminders of an unpleasant period. "As you probably know," she wrote, "as a rule your letters are published here. I defended myself as best I could, justifying myself with the 'intimacy' of the content, but in the end I relented and the excerpt about Jewish children in Zakopane found its way into the Bulletin."[23] Appenszlak's relations with Polish circles in Palestine had cooled, as she lacked the strength to fight against all the negative things that were being said about Poland. Moreover, she had no defense when she heard the news of antisemitism there. "It terrifies me a bit," she wrote, "that I'll never again come to Poland."[24] Her daughter, studying at a Polish-Jewish school in Palestine, had never heard of Jan Lechoń or Kazimierz Wierzyński—and this saddened her. Instead Appenszlak's daughter spoke constantly of Jerzy Putrament—of whom Appenszlak herself knew nothing.[25] Appenszlak was not alone in missing Broniewski. His old correspondent from prison, the then-aspiring poet Stanisław Wygodzki, wrote to Broniewski from a west European hospital where he was recovering from tuberculosis following his time in Auschwitz and Dachau. Wygodzki was overjoyed to learn that Broniewski had returned home to Poland, and that their correspondence, interrupted for so long, could now resume. Wygodzki, the lone survivor among his family, had plans to return to Poland in the spring.[26]

Broniewski had not been the only one of his circle to find himself in Palestine by way of the Anders army. In March 1946, Broniewski received a letter from Janina Broniewska's now-former husband. Gadomski wrote

that he had received Broniewski's letter from Zakopane, which had evoked
a general mood of jealousy in Palestine, where there reigned "sadness and
lethargy." Anatol Stern was there as well, and Gadomski wrote of Stern's
reaction to Broniewski's letter: he "simply turned green, and not knowing
what to say he purchased two large shots [of vodka]."[27] In Palestine Stern
roamed about, coordinating the Palestinian branch of the communist
Union of Polish Patriots. His sympathies vacillated between Polish communism and Jewish nationalism, he identified himself "sometimes as a
Zionist, sometimes as Polish as the occasion arises."[28] In January 1948,
Stern wrote to Wat, his former futurist co-author; they had last seen each
other at the restaurant in Lvov on the evening of their arrests. Stern had
seen Peiper in Kuibyshev and Broniewski in Palestine, he told Wat. He
had not written to old friends, for fear of "complicating his life," but now
he wanted to return to Poland, to Polish—the only language in which
he could think and write. He was afraid. He was afraid to return to the
enormous Jewish cemetery, afraid to find himself amidst an image of
what had happened there that was still so fresh. Yet he wanted, and felt it
his obligation, to work for the "new democracy in Poland."[29] Almost three
years had passed since the end of the war; the Anders army no longer
existed and there were no longer any repatriation transports. Stern did not
have money for the trip, and turned to Jerzy Borejsza. "Remembering our
warm and friendly relations in Lvov and knowing how you nurture literature at home, I would be greatly obliged and grateful to you if you were to
regard it as possible to endorse my request to the Ministry of Navigation
and in this way assist a Polish writer in returning and participating in
the common work of writers and artists in reborn Poland." Borejsza did
not ignore the letter; within that same year, Stern was home.[30] He threw
himself into the new People's Poland. Yet the Party had not forgotten his
flirtation with Zionism, and soon after his return to Poland, he became
an object of secret police surveillance.[31]

JULIAN TUWIM'S (ANTICIPATED) HOMECOMING
As the war reached its end, Tuwim waited anxiously in New York for his
opportunity to return to Poland, now as a decidedly *engagé* poet. In July
1945, he wrote to Józef Wittlin, an old friend of the Skamander poets,
urging him to return to Poland, too, and promising that no one in the
new Poland would force a literary agenda upon him, that these were only

hostile rumors. "Don't think that 'they don't want' you at home," Tuwim wrote, "and rid yourself of the bad habit of pointless considerations about your 'sins' or 'guilt' because of your absence during these six years." Tuwim assured Wittlin that nothing would be held against him—neither his absence during the war nor his failure to sign pro-Soviet and pro-Lublin government declarations, nor even his having signed some anti-Lublin ones. In Tuwim's mind that was all over now and the important thing was to return to their home and contribute to its reconstruction. "Of course," Tuwim qualified, as if as an afterthought, "if you start to work against the government, against its political orders and so forth or if you conspire with fascist sons of bitches who are still, constantly conducting so-called underhanded dealings—you'll go to prison."[32]

Tuwim corresponded prolifically with old friends with whom he hoped soon to be reunited. In September 1945, he wrote to Iwaszkiewicz, calling him "beloved" and asking him to recognize what an enormous investment of "love, longing, brotherhood and many other feelings—entangled, unexpressed, inexpressible" were contained in that word. This was true all the more, Tuwim explained, as he had seen neither Lechoń nor Wierzyński for three years, nor was Grydzewski any longer communicating with him. He was pained at having been away for so long; he had never managed to feel connected to America. Moreover, he was afflicted by various "complexes"—of "'nonparticipation,' 'absence,' 'safety,' 'satiety' . . . one great 'complex of survival,' mainly with a feeling of guilt (?) and sin (?) towards the murdered Polish Jews." Tuwim believed that only his return to Poland would free him from these feelings. "In all of your eyes, as soon as we see one another the first time," he told his old friend, "will be the verdict. Remember this!" Tuwim added that he knew—although no one had told him—that he had lost his mother. He wanted no one to speak of this to him, but asked Iwaszkiewicz if he would—should any grave exist—care for that piece of Polish ground until the time of Tuwim's return.[33]

Tuwim was full of plans for his future in Poland. In December 1945 he wrote to Jerzy Borejsza that he was in the process of compiling a "roguish and mischievous" dictionary of Polish humor, satire, irony, sayings, dialects, vulgarities, and so forth.[34] Two months later, still from New York, Tuwim wrote to Leon Kruczkowski, himself recently returned from long years as a prisoner of war and now a leading figure in the Stalinizing cultural sphere.[35] While promising that nothing would alter his intention to return to Poland, Tuwim wrote of how much news reaching him from people returning to the United States from Poland upset him. "Where is the Polish Mayakovsky," Tuwim asked, "even if only if in a pocket edition? Where is that young, new bard of young, new Polish history?" Yet what disturbed him most was something else: "The heaviest stone in my heart is the news of antisemitism at home. I know who is doing this and why it has lasted, but that's of small consolation."[36]

As for his host country, Tuwim had adopted the communist critique of capitalist society; he saw the United States as an industry-obsessed society for which even the war was "an industrial phenomenon, actually without any ideological roots. It was a business they had to do. The business was done—and Hitler had ceased to be an enemy." Now the Americans were setting off for the moon and had already calculated the cost in dollars of a trip for one person. "Macy's will establish a branch of its Babylonian enterprise there," Tuwim wrote in a letter to Słonimski, "and the Coca-Cola company (which spends more annually on advertisements than prewar Poland spent on new schools and hospitals) will sell its insipid wish-wash to the Martians. Moreover, it will turn out that from the moon an atom bomb is best aimed at the Kremlin."[37] In January 1946 Tuwim wrote to Słonimski of how emigration had aged him, and reminisced about the times, thirty years earlier, when they had read their poetry to each another. The previous year, even as the Germans were being driven from Łódź and Warsaw, Tuwim had become afflicted with nervous disorders, with agoraphobia in particular. Now he would spend days at a time lying in bed, rarely leaving his apartment, and when he did it was only with his wife Stefania.[38]

In May 1946 the Tuwims sailed for London. They were there only for two weeks, departing in early June on the ship *Śląsk*, which arrived at the Polish port of Gdynia some four days later.[39] When greeted by his friends and various government representatives, Tuwim was so moved that he broke into tears, unable to speak. Everything—the people, the air, the food, the coffee—seemed inexpressibly wonderful to him. When asked when he had decided to return to Poland, Tuwim answered that he had decided before he had ever set foot in America; through all his wanderings he had dreamt only of coming home. He passed along passionate greetings to all of his fellow countrymen, and especially to the remaining Polish Jews.[40] Now more than ever before Tuwim identified himself with Polish Jewry. When he saw Iwaszkiewicz's wife, who had done much to save Jews in the days of Nazi occupation, Tuwim embraced her and said, "Thank you, Hania, for protecting my little Jews!" To this she calmly replied: "But my Julek, those were *my* little Jews."[41]

Tuwim was embraced with open arms by the new government, who provided him with an apartment in Warsaw, a paid secretary, a privileged life.[42] Of devastated Warsaw Tuwim said desperately to Jakub Berman, "But you will rebuild her!"[43] In October 1947 when a delegation of Soviet writers came to Poland, Tuwim eagerly guided his friend Ilya Ehrenburg day and night around the ruins of Warsaw, saying again and again, "Look—how beautiful it is!"[44] Tuwim wanted to do his part; he threw himself into the cultural rebuilding of Poland. When he had fled Warsaw in September 1939, he had buried a trunk full of manuscripts in the basement of a building on Złota Street, home of the editorial offices of *Wiadomości Literackie*. Now, almost seven years later, he sought out his trunk. The contents had been partially destroyed by moisture, but some things had survived—in the company of "a macabre escort": on top of the trunk lay the corpse of a woman with her arm raised; a second dead woman lay at the feet of the first.[45] In compensation, perhaps, for so much death, Tuwim and his wife adopted a child, the six-year-old Ewunia, orphaned by the war. Now, along with helping to rebuild the new socialist Poland, raising little Ewunia became Tuwim's greatest postwar passion.[46] He embraced parenthood and his new life in the city that had been burned to ashes; even living amidst the ruins Tuwim insisted that no Rio de Janeiro could ever compare, for him the most beautiful spot on earth was Warsaw.[47] By autumn 1947 Tuwim was among the directors at the New Theater, and told an interviewer emphatically that there would be "no Sartres—God forbid!" in his repertoire. While Sartre had become very much a fan of communism, Tuwim was not a fan of existentialism. To emphasize this, he called over his new fair-haired, blue-eyed daughter, who obligingly trotted towards Tuwim and onto his lap.

> "Ewunia, what is it you say, when does it become dreadfully boring here at home?"
>
> Ewunia is embarrassed, she shakes her little head and is silent.
>
> "Go ahead, say it Ewunia."—I'm asking as well—"Say it into her ear."

I lean forward, the little girl stands on her tiptoes and with a warm, clean breath whispers clearly into my ear: "Existential-ism." And then she smiles playfully and is no longer in the room. And so Ewunia in her own way resolves the problem of Sartre.[48]

THE HOMECOMING OF BROTHERS

When Wanda Wasilewska declined to return to Poland, she left open a space in cultural politics, which required at least two men to fill. The first was Jakub Berman, who in 1949 found himself once again in Russia, this time dancing with Molotov. They were dancing to Georgian music, which Stalin especially liked, although he tended not to dance very much himself. "Surely," asked Berman's interviewer, "you mean with Mrs. Molotov?" But no, Jakub Berman explained, Mrs. Molotov was not there, she had already been sent to the gulag. It was Mr. Molotov with whom Jakub Ber-man was dancing, most likely a waltz, in any case something very simple because Jakub Berman knew not the slightest thing about dancing.[49] These were the years when Jakub Berman, together with Bolesław Bierut and the economist Hilary Minc, formed a triumvirate of Stalinist leaders in postwar Poland. Once the power behind the throne to Wasilewska, Jakub Berman now played this role for the less extraordinary Bierut. To this he added the position of postwar dictator of cultural policy in the harshest years of socialist realism. As he had once done in the role of KPP liaison in the interwar wars, Berman now again personally reached out to writers, attempting to influence them via "every conceivable means." He cultivated personal relationships. "I tried to create an atmosphere in which they would be eager to work, to be active," he said, "And I succeeded."[50]

Yet Jakub Berman had no illusions about the precariousness of his own position. It was Khrushchev who soon after the war cautioned Bierut about his choice of advisors, mentioning rumors of dissatisfaction with the ethnic composition of the Party leadership: Berman and Minc were both Jews.[51] In 1948, an "anticosmopolitan" campaign initiated in the Soviet Union coincided with the formation of the state of Israel. After having supported the creation of a Jewish state in the period 1944–1947, Moscow changed its position when Israel failed to place itself in the communist camp. Despite his warm gestures in Moscow, Stalin regarded Jakub Berman as a cosmopolitan.[52] Moreover, Jerzy Putrament informed a Soviet official that the younger brother, Adolf, was compromising the older one, Jakub, with his Zionism, that their relations had become tense.[53] Jakub Berman was well aware that he was an ideal candidate for the role of a Polish Rudolf Slánský, a leading Czech communist of Jewish origin executed after a 1952 show trial in Prague. That year Wanda Wasilewska, having learned—perhaps through Khrushchev—of Stalin's desire to prepare a trial on the model of the Slánský affair and to liquidate Jakub Berman, traveled from Kiev to Warsaw to warn him.[54]

The younger brother was indeed compromising the older one. Adolf Berman was chairman of the Central Committee of Polish Jews during the brief moment following the Second World War when the Zionist Left and the Jewish communists found a point of unity. By late 1948, that moment that passed. After the April 1948 ceremony unveiling Natan Rapaport's enormous granite monument on the fifth anniversary of the Warsaw Ghetto Uprising, Adolf Berman was accused of sabotage, of co-opting the unveiling ceremony for a Zionist demonstration.[55] In April 1949 he was deposed from the chairmanship of the Central Committee of Polish Jews by his communist comrades.[56] That same year Władysław Bartoszewski, to whom Adolf and Basia Berman owed, in part, their survival, was arrested for the third time—and now remained in prison.[57] Jakub Berman was familiar with such arrests; the security apparatus during the bloodiest years of Stalinism fell under his jurisdiction. He worked closely with Jerzy Borejsza in the cultural sphere, and in his other role as overseer of the security apparatus with Borejsza's brother, the security officer Jacek Różański. Upon arriving in Lublin from the Soviet Union in September 1944, Różański had been proposed work in security. He advanced quickly as a security officer, particularly after coming to the conclusion that "my inhibitions must be the result of my intelligentsia character, of too little militancy, of a lack of fortitude."[58] His efforts to liberate himself from such inhibitions were effective, and he became one of Jakub Berman's most notorious charges. He had much support, including that of Tuwim, who told him, "In you I see the avenger of my mother."[59]

The second person succeeding Wasilewska was Borejsza, "the Boss," who dangled a cigarette from his lips, wore a trench coat and his shirt unbuttoned, and flaunted his closeness to Jakub Berman.[60] Borejsza's role during the immediate postwar years granted him exceptional maneuverability, which he exploited, throwing himself into his various projects with tremendous energy. Those in Lublin at the time remember him with red eyes, full of energy and ideas, drinking great quantities of black coffee. Among his successes was the repatriation of many of the Ossolineum collections from Lvov, which had been annexed by the Soviet Union.[61] In October 1944 in Lublin the publishing collective Czytelnik (The Reader) was called to life.[62] It was a collective in name only; it functioned rather as a state enterprise and above all as Borejsza's personal project. He wanted to gather around him experts, cultural figures, and activists devoted to literature, people who supported the state's cultural politics, but were not necessarily part of the state apparatus. Borejsza worked hard to recruit the intelligentsia's support for the new government, offering good jobs, apartments, and stipends to go abroad. Moreover, it was Czytelnik that took care of the otherwise homeless writers in the year or two just after the war.[63] Among Borejsza's recruits was the antisemitic right-wing Catholic politician Bolesław Piasecki; Borejsza convinced Party authorities that if they were to release Piasecki from prison he could serve a useful function in organizing a "loyal opposition." The Party agreed; Piasecki was released with the understanding that he was to be part of a Catholic opposition but a legal, constructive one that recognized the new government.[64] Tuwim, though friendly with Borejsza, devoted a rather unfriendly poem to this bizarre flirtation, symbolizing the relationship in their rendezvous "In a certain quiet café / At the intersection of Stalin and Three Crosses."[65]

The communist-dominated but pluralist line Borejsza represented was articulated in his 1945 article "The Gentle Revolution"—which began with an unsigned letter that said "Liberté! Egalité! Fraternité!" and noted that the current situation in Poland was reminiscent of the Jacobins, with only the guillotine for the bourgeoisie missing. Borejsza responded to the unknown author: there would be no guillotine. Theirs would be a "gentle revolution." It had come late, but was the richer for having learned from the experiences of others. Its "gentleness" made it no less decisive: "Political and social reactionaries have lost the battle for Poland and that loss is complete and final. Among the intelligentsia there followed a division into a small group—which is and will most likely remain ensconced in reactionary prejudices—and the enormous majority, which clearly realizes that the path of broad reforms opens for Poland the window to Europe. We can and we must cease to be a musty, provincial, egocentric, out-of-the-way locality of snobs imitating foreign countries. We can and we must achieve an independent expression of our national culture, as we have achieved an independent path to great social and political reforms." The task of achieving that independent expression fell to the progressive intelligentsia. State control and coercion in the cultural realm would undoubtedly not be necessary; the character of "reborn Poland" and the composition of social forces would naturally give impetus to a literary transformation. In short, Borejsza promised a "gentle revolution" in the cultural sphere, a revolution protecting open discussion, a revolution devoid of any mandate to follow the Soviet model, a revolution respectful of Polish culture.[66]

Yet this space for pluralism lasted for only a short while. In October 1947 the Central Committee of the Polish Workers' Party passed a resolution concerning Czytelnik, accusing the institution of failing to adapt to the new conditions—that is, failing to recognize the Party's consolidation of power. Czytelnik's methods of influence, which in the earlier period had played the role of neutralizing hostile milieus, "presently on more than one occasion have started to become a riverbed of reactionary ideological influence on the non-Party masses reading Czytelnik's publications."[67] The resolution called for Czytelnik to expand Party cadres in leading positions; increase political control over periodicals; and in general shift to the left. Czytelnik was attacked as well for "growing above the Party"; for adopting Western press models; for "pseudo-neutralism"; for the "programlessness" of which Wat had once accused the Skamander poets in *Miesięcznik Literacki*.[68]

Now under attack, Borejsza crossed over to a hyper-leftist position. "He played," Ważyk observed, "a very complicated game."[69] It was a game with high stakes. Borejsza desired to provide some kind of fantastic evidence that he was one with the new, post–"gentle revolution" era. The idea came to him in the middle of the night, in the editorial offices of Czytelnik: he would organize a world congress of "Intellectuals in Defense of Peace" in the city of Wrocław, in the new territories postwar Poland had acquired from Germany.[70] And so it came to pass. In August 1948 Borejsza gathered some five hundred participants from forty-five countries—including Ilya Ehrenburg, Julien Benda, Paul Éluard, and Pablo Picasso—in the newly Polish city of Wrocław. The French participant Dominique Desanti, a correspondent from *L'Humanité,* described Borejsza at the congress: "Corpulent, excited, feverish, with blue eyes and an oblong glance, with wiggling ears and a face prematurely lined with wrinkles. . . . Heavy in the hips, with disheveled hair, taking off his rimless spectacles time after time in order to wave his arms, holding the glasses in fleshy fingers, he simply dissolved in one big smile. A person knowing no rest, capable of everything with the exception of maintaining calm."[71]

Iwaszkiewicz and Tuwim, who had not even been invited to the Lwów Congress twelve years earlier, now appeared as decidedly *engagé* poets on the correct side of the "red barricade." Iwaszkiewicz, Borejsza's co-organizer who looked upon Borejsza as an "eccentric, powerful, high-handed" figure, spoke at the congress's opening in a way he later thought overly idealistic, perhaps overly mystical. Ilya Ehrenburg assured him that what he had said was beautiful.[72] Tuwim began his speech by expressing hopes "of a political nature": the participants at this congress must now see that Poland was not separated from the rest of the world by an Iron Curtain. They had all been able to travel there freely and express themselves on the most press-ing topic: the threat of a new war to which fascist remnants were aspiring. Tuwim spoke critically of the interwar years, when intellectuals had tended to pass over political and ideological topics, and "being apolitical passed for a virtue of a writer, especially if he was a poet." The genocide of Polish Jewry had affected Tuwim deeply, and he spoke explicitly of the impetus for his politicization, of his reasons for embracing the Stalinist conception of the writer as an "engineer of human souls": "After the ghastly years of burning people in ovens, of breaking the tiny heads of infants on walls and murdering defenseless people—a new, vigorous consciousness must embrace all of us, a new sense must direct our actions. It is not permis-sible for us, people of the mind and heart, to remain in a position of neutrality, which is grist for the mill of people of the knife and fist. The enemy is unequivocal. Let our words be just as unequivocal. . . . let us be combative, revolutionary. Let our voice resound aggressively in defense of peace. Let the resolutions of this congress leave no doubts as to where these engineers of human souls can be found."[73]

Despite such articulate support by people of Tuwim's stature, the congress nearly ended in disaster. Leningrad Party leader Andrei Zhdanov had received the Soviet delegates before they set out for Wrocław. Jakub Berman later speculated that Zhdanov must have given the delegates some last-minute instructions, because the Soviet delegation arrived "bristling with tension and fiery speeches, and was clearly putting pressure on us to support their hurrah-style attack on the Western countries."[74] A speech by the Russian novelist Aleksandr Fadeev, who during the war had sent a very warm telegram to Tuwim, provoked a scandal. Fadeev spoke about the threats to peace in the contemporary world—namely imperialism in general and American expansionism in particular. He saw the world, as per Zhdanov, as divided into two camps: the antifascist, anti-imperialist camp with the Soviet Union at its head, and the reactionary, imperialist camp aspiring to a new war in the name of preserving the capitalist system.[75] The French writer Desanti was there and listened to

> lightning war against the decadence of literature and art in the West; the appearance of the new man bringing socialist realism and aligned with the position of the working class. Every intellectual worthy of the name should oppose that decadence. . . . Vercors, Éluard, Picasso, and I exchanged ironic glances: Ach, those Soviets and their dogmas! We felt safe in our French shell. Until suddenly: "Sartre, that hyena writing on a typewriter, that vulture armed with a fountain pen . . ." Picasso tears off his headphones, during which there resounds an echo of scurrying. Éluard takes his off slowly and starts to note something. Vercors and Léger remain motionless. For me it's a shock. . . . I see Borejsza alone, walking with a lowered head. When he reaches me, he says: "This is it, they've smashed my congress to pieces."[76]

Julian Huxley submitted a declaration of protest, walked out of the congress, and left for London. Jakub Berman made the decision to censor parts of some speeches in the Polish press.[77]

On the day of Fadeev's speech, Jakub Berman was in Warsaw, where he received a call from a despairing Borejsza. Berman spoke to Bierut, and then left by car for Wrocław. Once he had arrived and surveyed the situation, he telephoned Molotov, "applying the principle, well known—to speak parabolically—in the Catholic world, of appealing 'from an ill-informed pope to a well-informed pope.'" The conversation was a difficult one, but Berman sensed that Molotov might be of a different opinion than Zhdanov, and tried to persuade him that breaking up the congress would be detrimental to the communist cause. Afterwards Ilya Ehrenburg gave a speech that mitigated much of the tension provoked by Fadeev's. "We do not want to emphasize what divides us," Ehrenburg told the congress, "on the contrary, we are searching for what could unite us."[78] Following the congress in Wrocław there was an elegant reception in Warsaw, where the men were dressed in dark suits and Pablo Picasso was among the guests. It was late August in Warsaw and the French poet Paul Éluard grew hot, he took off his jacket, and later his shirt, and proceeded to parade around "with the naked, wonderful torso of an athlete."[79]

ALEKSANDER WAT'S HOMECOMING

Aleksander Wat, at the war's end still in Soviet Kazakhstan, had not been forgotten in Poland. In January 1945, as the Red Army approached Warsaw and the war drew to an end, Wat wrote to Iwaszkiewicz from Kazakhstan, pleading with him to learn the fate of his sister, the actress Seweryna Broniszówna.[80] Unlike Wat's younger brother, who had returned from Lvov to Warsaw to be murdered in the Holocaust, Seweryna Broniszówna had survived the war and remained in Poland. Nearly two years then passed before Wat himself received hopeful signs of returning to Poland. Paradoxically, it was Ola Watowa and their son Andrzej, who had relented and accepted Soviet passports, who received permission to leave the Soviet Union sooner than did Wat. That the family was eventually repatriated together owed much to Adam Ważyk, who published an open letter calling on the Ministry of Art and Culture to assist the Writers' Union in bringing one of its members back to Poland. In the letter, Ważyk did not dissimulate regarding Wat's lack of sympathy for communism or his recently adopted Catholicism; Ważyk only insisted that the issue was not ideology but rather a writer of exceptional intelligence who, far away in Central Asia, was dying of heart problems and homesickness.[81]

In 1946, some six and a half years after they had fled Warsaw, Wat and his family left the village of Ili. As they traveled through Alma-Ata to Moscow in rags, people asked from which camp they were returning. In Moscow they were cared for by the Polish embassy; and Wat took Andrzej to see Lenin's body at the mausoleum.[82] Finally they acquired their papers and boarded a train heading west. It was a train filled with Poles, who cried when they crossed the Polish border. Wat and his wife did not realize how Warsaw would look; they knew neither that it had all been destroyed nor what had happened to their families. They only knew, from a newspaper at the Moscow Polish embassy, that Wat's sister Broniszówna, whose former fiancé's bed Wat had inherited at Lubianka prison, was performing at the Polish Theater. In those first moments Ola Watowa "saw how my Warsaw was no longer, how something irrevocable had come to pass and how, like two halves of a cracked nut, the old life and the new life now approaching would not merge."[83] Wat felt more hopeful; after his years in the Soviet Union, he saw Poland as a land of freedom—and the ruins of Warsaw as the price of that freedom.[84]

Wat had been in Warsaw for only a few days when Borejsza's secretary came looking for him. Borejsza, who had given damning testimony against Wat to the NKVD in Lvov, now greeted his old colleague warmly. He was full of proposals for their work together: Wat could be a minister, an editor, could fill any position he liked. Wat demurred, saying he was too tired from the journey to make any decisions. When he returned from Czytelnik and related his conversation with Borejsza to Ola, she sensed an ominous subtext, and proposed that they escape across the border. It was a spontaneous, unrealistic sentiment; after nearly seven years of exile they had finally returned to Warsaw and were too exhausted to contemplate any further wanderings. In the end, Wat declined Borejsza's offers. Rather, he immediately publicized his break with communism by making contact with noncommunist, Catholic literary circles. Borejsza understood the message and issued no further invitations—with the exception of one to the Wrocław conference.[85] The precariousness of the situation Wat had consciously entered was mitigated somewhat by a chance happening: Wat ran into the director of the State Publishing Institute, who immediately offered him a job. Wat responded by telling him to first ask Jakub Berman, who would certainly not agree. But Wat had misjudged his Party tutor of times past; Jakub Berman did grant his permission, and Wat began to work as the chief editor at the State Publishing Institute.[86]

Wat was among the beneficiaries of Borejsza's "gentle revolution." He was, for a time, not cast out of the literary world even though he protested when called "comrade."[87] In 1947 Wat traveled with the Polish PEN Club to Zurich, where he spoke about the moral catastrophe the war had wrought in Europe. It was difficult, Wat told the PEN Club congress, for Polish writers to say what Leonhard Frank had said after the First World War: "Der Mensch ist gut." He asked that the delegates not be surprised when Polish writers now asked: "and what is the West?" After all, what had just come from the West but gas chambers and crematoria? The division into West and East was in any case a false and sinister one, Wat said. He went on to speak of the remarkable rebuilding occurring in Poland despite the enormous destruction, and of the moral responsibility felt by Polish writers. He told the writers gathered in Switzerland: "Do we, writers, have the right to approach people with words of despair, discouragement, catastrophism? Because what does he want, the ordinary Polish person? Only that the world not obstruct him in his peaceful and constructive, in his European, work. Despite everything and everyone I want to affirm my own optimism: man is good. And if one is again deluded, that is an illusion that brings humanity closer to the ideal of the common good. Our obligation as writers is to assist him in that hope. Because the cause of the writer is the cause of moral responsibility for the future." Wat added that never before had Polish literature been so animated and multivalent, never before had it contained such a mosaic of worldviews and literary forms. Now in Poland there was Catholic literature, Marxist literature, existentialist literature, and so forth; now realists coexisted with avantgardists.[88]

The previous year, shortly after their return to Poland in April 1946, Wat and his wife had gone to Łódź for a Writers' Union conference. Leon Schiller, with whom Wat had worked on his first socialist theatrical production in the 1920s, was putting on plays at the theater there, and Daszewski was designing the sets and costumes. After one performance Schiller invited the Wats to dinner. He asked Wat to try to understand Daszewski's role that fateful evening in Lvov, to believe that Daszewski had failed to realize what he was being used for at the time. Schiller believed that Daszewski had been told only that there would be a Soviet art historian at the restaurant who wanted to meet some Polish writers, and that if he arranged a meeting the authorities would help bring his wife to Lvov. Broniewski had forgiven their artist friend, but Wat had not. He remained haunted by the image of Daszewski's flying out the door of the restaurant that January evening.[89] Following the Writers' Union conference Ola Watowa decided to remain in the city for a few days. In Łódź after Wat's departure she was invited to dinner at a restaurant where she saw Daszewski, pale, moving towards her. He told her that he had to speak with her, but her host warded him off, guiding her to a table where Broniewski was gesturing to them. Daszewski, "like a robot," followed them. Before they had even sat down, Broniewski called out with laughter, "Ola, let's hope that Lvov doesn't repeat itself for us here!" Yet even then Daszewski did not leave them. After dinner he followed Ola Watowa in silence as her host escorted her back to her hotel. In the hallway Daszewski again insisted that he had to speak with her. She silently refused.[90]

ADAM WAŻYK'S HOMECOMING

Among the ventures Jerzy Borejsza initiated in Lublin was the literary newspaper *Odrodzenie*. In December 1945 the weekly printed a picture of a very tanned Broniewski who had come home to Poland.[91] There followed shortly the beginning of *A Balloon with Poetry,* telling of the house with a garden in Żoliborz that was no more.[92] There were no strict divisions into those who were and those who were not Party members, and the first few years of the weekly's existence saw varied contributions by Putrament, Stryjkowski, Wygodzki, Krzywicka, Ważyk, Stawar, Wasilewska, Tuwim, Przyboś, Peiper, and Stefan Jędrychowski's friend from their student days in Wilno, Czesław Miłosz. It was understood from the beginning that *Odrodzenie* could not be a revival of *Wiadomości Literackie;* the latter belonged to an era closed forever by the war.[93] *Wiadomości Literackie's* cosmopolitan legacy was nonetheless felt in the new paper. The editors published Vladimir Mayakovsky, Ilya Ehrenburg, Julien Benda, and Karel Čapek. Czesław Miłosz contributed translations of poetry by Pablo Neruda and various African-American authors. There was nostalgia, too, for Café Ziemiańska, which had perished with the rest of the city. A satirical cartoon in *Odrodzenie* pictured a woman ascending the stairs to the upper level of Ziemiańska where the Skamander poets sat. The caption read: "In its time a greater attraction than doughnuts with gold coins was our then young Parnassus 'upstairs' at Ziemiańska. Perverse Iwaszkiewicz, passionate Wierzyński, unkempt, daydreaming Lechoń, elegant Tuwim with his birthmark, oh, how the figures of these rising stars of our litera-ture impressed ladies young and old! We women feel a violent need to revive such a new 'upper level' in Warsaw."[94]

Soon after he had arrived in Poland, in November 1944 on the pages of *Odrodzenie,* Adam Ważyk offered a recantation of the futurism of times past. "In our times," he wrote, "respect for cultural traditions is spreading among perhaps even the whole of the intelligentsia. It is simply impos-sible in today's intellectual atmosphere to imagine such a manifestation against tradition as futurism once was." He was certain that this respect for tradition would not impede artistic progress; in this new society he saw artistic tendencies moving towards unity.[95] At the First Congress of the Polish Writers' Union, which took place in Cracow in late summer of 1945, Ważyk spoke about the cultural ideologies of interwar Europe: their defining trait was being cut off from life. Now the war had demonstrated that being cut off from life would have fatal results.[96]

Ważyk soon became the central figure in a second literary paper that coexisted with *Odrodzenie,* a less gentle—and less compromising—alternative. Unlike *Odrodzenie, Kuźnica* (The Forge) made little attempt to unite Party and non-Party writers, and made no pretense of embracing pluralism. This became still more true following the Tito-Stalin split of 1948, when the Party took an increasingly hard line towards culture. Now on the pages of *Kuźnica* Ważyk played out his new postwar role as "terroretician" of socialist realism, Jakub Berman's closest ally on the editorial staff.[97] He retold the history of the avant-garde for the benefit of those too young to remember, and explained that the thrill of discarding all formerly obtaining rules about literature was the thrill of remaking the world. Ważyk did not go as far in belittling his avant-garde years as he might have; his younger colleague Jan Kott suspected this was because "Ważyk never could have renounced Apollinaire—he would sooner have slashed his own veins."[98] Despite himself, Ważyk harbored a lingering attachment to Apollinaire, he saw in the French avantgardist's writing "the brilliant introduction to almost all of innovative poetry." Yet Ważyk qualified: words were only a substitute for people, avantgardism in literature a substitute for revolution. "In a word," Ważyk concluded, "unable in the realm of art to carry through battles for upheaval in social life, [the avant-garde] enacted upheavals in the forms of art."[99] Mayakovsky was the exception. His poetry stood as "an example of great revolutionary passion," he had understood the strength of words and the responsibility a writer must bear for them.[100] Ważyk took an accordingly hard line on responsibility. During a roundtable discussion with Andrzej Stawar, Jan Kott, and other *Kuźnica* writers, Ważyk spoke out against expressionism and "the amorphous ones," those whose writing was shapeless. "Naturally," Ważyk remarked, "we will shoot them with machine guns." One of the other *Kuźnica* writers was quick to answer that in such a case the first bullet would hit Ważyk's own heart.[101]

Julian Przyboś, the former avant-garde poet who in the interwar years had kept his distance from Warsaw, now became the focus of a literary debate. Przyboś unhesitatingly accepted the postwar political reality, considering himself a leftist and progressive. He saw himself as a bearer of the Revolution—yet the gift he bore was not necessarily well received by those who saw the future of communist literature not in a continuation of the avant-garde, but rather in a return to realism. Przyboś opposed Ważyk's self-annihilating theory about the backward, obscurantist, reactionary character of the avant-garde. At the center of their polemic was the notion of "comprehensibility." Przyboś came under attack for his failure to embrace realism, for the insufficient comprehensibility of his work to the masses.[102] For his part, Przyboś was skeptical about the Party's slogan of "universalizing culture." In a December 1945 article in *Odrodzenie*, Przyboś defended himself, criticizing the slogan "poetry for everyone" as hyperbole, as equivalent to the slogan "everyone into the ranks of the Polish army!" Children, the elderly and handicapped were not called to serve in the army, Przyboś argued, just as poetry was not written for illiterates. He continued: "'Lowering oneself' to the tastes of the reader *is the poet's downfall.*"[103] Socialist convictions notwithstanding, Przyboś maintained the elitist position that aesthetic tastes were always the privilege of a small number.[104] The times were against him. In 1946 Andrei Zhdanov gave a policy-setting speech about the Soviet journals *Zvezda* and *Leningrad*, castigating the poet Anna Akhmatova as well as Wat's friend from Alma-Ata, the Freud expert Mikhail Zoshchenko.[105] The following year, in November 1947, Bierut gave a radio speech in Wrocław, which effectively announced a radical policy change in culture: now the mandate came to follow the previously rejected Soviet model. This was the beginning of the end of Borejsza's "gentle revolution," and Przyboś was dispatched to a diplomatic post in Switzerland.[106]

As the cultural climate was transformed, the Ministry of Art and Culture organized a January 1948 seminar on the former noble estate of Nieborów, in an eighteenth-century palace decorated with Greek vases and family portraits.[107] The ministry wanted to introduce younger writers such as Wiktor Woroszylski and Tadeusz Borowski to the older generation, to Wat, Stawar, and Iwaszkiewicz.[108] At Nieborów, Wat spoke out against overly simplistic oppositions in literature—such as that between "optimistic" and "defeatist" categories. He opposed the idea that all literature should be adapted to the confines of realism, and insisted that literary style was a much more complicated matter. "The danger," Wat elaborated, "lies in something else as well. Socialist realism in particular, which makes use of the schema good versus evil, reaction versus progress, and creates a positive (chosen) and negative (condemned) hero, reinvokes a Christian eschatological schema."[109] In the end, the seminar revealed a generational conflict, with the radical young writers attacking the liberalism of the older writers and their sympathy for modernist trends such as cubism and postsurrealism.[110] The young generation launched a frontal attack, throwing insults by calling this one a symbolist and another one a *passéiste*—once a favorite accusation leveled by the avant-garde of the 1920s, which the older writers themselves represented.[111]

The Sovietization of the literary sphere—and the battle against bourgeois aestheticism—continued. In September 1948 Zhdanov appeared on the front page of *Odrodzenie* with the declaration that Soviet writers took pride in accusations of tendentiousness.[112] Borejsza, chastised for his liberalism and cosmopolitanism in cultural policy, composed a gentle negation of his gentle revolution.[113] Broniewski, the revolutionary poet, neither opposed nor embraced Zhdanov's mandates. Rather he spoke somewhat abstractly about how, on one hand, "commissions" for creative work derive from society, from the working masses—yet on the other hand, the poet must experience that content internally and not simply write to order; he must reach the same consciousness himself as opposed to producing on demand. About socialist realism Broniewski remained ambivalent: it was a good thing—which had its dangers.[114] At the 1949 Polish Writers' Congress in Szczeciń, socialist realism was formally mandated in Poland.[115] Now the once avant-garde poet who loved Apollinaire, "Ważyk with the ugly little face," became "our little Zhdanov." Like Zhdanov, Ważyk was harsh, dogmatic, and not without malice.[116] He had assistance from Jakub Berman, who at that time "personally took everything into his own hands, he dragged everyone to Central Committee meetings and enforced the style of socialist realism."[117]

The year 1949 saw the clear politicization of *Odrodzenie*. In December 1949 Borejsza organized a special issue in commemoration of Stalin's seventieth birthday, including Mayakovsky's poem "1917" in Ważyk's translation and a drawing of Picasso holding a glass with the inscription "A ta santé, Staline!"[118] The centerpiece was Władysław Broniewski's "Słowo o Stalinie" (A Word about Stalin), an eclectic poem of nine parts in different meters, bearing no traces of any resentment Broniewski might have harbored after his time in Soviet prison. "A Word about Stalin" began with an image of the nineteenth century. The century of Marx's "Communist Manifesto," of steam engines, of the defeat of the Paris Commune was now dying out like a gas lantern. "'Revolution—the locomotive of history,' / Marx said, Lenin enacted," Broniewski wrote. The fifth section continued:

> The train of history rushes forward,
> the century-signal flashes
> The Revolution does not need glory,
> it does not need noisy metaphors,
> it needs an engine driver,
> which is He.

Broniewski wrote of Stalin's name as the hope of a new world being born as the old world burst like an atom. He returned then to Poland:

> In my land
> millions of graves
> through my land
> passed a fire,
> through my land,
> passed ill fortune,
> in my land
> was Auschwitz.

Yet the unhappy land where Warsaw lay was being rebuilt: "Warsaw, cruelly destroyed, raises its blood-stained bricks all the more quickly with the name of STALIN."[119] This birthday issue devoted to Stalin was among *Odrodzenie*'s last. In 1950 *Odrodzenie* merged with *Kuźnica* to form *Nowa Kultura* (New Culture); these were now different times.

In February 1950, Jakub Berman expressed further thoughts on the socialist realist mandate: the deepening of Marxist consciousness among writers was resulting in progress, yet Polish literature remained burdened by the "the omnipotence of spontaneity."[120] Reports reaching Berman suggested that resistance to the Party line in culture was fading, that the "old worldview" was no longer on the ideological offensive. Aleksander Wat was the exception. He alone, "in a quite perfidious way, creating the superficial appearance of intellectual depth, attempted to proffer an idea of the catastrophic state of contemporary Polish literature, polemicizing against the Marxist thesis about the class and ideological causes of a certain crisis of literary creation."[121] In fact Wat was not on the ideological offensive; he was withdrawing from cultural life.[122]

In July 1950, Adam Ważyk gave a speech at the Fifth Congress of the Polish Writers' Union, held in Warsaw for the first time after the war. He began by announcing two tasks: the battle for world peace and the reshaping of the country. Ważyk's wartime reeducation in the Soviet Union revealed itself; he spoke in the Stalinist language of "the people," "building," "objective," "concrete," "errors," "bourgeois," and "consciousness." There could be no "objective" evaluation of art apart from its social and ideological function, he emphasized. "In the battle for the future," he said, ". . . every truth is passionate and political. The true intellectual and moral value of a literary work can be appraised in accordance with its force in mobilizing to battle for peace and for the future." The secret of socialist realism's mass appeal was its ability to provide the people with "the constructive and formative truth that they desire."[123] Now Ważyk passed judgment on his friends and colleagues in good Stalinist style, handing out praise and condemnation: recent poems by Tuwim, Słonimski, and Iwaszkiewicz, and certain poems by Miłosz, attested to the progress made in the development of ideological-political consciousness since the Szczeciń congress. Following a postwar transition period during which his poetry was weak, Broniewski's ideological and emotional ties to the developing new reality had led to a new blossoming of his artistic potency. Ważyk did not fail to articulate his own self-criticism, replete with the motif of "insufficiencies," regarding his 1949 essay collection *W stronę humanizmu* (In the Direction of Humanism). *Kuźnica* had published a review speaking of the important role these essays played in preparing the ground for socialist realism. Ważyk, however, was quick to point out that his essays played only a limited role, and even then not a consistent one: "I failed to see sufficiently clearly the perspectives for the evolution of literature in People's Poland. I failed to appreciate the value of innovative Soviet literature. In characterizing the literature of the imperialist period, I failed sufficiently clearly or sufficiently precisely to connect the ideological processes occurring in the womb of the bourgeoisie with the concrete course of the class war. As a consequence I did not appreciate the decisive influence of that battle on the formation of declining bourgeois ideologies."[124]

The years following the Szczecin congress were years of socialist realism and Stalinist court poetry, a new genre bearing few traces of the native
Polish proletarian poetry of the late 1920s. Broniewski was far from alone
in writing a poem for Stalin. Ważyk composed his own, comparing the
wisdom of Stalin to a wide river that watered the steppes and the tundra,
bringing forests and wheat and leaving gardens in its wake.[125] The younger
generation was now discovering Mayakovsky in a way all but divorced from
the Russian poet's futurist origins. In a January 1950 piece in *Odrodzenie*,
Wiktor Woroszylski wrote of how "Mayakovsky's poetry is and will be
the natural, classical poetry of the new society." Those who, in defense
of "cultural tradition," dismissed Mayakovsky as being "un-Polish and
unrepeatable" were only anti-Soviet nationalists and bourgeois cosmopolitans.[126] Borejsza responded to Woroszylski, criticizing his insistence that
Mayakovsky's form was the only suitable one. Woroszylski, Borejsza wrote,
had forgotten Broniewski, and forgotten about Poland's own heritage of
revolutionary poetry.[127] Some ten days after Borejsza's article appeared,
Tuwim wrote to a fellow poet and essayist, saying that they needed to talk
about "the unimportance of lyricism in the project of the socialization of
minds and in general about the exceedingly limited influence of poetry on
transformations of historical significance in humanity's history." Tuwim
added, "I write this without a shadow of irony, bitterness or regret. On
the contrary: with some joy. . . . I believe in fighting songs with drums,
trumpets, with a whole orchestra (such is the ingenious Mayakovsky).
. . . But Mayakovsky—in truth that's once in a hundred years, or perhaps
longer still."[128]

In 1952, Wat made an exception to his withdrawal from cultural life
and spoke out against socialist realism at a Writers' Union meeting. He felt
that someone had to speak, and that the obligation fell to him because of
his own accounts to settle: so many among the Party leadership had been
formed by *Miesięcznik Literacki*, now Wat had to redeem himself, to pay
for his sins of times past. Jerzy Putrament responded to Wat with hostility,
concluding his own speech in Russian: "when the bear is grumpy, you give
him a bat on the head and then he'll shut up." Another Party writer added
that everyone was united with the exception of one enemy—Aleksander
Wat. Woroszylski grew enraged as he listened to Wat say things "completely unacceptable"—so much so that he resolved to travel to the Soviet
Union so as to gain more knowledge to fight against Wat's heresy.[129] None

of Wat's friends spoke out in his defense. He returned home from the meeting feverish and chilled.[130]

TUWIM'S HOMECOMING (AS AN *ENGAGÉ* POET)

Tuwim, absent during the whole of the war, was deeply affected by it. The war, and above all the Holocaust, had made him a Polish Jew, a supporter of communism, an activist, and an *engagé* poet in a way he had never been before. In the spring of 1947 Stanisław Wygodzki, who had once written desperate letters to Broniewski from prison, was in a Warsaw café when he saw Tuwim sitting by the wall, looking at him uncertainly. They had met before the war, when Wygodzki, before his days in Auschwitz and Dachau, had looked quite different. Tuwim did recognize him, though. He stood up and called out the name of Wygodzki's hometown, "Będzin!" The younger poet was moved to tears. Tuwim asked him, "Do you know what they did with my mother?" Wygodzki was silent. "They threw her from the window onto the pavement."[131] After the war, Tuwim published a poem in *Odrodzenie* about his mother's grave in the Łódź cemetery, "the Polish grave of my mother / of my Jewish mother."[132] When he returned to Poland from New York, Tuwim began to sponsor a provincial elementary school library near Łódź through a fund in memory of his mother. He became intensely interested in the children there; he asked that they write to him with detailed descriptions of the area: the pharmacy, the houses, the woods, the smells. He sent them books and told them of the horrors of fascism, of his mother's death at the hands of Nazi bestiality, and of his hopes for the new People's Poland.[133]

Tuwim wrote a poem to the Soviet nation, speaking of the Revolution as an eternal beauty, and of Stalin as an immortal hero.[134] He published excerpts from his American notebooks: "Political disengagement has become for me a concept equivalent to unmusicality: I—a poet!—cannot understand it."[135] "Poland without social revolution: a childless mother. You can't make an omelet without breaking eggs."[136] He raised his voice in literary politics as well. In an autumn 1947 open letter to the poet Konstanty Gałczyński, Tuwim wrote of the responsibility of the poet. He condemned Gałczyński's recently published verse for its careless praise of saints and sinners alike. "We, poets," Tuwim wrote, "are not permitted today to go around the world with our eyes closed and fall into a blissful Franciscan state of love and forgiveness for all. Leave that to the hypocrites." He continued on a very personal note: "Because you should know, Konstanty, that sixteen months after my return to Poland I am full of such banalities like faith, hope, love for the noble, hatred for the villainous, youthful (for old age) optimism, in such degrees as I never experienced during my youth. You will perhaps ask, how do I distinguish the noble from the villainous? The sinners from the saints? I distinguish, my friend. It happened slowly and with difficulty. Until it happened decisively, without any vacillation, once and for all. It happened over the grave of my Mother, murdered by the fascists. They were sinners, Konstanty, terrible sinners."[137]

Nearly two decades after he received a kiss from Janina Broniewska for his intervention upon Ważyk's arrest, Tuwim intervened with the security apparatus on behalf of one of the "sinners": the poet Jerzy Kozarzewski, an officer in the Home Army and the great-grandson of the poet Cyprian Norwid. He was arrested in September 1945, and sentenced to death. Kozarzewski's wife Magdalena, whose family had aided Tuwim's mother during the war, turned to Tuwim with a plea for him to intervene with President Bierut on her husband's behalf. Despite his newly acquired political dogmatism, Tuwim was shaken and did not refuse her. To Bierut he wrote that this matter was perhaps the gravest he had ever experienced as it involved saving the life of a person—in fact of six people, as Tuwim did not neglect to plead on behalf of those sentenced together with Kozarzewski. He had agreed immediately to Magdalena Kozarzewska's request, he told Bierut, because how could he have responded otherwise?

> I agreed, although I breathe hatred for the ideology of the condemned; although their crimes are obvious to me; although I know that as a result of their activity hundreds of people have perished and are perishing. I even know that if they were to catch me—the one intervening on their behalf—they would murder me—they themselves or their supporters—mercilessly, because for them I'm "a Jew and a Bolshevik." Whatever else one can suspect me of, one cannot suspect me of sympathy for the condemned. But with that much greater passion, with that much greater fervor, I come to you, a person to a person, a Pole to a Pole, a democrat to a democrat, and I plead

with you to spare the life of Kozarzewski and the five other
condemned.

Tuwim spun a web of philosophical arguments. His intervention was the
intervention of a poet, and "what, after all, is the predestination of the
poet in that final, most essential meaning of that word? It is the doing
of good. That good is sometimes called beauty, sometimes knowledge,
sometimes truth." Moreover, he was intervening on a poet's behalf. "The
bullet that would kill Kozarzewski," Tuwim wrote to Bierut, "would rico-
chet and strike the heart of every Polish poet." He reminded Bierut of
what Dostoevsky had once written: if the salvation of humanity were to
depend on a single child's being put to death, we would have to relinquish
that salvation. These were not children, Tuwim acknowledged, and they
should be punished—but not with death, death would only grant them
dignity, transform them into martyrs. In conclusion Tuwim added that
Magadalena Kozarzewska's family had aided his mother during the occupation, despite the fact that they knew neither his mother nor Tuwim
personally. "They helped her for the reason that my Mother the Jewess
gave the world a Polish poet," he wrote. Tuwim's request was granted. The
death sentence was commuted to ten years of imprisonment.[138]

His humanitarian defense of Kozarzewski notwithstanding, Tuwim
now identified unambiguously as a political poet. When in 1949 the left-
wing Chilean poet Pablo Neruda paid a visit to Poland, Tuwim wrote a
long letter welcoming the Latin American visitor:

> Dear poet!
>   We are sons of different races, of different continents,
> different histories; different are our languages, our customs;
> for me your homeland is an "exotic" country—doubtlessly to
> the same degree that Poland is "exotic" for you. . . . And yet,
> when I learned that Pablo Neruda had come to Warsaw, my
> heart beat with more fervor, more joy from being so moved—
> just as if upon the news of the arrival of someone close and be-
> loved whom I had not seen for a very long time. Why? So much
> seems to divide us, we differ so much between ourselves, and
> so where is the source of so much joy at your arrival? Is it only

that we both represent that odd tribe that is the poet? No, not
for that reason. The cause is other: what joins us a hundred
times more than divides us lies in one qualification, which
up to this time has passed for "prosaism," yet which in the
essence of the matter resounds with beautiful poetic content:
a common *political* path, a path of conscious, decisive, and
ideologically explicit battle for a new, more beautiful life of
humanity. More beautiful by a complete justice, violated until
now at each step by greedy people, beasts of prey wreaking
injury on millions of paupers. More beautiful by the complete
defeat of all those who in their own interest are ready to burn
and murder three-quarters of the earth, if only on the remaining one-fourth they would live well.

Tuwim spoke to Neruda as one fellow-traveling poet to another, writing
of how they were united by their faith that wherever in the world a cry
of pain was heard, it would no longer pass without an echo—for Neruda
in Chile, Éluard in France, Broniewski in Warsaw, Venclova in Lithuania
would sound the alarm through their poetry. "Because we, poets," Tuwim
concluded, "in former times roaming around the world in solitude, today
have become one great family, one great community of brothers, calling
to one another not only by name, not only by the singing of words (whose
beauty and charm I do not at all reject)—but above all by the slogans of
the battle we are waging and will wage to its victorious end."[139]

JANINA BRONIEWSKA'S HOMECOMING

In the summer of 1946, Wasilewska formally brought the era of the Union
of Polish Patriots to a close, instructing her comrades and colleagues
not to forget "those who extended to us a fraternal hand, who helped us,
who took care of us, who—and how wisely and deeply—understood our
longings, dreams, desires, and battle." She paid tribute to the memory
of those who did not live to return to Poland, to Alfred Lampe who had
given them so much.[140] In October of that year Bolesław Bierut wrote to
tell Wasilewska that she had been awarded a Grunwald medal for all of
her work on behalf of Poland.[141]

Wasilewska became a permanent Soviet citizen. Khrushchev recalled
that her daughter Ewa, who after the war went to university and worked

at a library in Moscow, once came to her mother and said to her: "I found Grandpa's books and I ordered them all to be removed to the basement. They're blatantly anti-Soviet."[142] Wasilewska's own career expanded to include Soviet opera. In the late 1940s she co-authored with her husband Korneichuk a libretto in Ukrainian for Konstantin Dankevich's opera *Bohdan Khmel'nytsky.* The opera, telling the story of the seventeenth-century Cossack rebel leader, was simultaneously a socialist and Ukrainian nationalist one, drawing attention to the "heroic struggle" of the Ukrainian peasants against their Polish aristocrat landlords as well to the eternal friendship of the Ukrainian and Russian peoples. A chorus announced: "O, do not rejoice, mighty Poles, that you have bound and chained us. Soon you too shall die. The hour of vengeance is close upon you!. . . . O, do not boast, that you have crucified the Ukraine." The libretto included a feminist subplot in which Solomiya, the daughter of a Ukrainian killed by Polish lords, took up her father's saber to deliver Ukraine from bondage. At the conclusion of the libretto, the hero Bohdan declared: "Great Russia! Our great brother! Accept our deepest respects, our thanks, and our eternal love! Henceforth we shall be invincible with you at our side!"[143]

In 1947 the American writer John Steinbeck visited Soviet Ukraine, where he received an invitation to lunch from Korneichuk and Wasilewska, "a Polish poetess who is known in America." He described their home as pleasant with a lovely garden of vegetables and flowers. Wasilewska served lunch on a vine-shaded porch: "It was delicious, and there was a great deal of it. There was a vegetable caviar made of eggplant, a fish from the Dnieper cooked in a tomato sauce, strange-tasting stuffed eggs, and with this an aged vodka, yellow and very fine. Then came strong, clear chicken soup, and little fried chickens, rather like our Southern-fried chicken, except that they were dipped in bread crumbs first. Then there was cake, and coffee, and liqueur, and last Korneichuk brought out Upmann cigars in aluminum cases."[144]

It may well have been her friendship with Wasilewska that catapulted Janina Broniewska from being the wife of a revolutionary Polish poet to being an activist in her own right. After the war, she became the secretary of the Party circle in the Writers' Union.[145] The 1950 evaluation in her Party file noted that "Comrade J. Broniewska holds her own in a Bolshevik-like manner."[146] In addition to her political career, following her return to Poland Broniewska had three children under her care—the third being

Broniewski's stepdaughter Majka whom Broniewska had found in an orphanage when Marysia Zarębińska was in Auschwitz. Zarębińska soon after returned, but she had only seemingly survived Auschwitz. In 1947, she
died. Now Janina Broniewska, together with her new husband, General
Leon Bukojemski, again took in Majka. When she was unable to attend
one of Majka's school conferences she sent Bukojemski in her place. He
hesitated, asking how he was to explain his relationship to Majka to her
teacher. Broniewska replied that it was very simple: Majka was the daughter of his wife's first husband's second wife and her first husband—and
with that she set off to a Party meeting.[147]

In 1947, Janina Broniewska became the editor of the new magazine
Kobieta (Woman). The eccentric disjointedness of *Kobieta* included wild,
colorful covers with illustrations combining socialist realism and the aesthetics of American suburban housewives. Articles such as "The Demonstration of Polish Women on Behalf of Peace," "Leningrad in Battle,"
"There Can Be No Victorious Battle for Socialism without the Participation
of Women," and "Soviet Women—The Avant-garde in the Battle for Peace"
were juxtaposed with columns such as "The Art of Laundry," "How to
Cook," and "Cosmetics in a Woman's Life."[148] Wasilewska and her now-
grown daughter, Ewa, received *Kobieta* in Kiev, and wrote enthusiastically
to the editor: "All of us are living according to *Kobieta*. Ewa has already
tried all the cosmetic suggestions, I've enriched my culinary knowledge.
. . . we're all dressing according to Zuzanna's prescriptions."[149] *Kobieta*
was to be short-lived however; the venture was "liquidated" at the end of
1949, with the last issue dedicated to Stalin's seventieth birthday—and
including a picture of his mother.[150] Ewa Wasilewska's feelings were com-
municated by her mother: "How to live now without weekly instructions
about dressing, eating, washing out stains, and so forth?"[151]

Janina Broniewska was not entirely content that her closest friend
had chosen to remain far away. Despite that, their friendship remained a
remarkable one. They had become each other's family. Broniewska kept
a room in her postwar home, furnished with Wasilewska's furniture, always ready for her friend's arrival. Julian Stryjkowski, after his first awkward meeting with Wasilewska in Moscow, subsequently saw her more
than once at Janina Broniewska's villa. In postwar Warsaw, Stryjkowski
noted, Wasilewska still had "that same gloomy and lofty facial expression

she had had in Moscow."[152] After returning home to Kiev from a visit in 1947, Wasilewska wrote to her friend, "I have to tell you, despite the fact that I had thought that I was already a complete 'miednik i cynik' [hardened and cynical], it was very difficult for me to leave, not in general, but to leave all of you in particular."[153] In a letter written the following summer Wasilewska asked Broniewska to give a gentle hug from her to Anka.[154] Janina Broniewska's daughter was pregnant; and two months later Wasilewska sent a letter addressed to "Dearest Grandma":

> I understand that Warsaw is being rebuilt at an accelerated tempo. I understand that factories are rising and ports are expanding at lightening speed. But explain to me by what means you were able to master nature, or human nature, so as to produce children with such incomprehensible speed? How can it be done so that one isn't yet pregnant in May, yet in September has already borne an infant? If you clarify that mystery for me, who knows, maybe I, too, in my older years will want to be a *macia-heroinia*—at such a pace it's completely realistic. . . .
>
> I only worry about our baby linens for newborns—by November when I should be able to deposit the gifts personally at the feet of the heir to the throne, they could—all the more so as where you are children will probably grow as well at some unnatural rate—turn out to be too small. Let me know if by November the little one has already become a writer, doctor, or engineer so that instead of diapers I can bring a typewriter, dentist's chair, or a small Eiffel tower. Moreover, before you relate everything to me in person, don't torment my woman's soul but write how everything happened. How much does she weigh, how did Anka feel, how does she feel, her little head, little legs, in general everything.[155]

On that September day, as she was preparing to send this letter, Wasilewska received a letter from Broniewska in Warsaw, and so immediately began a second one herself, again lamenting her distance. "Jasieczka," she wrote, "if only it were possible to go to the airport, get on a plane, and be at your place just in time for lunch. . . . I wouldn't have to think it over for even a moment."[156]

ANTONI SŁONIMSKI'S HOMECOMING

Jarosław Iwaszkiewicz saw Antoni Słonimski in 1945, when Słonimski came to Poland for the first time after the war. Słonimski, the Iwaszkie-wiczes, and Irena Krzywicka were among the prewar friends who met for dinner at Warsaw's Hotel Polonia, which stood out alone among the ruins, amidst the lingering smells of burning and decaying bodies. They spoke about those who had been taken to Auschwitz, about those who had been killed, about Krzywicka's lover Boy-Żeleński. And every so often Słonimski or the others who had been absent during the war would ask: Why? Shot for what? These were questions that testified only to their fundamental lack of understanding, and they saddened Iwaszkiewicz. After the dinner, which lasted late into the night, Iwaszkiewicz together with his wife and Irena Krzywicka retired to a communal room in the hotel. Many people were sleeping on plank beds, they chose one for the three of them near the window. Iwaszkiewicz could not sleep. He lay awake between his wife and Krzywicka, and they began to whisper to one another:

> "I have the impression," I said, "that what we experienced during the occupation, the Warsaw uprising, the months after the uprising, the months of an empty Warsaw, it's weighed upon our dispositions, our characters, on that which is called the soul, a burden that cannot be cast off. It's a hallmark distinguishing us from all others. And that moment of difference will always remain a trifling, but essential element between us and them. We are marked for the ages."
> "I'm afraid that it's a very big difference," said Krzywicka.
> "It will probably balance out someday," my wife consoled us.
> "Perhaps," I said.[157]

And perhaps Słonimski felt this difference as well. Despite his formal repatriation to Poland in 1946, he soon returned to London, where he served first as chairman of the literary section of UNESCO and then as director of the Polish Culture Institute.[158] In 1949 Tuwim wrote tauntingly to his old Skamander friend, suggesting that Słonimski's correspondence—sparse yet filled with vulgarity, nonsense, and other foolishness "at odds with the beautiful and lofty creative work of the illustrious poet"—might well become a collector's item.[159] The following year Tuwim sent Słonimski a similarly jocular letter. "I dreamt of you," Tuwim wrote,

"With regret I affirm that you have many objections as to my character and abilities; yet you were enchanted by my beauty and you expressed that quite passionately. But this, too, wasn't very pleasant." He asked when his friend was finally planning to return to Poland, as "Ewunia often asks: 'when is that silly uncle coming from London?'"[160]

Słonimski returned permanently only in 1951. That same year Czesław Miłosz, who had been serving as Polish cultural attaché in Paris, defected from People's Poland. Now Słonimski wrote a vicious open letter to his fellow poet, the former catastrophist from Wilno:

> You agitate against the planned work encompassing the ever broader Polish masses, you strike a blow against the building of factories, universities, and hospitals, you are an enemy of workers, peasants, and the intelligentsia, who for the first time in the history of our country have stood in battle to cast off the harm and exploitation of the capitalist system. You are an enemy of our workers' and peasants' sons, who fill the schools of higher education, who crave learning and work, you are the enemy of the architects and bricklayers who are rebuilding the capital, of engineers who are working out plans for new factories, of Party workers who are fighting against ignorance. . . . Each Polish success, each stage victoriously overcome, each new factory, new collective, each good book by a Polish writer evokes your hatred. You feel joy at every adversity that the ravaged country encounters on the path to socialism.

That Miłosz had once upon a time been a "progressive" who included "revolutionary" slogans in his literary repertoire made his betrayal all the more hateful. Słonimski, the satirist who had harbored no illusions following his 1932 visit to the Soviet Union, now had mastered Stalinist discourse:

> You are an enemy of our present, but what frightens you most is our future. You know that the fulfillment of the six-year plan will make a great and strong socialist country of Poland. You don't want every person in Poland to have work, bread, and education. You don't want hundreds of new factories and hospitals, dozens of new universities and laboratories to arise in

this land, you don't want the works of the great writers of the world to reach the working masses in hundreds of thousands of copies, you don't want the liberation of your own nation from the capitalist yoke.

What do you want? What is your program? Let's be honest. You want only one thing. You want war. A war more terrible than all past wars. On the new corpses of millions of children, women, and men, on the new ruins of cities today rebuilt do you rest your hopes. Those bloody calculations bear various names, but you most often and most willingly call them "patri- otism." And so your "patriotism" desires the domination of reactionary neo-Nazi Germany over Europe, your patriotism aspires to the loss of half of the territory of the Republic and to the delivering of the whole of the Polish population into the vassalage of industrial barons, Junkers and Nazis.

At times you give your bloody schemings the name "crusade of freedom." What kind of allies do you have in this crusade? By now you sit down at one table, although at the far end, barely tolerated, with yesterday's executioners of the Polish nation. Your allies are the Nazi ghosts restored to life, the black Spanish Falanges, the dark reactionary forces of the entire world paid and armed by American capitalists.[161]

In the pages of the émigré Paris journal *Kultura* (Culture), Miłosz published his reply. His open letter to Słonimski was pained, reflective, and patronizing. Miłosz began with the observation that Słonimski's at- tack on him was composed in the tradition of the Moscow show trials, and reminded his attacker that there had been a time when Słonimski himself had been indignant at the servility of Russian writers who shouted on cue "kill him!" Now Słonimski was fulfilling the same role, and Miłosz would have had nothing to say to him were it not for his past as a poet. "I will answer you," Miłosz wrote, "in a way deserved by the old poet from Pikador, and not the author of feuilletons in the Polish version of *Pravda*." "You were never a communist," Miłosz continued:

When Polish communists were rotting in prisons, you sat in the café and wrote weekly chronicles for small-town liberals. When those liberals were dying in front of firing squads and in

gas chambers, you were in London. And you were in London
when Polish communists were then rotting in Soviet prisons
and when they forgave those prisons, when they took upon
their own conscience the deportations organized by Russians,
the destruction of Warsaw, the planned—under the disguise
of wartime operations—burning of cities and the pillaging of
factories in the western territories; they took it upon their own
conscience in the name of their own ideal. And now you have
chosen orthodoxy by the force of facts that you yourself did not
create and that you did not want.

Miłosz speculated that Słonimski's "conversion to orthodoxy" had its
source in a fear of his own emptiness. He reminded Słonimski of who
he had once been, of what he had once written. "Your voice sounded more
sincere," Miłosz told him, "when you wrote:

'Our people!' they cry glibly
Our people are as stupid as a block.
I prefer lemonade with ice
On a hot summer's day."

Miłosz added that he hoped Słonimski, in attacking him, had improved
his situation in Warsaw, for Miłosz wished him well. He further reminded
Słonimski of what someone they both knew had once said: "'If you have
to be in hell, then be the devil pushing the souls into the boiling tar, and
not a poor soul who is sizzling in the tar.' So push them into the tar, Antoni. Push them into the tar and may you have for that price a moment
of pure aesthetic delight in your apartment adorned with books. But the
taste must be bitter to you when you remind yourself of your past as a
humanist."[162]

MIESIĘCZNIK LITERACKI'S HOMECOMING

Adam Ważyk, whose open appeal had brought Wat home to Poland, was
convinced that Wat returned as a believing Catholic. Ważyk had not been
misled: in 1953 Wat and his wife were secretly baptized at a small church
on Piwna Street.[163] Ważyk had thrown himself into communism, and he
and Wat saw each other only rarely. Twice they found themselves together
abroad—once in 1949 in Weimar for the bicentennial of Goethe's birth,

and once in Venice for a PEN Club congress. Away from Poland, they had occasion to talk. Wat told Ważyk of how he had become religious in prison. Ważyk asked no questions, but was struck by Wat's mysticism, his "God-searching." In East Germany, Wat concluded his speech, in German, with an obligatory toast in honor of Stalin, and the next day told Ważyk that West Berlin radio had seized upon that toast and "reminded" Wat of his time in Stalinist prison.[164]

The legacy of *Miesięcznik Literacki,* which had once brought Jakub Berman and Wat together, remained with Wat in Stalinist Poland. Although he had given signs upon his return of not being "with them," the Party did not entirely reject him, and rather people like Jakub Berman hovered in the background as his protectors. In 1948, at the last reception Wat attended at the palace of the Council of Ministers, a stranger approached him and said: "'What, don't you recognize me? But I was in the editorial offices of *Miesięcznik Literacki* so many times. That was an incredibly memorable period for me! Those were my beginnings. *Miesięcznik Literacki* introduced me to the world of communism.' And he looked into my eyes with such affection that it would have felt stupid to say that I didn't recognize him."[165] From Putrament's memoirs Wat learned that Putrament had dedicated a poem to him, or rather to Aleksander Wat, editor of the legendary *Miesięcznik Literacki.* And Wat supposed that this cast light on Putrament's persecution of him as a renegade, that this was "a case of disappointed love." Yet despite the constant evidence of the power of *Miesięcznik Literacki*'s legacy, Wat never invoked that history to his advantage. In Russia, in Soviet prison, he had acknowledged *Miesięcznik Literacki* as his greatest sin.[166]

Perhaps then it was in partial atonement that Wat wrote the poem "Imagerie D'Epinal" in memory of the show trial deaths of Rudolf Slánský, László Rajk, and many others:

> The executioner yawned. From his axe blood was still dripping.
> "Oh don't cry, little one, no need for tears, here's a lollipop."
> He took her in his arms. Stroked her. And she stared at
>   the head.
> At the eyes no longer seeing. At the mute lips.
> It was the head of her father. Later, embalmed,
> washed, it was put on a pole and attractively painted.

With that pole the little girl marched in a parade on a crowded
   sunny road,
under her school banner:
      "In the name of happiness for all—death to enemies."[167]

Wat ceased going to May Day parades, after having attended almost all of
them in the prewar years. Only once did he make an exception, when it
seemed that he might be arrested. Janina Broniewska—whom Wat rather
disliked—blushed with pleasure at seeing him there. She took him by the
hand and pushed him towards the front, until Wat found himself in the
first row with Broniewska and Ważyk. Broniewska held one of his hands,
someone else held the other, and they paraded him in front of Bierut and
Jakub Berman.[168]

Janina Broniewska was happy to march together with Wat. She was
dogmatic and fearless; but many others avoided Wat in the Stalinist years.
Broniewski was another exception; he came to see Wat and spoke openly
of his late friends Jan Hempel, Stanisław Ryszard Stande, and Witold
Wandurski, executed by the Soviets.[169] Alongside his generous poem about
Stalin, Broniewski wrote a poem about Wandurski:

Wandurski taught me how I should write without compromise,
which poems were worse, and which were better.
Witold, if you appreciate only horseradish with mustard,
   don't come to Ziemiańska, because I'll pepper the pastries.[170]

Broniewski's alcoholism made him an increasingly difficult guest. Once
he stopped by the Wats' apartment unannounced and demanded vodka.
They did not refuse him; in the end it grew late, Broniewski had drunk
too much to go home, and Ola Watowa made a bed for him. He refused
to accept pajamas, insisting that he slept naked. Then, naked, he began to
fly around the apartment, chasing their fat maid, who ran away from him,
snickering.[171] Broniewski, prone to drunken phone calls in the middle of
the night, on another occasion telephoned Wat and said, "Don't think,
Aleksander, that I'm such a swine as everyone thinks I am."[172]

Andrzej Stawar was also often at Wat's apartment. He had made his
way back to Poland after having spent the war in Hungary. Upon his return
to Warsaw, he unexpectedly encountered Irena Krzywicka in the corridor
of a government building in Praga. They had been very close in the 1920s,

and Stawar was so moved to see her now that his hands began shaking. Their friendship began anew.[173] For a time after the war, during the "gentle revolution," the editors of *Odrodzenie* and even *Kuźnica* could publish his writing, but that time came to an end. The Party was watching him, and had not forgotten that Stawar was a former Trotskyite connected to Isaac Deutscher and Wiktor Alter, that he had published *Pod Prąd* and written for *Nurt*.[174] The younger writer Jan Kott was among the representatives of *Kuźnica* who took Stawar's case to Jakub Berman. Berman had little sympathy for the former *Miesięcznik Literacki* author. "Let him get down on his knees," he told Kott, "and take back all the lies he has spread about us."[175] Stawar refused. He moved about in silence, unobtrusively. His own writing remained unpublished, although after some time had passed Berman allowed him to publish translations under a pseudonym so that he could support himself.[176] When he was without an apartment, he lived at times with the Wats, at times with Irena Krzywicka.[177]

The Wats also received visitors from the younger generation of writers. At the height of the Stalinist era Tadeusz Borowski would come "to talk about his own schizophrenia, his profound disenchantment, his excessive zeal as a communist, his fanaticism as a means of destroying himself."[178] Once in 1950 Tadeusz Borowski was visiting when Stanisław Wygodzki telephoned, distraught, and asked Ola Watowa if he could come by right away. Life had not been easy for the poet who had been so enthralled by Broniewski and Wat when he was a young man sitting in prison and writing proletarian verse. In August 1943, while on a transport to Auschwitz, Wygodzki had poisoned his wife and daughter to spare them the gas chambers.[179] Now a friend of Wygodzki, whom Wygodzki had persuaded to return to Poland from Israel, had taken his own life in Wygodzki's home. Wygodzki's new wife sat beside him and pleaded with her husband not to cry. Suddenly, listening to this, Borowski flew into a passion and Ola Watowa listened as he shouted: "'What are you sniveling to me about, control yourself, if we're here now together, it's only because there in Auschwitz we took bread from the dying who no longer had the strength to raise a piece of bread to their mouths. We didn't cover them with blankets! We took their blankets, because we knew that they would no longer need them. It was largely their deaths that rescued us from ours, it was over their corpses that we left Auschwitz. Your friend killed himself, he lacked the strength and patience to fight and the desire to bear human generosity, to accept kindness, in which he had long ago ceased to believe. He didn't have the strength to go out into the jungle in which we've already struck roots and made ourselves comfortable.'"[180] The following year Borowski turned on the gas burners in his apartment and inhaled until he was dead. For Wat Borowski's suicide was reminiscent of Mayakovsky's, perhaps in their disillusionment, their disgust with themselves, their betrayed love.[181]

Following Borowski's suicide, and not long after the 1952 Writers' Union meeting at which Putrament attacked him, Wat fell seriously ill. He was in the hospital in March 1953 when Stalin died. Ola Watowa went to visit him and found a group of doctors and nurses gathered in front of Wat's room, where the hospital workers had made a little chapel of mourning for Stalin, with candles, flowers, and a large portrait. A young doctor had donated three meters of black material, which her husband had brought for her from a trip abroad.[182] On the small calendar he kept on the table by his bed Wat wrote "finally."[183] It was a difficult time for Ola Watowa. One day she walked away from a visit to Wat's doctor with tears in her eyes. It was winter, and she was walking quickly home when she was stopped by Jakub Berman's wife, who noticed that she was upset. Watowa told Guta Berman about Wat's illness, and Guta Berman said at once that this had to stop, that something had to be done so that Wat could spend the winter in southern Europe where it would be warmer and better for his health. Ola Watowa then applied to the Ministry of Health for permission for the trip. When she did, it was clear Jakub Berman was backing her request. Memories of his days as Wat's Party liaison, of *Miesięcznik Literacki* still held meaning for Jakub Berman.[184]

JERZY BOREJSZA'S DEPARTURE

In August 1948, Jerzy Borejsza went directly from the Wrocław congress to a Central Committee plenum where a resolution opposing "right-wing and nationalist deviation" was passed and Władysław Gomułka was removed from his leading role in the Party.[185] The era of the "gentle revolution" was then formally closed. Borejsza embodied the accusation of supporting cosmopolitanism in culture, and he quickly acquiesced, offering self-criticism of his "mechanical, undialectical approach to the arrangement of class forces in Poland, and even accommodating culture of a petty bourgeois type." He confessed further to prolonging the period of "neutralization of the petty bourgeoisie without boldly and courageously advancing elements of socialist culture," as well as to justifying liberalism in relation to "snobbish intellectuals becoming snobs" and to allowing "pseudo-Marxist" voices to reach the press.[186] In 1948 Borejsza was removed from the directorship of Czytelnik; he took over the editorship of *Odrodzenie,* but was no longer invited to the most prestigious cultural events.[187] The Wrocław congress was his last great success, despite the fact that it nearly collapsed in the spirit of the Cold War. By 1949, he was no longer the same person. At the beginning of that year he was involved in a serious car accident. Then he fell very ill with stomach cancer. By the time *Odrodzenie* dissolved in 1950, the period of Borejsza's glory had passed. The accusation of right-wing deviation hung over him. A younger writer on *Odrodzenie*'s editorial staff said of his boss: "The new time was not his time. It was the time of his brother, but not his. That wonderful Polish communist outlived his day. He was cast aside. Condemned."[188]

In April 1950, in an angry, desperate letter to Bolesław Bierut, Borejsza demanded to know all the accusations and complaints against him and insisted that he be given the opportunity to defend himself. He requested permission to travel to Moscow, "the capital of every communist," so as to gather the evidence to refute all the denunciations against him. He had spoken to Jakub Berman and declared his withdrawal from all creative work, including his film project, as work of such importance could be done only by someone who enjoyed the confidence of the Party—which, as upset him deeply, he did not have at the moment. Moreover, Berman had informed him that he was being removed as general secretary of the Committee for Peace due to some objections by the Soviet and French delegations and more generally due to certain of his disturbing character traits. He protested against being deposed from the leading position in a movement that had been his own brainchild. "I was, I am, and I will remain to the end of my life," Borejsza told Bierut, "a disciplined member of the Party, submitting to each pertinent Party authority. If I commit errors, I have the right to demand criticism."[189]

Antoni Słonimski saw Borejsza for the first time after the war in 1951. When Słonimski asked after Borejsza at Czytelnik, he was told that it was best to look for him early in the morning, by four or five A.M. he was already awake and drinking coffee. When Słonimski found him, Borejsza

told Słonimski that he needed his help in saving Stefan Żeromski. Borejsza wanted to continue to publish Żeromski, but the young hardliners
were opposed, and Borejsza could not bear to see his right to publish the
old master revoked; for him Żeromski was for Poland what Tolstoy was
for Russia. Słonimski did not entirely understand what was going on, he
had only recently returned to Poland. He agreed, however, to write something supportive of Żeromski. Then Borejsza told Słonimski that Stawar
had fallen into disgrace. Słonimski was confused: "I understood only one
thing, that in general things were different from how I had imagined
them, different from how my British friends had explained them, and
completely different from when I had first visited the country in 1945,
when the harpoon of return struck my heart and stayed tethered there for
a few years." When Słonimski arrived in 1951, it was still the case that some
activities in the cultural sphere began with Borejsza. What Słonimski
did not understand was that "Borejsza himself then, unfortunately, was
already coming to an end."[190]

Jerzy Borejsza died the following year. Putrament was asked to
speak at his funeral, which took place on a day that was sunny but cold.
Jakub Berman and other leading Party figures were there, as was all of
Czytelnik.[191] Despite Tuwim's sarcastic comments about Borejsza's opportunistic alliance with the antisemite Piasecki, Tuwim wrote a warm poem
to the cultural activist upon his death: "Jerzy! There were no red roses! /
Red roses were missing from Warsaw!" The poem's refrain told of how
the author was unable to find red roses to place on the grave of his communist friend. In their place he would put a word: battle, faith.[192] After
Borejsza's death, Jacek Różański said that his brother had never been
a true communist in the Stalinist sense because he was insufficiently
capable of hatred.[193]

SKAMANDER'S DEPARTURE

Following his return to Poland, Julian Tuwim received an unsigned letter
from a Polish Jew, a KPP activist from the interwar years who had spent
long years in Polish prisons, who was a veteran of hunger strikes and beatings from Polish counterintelligence. Now the Polish-Jewish communist
was broken and bitter. He longed for Poland even as he felt Poland reject
him, and posed obsessively the question of why he had been cast out:

Why must I emigrate from my country? Why is there no place
for me here? In this country to which I devoted the whole of
my youth. I want to emphasize that I bear no resentment towards the government. Unfortunately, even an appropriate
stance by the Polish government towards the Jewish question
could not change the nature of the problem. The nation has
been poisoned with the venom of hatred and does not want us.
It was not by coincidence that the Germans chose Poland as
the site of the murders and executions of millions of innocent
victims. As is presently revealed, here were the most favorable
conditions, for no other nation would have tolerated it. . . .

And even today, when my decision to leave has reached
maturity, even today at the very thought of what must follow
there swells in me a cruel, terrifying pain. Why?

Why must I leave the country in which I was born and
in which I grew up, whose language is my mother tongue, to
which I dedicated so many of the most beautiful years of my
life and with the thought of which I have lived through the past
several, difficult years of war. Why must I throw away everything and go out into terrible wandering in the unknown.[194]

Julian Tuwim, perhaps at a loss as to how to answer, gave the letter to
Adolf Berman. And Adolf Berman took it with him in 1950, when he left
Warsaw for Israel. He had maintained hopes of solidarity with his communist comrades until the very end.[195] In 1952, now far away in Tel Aviv, Adolf
Berman saw his relations with his Israeli Marxist Zionist party MAPAM
become unstable in the wake of the Stalinist show trials in eastern Eu-
rope. His life, like that of his brother, was shaken by the Slánský trial in
Prague. MAPAM leader Mordechai Oren was put on trial in Prague for
his connection with Slánský. While most of MAPAM's Central Commit-
tee insisted on Oren's innocence, Adolf Berman, now a member of the
Israeli Knesset, refused to take an anti-Soviet line against the Czechoslovak
Communist Party.[196] Soon afterwards, Adolf Berman broke with MAPAM.
In time he became a member of the Israeli parliament representing the
Communist Party of Israel.

Following his brother's emigration to Tel Aviv, and even after his
brother was the bearer of his own Communist Party card, Jakub Berman

was largely silent. He was then at the height of his career. And potentially the next in line to be purged. From New York Chaim Finkelstein, a friend of all the Berman siblings since before the First World War, wrote to Adolf Berman in response to the news of Jakub Berman's successful political career: "It's understood that I'm happy about the news that Jakub has acquired a 'higher rank.' But I'm afraid that my pleasure doesn't originate from the same source as does yours. For me this was only a confirmation that Jakub is still managing to survive, because truth be told, what kind of a life is it and how much value do those offices have, if even a man of Jakub's merit and position does not have the right, or the courage, to write to his brother?"[197]

Others did write. In 1951, Adolf Rudnicki sent a letter to Adolf Berman to discuss the translation of his stories into Hebrew. Rudnicki was not entirely happy in the new Poland. When they worked together on *Kuźnica*, Rudnicki had told Jan Kott that they were digging their own graves.[198] Now he wrote to Adolf Berman, "I definitely should have been born in a different time." He sent news of their mutual friends: Ważyk was translating Pushkin's *Eugene Onegin*.[199] In a second letter Rudnicki asked Berman and his wife not to forget the old Warsaw friends they had left behind at home.[200] Tuwim wrote as well, sending greetings not only to Adolf Berman, but also to all the citizens of Israel "who fight for a cause close to my heart: the cause of peace and liberation from the bonds of American capitalist gangsterism."[201]

Ważyk's translation of *Eugene Onegin* tormented Tuwim, whose engagement with Russian culture long predated his engagement with Soviet-style communism. If his attitude towards the Soviet Union was born in the war, his relationship to Russian literature was lifelong. He translated Mayakovsky as well as Pushkin—and was extremely proprietary in this role. When Ważyk embarked on the translation of Pushkin's *Eugene Onegin*, Tuwim was much offended. In the middle of the night he would awaken his wife to point out to her one of the hundreds of imperfections in that much-resented translation.[202] In spring of 1948 he was touched to receive an invitation to Moscow from the Soviet Writers' Union.[203] It was Tuwim's first trip to the Soviet capital, and Ilya Ehrenburg felt Tuwim's great enthusiasm as they sat in a restaurant and Tuwim spoke of all he wanted to see there. That evening, however, Tuwim fell ill and was taken to a hospital.[204]

Now, so many years after Pikador, Stalinism was destroying the ties of the Skamander poets. After the war, Iwaszkiewicz, once a diplomat for the interwar Polish government, became an activist for Borejsza's movement of Intellectuals in Defense of Peace, a representative in the Sejm, the author of a poem dedicated to President Bierut, and a leading figure in the Polish Writers' Union.[205] Less passionate and dogmatic than Tuwim, Iwaszkiewicz did maintain contact with his old friends "on the other side of the red barricade." In 1947 he visited Grydzewski in London. Afterwards, from Paris in July, Iwaszkiewicz wrote to Grydzewski that he was glad he had not read Grydzewski's newspaper before his visit, for then he might not have spoken so sincerely with him in London. Iwaszkiewicz wrote to his former editor of the "unusually injurious and disregarding relationship to my person to which you many times gave expression on the pages of Wiadomości—whether it was you or your dogs, it's all the same." Iwaszkiewicz reminded him that nothing negative about Grydzewski had ever appeared in Iwaszkiewicz's own publication in Warsaw, that on the contrary Iwaszkiewicz—in the hope that Grydzewski would decide to return to Poland—had tried to lay the groundwork for his return with favorable references to the legacy of Wiadomości Literackie. Now Iwaszkiewicz was saddened that the gesture had not been reciprocated, that Grydzewski had been "so unjust" in relation to his old friend, and he thanked Grydzewski only for having kept from Iwaszkiewicz what he truly thought of him during their visit in London. Now at least Iwaszkiewicz would have the good memories of their time together there.[206]

In response Grydzewski denied having expressed disregard towards Iwaszkiewicz, and justified what was written in Polskie Wiadomości: any kind of public engagement inevitably generated criticism.[207] Iwaszkiewicz responded that he remained glad they had reestablished contact after having lost touch during the wartime years.[208] Their correspondence continued in this spirit—filled with tension, ambivalence, and sadness. Both clung to this remnant of Skamander's legacy. Later that year, in November 1947, Iwaszkiewicz wrote that it was "with true pleasure that I receive letters from you from time to time—I'm glad that, despite everything, you write to me."[209] Grydzewski then asked him: Why the "despite everything"? He insisted that their old friendship had greater meaning than any present "differences."[210] Nevertheless, their relationship remained unstable. After Grydzewski sent Iwaszkiewicz a criticism of his recent work, Iwaszkiewicz responded, "The last package opened my eyes to the whole of your relationship to me and my work over many years. . . . I feel very sorry for you, and for myself, because at one time I considered you a friend."[211] Grydzewski replied: he did not understand "what criticism of this or that work has in common with friendship."[212]

Jan Lechoń never returned to Poland. Słonimski sensed that despite this decision, Lechoń had never been able to reconcile himself to life in exile: "He, who wrote, 'And in spring—let me see spring, not Poland' had her constantly before his eyes in the summer, and in the fall, and in the winter."[213] Lechoń had severed ties with Stern and Wat as well as with Tuwim; and his broken relationships with old friends haunted him in New York.[214] In 1950 Lechoń wrote of Słonimski's recent work, "It's astounding that someone can reach so high, and later become so entangled in a web of lies and so poetically lame."[215] Most painful to Lechoń was his break with Tuwim. In January 1950 he wrote in his diary, "Everything between myself and Tuwim is broken forever with the exception of poetry. In this will be his pardon."[216] Lechoń remained, despite everything, enchanted by Tuwim's poetry. Late in 1951 he wrote in his diary, "I'm not at all indifferent to the fact that the name "Leszek" has remained on the pages of "Polish Flowers." My accounts with Tuwim are not at all settled by the fact that I am not speaking to him and until death do not want to speak to him. There is between us—still another matter existing on a higher level, a Romantic poet would say 'among the stars.'"[217]

In 1952 Lechoń sent an excited letter to Stanisław Baliński, who had fled Warsaw in September 1939 with Mickiewicz's letters: Lechoń had miraculously recovered almost his entire library from Paris, including his correspondence. "I want you one day to see, to read, what not only Tuwim and Słonimski, but also Broniewski, Przyboś, Kruczkowski, once wrote to me," he told Baliński.[218] On November 29, 1953, the thirty-fifth anniversary of Skamander's debut at the café Pod Pikadorem, Lechoń wrote in his diary:

> The first evening the hall was full, which after all wasn't difficult—it was a small room, just for such performances, and immediately it was a true triumph, the feeling that something successful, almost a necessity, had happened. How much separated me from Tuwim and Słonimski was revealed only a few

years ago. At that time we could recite poetry, speak of mis-
chief, and tell jokes for whole days and not hit upon those
differences, which perhaps did not then exist. I think that
I yielded to them and they to me—that we tried to adapt to
one another so as only not to ruin for ourselves the occasion to
recite poems and mock everything and everyone. Słonimski
once wrote about our meeting: 'And from that time on we
spent ten years together with breaks for sleeping and writing
poems.' And he was exaggerating very little.[219]

In 1952 Tuwim sent Aleksander Wat and Ola Watowa a telegram on
the occasion of the twenty-fifth anniversary of their wedding on Hoża
Street, at which, Tuwim reminded them, he had been a witness.[220] Soon
afterwards—after they had known each other for so many years—Tuwim
asked Wat to drink *Brüderschaft* with him, to shift from the formal to the
informal mode of address.[221] In November 1953 Tuwim came to Iwaszkiewicz's lecture on Tolstoy at the Writers' Union. Afterwards they went for
drinks at the Hotel Bristol, where they reminisced about the Iwaszkie-
wiczes' post-wedding "breakfast" held there so many years ago. It was their
last conversation.[222] Julian Tuwim died the following month, in December
1953, almost before his friends had noticed his failing health. His final
words were written on a napkin in the restaurant where he collapsed: "'For
the sake of economy, please turn out the eternal light: I may need it some
day to shine for me.'"[223] Upon Tuwim's death Leon Kruczkowski gave a
speech saying that as much as Tuwim loved, he also hated: ugliness, indo-
lence, the spiritual nihilism of bourgeois society, domestic obscurantism,
and the cosmopolitan oligarchy of capital."[224] When in New York Lechoń
learned of Tuwim's death, he wrote in his diary,[225] "May the Polish ground
rest lightly over you, Julek, the Polish ground you so poorly, so foolishly,
but still truly loved."

CHAPTER NINE

Ice Melting

It calls to me, summons with a soft song
from behind a branch, as if from behind bars
Swollen with tears, trembling with anger
My own voice from many years ago.

—*Antoni Słonimski*

STALIN DIED IN MARCH 1953; in Moscow people were smothered in the mob desperate to say goodbye. The death of Stalin was the beginning of the end of Stalinism. As early as July 1953, the Central Committee of the United Polish Workers' Party voiced its concern about "cases of a lax attitude towards the violation of legal regulations in prisons."[1] There was talk as well—and pressure from Moscow—about reducing the number of comrades of Jewish origin in high-profile positions.[2] Jakub Berman's own expulsion was a gradual one. In 1954 the security apparatus was removed from his supervision; Berman believed it was Khrushchev who decided that in allowing him to be the scapegoat for the Stalinist era, discord could be mollified. Bolesław Bierut agreed to the Kremlin's suggestion that, in the interest of preserving appearances, Jakub Berman be made deputy premier. It was a deceptive promotion; everyone understood that.[3]

In February 1956, Jakub Berman traveled to Moscow with Bierut for the Communist Party of the Soviet Union's Twentieth Congress. On the evening of 24 February 1956, Khrushchev gave his "secret speech" concerning the "cult of personality" and "brutal violations of revolutionary legality" that had prevailed under Stalin. An era had now come to an end. The session was closed, foreign guests were not invited, but Bierut did receive a paper copy of Khrushchev's address. He had already been ill, the congress exhausted him, and now he was devastated. Afterwards

Berman returned to Warsaw, leaving behind Bierut, who was too weak to travel. At home in Warsaw, Berman's comrades attacked him in the wake of Khrushchev's revelations of crimes and "excesses." Disconcerted by the potential reverberations of Khrushchev's speech, Bierut phoned often from Moscow. Berman tried to reassure him that although the situation was a difficult one, it was not catastrophic. Then came another phone call. Bierut—Berman's ally, patron, and friend—was dying. Berman left Warsaw at once to say goodbye, but upon his appearance in Moscow, the doctor refused to allow him into the patient's room. When he arrived for the ceremony at the House of Soviets where Bierut's coffin was displayed, Jakub Berman was given a seat in a distant row, and he understood that this was the end for him.[4]

VOMITING SEAWATER

Even before Khrushchev spoke, Adam Ważyk had pulled the curtain on his own performance. Jerzy Borejsza was already dead. As was Ważyk's rival translator of Pushkin, Julian Tuwim, as were Witold Wandurski, Stanisław Ryszard Stande, and Bruno Jasieński. When Apollinaire's translator turned "terroretician" of socialist realism began the revolt against his own reign, he did so with an impassioned bitterness. "Poemat dla dorosłych" (A Poem for Adults), which Ważyk published in *Nowa Kultura* in August 1955, was a eulogy for a lost Poland. Its motif was the unrecognizability of Warsaw; its tone was one of dislocation; its refrain: "give me a piece of old stone / let me find myself again in Warsaw." The long poem opened with the narrator's inadvertently jumping on the wrong bus and finding himself on an unfamiliar street:

> I returned home
> like one who had gone out for medicine
> and returned after twenty years.
>
> My wife asked, where have you been.
> My children asked, where have you been.
> I was drenched in sweat, silent like a mouse.

The lost narrator grew increasingly harsh. He spoke of "vultures of abstraction" who "devour our brains," of language "reduced to thirty incantations," of a "lamp of imagination extinguished." The narrative topos in "A Poem for Adults" was drawn from an old fable: the emperor was wearing no clothes. Ważyk said this not triumphantly, but with disgust:

Fourier, the dreamer, charmingly foretold
that the sea would flow with lemonade.
And does it not?

They drink seawater,
and cry out—
lemonade!
They return home furtively
to vomit.
to vomit.

Ważyk's rhythm was relentless. Dislocation transposed itself into lies, lies into persecution, persecution into tragedy. The narrator began to tell stories of the victims of these illusions, of the girl expelled from art school for want of socialist morality: "She poisoned herself a first time—and was saved. / She poisoned herself a second time—and was buried."[5]

Ważyk's was a despondent appeal. His arrogant tone only thinly concealed self-disgust. "A Poem for Adults" was in some way a continuation of the communist genre of self-criticism—in this case one articulated as if collectively, on behalf of the Party. For in the end Ważyk did not here break with the Party; and the entire poem would have been a different one were it not for the final stanza demanding a redress of grievances and concluding with the lines: "we appeal every day, / we appeal through the Party." Ważyk affirmed his loyalty to Lenin's original revolution in a verse written several months later, in late 1955, and concluding with the stanza:

From medieval eyes,
from medieval ears,
from medieval noses,
from medieval minds,
from medieval methods
the Party will free the current of revolution
and become as Lenin saw it.[6]

It was the editor in chief of *Nowa Kultura* who made the decision to publish "A Poem for Adults." He paid for that with the loss of his position, as he knew he would—after all, as he remarked to a friend, "I was the sous-chef in this kitchen."[7] It was a scandal for the Party leadership, and a scandal for Jakub Berman in particular, this betrayal by Ważyk, the hitherto loyal cultural ideologue. Berman was indignant.[8] The result was "ferment," and the writers were divided. Some attacked Ważyk for vulgar "naturalism," the dark alter ego of "realism." Leon Kruczkowski accused Ważyk of irresponsibility, duplicity, a betrayal of his vocation. In Kruczkowski's reading, "A Poem for Adults" overflowed with "contempt for man," it presented half-truths, which were worse than lies.[9] Wat felt otherwise. That summer Wat was sitting on the steps of the palace in Nieborów with a Party official hovering nearby, when someone brought him the issue of *Nowa Kultura* with Ważyk's "A Poem for Adults." Wat recited the poem with a certain delicate pleasure. When he had finished, a colleague remarked that it was a crime to be wasting such theatrical talent.[10] In September Jakub Berman intervened, calling a meeting with various writers; in the Party's nocturnal tradition—and predilection for long meetings—it lasted from six in the evening until two in the morning. Someone inquired why the recent rehabilitations of KPP leaders purged by Stalin had occurred in silence, as if in secret. Another writer spoke about the crimes of Borejsza's brother Różański; many of the writers defended Ważyk and his ferment-inducing poem. Jakub Berman's violently theatrical concluding speech failed to provoke the reaction he desired.[11]

Ważyk had been made editor in chief of the literary magazine *Twórczość* (Creativity) in 1950. At the end of 1954, he was replaced by Iwaszkiewicz, who made use of Stawar's recent rehabilitation to solicit his contributions for *Twórczość*. Stawar's good graces in the Party remained, though, somewhat precarious; Iwaszkiewicz still needed Jakub Berman's permission, and so sent someone from his editorial board to persuade him. The editorial board member found Berman sitting hunched up behind his desk under Stalin's portrait in a deteriorated state, his former dynamism absent. In the end Berman gave his permission, on the condition that Stawar include a self-criticism in his first article. Yet Stawar did nothing of the sort, and Iwaszkiewicz published him regardless—with impunity.[12] The Party continued to consider Iwaszkiewicz among the unproblematic ones.[13]

So even before the Twentieth Party Congress did the ideological atmosphere begin to depart from what it had been only a few years earlier. Jakub Berman's statement on cultural policy in January 1956 announced that a climate of freedom was a necessary precondition for literary development, and that the Party wished to avoid interfering in the minutiae of literary creation, in favor of limiting itself to a more general ideological influence.[14] In April 1956—now safely after Khrushchev had spoken first—Antoni Słonimski published "For the Restoration of Citizens' Rights," calling for the democratization of public life. His criticism of the hitherto prevailing climate was severe: "The persecution of critical thought at the beginning of the Renaissance or later, in the 17th and 18th centuries, appears virtually idyllic when compared to the times we have recently lived through." Yet Marxism itself he exculpated. It was not Marxism, but rather the departure from Marxism that bore responsibility for the oppression of the Stalinist years. Nor was the Revolution itself to blame, for in the 1920s the Soviet Union had cultivated innovations in the cultural realm. Słonimski blamed rather the doctrine of socialist realism for destroying two decades of art and literature. His tone remained a mediated one, he did not return to the sharpness of his interwar feuilletons, yet there were shadows here of the sarcasm that had once won his weekly column in *Wiadomości Literackie* so many readers: "The 20th Congress, which contributed so significantly to cleansing the poisoned atmosphere, has unfortunately brought us little in the field of literature. The salvation of literature was seen there to lie in decentralization and in sending writers out into the field. I would gladly send a few of our writers to the devil, but I do not think they would return from their travels through hell bearing Dante's tercets."[15]

After "A Poem for Adults" appeared, Ważyk walked around repeating "I've been in an insane asylum."[16] Existentialism with its premise that existence precedes essence and its insistence on free choice—and therefore a potentially infinite, and devastating, responsibility—made its way into Marxist literary circles.[17] At Jean-Paul Sartre's invitation, Jan Kott put together an anthology of texts from the so-called Polish Thaw for an issue of *Les Temps Modernes*, opening with Ważyk's "A Poem for Adults." As 1956 came to an end, Kott and Ważyk were among those who came together with the idea of beginning a new literary monthly called *Europa*. The Party was unhappy about this. When it refused to consent to *Europa's* existence, Kott and Ważyk returned their Party cards.[18] Upon learning of this, Julian Przyboś condemned his colleagues who had "betrayed

FIGURE 14 Adam Ważyk. Caricature by Julian Żebrowski;
courtesy of Muzeum Literatury imienia Adama Mickiewicza.

the Party and communism" by leaving the Party. Broniewski, too, was harsh—although he himself had always remained a fellow traveler and did not even have a Party card to (not) return.[19] The following year Przyboś turned in his own Party card.[20]

THE ONE CAST OUT

When Jakub Berman returned to Poland after Bierut's funeral, he asked that he be allowed to submit his resignation from the Politburo.[21] His gesture of resignation was seemingly generous: he offered himself as the one to absorb the blame for the Stalinist era so that the Party could remain strong. Yet his own self-criticism was a qualified one, and there were limits to the recriminations he was willing to accept. He reminded his comrades that Stalin had aspired to his liquidation, that it was only Bierut's loyalty that had protected him. Moreover, even though he was in a "particular situation," he had done all he could to assure that Poland was spared the show trials that had occurred in other People's Democracies—and in this he had succeeded. There had been no such trials of Władysław Gomułka and Marian Spychalski; there had been no death sentences in the Tatar trial. The thousands of others tortured and executed he only alluded to—he was guilty above all, he said, of having placed too much trust in his comrades working in security, of not having suspected the methods employed in Polish interrogation chambers. Yet it had never been he who orchestrated the "dirty tricks" that had been played there, Berman insisted. He asked that his resignation be accepted unanimously, as he did not want to be the cause of divisiveness among the Party leadership. "I would like," Berman added in conclusion, "to devote the rest of my life to the cause of the Party, regardless of where and in which position I am working."[22]

It was, perhaps, the issue of cadres that finally coalesced the consensus against Jakub Berman. It was he who had been responsible for security, he who had poorly chosen those who worked under him. It was he who had allowed the violent and undoubtedly sadistic Różański to direct the security apparatus; and he who had allowed Różański's brother Borejsza to become a cultural dictator. Allusions arose to Jakub Berman's past, his "origins," his filling of the security apparatus with communists of Jewish descent. One of his comrades had first raised the issue the day before, in Berman's absence: "All of the leading positions Berman filled with Jewish comrades, and not only with old, good comrades. . . . I gazed at the figure of Comrade Berman, a Jewish intellectual from a bourgeois family who did not grow up in revolutionary conditions."[23] In the end the Central Committee accepted Jakub Berman's resignation.[24] Stefan Jędrychowski spoke to Berman during a break in the plenum, and Berman told him that he was not worried about himself, he was worried only about the fate of socialism. Jędrychowski assured him that his departure would not mean the end of socialism.[25] Now cast out, Jakub Berman was also ostracized.[26] The exception was Janina Broniewska. She did not abandon her wartime comrade.[27]

Jakub Berman was made an editor at a publishing house. It was not an atypical solution. In March 1954 Różański was removed from his position in the security services, and then appointed director of the State Publishing Institute. Yet in Różański's case, his editorial career was short-lived, and later that same year he was arrested. His self-criticism under interrogation was, like Jakub Berman's before the Central Committee, a qualified one. He admitted that he had beaten people, but insisted that he had always been faithful to the Party. Różański was found guilty and sent to prison.[28] Such was not the case for Jakub Berman, who was removed from the government but never arrested. Yet this was not the end, and for Jakub Berman the worst was still to come. In June 1956 the government violently suppressed workers' demonstrations in Poznań. In October, Władysław Gomułka, who had been silently released from house arrest in December 1954, became general secretary of the Party. On 18 May 1957 the Central Committee of the PZPR, now led by Gomułka, decided to revoke Jakub Berman's Party card. This he could not bear. He had never needed—or perhaps even wanted—to be in the spotlight, but he did need to belong to the Party. In an appeal to the PZPR he acknowledged that he understood the need for the sanctions against him, but he could not accept the loss of his Party card. "I cannot reconcile myself to the thought of exclusion from the Party," he wrote, "to which I have been joined for 34 years. I did commit errors, but from the time I became a communist I have lived only with the desire of serving our cause."[29]

THE VINDICATION OF SPECTERS

The expulsion of people such as Jakub Berman was accompanied by re-habilitations of the Terror's victims. The slow, bureaucratic process of returning disgraced and executed comrades to favor began after Stalin's death. After Gomułka assumed Party leadership, the PZPR even made informal overtures to Isaac Deutscher in London, inviting him to return to Poland after nearly two decades. Deutscher agreed—on the condition that he be allowed to deliver a series of lectures, to be collected as a book, on Polish communism. The matter was then dropped.[30] Many of those in prison, in particular communists, were released. In the Soviet Union posthumous rehabilitation commenced even before Khrushchev's February 1956 speech. It was only then that Adolf Warski's grandson, Zofia Warska's son Władysław Krajewski, understood that his father, his mother, his grandfather, and his onetime stepfather, Stande, had not been sent to camps without the right of correspondence. They had been executed. For nearly two decades after their executions, he had waited for someone to return.[31] He was not the only one who had waited. In March 1956 Stande's daughter from his first marriage, Olga, wrote to the Party's Department of History asking if, in the wake of her father's rehabilitation, they had any information about his fate. She hoped perhaps somewhere he remained alive. "From what I know," she wrote, "the news of his death is—quite justified—but only a conjecture."[32] She received the following reply: "Esteemed Comrade! The Department of History of the Central Committee of the PZPR . . . communicates with deep regret that we have been officially informed of the death of Comrade Stanisław Ryszard Stande. Your father was rehabilitated in full posthumously."[33]

Jan Hempel, Witold Wandurski, Stanisław Ryszard Stande, and Bruno Jasieński were all restored to favor. In December 1955, a Soviet military prosecutor produced a statement regarding Jasieński's execution, having investigated the case at the request of Anna Berziń, who was then still herself in the camp where she had been sent following Jasieński's arrest. The document revisited the original NKVD protocols of Jasieński's arrest on 31 July 1937 and his subsequent interrogations, noting that Jasieński was sentenced on 17 September 1938 under article 58 for having been brought by T. Dąbal into the conspiratorial terrorist and diversionary Polish Military Organization. His execution by shooting took place the same day. The report cited Jasieński's retraction of his confession, in which he insisted he had never been connected with the Polish Military Organization and was guilty only of not having seen in Dąbal a Polish spy. He asked to be shot not as a Polish spy but as someone not deserving the confidence of the Soviet government. In the course of the reinvestigation, no "objective evidence" was found to confirm Jasieński's guilt. Further, a 1955 security apparatus investigation regarding the cases of Adolf Warski and other Polish emigrants in the Soviet Union found that the NKVD had conducted the original investigations "in cardinal violation of the principles of socialist legality"; that those arrested had been subjected to beatings, sleep deprivation, and other such methods; and that given these circumstances the results of Jasieński's interrogation could not be regarded as evidence of his guilt and the 17 September 1938 verdict should be annulled.[34] In Moscow on 14 February 1956 a death certificate was belatedly issued for Jasieński, incorrectly dating his death 20 October 1941; the line after "cause of death" remained blank.[35]

Bruno Jasieński's first wife Klara Arem had been shot on 19 January 1938. Following the arrest of his parents, Jasieński's eight-year-old son Andrei was sent to a children's home. In time he ran away, changed his name, and found work as a stoker on the Trans-Siberian railway, eventually becoming an engineer.[36] In 1957, after the Twentieth Party Congress and his father's rehabilitation, Andrei Iasenskii joined the Communist Party. Some time later he wrote to Khrushchev, enclosing the last stanzas written by his father. "Having been convicted by false accusations," Iasenskii wrote, "[Bruno Jasieński] wrote these verses full of the clear faith of a communist in the vitality and force of the idea of Marxism-Leninism, full of love towards the Soviet Union, his second homeland. This poem by my father is a worthy conclusion to his path as a writer-communist. I believe further that the voice of those who perished innocently, but who preserved to the end a devout faith in the Party, in communism, can today have a positive meaning."[37]

In late 1955, the Soviet Writers' Union invited Anatol Stern to Moscow in the role of Mayakovsky's friend and translator.[38] There Stern met Mayakovsky's muse, the famous Lilia Brik, who years earlier had become a close friend of Anna Berziń. Stern had arrived at a fortuitous moment: only several days before Berziń had returned to Moscow after a seventeen-year stay in a gulag in Komi, a southeastern region of European Russia. It was through Lilia Brik, in December 1955, that Stern met Anna Berziń. She remained passionately devoted to her late husband, to the restoration of his memory and his work. She showed Stern the prosecutor's letter regarding Jasieński's rehabilitation; Stern copied it by hand.[39] When he returned to Poland, he wrote a poem to his former futurist friend, now no longer living for almost two decades: "And so perhaps you curse none of your travels, / nor the maddest of your rebellious dreams."[40]

THE FORTUNES OF FRIENDS

In 1938 Marysia Zarębińska had written to Władysław Broniewski that vodka was the only rival she feared for his love.[41] She did not lose him then, yet her fears were prescient. Only after the war was Broniewski truly lost to alcohol. In the fall of 1954, Broniewski's daughter Anka—herself already a filmmaker and the mother of a young daughter named Ewa—died tragically. Anka had been her father's greatest, most enduring love, and her death broke Broniewski in a way that prison had not. Seeing Broniewski in 1957, one of his young admirers from the interwar years found him no longer the same person. The Broniewski he now saw was tired and ill, his voice broke and his hands trembled as he read his poems, there were deep wrinkles on his sunburnt face, his nose was more conspicuous. Only the hat with the wide, wrinkled brim was reminiscent of prewar times.[42]

In March 1956 the literary scholar Stefan Żółkiewski wrote to Broniewski, enclosing something Broniewski had asked him for: the unpublished material given to delegates at the Twentieth Party Congress in Moscow concerning the "cult of personality." Żółkiewski asked that Broniewski read it. He wrote then, with respect to Broniewski's plans to republish "A Word about Stalin": "Of course I have no reservations about your decision to publish your poem about Stalin. It is in essence one of your most beautiful verses. But given the present moment do you yourself want to publish it? It's a very difficult and complicated decision. Act in such a way as to be persuaded that you're lying neither to yourself nor to others."[43] In the end, Broniewski decided to withdraw his poem from the coming edition of his collected works. To an audience in Wrocław, Broniewski explained that he had written that poem honestly, with the knowledge of Stalin's merits, and that he had now withdrawn it because he "had not supposed that alongside such a contribution of labor, blood, and energy, so many people could have incurred an undeserved death, and this is irrevocable."[44]

The twentieth anniversary of the 1936 Congress of Cultural Workers in Lwów came and went. Leon Kruczkowski, as president of the Writers' Union, collected material for the commemoration.[45] Broniewski remembered 1936 as a magical year, the time of Popular Front cooperation, and recalled the Congress as a magical moment, when Poles, Ukrainians, and Jews came together and crowds of workers ruled the streets.[46] Broniewski's heart remained with the Marxism that had preceded that congress, above all the Marxism of the 1920s. When a book of his poetry appeared in Russian translation, he wrote in the introduction that Mayakovsky's poetry had "made of him a socialist poet." Mayakovsky's verse "Poèt-Rabochii" (The Poet-Worker) had become Broniewski's own "life program and poetic program," it had completed his hitherto superficial education in Marxism.[47] After the war he spoke time and time again of Hempel, Stande, Wandurski, and Jasieński, he could not reconcile himself to their lives' having been wasted.[48] He wrote about them warmly, about the days in the 1920s when they had all just met and were absorbed in creating workers' theater. In November 1959, when Broniewski received a telephone call from a representative of the Institute of Party History interested in gathering material about Hempel, Broniewski recalled the brief time in 1924 when they had worked together on *Nowa Kultura*. Hempel had asked him then why he had not joined the KPP, and Broniewski had answered, "because I'm afraid." Hempel was surprised: after all Broniewski had been a soldier, he had faced death. Why now, when he was already ideologically attached to the Party, would he suddenly become afraid? And Broniewski had replied: "I'm afraid of you."[49]

Broniewski avoided black coffee because it was not good for his heart, but wrote only with a cigarette, most often by night.[50] He was not the only one. Wasilewska, too, remained an incurable chain-smoker. When, following an operation in the late 1950s, her doctors forbade her to smoke, she fell into a helpless state, unable to sleep, to write, to eat.[51] Moreover, life far away from Warsaw was difficult for her. She was grieved by Tuwim's death, and pored over every article about him that reached her from Poland. One of these was an essay in *Nowa Kultura* by Adolf Rudnicki, who wrote of the miserable weather on the day of the funeral, the snow that soaked his beret, and the people in Zakopane who approached the coffin only out of curiosity. Most painful to Wasilewska was Rudnicki's description of how "Zakopane received the death of the poet expressionlessly." He moreover confessed that he himself had not liked Tuwim's language, that he had found in Tuwim's poetry "a constant striking of the pedal, noisiness, lack of nuance, coarseness of feeling." It was only three weeks after Tuwim's death that Rudnicki reread Tuwim's poetry, and finally understood it, finally understood whom Poland had lost—and now belatedly brought a branch of lilacs to Tuwim's still-fresh grave.[52]

Wasilewska was enraged, and sent a letter to *Nowa Kultura* saying she did not believe Rudnicki:

> Perhaps it was the case that Rudnicki was not moved. . . . I
> didn't see Zakopane at the time of Tuwim's death. But I did
> see the hall filled with people at the Writers' Union in Moscow
> —thousands of kilometers from Zakopane, people far away,
> people of a different nationality shed real tears. The majority
> knew Tuwim only from (unfortunately) bad translations, and
> they found in themselves authentic emotion and authentic
> tears, and felt in their hearts authentic mourning because

thousands of kilometers away an authentic poet died. And in Zakopane, in Poland, Poles found *only*—as Rudnicki carefully emphasizes—curiosity? I very much fear that the author has transposed his own feelings onto the whole. I don't believe it, it's not true that people could stand and stare curiously in the face of a corpse in which song and blaze congealed. People speaking the language out of which the deceased conjured up colors and sounds like few before him. People living in the country that the one who died loved with a passionate, violent, choking love. And I very much doubt whether "not everyone knew to whom they were paying respects." . . . Tuwim was too unusual, he too much contrasted with the general background, he too much distinguished himself to be able to pass by and live among people unnoticed, to not draw the attention of even the most indifferent.

For Rudnicki himself Wasilewska expressed only pity that he "did not experience what was given to his generation—to be dazzled by the splendor of Tuwim's poetry." Her wrath was directed rather against *Nowa Kultura*. What Rudnicki had written was entirely permissible for a private journal entry, for memoirs, or even for publication—not in a year, but perhaps in ten years, and certainly in twenty. "But not today," Wasilewska wrote. "In the house where the deceased lies a certain tact obliges even those who are indifferent. An atheist entering a church takes off his hat so as not to offend the feelings of others. In this case the beret was taken off only upon leaving the church."[53]

Neither did Wasilewska's attachment to Janina Broniewska diminish as the years passed. In late summer of 1954 Wasilewska wrote to Broniewska of how acutely she felt the passing of time and the coming of old age. Four years earlier, in response to her friend's reflections about aging, Wasilewska had insisted that what she had to do in life remained still before her.[54] Now her energy had faded. She fell into a depression. She had been feeling "more or less as were you on a certain day when I laid you on the sofa and fed you tea—which is to say, without a single drop of strength. As to the rest, do you ever have attacks of dark melancholy? But so dark, like coffee in the stomach of a black man on a dark night? If so, then multiply that ten times and you'll more or less be able to imagine how it looked. . . . In a word, at the beginning of the summer I had something that in medicine is called a nervous breakdown, towards which for my entire life I have felt deep disgust and disbelief—and yet it exists."[55] Soon afterwards Wasilewska turned fifty. Jakub Berman and Bolesław Bierut sent warm birthday wishes; Berman wished her hoards of fat grandchildren and many good books to come.[56] Wasilewska did continue to write, including a long introduction that year to the Russian translation of Janina Broniewska's war correspondent's notebook.[57] The two women visited each other, and worried about each other in each other's absence. After one of Broniewska's trips to Kiev, Wasilewska wrote to her friend complaining that her visit was terribly short and pleading with her, "take care of your precious health, for without me, who will drag you to the doctor."[58]

Despite painful moments, Wasilewska continued to write with all the passionate faith in the Revolution she had always had; she wrote ecstatically of the peasants who now ate in their own restaurants, of pig farms where not a single worker had anything less than a secondary school education. "Because I've seen," she wrote to Broniewska in 1955, "I've seen with my own eyes how hundreds and thousands of people are living in the epoch of communism and not on the moon, but a mere thousand kilometers from Kiev. . . . What to do with this, because even so no one will believe you and will say that you're an old, blinded, crazy woman."[59] She discovered two other passions during her postwar life in Kiev. The first—a rediscovery—was her childhood love of fishing.[60] The second was her adoration for her young grandson, Piotr, whom Ewa Wasilewska often left under her care. When he was away with his mother in Moscow, Wasilewska's letters to Broniewska reveal her despair at his absence.[61]

SKAMANDER LOSES A POET

The Skamander poets had been the darlings of Polish readers in their youth; it seemed to their colleagues that this need to shine never left them. Słonimski was no exception.[62] He—the most irreverent of all of them—could not fade into the backdrop of postwar literary life, just as he had not been able to reconcile himself to life in exile. In 1956, in the atmosphere of emergent freedom brought by the Thaw, he was elected president of the Polish Writers' Union. In memoirs published a year later, he wrote of the Thaw as justifying his decision to return to Poland: "I don't know what is still to come, what fate will bring us, but I do know that the decision to return home was the right one. It was worth agreeing to small compromises, experiencing humiliations and disappointments so as to live and fight in Warsaw."[63]

Słonimski was now harsh on those of his literary colleagues whom he considered servile, whose work in previous years he compared to that of firing squads. Kruczkowski was resentful, and in December 1956 sent Słonimski a letter accusing him of hypocrisy, and reminding Słonimski that he had declined to make such strong statements during the years when doing so would have been an authentic act of courage. Perhaps, Kruczkowski suggested, those who "would like to persuade their colleagues that they had been the righteous of Sodom might exercise a bit more modesty."[64] As recently as 1954 Słonimski had written a poem bemoaning the historical woe of the peasantry and exalting Bierut and the coming of the new, better world. Like others, he, too, had written in the Stalinist years of the "victorious rhythm of history," of the May Day parades and the red banners—alongside the puddles of blood and the ashes that burned bare feet.[65] A fellow writer marveled: "How is it possible to unite in oneself nobility and intelligence with courtliness and compromise, tossing the compromise up into the air like a delicate cane with a handle made of elephant tusk."[66]

Słonimski's reign as Writers' Union president was short. Within three years after the Thaw had begun, the Party had grown disconcerted by the "ferment" it had generated. Once again the climate began to change.[67] After the Ninth Congress of the Polish Writers' Union held in Wrocław in December 1958, the Party decided to quell the "revisionist tendencies" within the union. Those in the "Europa" group were to be treated as political opponents, all efforts were to be made to circumscribe their influence on "loyal writers."[68] In 1959, Słonimski was replaced as president by the more placid Iwaszkiewicz, whom the Party saw as less inclined to direct the Writers' Union against the Party leadership.[69] In 1956, when in Italy Wat saw Mieczysław Grydzewski for the first time after the war, Grydzewski lamented Iwaszkiewicz's new incarnation, believing him a swine for having suddenly become a regime poet when he had never even been a communist before the war. In Grydzewski's mind, it was something else for someone like Broniewski who had been a prewar communist, but for Iwaszkiewicz it was inexcusable. Wat thought otherwise, and told Grydzewski so: "I convinced him that he was committing a fundamental error. Iwasz-kiewicz was always a court writer, he had always been in well with the government, with those on top, with the elite, he was an elitist. And it can be understood that when the government changed, he continued to be in with the elite. But Broniewski, the bard of the proletariat, the revo-lutionary, has absolutely no right to be following such a regime, seeing how the proletariat is so horribly exploited."[70] It was nonetheless painful for Grydzewski, who wrote to Iwaszkiewicz in March 1956, "What does it mean, that we won't be able to understand each other? You won't make me believe, will you, that you've changed, because I haven't at all."[71] Some six weeks later Grydzewski wrote to Iwaszkiewicz again, asking: "What does it mean, that Kazio [Wierzyński] and Leszek [Lechoń] wouldn't want to see you? That's certainly an unjust supposition. After all it wasn't I who broke with Julek and Antoni, but they with me."[72] Such was the case. Yet in 1957, when Wierzyński saw Słonimski in Tokyo, Słonimski told him in parting, "All the same, tell Grydz that I send my greetings."[73]

It was painful for all of them. Upon hearing in 1954 that Słonimski had had a heart attack, Lechoń wrote in his diary, "What else did he ex-pect, going to Warsaw two years ago when it was already clear what was going on there? I know one thing—if he had stayed here, I would have given him regularly something from my pension. And after a couple of years I would have forgiven him that Bolshevik UNESCO, which after all was in the style of his previous life."[74] For Lechoń those "bombastic and insincere" verses Słonimski had written in the Stalinist years were Słonimski's "falsetto" voice, the falsetto they had found so offensive on many occasions sitting around the table at Ziemiańska, when Słonimski would "announce to them some hundred-year-old novelty."[75] It was only in late 1954 that Lechoń finished his poem to his other great onetime friend, the poem he had begun upon Tuwim's death:

I see your gray hair and your sharp face,
And your hand, like an oar, contrasts with consciousness
So here you dream by night, ill-fated Cagliostro,
By the empty streets of a Warsaw not your own.

Your senses kidnapped by the gale eternal
You want to inhale from new streets the time of dead scents
Amidst the lights of new lanterns shining down on them

With a crazed look you raise up the shadow of bygone
  buildings.

And you cry, because you hear the rain falling from an
  old gutter
And yourself not yet believing that no one forbids you
You, innocent offender, reach out your hand in the dusk
To the helping hand extended, once again, from afar.[76]

It was just after one-thirty in the afternoon on Friday, 8 June 1956, when Jan Lechoń, the Skamander poet, threw himself from a twelfth-floor window of the Hudson Hotel onto the Manhattan sidewalk. He died at once. A week later from New York, Wierzyński wrote to Grydzewski in London, describing how Lechoń had been in a depression for the past few months; he had applied for American citizenship, but the process was not going smoothly: Lechoń's file included testimonies regarding his homosexuality.[77] The suicide softened Iwaszkiewicz, who wrote to Grydzewski as soon as he heard: "Yesterday evening the news reached me of Leszek's tragic death. . . . At such moments one forgets about what divided us—and remembers what once connected us, and there was much that connected us." Once, before the war, Iwaszkiewicz had written Grydzewski a letter about Lechoń. Grydzewski had kept the letter in his archive, and now Iwaszkiewicz was grateful that the archive had burned. Whatever Iwaszkiewicz had said in that letter, he was thankful it was no more.[78] He and Grydziewski continued to correspond. Two and a half years later, in November 1958, Iwaszkiewicz wrote to Grydzewski on the fortieth anniversary of their first appearance at Pikador. He recalled it with tears.[79]

NOSTALGIA

In Tel Aviv in 1953, Adolf Berman was pained by the news of Tuwim's death. In February 1954, Rudnicki wrote to Adolf Berman, mentioning his article about Tuwim; he was certain it would reach Berman in Israel. Rudnicki added news of others Adolf Berman had known: "You left behind at home a few people who remember you warmly, among them—Wat has unfortunately been seriously ill for a time now; a second child, a son, was born to Kott . . . Ważyk with the ugly little face has written a screenplay . . . In the coming days we will be celebrating the 60th birthday of our emissary for peace—Iwaszkiewicz; Słonimski is not feeling well due to his heart, he's resting now in Ciednocinek; lately the hearts of many people are causing trouble."[80]

In June 1956, Adolf Berman resumed a correspondence with his old friend Michał Mirski, a KPP activist "on the Jewish street" during the interwar years, and in the postwar years one of those who had attacked Adolf Berman most harshly for nationalist deviation.[81] The occasion was the twentieth anniversary of the Lwów congress, when Adolf Berman and Mirski had been among a group of Wasilewska's Jewish interlocutors who had created a subsidiary Front of Progressive Jewish Culture. Now Adolf Berman's tone was nostalgic; he addressed Mirski in the second person plural form used among comrades and reminisced about their visits with Wasilewska and Wiktor Alter in the years before the war: "Dear Comrade Mirski! Twenty years ago, in 1936, we met for the first time. As you remember, this was during the time when together we created the Progressive Cultural Front. In my consciousness it is as if it had happened in a former life, before the bloody deluge. Yet it happened and it had its own meaning. Do you remember our visits together to Wanda Wasilewska, to Wiktor Alter. . . ."[82]

LEAVE-TAKING

In the 1950s Wat told Stawar, somewhat in jest, "Listen, I really owe all this to you. You're to blame; you got me into communism." With his characteristic "grimace of contempt," Stawar answered that Wat would have ended up there anyway.[83] On New Year's Eve of 1954 Stawar presented Wat with a complete collection of the short-lived *Miesięcznik Literacki* dedicated "To Olek, In memory of the shared sins of our youth." On the first page of the first issue Wat scribbled "the corpus delicti of my degradation . . . in communism, by communism."[84] He did not recover from his illness. With the help of his old friends who were now in positions of power, people such as Iwaszkiewicz and Jakub Berman, Wat began to spend more time abroad, in warmer west European climates. In 1955 Iwaszkiewicz arranged to send him to France as a special correspondent for *Twórczość* and *Nowa Kultura*.[85] For the next few years he and Ola Watowa moved between France, Italy, and Warsaw; as Wat became disengaged from Polish literary politics, he began to write again after a hiatus of decades, preoccupied—like Hannah Arendt, Theodor Adorno, and Max Horkheimer, like so many intellectuals of their generation—with Nazism and Stalinism, with the question of where history had gone so wrong. He was now convinced that the past was always more powerful than the future. He reflected on the origins of the German impulse towards unity, and began work on a novel about totalitarianism.[86] At variance with a communist policy that insistently divided Germany into two entities and carefully distinguished between good and bad Germans, Wat's premise was the guilt of the whole German nation.[87]

Wat thought as well of how Hitler had benefited from Stalin's example, from the idea that in the interest of the happiness of all, the enemies must die. Yet in the case of Stalinism, whoever was included in the first part of the formula would eventually find himself in the second; the enemy came from the inside. Wat belonged to those who believed in Stalin's uniqueness, in Stalinism as a phenomenon of modernity unprecedented in history. None of the other conquerors in history had ever "plowed as thoroughly, as deeply as did Stalin the lives, psychology, ways of thought of hundreds of millions of people (even his enemies), no one had ever seized their entire existence in all its forms." Wat reflected on Stalin's biography, on his studies at an Orthodox seminary, where Stalin had found his atheism—an aggressive atheism that could only be a variation of fanatical religiosity, that could only be hatred towards God, the father. The Orthodox seminary was set amidst the influence of Islam, and Wat hypothesized an Islamic influence on Stalinism, the Islamic fatalism that could lie beneath Stalin's calmness towards the chopping off of heads.[88]

That Stalin forbade the reading of Dostoevsky was, Wat speculated, an attempt to "efface the traces" that reading the Grand Inquisitor in his youth must have left on him. Wat returned more than once to the great Russian writer, to Dostoevsky's idea that if there was no God, then all was permissible, and the only dignified gesture was suicide. Throughout these writings, Wat struggled with the existence of God, he vacillated between Christianity and existentialism. If there was no God, then every life was pointless. If there was, then none was. If there was no God, then everything was permissible—but each person must discover that for himself. It was all a matter of desire, of choice; Wat could accept the existence of God or reject it. It was a choice between the crucifix and nothingness. He chose guilt. He believed that between life and death there was a third state, a state of dying that was his own present existence, and perhaps as well the existence of the contemporary world. If so, then what he suspected—that his illness had a demonic etiology—was true, and it was exorcists he needed to cure him. He tried something of the sort in a visit to Padre Pio—a healer, stigmatic, mystic—but after the visit Wat's illness was no less present.[89]

In his writings Wat meditated as well on his friends, on their shared past. He remembered that in Lvov, on the eve of his arrest, Borejsza had greeted him so ostentatiously, with such strange warmth. He wrote of how Ważyk, after Wat's many attempts to persuade him, had been brave enough to give Wat a short book review for *Miesięcznik Literacki*, signing it with a pseudonym; of how Słonimski, after vacillating, signed a protest against the Polish government, while Tuwim could not be convinced, citing his friendship with Colonel Wieniawa-Długoszowski. He wrote as well of Piłsudski, whom he had so much opposed, and yet "that dictator's unusual . . . personal charm" had affected Wat as well.[90] He wrote of how Tuwim, as much as he was an innovator, had nurtured infantile dreams of finding a treasure or a cloak of invisibility, and had harbored an old-fashioned conception of the devil, failing to grasp the "demonism of contemporaneity."[91] He wrote of Broniewski, whose poetry was so tied to his soldierly self: "Lyric poetry begins when the platoon leader said, 'fall out,' when it was possible to sit down in the grass, roll a cigarette, absorb the sound of the trees, the rippling of the cornfields, the song of the oriole. Here is still a place for a soldier's humor and a soldier's smile. B.'s poetry . . . is written on that principle—a sharp march and a rest—a break in the field, in the woods. A soldier unifies the world just like a criminal, like a primitive: 'ours—the enemy.' Lyric poetry unifies the world, identifying it with itself."[92] Wat reflected as well on Broniewski's degeneration. It was the degeneration of a great revolutionary poet, now lying naked on the grass, two empty half-liter bottles beside him, telling the young writers: "'To hell with Ważyk. When I die, write on the tombstone: 'Here lies someone who said to hell with everyone and everything.'"[93]

In April 1956, Wat, himself disengaged from Polish literary politics, dedicated a poem to his friends who had worked to bring about the Thaw:

And so you pump your own blood
into the dark chimera of illusion

and sing to her Hallelujah,
and adorn her in scarlet and gold.

Now strong, as you are weak, she
jumps onto Jagganath's cart.
So does history, facetious,
play the jester to you.[94]

In 1957 Wat returned to Poland from France. It seemed to him that Iwaszkiewicz and his friends from *Twórczość*, who had been so supportive in
facilitating his stay abroad, had now grown cold. Ill and feverish, he
wondered aloud to Ola Watowa about the source of their rejection. She
could not bear her husband's pain, and that very day—Christmas Day of
1957—sent a bitter letter to Iwaszkiewicz. "From the moment when I read
your first stories," she wrote to him, "I became an adoring admirer of your
talent—and I've always wanted to believe that great talent goes together
with greatness of heart.—Yet everything now denies that.—Your (incomprehensible to us) embittered silence—absence of any kind of interest
in a man as severely tried by fate as Aleksander. Has that one ugly vessel
filled with bile and haughtiness really managed to infect with distaste you
and the rest of our friends from *Twórczość* who were so recently full of
goodwill towards Aleksander."[95]

On New Year's Day Iwaszkiewicz answered generously, if defensively,
forgiving her for her peculiar New Year's greetings, and assuring her he
understood that Wat's long-lasting illness and its recent complications had
been upsetting her, that this was the only way he could understand her
unjust words. Yes, Wat had been "severely tried by fate," but alas, so had
so many people. "Of course I am guilty of coolness or neglect in relation
to him, I admit my guilt—yet this is not a reason for you to accuse me
and the whole editorial staff of *Twórczość* of bile and haughtiness. You
know well that I possess neither haughtiness nor bile." He was confident
that in time she would see things differently, that she would regret what
she had written. In any case, he assured her, she need not worry—he had
already forgotten it, already forgiven her.[96] A week later she wrote to Iwaszkiewicz a second time, now in an entirely different tone, sincerely full of
joy at the forgiveness for which she had not even asked. "I knew that you

would understand and forgive," she wrote, "Only one thing astonished me, that you—such a beautiful man—(and you know this well!)—could have thought for a moment that in writing, 'an ugly vessel . . . ,' I could have had in mind you!" She did regret her impulsive angry words. It had been her husband's pain that she could not endure.[97]

Paradoxically, Wat's sense of his old friends' coldness came at the moment when the poems Wat had begun to publish in 1955 and 1956 after decades of silence had been chosen for *Nowa Kultura*'s prestigious literary prize. Wat was then in the hospital. It was Słonimski who telephoned close to midnight with the news that the jury had unanimously chosen his recent collection of poetry as the best book of 1957. Wat had a high fever, Ola Watowa repeated to him what Słonimski had said, "which sounded then in my ears like the sound of the waves of a faraway sea, pleasant and refreshing—but not me, not me—but someone foreign, a stranger, although one evoking sympathy."[98] At least one person did not think the recipient to be worthy of sympathy. Julian Przyboś believed Wat had been undeserving, and said as much in the literary press. Wat was irritated and immediately replied in a short feuilleton describing Przyboś as an intellectually vacant poet with a hollow imagination; when it appeared, Iwaszkiewicz and the editorial staff of *Twórczość* sent Wat flowers.[99] Wat was not alone in having been offended by Przyboś's attitude towards his colleagues. In addition to the flowers for the feuilleton, Wat heard from many friends who wanted to congratulate him on the literary award. Słonimski sent a note saying, "I love you very much."[100] Wat also received a letter from Stanisław Baliński in London, who was ecstatic that Wat had been chosen and disconcerted only by the fact that in the press report Wat had been called "a poet of the older generation." Had they all really grown so old? "I had wanted to write something 'cheerful' in this letter," Baliński continued, "but I cannot, nothing comes out, only something tightens in my throat when I think about you, about Warsaw, about so many things, people; and the present and the past become entangled and in that entanglement I sometimes feel lost . . ."[101]

It was a time for reminiscences. Later that year, in 1958, Stanisław Wygodzki published a memoiristic essay about *Miesięcznik Literacki*—how it had disappeared quickly from kiosks, had been passed from person to person, had been smuggled into prisons.[102] It was a nostalgic piece; the

FIGURE 15 Władysław Broniewski at his family home
in Płock at the end of the 1950s. Courtesy of Muzeum
Władysława Broniewskiego.

despair beneath the nostalgia emerged from a letter his wife had written
to Ola Watowa the year before: "I'm experiencing now a period of much
sadness. Even in the camp I didn't feel so hopeless. For then I believed in
some kind of better future. Do you know how life now looks in our country? The worst thing is that I'm unable to resuscitate even a bit of faith and
hope for change. Together all of it is a monstrous nightmare. I see absolutely no possibility of life here either for myself or for our children. And
Stasiek [Wygodzki] can't imagine life outside of Poland. I understand him
well, but I'm unable to reconcile myself to that. I'm passing over the issue
of antisemitism, which is very painful, but I believe that it's necessary

to give the children some kind of truth, to teach them what is good and what is evil, and in our conditions this is completely impossible."[103] In July 1959 Aleksander Wat and Ola Watowa left Poland permanently.[104]

AGING

Tadeusz Peiper had grown old. The young Peiper of Cracow had worn a black beard like a Spaniard. Now the Peiper sitting at a café in the summer of 1957 was an old man, thin, graying, unshaven.[105] In fact they had all begun to age. The fixation on the future that had been their motif and their passion in the interwar years had faded. Now they were drawn more and more to painful, nostalgic reflection on the past. In 1957 Stern and Ważyk, together with two colleagues, published an anthology of Mayakovsky's poetry, translated by Jasieński, Stande, Broniewski, Słonimski, and themselves, among others. In his introduction, Stern reminded his readers that Mayakovsky and Revolution were one. He added, "And if to her he devoted at times even his own poetry, he did this as a man who was ready to do anything his beloved demanded of him—even at those times when he sees her claiming that to which she has no right and that which she should not demand."[106] Wat, who in his days as the editor of *Miesięcznik Literacki* had written of Polish futurism as "the crooked mirror in which Caliban looked at himself with a grimace of abomination," now returned to the same metaphor to describe the peculiarity of his century: "Caliban, upon seeing his own face in the mirror, fell in love with himself."[107]

Such was, perhaps, the case. The war and the Stalinist era had broken all of them, each in different ways. Wat could not free himself from his prison experiences.[108] Broniewski had forgiven Daszewski; he had accepted Daszewski's explanation that he had only invited them to meet a man whom he thought was a Soviet art historian, that he had not known it was an organized provocation. Broniewski even forgave Putrament when, in the wake of 1956, he came to Broniewski to try to explain his behavior in Lvov; but he could not forgive Putrament's rewriting of that story in his memoirs.[109] Yet Broniewski's generosity did not save him from alcoholism. Wasilewska descended into a depression she never had known possible, Wat into an agonizing, relentless illness. Lechoń took his own life. Jakub Berman was reduced to begging for his Party card back. From this generation Isaac Deutscher, now for many years far away in emigration in England, was one of the very few who remained hopeful. For the Trotskyite who had once wanted Ola Watowa to sit on his lap, 1956 was a resurrection of the spirit of the interwar KPP almost twenty years after its violent dissolution—and perhaps a resurrection of something of Rosa Luxemburg's old tradition as well. Of the Thaw, the Polish October, Deutscher wrote,[110] "Nothing in nature perishes."

CHAPTER TEN

The End of the Affair

The lapses in our conversations are mostly the result of the pain killers I have to take to be able to talk with you at all. And I'm afraid there's yet another danger here: I could easily slip into confessions. Confessions of an ex!

—*Aleksander Wat*

THE YEAR AFTER THE Party expelled Jakub Berman, Antoni Słonimski went to see a screening of a Russian film based on a play by Mayakovsky. Jakub Berman was sitting in one row, Władysław Gomułka in the next. The photographers were forced into tricky maneuvers, so as not to accidentally include the now purged Berman in their photographs of the Party leadership.[1] When the Central Committee passed its resolution to expel Jakub Berman, it had included a provision allowing him to appeal for the return of his Party card after three years had passed.[2] And so he did. In a letter to General Secretary Władysław Gomułka on 9 May 1960, Jakub Berman pleaded for his Party card back. "In the course of these three years," he wrote to the man whose imprisonment he had overseen, "I have felt, as in the years preceding, indissolubly joined to the Party, to the Party's daily efforts. . . . I beg to be accepted back into the Party, so that in the ranks of the Party I can serve the cause that is the essence of my entire life."[3]

DEATH IN PARIS, IN WARSAW, IN KIEV

Władysław Broniewski continued to drink heavily and to live nocturnally. In the early 1950s, during one of Broniewski's late night phone calls to Aleksander Wat, Broniewski asked, "Listen, you have an influence on Edward [Stawar], why doesn't that fool submit self-criticism? After all he could write, he could write about me. No one is able to write about me. Only Stawar. He could live peacefully. The point was for him to write that 'idiotic' self-criticism, they're not demanding anything more from him. And he says to hell with the self-criticism.'"[4] Such was the case. Stawar declined to issue self-criticism. Having been cast out of the literary world during the Stalinist years, he was allowed to return only in 1955. His work was again published; he occasionally appeared at the literary cafés in a trench coat, his mustache closely trimmed.[5] These were better years for him, yet by the end of the decade he was ill and would spend months at a time at the writers' retreat in Zakopane. In late 1960 he was given permission to go to the West to gather material for a book on aesthetics. Wat and his wife were in Italy in late spring and summer of 1961, and Stawar was anxious to see them. Wat was in no state to travel, but he was alarmed at the news of his friend's poor health: Stawar had lost over twenty pounds.[6] A Polish embassy representative came to visit him, but Stawar declined the embassy's offers of assistance. In a letter dated 25 July 1961, Stawar wrote to Wat that the following day he was leaving for Paris and he believed they would manage to meet there.[7] He went to the Paris suburb of Maisons-Laffitte, home of Jerzy Giedroyc's émigré monthly *Kultura*. There he spoke to Giedroyc about Trotskyism; in some way Stawar felt himself to be a Trotskyite still.[8]

Stawar had gone to Paris to publish his collection of essays. He did not intend to remain abroad, he wanted to die in Warsaw. In this he failed. Shortly after Stawar posted his letter of 25 July, Jerzy Giedroyc called Wat to tell him that Stawar was in the hospital, dying. But Wat was too ill to go out that day, and afterwards it was too late. The man who had once professed his love to Janina Broniewska in the glow of a Warsaw lantern died in Paris in August 1961. His body was cremated. He never had the last conversation with Wat that he had so hoped for; instead the Wats arrived at the airport in Paris in time to see the urn with Stawar's ashes being loaded onto a flight to Warsaw.[9] In Poland Jerzy Putrament organized Stawar's funeral. He sent to the airport three young writers who, after some searching, found the urn with Stawar's ashes in the storage area for unclaimed packages, in a small box marked "Duty-Free." Stawar was given a state funeral, with a military band, Party delegates, and a prestigious burial site at Powązki cemetery; Putrament spoke of "Comrade Stawar, the model Marxist writer and activist, faithful to the Party to the very end."

"The whole funeral," wrote Jan Kott, "was like a nightmare from which we could not wake up."[10]

Five years later, in a long article for Radio Free Europe, Wat wrote of how his friend had remained a believer in communism—a different communism from the one that existed—until the very end. For all that Wat himself spoke out against the Party's cultural policy in the Stalinist years, Stawar's silence during that time, his quiet refusal to give self-criticism, was for Wat an act of greater courage.[11] It was only after his death that Stawar's *Pisma ostatnie* (Last Writings) were published in Paris; and thus Stawar's ashes reached Warsaw before his last book. These "last writings" were actually a collection of articles and essays he had published years earlier, some of them in *Pod Prąd* in the 1930s. In Wat's understanding, Stawar had published them now so that the Party could not, after his death, appropriate him as one who had been "theirs." Like Kott, Wat believed this state funeral with a military band—orchestrated by someone Stawar could not have respected—was exactly what his friend had not wanted.[12]

Władysław Broniewski had also fallen ill. His face now appeared tired and old, he was rarely sober, he coughed and spoke with difficulty.[13] Suffering from insomnia, time and time again he awoke his friends in the middle of the night and insisted they listen as he recited his poetry—as he had insisted years earlier in the prison cell in Centralniak. When the doctors told Broniewski he had cancer of the larynx, he was reluctant to accept the diagnosis. Until the very end, without dissimulating Broniewski remained in the Party's good graces. Broniewski, whom Janina Broniewska called "the prodigal husband," and Wat called "the prodigal son," was also, as Wat put it, the only one of their original circle to die *in odore sanctitatis*.[14] The Ministry of Art and Culture sent him gifts. This was in contrast to the Party's generosity towards Stawar after his death, which came to an abrupt end when news of his *Last Writings* and his close relations with *Kultura* reached Warsaw.[15] Some two months after Stawar's death, Broniewski wrote to the Minister of Art and Culture thanking him for the kind words and the abundant gifts, and adding that they were presumably in place of flowers for Stawar's grave. "With respect to the latter," Broniewski wrote, "I have certain ideas and would gladly converse with you on that subject."[16] Broniewski, who was vain and self-absorbed and unfaithful to his wives, had proven very loyal to his friends. In 1960 he published an anthology of his Polish translations of foreign poetry titled *Moje przyjaźnie poetyckie*

(My Poetic Friendships), including Pushkin, Mayakovsky, Brecht, Esenin, and Pasternak.[17] The poems he wrote of his own in these last years were among his most moving, especially those to his daughter Anka, whose death—he wrote—had left him an orphan. He wrote of how he thought of her before he fell asleep and when he awakened; of how he no longer knew how to write, because she was not there; of how she surpassed any lover and was always first in his heart. In the end, he awaited death to be with her. In November 1961 he wrote of how he had brought a pansy from Anka's grave to his hospital room, and of how he would now like to die. Three months later, on 10 February 1962, he did.[18]

In London, Mieczysław Grydzewski gathered information for a memorial article about Broniewski for *Wiadomości*; he wrote to Wat asking about the circumstances of his and Broniewski's 1931 imprisonment, about *Miesięcznik Literacki*.[19] Wat answered in detail: Broniewski had been a burdensome, egotistical cell mate, but he had conducted himself fantastically well under interrogation. Wat added, "Overall, of the first seven revolutionary writers, four (Hempel, Wandurski, Stande, Jasieński) were murdered over there. Now Stawar and Broniewski have died suddenly in rapid succession, there remains only myself, sick, wrecked, but for a long time now the most radically cured of that degeneration."[20] Wat wrote, too, of how Broniewski had died in a sorrowful state of moral and intellectual deterioration, yet reminded those who were listening of how "that valiant poet" had behaved more admirably in occupied Lvov than had any of their friends and colleagues.[21]

Like Wat and Grydzewski, the surviving Skamander poets wrote of the former Legionnaire. Iwaszkiewicz spoke of Broniewski's "eternal Polishness." "Nothing," Iwaszkiewicz wrote, "is more sad or more moving than the Polishness of those poems."[22] Wierzyński, for a long time now an émigré in the United States "on the other side of the red barricade," wrote his own poem about the death of this Polish poet who had once been his friend. They had broken only after the war, when Broniewski had decided to return to Poland. Now Wierzyński forgave "the romantic" everything and wrote of his "ex-friend's" individualism, his integrity, his "rebel's honor."[23]

Janina Broniewska mourned for her former husband. In writing her memoirs, she placed before her the letters Broniewski had written to her during their courtship. The letters were yellowed, brittle, too intimate for publication. Yet through them she called back to life those bygone years: "The dead returning to life. Dead? And perhaps everything that has passed behind us in life isn't dead at all?"[24] She mourned as well for their daughter. When Anka had died tragically in 1954, Janina Broniewska had followed Wasilewska's example upon her father Leon Wasilewski's death of almost twenty years earlier, and did not cry at her daughter's funeral. She was disgusted at the behavior of Broniewski, who flung himself, choking with sobs, at Anka's coffin.[25] Now when Wasilewska would come to Warsaw, they would visit Anka's grave as well as the grave of Leon Wasilewski. During one of these visits to the cemetery Wasilewska "divided her enormous bouquet of flowers. She said in a warm voice, without that frigid restraint she had had that day of her father's death: 'Take these, Jasieczka. They'll be from Grandpa for our Ania.'"[26]

When Wasilewska was not in the room Janina Broniewska kept for her friend in her Warsaw home, she shared with Korneichuk an apartment in Kiev and a dacha just outside the city, where she continued to write and participate in the government as a Soviet deputy. In March 1963 she traveled to Latin America, where Fidel Castro took her fishing.[27] Yet nothing Wasilewska did in the postwar years could compare to her extraordinary role during the war. Now her time had passed. In the 1960s, she began to devote more time to memoirs and reminiscences; she confessed to the painful shyness she had always felt when meeting new people and to the absence of imagination in her literary work. She was only able to write of what she herself had seen and heard; this was, she believed, both her weakness and her strength.[28] Khrushchev's revelations about Stalin mitigated neither her nostalgia nor her idealism. In a 1963 article on the occasion of the twentieth anniversary of the Kościuszko Division she wrote of the intimate, "homemade" way the division had come into being; its founding was one of the happiest moments of her life, and she now described that time as a crazed but beautiful one, a time when everything was happening as if in a feverish dream.[29] Until the very end that essential contradiction—harsh dogmatism and extreme sentimentality—remained in her.

In 1964 Wanda Wasilewska traveled to Warsaw to record her memoirs for the Institute of Party History. There she told her interviewers that she had never been inclined towards leadership, that during the war she had played the role she did because she was able to—and others were not. She understood that as much as she tried, some communists—members

of the then-dissolved KPP who had devoted themselves for years to communism and to the Soviet Union, who had long prison terms behind
them—would resent that it was she whom the Soviet leadership trusted,
she who had become their necessary intermediary. She had done what
she could.[30] Wanda Wasilewska did not live long enough to authorize
the transcripts of her memoirs; in July she died unexpectedly in Kiev. In
Warsaw, the Party leadership sent telegrams of condolences to Korneichuk; Janina Broniewska led a delegation to Kiev for the funeral.[31] On 31
July 1964, a hagiographic obituary of "this brave daughter of the Polish
nation whom the Soviet nation joyously accepted into their family" appeared in *Izvestiia*. It was signed by, among others, Nikita Khrushchev,
Ilya Ehrenburg, and the two men whom Khrushchev had sent in 1940
to ask for her understanding concerning her husband Marian Bogatko's
murder: Oleksandr Korneichuk and Mykola Bazhan.[32]

IN PARISIAN EXILE

Living abroad in west European exile, Aleksander Wat fell into bouts of
self-hatred—the theme of *le moi haïssable* ("my detestable self") appeared
again and again in his diary from those years. His thoughts returned to
his earliest childhood, his enthusiasm for drawing, and his shock when
one day—when he was no more than two years old—he saw a human
face emerge from the lines he had drawn on a piece of paper. At that time
the human face was what he most feared—yet upon seeing this image
on the paper, his fear of faces melted, or rather turned against himself.
Now he was struck by the fact that he could produce a human face at will,
and so did the threat transpose itself into an internal one. Wat struggled
as well with questions of identity. At moments he felt he was—and had
always been—a Jew, a Polish-speaking cosmopolitan. At other moments
he felt strongly that as a Polish poet, his homeland was his language, and
he belonged in Poland, where his father and his father's fathers were
buried.[33] In 1963 he wrote in his diary, "In the end I've found myself in
a fine place: not at home, not with the emigration—in a void."[34] He felt
isolated, and closer to those back in Poland who supported the communist
regime than to the émigré Poles who shared his anticommunism. When
Słonimski visited Paris in November 1963, Wat was terribly happy to see
him. For with those who had attacked him as an "enemy of the people"
during the Stalinist years, he shared a history, a long intimacy.[35] With

respect to Jerzy Giedroyc's émigré journal *Kultura,* Wat was reluctant to contribute to anything that would engage him in politics per se, and firm in his refusal to be portrayed as someone who had "converted" from communism, to be used as anticommunist propaganda, or to contribute to any political manifestos. In any case, he believed that *Kultura*'s influence would penetrate further if the journal's pages remained free from politics in the strict sense of the word.[36] If Wat spoke often about himself, his own story as the last of the group around *Miesięcznik Literacki* who remained alive—he explained to Giedroyc—it was because he wanted to illuminate the tragic fate of his generation of communist intellectuals; if he spoke of his experiences in prison, it was to show that his reflections on communism were the results of rich personal knowledge.[37] On the pages of *Kultura* Wat fulfilled an Old Bolshevik's final request: he told the story of how old Steklov died.[38]

In Parisian exile, Wat maintained correspondence with many who were still in Poland. Now his interlocutors included Adolf Rudnicki and Wiktor Woroszylski; the latter, who had been among Wat's harshest critics during the Stalinist era, was now full of affection and admiration for the Wats—and committed to reviving the legacy of Mayakovsky.[39] Wat himself wrote long, reflective letters, which he would sometimes revise before sending, or sometimes not send at all. He was now among the last of his generation, and his thoughts turned more and more to his friends, both those who were still in Poland and those who were no longer living. Wat reflected on how Jasieński's perfect memory for poetry impeded his talent; how Wasilewska was impassioned and blind, but always full of authentic concern for her colleagues; how Przyboś was brutal, arrogant, simplistic; how Janina Broniewska and Leon Kruczkowski hated Ważyk—Ważyk, whose beautiful wife was killed by Nazis and Polish *szmalcownicy,* who believed in the inexorable march of History, who in the Stalinist years had tried to save Wat by portraying him as a lost nineteenth-century liberal not possessed of full reason.[40] Wat thought about Iwaszkiewicz's duality—how the Jarosław who was so deeply rooted in nature and darkness had so long coexisted with the master of his court at Stawisko, the Polish ambassador, the poet laureate, the Writers' Union president. There were moments when Wat had the impression still that he was "among Witkacy's old aunts, in the times when that same Jarosław seemed to me a (perverted) simpleton from Ukraine."[41] Wat reflected, too, about the purity of Tuwim's love for words, and how this was, perhaps, connected with his adoration of one leader after another: first Piłsudski, then Stalin. Słonimski remained for Wat, as always, youthful and charming and quick in his humor; gentle but at moments malicious; courageous but self-absorbed, desirous of constant admiration. This need, Wat felt, was the tragic flaw of all of the Skamander poets, spoiled by their early fame. Wieniawa had befriended Tuwim, "the lion of the Warsaw salons"; the American ambassador had paid a visit to the twenty-year-old Lechoń. They, not the futurists—Wat felt—should have been the poetic avant-garde, but "the *beau monde* ruined them." As for Mayakovsky, Wat thought of how his Russian friend had realized the slogan of "poetry to the streets," but the streets had never understood him.[42]

There was someone else whom Wat could not forget. This was the man who, in the cell they shared in Lubianka, had taught him so much about Marxism. In 1965 the Russian poet Semën Kirsanov, the friend of Wat's cellmate Misha Taitz, came to Paris with a Soviet writers' delegation. Wat invited himself to the reception, he wanted desperately to learn from Kirsanov what had happened to Taitz. Wat was gentle, he did not speak of Lubianka or of prison, he said only that they had a mutual friend, a wonderful, brave person, and that for twenty years Wat had wanted to learn of his fate. Yet though Wat spoke "in half-words," as Russians do, Kirsanov felt the ominousness of the question; he insisted he knew nothing, only that cruelty had been ubiquitous in the world. In the end, he would say only that Misha Taitz was no longer alive—and that Wat should not poke his finger in other people's wounds. Wat defended himself: the wounds were his own.[43]

Even as the war receded further into the past, Wat continued to live ensconced in the nightmare of his encounter with totalitarianism. In his diary, his notes, his poetry, he revisited over and over his time in prison, the twenty-eight prisoners squeezed into an eleven-meter cell, the counting of the lice, the shouting of the interrogators, the torturing of Taitz. He revisited time and again his near-death in Kazakhstan, in Ili, his desperate wish not to be buried there, in the ground of Bolshevism. That he himself had come to Marxism before Stalinism was of no consolation to him. Wat was convinced that Stalin was not an aberration, that Stalinism was an inescapable consequence of Lenin and Leninism. During his time in the Soviet Union, nearly everyone in his family had died in the Holocaust, and this haunted him now as well. He had lived in a time and space defined by Stalinism and Nazism and now was consumed by the attempt to make sense of both of them. For Wat, the essential distinction between Bolshevism and Nazism was not in the quantity of the crimes but rather in the fact that the Germans had chosen Hitler, had supported him, had reaped the benefits of his rule; in contrast the crimes of Bolshevism fell upon its own Russian nation, a nation enslaved by a handful who had usurped power. He was deeply convinced that, on the contrary, never before in history had a whole nation borne such concrete, irrefutable guilt as did the Germans.[44]

In 1962, Adam Ważyk came to Paris. There he and Wat sat in a café and spoke about Stalinism. "I didn't know," Ważyk said.

> "You, you didn't know?! You, who were in Russia for five
> years?!"
> "I believed!"
> "You believed, after everything that you saw with your own
> eyes, the suffering and the humiliation of the working people,
> the boorishness and the villainy and the haughtiness of the
> elite?!"
> "I suffered from a splitting of the self."[45]

Wat believed this. He became increasingly preoccupied with the relationship between knowing and believing, between knowledge and faith. These questions haunted him both in his relationship to communism and in his relationship to God. For Wat the memory of his experience in communism, in communist prison, was intimately connected to his experience of religious faith. It was in Soviet prison that he had become a believer. In the beginning, in Zamarstynów, he had not known how to pray, he had sat alone, trembling, crying, while the others in his cell prayed. Then in Saratov he had seen the devil, understood the devil in history, and felt the demonic nature of communism.[46]

Now in France some two decades later, he had lost that faith. In the same poem in which he wrote of Taitz's being tortured, Wat spoke to the God whose presence he no longer felt:

And now again I don't see you, don't hear you
Yet suddenly an echo of that bygone breath jostles me

when the wind will wander to a hanging olive branch
when I wander, somber, inside my somber recollections.[47]

Yet Wat was uncertain about God's absence as well; he wondered if he could truly be an unbeliever given that he had once, in Kazakhstan and afterwards in Poland, believed so completely. Even in his unbelief he continued every night to say the prayer he had learned from the Ukrainians in Zamarstynów. He feared the nothingness that was the alternative to faith and understood Christianity as the antithesis of Stalinism. For Christianity had as its premise a negative philosophy: man was in essence evil and only circumstances, conditions—Love, Mercy, Suffering—made him good. The inversion of that philosophy—that man was good and only conditions rendered him evil—was Stalinism. Wat saw no third path. And so he continued to vacillate between belief and its absence, between desire and failure to believe. The same fear—of nihilism, of nothingness—that had once propelled him from futurism to Marxism now returned. "To my friend—the Catholic," he wrote in his diary in October 1963, "You place me before the alternative: the crucifix or nothingness. But when, being on the crucifix, one sighs into nothingness? Only into nothingness? Exclusively? And not into such nothingness that one will no longer ever be, but into such nothingness that one never was."[48] Józef Wittlin now reminded Wat of the night in 1929 when they had been walking along the Seine in Paris, and Wittlin had told Wat that in the end, Wat would become a Catholic. Yet the materiality of Catholicism pushed Wat away. He could only believe in a metaphysical Christianity; the personhood of God, the resurrection of bodies, the transfiguration all repelled him. So it was through Christianity that Wat began to return to Judaism. More and more he felt a part of his Jewish ancestry, felt that what was Jewish could not be alien to him. The fate of his ancestors who had been persecuted by the Catholic Church—the mandate to remember their suffering—now began to separate him from Catholicism. Yet even as he felt an increasing sense of closeness to his forefathers, the great rabbis, he returned to both the dialectical thinking of Marxism and the language of the futurists, believing Judaism to be "passé," a religion that had done its part and ended in Christianity.[49]

Even in his uncertainty about faith, Wat was deeply persuaded that he was possessed by demons, that his illness was a punishment for his sins: for not having loved his mother; for having been the force behind *Miesięcznik Literacki;* for having lied during those months in Lvov. At once he had a sense of having been blessed by fate, in particular with Ola, whose presence he saw as proof of God's intervention in his life. Even as they both aged, she continued to be the object of his most intense idealization, the embodiment of all that was good, beautiful, and pure. She was also the obstacle to his desired suicide, for Wat believed he would not be at peace after his death if she were to despair. He believed as well that they were so completely joined to each other that as long as one of them lived, the other could not cease to exist, even in death. Again and again in Paris in the 1960s, he relived in his mind the day in the prison in Alma-Ata when the NKVD oblast chief had brought Ola Watowa from Ili to tell her husband that the Polish ambassador had been expelled from Kuibyshev and there was no one to help him now, that his situation was hopeless, that he must accept the Soviet passport. She had asked him: Would he take the passport? And when he had answered no, they began to talk about something else. She did not ask a second time, although she knew his answer most likely meant his death in the gulag, and her own and their son's death in Kazakhstan. "It was the highest moment of our love," Wat wrote, "on that Russian porch, the enormous, littered courtyard of the Third Division, the detention barracks, I was brought there from the bandits' dungeon, it was sunny, I was blinded by the glare and blinded by the beauty of Ola, so wretched, so hunted, and so calm."[50] He prayed that if his illness caused him to forget all else that had happened in his life, let him not forget that one moment in Alma-Ata in April 1943.[51]

These were the years when Czesław Miłosz became one of the most important figures in Wat's life. Their relationship was at times a difficult—and for Wat a painful—one. Miłosz became in some sense Wat's patron, and Wat was enormously grateful, and yet often hurt by what he felt as Miłosz's condescension, his disregarding attitude towards Wat as a poet.[52] On one occasion in Paris Miłosz introduced Wat to an American poet, telling the American that Wat was a good poet—then after a short pause adding, "I think so."[53] Wat was intensely sensitive; at times he felt that Miłosz held something—philosophically, perhaps—against him.[54] It was Miłosz who arranged for the Wats to come to Berkeley on a fellowship. In his letters to Wat from California, Miłosz wrote that America was something entirely different, inexplicable in any terms available to Europeans. "Because we're so peculiar," Miłosz wrote to Wat, "that sometimes an American Jew can understand us, but even so, only to a small extent . . . I know cases of people who fled from America because 'there are no cafés'—and this is a symbolic formulation of something deeper."[55] Miłosz was didactic and at times chastising in his directions to Wat as to how to proceed with arranging their trip. Do not try to make yourself sound like a scholar—Miłosz instructed—"scholars are those who don't know how to become writers." Above all Miłosz insisted that Wat not think about—and at all costs not voice—the possibility of staying longer than a year.[56]

In the end the formalities were successfully arranged; Wat was hopeful that the climate in California would alleviate his illness, and he looked forward to interacting with the students at Berkeley. In December 1963 the Wats arrived in California. Their initial experience was an almost euphoric one; the Slavicists at Berkeley gave them a very warm welcome, the young women were drawn to Watowa, they treated her like an older, attractive sister—perhaps because, Wat speculated, despite their beauty and energy they had lost something of the feminine in themselves, something they saw in this older woman.[57] Wat was charmed by the young, bright graduate students who surrounded him with interest.

Yet this was a capriciously ephemeral interlude, lasting no more than a few weeks. Miłosz cautioned the Wats not to importune, not to do anything that would lead anyone to fear they might try to stay in the United States permanently. Wat felt as if struck; he sensed that Miłosz felt their presence at Berkeley as a burden to himself. Wat was hurt by Miłosz, but hurt more by his sense of being rejected by those around him. He met with a Polish émigré who worked at the Hoover Institute at Stanford, and realized that many among the émigré community saw in him only żydokomuna. He sensed that others at Berkeley feared Wat would try to find a way to stay in the United States, and so treated him coldly; their fears humiliated him. In any case, he did not see a life for himself in the American professoriate.[58] His initial impression had been an idealized one; the same young people who had been so embracing and attentive disappeared from his and Ola Watowa's lives; their curiosity having been satisfied, their interest now waned, they avoided him when they passed on the street. He began to see American intellectual life as something professionalized in a way it was not in Europe; it was a career like any other.

Even the young man working on a dissertation on the Russian poetess Marina Tsvetaeva now avoided him, passing over Wat's offer to provide him with material about Tsvetaeva's suicide. As Wat watched the students turn the other way, he began to understand not only the superficiality of their initial warm reception, but also their fear of being "contaminated" by someone like himself who would surely not manage to make a career in America; he felt the division of American society into the "losers" and the successful ones. He reflected on his own choices, how he had by-passed success, how he could have remained free in Lvov had he written an exhaustive self-criticism and a poem about Stalin, how he could have been vice minister of culture in communist Poland had he been more obedient, less difficult.[59] "Now I, too, am a *loser*," he wrote in his diary six months after having arrived in Berkeley.[60]

The sense of being boycotted and ostracized was all the more painful as it was reminiscent of the worst years of Polish Stalinism. He remembered how he would come to the Warsaw Writers' Union and no one would speak to him. The fault was his own, though, he wrote in a letter back to Paris; he suffered from an "undoubtedly pathological hypersensitiv-ity."[61] To Miłosz he wrote despairingly some two months into his stay at Berkeley, asking why people's relations to him had changed so suddenly, asking what he had done wrong and reminding Miłosz that he had earlier asked him what kinds of behaviors were taboo in America, what he should avoid doing or saying. Miłosz had answered that there were no taboos, that Wat should only act naturally, should be himself. Now an anguished Wat wrote to Miłosz asking, "Perhaps this is fundamentally true and it's just my nature and naturalness that repel people here?"[62]

Against the hopes of Wat's doctors and friends, Berkeley's psycho-logical and meteorological climate only caused his illness to worsen. He was in constant pain and unable to write. It was at this point that Miłosz performed his greatest act of generosity: he offered himself as Wat's in-terlocutor in speaking about his past. Miłosz turned on a tape recorder; they began to talk. Miłosz, whose friendship had often been a difficult one for Wat, revealed himself to be the ideal listener. He was intensely interested, and familiar with Wat's otherwise obscure references. As for Wat, he was deeply convinced that his illness was of demonic origin, that it was induced by communism, by guilt, and he came to see their dialogue as an act of exorcism and Miłosz as the exorcist. Guilt was the motif of their long conversations, and Wat speculated that it was his burden as a Jew that caused him to perceive the world through the prism of guilt and punishment.[63] He returned obsessively to *Miesięcznik Literacki* as his greatest sin: "the *corpus delicti* of my degradation, the history of my degradation in communism, by communism. It was in a communist prison that I came fully to my senses and from then on, in prison, in exile, and in communist Poland, I never allowed myself to forget my basic duty—to pay, to pay for those two or three years of moral insanity. And I paid, and paid."[64] In revisiting those—the most blind and fanatical—years, Wat had only one moment of comfort: he picked up the issue of *Miesięcznik Literacki* with his eulogy to Mayakovsky and saw that no, thank God, he had not reproached his Russian friend for his suicide.[65] "When a person who can't swim is in the water," Wat told Miłosz, "the worst thing for him to do is to flail around. And I kept moving. Enormous History, a mighty machine, and I had stuck my little foot in."[66] In June 1965 the Wats returned to Paris, and Ola Watowa began to transcribe the tapes.[67]

THE KOŁAKOWSKI AFFAIR

Adolf Rudnicki sent news to Wat of his old friends in Warsaw. Słonimski had now begun to return to the role of acerbic commentator he played in the interwar years, publishing feuilletons again in a journal called *Szpilki* (Needles). These were, Rudnicki wrote to Wat, "sad and lamentable—Słonimski hasn't changed but the world has changed. People speak badly about those feuilletons, because—how can they be good, you yourself know best that they can't be. I feel sorry for Antoni, although better that he write bad feuilletons and in some way feel needed than that he do nothing."[68] The knowledge of having colluded with the Stalinist regime was particularly painful for Słonimski—not because the regime had betrayed Marxism, but because he had betrayed his own self-identification as the iconoclastic critic who held nothing sacred, who feared offending no one, who always stood aside. His poetry now, like Wat's, revealed influences of existentialism and an irony now turned against himself as well.[69] His 1963–1965 poem "Sąd nad Don Kichotem" (Judgment on Don Quixote) ended:

> Because I was fainthearted once,
> Because I once lacked courage
> And kept silent against my conscience,

I wish to be naked when I die.
I wish to throw the oppressive burden off my chest
And I prefer to lie in oblivion,
In ashes and wayside dust,
Rather than on a tall catafalque
In the church of your false gods.[70]

In the spring of 1964, Słonimski, together with Rudnicki, Ważyk, and others, signed the Letter of the Thirty-four to premier Józef Cyrankiewicz, demanding a liberation of cultural policy and a relaxation of censorship. The Party reacted by not allowing the signatories to publish or to leave the country.[71] Słonimski was unintimidated, he was coming into his own again. In 1929 he had written in one of his weekly columns of how he disliked being addressed "you Skamandrites," of how he disliked being addressed as one of a group, of how he felt himself to belong to no collectivity.[72] Now he returned to his ethos of individualism and irreverence.

The hopes for a kinder, freer, more prosperous Marxism inaugurated with Jakub Berman's departure and Gomułka's ascension to power had not been realized. The following year at the 1965 Cracow congress of the Polish Writers' Union Słonimski spoke about the liquidation of the cultural accomplishments brought by the Polish October. In particular, he protested the Party's liquidation of both the discussion group Klub Krzywego Koła (the Crooked Wheel Club) and the periodicals *Przegląd Kulturalny* (Cultural Review), *Nowa Kultura,* and *Po Prostu* (Simply), and its replacement of these with a single journal called *Kultura*—whose contributors consisted entirely of writers whom the rest of the literary community did not hold in especially high esteem. He had not come there to complain about his own situation, Słonimski noted, "on balance I'm somehow managing and with full gratitude must say that my poetry was published twice in very beautiful editions, so as a poet I'm exculpating myself, but as a writer of feuilletons—I must say frankly—I wouldn't want to write feuilletons for *Szpilki,* because the affair of the 34 has placed me in such high moral esteem in society that it wouldn't behoove me to write for *Szpilki.*" Słonimski's old sarcastic tone had returned; he went on to name those among the Writers' Union members who were *not* writing for *Kultura,* a long list of essentially anyone of any importance, including himself, Rudnicki, Ważyk, and Woroszylski. Słonimski noted further that it seemed even Iwaszkiewicz, president of the Writers' Union, was not writing for *Kultura*—at which point Iwaszkiewicz asked him to please remember himself. This was precisely what Słonimski had done.[73]

Słonimski was not the only one creating difficulties for the Party. In early 1966, a group of Party members including Karol Modzelewski and Jacek Kuroń were convicted in closed trials and imprisoned for circulating "false information detrimental to the State." One of those convicted, Ludwik Hass, was a prewar communist who had spent seventeen years in the Soviet gulag for Trotskyism. Upon his release in 1957, he returned to Poland and, still a convinced communist, joined the Party. When Hass was brought into the courtroom, he and his co-defendants raised their handcuffed fists in a communist salute and sang the *Internationale*. Now from London, the man who had once thrown parties where herring was served on newspaper, and women sat on the laps of men who were not their husbands, sent an open letter to Gomułka. Isaac Deutscher broke his self-imposed stance of nonintervention in Polish politics with a defense of Hass and his comrades who were, Deutscher pointed out, perhaps among the last in Poland who continued to nurture such a sincere faith in Marxism.[74]

Revolt was now coming from within. In the realm of irreverence, Słonimski had some competition from a younger Marxist philosopher named Leszek Kołakowski, who at this point in his ideological evolution was committed to a reformed Marxism. In October 1966, Kołakowski gave a lecture at the University of Warsaw; the occasion was the tenth anniversary of the Polish October. Kołakowski revisited the rare feeling of national unity present in 1956—and went on to describe the abysmal state of the country ten years later. He began by speaking about "lawlessness," a salient term during the Polish October, when it became possible to talk about law's being so abstract and all-encompassing that it could be applied rather arbitrarily against anyone at any time. This resulted in law's being regarded as an instrument of repression, which in turn provoked a general contempt for law—something that ten years later remained a source of demoralization. This was only the beginning of Kołakowski's litany. He went on to note the country's material poverty, its low rate of housing construction, its miserable automobiles, and its high rate of infant mortality. Party representatives were chosen on the principle of "negative selection," according to which "fawning, cowardice, absence of initiative, [and] willingness to eavesdrop" were qualifying factors. At least in the Stalinist period, Kołakowski suggested, the ideological sincerity of so many in the Party apparatus worked against this particular kind of negative selection. The result of the present negative selection, continued feeling of lawlessness, and material poverty was a "spiritual pauperization," an absence of hope in the face of the failed promises of October. Poland continued to be a country in which there were no free elections, no freedom of association, no freedom of criticism, no freedom of information. Here Kołakowski adopted a Słonimski-like tone: "The very word freedom has become suspicious. It's true that in the Stalinist period the word freedom was incredibly fashionable, it was quite widespread and indicated more or less the same thing as the absence of freedom. In this respect the situation now is perhaps simpler. In the law about higher education from the Stalinist period there are words about the freedom of scholarship. In the law passed after 1956 that expression is no longer there."[75]

Six days after Kołakowski's lecture, on 27 October 1966, the Central Commission for Party Control passed a resolution to expel Kołakowski from the PZPR for taking a position against that of the Party; propagating revisionist concepts; negating the leading role of the Party in cultural policy; aspiring to turn the Party intelligentsia and youth against the Party's leadership; and endeavoring to weaken the existence of socialist democracy from a liberal-bourgeois position. In a letter to Gomułka written the following month, Kołakowski appealed for his Party card back, insisting that criticism of phenomena that opposed the ideals of socialism was his right and obligation as a Party member—and that moreover the "disastrous social results of deceitful acts in cultural and political life will not be removed by applying repression to those who reveal them."[76] He was not the only one to protest. A few days earlier the Politburo had received a letter from fifteen writers, including Julian Stryjkowski and Wiktor Woroszylski, asking that Kołakowski be reinstated in the Party. Adolf Berman's and Wanda Wasilewska's friend Michał Mirski endorsed their protests.[77]

Kołakowski was not reinstated. On 21 January 1967 Julian Stryjkowski returned his Party card, enclosing a letter noting that his own views were similar to those of Party members who had been expelled or who had left voluntarily.[78] Stryjkowski had for some time been waiting for the right moment; his book *Czarna róża* (The Black Rose), published in 1962, was his farewell to his communist past.[79] Among those who did not resign, and were not prepared to part with the past, was Janina Broniewska. At a Writers' Union meeting held that February of 1967 she protested Kołakowski's demand at the December 1965 Writers' Union congress that all of Władysław Broniewski's work now be published—including those poems composed during his stay in Soviet prison. Kołakowski's point had been unambiguous. "And when I say the complete works," he had told the congress, "I have in mind the complete works."[80] Broniewska called this proposal evidence of Kołakowski's "uncommon impudence and rare impertinence," and a case of exploiting the tragedy of a great poet for personal political aims. She reminded those present that this same great poet had later written a poem about Stalin—and had done so with full sincerity, in the absence of any opportunistic aims—and that later Broniewski had been hurt by those now allegedly his friends, who for a long time maliciously reproached him for that poem.[81]

REFLECTIONS ON A FUTURIST YOUTH

In the 1960s, Anatol Stern wrote a hagiographic book about his old futurist collaborator, the same one who, in 1928, had insisted to Broniewski that Stern had no right to speak for him. In the book, Stern described Bruno Jasieński's "battle with God," a battle often taking the form of a bitter grotesque, but one intimately connected with the tragic rebellion of romantic poetry.[82] Stern wrote of the influence of Apollinaire and Mayakovsky, and even Stefan Żeromski, on Jasieński's work. At the center of Stern's text was his desire to present a certain narrative of their shared past, to show that Polish futurism—in contrast to Skamander—had contained within itself a revolutionary impulse from the outset, that while Marinetti had wanted to awaken his nation with a cult of strength, and the French futurists had declined political engagement, the Polish futurists—like their Russian counterparts—had declared rebellion in the name of social justice. These immature currents admittedly took time to develop, but were nonetheless present from the beginning. In this sense, Stern's polemic was, in a sense, with the very object of his hagiography; the author insisted that Jasieński's own criticisms and recantations of his early work later in his life were often misguided and excessively harsh, that Jasieński himself did not always appreciate his own contribution. In an article on Jasieński's stay in Paris, Stern revisited a letter Jasieński had sent from France in November 1926. "Traveling is a disease," Jasieński had written then, "which has always consumed me and from which I will surely die." Now Stern speculated: Had Jasieński been able to see into the future and learned what awaited him in ten years, would he have come home to Poland? Or would Jasieński's fanatical nature not have allowed for a change in itinerary even if he were to have had forebodings of the tragic ending?[83]

Stern had solicited Wat's contribution to his work on Jasieński, but Wat had declined. Stern was disappointed—he envied Wat his memory, which preserved details so much better than Stern's own. Their common "prehistoric literary youth" was being distorted by other literati, not only by "enemies," but, still worse, also by "friends." Stern was unable to correct all the false information on his own; nevertheless he was determined to proceed. If he were not to do so, Jasieński's memory, "the memory of yet one more great and uncompromising artist, and at once a person so vehement and passionate, that he himself condemned his own work to destruction when it ceased to satisfy him" would perish.[84] Even in his sixties, Stern continued to be moved by the memories of their futurist antics of long ago. "Whatever happened to those times," he wrote to Wat, "when everything was settled beyond appeal with one short 'Yes'?"[85]

In 1965 Stern wrote a letter to the regime journal *Kultura* whose existence Słonimski found so objectionable. In it he attacked the author of a recent book dismissing—in part in Tadeusz Peiper's name—Polish futurism in general and Stern's work in particular as "mockery and short-lived rabble-rousing."[86] Stern was enraged, and cited at some length Peiper's interwar writings attesting to Peiper's respect for Stern and his then collaborators and to Peiper's appreciation of futurism's literary innovations. This open letter came at a time when Stern was lamenting that the censors were not allowing him in his book in Polish futurism to write about Wat—who had defected to the West and betrayed socialism. "I received that news with quite some contentment," Wat wrote to the object of Stern's attack, in the first draft of a letter he later softened before posting, "perhaps I will finally detach myself from the importunate tandem: Stern-Wat, Wat-Stern." Wat continued to harbor some sentiment for Stern, but felt compelled to give his own—unkind yet at once nostalgic—testimony:

> Peiper (like Witkacy) regarded Stern as the misfortune of an
> innovative movement. He reproached him for self-promotion,
> for the complete absence of any kind of aesthetic principles

and scruples, for ostentatiously vulgar tawdriness. These aren't
Peiper's exact words, but *the sense is the same,* my memory isn't
bad, which Stern has learned on more than one occasion. So
much for judgment.

   Both Peiper and especially Witkacy pressured me to break
with Anatol. Witkacy placed me before the alternative: either
him, or Stern. I chose Stern for those very reasons that estranged them, the aesthetes: with Stern I had marvelous fun,
refinedly intelligent literary, philosophical, intellectual hooli-
ganry. Today that means nothing to anyone, too much of that
is everywhere, but in 1920, 1921, 1922, in Poland! Two kids
(Jasieński joined later and brought . . . dandyism à la Severia-
nin), the only ones in Poland at that time, mocking absolutely
everything, and above all poetry. And without today's taste for
assault, it wasn't a discharging of aggressive instincts as it is
today, as it was then among the dadaists. It wasn't the result of
social resentments (or of despair, as it was among those others)
as it was for Gombrowicz. Pure disinterested mockery. In this
lay the whole value, sense and harbingership of so-called Polish
futurism, because the rest, all of it, was a wretched imitation
of what had been already been done for a couple of decades
abroad ("plagiaristic character"). That "pontifical" fool under-
stands nothing of that.

Wat did not disparage this period in its entirety; as in his memoirs of
futurism in *Miesięcznik Literacki,* here, too, his judgment remained an
ambivalent one. He thought Stern foolish to have passed over in silence
their only truly original achievements: their prefaces to *GGA* and *A Jew-
Boy of Letters,* Stern's strikingly forthright sensual—and sexual—longings
in his early poetry. "But even though Stern and I had untimely and apt
intuition (of antiliterature)," he wrote, "we were kids and we ourselves got
lost in it." Wat added about his one-time futurist co-author, alluding to the
intentional misspellings that the futurists had once delighted in: "he was
already back then 'pontifical,' but—then—it added charm to his impudence. But a 67-year-old Kingg of New Art!—it's a sorry sight. It's difficult
today to imagine the freshness and luster of the boasting intelligence, the
wit he had then."[87]

Wat was also disappointed by Ważyk's memoirs of the avant-garde.[88] Ważyk, Wat felt, had written of him in these memoirs as if they had encountered each other for the first (and last) time at a futurist poetry reading. In a letter to Miłosz in 1966, Wat contested this perception: Wat had known Ważyk since they were fifteen and ten years old, respectively. At that time Wat was at Ważyk's home almost every day with Ważyk's older brother Tristan, Wat's closest friend from school, who along with one of Ważyk's sisters, "stood out for their beauty in that family of exceptionally ugly faces." Ważyk's brother Saul [Wagman] was writing Zionist poetry; Ważyk's older sister was engaged to an ugly medical student; on summer evenings she would flirt with Wat on the balcony. "Their father was a frightful Jew," Wat continued, "everyone feared him, fortunately he rarely left his office, in the hallway characters from 'Secrets of Nalewki' would meet, he was not a notary, as the official biography goes, but a clandestine advisor, a trickster; their home was nouveau riche, absolutely Jewish, but also with all of the pluses of having been highly intellectualized: in the salon abstract discussions, judgments of Raskolnikov, Russian Jewish students, admirers of Volynskii, Merezhkovskii, and Blok. There were no goys. I knew Adam Ważyk's friends from school—not a single goy." Wat attributed Ważyk's "mystification" of his family, his rewriting of his past to include only gentiles, to the need for *respectabilité* so endemic to the Polish-Jewish intelligentsia.[89]

THE LAST OF THE SEVEN

On Friday, 29 July 1967, Ola Watowa went into the room where her husband was sleeping, took him in her arms, and said to him, "Ol, wake up!" His head was turned to the side, he was cold and calm. It was only then that she saw the notebook and two sheets of paper by his feet. On the first Wat had written in large letters "DO NOT SAVE ME." On the second he had written a letter to her—"my life, my everything"—pleading with her to forgive him this crime, and above all not to save him and not to despair.[90] Early that evening he had swallowed forty tablets of Nembutal. He was buried in France, in the cemetery in Montmorency. Miłosz, Wierzyński, Grydzewski, and Stern were among those who sent letters and telegrams to Ola Watowa. Iwaszkiewicz wrote to Wat's sister, the actress Seweryna Broniszówna, of his and Wat's half-century-long friendship.[91] Ola Watowa struggled not to despair. Some six weeks after Wat's death she wrote to a friend, "I look into the eyes of my friends, searching for confirmation that I did what I could to be a comfort to Aleksander, that I did everything possible to the best of my strength. And I'm horribly tormented. For after all it's always possible to do more, more. And that very much pains me now."[92] In a letter to Broniszówna, Ola Watowa copied several passages from Wat's last notebook, and asked her sister-in-law to share them, discreetly, with those among Wat's close friends who were still in Poland.[93]

The "last notebook" had been filled largely in May; Wat had been prepared to depart since then. In its pages he said goodnight and goodbye to his wife over and over again; begged their son Andrzej not to be broken by his death; and pleaded with everyone to take care of Ola. He told of abominable pain, of nights of torture, of relentless "vegetation in Hell," and begged them to think that his pain was now over, pain whose depths even Ola could not have understood. He insisted he would remain present in them, and that he would not have peace after his death if they were to despair. For eleven years everything selfish in him had demanded death, only Ola and Andrzej had prevented him from succumbing, he had wanted to be with his wife for as long as he could.

In other pages, in a handwriting decipherable by few besides Ola Watowa, Wat mixed poetry and prose in a kind of stream-of-consciousness prose poem evoking traces of his *I from One Side and I from the Other Side of My Cast-Iron Stove* from nearly half a century earlier. He sketched as well several versions of a poem titled "Zejście" (The Descent), reflecting on his descent into death. His memory he compared to a bombarded city, but he insisted that what he remembered he remembered faithfully. His mind wandered over the rabbinic commentators and Kabbalists who were his ancestors; he wrote of beginning to read Shakespeare at the age of five; of discovering Nietzsche when he was still a child, because his father, the Kabbalist, read German philosophy. His had been a large household full of both books and visitors, as his father was very tolerant and his mother adored young people. His parents loved one another, and they all loved the theater, especially his mother who would sing "I, I the beautiful Helena." He had not been a good son to his mother, who loved her children as only Jewish mothers were able to love, but he was there in the last week of her life, when she was dying of cancer. His nanny Anusia used to take him secretly to church. On Passover Wat would open the door, looking out on

FIGURE 16 Aleksander Wat and Ola Watowa, early 1967. Reproduction by the Beinecke Rare Book and Manuscript Library, Yale University.

the dark stairs for the prophet Elijah, and watch "greedily as a drop of wine disappeared from the full silver jug." His father would end the seder with the words "next year in Jerusalem." He spoke with his father rarely, they understood each other without words. When his father died it was already the beginning of the war, Wat had fled Warsaw without saying goodbye, now his father asked as he lay dying, "Olek, Olek, where is Olek?" His uncle, the ascetic, went to Palestine; his brother and sister-in-law died in Auschwitz. From the age of eight Wat was a Darwinist and an adamant atheist, and would tease his nanny Anusia that people were descended from apes, and she would answer him, "then go, my little son, and climb trees"—Anusia, who had been killed by the Germans and whose body lay in a common grave, after their family had always promised her a Catholic funeral with many crosses. In Kazakhstan the only book he had had with him was *The Imitation of Christ,* which some wise person had sent from London for the Polish refugees. It was magical that he had become an authority to the Jews in Ili, that he had raised them up in rebellion—to their own great detriment. A merchant in Ili, a religious Jew, had shyly proposed that Wat say kaddish for his father on the Jewish New Year, and on a small piece of paper the merchant had written out for Wat the Jewish prayer of mourning in Polish transliteration. Wat felt he had reached the height of his religious unity, his sense of Christianity as the religion of his Jewish ancestors. When he and Ola returned to Warsaw in 1946, they were both ready for baptism, having come to this separately, during their two years apart, and yet mysteriously together. Now as he was dying his faith had left him, he knew he would be buried neither in a Christian cemetery in Israel nor in Warsaw, and he felt the bitterness of dying in a foreign land.[94]

Wat returned now to his first poetic work, *I from One Side and I from the Other Side of My Cast-Iron Stove,* written in a trance-like state of high fever in January 1919, and taken to the printer without ever having been read. He had written nothing before then, no poetry, only short philosophical essays in German, and *Cast-Iron Stove* bore traces of his reading of Kierkegaard. It was a "psychoanalytic confession of a troubled soul"; the young Wat had intended to take his own life, by the age of twenty-five at the latest. Now he asked, "Is it so that a young poet was the seer of his own future fate, a prophet to whom were given words he was to understand only in his old age, as his long life came to a close?" Now he corrected some grammatical mistakes, some words that the printer had misread. Miłosz had shrunk from *Cast-Iron Stove,* had said to him, "but that's art nouveau." Wat had been wounded, that piece remained close to him. Now Wat defended *Cast-Iron Stove,* its subtle tricks, its innovations, its detaching of poetic discourse and poetic syntax from rational discourse and logical syntax, its pushing of syntax to its final limits, beyond which there was only gibberish; its yoking of individual sentences and words, not on the basis of logical continuity or associations, but through an "eruption or invasion in the course of normal speech—in a state of the eclipsing of consciousness." *Cast-Iron Stove* was not "pure nonsense," Wat now insisted: it was not the obscuring of meaning, but rather "the casting of a beam of light on things dark by their nature."[95]

The erratically written pages of the "last notebook" told a remarkable love story that had lasted nearly half a century. Ola's love was, for Wat, the one source of purity in his anguish-laden life. He did not believe he had ever deserved her.[96] Now in his final pages he wrote poetry to her, for her, about her:

> The faithfulness and devotion of [my] wife
> make sublime our
> male debacles . . .
> The purity and devotion of [my] wife
> sanctifies existence.

On the last page, he wrote to her as if already from beyond the grave, telling her he was better now, saying goodnight. To his daughter-in-law, Andrzej's wife Françoise, Wat left in the pages of his last notebook a letter in French. In it he spoke mostly about Ola, about her "extraordinary strength of soul," about the miraculous way she had saved Andrzej in Kazakhstan—and had saved Wat from the seductions of power, glory, and money. "She accepted the loss of us all," Wat wrote in reference to that April day in 1943 in the Alma-Ata prison, "when honesty, dignity demanded this sacrifice." Wat feared that Françoise had misunderstood his wife, and begged his daughter-in-law to raise his grandchildren with love and respect for their grandmother; to do everything in her power to prevent her husband's falling into despair; and to ensure that Andrzej watched over his mother. "I beg you," Wat wrote, "I demand, I admonish you, for the love of God—and thank God you are a believer—to never lack the *supreme respect* you owe to your mother-in-law, which she deserves entirely." He concluded, "Farewell, my dear ones, farewell. May you all be happy. See to it that my wife, my light, has a sweet old age, and that my memory does not haunt you."[97]

THE LAST CHILDREN TO BE EATEN

Stawar's were not the only ashes to be brought back to Warsaw. In October 1964 another urn arrived, this time not from Paris but from Moscow. Some twenty years after Alfred Lampe's death, the ashes of the man who long before had come to Polish communism from the young Zionists were brought to Warsaw for a funeral at Powązki cemetery.[98] Wasilewska, whom in December 1943 Lampe's wife had summoned in desperation to revive her husband, was no longer living. An era of Polish—and Polish-Jewish—Marxism was reaching its end. Polish communism was being domesticated in a way the old KPP vanguard had never anticipated. Like Wat, Broniewski, Stawar, and Deutscher, Wanda Wasilewska did not live to see the "anti-Zionist" campaign of March 1968. Jakub and Adolf Berman, however, did. Even as he became Israeli, Adolf Berman's emotional ties to Poland never faded. In the spring of 1962 he became absorbed in planning memorial celebrations for Broniewski.[99] In late 1963 he wrote enthusiastically of a successful evening in Israel devoted to the memory of Stefan Żeromski.[100] Now in his old age, Adolf Berman would encounter a world that no longer had a place for those such as himself who had remained throughout their lives committed to Jewishness, to Polishness, to Zionism, and to Marxism.

In 1967 the outbreak of the Six-Day War became the pretext for purging the Polish military of officers of Jewish descent. In November 1967, a theater director staged Adam Mickiewicz's play *Dziady* (Forefathers' Eve); students attended the performances in large numbers, some cheering at those parts protesting the tyranny of the Russian tsar. In January 1968 the government forced the play to close. The Polish Writers' Union protested, as did the students.[101] The communist authorities claimed the demonstrations were incited by Zionist conspirators and responded with brutal repression against the student protesters. Władysław Broniewski and Janina Broniewska's granddaughter, nineteen years old and in the last trimester of her pregnancy, was among those students chased by troops in riot gear. When she returned home, her grandmother warned her that she and her young husband, like the other students involved in the protests, were merely pawns in a "complicated political shoving match in the Politburo." Janina Broniewska herself stood aside; her era of revolution had come to an end. When one of her granddaughter's friends was arrested in March, Broniewska took into her home his infant daughter and young wife, who had been evicted from the room where she lived following her husband's arrest.[102] The Party purged the universities and its own ranks; at the University of Warsaw, the philosophy department was forced to close for lack of instructors. Leszek Kołakowski was among those expelled. There followed a collusion of the weltanschauung of the antisemitic Right with the communist Party, and the popularization of a theory of a Nazi-Zionist conspiracy. Newspaper cartoons depicted U.S. President Lyndon Johnson joining the anti-Polish campaign led by American Zionists; Nazis saluting Israeli tanks; and Israeli occupiers of the Gaza Strip reading the works of Adolf Eichmann and thinking, "One should profit from experience."[103] In the same speech in which he spoke about opening the borders in order that those who "regard Israel as their homeland" could leave Poland, General Secretary Gomułka cited Antoni Słonimski's 1924 article "On the Petulance of Jews" as evidence of both Słonimski's antisemitism and his lack of Polishness. Gomułka quoted what Słonimski had written some forty-four years earlier, "'With my hand on my heart I must confess that I have no national feelings at all. I don't feel like either a Pole or a Jew.'" Such cosmopolitans, Gomułka went on to announce, should avoid the kind of work for which national affirmation is indispensable.[104] Słonimski, for his part, was outspoken in defending the students—as he had been increasingly outspoken in various protests throughout the decade. "In former times this was called—*żydokomuna*. Now there's appeared the new concept *żydoantykomuna* (Jewish anti-Bolshevism)," he commented.[105]

Jakub Berman, now suspected of involvement with a group espousing "Zionist-revisionist" views, had become object of secret police surveillance. A forged transcript dated April 1945 was circulated in which he allegedly spoke of how the Jews now had the opportunity to take state power into their own hands—not overtly, but rather from "behind the scenes" by assuming Polish names and concealing their Jewish origins.[106] In 1969 Jakub Berman retired from his position as editor at a publishing house. That year Michał Mirski sent a letter to the Polish Writers' Union saying that he was endeavoring to leave the country and asking that he be removed from the list of members of the United Polish Workers' Party.[107]

In 1963, when *Tygodnik Powszechny* (The Universal Weekly) agreed to publish the initial results of Władysław Bartoszewski's questionnaire about Poles who had helped to hide Jews during the Nazi occupation, Bartoszewski decided to conduct the research under a name taken from the title of Słonimski's poem "Ten jest z ojczyzny mojej" (He is from my homeland). This was the title under which Bartoszewski's book was published in 1967. It sold out quickly; when the publisher requested permission for a second printing, state authorities demanded that Bartoszewski change the title. By

FIGURE 17 Antoni Słonimski and his wife in Warsaw; photograph taken by a security service informant, November 1966. Courtesy of Instytut Pamięci Narodowej.

then it was 1968, Słonimski had contributed to a protest by Polish writers and had himself become a target of Gomułka's attacks. Słonimski, his work, and even his titles were now on a blacklist.[108] Bartoszewski spoke to Słonimski—by now they had become friends; Słonimski told Bartoszewski to change the title and publish the book, but Bartoszewski refused, for him it was a matter of principle. In the end the publisher supported the author against the censors, and when the book reappeared in print in October 1969 it was with the same title—and on the dedication page the poem "He Is from My Homeland," ending with the stanza:

> He who opens his heart to all is
> French when France suffers is
> Greek when the Greek nation withers from hunger.
> He is from my homeland. He is a human being.[109]

It was the first sign of Słonimski's return to print, somewhat—as Bartoszewski wrote—"through the back door."[110]

Adolf Berman was among the contributors to *He Is from My Homeland*.[111] In October 1968, during a trip abroad to Austria, Bartoszewski wrote to Adolf Berman, expressing his pain and regret at the antisemitic campaign of 1968 being conducted under the pretext of a "battle against Zionism." Nothing, he wrote, could shock him any longer.[112] Ten months later Bartoszewski wrote again from abroad, this time from London, returning to the same theme: "I am getting in touch once again, taking advantage of the occasion of being abroad—that which it's possible to write from Poland is not at all worth writing, and that which it's necessary to write—is not possible to write. I send you heartfelt expressions of remembrance and greetings together with expressions of my deepest shame for what the communists who rule Poland are doing."[113]

In 1970, Adolf Berman's onetime student from before the war, Aleksander Masiewicki, contacted his former teacher after many years. Masiewicki, a Polish communist since his youth in the 1930s, was now, in the wake of the "anti-Zionist" campaign, a Polish-Jewish émigré in New York. In his letter he told Adolf Berman the story of the day he returned his Party card. It was a beautiful, sunny morning, 13 March 1968. On that day Masiewicki looked at himself in the mirror and saw the face gazing back at him as one of a man who in moment would take his own life—or hurl a bomb. It was then that he came to a Party committee meeting:

In silence I placed before [the committee secretary] my Party card together with a declaration composed earlier on a sheet of paper saying the following: "In connection with the campaign being conducted by the Party concerning student activities, a campaign unworthy of the great traditions of our Party and hence villainous, I ask that you remove my name from the list of members of the PZPR." I submitted my resignation and signature and without a word left the room of farewells in deep silence. I felt then a tremendous relief, the nightmare that had throttled me for many years departed. Already long ago I had entertained the thought of finally tearing from myself that "burning shirt of Deianeira," I lived in unceasing conflict with my conscience which was choking me with disgust. The decision was a difficult one, as it meant self-annihilation, the negation of my entire life. Yet now that this was behind me, I felt absolutely indifferent as to the consequences. I could not have acted differently. I called my wife. I said: "You can congratulate me!" She did not ask what for, at once she understood. For a moment she was silent, then she spoke: "If you've made your decision, then good. Now it's my turn!"[114]

Adolf Berman reproached Masiewicki then for his negativism, for abandoning his faith; and Masiewicki partially concurred—for it was true that he no longer harbored illusions that the utopia they had fought for and dreamed of their whole lives would ever come about.[115] "I have my doubts," he concluded to his former teacher, "as to whether 'history goes on.'"

Epilogue

It will be like going from one room to another
like moving to another apartment
like a transfer to a neighboring town
like a journey across the ocean
like a flight to another planet
It isn't so, there will be no comparison
Neither the fate of Odysseus nor the fate of a great outcast
    was I given.

—*Adam Ważyk*

WŁADYSŁAW BARTOSZEWSKI WAS IN prison between 1949 and 1954, while Adolf Berman, his old partner in Żegota, was apparently silent. Yet by the time Bartoszewski was elected a senator in Poland in the 1990s, he spoke of Adolf Berman with nostalgia rather than bitterness. Whether he attributed Berman's silence to communist loyalty or tragic impotence, Bartoszewski accused him of nothing: "I never expected that he would 'stand on his head' or that he would change my fate in Poland. Yet even to his brother I never would have turned for anything. I regard his brother as responsible for the deaths of thousands of people: my friends and acquaintances, strangers, decent people."[1] Only once did Bartoszewski meet Adolf Berman's brother Jakub in person. It was years after Bartoszewski's imprisonment and Jakub Berman's expulsion from the Party. "There were many times when [Adolf] Berman came to Poland during the '60s and '70s. And even after Poland had broken off diplomatic relations with Israel, he still came (as a trusted 'comrade'), he would stay in a hotel, he always called me, we always saw each other. But he never invited me to see his family, although I knew he was in contact with them. Once he arranged to meet with me at some kind of performance or event at the theater. I saw him in the foyer, he was standing with his brother Jakub. And so I hesitated—they were talking to each other, as family, I had no place there. But he ran over to me and said, '*Panie Ludwiku* (as he called me until the end of his life), allow me to introduce my brother.'"[2] The two men shook hands in silence.

In an interview conducted shortly before Jakub Berman's death in 1984, Teresa Torańska asked Jakub Berman about the communists' postwar persecution of Żegota, and specifically about Bartoszewski's long imprisonment. How was it possible that his brother said nothing then? He only spoke about it many years later, Jakub Berman answered her.[3] Torańska was on "the other side of the red barricade," a member of Solidarity and the underground, bitterly resentful of the communist regime. When in the winter of 1981–1982 Torańska resolved to contact Jakub Berman, Poland was under martial law and Torańska was in a state of despair. What she demanded from Jakub Berman was an explanation: Why had he done what he had—and caused so much suffering?[4] Beginning in the summer of 1982, Torańska visited Jakub Berman every Tuesday. "He was absolutely aware," Torańska recalled, "that this was his last conversation about the past. . . . He was absolutely aware that he was speaking to history."[5] A curious respect grew up between them, transcending her viciousness and his condescension. Time and again she reminded him that he was hated in Poland. Berman was unflustered. He had not done what he had to be loved; he even accepted that he had been deleted from the encyclopedia following his expulsion.[6] This was, after all, a revolution and not a tea party.

Jakub Berman understood that the end of his life was near, and to the very end believed that communism would prevail, that it would bring people a better life—even if he would no longer be there to see this.[7] In his unpublished memoir of the 1948 Wrocław congress that had been Jerzy Borejsza's last great act, Berman wrote in 1978 of how lingering in his memory were the shadows of the congress's participants, their unfulfilled hopes, their dilemmas and their passions. He wrote down then some lines from Ilya Ehrenburg's poetry:

> But the long day was not lived in vain
> I was able to make out the evening star.
>
> I lived so much, but not to the end
> I didn't see enough, didn't love enough.[8]

By then, few of his generation remained. Mieczysław Grydzewski died in London in 1970. When the editor of a Warsaw newspaper refused to publish Grydzewski's obituary, Słonimski called it a scandal: Grydzewski, the devoted editor, had never even involved himself in politics, the government should have nothing against him.[9] Not long afterwards, Słonimski gave Bartoszewski a copy of his book *Jedna strona medalu* (One Side of the Coin) with the dedication "To him who is from my homeland."[10] By this time Słonimski had become the grand old man of the political opposition. He was continually at odds with his old friend Iwaszkiewicz, still president of the Writers' Union, whose eternally reconciliationist posture towards the Party Słonimski found odious. Instead, he turned to younger generations; among his most frequent interlocutors in the last decade of his life were Bartoszewski and Adam Michnik. By this time Słonimski was under constant surveillance by the Ministry of Internal Affairs. He was not terribly disconcerted. After all, he said, "I'm no longer young, what can they do to me?"[11]

Among Słonimski's last dissident ventures was the December 1975 "Letter of the Fifty-nine," whose signatories included Leszek Kołakowski and Julian Stryjkowski (and, the following month, Adam Ważyk), protesting projected amendments to the Polish constitution that would have formalized the leading role of the Party.[12] In January 1976 Słonimski gave an interview to *Les Nouvelles Littéraires* in which he chastised French writers for their silence, accusing them of naïveté and a willful refusal to recognize the reality obtaining in the communist bloc. Bitterly Słonimski recalled how in 1956 Sartre had not wanted to see Polish writers break from socialist realism, for fear this would weaken the socialist camp against the United States. "Freedom for him, every limitation for us!" Słonimski told his French interviewer. He believed that because French intellectuals enjoyed freedom, they left others to their own fate, and insisted that "for the soul no borders exist," that intellectuals must speak up regardless of the danger.[13] Now Czesław Miłosz, the object of Słonimski's vicious attack in 1951, published an open letter telling Słonimski that he had read his "truthful and acrid interview" with a feeling of pride.[14] Later that same year Słonimski presented Bartoszewski with a second gift: the original version, complete with the censor's marks, of his memoir *Alfabet wspomnień* (An Alphabet of Memories).[15] It was among Słonimski's last acts. In summer of 1976 he died of injuries suffered in an automobile accident. Jarosław Iwaszkiewicz and Jakub Berman were among some eight hundred mourners at the July funeral held at a neglected Catholic cemetery; after Słonimski's body was lowered into the ground, the mourners sang "Poland has not yet perished."[16] Six years later, Bartoszewski published the censored fragments of Słonimski's *Alphabet of Memories* in a Catholic journal.[17]

As for the others, Iwaszkiewicz remained president of the Polish Writers' Union all through the 1970s. His wife Anna, the heart of their court at Stawisko for half a century, died in late 1979. Iwaszkiewicz soon followed her to the grave.[18] This was the year of Ważyk's seventy-fifth birthday. Jakub Berman, so infuriated at Ważyk's "A Poem for Adults" a quarter-century earlier, wrote to him now: "For decades your writing has been interwoven with the path of my life and my pursuits, consonantly or disconsonantly, but always evoking response and reflection."[19] Berman wished Ważyk a quick return to good health. This was not to be. Ważyk died in August 1982, nine months after the Party and the military had subdued the Polish labor movement Solidarity by imposing martial law. After Ważyk's death, Julian Stryjkowski told a younger writer of his days working with Ważyk at *Czerwony Sztandar* in Lvov: "After Wat's disappearance, Ważyk waited for his turn. . . . I was glad that he survived. In all the long years of our friendship I never told him that."[20]

Writing to her sister-in-law Seweryna Broniszówna just after Wat's suicide, Ola Watowa described her husband's "last notebook": "Everything written by hand, despite his suffering he wanted to preserve everything that lived in him until the last moment. All of the faiths and disillusionments of our existence. I desire now only one thing: to manage to preserve what's there, what he wrote up to his last moment."[21] She did manage. It was this dedication that dissuaded her from her own thoughts of suicide; her life without her husband felt empty and devoid of meaning, it was only a shadow of a life, as she wrote to Broniszówna.[22] She lived in memories. When in May 1973 Iwaszkiewicz gave a poetry reading in Paris, Ola Watowa was overcome by a longing for the past. The following day she wrote to him in a flush of emotion:

> Memories assailed me. Your presence, Witkacy, who bestowed
> his friendship upon Aleksander, his visits to us, his portraits of
> myself and Aleksander—unfortunately lost during the war—
> his death. . . . Your home in Stawisko, your melodious voice . . .

I hadn't then yet met Aleksander and like a typical schoolgirl, very shyly but spontaneously, I began to talk to you about the beauty of *Panny z Wilka* [The Young Women of Wilko], about *Brzezina* [Birchwood]. . . .

So many memories—all now imbued with pain, with regret, with longing for Aleksander.

I show to the world a "smiling face." I've learned here always to answer: *ça va, ça va,* although it's so lonely and difficult, so without hope for me—as it will be now until the end of my life and one so feels like *departing* and only Aleksander's unorganized papers—which I'm suffering over, trying to decide what to keep and what to throw out so as not to do him injury —give me no right to depart. And also my Andrzej.

In April I turned 70. Time has suddenly contracted and the feeling of guilt increases. Which is good. A feeling of guilt leavens an *authentic* perception of our life, our relationship to people, to the world and its issues. And perhaps for that reason those several final verses concluding your poem in the March issue of *Twórczość* so affected me:

"Why has Golem entered my home?
Why is Mr. Hyde sitting at my desk?
Why is a demon's funeral taking place outside my window?"

And you end:

"It all must be destroyed
Let there be a quiet beach and the complete absence of
   questions.
No questions."

No questions? Is it so?[23]

For Ola Watowa, questions—things unsaid—remained. She regretted having refused to talk to Władysław Daszewski that evening in Łódź, she regretted having never learned what Daszewski had to say. In the "last notebook," Wat had urged his wife to write her own story. When in her old age, many years after his suicide, she did, she began: "Everything that is most important in my life is connected to Aleksander."[24] She wrote that she would get goose bumps whenever she thought of how she might not have been at that drama school ball, she might never have met him, and her life would have been wasted.

Conclusion

All the demons took them all
    demons took them all
        demons took them all
Until from laughter monkeys fell
From the astral carousel.

—*Julian Tuwim*

WHILE THE POLISH AVANT-GARDE was all but forgotten, its Russian counterpart, to which it was so closely tied, long received sympathetic attention as a casualty of the Bolsheviks. As the era of East European communism came to a close, however, some studying the relationship between the avant-garde and Stalinist culture began to question the former's presumed innocence. The Russian artist Boris Groys indicts the avant-garde, even while empathetically conveying its philosophy: "If the avant-garde followed Nietzsche's maxim to the effect that what was falling should still be pushed, it was only because it was deeply convinced that the fall could not be broken. The avant-garde regarded the destruction of the divine work of art that had been the world as an accomplished and irreversible fact whose consequences had to be interpreted as radically as possible if any compensation were to be made for the loss." It was the avantgardists who first recognized the naïveté of the notion that art is independent of power. It was they who created the precedent for conceiving of art as the will to power, they who were the first to be enraptured by the violation of thresholds and the pursuit of liminality. Later, Groys argues, Bolshevik elites formulated socialist realism in the name of the masses, having come to socialist realism through the avant-garde. The Stalinist era then consummated this "fundamental avant-garde demand that art cease representing life and begin transforming it by means of a total aesthetico-political project."[1]

The fatal step was thus not the imposition of Marxism per se, but rather the leap from art as representation to art as transformation. The Bolsheviks realized the implications of such a crossing, but it was the avantgardists who first transgressed the boundary. Mayakovsky was often quoted as saying that art was not a mirror to reflect the world, but a hammer with which to shape it. Art as representing life came to be seen by both the avantgardists and the Bolsheviks as a bourgeois aesthetic, a stark contrast to the revolutionary aesthetic of art as building life. It was the avantgardists who first embodied the drive to separate space like time into the old and the new, with a beginning in black chaos, at absolute zero, where God was dead. For Groys, Stalinist aesthetics were the logical culmination of the program the avant-garde had set in motion: "Stalinist culture both radicalizes and formally overcomes the avant-garde; it is, so to speak, a laying bare of the avant-garde and not merely a negation of it." Moreover, the Russian avant-garde was complicitous in the appropriation of its ideas by the Bolsheviks, since "the central issue to these artists was the unitary nature of the politico-aesthetic project."[2]

In June 1965 Stefan Kordian Gacki, once the editor of the avant-garde *Almanach Nowej Sztuki,* wrote to Aleksander Wat from the United States. He had been reflecting on the causes of what Wat had called the "sinking into the sand" of their generation:

I agree with your evaluation: we were kids, we lacked crafts-manship, patience. . . . But literary shortcomings and personal faults don't explain in full what happened. The fascinating question remains: Where did we get an "intuition of today's man"? What inclined so many to search for salvation in the womb of reactionary Moscow? The answer must embrace the fact that Poland at that time strayed from the remainder of the West in its understanding of social problems, in science and technology, and in imagination. But even that—while fascinating for us, and perhaps as well for historians of those times— would not adequately justify taking up (by myself as well) this question at this moment. . . . In other words, it seems to me

that the conflict between ourselves and Skamander from the
1920s (and everything connected with it: the role of poetry,
its scope, its vision of the world) is *to this day unresolved.*[3]

How was it that this generation of avant-garde poets of the early 1920s
became the revolutionary Marxists of the late 1920s? How did they make
the leap from radical nihilism and radical contingency to radical utopianism and radical determinism? They bore some of the qualities of their
west European counterparts, the "generation of 1914" who harbored "the
conviction that they represented the future in the present."[4] The future
was everything because the old world, they deeply believed, was spiraling into an irrevocable abyss. A philosophy of despair—what Wat called
"that entire ballast of weltschmerz"—penetrated Polish futurism, as did
the poets' painful awareness of their alienation from, and ostracism by,
the amorphous masses.[5] At a moment of historical optimism and faith
in national self-determination, the young avantgardists were deeply persuaded that life could not continue as it had—but they embraced this
conviction more with a sense of impending catastrophe than with hope
for a hereafter. Ultimately their nihilism proved unbearable, their belief
in radical contingency existentially unsustainable. Wat came to see his
inability to endure nihilism as the fatal weakness that propelled him towards communism.[6] Adolf Warski's great-grandson Stanisław Krajewski
writes of Wat and his contemporaries: "They found themselves in a void,
without footing, because they had already undermined everything. But
that emptiness, anarchy, senselessness, they could not endure, and just
then they made the jump from the kingdom of freedom to the kingdom
of necessity."[7] The catastrophism of the 1920s arose from this sense of a
void, an abyss of nothingness, the degeneration of civilization; the simultaneous utopianism and catastrophism of the 1930s arose from a sense
of impending horror, the rise of fascism—and of Stalinism. Wat and his
friends' *engagement* was a desperate flight from their nihilism, a revolt
against it, and yet at once a desperate attempt to sustain a state of dizzying
liminality. Together with the inability to endure nihilism and contingency
was a certain impulse towards transgression, a desire to maintain the
headiness of it all, to remain on the edge, hovering at the threshold—only
now with a certainty as to what fantastic things would materialize on the
other side.

Wat believed that the choices were few, and it is true that as the inter-war years wore on the spectrum of choices appeared ever more circum-scribed.[8] In a polarizing political spectrum, the Right was becoming more radical, the Left was becoming more radical, and the center was rapidly disappearing. For "Poles of Jewish origin," there was no place on the Right. Yet such a pragmatic conceptualization perhaps fails to capture the zeitgeist, the existential imperative to make a choice, to take some decisive action as a means of realizing oneself. Hans Ulrich Gumbrecht invokes the German word *Tat* for such direct action in the 1920s: "*Taten* do not emanate from principles of legitimacy or from generally acceptable rea-sons. . . . The individual strength of those who act lies not in rationality, but in their determination to do whatever they intuitively encounter and identify as an absolute, fated obligation. Once they make such eminently subjective decisions, the agents' subjecthood, paradoxically, is absorbed in an overwhelming flow of vitality."[9] Revolution, as Witold Wandurski's correspondence with Władysław Broniewski of the 1920s expressed so forcefully, was above all a grasping at self-actualization—that this was to be achieved through self-negation made it no less true.

Remembering how, at a party in the 1920s, her husband watched as Isaac Deutscher pulled her onto his lap, Ola Watowa wrote, "So that drama, as they say, of a communist began very early, some kind of maso-chistic self-annihilation, in the name of what?"[10] Her observation of maso-chistic self-annihilation speaks not only to the role of Marxist intellectuals vis-à-vis the proletarian revolution, but also to Slavoj Žižek's observation about the differing natures of Stalinist and fascist totalitarianism: "After the Fascist Leader finishes his public speech and the crowd applauds, the Leader acknowledges himself as the addressee of the applause (he stares at a distant point, bows to the public, or something similar), while the Stalinist leader (for example, the general secretary of the Party, after finishing his report to the congress) *stands up himself and starts to applaud.* This change signals a fundamentally different discursive position: the Stalinist leader is also compelled to applaud, since the true addressee of the people's applause is not himself, but the big Other of History whose humble servant he is."[11] The distinction is a meaningful one. The Frank-furt School theorists Theodor Adorno and Max Horkheimer attempted to draw a line between Enlightenment and totalitarianism. Inherent in the Enlightenment, they maintained, was the sacrifice of the self to the self, the surrendering of subjectivity as a means of achieving subjectivity.[12] A Marxist understanding of the fulfillment of subjectivity is oneness with objectivity, with the grand narrative, with the momentum of History. For the poets of Café Ziemiańska and their friends, the desire to become one with History was at once the fulfillment of their narcissism, their altruism, and their self-hatred—all extreme, sincere, inextricably intertwined.

Their rendezvous with Marxism was not simply—or not only—an extension of the liberalism and the leftism that might seem a natural emanation of their cosmopolitanism. For in opting for Marxism they opted for determinism, and hence a radical transformation of responsibility, a wholly different moral standpoint from that of an intellectual in a contingent world. Now as Marxist intellectuals they were to play out in a particularly poignant way the tension between telos and subjectivity—or rather, between fate and individual agency—inherent in their experience of modernity. The burden of responsibility was all the heavier because of the enormous role of intellectuals, and the extraordinary resonance of poetry, in their world. When Jakub Berman wrote in 1980 that Tuwim's poetry would continue to accompany them all, he was very much correct—as were Tuwim and his friends when they sat in Café Ziemiańska and truly believed that the world moved on what they discussed there.[13] In a sense, it did. Wat's recantation of futurism on the pages of *Miesięcznik Literacki* was a step towards the communist art of self-criticism, which the poets would eventually embrace. The preoccupation with criticism and self-criticism that emerged on the pages of *Miesięcznik Literacki* was something they learned before socialist realism—and something much more fundamental to their Marxist consciousness.

The communist ritual of self-criticism reveals Marxism's origins in the rationality of the Enlightenment on one hand, and in modernity's emphasis on linear temporality on the other. When Robespierre declared that "we have raised the temple of liberty with hands still withered by the irons of despotism," he encapsulated a problem that would be fundamental to Marxism as well: how was it possible to move from the old world to the new world when the makers of the new world were "always already" contaminated by having been born into the old?[14] The Marxist intellectuals in Poland, as elsewhere, were afflicted with a subjectivity a priori made impure by their origins in the bourgeois world. Self-criticism responded to this "existential condition" of revolution and revolutionaries—an existential condition these intellectuals felt with particular intensity. This new language of self-criticism was predicated on the condemnation of the subjective in favor of the objective—and in fact self-criticism tended to be directed at one's failure to recognize objective truth, that is, a failure to align oneself with the inevitable direction of History. If their early self-hatred was expressed in a drowning confusion, self-criticism was its complement: a confession of past uncertainty as sin, spoken from the position of having achieved that certainty. That constant vigilance was necessary in order to safeguard what was ostensibly an inexorable path towards communism alluded to a fear that perhaps the "iron laws of History" were subject to some contingency after all.[15]

Self-criticism was one instance revealing the complicated interaction between the individual and collective levels of the communist project. Another such instance is what Jan T. Gross in his book on the Soviet occupation of Poland's eastern territories describes as the privatization of the public sphere. Unlike Wat's and Broniewski's first experience of prison in Warsaw in 1931, their first experience of Soviet prison was one of collaboration and betrayal. For those like Wat, Broniewski, Stern, and Ważyk, newly Soviet Lvov was their first real encounter with communism in power, a communism much different from the one they had imagined in Café Ziemiańska and on the pages of *Miesięcznik Literacki*. Here was a communism in which close friends betrayed one another, a communism not devoid of the grotesque. Gross contextualizes this new form of *engagement* in a regime that believed that "the population must subdue itself and that with a little encouragement it generally would."[16] He argues that the essence of Soviet totalitarianism in this case lay not in the obliteration of the private sphere but rather in the privatization of the public sphere. The result was a society in which everyone had immediate access to the apparatus of the state and was encouraged to use it against one another. Denunciations were integral because "the real power of a totalitarian state," Gross writes, "results from its being at the disposal of every inhabitant, available for hire at a moment's notice." As a result "the distinction was lost between those responsible for and those subject to public order."[17] The effacing of the distinction between public and private came together with the effacing of the distinction between victim and oppressor. This period saw the great fall of people like Aleksander Wat, Anatol Stern, Tadeusz Peiper, and Władysław Broniewski, and at once the great rise of Jerzy Borejsza, Adam Ważyk, Janina Broniewska, and Wanda Wasilewska—who herself was not protected from the murder of her husband. No position was a stable one.

That a private space was never obliterated is revealed as well by the surviving photographs of Wanda Wasilewska. In some she wears a colonel's uniform, a man's tie, her hair cropped short. In another she is holding a cigarette, glancing back over her shoulder, looking beautiful and not unlike a young Margaret Hamilton.[18] After Wasilewska's death, Janina Broniewska wrote, "In my home there remain her books, her furniture, and so very often I have the impression that she still lives. I know the beating of Wanda's heart, I know her personal affairs. It was proposed to me that I write her biography, but I couldn't do it. She's just too close."[19] Later Broniewska would emphasize that family members, sisters, do not choose one another, whereas theirs was "a love by choice."[20] In her memoirs she referred often to the private language she and Wasilewska shared, with phrases sometimes appropriated from their enemies and used mockingly; their correspondence often reads as if encrypted. Theirs was a relationship revealing that the private sphere, even under communist totalitarianism, and even among communists, was never entirely eclipsed. These women were comrades in political battle, but also intimate friends who spoke to each another in a language clearly departing from a communist idiom that was their public language.

The observation speaks as well to the young Władysław Broniewski, who in the 1920s was writing proletarian poetry in a new language of battle and letters to Janina Kunig in a language of premodern chivalry. As with the two women, Broniewski's multilingualism ran deep. In fact it is so that among all of these figures an internal polyphony of voices never disappeared. Throughout his life, Broniewski maintained perhaps four great passions: for women, for poetry, for Poland, and for socialism. Their accompanying discourses—romantic and literary, patriotic, and communist—while sometimes distinct, nonetheless coexisted even in the most improbable, and inauspicious, circumstances. So did Wat's love for his wife transcend all of his ideological choices—even at the height of his communist engagement, he rejected Isaac Deutscher's accusation that he was harboring foolish bourgeois prejudices and whisked Ola from Deutscher's lap. Theirs was a love story.

Janina Broniewska and Wanda Wasilewska embodied as well a seem-

ingly improbable yoking of extreme harshness with extreme sentimentality. Both came to be despised in Poland as traitors who ushered Stalinism
into Poland, who sold their homeland to the Soviets. And so it was. Perhaps it is even true that Wanda Wasilewska was Stalin's lover as well as his
confidante. Yet this makes her relationship with Janina Broniewska no less
moving in its undying affection, no less persuasive in its claims of loyalty.
"I kiss you (in our younger years one would write: a hundred thousand, a
million times)," Wasilewska wrote to Broniewska from Kiev in 1948.[21] It is
among the ironies of their circle and their times that the language of their
correspondence is reminiscent of a Victorian friendship between women
—a pastiche of love, sensuality, sexuality, and romanticism in which all
those elements are no less poignant for being amorphous, entangled.[22] To
neither one of these women should be ascribed an idealized Victorian-era
innocence (with respect to sexuality or otherwise), yet neither can they
be understood in monovalent—or exclusively political—terms. In her
relationship with Janina Broniewska, Wanda Wasilewska proved capable
of an unusual, and very sincere, loyalty and human affection. This excuses nothing, of course, yet it does offer another picture of those circles
and those times. Their friendship, moreover, revealed a space within the
Revolution for embracing the varied meanings of femininity. While Wanda
Wasilewska might have been masculine to her male comrades, she was
always a woman to Janina.

The stories of these two women and their friends reveal the complexity of human identity, and the extraordinary complexity of human relationships. For all of these figures, identity was not an essence, but rather
an ever-shifting process, a contingent choice, the contours of which were
continually in flux.[23] A reality of "underdetermination" always obtained.
Like the Berman family, the families of both Stryjkowski and Ważyk were
split between communism and Zionism, a potent testimony to the space
for making choices. Most of these intellectuals came of age in what was at
a minimum a Russian-Polish bicultural space, and most often a Russian-
Polish-Jewish tricultural space. This was true even for many of those not
"of Jewish origin." Broniewski was quickly taken in by the Polish Jews
in Palestine; his identification with the Warsaw Ghetto Uprising was an
expression of his Polishness, a Polishness that contained a nontrivial
element of Polish-Jewishness as well. Wasilewska absorbed the Jewish
references around her, this was part of her milieu as a writer, a socialist,

an activist, a Pole. Later she embraced a Soviet identity, an identity that was sometimes more and sometimes less a Ukrainian one.

For all of them, notions such as Polishness and Jewishness were far from monolithic and mutually exclusive; and the question of whether writers like Julian Tuwim, Antoni Słonimski, and Aleksander Wat should be "read" as Poles or "read" as Jews obscures the polyvalence and the fluidity of their sense of self. They identified in different ways and in different roles at different moments in their lives—choices that at each moment were contingent upon their memories of the past, their position in the present, their vision of the future. Stryjkowski grew up trilingual in Hebrew, Yiddish, and Polish; like so many others, he had been a young Zionist before he became a communist, and he may well have remained a Zionist had it not been for a personal rejection. In some way Stryjkowski never recovered from having been cast out of his Zionist youth group—by adolescent boys who sensed his homosexuality and felt uncomfortable around him.[24] Of his communist years Stryjkowski wrote that he ceased to feel like either a Jew or a Pole, and became rather a cosmopolitan—who defended himself against his "double—Jewish and Polish—sentimentality."[25]

Tuwim's coming to Jewishness converged with his coming to communism, while Wat's longings to return to Judaism converged with his sense that his engagement in communism was his greatest sin. Even as he delved further into the religion of his ancestors, Wat employed the same antisemitic epithet, *gudłaj* (kike), that Wandurski had used with Broniewski in the 1920s in reference to Wat and his friends.[26] Tuwim, having spent the interwar years unyielding in his conviction that he was a Pole, became in wartime exile a Polish Jew longing to return to Poland. He insisted that the blood effecting this solidarity was not the blood of his own origins, but rather the blood spilled by those Jews who were murdered in his country. In "He is from My Homeland," Słonimski echoed this identification with the one who suffers. After the war he wrote a poignant elegy to the Jewish shtetl that was no more, lamenting the destruction of the same world whose existence he had assailed in the interwar years.[27] To categorize figures such as Wat, Tuwim, and Słonimski as self-hating Jews would obscure the extent to which their antisemitism was inseparable from their all-encompassing self-hatred, and the extent to which this was inseparable from their narcissism. Adam Ważyk called Wat "the most disintegrated individual I ever met in my life."[28] Perhaps this was true, but it was also true that Wat was the most introspective of all of them. At the end of his life, he wrote that he had never felt himself to be a Polish Jew or a Jewish Pole, but rather had always been both a Pole and a Jew—two identities in which he had always taken pride, and of which he had always despaired.[29]

As socialist realism shifted into the past, the coming of existentialism—with its insistence that "existence precedes essence"—into literary circles brought with it an increasing self-consciousness of the role of choice. When Stern discovered the letter Barbusse had written in 1929 protesting Jasieński's expulsion from France, Stern wondered if Jasieński had known of it. He wondered further: if Jasieński had known of it, would he have softened his attack on Barbusse two years later at the writers' congress in Kharkov? Or by that time was there nothing that would have restrained Jasieński in his pursuit of the idea to which he had given himself?[30] Stern's wife, Alicja Sternowa, had similar thoughts. At times she and her husband had been very poor, at times very rich, at times entirely isolated, at times surrounded by friends. "Our life is composed of individual artistic adventures," she wrote, "everything in it conditioned by what impassioned Anatol at a given moment."[31] Wat, too, at the end of his life described the moment of his engagement with communism in similar terms: "But you know, that was a certain central moment in my life, the moment of choice that created all the consequences. . . . But mine was a pure choice, subjective, not especially conditioned by anything outside my own will, my own outlook, my own sense of the world, my own spiritual needs. Do you understand? It was a free, pure choice!"[32] Ważyk agreed, noting after Wat's death that while fate had been harsh towards Wat, Wat had done his part to assist fate.[33] In turn, Wat remained unconvinced that Ważyk's Stalinism was an exercise in self-delusion in the interests of either comfort or opportunism—such an explanation, Wat insisted, explained nothing.[34] This also held true for others. "Among the communists I knew," Wat related in his memoirs, "were some of the most attractive people I have ever met, people whose motives were incredibly pure. They made their choice with intentions that were pure—I would use that monstrous distinction—subjectively pure. Objectively, they made a choice for Stalin."[35] After the war, while Wat suffered from the memory of *Miesięcznik Literacki* as his greatest sin, Stanisław Wygodzki described to Tadeusz

Borowski the *Miesięcznik Literacki* period as the most beautiful years of his youth, years that belonged to Broniewski, to Stande, to Wat.[36]

In the end, the subjects of this book lived their lives ensconced in angst, the creators as well as the victims of tragic fate. And here "tragic" must perhaps be understood in its nonclassical meaning of the 1920s—that is, not as that which was preordained by the gods and wrought through the tragic flaws of heroes, but rather as the preservation of the beauty of a disastrous action.[37] They suffered all the more painfully for their self-consciousness of the tension between subjectivity and telos.[38] They suffered intensely personally as well, by the force of their private relationships. Together they experienced Mayakovsky's 1927 visit as the ecstatic beginning of the Revolution, the new world—yet in fact it was the climax, the beginning of the end. For these writers, faith and betrayal referred not only to Marxist ideology, but more poignantly to Mayakovsky, the greatest of all their loves. The choices they made to opt for Marxism framed their lives. They were a particularly sad generation, pursued in their old age by a demon of communism, who haunted their old city, burnt to ashes by Nazis and now rebuilt with Stalinist architecture. All of them died consumed by their pasts. Ultimately these poets were destroyed by Marxism, by the choices they made to embrace Marxism. Their story contains no possibility of an aesthetically pleasing ending. They did not become revisionist Marxists, they did not try to sift through the layers of Stalin, then Lenin, and return to Marx. They were too old, too crushed; this was left for the next generation, the generation of Leszek Kołakowski.[39] For the Polish generation born at the fin de siècle, the young avant-garde poets of the 1920s, after Marxism there was nothing.

Years after Wat had taken his own life, when Ola Watowa had long been living in Paris, she went to Warsaw and paid a visit to Adam Ważyk, by then an old man and the last of his avant-garde circle among the living. Like Słonimski, Ważyk had become the object of government surveillance. In the 1960s and 1970s, informers noted that he corresponded with the émigré Poles in Paris who published *Kultura;* that he met with Leszek Kołakowski for coffee; that he was somehow involved in Słonimski's dissident plots.[40] This was all true, yet unlike Słonimski, Ważyk was broken and passive. Now as soon as Ola sat down in his apartment, Ważyk hastened to remind her that he had also once been a Stalinist. "I know, I know," she answered.[41] She had not forgotten. The guilt was not the only source of pain. The Polish PEN Club had recently dedicated an evening to the French futurist Apollinaire; Ważyk had not been invited. "'I was the first one in Poland to translate Apollinaire,'" he told her, "'and they didn't even invite me to say a few words.'"

NOTES

The following abbreviations are used in the notes.

AAN   Archiwum Akt Nowych, Warsaw

AABB   Abraham A. Berman Bequest, Diaspora Research Institute, Tel Aviv

ADH   Archiwum Dokumentacji Historycznej Polskiej Rzeczypospolitej Ludowej, Warsaw

AM   Arkhiv Maiakovskogo, Moscow

AW   Archiwum Wschodnie, Warsaw

AWPB   Aleksander Wat Papers, Uncat MS Vault 526, Beinecke Rare Book and Manuscript Library, Yale University, New Haven

BJSW   Krzysztof Jaworski, ed., *Bruno Jasieński w sowieckim więzieniu: Aresztowanie, wyrok, śmierć* (Kielce: Wyższa Szkoła Pedagogiczna im. Jana Kochanowskiego, 1995)

IPN   Instytut Pamięci Narodowej, Warsaw

KWB   Feliksa Lichodziejewska, ed., *Od bliskich i dalekich: Korespondencja do Władysława Broniewskiego*, vols. I and II (Warsaw: PIW, 1981)

LPP   Julian Tuwim, *Listy do przyjaciół-pisarzy*, ed. Tadeusz Januszewski (Warsaw: Czytelnik, 1979)

MB   Muzeum Broniewskiego, Warsaw

MieL   *Miesięcznik Literacki*

ML   Muzeum Literatury, Warsaw

PAN   Archiwum Polskiej Akademii Nauk, Warsaw

RGALI   Rossiiskii Gosudarstvennyi Arkhiv Literatury i Iskusstva, Moscow

RGASPI   Rossiiskii Gosudarstvennyi Arkhiv Sotsial'no-politicheskoi Istorii, Moscow

TsDAMLM	Tsentral'nyi Derzhavnyi Arkhiv-Muzei Literatury i Mystetstva Ukraïny, Kiev
WAS	Paweł Kądziela and Artur Międzyrzecki, eds., *Wspomnienia o Antonim Słonimskim* (Warsaw: Biblioteka Więzi, 1996)
WJT	Wanda Jedlicka and Marian Toporowski, eds., *Wspomnienia o Julianie Tuwimie* (Warsaw: Czytelnik, 1963)
WL	*Wiadomości Literackie*
WWW	Eleanora Syzdek, ed., *Wanda Wasilewska we wspomnieniach* (Warsaw: Książka i Wiedza, 1982)
ŻIH	Archiwum Żydowskiego Instytutu Historycznego, Warsaw

INTRODUCTION

Epigraph: Aleksander Wat, *My Century: The Odyssey of a Polish Intellectual*, trans. Richard Lourie (New York: Norton, 1988), 5. The English version, beautifully translated by Richard Lourie, is significantly abbreviated from the original two volumes published in Polish. I will reference Lourie's translation when possible, and when citing passages not included in the English version will use my own translations.

1. Adolf Warski, "Stanowisko Róży Luksemburg wobec taktycznych problemów rewolucji," in *Wybór pism i przemówień*, vol. II (Warsaw: Książka i Wiedza, 1958), 149. Adolf Warski (1868–1937) was a co-founder of the Social Democratic Party of Poland and Lithuania as well as a leader of the interwar Communist Party of Poland (KPP).

2. Leszek Hajdukiewicz to Celina Budzyńska, 23 February 1966, Cracow, 9889, AAN. On introducing Warski to his future wife: Władysław Krajewski (son of Zofia Warska), interview, 28 July 2003, Warsaw.

3. Wat, *My Century*, 293.

4. Julian Tuwim, "Wspomnienia o Łodzi," *WL* 33 (12 August 1934): 11.

5. See Janusz Maciejewski, introduction to Mieczysław Braun, *Mieczysław Braun: Wybór poezji* (Warsaw: PIW, 1979), 10.

6. See Brian Porter, *When Nationalism Began to Hate: Imagining Modern Politics in Nineteenth-Century Poland* (Oxford: Oxford University Press, 2000), 212. On interwar Polish politics, see Antony Polonsky, *Politics in Independent Poland: The Crisis of Constitutional Government* (Oxford: Clarendon Press, 1972).

7. C. Budzyńska, "Stanisław Ryszard Stande: Poeta—działacz—komunista," 9889, AAN; Władysław Krajewski (son of Zofia Warska), interview, 28 July 2003, Warsaw.

8. Copy of article by Antoni Słonimski for Jerzy Turowicz, editor of *Tygodnik Powszechny*, postmarked 20 May 1975, in "Operacyjne rozpoznanie Antoniego Słonimskiego, 1955–1976," 0204/1203/t-11, IPN.

9. Aleksander Wat, *Dziennik bez samogłosek* (London: Polonia, 1986), 184.

10. On the Polish-Soviet War and its relationship to Piłsudski's understanding of the Polish nation, see Timothy Snyder, *The Reconstruction of Nations: Poland, Ukraine, Lithuania, Belarus 1569–1999* (New Haven: Yale University Press, 2003).

11. Mieczysław Braun entered the army after completing secondary school in 1920; he was wounded seriously on 19 August 1920. Janusz Maciejewski, introduction to Braun, *Mieczysław Braun*, 13.

12. Quoted in Czeslaw Milosz, *The History of Polish Literature* (London: Macmillan, 1969), 385.

13. Tony Judt, *Past Imperfect: French Intellectuals, 1944–1956* (Berkeley: University of California Press, 1992), 38.

14. Isaac Deutscher, *The Non-Jewish Jew and Other Essays* (London: Oxford University Press, 1968).

15. I tell the story of the Berman brothers in more detail in Marci Shore, "Children of the Revolution: Communism, Zionism, and the Berman Brothers," *Jewish Social Studies* 10:3 (spring/summer 2004): 23–86.

16. While Michel Foucault's name does not appear in the chapters that follow, his observations about the nature of power—emanating not from a single point downwards but rather omnipresent, radically dispersed, implicit in all relations—comprise an ever-present subtext in my reading of the past. I owe much as well to recent Soviet historiography—that which I would call "postrevisionist," embodying a kind of neo–totalitarian school synthesis of Hannah Arendt and Michel Foucault—especially that by Stephen Kotkin, Igal Halfin, Jochen Hellbeck, Eric Naiman, Peter Holquist, and Amir Weiner, who examine the ways in which Stalinism ultimately was as creative (in the nonnormative sense of the word) as it was repressive.

17. I owe much here to Mikhail Bakhtin's notions of polyphony and dialogism.

18. See Arthur Koestler et al., *The God that Failed*, ed. R. H. S. Crossman (London: Hamish Hamilton, 1950).

19. Julien Benda, *The Treason of the Intellectuals*, trans. Richard Aldington (New York: Norton, 1969).

20. Judt, *Past Imperfect*, 11.

21. Ibid., 38.

22. These pseudonyms refer to Jerzy Andrzejewski, Tadeusz Borowski, Jerzy Putrament, and Konstanty Ildefons Gałczyński, respectively.

23. Czeslaw Milosz, *The Captive Mind*, trans. Jane Zielonko (New York: Vintage Books, 1981).

24. Jacques Derrida, *Specters of Marx: The State of the Debt, the Work of Mourning, and the New International*, trans. Peggy Kamuf (New York: Routledge, 1994).

25. Wat, *My Century*, 16.

26. Michel Foucault, *The Archaeology of Knowledge and the Discourse on Language*, trans. A. M. Sheridan Smith (New York: Pantheon Books, 1982), 235.

CHAPTER 1. ONCE UPON A TIME, IN A CAFÉ CALLED ZIEMIAŃSKA
Epigraph: Vladimir Maiakovskii, "Oblako v shtanakh," in *Vladimir Maiakovskii* (Saint Petersburg: Diamant, 1998), 70.

1. Mieczysław Grydzewski, *Listy do Tuwima i Lechonia (1940–1943)*, ed. Janusz Stradecki (Warsaw: PIW, 1986); Janina Broniewska, *Maje i listopady* (Warsaw:

Iskry, 1967), 157; Ola Watowa, *Wszystko co najważniejsze* (Warsaw: Czytelnik, 1990), 13.

2. Watowa, *Wszystko co najważniejsze*, 13.

3. Czeslaw Milosz, *The History of Polish Literature* (London: Macmillan, 1969), 385–386.

4. On Grydzewski see Antoni Słonimski, *Alfabet wspomnień* (Warsaw: PIW, 1975), 70–72. On Tuwim and Esperanto, see R. B. [Roman Brandstaetter], "Rozmowa z Julianem Tuwimem," in *Rozmowy z Tuwimem*, ed. Tadeusz Januszewski (Warsaw: Wydawnictwo Naukowe Semper, 1994), 27–31, from *Gazeta Literacka* 6 (15 March 1927).

5. *WJT*, 14–16, 176, 435–436, 446.

6. Aleksander Wat's original surname was "Chwat," later shortened to "Wat." Jarosław Iwaszkiewicz, *Listy z Ostrowa* (Ostrów Wielkopolski: Muzeum Miasta Ostrowa Wielkopolskiego, 1991), 22.

7. Jarosław Iwaszkiewicz, "Tolek," in *WAS*, 55.

8. Ibid., 58. On Słonimski's first meeting with Jan Lechoń: Antoni Słonimski, *Kroniki tygodniowe 1927–1939*, ed. Władysław Kopaliński (Warsaw: PIW, 1956), 214.

9. Tadeusz Peiper, "Zakończenie," in *Tędy Nowe usta* (Cracow: Wydawnictwo Literackie, 1972), 312.

10. Władysław Broniewski, *Pamiętnik 1918–1922* (Warsaw: PIW, 984), 280.

11. C. Budzyńska, "Stanisław Ryszard Stande: Poeta—działacz—komunista," 9889, AAN.

12. Stanisław Ryszard Stande, Anketa, 495/123/212, RGASPI.

13. *WJT*, 173.

14. *WJT*, 173.

15. Krzywicka, "Nasza przyjaźń trwała pół wieku," in *WAS*, 104.

16. Irena Krzywicka, *Wyznania gorszycielki* (Warsaw: Czytelnik, 1998), 100–101, 272.

17. Aleksander Wat, *My Century: The Odyssey of a Polish Intellectual*, trans. Richard Lourie (New York: Norton, 1988), 115–116; Aleksander Wat, *Dziennik bez samogłosek* (London: Polonia, 1986), 183–196.

18. Aleksander Wat, *Mój wiek: Pamiętnik mówiony*, 2 vols. (Warsaw: Czytelnik, 1998), vol. I, 59.

19. Ważyk, "Przeczytałem *Mój wiek*," *Puls* 34 (1987): 53.

20. Filippo Tommaso Marinetti, "Destruction of Syntax, Imagination without Strings, Words-in-Freedom," *Futurist Manifestos*, ed. Umbro Apollonio (New York: Viking Press, 1973), 104.

21. Aleksander Wat, "JA z jednej strony a JA z drugiej strony mego mopsożelaznego piecyka," in *Poezje*, ed. Anna Micińska and Jan Zieliński (Warsaw: Czytelnik, 1997), 332.

22. Bruno Schulz (1892–1942) was among the most talented Polish short story writers and visual artists of the interwar years. His stories reflected life in the Jewish quarter of his Galician hometown of Drohobycz/Drohobych (which

belonged to the Austrian empire before the First World War and to Poland in the interwar years, and is presently part of Ukraine). Schulz, a Polish Jew, was murdered by the Gestapo in Drohobycz in 1942. Wat, "Zeszyt ostatni," Box 4, AWPB; Krzywicka, *Wyznania gorszycielki,* 272. See also Tomas Venclova, *Aleksander Wat: Life and Art of an Iconoclast* (New Haven: Yale University Press, 1996), 45–68; and Bogdana Carpenter, *The Poetic Avant-Garde in Poland, 1918–1939* (Seattle: University of Washington Press, 1983), 64–75. Stanisław Ignacy Witkiewicz (1885–1939), known as Witkacy, was a novelist, playwright, philosopher and painter. See Daniel Gerould, *Witkacy: Stanislaw Ignacy Witkiewicz as an Imaginative Writer* (Seattle: University of Washington Press, 1981).

23. Wat, *My Century,* 208.

24. Krzywicka, *Wyznania gorszycielki,* 274.

25. Watowa, *Wszystko co najważniejsze,* 9–10.

26. Wat, *Dziennik bez samogłosek,* 195; Wat, *Mój wiek,* vol. I, 51–52.

27. Stefan Napierski, "Ciekawy debiut poetycki," *WL* 39 (28 September 1924): 4.

28. See Czesław Miłosz, *inne abecadło* (Cracow: Wydawnictwo Literackie, 1998), 69. Saul Wagman became a leading figure in the Polish-language Jewish newspaper *Nasz Przegląd* (Our Review).

29. Jerzy Jasieński, "Wspomnienia o Brunonie Jasieńskim," 1963, 15523/II, Dział Rękopisów Biblioteki im. Ossolińskich, Wrocław. Also see Krzysztof Jaworski, "Kilka przyczynków do biografii Brunona Jasieńskiego," *Kieleckie Studia Filologiczne* 8 (1994): 47–60.

30. Anatol Stern, *Bruno Jasieński* (Warsaw: Wiedza Powszechna, 1969), 23–24.

31. Piotr Mitzner, "Śmierć futurysty," *Karta* 11 (1993): 61.

32. Jan Brzękowski, "Droga poetycka Brunona Jasieńskiego," *Kultura* [Paris] 4 (April 1956): 100.

33. Wat, *My Century,* 5.

34. "Cmentarz mojej matki," in Anatol Stern, *Poezje 1918–1968* (Warsaw: PIW, 1969), 116–118.

35. Stern and Wat, "GGA," in *Antologia polskiego futuryzmu i Nowej Sztuki,* ed. Helena Zaworska (Wrocław: Zakład Narodowy im. Ossolińskich, 1978), 3.

36. Ibid., 5–6.

37. Ibid., 6.

38. D. Burlyuk, A. Kruchenykh, V. Mayakovsky, and V. Khlebnikov, "A Slap in the Face of Public Taste," in *Russian Literature of the Twenties: An Anthology,* ed. Carl R. Proffer et al. (Ann Arbor: Ardis, 1987), 542.

39. On Stern's "Nagi człowiek w śródmieściu": Adam Ważyk, *Dziwna historia awangardy* (Warsaw: Czytelnik, 1976), 48.

40. Jarosław Iwaszkiewicz, *Książka moich wspomnień* (Cracow: Wydawnictwo Literackie, 1968), 231–232.

41. Anatol Stern, *Poezja zbuntowana* (Warsaw: PIW, 1964), 52; Ważyk, *Dziwna historia awangardy,* 54.

42. Peiper, "Zakończenie," in *Tędy Nowe usta,* 313–314.

43. Bruno Iasenskii, Aleksander Vat, and Anatol' Stern to Vladimir Maiakovskii, Warsaw, 1 July 1921, 2852/1/599, RGALI.

44. Zbigniew Jarosiński, "Wstęp," *Antologia polskiego futuryzmu*, lxix.

45. See Tadeusz Peiper, "Miasto. Masa. Maszyna," *Zwrotnica* 2 (July 1922): 23–31.

46. Quoted in Jarosiński, "Wstęp," lxxiv.

47. Bruno Jasieński, "Futuryzm Polski (bilans)," *Zwrotnica* 6 (1923): 177–181.

48. Karol Irzykowski, "Likwidacja futuryzmu," *WL* 5 (3 February 1924): 1.

49. Reprinted in *WJT*. Pod Pikadorem is spelled sometimes with a "c" and sometimes with a "k." On this early period of the Skamander poets, see Wanda Nowakowska, "Lechoń i Tuwim—dzieje przyjaźni," *Prace Polonistyczne* 51 (1996): 237–247.

50. *WJT*, 446–448.

51. Quoted in Milosz, *History of Polish Literature*, 385–386.

52. Stern, *Bruno Jasieński*, 15.

53. Stanislaw Baranczak, "Skamander after Skamander: The Postwar Path of the Prewar Polish Pleiade," *Cross Currents* 9 (1990): 331.

54. Ważyk, *Dziwna historia awangardy*, 38.

55. See, for example, "Nowy manifest Marinettiego," *WL* 18 (4 May 1924): 1; and "Wiktor Szkłowskij," *WL* 21 (25 May 1924).

56. Tomas Venclova names Jan Lechoń as the instigator in *Aleksander Wat*, 30. In his own account, however, Wat speaks only of "jeden z poetów przeciwnego obozu, mocno juz wówczas zaawansowany w karjerze antyszambrowej" ("one of the poets of the opposing camp, already powerfully advanced in his career of dancing attendance"). See Wat, "Wspomnienie o Futuryzmie," *MieL* 2 (January 1930): 76.

57. The booklet made fun of Skamander as well as the futurists themselves. A stanza in *Żydek-Literat* begins "Aleksander Wat / Komuś imię skradł / Kto spojrzy na niego / Ten widzi Mojszego." Anatol Stern, *Wiersze zebrane*, vol. I, ed. Andrzej K. Waśkiewicz (Cracow: Wydawnictwo Literackie, 1986), 525–530.

58. See Julian Tuwim, "Czyhanie na Boga," in *Dzieła*, vol. I (Warsaw: Czytelnik, 1955), 45–120.

59. Znamor [Roman Zrębowicz], "U Juliana Tuwima," in *Rozmowy z Tuwimem*, 16–21; from *WL* 5 (31 January 1926).

60. See Grzegorz Gazda, "Tuwim i Awangarda," *Prace Polonistyczne* 51 (1996): 23; and W. Majakowski, "Obłok w spodniach," in Tuwim, *Dzieła*, ed. Seweryn Pollak, vol. IV (Warsaw: Czytelnik, 1959), 227–253.

61. Wat, *Dziennik bez samogłosek*, 180.

62. Jarosiński, "Wstęp," xxxix. The petition was published in early January 1920 in *Kurier Poranny* 3 (1920) and in *Skamander* 1 (1920).

63. Jarosiński, "Wstęp," xxxix.

64. The text is from taken from *Sprawozdania stenograficzne z posiedzeń Sejmu Ustawodawczego*, posiedzenie 332, 28 July 1922; quoted by Jarosiński, "Wstęp," lxxv.

65. Jarosiński, "Wstęp," lxxv.

66. Wat, *Dziennik bez samogłosek*, 187.

67. Stefan Żeromski, *Snobizm i postęp* (Warsaw: Wydawnictwo J. Morkowicza, 1926), 1, 4, 73.

68. Broniewski, *Pamiętnik 1918–1922*, 324.

69. Stanisław Witold Balicki, ed., *To ja—dąb: Wspomnienia i eseje o Władysławie Broniewskim* (Warsaw: PIW, 1978), 275.

70. Wat, *My Century*, 6.

71. Broniewski, *Pamiętnik 1918–1922*, 27.

72. Balicki, *To ja—dąb*, 66–67.

73. Broniewski, *Pamiętnik 1918–1922*, 38.

74. Feliksa Lichodziejewska, ed., "Pamiętnik Władysława Broniewskiego 1918–1922," *Polityka* 6 (6 February 1965): 1.

75. Broniewski, *Pamiętnik 1918–1922*, 41.

76. 17 May 1919. Ibid., 96.

77. Citation from the manifesto *Federaliści* by Józef Rudolf Kustroń. Feliksa Lichodziejewska, ed., "Pamiętnik Władysława Broniewskiego 1918–1922," *Polityka* 7 (13 February 1965): 1; Broniewski, *Pamiętnik 1918–1922*, 93–96, 214.

78. Broniewski, *Pamiętnik*, 289.

79. Ibid., 267.

80. Feliksa Lichodziejewska, "Korespondencja Władysława Broniewskiego z Bronisławem Sylwinem Kencbokiem," *Pamiętnik Literacki* 62:4 (1971): 155. On Żeromski and Broniewski's generation, see Janina Dziarnowska, *Słowo o Brunonie Jasieńskim* (Warsaw: Książka i Wiedza, 1978); Wat, *Mój wiek*, vol. I, 52–53; Włodzimierz Sokorski, *Wspomnienia* (Warsaw: Krajowa Agencja Wydawnicza, 1990), 18; Jerzy Zawieyski, *Dobrze, że byli* (Warsaw: Biblioteka Więzi, 1974), 38–56; Helena Zatorska, *Spoza smugi cienia* (Cracow: Wydawnictwo Literackie, 1982), 18–32; Jan Hempel, "Szarzyzna," *Dźwignia* 1 (March 1927): 8–14.

81. Lichodziejewska, "Korespondencja Władysława Broniewskiego z Bronisławem Sylwinem Kencbokiem," 162–180.

82. Ibid., 188–189.

83. Stanisław Brucz (1899–1977) was a poet involved in the editing of *Almanach Nowej Sztuki* together with Stern and Ważyk. Broniewski, *Pamiętnik 1918–1922*, 323. In the original Broniewski uses the diminutive "Same Żydki." The phrase was edited out in the first version of that passage of the diary published in 1965: Lichodziejewska, "Pamiętnik Wł. Broniewskiego 1918–1922," *Polityka* 7 (13 February 1965): 9.

84. Lichodziejewska, "Korespondencja Władysława Broniewskiego z Bronisławem Sylwinem Kencbokiem," 197.

85. Ibid., 200–201; Stern, "Bruno Jasieński w Paryżu czyli trzy portrety pisarza," *Kamena* 2 (21 January 1968): 4; Wandurski, "Majakowski i polscy poeci," in *Włodzimierz Majakowski*, ed. Florian Nieuważny (Warsaw: Państwowe Zakłady Wydawnictw Szkolnych, 1965), 278.

86. Lichodziejewska, "Korespondencja Władysława Broniewskiego z Bronisławem Sylwinem Kencbokiem," 212–213.

87. Ibid., 207–213.

88. This and the following quote from Braun to Broniewski, Łódź, 22 October 1923, teczka Brauna, MB. The Latin phrase "Surgunt indocti et rapiunt coelos!" translates as "the unlearned men rise up and take heaven," and comes from St. Augustine's *Confessions*. "Cloaca maxima" means "main sewer" and originally referred to the first actual Roman sewer, which drained into the Tiber River.

CHAPTER 2. LOVE AND REVOLUTION

Epigraph: Mieczysław Braun, "Moje osobiste zdanie o poezji," *Nowa Kultura* 9 (1 March 1924): 206–207.

1. Braun to Broniewski, Łódź, 22 May 1923, teczka Brauna, MB.

2. Bruno Jasieński and Anatol Stern, *Ziemia na lewo* (1924; Cracow: Wydawnictwo Literackie, 1987). See also "Poezja t. zw. 'Nowej Sztuki,'" *WL* 11 (16 March 1924).

3. Jasieński and Stern, *Ziemia na lewo;* reprinted in *Antologia polskiego Futuryzmu i Nowej Sztuki,* ed. Helena Zaworska (Wrocław: Zakład Narodowy im. Ossolińskich, 1978), 74.

4. Jan Wiślak [Hempel], Anketa, 495/123/212, RGASPI. Also see Hempel's column "Dziesięcioro przykazań" beginning in *Nowa Kultura* 3 (15 August 1923); and Hempel, "Poszukiwanie boga," ibid., 1 (5 January 1924): 5–9.

5. "Od Redakcji," *Nowa Kultura* 1 (1 July 1923): 1–2. The phrase "the seed has not fallen on stony ground" is a reference to a parable by Jesus.

6. Aleksander Wat, *Mój wiek: Pamiętnik mówiony,* 2 vols. (Warsaw: Czytelnik, 1998), vol. I, 31.

7. Grzegorz Lasota, "Rozmowa z towarzyszem Broniewskim," *Nowe Drogi* 10: 5 (May 1956).

8. S. R. Stande, "Z za kraty," *Nowa Kultura* 3 (15 July 1923): 79–81; and Mieczysław Braun, "Pieśni o walkach," ibid., 6 (15 September 1923): 181–182.

9. Wi-ski [Witold Wandurski], "Scena robotnicza w Łodzi," ibid., 4 (15 August 1923): 103–109.

10. Witold Wandurski, "Upodobania estetyczne proletarjatu," ibid., 6 (15 September 1923): 173–178.

11. Witold Wandurski, "Do panów poetów," ibid., 15 (22 December 1923): 392. Also see Antoni Słonimski, "Do poetów-komunistów," *WL* 47 (22 November 1925): 1.

12. Aleksander Wat, "Prowokator," *Nowa Kultura* 1 (5 January 1924): 17.

13. Ibid., 18.

14. Anatol Stern, "Karnawały," ibid., 2 (12 January 1924): 39; Aleksander Wat, "Policjant," ibid., 3 (19 January 1924): 62; G. Apollinaire, "Nieomylność," ibid., 2 (12 January 1924).

15. See the review of *Ziemia na lewo,* ibid., 9 (1 March 1924): 212.

16. Piotr Mitzner, "Śmierć futurysty," *Karta* 11 (1993): 63.

17. Mieczysław Braun, "Moje osobiste zdanie o poezji," *Nowa Kultura* 9 (1 March 1924): 206–207.

18. B. K., "Nieporozumienia literackie," ibid., 11 (15 March 1924): 255–258.

19. H. K., "Telefoniczna rozmowa z Władysławem Broniewskim," 26 November 1959, 731, AAN.

20. Braun to Broniewski, Łódź, 22 October 1923, teczka Brauna, MB.

21. Braun to Broniewski, Łódź, 11 January 1924, teczka Brauna, MB.

22. Braun to Broniewski, 12 February 1924, *KWB*, vol. I, 115–116.

23. Wandurski to Broniewski, Łódź, 21 January 1924, A/2, MB.

24. Wandurski to Broniewski, May 1924, *KWB*, vol. I, 118–120.

25. Wat, *My Century*, 3. Stefan Kordian Gacki was also the founder of the journal *F 24* and an avant-garde publishing house. See Wat, *Mój wiek*, vol. I, 24. See also Barbara Stawiczak [Stanisław Baranczak], "Trzy złudzenia i trzy rozczarowania polskiego Futuryzmu," *Znak* 304 (1979): 995–1006; Nina Kolesnikoff, "Polish Futurism: The Quest to Renovate Poetic Language," *Slavonic and East European Journal* 1 (1977): 64–77; Bogdana Carpenter, *The Poetic Avant-Garde in Poland* (Seattle: University of Washington Press, 1983), 167–168; Jarosiński, "Wstęp," in Zaworska, *Antologia polskiego Futuryzmu*, lxxxi.

26. The Russian poet Sergei Aleksandrovich Esenin, born in 1895, committed suicide in 1925. Braun to Broniewski, 6 January 1925, Łódź; *KWB*, vol. I, 143–144.

27. Aleksander Wat, "The Eternally Wandering Jew," *Lucifer Unemployed*, trans. Lillian Vallee (Evanston: Northwestern University Press, 1990), 8. Also see L. Pomirowski, "'Bezrobotny Lucyfer' Wata," *WL* 10 (6 March 1927): 3; Witold Wandurski, "O źródłach zatrutych, skorpionach literackich, o mechanicznym witrjonie rewolucji i o znarowionym wyżle," *Dźwignia* 2–3 (April–May 1927): 48–55; Wat, *Mój wiek*, vol. I, 86.

28. Janina Broniewska, *Dziesięć serc czerwiennych* (Warsaw: Iskry, 1964), 66.

29. "Pionierom," in Władysław Broniewski, Stanisław Ryszard Stande, and Witold Wandurski, *Trzy Salwy: Biuletyn poetycki* (Warsaw: PIW, 1967), 22.

30. Broniewska, *Dziesięć serc czerwiennych*, 73.

31. Broniewski to Janina Kunig, 24 July 1925, teczka Broniewskiej, ML.

32. Broniewski to Janina Kunig, 26 July 1925, teczka Broniewskiej, ML; published in Barbara Riss, ed., *O miłości—listy pisarzy polskich* (Warsaw: Prószyński i S-ka, 1997), 179–180.

33. Broniewski to Janina Kunig, 9 February 1926, teczka Broniewskiej, ML.

34. Janina Kunig to Broniewski, 3 March 1926, *KWB*, vol. I, 252–253.

35. Krzywicka to Broniewski, 15 August 1926, *KWB*, vol. I, 300–302.

36. Broniewski to Janina Kunig, 10 September 1926, teczka Broniewskiej, ML.

37. Broniewski to Janina Kunig, 10 September 1926, teczka Broniewskiej, ML.

38. Broniewski to Janina Kunig, 11 September 1926, teczka Broniewskiej, ML.

39. Broniewski to Janina Kunig, 11 September 1926, teczka Broniewskiej, ML.

Poronienie is the Polish word for "miscarriage," and the phrase "to Poronin" here alludes to an illegal abortion.

40. Halina Koszutska to Broniewski, 8 November 1926, *KWB*, vol. I, 312.

41. Jadwiga Lubowidzka was the third wife of Broniewski's grandfather Lubowidzki, and Broniewski's godmother.

42. Jadwiga Lubowidzka to Broniewski, Płock, 19 November 1926, *KWB*, vol. I, 316–317.

43. Broniewski to Janina Kunig, 27 December 1926, teczka Broniewskiej, ML.

44. Irena Krzywicka, *Wyznania gorszycielki* (Warsaw: Czytelnik, 1998), 102; Halina Koszutska to Broniewski, 28 December 1926. *KWB*, vol. I, 323–324; Janina Broniewska, "Hipoteczna i Sandomierska," in *To ja—dąb: Wspomnienia i eseje o Władysławie Broniewskim*, ed. Stanisław Witold Balicki (Warsaw: PIW, 1978), 50.

45. See Wandurski, "Majakowski i polscy poeci," in *Włodzimierz Majakowski*, ed. Florian Nieuważny (Warsaw: Państwowe Zakłady Wydawnictw Szkolnych, 1965), 278; Broniewski, "Kilka słów wspomnień: Z tradycji robotniczego ruchu amatorskiego," in *Władysław Broniewski*, ed. Feliksa Lichodziejewska (Warsaw: Państwowe Zakłady Wydawnictw Szkolnych, 1966), 125. Wandurski was arrested as a Polish citizen during Piłsudski's march on Kiev. "Kilka szczegółów z biografii Witolda Wandurskiego," 25199, AAN; Wandurski's NKVD file, M/III/56, AW.

46. Krzywicka, *Wyznania gorszycielki*, 102.

47. Wandurski to Broniewski, Łódź, 7 July 1924, A/2, MB.

48. Wandurski to Broniewski, 12 February 1925, *KWB*, vol. I, 145.

49. Wandurski to Broniewski, Łódź, 17 February 1925, MB.

50. Wandurski to Broniewski, Łódź, 28 April 1925, MB. See "Śmierć na gruszy," in Witold Wandurski, *Wiersze i dramaty* (Warsaw: PIW, 1958), 41–215; and "Sensacyjna premjera Teatru im. Słowackiego: 'Śmierć na gruszy' Witolda Wandurskiego: Wywiad 'Wiadomości Literackich' z autorem," in *WL* 5 (2 February 1925): 3.

51. Wandurski to Broniewski, Łódź, [26 April 1925], MB; *KWB*, vol. I, 163.

52. Witold Wandurski, "Jak policja łódzka walczy z literaturą," *WL* 23 (7 June 1925): 1.

53. Broniewski, Stande, and Wandurski, *Trzy Salwy*.

54. *KWB*, vol. I, 155.

55. Stanisław Wygodzki, "Ankieta członkowska," 15191, AAN; *WJT*, 169.

56. Wygodzki to Broniewski, 3 December 1925, Będzin, *KWB*, vol. I, 211–214.

57. Wygodzki to Broniewski, 8 March 1926, Będzin, *KWB*, vol. I, 254.

58. Wandurski to Broniewski, Łódź, 4 November 1925, *KWB*, vol. I, 199.

59. Wandurski to Broniewski, Łódź, 11 November 1925, A/2, MB.

60. Wandurski to Broniewski, Łódź, 11 November 1925, A/2, MB.

61. Wandurski to Broniewski, Łódź, 9 January 1926, A/2, MB; Władysław Broniewski, "O twórczości Sergiusza Jesienina: Po zgonie znakomitego poety," *WL* 3 (17 January 1926): 3.

62. Emphases in original. Wandurski to Broniewski, Łódź, 22 January 1926, A/2, MB; *KWB*, vol. I, 232–238.
63. "Gudłaje" in original. Wandurski to Broniewski, Łódź, 22 January 1926, A/2, MB.
64. Emphasis in original. Wandurski to Broniewski, 19 February 1926, *KWB*, vol. I, 245–246.
65. *KWB*, vol. I, 249.
66. Wandurski to Broniewski, Łódź, 23 March 1926, A/2, MB.
67. Antoni Słonimski, "Kronika tygodniowa," *WL* 23 (9 June 1935): 12.
68. Stalin later instructed Polish communists to condemn this strike as "the May error." On the "May Error," see Isaac Deutscher, "The Tragedy of the Polish Communist Party," in *Marxism, Wars and Revolutions: Essays from Four Decades*, ed. Tamara Deutscher (London: Verso, 1984), 91–127. Also see Gabriele Simoncini, *The Communist Party of Poland, 1918–1929: A Study in Political Ideology* (Lewiston: East Mellen Press, 1993); and M. K. Dziewanowski, *The Communist Party of Poland: An Outline of History* (Cambridge: Harvard University Press, 1976).
69. Wandurski to Broniewski, Łódź, 21 July 1926, MB.
70. Anatol Stern, "Czyżby śmierć poezji?" *WL* 30 (25 July 1926): 1.
71. Antoni Słonimski, "Historja 'Pikadora,'" *WL* 51–52 (26 December 1926): 2. Słonimski writes, "Following the example of the Burliuks and Mayakovskys we decided to open such a café in Warsaw. And so the idea came from Russia."
72. Julian Tuwim, "Nasz pierwszy wieczór," *WL* 51–52 (26 December 1926): 2.

CHAPTER 3. A VISIT FROM MAYAKOVSKY
Epigraph: Wiktor Woroszylski, *Życie Majakowskiego* (Warsaw: Czytelnik, 1984), 534.
1. Wandurski to Broniewski, 15 April [1928], więzienie śledcze w Łodzi, MB; *KWB*, vol. I, 386.
2. Wandurski to Broniewski, 15 April [1928], więzienie śledcze w Łodzi, MB. Reference to Paweł Hulka-Laskowski, a writer, critic, translator and social activist whose position towards "proletarian poetry" was critical. See Władysław Broniewski, "Wczoraj i jutro poezji w Polsce," *WL* 4 (22 January 1928): 1; and Pawel Hulka-Laskowski, "O t. zw. 'Poezję proletarjacką': Teorja a rzeczywistość," *WL* 7 (12 February 1928): 1.
3. Wygodzki to Broniewski, Będzin, teczka Wygodzkiego, MB.
4. Wygodzki to Broniewski, Będzin, 18 February 1927, teczka Wygodzkiego, MB.
5. Wygodzki to Broniewski, Będzin, 12 April 1927, *KWB*, vol. I, 348.
6. Wygodzki to Broniewski, Będzin, 20 May 1927, *KWB*, vol. I, 351.
7. Wygodzki to Broniewski, Będzin, 23 June 1927, *KWB*, vol. I, 357.
8. Wygodzki to Broniewski, Będzin, 20 December 1927, teczka Wygodzkiego, MB.

9. Wygodzki to Broniewski, Będzin, 9 January 1928, *KWB*, vol. I, 374–376.

10. See Stanisław Wygodzki, "Zadania Poezji w Polsce dziejsiejszej: O zmianę frontu," *WL* 29 (15 July 1928): 1.

11. Anatol Stern, "O zmianę metod naszej krytyki," *WL* 31 (29 July 1928): 1.

12. Paweł Merlend, [wspomnienia o Broniewskim], 731, AAN.

13. Janina Broniewska, *Dziesięć serc czerwiennych* (Warsaw: Iskry, 1964), 250–253.

14. Ibid., 186.

15. Aleksander Wat, *Mój wiek: Pamiętnik mówiony,* 2 vols. (Warsaw: Czytelnik, 1998), vol. I, 39–41.

16. Redakcja, Untitled, *Dźwignia* 1 (March 1927): 1.

17. Witold Wandurski, "O źródłach zatrutych, skorpionach literackich, o mechanicznym witrjonie rewolucji i o znarowionym wyźle," ibid., 2–3 (April–May 1927): 48–55. See also Stanisław Ryszard Stande, "Towarzysz" and "Plakat," ibid., 2–3 (April–May 1927): 26–27; and Bruno Jasieński, "Zakładnicy," ibid., 5 (November 1927): 32–34; Bruno Jasieński, "Do proletarjatu francuskiego," ibid., 8 (July 1928): 26–28; Witold Wandurski, "Scena robotnicza w Łodzi," ibid., 4 (July 1927): 19–31.

18. Andrzej Stawar, "Poezje Broniewskiego," ibid., 4 (July 1927): 35. Also see Stawar's review of Jasieński's *Słowo o Jakubie Szeli, Dźwignia* 1 (March 1927): 44, and of Stern's *Bieg do bieguna,* ibid., 1 (March 1927): 44–46.

19. Andrzej Stawar, "Kryzys prozy," ibid., 2–3 (April–May 1927): 1–10.

20. Andrzej Stawar, "Zachód w Polsce," ibid., 4 (July 1927): 1.

21. Broniewska, "Hipoteczna i Sandomierska," in *To ja—dąb: Wspomnienia i eseje o Władysławie Broniewskim,* ed. Stanisław Witold Balicki (Warsaw: PIW, 1978), 63.

22. Broniewski to Broniewska, 25 April 1927, Warsaw, teczka Broniewskiej, ML.

23. Broniewska, *Dziesięć serc czerwiennych,* 172–174; Broniewska, *Tamten brzeg mych lat* (Warsaw: Książka i Wiedza, 1973), 199; Broniewski to Broniewska, 17 April 1928, Warsaw, teczka Broniewskiej, ML. *Żydokomuna* is a virtually untranslatable term referring to Jewish communism; the tendency of Jews to become communists; or a Polish perception of a Jewish-Bolshevik conspiracy.

24. Broniewska, *Dziesięć serc czerwiennych,* 186.

25. Ibid., 186–188.

26. See Isaac Deutscher, "The Tragedy of the Polish Communist Party," in *Marxism, Wars and Revolutions: Essays from Four Decades,* ed. Tamara Deutscher (London: Verso, 1984), 113.

27. Broniewski to Broniewska, 1 May 1928, Warsaw, teczka Broniewskiej, ML; in *Polityka* 7 (12 February 1972): 6.

28. Witold Wandurski, "Majakowski i polscy poeci," in *Włodzimierz Majakowski,* ed. Florian Nieuważny (Warsaw: Państwowe Zakłady Wydawnictw Szkolnych, 1965), 277–286.

29. The title was *Prostoe kak mychanie* (Petrograd, 1916). Julian Tuwim,

"Majakowski po raz pierwszy," in *Włodzimierz Majakowski*, 290–291; from *Odrodzenie* 45 (1949): 2.

30. Wandurski, "Majakowski i polscy poeci"; "Levyi marsh," in Vladimir Maia-kovskii, *Vladimir Maiakovskii* (Saint Petersburg: Diamant, 1998), 139–141.

31. Vladimir Maiakovskii, "Ezdil ia tak," in *Polnoe sobranie sochinenii*, vol. II (Kaliningrad: FGUIPP Iantarnyi Skaz, 2002), 82; Broniewska, *Dziesięć serc czerwiennych*, 156.

32. Broniewski to Broniewska, 13 or 15 April 1927, Warsaw, teczka Broniewskiej, ML; *Polityka* 7 (12 February 1972): 6.

33. Wandurski, "Majakowski i polscy poeci," 282.

34. Broniewski to Broniewska, 13 or 15 April 1927, Warsaw, teczka Broniewskiej, ML.

35. Maiakovskii, "Poverkh Varshavy," in *Polnoe sobranie sochinenii*, vol. II, 90.

36. Wandurski, "Majakowski i polscy poeci," 283.

37. Woroszylski, *Życie Majakowskiego*, 534.

38. Wandurski, "Majakowski i polscy poeci," 283; Maiakovskii, "Ezdil ia tak," 84. The group Lef, or Left Front of the Arts, was formed in 1923 for the purpose of joining revolutionary politics and progressive art. The group included the literary figures Mayakovsky, Shklovsky, Nikolai Aseev, Osip Brik, Sergei Tret'iakov, the filmmakers Sergei Eisenstein and Dziga Vertov, and theater director Vsevolod Meyerhold. Lef existed between 1923 and 1925; subsequently Novyi Lef came into being in 1927 and lasted until 1928.

39. Ola Watowa, *Wszystko co najważniejsze* (Warsaw: Czytelnik, 1990), 15.

40. Woroszylski, *Życie Majakowskiego*, 534.

41. Wandurski, "Majakowski i polscy poeci," 284.

42. Stanisław Ryszard Stande, "Mój przyjazd do Moskwy," 1927, 245/2, AAN; C. Budzyńska, "Stanisław Ryszard Stande," 9889, AAN.

43. Wandurski, "Majakowski i polscy poeci," 284.

44. Maiakovskii, "Ezdil ia tak," 85.

45. Maiakovskii, *Vladimir Maiakovskii*, 139–141; Watowa, *Wszystko co najważniejsze*, 16.

46. Broniewska, *Dziesięć serc czerwiennych*, 157.

47. Ibid.

48. Ibid.

49. Watowa, *Wszystko co najważniejsze*, 16.

50. Aleksander Wat, *My Century: The Odyssey of a Polish Intellectual*, trans. Richard Lourie (New York: Norton, 1988), 44.

51. Ibid., 44.

52. Copy of Broniewski, *Dymy nad miastem*, R5477 RD 5424, AM.

53. Copy of Jasieński, *Słowo o Jakóbie Szeli* on display at AM.

54. Copy of Stern, *Bieg do Bieguna*, R5473 RD 5420, AM.

55. Copy of Wat, *Bezrobotny Lucyfer*, R5478 RD 5425, AM.

56. Copy of Ważyk, *Semafory*, R5475 RD 5422, AM. See also copies of Wandurski *"Nowa Scene Robotnicza": Utwory sceniczne Władimira Majakowskiego, Iwana Golla, Mieczysława Brauna:* "To Vladimir Vladimirovich Maiakovskii the poet

from the translator of his works 2 X 1923," 9241 RD 6267, AM; Stern, *Aniel-ski Cham:* "To Mayakovsky, the uncle of Polish futurism 14 V.27," R5474 RD 5421, AM; Ważyk, *Oczy i usta:* "To Vladimir Maiakovskii—from the author 14 V 1927," R5476 RD 5423, AM.

57. V. A. Arutchev, "Zapisnye knizhki Maiakovskogo," *Literaturnoe nasledstvo* 65 (1958): 384.

58. Vladimir Maiakovskii, "Naruzhnost' Varshavy," in *Polnoe sobranie sochinenii,* vol. II, 88.

59. Wat, *My Century,* 23–25, 44–47; Watowa, *Wszystko co najważniejsze,* 15–17. In their memoirs Aleksander Wat and Ola Watowa write about a second visit Mayakovsky made to Warsaw in 1929. Biographical sources on Mayakovsky mention nothing about a second visit to Warsaw, nor do any of the other Polish poets. Mayakovsky was in Prague and Paris in 1929; he might have come to Warsaw inconspicuously, or Wat might have met Mayakovsky this second time when they were both traveling in western Europe that year. See also Tomas Venclova, *Aleksander Wat: Life and Art of an Iconoclast* (New Haven: Yale University Press, 1996), 80–83.

60. Wat, *My Century,* 44–45. RAPP (the Russian Association of Proletarian Writers) effectively held dictatorial power in Soviet literary affairs between 1928 and 1932.

61. Watowa, *Wszystko co najważniejsze,* 17.

62. Roman Jakobson, *My Futurist Years,* ed. Bengt Jangfeldt, trans. Stephen Rudy (New York: Marsilio Publishers, 1992), 91–92.

63. Francine Du Plessix Gray, "Mayakovsky's Last Loves," *The New Yorker* (7 January 2002).

64. Wat, *Mój wiek,* vol. I, 143.

65. Wat, *My Century,* 24.

66. Władysław Broniewski et al., "Co zawdzięczają pisarze polscy literaturom obcym?" *WL* 47 (20 November 1927): 3.

67. Anatol Stern, "Poeta stu pięćdziesięciu miljonów: Włodzimierz Majakow-skij," *WL* 21 (22 May 1927): 2.

68. Wat, *My Century,* 46.

69. Jasieński to Broniewski, 18 March 1928, Paris, *KWB,* vol. I, 383–384.

70. Jasieński to Broniewski, 22 April 1928, *KWB,* vol. I, 392.

71. Jasieński to Broniewski, 22 April 1928, Paris, *KWB,* vol. I, 392.

72. Quoted in Anatol Stern, "Bruno Jasieński w Paryżu czyli trzy portrety pisarza," *Kamena* 2 (21 January 1968): 4.

73. Wat, *Mój wiek,* vol. I, 33–34.

74. Quoted in Stern, "Bruno Jasieński w Paryżu," 4.

75. Paweł Merland, Relacja o Władysławie Broniewskim, 731, AAN.

76. Julian Tuwim, "Słowo o Kubie Rozpruwaczu," *Cyrulika Warszawskiego* 26 (1926). Also see Julian Tuwim, "Sprawozdanie z książki Jasieńskiego 'But w butonierce,'" in *Księga parodii,* ed. Danuta Sykucka (Warsaw: Wydawnictwo Artystyczne i Filmowe, 1985).

77. Stern, "Bruno Jasieński w Paryżu," 4.

78. Quoted ibid.

79. Quoted ibid. Barbusse (1873–1935) was the editor of *L'Humanité* and a member of the Communist Party beginning in 1923.

80. Wat, *My Century*, 8.

81. Ibid.; Wat, *Mój wiek*, vol. I, 34.

82. On Morand see also Anatol Stern, *Bruno Jasieński* (Warsaw: Wiedza Powszechna, 1969), 126–138; M. Zhivov, "Bruno Iasenskii (k ego priezdu v Sovetskii Soiuz)," *Izvestiia* 113 (21 May 1929), copy in 1861/1/13, RGALI.

83. Bruno Jasieński, *Palę Paryż* (Warsaw: Czytelnik, 1957). See also Nina Kolesnikoff, *Bruno Jasieński: His Evolution from Futurism to Socialist Realism* (Waterloo: Wilfrid Laurier University Press, 1982), 74–85.

84. Jan Brzękowski, "Droga poetycka Brunona Jasieńskiego," *Kultura* [Paris] 4 (April 1956): 103.

85. See Antal Hidas, "Wspomnienia o Brunonie Jasieńskim," *Literatura na świecie* 11 (1975): 149–167; Bruno Jasieński, "Dżuma w Paryżu," *WL* 7 (17 February 1929): 1. Barbusse was under the false impression that Jasieński had earlier been deported from Poland. See Stern, *Bruno Jasieński*, 166. Also see Krzysztof Jaworski, *Bruno Jasieński w Paryżu 1925–1929* (Kielce: Wydawnictwo Akademii Świętokrzyskiej, 2003).

86. Wat, *My Century*, 18; Julian Tuwim, "Wieniawa," in *Jarmark rymów*, ed. Janusz Stradecki (Warsaw: Czytelnik, 1991), 139–140. Józef Beck (1894–1944) was Poland's minister of foreign affairs in the 1930s. Bronisław Pieracki (1895–1934) was minister of internal affairs between 1931 and 1934. He was assassinated in 1934 by Ukrainian nationalists.

87. Władysław Krajewski, interview, Warsaw, 28 July 2003.

88. Wat, *My Century*, 27–30.

89. Wat to Wittlin, 26 June 1965, [Berkeley]. "'Twarzą zwrócony do śmierci . . .' Listy Aleksandra Wata do Józefa Wittlina," *Znak* 43 (February 1991): 3–16; Wat, *Mój wiek*, vol. I, 321.

90. M. K. Dziewanowski, *The Communist Party of Poland: An Outline of History* (Cambridge: Harvard University Press, 1976), 96.

91. Wat, *My Century*, 15–16.

92. According to Stande *Dźwignia* was liquidated by the government after eight issues. Stanisław Ryszard Stande, "Polska literatura proletariacka," *Kultura Mas* 1 (1931): 22–26. Reprinted in Krystyna Sierocka, *Z dziejów czasopiśmiennictwa polskiego w ZSRR ('Kultura Mas' 1929–1937)* (Warsaw: Książka i Wiedza, 1963), 183–190.

93. Wat, *My Century*, 19.

94. On Deutscher see Daniel Singer, "Armed with a Pen," in *Isaac Deutscher: The Man and His Work*, ed. David Horowitz (London: Macdonald, 1971), 19–56; and Perry Anderson, preface to Deutscher, *Marxism, Wars and Revolutions*, i–xx.

95. Wat, *Dziennik bez samogłosek*, 25; Ważyk, "Przeczytałem *Mój wiek*," 50–51.

96. Wat, *Mój wiek*, vol. I, 172.

97. Anatol Stern, *Wiersze zebrane*, vol. I, ed. Andrzej K. Waśkiewicz (Cracow: Wydawnictwo Literackie, 1985), 169–171.

98. Ibid., 232.

99. Wat, *My Century*, 35.

100. Jakub Berman, "Jakub Berman," 325/1, AAN.

101. Wat, *Mój wiek*, vol. I, 164.

102. On Shklovsky see Henryk Drzewicki, "Etap Formalisty," *MieL* 1 (December 1929): 46.

103. Jerzy Szymański, "Palę Paryż," ibid., 33.

CHAPTER 4. A FUNERAL FOR FUTURISM
Epigraph: Aleksander Wat, "Metamorfozy Futuryzmu," *MieL* 3 (February 1930): 126.

1. Antoni Słonimski, "Kronika tygodniowa," *WL* 49 (8 December 1929): 4.

2. Ibid., 4. See also "Kłusownictwo Frazesów," *MieL* 2 (January 1930): 117–119.

3. Aleksander Wat, *My Century: The Odyssey of a Polish Intellectual*, trans. Richard Lourie (New York: Norton, 1988), 52. See also Antoni Słonimski's "Zakuty Łeb," *WL* 4 (27 January 1929): 5.

4. "Metody przedrzeźniania się P. Słonimskiego," *MieL* 2 (January 1930): 117.

5. Antoni Słonimski, "Kronika tygodniowa," *WL* 2 (12 January 1930): 4.

6. Aleksander Wat, "Łosoś w majonezie, Liga Narodów i radosny cień króla Stasia," *MieL* 9 (July 1930): 410–412.

7. "Shmoncesman zagranicą: Co P. Słonimski widział w Londynie," *MieL* 9 (July 1930): 421.

8. "A jak o tem pisał w 'Wiadomościach Literackich,'" *MieL* 10 (July 1930): 421–422. Also see *WL* 20 (1930).

9. Antoni Słonimski, "Kronika tygodniowa," *WL* 27 (6 July 1930).

10. Natan Wistreich to Broniewski, 6 October 1930, Rzeszów, *KWB*, vol. I, 546–548.

11. Janina Broniewska, *Maje i listopady* (Warsaw: Iskry, 1967), 10, 35–37, 53–54, 85.

12. Tuwim, "Do prostego człowieka," 245/2, AAN; Julian Tuwim, *Poezje*, ed. Tadeusz Januszewski (Wrocław: Zakład Narodowy im. Ossolińskich, 2004), 347–348; from *Robotnik* 305 (1929).

13. Broniewska, *Maje i listopady*, 96.

14. *WJT*, 166–167.

15. Julian Tuwim, *Pisma Prozą*, ed. Janusz Stradecki, vol. V of *Dzieła* (Warsaw: Czytelnik, 1964), 677.

16. Tuwim, "Klasa robotnicza a literatura," in *Rozmowy z Tuwimem*, ed. Tadeusz Januszewski (Warsaw: Wydawnictwo Naukowe Semper, 1994), 32–33; from *Robotnik* 29 (29 January 1928).

17. Tuwim to Broniewski, 21 February 1931, Krynica, *LPP*, 113; *KWB*, vol. II, 38.

18. Aleksander Wat, "Wspomnienia o Futuryźmie," *MieL* 2 (January 1930): 68–77.

19. Ibid., 70–75.
20. Wat, "Metamorfozy Futuryzmu," 122–127.
21. Ibid., 122–123.
22. Ibid., 125. Polish positivism: Jerzy Jedlicki, *A Suburb of Europe: Nineteenth-Century Polish Approaches to Western Civilization* (Budapest: CEU Press, 1999); Norman Naimark, *The History of the "Proletariat": The Emergence of Marxism in the Kingdom of Poland, 1870–1887* (Boulder: East European Monographs, 1979); Stanislaus A. Blejwas, *Realism in Polish Politics: Warsaw Positivism and National Survival in Nineteenth-Century Poland* (New Haven: Yale Russian and East European Publications, 1984).
23. Wat, "Metamorfozy Futuryzmu," 126.
24. Wat, "Wspomnienia o Futuryźmie," 71.
25. Tadeusz Peiper, "List do Redakcji," *MieL* 5 (April 1930): 278–280.
26. Aleksander Wat, "Odpowiedź Redaktora," *MieL* 5 (April 1930): 280.
27. Broniewska, *Maje i listopady*, 47–48; Wat, *My Century*, 44; Ola Watowa, *Wszystko, co najważniejsze* (Warszawa: Czytelnik, 1990), 16–17.
28. Aleksander Wat, "Poeta Rewolucji Majakowski," *MieL* 6 (May 1930): 281–288.
29. Władysław Broniewski, "14 Kwietnia," *MieL* 6 (May 1930): 289. Also see Stanisław Ryszard Stande, "Majakowski," ibid., 288–289, and Stanisław Wygodzki, "'Lewa Marsz,'" ibid., 289–291.
30. Maiakovskii, "Ezdil ia tak," in *Polnoe sobranie sochinenii*, vol. II (Kaliningrad: FGUIPP Iantarnyi Skaz, 2002), 84; Maiakovskii, "Poverkh Varshavy," ibid., 92; Antoni Słonimski, *Alfabet wspomnień* (Warsaw: PIW, 1975), 134–135; mg [Mieczysław Grydzewski], "Prawda i Kłamstwo," *WL* 13 (21 March 1937): 7.
31. Antoni Słonimski, "Na śmierć Majakowskiego," *WL* 18 (4 May 1930): 1.
32. Aleksander Wat, "Reportaż jako rodzaj literacki," *MieL* 7 (June 1930): 330–334.
33. Aleksander Wat, "Jeszcze o reportażu," *MieL* 10 (August 1930): 425.
34. Ibid., 426; see also Aleksander Wat, "Literatura Faktu," *WL* 35 (1 September 1929): 1.
35. Wat, *My Century*, 50–51.
36. Andrzej Stawar, "O krytyce," *MieL* 2 (January 1930): 57–65.
37. Wat, *My Century*, 57.
38. Stanisław Ryszard Stande, "O krytykę marksistowską," *MieL* 5 (April 1930): 232.
39. Natan Wistreich to Broniewski, 6 October 1930, Rzeszów, *KWB*, vol. I, 546–548.
40. Wat, *My Century*, 50–51.
41. Ibid., 53.
42. Jan Trusz, *Z doświadczeń pokolenia* (Warsaw: Książka i Wiedza, 1981), 22.
43. Wat, *My Century*, 55; Watowa, *Wszystko co najważniejsze*, 12.
44. Broniewska, *Maje i listopady*, 109.
45. Wat, *My Century*, 60–61; Wat to Grydzewski, 2 March 1962, La Messuguière, C-219, AWPB.

46. Broniewska, *Maje i listopady*, 110.
47. Ibid., 112–113.
48. Wat, *My Century*, 61.
49. Tomas Venclova, *Aleksander Wat: Life and Art of an Iconoclast* (New Haven: Yale University Press, 1996), 123.
50. Broniewska, *Maje i listopady*, 116–117.
51. Watowa, *Wszystko co najważniejsze*, 18.
52. Ibid., 18; Wat to Grydzewski, 2 March 1962, La Messuguière, C-219, AWPB.
53. Broniewska, *Maje i listopady*, 121–123.
54. Antoni Słonimski, "Kronika tygodniowa," *WL* 38 (20 September 1931): 4.
55. Wat to Grydzewski, 2 March 1962, La Messuguière, C-219, AWPB; Broniewski to "Kochana Jasieńko, Mario, Janko," teczka Broniewskiej, ML.
56. Wat, *My Century*, 67.
57. Emil Herbst, "O Władysławie Broniewskim," 14 March 1962, 731, AAN.
58. Wat, *My Century*, 67.
59. Broniewska, *Maje i listopady*, 141; Władysław Broniewski, "Magnitogorsk albo rozmowa z Janem," in *Poezje zebrane*, vol. II, ed. Feliksa Lichodziejewska (Płock: Algo, 1997), 130–131. On Magnitogorsk, see Stephen Kotkin, *The Magnetic Mountain: Stalinism as Civilization* (Berkeley: University of California Press, 1995).
60. Broniewski to "Kochana Jasieńko, Mario, Janko," teczka Broniewskiej, ML.
61. Wat, *My Century*, 66.
62. Ibid., 67.
63. Ibid., 67–68.
64. Ibid., 68.
65. Emil Herbst, "O Władysławie Broniewskim," 14 March 1962, 731, AAN.
66. Wat, *My Century*, 69–73.
67. According to Herbst Wat received a salary of twelve hundred złotys a month as editor of *Miesięcznik Literacki*. Emil Herbst, "O Władysławie Broniewskim," 14 March 1962, 731, AAN.
68. Wat, *My Century*, 77.
69. Emil Herbst, "O Władysławie Broniewskim," 14 March 1962; Leon Kasman, "O Władysławie Broniewskim," 14 March 1962; Lucjan Marek, "O Władysławie Broniewskim," 14 March 1962, 731, AAN.
70. Wat, *My Century*, 15, 64–65. On communists in Polish prison, see Jaff Schatz, *The Generation: The Rise and Fall of the Jewish Communists of Poland* (Berkeley: University of California Press, 1991), 128–138.

CHAPTER 5. ENTANGLEMENTS, TERROR, AND THE FINE ART OF CONFESSION

Epigraph: Ola Watowa, *Wszystko co najważniejsze* (Warsaw: Czytelnik, 1990), 13–14.
1. Janina Broniewska, *Maje i listopady* (Warsaw: Iskry, 1967), 116.
2. Aleksander Wat, *My Century: The Odyssey of a Polish Intellectual*, trans.

Richard Lourie (New York: Norton, 1988), 34; Jan Wiślak [Jan Hempel], Anketa, 495/123/212, RGASPI.

3. *KWB*, vol. II, 42.

4. Broniewska, *Maje i listopady*, 141.

5. Aleksander Wat, *Mój wiek: Pamiętnik mówiony*, 2 vols. (Warsaw: Czytelnik, 1998), vol. I, 190.

6. Aleksander Wat, *Dziennik bez samogłosek* (London: Polonia, 1986), 185.

7. Watowa, *Wszystko co najważniejsze*, 14.

8. Wat, *My Century*, 41.

9. Wat, *Mój wiek*, vol. I, 230; Watowa, *Wszystko co najważniejsze*, 19.

10. Untitled report, 26 March 1953, 0246/1031, IPN.

11. Broniewski—police commissariat, document of house search, 12 October 1934; wezwanie Broniewskiego 17 October 1934, *KWB*, vol. II, 164–165. Broniewska, *Maje i listopady*, 164; Antoni Borman and Broniewski to Iwasz-kiewicz, 16 December 1932, quoted in Stanisław Witold Balicki, ed., *To ja—dąb: Wspomnienia i eseje o Władysławie Broniewskim* (Warsaw: PIW, 1978), 435–436.

12. Broniewska, *Maje i listopady*, 185.

13. Watowa, *Wszystko co najważniejsze*, 15.

14. Wat, *My Century*, 47.

15. "Kilka szczegółów z biografii Witolda Wandurskiego," 25199, AAN; also see Marian Stępień, *Polska lewica literacka* (Warsaw: Państwowe Wydawnictwo Naukowe, 1985), 203.

16. Vitold Vandurskii, introduction to Bronevskii, *Izbrannye stikhi* (Moscow: Gosudarstvennoe Izdatel'stvo Khudozhestvennoi Literatury, 1932).

17. Photographs in Bruno Jasieński, *The Mannequins' Ball*, trans. Daniel Gerould (Amsterdam: Harwood Academic Publishers, 2000); Wat, *Mój wiek*, vol. I, 35.

18. Antal Hidas, "Wspomnienia o Brunonie Jasieńskim," *Literatura na Świecie* 11 (1975): 150.

19. Piotr Mitzner, "Śmierć futurysty," *Karta* 11 (1993): 59.

20. M. Zhivov, "Bruno Iasenskii (k ego priezdu v Sovetskii Soiuz)," *Izvestiia* 113 (21 May 1929); copy in 1861/1/13, RGALI.

21. These attachments are described in Jasieński's letter, but are missing from the file in the archives.

22. Bruno Jasieński to Sekcja KPP przy Kominternie, Moscow, 9 November 1929, 495/123/130, RGASPI.

23. See Witold Wandurski, "Jak policja łódzka walczy z literaturą," *WL* 23 (7 June 1925): 1.

24. Jasieński to Sekcja KPP przy Kominternie, Moscow, 9 November 1929, 495/123/130, RGASPI.

25. The reference is to Stawar's review of *Słowo o Jakóbie Szeli* in *Dźwignia* 1 (March 1927): 44.

26. Jasieński to Sekcja KPP przy Kominternie, Moscow, 9 November 1929, 495/123/130, RGASPI.

27. Anatol Stern, *Wiersze zebrane*, vol. I, ed. Andrzej K. Waśkiewicz (Cracow: Wydawnictwo Literackie, 1985), 233–244.

28. Stanisław Ryszard Stande, Anketa, 495/123/212, RGASPI.

29. Stande's Party "anketa" lists his date of arrival in the Soviet Union as 1932, but it seems from other sources more likely that he actually arrived in 1931. Zofia Warska, following a brief "teenage rebellion" during World War I when she joined Piłsudski's Polska Organizacja Wojskowa (Polish Military Organization), joined the KPP in 1918. Władysław Krajewski, personal interview, 28 July 2003, Warsaw; Zofia Warska, Anketa, 495/123/212, RGASPI.

30. Stande to Broniewski, Moscow, c. 24 December 1932. *KWB*, vol. II, 48.

31. C. Budzyńska, "Stanisław Ryszard Stande: poeta—działacz—komunista," 9889, AAN.

32. Quoted in Krystyna Sierocka, *Z dziejów czasopiśmiennictwa polskiego w ZSRR ("Kultura Mas" 1929–1937)* (Warsaw: Książka i Wiedza, 1963), 33.

33. Jasieński to Broniewski and Stawar, Moscow, 11 June 1929, teczka Jasieńskiego, MB.

34. Sierocka, *Z dziejów czasopiśmiennictwa polskiego w ZSRR*, 145–149; Bruno Jasieński, "O rewolucję językową," *Kultura Mas* 1/2 (1929): 11–13. See also Bruno Jasieński, "Twórzmy polski język radziecki," *Kultura Mas* 2 (1930): 5.

35. Witold Wandurski, "Kręćmy polski film rewolucyjny," *Kultura Mas* 3 (1929): 23–29; reprinted in Sierocka, *Z dziejów czasopiśmiennictwa polskiego w ZSRR*, 163–177.

36. Witold Wandurski, "Polska pracownia teatralna w Kijowie," *Kultura Mas* 1 (1930): 8–9; reprinted in Sierocka, *Z dziejów czasopiśmiennictwa polskiego w ZSRR*, 178–182. Also see "Chronology of the Life and Work of Witold Wandurski (1891–1937)" and Witold Wandurski, "The Mass Amateur Theatre Needs the Dramatist! The Dramatist Needs the Mass Amateur Theatre!" in *Slavic and East European Performance* 22:1 (winter 2002): 61–74.

37. Sierocka, *Z dziejów czasopiśmiennictwa polskiego w ZSRR*, 183–190; from Stanisław Ryszard Stande, "Polska literatura proletariacka," *Kultura Mas* 1 (1931): 22–26.

38. Jan Wiślak [Hempel], "Na polskim odcinku frontu kulturalnego," *Kultura Mas* 1 (1933): 3–7; reprinted in Sierocka, *Z dziejów czasopiśmiennictwa polskiego w ZSRR*, 202–210. *Kultura Mas* published much from Poland, including Julian Tuwim, "Do prostego człowieka," 4/5 (1930): 100–101; Aleksander Wat, "Pacyfistyczna literatura w Niemczech," 4/5 (1930): 26–31; and Władysław Broniewski, "Kongres w obronie kultury," 2/3 (1936): 91–93. Also see "Miesięcznik Literacki," 4/5 (1930): 104; Władysław Broniewski, Jan Hempel, Stanisław Ryszard Stande, Andrzej Stawar, Aleksander Wat, et al., "List otwarty do Międzynarodowego Zjazdu PEN Klubów w Warszawie," 6/7 (1930); J. Sosnowicz, "Słonimski w faszystowskiej 'Rodzinie,'" 1 (1934): 50–51.

39. Tomasz Dąbal was also forced to sign such a declaration. Ministerstwo Spraw Zagranicznych, Departament Polityczno-Ekonomiczny, Wydział

Wschodni, "Biuletyn Narodowości," 26, 1931, I.303.4.1787, Centralne Archiwum Wojskowe, Rembertów, Poland. Timothy Snyder provided a copy of this document. See also Stanisław Stępień, ed., *Polacy na Ukrainie: Zbiór dokumentów,* pt. 1: *Lata 1917–1939,* vol. II (Przemyśl: Południowo-Wschodni Instytut Naukowy w Przemyśle, 1998), 257–301. On Soviet nationalities policy under Stalin see Terry Martin, *The Affirmative Action Empire: Nations and Nationalism in the Soviet Union 1923–1939* (Ithaca: Cornell University Press, 2001); Ronald Grigor Suny, *The Revenge of the Past: Nationalism, Revolution, and the Collapse of the Soviet Union* (Stanford: Stanford University Press, 1993); and Yuri Slezkine, "The USSR as a Communal Apartment or How a Socialist State Promoted Ethnic Particularism," *Slavic Review* 53:2 (summer 1994): 414–452.

40. Wat, *Mój wiek,* vol. I, 242–243. Colonel Jan Kowalewski (1892–1965) was the Polish military attaché in Moscow.

41. Anatol Stern, *Bruno Jasieński* (Warsaw: Wiedza Powszechna, 1969), 81.

42. Bruno Jasieński, "Coś w rodzaju życiorysu," *Przegląd Kulturalny* 17 (26 April–2 May 1956): 5; originally published in Russian in May 1931.

43. Ibid., 5.

44. Bruno Jasieński, *The Mannequins' Ball,* trans. Daniel Gerould (Amsterdam: Harwood Academic Publishers, 2000), 9.

45. Ibid., 11.

46. Ibid., 68.

47. Anatolii Lunacharsky, introduction to the 1931 Moscow edition, ibid., xxxi. See also Nina Kolesnikoff, *Bruno Jasieński: His Evolution from Futurism to Socialist Realism* (Waterloo: Wilfrid Laurier University Press, 1982), 120.

48. *BJSW,* 67–73.

49. Quoted in Kolesnikoff, *Bruno Jasieński,* 117.

50. Quoted in Stern, *Bruno Jasieński,* 200–201.

51. Quoted ibid., 223–225.

52. Ibid., 10.

53. Mitzner, "Śmierć futurysty," 62.

54. Quoted in Krzysztof Jaworski, "Kilka przyczynków do biografii Brunona Jasieńskiego," *Kieleckie Studia Filologiczne* 8 (1994): 57–58. See also Bruno Jasieński, "O znaczeniu i roli pisarza w Rosji sowieckiej," *WL* 28 (14 July 1935): 7. See also G. S. Smith, *D. S. Mirsky: A Russian-English Life, 1890–1939* (New York: Oxford University Press, 2000), 224, 314–317.

55. See Bruno Jasieński, "Książka odarta ze skóry," *WL* 26 (24 June 1934): 4. On Jasieński's Polishness, see also Wojciech Orliński, "Bolszewik z monoklem," *Gazeta Wyborcza* 303 (30 December 2000–1 January 2001): 18 (Gazeta Świąteczna).

56. Hidas, "Wspomnienia o Brunonie Jasieńskim," 149–167.

57. A. Ia. Vishnevskii and B. A. Rudnitskii, "Pod znamenem proletarskogo internatsionalizma i edinstva," 9328, AAN; Iasenskii, "Pis'mo Bruno Iasenskogo," 9328, AAN.

58. Bruno Iasenskii, "Nash otvet kolonizatoram-imperialistam," 17 June 1931, 9328, AAN.

59. Bruno Iasenskii, "Iz rechi Bruno Iasenskogo na V s"ezde sovetov Tadzhikskoi SSR," 11 January 1935, 9328, AAN.

60. Bruno Iasenskii, "Rech' Bruno Iasenskogo na torzhestvennom zasedanii Tadzhikskogo studenchestva v Moskve, posviashchënnom dosrochnomu vypolneniiu Tadzhikistanom plana zagotovok khlopka," 1936, 9328, AAN.

61. Wat, *Mój wiek*, vol. I, 126, 157, 224–227; Jakub Berman, "Na marginesie dyskusji wokół projektu programu KPP w latach 1932–1933," Warsaw, April 1974, 325/31, AAN.

62. *KWB*, vol. II, 65–66.

63. Henryk Dembiński to Broniewski, Około, 10 December 1935, *KWB*, vol. II, 219.

64. Wat, *Mój wiek*, vol. I, 231–232.

65. Ibid., 244–245; Janina Broniewska, *Tamten brzeg mych lat* (Warsaw: Książka i Wiedza, 1973), 109–113. Wasilewska was also a leading figure in the short-lived *Dziennik Popularny*, which existed between October 1936 and March 1937 and was co-edited by the KPP activist Szymon Natanson.

66. "Na Wolności," reprinted in Broniewska, *Tamten brzeg mych lat*, 109–113.

67. Watowa, *Wszystko co najważniejsze*, 20; Wat, *Mój wiek*, vol. I, 12.

68. Wat, *Mój wiek*, vol. I, 230.

69. Ibid., 229–230. See also "O bonapartyzmie i faszyzmie," "O biurokracji sowieckiej," "Planiści i państwowcy na lewicy socjalistycznej," and "'Historia' Trockiego," in Andrzej Stawar, *Pisma ostatnie* (Paris: Instytut Literacki, 1961). The other major figure in *Pod Prąd* was Roman Jabłonowski. "Notatka służbowa dot. sprawy Janusa Edwarda i Jabłonowskiego Romana-Jana krypt. 'Literaci,'" Warsaw, 10 April 1954, 0298/200, t. 1, IPN.

70. Isaac Deutscher, "U źródeł tragedii KPP," 1957, S V/7 K. 42, ADH.

71. See Isaac Deutscher's "The Moscow Trial," in *Marxism, Wars and Revolutions: Essays from Four Decades*, ed. Tamara Deutscher (London: Verso, 1984).

72. "Notatka służbowa dot. sprawy Janusa Edwarda i Jabłonowskiego Romana-Jana krypt. 'Literaci,'" Warsaw, 10 April 1954, 0298/200, t. 1, IPN. The Party succeeded in acquiring Jabłonowski's testimony about these projects after World War II. See "Streszczenie sprawy kryptonim 'Literaci,'" Warsaw, 11 February 1953, 01224/1426 (microfilm 12366/2), IPN. See also Daniel Singer, "Armed with a Pen," in *Isaac Deutscher: The Man and His Work*, ed. David Horowitz (London: MacDonald, 1971), 54n.

73. Wat, *Mój wiek*, vol. I, 231.

74. Broniewska, *Tamten brzeg mych lat*, 25–27.

75. Barbara Fijałkowska, *Borejsza i Różański: Przyczynek do dziejów stalinizmu w Polsce* (Olsztyn: Wyższa Szkoła Pedagogiczna, 1995), 27–31, 58.

76. Wat remembered the date as having been 1936; Stawar's secret police file gives the date 1938. "Streszczenie sprawy kryptonim 'Literaci,'" Warsaw, 11 February 1953, 01224/1426 (microfilm 12366/2), IPN.

77. Fijałkowska, *Borejsza i Różański*, 27–31, 68–69.

78. Aleksander Wat et al., "Za porozumieniem," *Lewar* 11 (1935): 2; Venclova, *Aleksander Wat*, 127.

79. Wat, *Mój wiek*, vol. I, 231–239, 246–247.

80. Antoni Słonimski, *Moja podróż do Rosji* (Warsaw: Literackie Towarszystwo Wydawnicze, 1997), 5–6. Originally published in *WL* in 1932.

81. Ibid., 125, 107–108, 100, respectively.

82. Ibid., 132–133.

83. Ibid., 138.

84. Jan Hempel, *Listy do siostry*, ed. Roman Rosiak (Lublin: Wydawnictwo Lubelskie, 1961), 65.

85. Słonimski, *Moja podróż do Rosji*, 140.

86. Broniewska, *Maje i listopady*, 175, 192.

87. Broniewski to Irena Hellman, 15 March 1933, Warsaw; in Barbara Riss, ed., *O miłości—listy pisarzy polskich* (Warsaw: Prószyński i S-ka, 1997), 183–184.

88. Broniewska, *Maje i listopady*, 194–199; Jadwiga Weissenburgowa to Broniewski, Kalisz, 13 August 1933 and 28 August 1933, *KWB*, vol. II, 80–83.

89. Irena Hellman to Broniewski, 13 November 1933, *KWB*, vol. II, 91–97.

90. *KWB*, vol. II, 97.

91. Broniewska, *Maje i listopady*, 211–213.

92. Ibid., 214.

93. Władysław Broniewski, "W drodze do Dnieprogesu," *WL* 25 (17 June 1934): 3.

94. Wat, *My Century*, 85–86.

95. Ważyk, "Przeczytałem *Mój wiek*," 50.

96. Stande to Broniewski, Moscow, 14 February 1934, *KWB*, vol. II, 114.

97. Jasieński to Broniewski, Tadzhikistan, teczka Jasieńskiego, MB.

98. Hempel to Wanda Papiewska, 19 April 1934, MB.

99. Hempel to Wanda Papiewska, Kislovodsk, 11 August 1934, MB.

100. The Polska Organizacja Wojskowa was created by Piłsudski alongside his Legions during World War I and ceased to exist after the Polish-Bolshevik War. On the POW as both reality and specter, see Timothy Snyder, *Sketches from a Secret War: A Polish Artist's Mission to Liberate Soviet Ukraine* (New Haven: Yale University Press, 2005).

101. Protokół przesłuchania Witolda Wacławowicza Wandurskiego przeprowadzonego 13 i 14 września 1933 przez Nacz. II sekcji Wydziału Specjalnego OGPU Giendina, M/III/56, AW (mostly in Polish, partly in Russian); published in Maria Wosiek, ed., "Zeznania Witolda Wandurskiego w więzieniu GPU," trans. Ewa Rybarska, *Pamiętnik Teatralny* 3/4 (1996): 487–510.

102. Wosiek, "Zeznania Witolda Wandurskiego w więzieniu GPU," 487.

103. Broniewska, *Maje i listopady*, 86.

104. Wat, *Mój wiek*, vol. I, 241.

105. Władysław Broniewski, *Poezje zebrane*, ed. Feliksa Lichodziejewska, vol. II (Płock: Drukarnia Kujawska 'POLKAL' w Inowrocławiu, 1997), 683–684;

Broniewski, "Prztyczek 'smalonemu dubkowi,'" ibid., 281. Światopełk Karpiński's "Do poety-komunisty" was originally published in "Duby Smalone," supplement to *Kurier Poranny* 320 (1934).

106. Janina Broniewska, "Przedmowa do 'Utworów dla młodzieży' W. Wasilewskiej," in *Wanda Wasilewska*, ed. Helena Zatorska (Warsaw: Wydawnictwa Szkolne i Pedagogiczne, 1976), 341–344. See Jan Hempel, "Oblicze dnia, Wandy Wasilewskiej," *Kultura Mas* 1/2 (1935): 71–73.

107. Wanda Wasilewska to Wanda Maria Wasilewska, 6 October 1932. Zofia A. Woźnicka and Eleonora Syzdek, eds., "Listy Wandy Wasilewskiej," *Zdanie* 6 (1985): 38.

108. *WWW*, 33, 47; Wanda Wasilewska, "Dzieciństwo," in Zatorska, *Wanda Wasilewska*, 111–113.

109. 15 October 1919, "Dziennik 1919–1924," 73/1/323, TsDAMLM.

110. 29 February 1920, "Dziennik 1919–1924," 73/1/323, TsDAMLM.

111. *WWW*, 47.

112. Zofia A. Woźnicka and Eleonora Syzdek, eds., "Listy Wandy Wasilewskiej," *Zdanie* 6 (1985): 33–34.

113. 6 May 1923, 'Dziennik 1919–1924,' 73/1/323, TsDAMLM.

114. Zofia Aldona Woźnicka, "O mojej siostrze," in *WWW*, 55.

115. 19 October 1919, "Dziennik 1919–1924," 73/1/323, TsDAMLM.

116. Quoted in Woźnicka, "O mojej siostrze," 55–56.

117. Wanda Wasilewska, "Wspomnienia Wandy Wasilewskiej," *Z pola walki* 1 (1968): 121–122.

118. Janina Broniewska, "Przedmowa do 'Utworów dla młodzieży' W. Wasilewskiej," in Zatorska, *Wanda Wasilewska*, 341–344. Also see Broniewska, "Poprzez maje i listopady," in *WWW*, 95.

119. Broniewska, *Tamten brzeg mych lat*, 96–97.

120. Wasilewska, "Wspomnienia Wandy Wasilewskiej," 158.

121. Wanda Wasilewska, "Przesłuchania," "Praca w Związku Nauczycielstwa Polskiego," in Zatorska, *Wanda Wasilewska*, 148–149.

122. Ibid.

123. See Adam Ciołkosz, *Wanda Wasilewska: Dwa szkice biograficzne* (London: Polonia Book Fund, 1977), 47.

124. Wasilewska, "Wspomnienia Wandy Wasilewskiej," 133.

125. Broniewska, *Tamten brzeg mych lat*, 191–194.

126. Ibid., 199–217.

127. Wasilewska, "Praca w Związku Nauczycielstwa Polskiego," 140.

128. Broniewska, *Tamten brzeg mych lat*, 202–203; Wanda Wasilewska, *Historia jednego strajku* (Warsaw: Nasza Księgarnia, 1950), 17.

129. Broniewska, *Tamten brzeg mych lat*, 230, 238.

130. Wasilewska, *Historia jednego strajku*, 163.

131. Broniewska, *Tamten brzeg mych lat*, 248–253.

132. Ibid., 235–237. On Jędrychowski, see Czesław Miłosz, *abecadło miłosza* (Cracow: Wydawnictwo Literackie, 1997), 130–133.

133. Włodzimierz Sokorski, *Wspomnienia* (Warsaw: Krajowa Agencja Wydawnicza, 1990), 64; see also Wasilewska to Broniewski, Warsaw, 13 August 1936, xf B 143, Muzeum Niepodległości, Warsaw.

134. Broniewska, *Tamten brzeg mych lat*, 124.

135. Jerzy Putrament, "Poeta, język, kraj," in Balicki, *To ja—dąb*, 288. Władysław Broniewski, "Zagłębie Dąbrowskie," in *Władysław Broniewski: Poezje 1923–1961*, ed. Wiktor Woroszylski (Warsaw: PIW, 1995), 140–142.

136. Broniewski, "Kongres w Obronie Kultury," *WL* 24 (31 May 1936): 2; Leon Kruczkowski, "Wojna a przyszłość kultury," *Trybuna Robotnicza* 3:21 (24 May 1936): 3.

137. Broniewski, "Kongres w Obronie Kultury," 2; "Rezolucja," *Trybuna Robotnicza* 3:21 (24 May 1936): 5.

138. Julian Stryjkowski with Piotr Szewc, *Ocalony na wschodzie* (Montricher: Les Editions Noir sur Blanc, 1991), 27–44.

139. Ibid., 94.

140. The Bund was a Jewish socialist Yiddishist (anti-Zionist) party/workers' movement formed in Vilna in 1897. Wasilewska, "Wspomnienia Wandy Wasilewskiej," 165; Adolf Berman to Michał Mirski, 10 July 1956; Adolf Berman to Michał Mirski, Tel Aviv 22 August 1956; Adolf Berman to Michał Mirski, Tel Aviv, 10 January 1959, 330/35, ŻIH; Michał Mirski to Adolf Berman, Warsaw, 25 February 1959, P-70/59, AABB.

141. Wanda Wasilewska, "Wspomnienia Wandy Wasilewskiej (1939–1944)," *Archiwum Ruchu Robotniczego* 7 (1982): 393.

142. Broniewski, "Kongres w Obronie Kultury," 2.

143. Wanda Wasilewska to Wanda Maria Wasilewska, 21 May 1936. Copy provided by Eleonora Syzdek.

144. Antoni Słonimski, "Kronika tygodniowa," *WL* 26 (14 June 1936): 6.

145. On interwar Polish-Jewish relations and antisemitism, see Ezra Mendelsohn, "Interwar Poland: Good for the Jews or Bad for the Jews?" in *The Jews of Poland*, ed. Chimen Abramsky, Maciej Jachimczyk, and Antony Polonsky (Oxford: Basil Blackwell, 1986), 130–139; William Hagen, "Before the 'Final Solution': Toward a Comparative Analysis of Political Anti-Semitism in Interwar Germany and Poland," *Journal of Modern History* 68:2 (June 1996): 351–382; Joseph Marcus, *The Social and Political History of the Jews in Poland, 1919–1939* (New York: Mouton, 1983); Szymon Rudnicki, *Obóz Narodowo-Radykalny: Geneza i działalność* (Warsaw: Czytelnik, 1985).

146. Antoni Słonimski, "Listki z drzewa czarodziejskiego," *WL* 52/53 (26 December 1937): 21.

147. Antoni Słonimski, "Wspomnienia," *WL* 36 (2 September 1928): 4.

148. Antoni Słonimski, "Rozmowa z rodakiem," in *Liryki najpiękniejsze*, ed. Aleksander Madyda (Toruń: Algo, 1999), 23.

149. Antoni Słonimski, "O drażliwości Żydów," *WL* 35 (31 August 1924): 3.

150. See Wanda Melcer, "Dziecko żydowskie rozpoczyna ziemską wędrówkę,"

WL 14 (1934): 1; Wanda Melcer, "Młodzieniec żydowski wstępuje w świat," *WL* 22 (1934): 2.

151. Antoni Słonimski, "Kronika tygodniowa," *WL* 23 (10 June 1934): 10.

152. Antoni Słonimski, *Kroniki tygodniowe 1927–1939*, ed. Władysław Kopaliński (Warsaw: PIW, 1956), 333, 359.

153. Antoni Słonimski, "Kronika tygodniowa," *WL* 17 (29 April 1934): 6.

154. Antoni Słonimski, "Kronika tygodniowa," *WL* 13 (1 April 1934): 14.

155. Antoni Słonimski, "Kronika tygodniowa," *WL* 10 (28 February 1937): 6.

156. Broniewska, *Tamten brzeg mych lat*, 79–80.

157. Wat, *My Century*, 52; see also Krzywicka, "Nasza przyjaźń trwała pół wieku," in *WAS*, 106.

158. Antoni Słonimski, "Kronika tygodniowa," *WL* 34 (9 August 1936): 5.

159. Słonimski, *Kroniki tygodniowe*, 471–472.

160. Antoni Słonimski, "Kronika tygodniowa," *WL* 44 (18 October 1936): 6.

161. Antoni Słonimski, "Kronika tygodniowa," *WL* 1 (5 January 1936): 6.

162. Antoni Słonimski, "Kronika tygodniowa," *WL* 5 (31 January 1937): 6.

163. Antoni Słonimski, "Kronika tygodniowa," *WL* 49 (28 November 1937): 6.

164. Antoni Słonimski, "Kronika tygodniowa," *WL* 20 (9 May 1937): 6.

165. Antoni Słonimski, "Kronika tygodniowa," *WL* 45 (30 October 1938): 6.

166. Antoni Słonimski, "Kronika tygodniowa," *WL* 49 (27 November 1938): 5.

167. Słonimski, *Kroniki tygodniowe*, 568–570.

168. Ibid., 515.

169. Julian Tuwim, *Rozmowy z Tuwimem*, ed. Tadeusz Januszewski (Warsaw: Semper, 1994); from *Czas* 131 (14 May 1935).

170. "Pod bodźcem wieków," quoted in Janusz Dunin, "Tuwim jako Żyd, Polak, człowiek," *Prace Polonistyczne* 51 (1996): 88.

171. Dunin, "Tuwim jako Żyd, Polak, człowiek," 89.

172. Julian Tuwim, "Żydzi," *Wiersze*, vol. I, ed. Alina Kowalczykowa (Warsaw: Czytelnik, 1986), 247–248; from *Czyhanie na Boga* (1918).

173. Januszewski, *Rozmowy z Tuwimem*, 14–15; from *Nasz Przegląd* 6 (6 January 1924).

174. Januszewski, *Rozmowy z Tuwimem*, 25–26; from *Dziennik Warszawski* 34 and 35 (6 and 7 February 1927).

175. Ibid.

176. Ibid., 53–55; from *Nasz Przegląd* 46 (15 February 1935).

177. Julian Tuwim, "Wspomnienia o Łodzi," *WL* 33 (12 August 1934): 11.

178. Januszewski, *Rozmowy z Tuwimem*, 53–55; from *Nasz Przegląd* 46 (15 February 1935). Also see Tuwim's 1936 "List do Przyjaciela-poety (aryjczyka, katolika i 'gazety polskiej' współpracownika)" in Julian Tuwim, *Dziela*, vol. V, ed. Janusz Stradecki (Warsaw: Czytelnik, 1964), 691–694.

179. Janusz Maciejewski, introduction to Mieczysław Braun, *Mieczysław Braun: Wybór poezji* (Warsaw: PIW, 1979), 17–22.

180. Mieczysław Braun, "Powieść żydowska po polsku," *Nasz Przegląd* 13 (13 January 1929): 8.

181. Quoted by Maciejewski, introduction to Braun, *Mieczysław Braun: Wybór poezji*, 27; originally "'Pisarze polscy' czy 'pisarze żydowscy piszący po polsku' albo pisarze 'polsko-żydowscy'?" *Ster* 16 (1937).

182. Watowa, *Wszystko co najważniejsze*, 20–21.

183. Ibid., 21; Irena Krzywicka, *Wyznania gorszycielki* (Warsaw: Czytelnik, 1998), 326. Also see Krzywicka to Iwaszkiewicz, 23 December 1938, Zakopane, in Riss, *O miłości*, 220–221.

184. Wat, *Mój wiek*, vol. I, 252.

185. Ellipses in original. "Goy" here is antiquated Russian for "hail" or "good health to you"; the sentence is paraphrased from the Russian folk song, "Il'ia Muromets i Solovei-Razboinik." Alexander Zeyliger researched this reference. Tuwim to Iwaszkiewicz, 14 June 1933, Warsaw, *LPP*, 29.

186. Andrzej Stawar, "Jeszcze o Antysemityzmie," *WL* 22 (23 May 1937): 2. On *Wiadomości Literackie* and the Jewish question see Magdalena M. Opalski, "*Wiadomości Literackie*: Polemics on the Jewish Question," in *The Jews of Poland between Two World Wars*, ed. Yisrael Gutman et al. (Hanover: University Press of New England, 1989), 434–449; Jan Błonski, "*Wiadomości Literackie*, 1924–1933: A Problem for the Poles, a Problem for the Jews," *Gal-Ed on the History of the Jews in Poland* 14 (1995): 39–48.

187. Wanda Wasilewska, "Szukam antysemityzmu," *WL* 40 (26 September 1937): 3.

188. Broniewska, *Maje i listopady*, 145.

189. Broniewska, *Tamten brzeg mych lat*, 87.

190. *BJSW*, 85. All material, originally in Russian, from Jasieński's NKVD file is from M/III/55, AW. Polish translations were published as a collection in *BJSW*. I have translated the original Russian, in consultation with the Polish version; page number references, however, are to the documents as they appear in Jaworski's collection.

191. *BJSW*, 87.

192. Bruno Jasieński to Stalin, 25 April 1937, *BJSW*, 88–89.

193. *BJSW*, 93–94.

194. The phrase "i mne stydno" here is written unclearly in the original Russian, and so it is not possible to be certain whether the phrase was originally "i mne stydno" or "i mne nestydno." The difference is between "but I am ashamed" and "so I am not ashamed," respectively. I concur with Jaworski that the former is the more likely.

195. Bruno Jasieński to Stalin, 28 April 1937, *BJSW*, 95.

196. *BJSW*, 95.

197. *BJSW*, 97.

198. *BJSW*, 99.

199. *BJSW*, 102.

200. *BJSW*, 102.

201. *BJSW*, 105.

202. *BJSW*, 107–110.

203. *BJSW*, 107–110.

204. *BJSW*, 119.

205. *BJSW*, 127–128.

206. *BJSW*, 131.

207. *BJSW*, 132–133.

208. *BJSW*, 135–137.

209. *BJSW*, 141–142.

210. *BJSW*, 178–179.

211. Quoted in Piotr Mitzner, "Śmierć futurysty," *Karta* 11 (1993): 76.

212. Jan Hempel to Wanda Papiewska, 6 December 1936. Wanda Papiewska, *Jan Hempel: Wspomnienia siostry* (Warsaw: Książka i Wiedza, 1958), 146.

213. Władysław Krajewski, personal interview, Warsaw, 28 July 2003. See also Władysław Krajewski, "Facts and Myths: About the Role of Jews in the Stalinist Period," special English issue of *Więź* titled *Under One Heaven* (1998): 93–108.

214. Ignacy Loga-Sowiński, "Wspomnienia 1988," K. 193, ADH; Wat, *Mój wiek*, vol. I, 124; A. Lampe, "Avtobiografia," Moscow 1940, 250/1, AAN; "Lampe Alfred—ps. Alski, Marek, Nowak," 250/1, AAN.

215. The KPP list was kept in an undated Russian address book; 495/123/211, RGASPI.

216. *BJSW*, 204.

217. Mitzner, "Śmierć futurysty," 76.

218. *BJSW*, 204; quotation from Daniel Gerould, introduction to *The Mannequins' Ball*, xvii. A death certificate issued in Moscow in 1956, however, gave the date of death as 20 October 1941, while leaving the cause of death blank. Svidetel'stvo o smerti II-A, No. 910123, Moscow, 14 February 1956, 1861/2/20, RGALI. The 1941 date seems unlikely to be accurate given the information in the NKVD file.

219. Broniewska, *Tamten brzeg mych lat*, 270.

220. Tadeusz Tomaszewski to Władysław Broniewski, 31 May 1938, Warsaw, *KWB*, vol. II, 291.

221. Maria Zarębińska to Władysław Broniewski, 30 December [1938], *KWB*, vol. I, 326–328.

222. Broniewska, *Tamten brzeg mych lat*, 287–288.

223. Maria Zarębińska to Broniewski, Horochów, 8 April 1939, *KWB*, vol. II, 347–350; Broniewska, *Tamten brzeg mych lat*, 302; Maria Zarębińska to Broniewski, 10 April 1939, *KWB*, vol. II, 351–354.

224. Antoni Słonimski, "Kronika tygodniowa," *WL* 38 (6 September 1936): 5.

225. Antoni Słonimski, "Kronika tygodniowa," *WL* 9 (21 February 1937): 6.

226. Antoni Słonimski, "Stalin Imperatorem Proletarjatu," *WL* 14 (28 March 1937): 12–13.

227. Antoni Słonimski, "Kronika tygodniowa," *WL* 13 (20 March 1938): 6.

228. Włodzimierz Sokorski, "Wspomnienia o Władku," in Balicki, *To ja—dąb*, 369; Sokorski, *Wspomnienia*, 66; Wat, *My Century*, 91.

229. Aleksander Wat, "Sny sponad Morza Śródziemnego," in *Poezje*, ed. Anna Micińska and Jan Zieliński (Warsaw: Czytelnik, 1997), 103.

230. Closing quote: Wat, *My Century*, 89.

CHAPTER 6. AUTUMN IN SOVIET GALICIA

Epigraph: Władysław Broniewski, "Rozmowa z Historią," in Feliksa Lichodziejewska, *Broniewski bez cenzury 1939–1945* (Warsaw: Wydawnictwo Społeczne KOS, 1992), 62.

1. Daszewski to Broniewski, Lwów, 16 September 1934, *KWB*, vol. II, 159–160.

2. Aleksander Wat, *My Century: The Odyssey of a Polish Intellectual*, trans. Richard Lourie (New York: Norton, 1988), 87.

3. Helena Zatorska, ed., *Wanda Wasilewska* (Warsaw: Wydawnictwa Szkolne i Pedagogiczne, 1976), 57.

4. Agnieszka Cieślikowa, *Prasa okupowanego Lwowa* (Warsaw: Wydawnictwo Neriton, 1997), 77; Paweł Merlend, relacja, 731, AAN; Inglot, "Spór o Wrzesień w poezji polskiej lat 1939–1941 we Lwowie," *Pamiętnik Literacki* 1 (1990): 206.

5. Jacek Trznadel, ed., *Kolaboranci: Tadeusz Boy-Żeleński i grupa komunistycznych pisarzy we Lwowie 1939–1941* (Komorów: Fundacja Pomocy ANTYK, 1998), 414; Shimon Redlich, *Propaganda and Nationalism in Wartime Russia: The Jewish Antifascist Committee in the USSR 1941–1948* (Boulder: East European Monographs, 1982), 16.

6. Mieczysław Inglot, *Polska kultura literacka Lwowa lat 1939–1941: Ze Lwowa i o Lwowie* (Wrocław: Towarzystwo Przyjaciół Polonistyki Wrocławskiej, 1995), 23.

7. Wanda Wasilewska, "Wspomnienia Wandy Wasilewskiej (1939–1944)," *Archiwum Ruchu Robotniczego* 7 (1982): 345.

8. Ola Watowa, *Wszystko co najważniejsze* (Warsaw: Czytelnik, 1990), 23–26.

9. Wat, *My Century*, 98–99.

10. Ibid., 97.

11. Ibid., 106–109.

12. Watowa, *Wszystko co najważniejsze*, 30.

13. Adolf Rudnicki, "Wielki Stefan Konecki," in *Żywe i martwe morze* (Warsaw: Czytelnik, 1956), 58–59.

14. Wat, *My Century*, 104.

15. Julian Stryjkowski, *Wielki strach* (Warsaw: ANTYK, 1989), 62, 68–69.

16. Ibid., 68–69.

17. Ibid., 70.

18. Wat, *My Century*, 102.

19. Stryjkowski, *Wielki strach*, 138.

20. Wasilewska, "Wspomnienia Wandy Wasilewskiej (1939–1944)," 344; see also Leon Pasternak, "Aresztowanie Władysława Broniewskiego," *Zapis* 16 (October 1980): 109.

21. Wat, *My Century*, 123.

22. According to Wasilewska, it was "immediately evident that such a collective declaration was out of the question and fortunately no one agreed individually to that kind of statement." Wasilewska, "Wspomnienia Wandy Wasilewskiej (1939–1944)," 341; Janusz Kowalewski, "Boy i Bartel we Lwowie w 1939 r.," *Kultura* [Paris] 15 (1949): 121; Wat, *My Century*, 123.

23. Wat, *My Century*, 104–105.

24. See Kowalewski's account in Trznadel, *Kolaboranci*, 245–246.

25. Wat, *My Century*, 99–100.

26. Aleksander Wat, *Mój wiek: Pamiętnik mówiony*, 2 vols. (Warsaw: Czytelnik, 1998), vol. I, 275.

27. Wat, *My Century*, 99–101; also see Kowalewski, "Boy i Bartel we Lwowie w 1939 r.," 119.

28. Cieślikowa, *Prasa okupowanego Lwowa*, 71.

29. Pasternak, "Aresztowanie Władysława Broniewskiego," 108; Wat, *My Century*, 124.

30. Wat, *Mój wiek*, vol. I, 304.

31. Pasternak, "Aresztowanie Władysława Broniewskiego," 108.

32. Wat, *Mój wiek*, vol. I, 284.

33. Cieślikowa, *Prasa okupowanego Lwowa*, 57–59; Władysław Daszewski, "Teatralne życzenia noworoczne," *Czerwony Sztandar* 62 and 63 (7 and 8 December 1939). See also Barbara Fijałkowska, *Borejsza i Różański: Przyczynek do dziejów stalinizmu w Polsce* (Olsztyn: Wyższa szkoła pedagogiczna, 1995); and Tadeusz Peiper, *Pierwsze trzy miesiące* (Cracow: Wydawnictwo Literackie, 1991).

34. Jerzy Putrament, *Pół wieku: Wojna* (Warsaw: Czytelnik, 1964), 25.

35. Cieślikowa, *Prasa okupowanego Lwowa*, 33–91; Klementyna Pytlarczyk, "Sprawy kultury polskiej na łamach lwowskiego 'Czerwonego Sztandaru' (wrzesień 1939–czerwiec 1941)," *Biuletyn Informacyjny Studiów z Dziejów Stosunków Polsko-radzieckich* 20 (October–December 1970): 35–47; Grzegorz Hryciuk, "Kolaboracja we Lwowie w latach 1939–1941," *Mówią Wieki* 1 (January 1996): 37–40.

36. Agnieszka Koecher-Hensel, "Władysław Daszewski—Prowokator czy ofiara sowieckiej prowokacji?" *Pamiętnik Teatralny* 46:1–4 (1997): 256.

37. Julian Stryjkowski, *Ocalony na wschodzie* (Montricher: Les Editions Noir sur Blanc, 1991), 103–104.

38. Venclova, *Aleksander Wat*, 137; Trznadel (interview with Stryjkowski), *Hańba domowa* (Warsaw: Agencja Wydawnicza Morex, 1997), 175.

39. Stryjkowski, *Ocalony na wschodzie*, 103.

40. Watowa, *Wszystko co najważniejsze*, 25.

41. Trznadel, *Kolaboranci*, 362–363.

42. Inglot, *Polska kultura literacka Lwowa*, 381; originally Adam Ważyk, "Do inteligenta uchodźcy," *Czerwony Sztandar* 38 (5 November 1939): 3.

43. Trznadel, *Kolaboranci*, 450; originally Adam Ważyk, "Radziecka choinka," *Czerwony Sztandar* 84 (1 January 1940).

44. Wat, *My Century*, 102.

45. Trznadel, *Kolaboranci*, 428; originally Wat, "Kobieta radziecka," *Czerwony Sztandar* 61 (5 December 1939).

46. Quoted in Inglot, "Spór o Wrzesień w poezji polskiej lat 1939–1941 we Lwowie," 213. Semën I. Kirsanov (1906–1971) was a Russian poet influenced by Mayakovsky.

47. Wat's article reprinted ibid., 231–233; originally "Polskie sovetskie pisateli" in *Literaturnaia Gazeta* 67 (1939): 4.

48. Wat, *My Century*, 112.

49. Ibid., 103.

50. Ibid., 103–104.

51. Ibid., 111.

52. Quoted in Trznadel, *Kolaboranci*, 326.

53. Wat's article reprinted in Inglot, "Spór o Wrzesień w poezji polskiej lat 1939–1941 we Lwowie," 231–233; originally Aleksander Wat, "Polskie sovetskie pisateli," *Literaturnaia Gazeta* 67 (1939).

54. Article reprinted in Inglot, "Spór o Wrzesień w poezji polskiej lat 1939–1941 we Lwowie," 229–230; originally "Poeta proletariatu," *Czerwony Sztandar* 54 (1939).

55. Lichodziejewska, *Broniewski bez cenzury 1939–1945*, 10.

56. "Żolnierz polski" reprinted in Inglot, *Polska kultura literacka Łwowa*, 320.

57. Lichodziejewska, *Broniewski bez cenzury 1939–1945*, 11–12. Leon Pasternak wrote a poem about the rejection of Broniewski's poem. See Inglot, *Polska kultura literacka Lwowa*, 399; published in Leon Pasternak, *Pamięć* (Warsaw: Czytelnik, 1969), 32–33.

58. Account of Jan Karol Wende cited in Inglot, "Spór o Wrzesień w poezji polskiej lat 1939–1941 we Lwowie," 216. Also see Trznadel, *Kolaboranci*, 222.

59. Broniewski, "Syn podbitego narodu," reprinted in Inglot, *Polska kultura literacka Lwowa*, 321. See also Inglot, "Spór o Wrzesień w poezji polskiej lat 1939–1941 we Lwowie," 210; and Cieślikowa, *Prasa okupowanego Lwowa*, 77.

60. See, for example, Jan Kott, *Still Alive: An Autobiographical Essay*, trans. Jadwiga Kosicka (New Haven: Yale University Press, 1994), 150–151.

61. Wat, *My Century*, 110. The song is most likely "Moskva Maiskaia," by Pokrass and Lebedev-Kumach, although Wat is slightly misquoting it: the chorus is "Strana moia, Moskva moia."

62. Trznadel, *Kolaboranci*, 414.

63. Władysław Broniewski, "Lotniczka," in Lichodziejewska, *Broniewski bez cenzury 1939–1945*, 13; copy in Broniewski's NKVD file.

64. Michał Borwicz, "Inżynierowie dusz," *Zeszyty historyczne* 3 (1963): 133.

65. Wasilewska, "Wspomnienia Wandy Wasilewskiej (1939–1944)," 352.

66. Watowa, *Wszystko co najważniejsze*, 31; Wat, *My Century*, 117–119; Ważyk, "Przeczytałem *Mój wiek*," *Puls* 34 (1987): 48–49. Accounts conflict as to the exact nature of the invitation. Wat wrote that he asked if it were perhaps Daszewski's birthday, but Daszewski refused to reveal the occasion for the

gathering. Ważyk wrote that Daszewski told them from the beginning that two people from Moscow, a filmmaker and a theater critic, were coming to Lvov and wanted to meet Wat, Broniewski, and Peiper. Daszewski had been asked to organize a gathering at the Intelligentsia Club, and he wanted to know Peiper's address. Wat expressed surprise that the Russians were interested in Peiper; Daszewski said they were interested only indirectly.

67. Watowa, *Wszystko co najważniejsze*, 33.

68. Pasternak, "Aresztowanie Władysława Broniewskiego," 111.

69. Story of the arrests reconstructed from four accounts: Watowa, *Wszystko co najważniejsze*, 31–35; Ważyk, "Przeczytałem *Mój wiek*," 48–49; Wat, *My Century*, 118–125; Pasternak, "Aresztowanie Władysława Broniewskiego," 105–115. Also see Borwicz, "Inżynierowie dusz," 134; and Koecher-Hensel, "Władysław Daszewski—Prowokator czy ofiara sowieckiej prowokacji?"

70. Ważyk, "Przeczytałem *Mój wiek*," 49–50.

71. Watowa, *Wszystko co najważniejsze*, 28–29.

72. Stryjkowski, *Wielki strach*, 85–94.

73. Witold Kolski, "Zgnieść gadzinę nacjonalistyczną!" reprinted in Mieczysław Inglot and Jadwiga Puzynina, "Dokument politycznego egzorcyzmu (W pięćdziesiątą rocznicę aresztowania pisarzy polskich w Lwowie przez NKWD)," *Polonistyka* 42:8 (October 1990): 390–391; from *Czerwony Sztandar* 104 (27 January 1940).

74. Stryjkowski, *Wielki strach*, 97.

75. Wasilewska, "Wspomnienia Wandy Wasilewskiej (1939–1944)," 346–352.

76. The other two collectors of signatures were Bolesław Piach and the illustrator Franciszek Parecki. See Trznadel, *Kolaboranci*, 338; Borwicz, "Inżynierowie dusz," 136–137; Lichodziejewska, *Broniewski bez cenzury 1939–1945*, 20–21; Wat, *Mój wiek*, vol. I, 305; Ważyk, "Przeczytałem *Mój wiek*," 51; Czeslaw Milosz, *The Captive Mind*, trans. Jane Zielonko (New York: Vintage Books, 1990), 152–153. Putrament appears in *The Captive Mind* under the pseudonym of Gamma. Also see Jerzy Putrament, *Pół wieku: Wojna*, 23. Putrament omits the episode of the petition in his memoirs and writes only of the terror generated by the news of the arrests.

77. Watowa, *Wszystko co najważniejsze*, 28–35; Erwin Axer to Zbigniew Raszewski, July 1987, quoted in Agnieszka Koecher-Hensel, "Władysław Daszewski—Prowokator czy ofiara sowieckiej prowokacji?" 239–240; Stefan Jędrychowski, rozmowa z Grzegorzem Sołtysiakiem, 17 February 1994, part II, K.143, W/R 5, ADH; Wasilewska, "Wspomnienia Wandy Wasilewskiej (1939–1944)," 349–350; see also Jan Karol Wende's account in Trznadel, *Kolaboranci*, 224.

78. Koecher-Hensel, "Władysław Daszewski—Prowokator czy ofiara sowieckiej prowokacji?" 257.

79. Wat, *My Century*, 106–108.

80. See Hryciuk, "Kolaboracja we Lwowie w latach 1939–1941," 37–40; and Wasilewska, "Wspomnienia Wandy Wasilewskiej (1939–1944)," 356–357.

81. Wat, *My Century*, 107.

82. Trznadel (interview with Stryjkowski), *Hańba domowa*, 179.

83. Trznadel, *Kolaboranci*, 276.

84. Redlich, *Propaganda and Nationalism in Wartime Russia*, 16.

85. Wasilewska, "Wspomnienia Wandy Wasilewskiej (1939–1944)," 351.

86. Quoted in Mykoła Bażan, "Indywidualność zadziwiająca i niepowtarzalna," in *WWW*, 217.

87. Wasilewska, "Wspomnienia Wandy Wasilewskiej (1939–1944)," 346.

88. Wanda Wasilewska, "Spotkanie z wyborcami," *Czerwony Sztandar* 150 (21 March 1940); in Trznadel, *Kolaboranci*, 398.

89. Zofia Zołątkowska, "Wanda Wasilewska," 21 April 1973, 9599/t. 1, AAN; Trznadel, *Hańba domowa*, 179.

90. Adam Ciołkosz quoted in Trznadel, *Kolaboranci*, 416–417.

91. Watowa, *Wszystko co najważniejsze*, 36.

92. Wat, *My Century*, 108–109.

93. Aleksander Wat, *Dziennik bez samogłosek* (London: Polonia, 1986), 218.

94. Adam Ciołkosz quoted in Trznadel, *Kolaboranci*, 416–417.

95. Ibid., 416–417, 423; Watowa, *Wszystko co najważniejsze*, 36; Zofia Zołątkowska, "Wanda Wasilewska," 21 April 1973, 9599/t. 1, AAN.

96. Zofia Zołątkowska, "Wanda Wasilewska," 21 April 1973, 9599/t. 1, AAN.

97. Wat, *My Century*, 108–109.

98. N. S. Chruszczow, "Fragmenty wspomnień N. S. Chruszczowa," *Zeszyty Historyczne* 132 (2000): 119, 118,.

99. Ibid., 140.

100. "Wielka demonstracja i wiec pracujących Lwowa," *Czerwony Sztandar* 302 (18 September 1940); reprinted in Trznadel, *Kolaboranci*, 401–402. Also see Jan T. Gross, *Revolution from Abroad: The Soviet Conquest of Poland's Western Ukraine and Western Belorussia* (Princeton: Princeton University Press, 1988), 142–143.

101. Stryjkowski, *Wielki strach*, 147.

102. Wasilewska, "Wspomnienia Wandy Wasilewskiej (1939–1944)," 350.

103. Ibid., 351, 363–364. On attempts to intervene with Stalin regarding former KPP members, see also Jakub Berman, "Interwencje na rzecz uwolnienia i repatriacji kapepowców oraz rehabilitacji KPP," Warsaw, September 1977, 325/31, AAN.

104. Bohdan Urbankowski, *Czerwona msza, albo uśmiech Stalina* (Warsaw: ALFA, 1995), 65.

105. See Grzegorz Hryciuk, "Kolaboracja we Lwowie w latach 1939–1941," 37–40.

106. Quoted in Michaił O. Głobaczow, "Życie kulturalne Polaków w tzw. okresie lwowskim (jesień 1939–lato 1941)," *Z pola walki* 1 (1986): 112; and Cieślikowa, *Prasa okupowanego Lwowa*, 93; from *Nowe Widnokręgi* 1 (1941): 3–6. On *Nowe Widnokręgi*, see Wojciech Śleszyński, *Okupacja sowiecka na Białostocczyźnie 1939–1941: Propaganda i indoktrynacja* (Białystok: Agencja Wydawnicza Benkowski, 2001), 393–394.

107. Cieślikowa, *Prasa okupowanego Lwowa*, 92; Wasilewska, "Wspomnienia Wandy Wasilewskiej (1939–1944)," 358–359.

108. Quoted in Cieślikowa, *Prasa okupowanego Lwowa*, 92–93.

109. Putrament, *Pół wieku: Wojna*, 48. Both Słonimski's and Ważyk's translations appear in the collection Włodzimierz Majakowski, *Poezje*, ed. Mieczysław Jastrun, Seweryn Pollak, Anatol Stern, and Adam Ważyk (Warsaw: Czytelnik, 1957).

110. Ważyk, "Biografia," *Nowe Widnokręgi* 4 (1941): 36; reprinted in Inglot, *Polska kultura literacka Łwowa*, 384–385.

111. Wat, *My Century*, 129.

112. Ibid., 123–126, 158–164; Wat, *Dziennik bez samogłosek*, 25.

113. Wat, *My Century*, 121–125.

114. Ibid., 137–138, 154.

115. Ibid., 132–133, 136.

116. Watowa, *Wszystko co najważniejsze*, 39.

117. Wat, *My Century*, 159–160.

118. Ibid., 160–161. See also Wat to Grydzewski, La Messuguière, 2 March 1962, C-219, AWPB.

119. Wat, *My Century*, 161.

120. Quoted in Inglot, *Polska kultura literacka Lwowa*, 325–326. Janina Broniewska later used the ending phrase "Tamten brzeg mych lat" as the title of one volume of her memoirs.

121. Broniewski composed "Rozmowa z Historią" in Zamarstynów prison in May 1940.

122. Wat to Grydzewski, La Messuguière, 2 March 1962, C-219, AWPB.

123. Vladislav Antonivich Bronevskii, NKVD interrogation protocol, 12 February 1940, Lvov, M/III/5, AW; copy at MB. In Russian.

124. Frantishek Paretskii [Franciszek Parecki], deposition for the NKVD, M/III/5, AW.

125. Wat, *My Century*, 113, 148.

126. Wat, *Mój wiek*, vol. I, 279.

127. Wat, *My Century*, 63, 195–196. See also Herminia Nagerlerowa's account of her interrogations regarding Wat, Broniewski, Jasieński, Stande, and Wandurski in Trznadel, *Kolaboranci*, 303–304.

128. Vladislav Antonivich Bronevskii, NKVD interrogation protocol, date missing, M/III/5, AW; copy at MB. The page that follows is missing from the NKVD file.

129. Lichodziejewska, *Broniewski bez cenzury*, 22.

130. Vladislav Antonivich Bronevskii, NKVD interrogation protocol, date missing, M/III/5, AW; copy at MB.

131. Watowa, *Wszystko co najważniejsze*, 35.

132. Ważyk, "Przeczytałem *Mój wiek*," 50.

133. Wat, *My Century*, 155–156; Wat, *Dziennik bez samogłosek*, 10.

134. Hryciuk, "Kolaboracja we Lwowie w latach 1939–1941," 37–40; Wat, *My*

Century, 110, 156. On these deportations, see Gross, *Revolution from Abroad*, Jan Tomasz Gross and Irena Grudzińska-Gross, *War through Children's Eyes: The Soviet Occupation of Poland and the Deportations, 1939–1941* (Stanford: Hoover Institution Press, 1981); Katherine Jolluck, *Exile and Identity: Polish Women in the Soviet Union during World War II* (Pittsburgh: University of Pittsburgh Press, 2002).

135. Watowa, *Wszystko co najważniejsze*, 39–42.

136. Ibid., 41–68.

137. Ibid., 67–68.

138. Quoted ibid., 66.

139. Stefania Skwarzyńska to Ola Watowa, [Lvov], 4 December 1940, 11, AWPB.

140. Wat, *My Century*, 175.

141. Ibid., 248.

142. Ibid., 189, 234.

143. Broniewski to Broniewska, Moscow, 21 August 1941, teczka Broniewskiej, ML.

144. Ibid., 219–220.

145. Ibid., 223–225.

146. Ibid., 238–263; Aleksander Wat, "Śmierć starego bolszewika," *Kultura* [Paris] 1–2 (1964): 37.

147. Wat, *My Century*, 266–268.

148. Ibid., 264–269; Wat, "Śmierć starego bolszewika," 27–31.

149. Wat, *My Century*, 271–273; Wat, "Śmierć starego bolszewika," 29–34; on Erlich also see Wat to Grydzewski, La Messuguière, 2 March 1962, C-219, AWPB.

150. Wat, *My Century*, 276.

151. Ibid., 291.

152. Wat, "Śmierć starego bolszewika," 37–38; Wat, *My Century*, 297–299. Also see Aleksander Wat, "La mort d'un vieux bolchévik: Souvenirs sur Stieklov," *Le Contrat Social* 7 (1963).

CHAPTER 7. INTO THE ABYSS

Epigraph: Julian Stryjkowski, *Ocalony na wschodzie* (Montricher: Les Editions Noir sur Blanc, 1991), 137.

1. Jarosław Iwaszkiewicz, *Notatki 1939–1945*, ed. Andrzej Zawada (Wrocław: Wydawnictwo Dolnośląskie, 1991), 9.

2. Słonimski, *Wspomnienia warszawskie* (Warsaw: Czytelnik, 1957), 96.

3. Meleniewski, "Odyseja Tuwima," Rio de Janeiro, 27 August 1940, in Julian Tuwim, *Rozmowy z Tuwimem*, ed. Tadeusz Januszewski (Warsaw: Wydawnictwo Naukowe Semper, 1994), 71.

4. Słonimski, *Wspomnienia warszawskie*, 98.

5. Ibid., 96–101.

6. Meleniewski, "Odyseja Tuwima," 71–72.

7. Antoni Słonimski, *Alfabet wspomnień* (Warsaw: PIW, 1975), 241–242.

8. Ibid., 120; Wanda Nowakowska, "Lechoń i Tuwim—dzieje przyjaźni," *Prace Polonistyczne* 51 (1996): 240.

9. Ilia Erenburg, "Tuwim Jestem," in *WJT*, 438.

10. Ibid.

11. Julian Tuwim to Bolesław Miciński, Paris, 3 April 1940, *LPP*, 192.

12. Stanislaw Baranczak, "Skamander after Skamander: The Postwar Path of the Prewar Polish Pleiade," *Cross Currents* 9 (1990): 336.

13. Meleniewski, "Odyseja Tuwima," 72–73.

14. Nowakowska, "Lechoń i Tuwim—dzieje przyjaźni," 241.

15. Meleniewski, "Odyseja Tuwim," 74.

16. Tuwim to Wierzyński, Rio de Janeiro, 10 September 1940, *LPP*, 73.

17. Nowakowska, "Lechoń i Tuwim—dzieje przyjaźni," 241.

18. Julian Tuwim, "Polish Flowers," in *The Dancing Socrates and Other Poems*, trans. Adam Gillon (New York: Twayne, 1968), 44–50.

19. Ewa Zawistowska, personal correspondence, Greece, 23 December 2000.

20. Janina Broniewska, *Maje i listopady* (Warsaw: Iskry, 1967), 235.

21. Ewa Zawistowska, personal correspondence, Greece, 13 May 2001.

22. Bohdan Urbankowski, *Czerwona msza, albo uśmiech Stalina* (Warsaw: ALFA, 1995), 65.

23. On *Sztandar Wolności*, see Wojciech Śleszyński, *Okupacja sowiecka na Białostocczyźnie 1939–1941: Propaganda i indoktrynacja* (Białystok: Agencja Wydawnicza Benkowski, 2001), 389–392.

24. Janina Broniewska to Feliks Kon, 11 April 1941, Minsk, 135/1/264, RGASPI. On Proletariat see Norman Naimark, *The History of the "Proletariat": The Emergence of Marxism in the Kingdom of Poland, 1870–1887* (Boulder: East European Quarterly, 1979).

25. Janina Broniewska to Feliks Kon, 5 May 1941, Minsk, 135/1/264, RGASPI.

26. Alfred Lampe to Ministerstwo Sprawiedliwości Rzeczypospolitej Polskiej, 31 March 1942, Białystok, 250/1, AAN. See also "Lampe Alfred—ps. Alski, Marek, Nowak," 250/1, AAN.

27. Teresa Torańska, *Oni* (Warsaw: Agencja Omnipress, 1990), 25–26; "Jakub Berman," 325/1, AAN.

28. Janina Broniewska, *Z notatnika korespondenta wojennego,* 2 vols. (Warsaw: Iskry, 1965), vol. I, 27.

29. Ibid., 27; Ewa Zawistowska, personal correspondence, Greece, 13 May 2001.

30. "Jakub Berman," 325/1, AAN; Jakub Berman, "Epizod grudniowy na przełomie 1943/1944," Warsaw, April 1973, 325/31, AAN.

31. Wanda Wasilewska, "Wspomnienia Wandy Wasilewskiej, (1939–1944)," *Archiwum Ruchu Robotniczego* 7 (1982): 372–374; Jerzy Putrament, *Pół wieku: Wojna* (Warsaw: Czytelnik, 1964), 64 [photograph].

32. The poems appeared in *Nowe Widnokręgi* 7 (1941). See Feliksa Lichodziejewska, *Broniewski bez cenzury: 1939–1945* (Warsaw: Wydawnictwo Społeczne KOS, 1992), 12; and [Jakub Berman], "O próbach utworzenia Batalionu pol-

skiego w czerwcu-lipcu 1941 r. dla walki z hitlerowskim najeźdźcą," 325/31, AAN.

33. "Przemówienie na wiecu mieszkańców Kijowa," 4 September 1941, in Wanda Wasilewska, *O wolną i demokratyczną: Wybór artykułów, przemówień i listów,* ed. Zbigniew Kumoś et al. (Warsaw: Wojskowy Insytut Historyczny im. Wandy Wasilewskiej, 1985), 34.

34. Wasilewska, "Odezwa polskich działaczy demokratycznych w ZSRR—uczestników wiecu radiowego w Saratowie," 27 November 1941, ibid., 36–38.

35. Barbara Fijałkowska, *Borejsza i Różański: Przyczynek do dziejów stalinizmu w Polsce* (Olsztyn: Wyższa Szkoła Pedagogiczna, 1995), 89; Putrament, *Pół wieku: Wojna,* 82.

36. Julian Stryjkowski, *Wielki strach* (Warsaw: ANTYK, 1989); *To samo ale inaczej* (Warsaw: Czytelnik, 1990), 241–246.

37. Stryjkowski, *To samo ale inaczej,* 245–261.

38. Stefania and Julian Tuwim to Irena Monique Wiley, 5 July 1940, Brazil; Wierzyński to Irena Monique Wiley, 11 July 1941, Forest Hills, New York; Wierzyński to Irena Monique Wiley, 18 July 1941, Forest Hills, New York, zbiór Moniki Wiley, 151, Instytut Badań Literackich, Warsaw.

39. Erenburg, "Tuwim Jestem," 439.

40. Tuwim to Irena Tuwimowa, 12 September 1941, *LPP,* 60–61.

41. Tuwim to Irena Tuwimowa, 15 November 1941, *LPP,* 69.

42. Tuwim to Irena Tuwimowa, 23 February 1942, *LPP,* 69.

43. Tuwim to Irena Tuwimowa, 12 September 1941, *LPP,* 60–61.

44. Lechoń to Tuwim, 29 May 1942, New York, *LPP,* 43n.

45. Tuwim to Józef Wittlin, New York, 5 June 1942, *LPP,* 251.

46. Tuwim to Irena Tuwimowa, 25 July 1942, New York, *LPP,* 60–61.

47. Broniewski to Broniewska, Moscow, 21 August 1941, teczka Broniewskiej, ML.

48. Broniewski to Broniewska, Alma-Ata, 7 August 1941, teczka Broniewskiej, ML.

49. Wasilewska, "Wspomnienia Wandy Wasilewskiej (1939–1944)," 375.

50. Ibid.

51. Broniewski to Broniewska, 21 August 1941, Moscow, teczka Broniewskiej, ML.

52. Quoted in Lichodziejewska, *Broniewski bez cenzury,* 29–30.

53. Quoted ibid., 30.

54. Broniewski to Broniewska, Moscow, teczka Broniewskiej, ML.

55. Quoted in Lichodziejewska, *Broniewski bez cenzury,* 28.

56. Ibid., 30.

57. Władysław Anders to Broniewski, 21 March 1942, Kuibyshev, M/III/5, AW.

58. Emil Herbst, "O Władysławie Broniewskim," 14 March 1962, 731, AAN.

59. Grażyna Pietruszewska-Kobiela, *Pejzaż dramatyczny Anatola Sterna* (Częstochowa: Wyższa Szkoła Pedagogiczna w Częstochowie, 1989), 11.

60. Władysław Anders to Broniewski, "Zaświadczenie," Kuibyshev, 21 March 1942, M/III/5, AW.

61. Władysław Broniewski, "Droga," Moscow, September 1941, 245/6, AAN; published in Bogdan Czaykowski, ed., *Antologia poezji polskiej na obczyźnie, 1939–1999* (Warsaw: Czytelnik, 2002), 50.

62. Słonimski, *Wspomnienia warszawskie*, 109.

63. Antoni Słonimski, "Pozdrowienia dla Władysława Broniewskiego," 20 April 1942, 245/6, AAN; published as "Pozdrowienia dla autora 'Drogi'" in Czaykowski, *Antologia poezji polskiej na obczyźnie*, 51. Czaykowski gives the date as November 1941, the archival copy is dated April 1942.

64. Władysław Bartoszewski, "Mój Słonimski," in *WAS*, 16–17; Antoni Słonimski, *Alarm* (London: M. I. Kolin, 1940).

65. Antoni Słonimski, "Popiół i wiatr," in *Poezje* (Cracow: Czytelnik, 1951), 312–330.

66. Słonimski, *Wspomnienia warszawskie*, 111.

67. Mieczysław Grydzewski to Julian Tuwim, London, 14 September 1941. Grydzewski, *Listy do Tuwima i Lechonia (1940–1943)*, ed. Janusz Stradecki (Warsaw: PIW, 1986), 62.

68. Grydzewski to Tuwim, London, 14 September 1941. Ibid.

69. Grydzewski to Tuwim, London, 14 September 1941. Ibid., 60.

70. Quoted in Grydzewski to Tuwim, London, 30 January 1942. Ibid., 66–67.

71. Here "fifth column" refers to the fifth item in Soviet identity documents, which contains the holder's nationality.

72. Grydzewski to Tuwim, London, 30 January 1942. Grydzewski, *Listy do Tuwima i Lechonia (1940–1943)*, 66–67. OZON, Obóz Zjednoczenia Narodowego, was a right-leaning formation organized on a military model following Piłsudski's death in the interest of uniting the nation around a central leader and the military. It existed between 1937 and 1942.

73. Grydzewski to Tuwim, London, 30 January 1942. Ibid., 68.

74. Tuwim to Słonimski, New York, July 1942, *LPP*, 213–214.

75. Słonimski, *Wspomnienia warszawskie*, 114.

76. Jan T. Gross, *Revolution from Abroad: The Soviet Conquest of Poland's Western Ukraine and Western Belorussia* (Princeton: Princeton University Press, 1988), 144.

77. Aleksander Wat, *My Century: The Odyssey of a Polish Intellectual*, trans. Richard Lourie (New York: Norton, 1988), 124–125, 307–309.

78. Ola Watowa, *Wszystko co najważniejsze* (Warsaw: Czytelnik, 1990), 68–71.

79. Ibid., 71; Aleksander Wat, *Mój wiek: Pamiętnik mówiony*, 2 vols. (Warsaw: Czytelnik, 1998), vol. II, 245–248.

80. Watowa, *Wszystko co najważniejsze*, 71–72.

81. Wat, *My Century*, 305–318.

82. Ibid., 319.

83. Ibid., 320–325.

84. Ibid.; Watowa, *Wszystko co najważniejsze*, 73.

85. Wat, *My Century*, 328.

86. Watowa, *Wszystko co najważniejsze*, 76; copy of letter in 11, AWPB.

87. Watowa, *Wszystko co najważniejsze*, 74–77.

88. Ibid., 77.

89. Ibid., 78.

90. Ibid., 82.

91. Wat, *My Century*, 329–330; Watowa, *Wszystko co najważniejsze*, 83; Wat and Watowa to "Kochana Pani," Alma-Ata, 17 June 1942, C-194, AWPB.

92. Watowa, *Wszystko co najważniejsze*, 71–72.

93. Wat, *My Century*, 330.

94. Watowa, *Wszystko co najważniejsze*, 85.

95. Wat, *My Century*, 328–345.

96. Ibid., 335–337.

97. Ibid., 162. Despite their own connection to the delegation, Wat and his wife were very critical of this Polish outpost that did much for many Poles who had been cast into the Soviet Union against their will; they accused the delegation of corruption, favoritism, and incompetence. See Watowa, *Wszystko co najważniejsze*, 85–86. See the polemic with Więcek: Wat, *My Century*, 339–341; Jacek Trznadel, "Głosy do wspomnień Aleksandra Wata," *Puls* 33 (spring 1987): 70–76; Kazimierz Więcek, "W Alma-Acie, w *Moim wieku* . . . ," ibid., 58–69.

98. Wat, *My Century*, 345–347.

99. Quoted in Lichodziejewska, *Broniewski bez cenzury*, 34.

100. Quoted ibid., 36–40.

101. Broniewski, "Mniejsza o to," in Lichodziejewska, *Broniewski bez cenzury*, 43.

102. Lichodziejewska, ibid., 43.

103. Wasilewska, "Wspomnienia Wandy Wasilewskiej (1939–1944)," 392.

104. Lichodziejewska, *Broniewski bez cenzury*, 44–47.

105. Quoted ibid., 46–47.

106. Quoted ibid., 46–47.

107. Quoted ibid., 47.

108. Quoted ibid., 38.

109. Ewa Zawistowska, personal correspondence, Greece, 13 May 2001.

110. Wanda Wasilewska to Janina Broniewska, 25 January [1942 or 1943]. Copy provided by Ewa Zawistowska.

111. Broniewska, *Z notatnika korespondenta wojennego*, vol. I, 28. Also see Wasilewska, "Wspomnienia Wandy Wasilewskiej (1939–1944)," 379.

112. Broniewska, *Z notatnika korespondenta wojennego*, vol. I, 31–32.

113. Ibid., 32–33; Wasilewska, "Wspomnienia Wandy Wasilewskiej," 379; Stefan Jędrychowski, rozmowa z Grzegorzem Sołtysiakiem, 17 February 1994, part II, K. 143, W/R 5, ADH.

114. "Lampe Alfred—ps. Alski, Marek, Nowak," 250/1, AAN.

115. Wasilewska, "Wspomnienia Wandy Wasilewskiej (1939–1944)," 376.

116. Stefan Jędrychowski, "O działalności ZPP," 3 June 1980, and "Związek Patriotów Polskich," 25 May 1972, JI/2, ADH; Putrament, *Pół Wieku: Wojna*, 146.

117. Broniewska, *Z notatnika korespondenta wojennego*, vol. I, 35.

118. Ibid., 44. See also Wasilewska's letters to Broniewska during this period from late 1942 and early 1943 in Helena Zatorska, ed., *Wanda Wasilewska* (Warsaw: Wydawnictwa Szkolne i Pedagogiczne, 1976), 175–176.

119. Janina Broniewska, *Tamten brzeg mych lat* (Warsaw: Książka i Wiedza, 1973), 263–264.

120. Wanda Wasilewska to Bolesław Drobner, Kuibyshev, 7 July 1942, 216/31, AAN; Putrament, *Pół Wieku: Wojna*, 151–152; Oleksandr Korneichuk, *Front* (Moscow: Voyennoye Izdatel'stvo Narodnogo Komissariata Oborony Soiuza SSR, 1942).

121. Stefan Jędrychowski, rozmowa z Grzegorzem Sołtysiakiem, 17 February 1994, part II, K. 143, W/R 5, ADH.

122. Wanda Wasilewska, *The Rainbow*, trans. Edith Bone, ed. Sonia Bleeker (New York: Simon and Schuster, 1944).

123. Wasilewska, "Wspomnienia Wandy Wasilewskiej (1939–1944)," 430.

124. Maria Iwaszkiewicz-Wojdowska and Włodzimierz Susid, "Azyl w Stawisku," *Midrasz* 11 (November 2000): 28. See also Watowa, *Wszystko co najważniejsze*, 21.

125. Iwaszkiewicz, *Notatki 1939–1945*, 101–102.

126. Wat, *My Century*, 120.

127. Lichodziejewska, *Broniewski bez cenzury*, 27–28.

128. Irena Krzywicka, *Wyznania gorszycielki* (Warsaw: Czytelnik, 1998), 361–369.

129. Jerzy Zawieyski, *Dobrze, że byli* (Warsaw: Biblioteka "Więzi," 1974), 133.

130. Janusz Maciejewski, introduction to Mieczysław Braun, *Mieczysław Braun: Wybór poezji* (Warsaw: PIW, 1979), 32. On the Warsaw ghetto, see Barbara Engelking and Jacek Leociak, *Getto Warszawskie: Przewodnik po nieistniejącym mieście* (Warsaw: Wydawnictwo IfiS PAN, 2001).

131. Adolf Berman, "Blok Antyfaszystowski (Ze wspomnień)," trans. Stefan Bergman, *Biuletyn Żydowskiego Instytutu Historycznego* 2–3 (1980): 79.

132. Yitzhak Zuckerman, *A Surplus of Memory: Chronicle of the Warsaw Ghetto Uprising*, trans. and ed. Barbara Harshav (Berkeley: University of California Press, 1993), 240, 463n.

133. Jakub Berman, Wspomnienia, 1949–1982, 325/33, AAN.

134. Adolf Berman, "Zagłada Getta Żydowskiego w Warszawie," 302/209, ŻIH; Basia Temkin-Bermanowa, *Dziennik z podziemia*, ed. Anka Grupińska and Paweł Szapiro (Warsaw: Wydawnictwo Książkowe Twój Styl and Żydowski Insytut Historyczny, 2000); Emanuel Ringelblum in his *Polish-Jewish Relations during the War* (Evanston: Northwestern University Press, 1992) describes Adolf and Basia Berman's lives on the Aryan Side.

135. Zuckerman, *A Surplus of Memory*, 348–349.

136. Władysław Bartoszewski, "75 lat w XX wieku: Pamiętnik mówiony (8)," *Więź* 40:9 (September 1997): 143.

137. Ibid., 141.
138. Władysław Bartoszewski, interview, Warsaw, 23 December 1997. Also see Bartoszewski, "75 lat w XX wieku: pamiętnik mówiony (8)," 141–142; and Władysław Bartoszewski to Ber Mark, 23 March 1958, 566, ŻIH.
139. Marek Edelman, personal interview, Łódź, 3 December 1997.
140. Lampe and Wasilewska to Molotov, 3 January 1943, Kuibyshev, in Wasilewska, *O wolną i demokratyczną*, 52–53.
141. Wasilewska, "Wspomnienia Wandy Wasilewskiej (1939–1944)," 383.
142. Broniewska, *Z notatnika korespondenta wojennego*, vol. I, 67–70.
143. Wasilewska, "Wspomnienia Wandy Wasilewskiej, (1939–1944)," 387.
144. Broniewska, *Z notatnika korespondenta wojennego*, vol. I, 67–70. *Wolna Polska* appeared as a weekly between 1 March 1943 and 15 August 1946. Wasilewska, "Wspomnienia Wandy Wasilewskiej," 380–382; Wasilewska, "Zadania Związku Patriotów Polskich w ZSRR," in *O wolną i demokratyczną*, 111–113.
145. Soviet sources have long since made clear that the Polish officers were murdered by the Soviets.
146. Wasilewska, "Przemówienie radiowe do Polaków w ZSRR, 28 April 1943," *O wolną i demokratyczną*, 54–55.
147. Wasilewska, "Wspomnienia Wandy Wasilewskiej (1939–1944)," 382.
148. Ibid., 387.
149. Stryjkowski, *To samo ale inaczej*, 348.
150. Stryjkowski, *Ocalony na wschodzie*, 161.
151. Stryjkowski, *To samo ale inaczej*, 352–356.
152. Ibid., 357–358.
153. Bolesław Gebert, "Tuwim w Nowym Jorku," in *WJT*, 223–227.
154. Erlich committed suicide in Soviet prison. See Gertrud Pickhan, "That Incredible History of the Polish Bund Written in a Soviet Prison," *Polin* 10 (1997): 247–272.
155. Grydzewski to Tuwim (in English), London, 22 March 1943. Mieczysław Grydzewski, *Listy do Tuwima i Lechonia (1940–1943)* ed. Janusz Stradecki (Warsaw: PIW, 1986), 71.
156. Julian Tuwim to Irena Tuwimowa, 14 April 1943, New York. Ibid., 72.
157. Tuwim to Stanisław Barski, White Plains, New York, 8 June 1944, in Piotr Chrzczonowicz, "Nieznana korespondencja Juliana Tuwima z działaczem robotniczym," *Archiwum Ruchu Robotniczego* I (1973): 341–347.
158. See Oskar Lange, "Conversations with Wanda Wasilewska," III-309/276, PAN; Wasilewska, "Wspomnienia Wandy Wasilewskiej (1939–1944)," 399–400; Teresa Toranska, *"Them": Stalin's Polish Puppets*, trans. Agnieszka Kolakowska (New York: Harper and Row, 1987), 233; Tuwim to Irena Lange, White Plains, 2 July 1944, III-309/280, PAN; Tuwim to Broniewska, New York, 6060, AAN.
159. Tuwim to Erenburg, New York, 24 July 1944, *LPP*, 269.
160. Tuwim to Lange, White Plains, 4 August 1944, III-309/280, PAN.

161. Tuwim to Słonimski, New York, 12 December 1944, *LPP*, 215–218.

162. Julian Tuwim, *My, Żydzi polscy* (Tel Aviv: Universum, 1944), 3.

163. Ibid., 3.

164. Ibid., 4.

165. Ibid., 5.

166. Ibid., 6.

167. Wasilewska, "Wspomnienia Wandy Wasilewskiej (1939–1944)," 371; Toranska, *"Them,"* 216–217; Stefan Jędrychowski, "O działalności ZPP," 3 June 1980, JI/2, ADH; Stefan Jędrychowski, rozmowa z Grzegorzem Sołtysiakiem, 17 February 1994, part II, K. 143, W/R 5, ADH.

168. Toranska, *"Them,"* 217.

169. Teresa Torańska, *Oni* (Warsaw: Agencja Omnipress, 1990), 147.

170. Włodzimierz Sokorski, *Wspomnienia* (Warsaw: Krajowa Agencja Wydawnicza, 1990), 98; Broniewska, *Z notatnika korespondenta wojennego*, vol. I, 187.

171. Broniewska, *Z notatnika korespondenta wojennego*, vol. I, 90.

172. Wasilewska to Stalin, April 1943, in *O wolną i demokratyczną*, 77–78.

173. Putrament, *Pół wieku: Wojna*, 164–165.

174. Stryjkowski, *To samo ale inaczej*, 349–351.

175. Broniewska, *Z notatnika korespondenta wojennego*, vol. I, 92–94.

176. Wasilewska initially believed that Andrzej Witos was his brother, the Polish Peasant Party leader Wincenty Witos, but seemed content even when the misunderstanding became clear. Stefan Jędrychowski, "Związek Patriotów Polskich," 25 May 1972, JI/2, ADH; Stryjkowski, *To samo ale inaczej*, 340; Toranska, *"Them,"* 237; Wasilewska, "Wspomnienia Wandy Wasilewskiej (1939–1944)," 384–395.

177. Wasilewska, "Wspomnienia Wandy Wasilewskiej (1939–1944)," 389.

178. Wasilewska, "Przemówienie na I zjeździe Związku Patriotów Polskich," Moscow, 9 June 1943, in Wasilewska, *O wolną i demokratyczną*, 61–63.

179. Ibid., 82–83.

180. Broniewska, *Z notatnika korespondenta wojennego*, vol. I, 144–145.

181. Stryjkowski, *Ocalony na wschodzie*, 163–164.

182. Wasilewska, "Wspomnienia Wandy Wasilewskiej (1939–1944)," 399.

183. Ibid., 426–427.

184. Broniewska, *Z notatnika korespondenta wojennego*, vol. I, 209–210; Gruppa Tovarishchei, "Alfred Lampe," *Pravda* 309 (17 December 1943), copy in 250/1, AAN.

185. Wat, *My Century*, 352.

186. Watowa, *Wszystko co najważniejsze*, 87–100.

187. Wat, *My Century*, 359–360.

188. Watowa, *Wszystko co najważniejsze*, 88.

189. Ibid., 103.

190. Wat, *My Century*, 113–114; Watowa, *Wszystko co najważniejsze*, 104.

191. Wat, *My Century*, 360.

192. Watowa, *Wszystko co najważniejsze*, 109–111.

193. Ibid., 112–113.

194. Ibid., 114–119.

195. Ibid., 115–116.

196. Aleksander Wat, "'. . . Jak upiór staję między wami i pytam o źródło złego' . . . ," *Na Antenie* 4:43 (6 November 1966): 1; Watowa, *Wszystko co najważniejsze*, 116–119.

197. Watowa, *Wszystko co najważniejsze*, 120.

198. Ibid., 120–124.

199. N. S. Chruszczow, "Fragmenty wspomnień N. S. Chruszczowa," *Zeszyty Historyczne* 132 (2000): 144.

200. Stefan Jędrychowski, "Na pierwszej linii spraw polskich," *WWW*, 174.

201. Jan Karaśkiewicz, "Wyrosła do rangi męża stanu," *WWW*, 140.

202. Wasilewska, "Wspomnienia Wandy Wasilewskiej (1939–1944)," 430.

203. Wasilewska to Stalin, August 1943, in *O wolną i demokratyczną*, 88–89.

204. Wasilewska, "Wspomnienia Wandy Wasilewskiej (1939–1944)," 388.

205. A Soviet news brief to this effect was published in *Pravda* on 14 March 1944. Wasilewska, "Wspomnienia Wandy Wasilewskiej (1939–1944)," 394–397.

206. Toranska, *"Them,"* 229.

207. Broniewska, *Z notatnika korespondenta wojennego*, vol. I, quotations at 136, 138, 159, respectively; Ewa Zawistowska, personal correspondence, Greece, 28 June 2001.

208. Broniewska, *Z notatnika korespondenta wojennego*, vol. II, 125. See also Jerzy Giedroyc, *Autobiografia na cztery ręce* (Warsaw: Czytelnik, 1994), 186.

209. Adam Ważyk, "Marsz I Korpusu," 245/6 AAN.

210. Broniewska, *Z notatnika korespondenta wojennego*, vol. I, 229.

211. Ibid., 256.

212. Ibid., vol. I, 44–45; vol. II, 78.

213. Stefan Jędrychowski, "O działalności ZPP," 3 June 1980, JI/2, ADH.

214. Stefan Jędrychowski, "Związek Patriotów Polskich," 25 May 1972, JI/2, ADH.

215. See Krystyna Kersten, *The Establishment of Communist Rule in Poland, 1943–1948*, trans. John Micgiel and Michael H. Bernhard (Berkeley: University of California Press, 1991).

216. Broniewska, *Z notatnika korespondenta wojennego*, vol. II, 151, 179, 180, 188.

217. Tuwim to Broniewska, New York, 6060, AAN.

218. Wasilewska, "Wspomnienia Wandy Wasilewskiej (1939–1944)," 404.

219. Chruszczow, "Fragmenty wspomnień," 158.

220. Wasilewska, "Wspomnienia Wandy Wasilewskiej (1939–1944)," 418.

221. Ibid., 418.

222. Iwaszkiewicz, *Notatki 1939–1945*, 113–114.

223. Edward Raczyński to Anthony Eden, 28 March 1944, Stanisław Mikołajczyk collection, 31, Hoover Institution Archive, Stanford.

224. "Most Urgent to President Raczkiewicz and Vicepremier Kwapiński,"

9 August 1944, Mikołajczyk collection, 34; Edward Raczyński to Sir Orme Sargent, 16 August 1944, Mikołajczyk collection, 32, both Hoover Institution Archive, Stanford. See also Stanisław Mikołajczyk, *The Rape of Poland* (New York: McGraw Hill, 1948); Stefan Korbonski, *Fighting Warsaw: The Story of the Polish Underground State, 1934–1945,* trans. F. B. Czarnomski (New York: Funk and Wagnalls, 1956); and Jan Ciechanowski, *The Warsaw Rising of 1944* (Cambridge: Cambridge University Press, 1974). For a colorful account of the uprising, see Norman Davies, *Rising '44* (London: Macmillan, 2003).

225. Wasilewska, "Wspomnienia Wandy Wasilewskiej (1939–1944)," 412–414.

226. Toranska, *"Them,"* 247.

227. Broniewska, *Z notatnika korespondenta wojennego,* vol. II, 201.

228. Iwaszkiewicz, *Notatki 1939–1945,* 114.

229. Broniewski, "Warszawa," in Lichodziejewska, *Broniewski bez cenzury,* 53.

230. Broniewska, *Z notatnika korespondenta wojennego,* vol. II, 260, 262.

231. Broniewski to Anka Broniewska, 15 March 1945, quoted in Lichodziejewska, *Broniewski bez cenzury,* 56.

232. Sławomir Kędzierski, personal correspondence, Warsaw, 7 December 2000.

233. Wasilewska, "Refleksje z pobytu w wyzwolonej Warszawie," *O wolną i demokratyczną,* 152–154.

234. Wasilewska, "Wspomnienia Wandy Wasilewskiej (1939–1944)," 419.

CHAPTER 8. STALINISM AMIDST WARSAW'S RUINS

Epigraph: Adam Ważyk, "Pozycja artysty (Uwagi ogólne)," *Odrodzenie* 8–9 (12 November 1944): 6–7.

1. Grzegorz Jaszuński, "Julian Tuwim w maju wyjeżdża do Polski," New York, March 1945, in Julian Tuwim, *Rozmowy z Tuwimem,* ed. Tadeusz Januszewski (Warsaw: Wydawnictwo Naukowe Semper, 1994), 75–77.

2. Quoted in Krzysztof Teodor Toeplitz, "Adam Ważyk—poeta i historia," *Gazeta Wyborcza* 45 (22 February 2002).

3. Adam Ważyk, "Sketch for a Memoir," in *Postwar Polish Poetry,* ed. Czeslaw Milosz (Berkeley: University of California Press, 1983), 54. From Ważyk's "Szkic pamiętnika."

4. Adam Ważyk, "Troska o człowieka," *Kuźnica* 3 (14 January 1946).

5. Julian Tuwim, "Modlitwa," *Odrodzenie* 1 (3 September 1944): 1; Jerzy Putrament, *Pół Wieku: Wojna* (Warsaw: Czytelnik, 1964), 277–292; Jacek Natanson, *Tygodnik "Odrodzenie" (1944–1950)* (Warsaw: Państwowe Wydawnictwo Naukowe, 1987), 18–19.

6. Agnieszka Koecher-Hensel, "Władysław Daszewski—Prowokator czy ofiara sowieckiej prowokacji?" *Pamiętnik Teatralny* 46:1–4 (1997): 269.

7. Ibid., 269.

8. See Jan Tomasz Gross, *Upiorna Dekada: Trzy eseje o stereotypach na temat Żydów, Polaków, Niemców i komunistów, 1939–1948* (Cracow: TAiWPN Universitas, 1998), 93–113.

9. See George H. Hodos, *Show Trials: Stalinist Purges in Eastern Europe,*

1948–1954 (New York: Praeger, 1987), 135–154; Andrzej Paczkowski, "Poland, The Enemy Nation," in Stéphane Courtois et al., *The Black Book of Communism: Crimes, Terror, Repression,* trans. Jonathan Murphy and Mark Kramer (Cambridge: Harvard University Press, 1999), 363–393.

10. Krystyna Domańska to Broniewski, 12 April 1945, "Krystyna Domańska," MB.

11. Broniewski to Stefania Zahorska and Adam Pragier, 18 August 1944 [sic—1945]. Quoted in Feliksa Lichodziejewska, *Broniewski bez cenzury: 1939–1945* (Warsaw: Wydawnictwo Społeczne KOS, 1992), 60.

12. Tuwim to Broniewski, 1945, *LPP,* 114.

13. Broniewski to Tuwim, Tel Aviv, 8 October 1945, "do Tuwima," MB.

14. Broniewski to Tuwim, Tel Aviv, 8 October 1945, "do Tuwima," MB.

15. Tuwim to Zarębińska-Broniewska, New York, 16 November 1945, *LPP,* 115–116. The "Andersonian weekly" was *Tygodnik Polski,* published by Jan Lechoń, Kazimierz Wierzyński, and Józef Wittlin between 1943 and 1947.

16. Tuwim to Zarębińska, New York, 16 November 1945, *LPP,* 115–116.

17. Zarębińska and Broniewski to Tuwim, Zakopane, 10 February 1946, "do Tuwima," MB.

18. Lucjan Marek, "O Władysławie Broniewskim," 14 March 1962, 731, AAN.

19. Zarębińska and Broniewski to Tuwim, Zakopane, 10 February 1946, "do Tuwima," MB.

20. Władysław Broniewski, "Żydom polskim," *Odrodzenie* 14 (4 March 1945): 2.

21. Appenszlak to Broniewski, Palestine, 11 December 1946, "z Palestyny," MB. Paulina Appenszlak (Appenszlakowa) was the editor of the Warsaw-based, Polish-language Jewish women's weekly newspaper *Ewa: Tygodnik* (1928–33); an advocate of contraception and women's reproductive rights; and the wife of Jakub Appenszlak, one of the editors of *Nasz Przegląd.* See Ewa Plach, "Feminism and Nationalism on the Pages of *Ewa: Tygodnik,* 1928 to 1933," *Polin* 18 (2005).

22. Appenszlak to Broniewski, Palestine, 11 December 1946, "z Palestyny," MB.

23. Appenszlak to Broniewski, Palestine, 2 April 1946, "z Palestyny," MB.

24. Appenszlak to Broniewski, Palestine, 20 May 1946, "z Palestyny," MB.

25. Appenszlak to Broniewski, Palestine, 5 July 1946, "z Palestyny," MB.

26. Wygodzki to Broniewski, 7 November 1945, "różne," MB.

27. Gadomski to Broniewski, Palestine, 12 March 1946, "z Palestyny," MB.

28. Appenszlak to Broniewski, Palestine, 7 September 1946, "z Palestyny," MB; Appenszlak to Broniewski, Palestine, 25 January 1947, "z Palestyny," MB.

29. Stern to Wat, 6 January 1948, A-4, AWPB.

30. Stern to Borejsza, Tel Aviv, 14 February 1948. Quoted in Barbara Fijałkowska, *Borejsza i Różański: Przyczynek do dziejów stalinizmu w Polsce* (Olsztyn: Wyższa Szkoła Pedagogiczna, 1995), 163.

31. Stern was suspected of Jewish nationalist activity; extant informers' reports on Stern date from 1951. See Stern's file: 01178/1319, IPN.

32. Tuwim to Wittlin, Toronto, 31 July 1945, *LPP,* 255–257.

33. Tuwim to Iwaszkiewicz, New York, 14 September 1945, *LPP*, 37–41.
34. Tuwim to Borejsza, 12 December 1945, *LPP*, 45–46.
35. Kruczkowski's correspondence to his wife during his years as a prisoner of war survives at ML.
36. Tuwim to Kruczkowski, New York, 9 February 1946, 1067/7, ML.
37. Tuwim to Słonimski, New York, 4 February 1946, *LPP*, 227–228.
38. Tuwim to Słonimski, New York, 17 January 1946, *LPP*, 222–225.
39. *LPP*, 232.
40. Tuwim, *Rozmowy z Tuwimem*, 79–81; from Z. S., "Powrót do kraju jest największym szczęściem," *Rzeczpospolita* 158 (9 June 1946).
41. Iwaszkiewicz, "Trzydzieści pięć lat," in *WJT*, 453.
42. Stanislaw Baranczak, "Skamander after Skamander: The Postwar Path of the Prewar Polish Pleiade," *Cross Currents* 9 (1990): 340.
43. Lucyna Tychowa [daughter of Jakub Berman], personal interview, 25 August 2003, Warsaw.
44. *LPP*, 266–267.
45. Tuwim, *Rozmowy z Tuwimem*, 85–89; from Maria Szczepańska, "'Najpiękniejsza ze wszystkich miast jest Warszawa . . .' Julian Tuwim o swej pracy pisarskiej i teatralnej," *Dziennik Literacki* 3 (14–21 November 1947).
46. Tuwim to Leopold Staff, Warsaw, 31 August 1947, *LPP*, 282.
47. Tuwim, *Rozmowy z Tuwimem*, 85–89.
48. Ibid., 85–89.
49. Teresa Torańska, *Oni* (Warsaw: Agencja Omnipress, 1990), 49–50. Jakub Berman remembered the year as having been 1948, but it must have been 1949, as only then was Molotov's wife purged.
50. Teresa Toranska, *"Them": Stalin's Polish Puppets*, trans. Agnieszka Kolakowska (New York: Harper and Row, 1987), 269–270; see also Jakub Berman, "Zagadnienie pracy partyjnej wśród inteligencji (referat wygłoszony na konferencji inteligencji PPR w Bydgoszczy 2 marca br.)," *Nowe Drogi* 2 (March 1947).
51. N. S. Chruszczow, "Fragmenty wspomnień N. S. Chruszczowa," *Zeszyty Historyczne* 132 (2000): 172.
52. Torańska, *Oni*, 135.
53. T. V. Volokitina et al., eds., *Sovetskii faktor v vostochnoi Evrope 1944–1953*, vol. II: *Dokumenty* (Moscow: ROSSPEN, 2002), 198. See also V. Z. Lebedev to A. Y. Vyshinskii, Warsaw, 10 July 1949 in T. V. Volokitina et al., eds, *Vostochnaia Evropa v dokumentakh rossiiskikh arkhivov 1944–1953*, vol. II (Moscow: Sibirskii khronograf, 1998), 172–178.
54. Jakub Berman, Wspomnienia, 1979–1982, 325/33, AAN; Torańska, *Oni*, 146–147. On the Slánský trial: Jiří Pelikán, ed., *The Czechoslovak Political Trials, 1950–1954: The Suppressed Report of the Dubček Government's Commission of Inquiry* (London: Macdonald, 1970); and Heda Margolius Kovály, *Under a Cruel Star: A Life in Prague, 1941–1968*, trans. Franci and Helen Epstein (Cambridge: Plunkett Lake Press, 1986).

55. Sprawozdanie z obchodu 5-ej rocznicy powstania w Gehtcie [sic] Warszaw-skim, 29 April 1948, 295/IX-407, AAN; CKŻP Prezydium, Protocol 56, 10 June 1948, 303/11, ŻIH; CKŻP Prezydium Protokol 57, 16 June 1948, 303/11, ŻIH, Warsaw; Dyskusja, 25 October 1948, 295/IX-407, AAN. For more detail see Marci Shore, "Język, Pamięć i Rewolucyjna Awangarda: Kształtowanie Historii Powstania w Getcie Warszawskim, 1944–1950," *Biuletyn Żydowskiego Instytutu Historycznego* 188:4 (December 1998): 44–61.

56. CKŻP Prezydium Protokół 21, 13 April 1949, 303/16, ŻIH.

57. Władysław Bartoszewski, interview, Warsaw, 22 December 1997; see also Torańska, *Oni*, 143, 328.

58. Quoted in Fijałkowska, *Borejsza i Różański*, 184–185.

59. Ibid., 189.

60. Jan Kott, *Still Alive: An Autobiographical Essay*, trans. Jadwiga Kosicka (New Haven: Yale University Press, 1994), 172–173.

61. Fijałkowska, *Borejsza i Różański*, 112, 152–153.

62. *LPP*, 376; Natanson, *Tygodnik "Odrodzenie" (1944–1950)*, 25.

63. Kott, *Still Alive*, 174; Toranska, *"Them,"* 144; Fijałkowska, *Borejsza i Różański*, 114, 125.

64. Fijałkowska, *Borejsza i Różański*, 118–133.

65. The reference here is to Café Ujazdowska, ironically located at the corner of the street then named Aleje Stalina (Stalin Avenue, formerly Aleje Ujazdow-skie) and Plac Trzech Krzyży (The Square of the Three Crosses); quoted ibid., 131–132n. See the dissertation by Mikołaj Kunicki, "The Polish Crusader: The Life and Politics of Bolesław Piasecki, 1915–1979" (Stanford University, 2004).

66. Jerzy Borejsza, "Rewolucja łagodna," *Odrodzenie* 10–12 (15 January 1945): 1.

67. Quoted in Fijałkowska, *Borejsza i Różański*, 122.

68. Natanson, *Tygodnik "Odrodzenie" (1944–1950)*, 142.

69. Adam Ważyk, quoted ibid., 148.

70. Fijałkowska, *Borejsza i Różański*, 141.

71. Quoted ibid., 142.

72. Quoted in Jakub Berman, "Wokół Kongresu Intelektualistów we Wrocławiu w obronie pokoju (25–28 sierpnia 1948), Warsaw, June 1978, 325/32, AAN. Iwaszkiewicz's recollections of the Wrocław congress were published in *Odra* (February 1978).

73. Julian Tuwim, "Nadzieje i życzenia," *Odrodzenie* 35 (29 August 1948): 3.

74. Toranska, *"Them,"* 290–291.

75. Fijałkowska, *Borejsza i Różański*, 144. Fadeev's telegram: Tuwim to Broniew-ska, New York, 6060, AAN.

76. Quoted ibid., 144–145. On Borejsza during this period, see also Czesław Miłosz, *abecadło miłosza* (Cracow: Wydawnictwo Literackie, 1997), 69–70.

77. Toranska, *"Them,"* 290–291; Jan Kott, *Still Alive*, 174; Jakub Berman, "Wokół Kongresu Intelektualistów we Wrocławiu w obronie pokoju (25–28 sierpnia 1948)," Warsaw, June 1978, 325/32, AAN.

78. Quoted in Jakub Berman, "Wokół Kongresu Intelektualistów we Wrocławiu w obronie pokoju (25–28 sierpnia 1948)," Warsaw, June 1978, 325/32, AAN.

79. Ola Watowa, *Wszystko co najważniejsze* (Warsaw: Czytelnik, 1990), 153.

80. Wat to Iwaszkiewicz, Alma-Ata, 18 January 1945, ML.

81. Ważyk, "Troska o człowieka"; Watowa, *Wszystko co najważniejsze*, 126.

82. Watowa, *Wszystko co najważniejsze*, 129.

83. Ibid., 132.

84. Aleksander Wat, *Dziennik bez samogłosek*, ed. Krzysztof Rutkowski (London: Polonia, 1986), 162.

85. Juliusz Starzyński to Wat, 20 August 1948, A-5, AWPB.

86. Watowa, *Wszystko co najważniejsze*, 135–136.

87. Ibid., 138; Wat to Borejsza, 12 March 1947, quoted in Fijałkowska, *Borejsza i Różański*, 160; Natanson, *Tygodnik "Odrodzenie" (1944–1950)*, 135–136; Iwaszkiewicz to Wat, 13 August 1947, Stawisko, A-86, AWPB.

88. Aleksander Wat, "Przemówienie Aleksandra Wata na zjeździe P.E.N. Clubów," *Odrodzenie* 23 (8 June 1947): 1.

89. Aleksander Wat, *My Century: The Odyssey of a Polish Intellectual*, trans. Richard Lourie (New York: Norton, 1988), 120–121; Koecher-Hensel, "Władysław Daszewski," 241.

90. Watowa, *Wszystko co najważniejsze*, 36–38.

91. See *Odrodzenie* 56–57 (23–30 December 1945): 16.

92. Władysław Broniewski, "Bania z Poezją," ibid., 1 (6 January 1946): 7.

93. See Wiesław Paweł Szymański, *"Odrodzenie" i "Twórczość" w Krakowie (1945–1950)* (Wrocław: Zakład Narodowy imienia Ossolińskich Wydawnictwo PAN, 1981), 6–7.

94. Maja Berezowska, "Na 'górce' w Ziemiańskiej," *Odrodzenie* 20 (18 May 1947): 8. One of the owners of the interwar Café Ziemiańska once began an advertising campaign announcing that one in every so many doughnuts (*pączki*) would contain a gold coin.

95. Adam Ważyk, "Pozycja artysty (Uwagi ogólne)," ibid., 8–9 (12 November 1944): 6–7.

96. Quoted in Grzegorz Wołowiec, *Nowocześni w PRL: Przyboś i Sandauer* (Wrocław: Wrocławska Drukarnia Naukowa PAN, 1999), 34. See also the response by Zbigniew Bieńkowski, "Pierwszy ogólnopolski zjazd literatów" in *Odrodzenie* 44 (1945).

97. Natanson, *Tygodnik "Odrodzenie" (1944–1950)*, 114–115, 213; see also Adam Ważyk, "Kilka słów o metodzie," *Kuźnica* 4:39 (26 September 1948): 1; Adam Ważyk, "Niedobry Klimat," ibid., 3:42 (20 October 1947): 2.

98. Kott, *Still Alive*, 186.

99. Adam Ważyk, "U źródeł nowatorstwa w poezji," *Kuźnica* 1:12 (18 November 1945): 2–3.

100. Adam Ważyk, "O właściwe stanowisko," ibid., 5:10 (12 March 1950): 1.

101. Paweł Hertz, Jan Kott, Andrzej Stawar, Ryszard Matuszewski, and Adam Ważyk, "Rozmowy Kuźnicy," ibid., 3:1 (7 January 1947): 6–7.

102. See Wołowiec, *Nowocześni w PRL,* 39–60.

103. Emphasis in original. Julian Przyboś, "Na linii poetyckiej," *Odrodzenie* 56–57 (23–30 December 1945): 14.

104. Julian Przyboś, "Upowszechnienie czego?" ibid., 26 (30 June 1946): 1–2.

105. Andrei Zhdanov, *Zhdanov's Speech on the Journals Zvezda and Leningrad,* trans. Felicity Ashbee and Irina Tidmarsh (Royal Oak: Strathcona Publishing, 1978).

106. Wołowiec, *Nowocześni w PRL,* 65–70; Natanson, *Tygodnik "Odrodzenie" (1944–1950),* 134.

107. Tadeusz Borowski, "Studium Literackie w Nieborowie," *Po Prostu* 2 (1–15 February 1948): 6; Kott, *Still Alive,* 191.

108. Czesław Miłosz, *Zaraz po wojnie: Korespondencja z pisarzami 1945–1950* (Cracow: Wydawnictwo Znak, 1998), 387.

109. Quoted in Borowski, "Studium Literackie w Nieborowie," 6; see also Aleksander Wat, "Antyzoil albo rekolekcje na zakończenie roku," *Kuźnica* 4:6 (8 Feburary 1948) and 4:7 (15 February 1948): 3–5, 9.

110. Zbigniew Żabicki, *"Kuźnica" i jej program literacki* (Cracow: Wydawnictwo Literackie, 1966), 39.

111. Jacek Trznadel (interview with Zbigniew Herbert), *Hańba domowa* (Warsaw: Agencja Wydawnicza Morex, 1997), 203.

112. Andrzej Żdanow, "Na pierwszej linii frontu ideologicznego (wyjątki z przemówień)," *Odrodzenie* 38 (19 September 1948): 1.

113. Jerzy Borejsza, "Na rogatkach kultury. Gościniec i pył przydrożny," *Odrodzenie* 48 (28 November 1948). Quoted in Natanson, *Tygodnik "Odrodzenie" (1944–1950),* 180.

114. Broniewski, "O zamówieniu społecznym i socrealiźmie," in *Władysław Broniewski,* ed. Feliksa Lichodziejewska (Warsaw: Państwowe Zakłady Wydawnictw Szkolnych, 1966), 160–161.

115. "Rezolucja Zjazdu Literatów w Szczecinie," *Odrodzenie* 5 (30 January 1949): 1. On socialist realism see also Katerina Clark, *The Soviet Novel: History as Ritual* (Chicago: University of Chicago Press, 1981).

116. See Trznadel, *Hańba domowa,* 285; Miłosz, *Zaraz po wojnie,* 370; Wołowiec, *Nowocześni w PRL,* 21; Artur Sandauer, *O sytuacji pisarza polskiego pochodzenia żydowskiego w XX wieku* (Warsaw: Czytelnik, 1982), 60–61.

117. Ważyk quoted in Natanson, *Tygodnik "Odrodzenie" (1944–1950),* 148.

118. Fijałkowska, *Borejsza i Różański,* 151.

119. Władysław Broniewski, "Słowo o Stalinie," *Odrodzenie* 51–52 (21 December 1949): 3; Władysław Broniewski, *Władysław Broniewski: Poezje zebrane,* vol. III (1946–1962), ed. Feliksa Lichodziejewska (Płock-Toruń: Algo, 1997), 50–56.

120. Jakub Berman, "Rola i zadania pisarza socjalistycznego," *Odrodzenie* 9 (26 February 1950): 1–2.

121. "Uwagi (na marginesie Zjazdu Literatów) (dla tow. Bermana)," 18 July 1950, 325/13, AAN.

122. Wat, "Zeszyt ostatni," 4, AWPB.

123. Adam Ważyk, "Perspektywy rozwojowe literatury polskiej (referat wygłoszony na V Zjeździe Związku Literatów Polskich)," *Nowa Kultura* 14 (2 July 1950): 1.

124. Adam Ważyk, "Referat na Zjazd Literatów," 325/13, AAN. See also "Uwagi (na marginesie Zjazdu Literatów) (dla tow. Bermana)," 18 July 1950, 325/13, AAN.

125. Quoted in Andrzej Roman, *Paranoja: Zapis Choroby* (Warsaw: Editions Spotkania, 1989), 95–96.

126. Wiktor Woroszylski, "Batalia o Majakowskiego," *Odrodzenie* 5 (29 January 1950): 6–7.

127. Jerzy Borejsza, "O niektórych zagadnieniach kultury socjalistycznej i o niektórych błędach," *Odrodzenie* 11–12 (19 March 1950): 3–5.

128. Tuwim to Mieczyław Jastrun, 30 March 1950, *LPP*, 421–422.

129. Trznadel (interview with Woroszylski), *Hańba domowa*, 121.

130. Watowa, *Wszystko co najważniejsze*, 138–139.

131. Stanisław Wygodzki, "Będzin!" in *WJT*, 170–171.

132. Julian Tuwim, "Matka," *Odrodzenie* 50 (11 December 1949): 1.

133. Franciszek Strojowski, "Poeta i dzieci," *WJT*, 296–307.

134. Julian Tuwim, "Do narodu radzieckiego," *Wiersze 2*, ed. Alina Kowalczykowa (Warsaw: Czytelnik, 1986), 344.

135. Julian Tuwim, "Z notesu," *Odrodzenie* 48 (27 November 1949): 4.

136. Julian Tuwim, "Z notesu amerykańskiego," ibid., 13 (30 March 1947): 4.

137. *LPP*, 405–407; from Julian Tuwim, "List do K. I. Gałczyńskiego," *Przekrój* 135 (9 November 1947): 11. Gałczyński's "Pochwalone niech będą ptaki" was published in *Przekrój* 132.

138. Tuwim to Bierut, 30 August 1946, in Piotr Chrzczonowicz, "Nieznany list Juliana Tuwima do Bolesława Bieruta," *Acta Universitatis Wratislaviensis* 2011 (1998): 123–129. Wat recalled that despite Tuwim's success, the security apparatus told him in the future he should not interfere in these matters. Five years later, however, in 1951, Tuwim did indeed interfere again on behalf of the same Polish poet, now appealing for Kozarzewski's early release. This time, however, Tuwim appealed not to Bierut but rather to Jacek Różański, writing that, although he saw Kozarzewski as an enemy, he could not deny Magdalena Kozarzewska's plea in the name of his late mother and live with his conscience. Wat, *Mój wiek: Pamiętnik mówiony*, 2 vols. (Warsaw: Czytelnik, 1998), vol. I, 223; Fijałkowska, *Borejsza i Różański*, 189–190.

139. Tuwim to Pablo Neruda, 1 July 1949, 1067/7, ML.

140. Wanda Wasilewska, *O wolną i demokratyczną: Wybór artykulów, przemówień i listów*, ed. Zbigniew Kumoś et al. (Warsaw: Wojskowy Instytut Historyczny im. Wandy Wasilewskiej, 1985), 157–160; from *Wolna Polska* 31 (15 August 1946).

141. Bierut to Wasilewska, 9 October 1946, Warsaw, 73/1/348, TsDAMLM.

142. Chruszczow, "Fragmenty wspomnień," 119.

143. Konstantin Dankevich, *Bohdan Khmelnytsky: Ukrainian Opera in Four Acts* (n.p.: Musicart International, 1964). Daniel Shore helped with this reference.

144. John Steinbeck, *A Russian Journal* (New York: Penguin Books, 1999), 85. Gabriella Safran pointed me to this source.

145. "Spis członków Koła Literatów PPR," 257/5, AAN; Natanson, *Tygodnik "Odrodzenie" (1944–1950)*, 130.

146. Lucjan Rudnicki et al., "Ankieta [J. Broniewskiej]," 31 March 1950, 730, AAN.

147. Ewa Zawistowska, personal correspondence, Greece, 6 January 2001.

148. See *Kobieta* 1 (October 1947) to 105–106 (December 1949).

149. Wasilewska to Broniewska, 24 July 1948, quoted in *Wanda Wasilewska*, ed. Helena Zatorska (Warsaw: Wydawnictwa Szkolne i Pedagogiczne, 1976), 180.

150. "W 70 rocznicę urodzin wodza obozu pokoju i postępu—Józefa Stalina," *Kobieta* 105–106 (December 1949).

151. Wasilewska to Broniewska, Kiev 8 January 1950, quoted in Zatorska, ed., *Wanda Wasilewska*, 180–181.

152. Julian Stryjkowski, *Wielki strach; To samo, ale inaczej* (Warsaw: Czytelnik, 1990), 359.

153. Wasilewska to Broniewska, 15 June 1947. Copy provided by Ewa Zawistowska.

154. Wasilewska to Broniewska, 24 July 1948, quoted in Zatorska, *Wanda Wasilewska*, 181.

155. Wasilewska to Broniewska, 28 September 1948. Cited in Ewa Zawistowska, personal correspondence, Greece, 15 December 2000; edited version in Zatorska, *Wanda Wasilewska*, 181–182. "Macia-heroina" is a reference to the Soviet term "mat'-geroinia"—an award and special status conferred upon Soviet women who gave birth to a large number of children.

156. Wasilewska to Broniewska, 28 September 1948, quoted in Zatorska, ed., *Wanda Wasilewska*, 182–183.

157. *WAS*, 68–70.

158. Baranczak, "Skamander after Skamander," 346.

159. Tuwim to Słonimski, Anin, 12 August 1949, *LPP*, 234–236.

160. Tuwim to Słonimski, Anin, 16 May 1950, *LPP*, 237–239.

161. Antoni Słonimski, "Odprawa," *Krytyka* 13/14 (1983): 242–243; from *Trybuna Ludu* (4 November 1951).

162. Czesław Miłosz, "Do Antoniego Słonimskiego," ibid., pp. 244–252; from *Kultura* 12 (1951).

163. Wat, *Dziennik bez samogłosek*, 501.

164. Adam Ważyk, "Przeczytałem *Mój wiek*," *Puls* 34 (1987): 53–54; Wat, *Dziennik bez samogłosek*, 15.

165. Wat, *My Century*, 59–60.

166. Ibid., 59.

167. Aleksander Wat, "Imagerie D'Épinal," *Poezje*, ed. Anna Micińska and Jan

Zieliński (Warsaw: Czytelnik, 1997), 169. The poem is dated by the editors 1949, although this seems unlikely given the dedication to Slánský and Rajk.

168. Wat, *Mój wiek*, vol. I, 247, 260.

169. Feliksa Lichodziejewska, "Broniewski i jego archiwum," in *To ja—dąb: Wspomnienia i eseje o Władysławie Broniewskim*, ed. Stanisław Witold Balicki (Warsaw: PIW, 1978), 439.

170. Ibid., 442.

171. Watowa, *Wszystko co najważniejsze*, 143.

172. Wat, *Mój wiek*, vol. I, 69–70.

173. Irena Krzywicka, *Wyznania gorszycielki* (Warsaw: Czytelnik, 1998), 408.

174. "Streszczenie sprawy kryptonim 'Literaci,'" Warsaw, 11 February 1953, 01224/1426, IPN, Warsaw; "Notatka służbowa dot. sprawy Janusa Edwarda i Jabłonowskiego Romana-Jana krypt. 'Literaci,'" Warsaw, 10 April 1954; 0298/200/t-1, IPN.

175. Quoted in Kott, *Still Alive*, 235.

176. Watowa, *Wszystko co najważniejsze*, 140.

177. "Streszczenie sprawy kryptonim 'Literaci,'" Warsaw, 11 February 1953, 01224/1426, IPN. In Hungary during the war, Stawar was involved in publishing the Polish weekly newspaper *Tygodnik Polski;* following the defeat of the Nazis in Hungary, Stawar helped to organize the Tymczasowy Komitet Polski (The Polish Temporary Committee).

178. Wat, *My Century*, 47.

179. Wygodzki to Tadeusz Borowski, Gauting, 31 December 1945, in Tadeusz Drewnowski, ed., *Niedyskrecje pocztowe: Korespondencja Tadeusza Borowskiego* (Warsaw: Prószyński i S-ka, 2001), 60.

180. Watowa, *Wszystko co najważniejsze*, 143–144. See Tadeusz Borowski, *This Way to the Gas, Ladies and Gentlemen*, trans. Barbara Vedder (New York: Penguin, 1992).

181. Wat, *My Century*, 47.

182. Watowa, *Wszystko co najważniejsze*, 145–146.

183. Wat, *Dziennik bez samogłosek*, 16. On the reactions of Tuwim, Ważyk, and Stryjkowski to Stalin's death see Michał Zarzycki, "Po Stalinie: To nie wiatr, to szloch," *Karta* 37 (2003): 54–87.

184. Watowa, *Wszystko co najważniejsze*, 146–147.

185. Fijałkowska, *Borejsza i Różański*, 145.

186. Quoted ibid., 146. See the protocol from this Plenum KC PPR 31 August– 3 September 1948 in *Nowe Drogi* 11 (1948).

187. Natanson, *Tygodnik "Odrodzenie" (1944–1950)*, 143; Kott, *Still Alive*, 176; Fijałkowska, *Borejsza i Różański*, 124.

188. Roman Bratny quoted in Natanson, *Tygodnik "Odrodzenie" (1944–1950)*, 149.

189. Jerzy Borejsza to Bolesław Bierut, 4 April 1950, Warsaw. Józef Stępień, ed., *Listy do Pierwszych Sekretarzy KC PZPR (1944–1970)* (Warsaw: Wydawnictwo FAKT, 1994), 68–69.

190. Antoni Słonimski, *Alfabet wspomnień* (Warsaw: PIW, 1975), 21–22.

191. Jerzy Putrament, *Pół wieku: Literaci* (Warsaw: Czytelnik, 1970), 106.

192. Julian Tuwim, "Do Jerzego Borejszy," in Kowalczykowa, *Wiersze 2*, 340–341.

193. Fijałkowska, *Borejsza i Różański*, 97.

194. Unsigned to Tuwim, Wałbrzych, 30 July 1946, P-70/110, AABB.

195. See Adolf Berman et al. to Centralny Komitet PZPR, 31 January 1950, 333/8, ŻIH; published in *Midrasz* 1 (May 1997): 37. Adolf Berman's notes for the original letter in P-70/11, AABB.

196. E. Rostal, "List otwarty do Dra A. Bermana i Geni Levi, członków C.K. 'MAPAM' w Izraelu," *Nowiny Izraelskie* 11 (30 November 1952): 3; copy in P-70/3, AABB.

197. Chaim Finkelstein to Adolf Berman, New York, 26 May 1954, P-70/58, AABB.

198. Kott, *Still Alive*, 185.

199. Rudnicki to Adolf Berman, 16 May 1951, P-70/57, AABB.

200. Rudnicki to Adolf and Basia Berman, Warsaw, 4 March [1953?], P-70/57, AABB.

201. Tuwim to Adolf Berman, Warsaw, 19 January 1952, P-70/57, AABB.

202. Anatol Stern, "Z niedomkniętej nocy," in *WJT*, 116; also see Putrament, *Pół wieku: Literaci*, 215–216; Julian Tuwim, "Eugeniusz Oniegin w przekładzie Adama Ważyka: Materiały do recenzji i dyskusji," in *Pisarze polscy o sztuce przekładu 1440–1974: Antologia*, ed. Edward Balcerzan (Poznań: Wydawnictwo Poznańskie, 1977), 302–377.

203. Tuwim to Leopold Staff, Warsaw, 21 April 1948, *LPP*, 284.

204. *LPP*, 266–267.

205. See Roman Loth, introduction to Mieczysław Grydzewski and Jarosław Iwaszkiewicz, *Listy 1922–1967*, ed. Małgorzata Bojanowska (Warsaw: Czytelnik, 1979), 5–10.

206. Iwaszkiewicz to Grydzewski, Paris, 4 July 1947. Ibid., 55–57.

207. Grydzewski to Iwaszkiewicz, London, 2 August 1947. Ibid., 59.

208. Iwaszkiewicz to Grydzewski, Stawisko, 13 August 1947. Ibid., 61.

209. Iwaszkiewicz to Grydzewski, Stawisko, 14 November 1947. Ibid., 67–68.

210. Grydzewski to Iwaszkiewicz, London, 19 November 1947. Ibid., 70.

211. Iwaszkiewicz to Grydzewski, Stawisko, 2 February 1950. Ibid., 71.

212. Grydzewski to Iwaszkiewicz, 8 November 1950. Ibid., 72.

213. Słonimski, *Alfabet wspomnień*, 120.

214. Wat, *Mój wiek*, vol. II, 209.

215. *WAS*, 109.

216. Quoted in Wanda Nowakowska, "Lechoń i Tuwim—dzieje przyjaźni," *Prace Polonistyczne* 51 (1996): 242.

217. Quoted in *LPP*, 61–62.

218. Lechoń to Stanisław Baliński, Margaretville, USA, 31 July 1952. Tadeusz Januszewski, ed., "Listy Jana Lechonia do Stanisława Balińskiego," *Kwartalnik Literacki* 35:3 (1998): 223.

219. *WAS*, 110–111.

220. Tuwim to Aleksander and Ola Wat [1952], B-179, AWPB.

221. Wat, *Dziennik bez samogłosek*, 35.

222. Iwaszkiewicz, "Trzydzieści pięć lat," *WJT*, 457.

223. Quoted in Baranczak, "Skamander after Skamander," 340.

224. Leon Kruczkowski, Przemówienie z okazji śmierci Juliana Tuwima, 1954, 1040, ML.

225. 28 December 1953, quoted in Nowakowska, "Lechoń i Tuwim—dzieje przyjaźni," 244.

CHAPTER 9. ICE MELTING

Epigraph: Antoni Słonimski, "Nie wołaj mnie," *Lyriki najpiękniejsze*, ed. Aleksander Madyda (Toruń: Algo, 1999), 45.

1. "Protokół Nr. 252 posiedzenia Sekretariatu Biura Organizacyjnego KC w dniu 24 lipca 1953 r.," in *Centrum władzy: Protokoły posiedzeń kierownictwa PZPR wybór z lata 1949–1970*, ed. Antoni Dudek et al. (Warsaw: Instytut Studiów Politycznych PAN, 2000), 124.

2. Artur Starewicz, relacja, part 4, W-R/26, ADH.

3. Teresa Torańska, *Oni* (Warsaw: Agencja Omnipress, 1990), 166.

4. Ibid., 170. "Protokół Nr. 82 posiedzenia Biura Politycznego w dniach 12 i 13 marca 1956 r." in Dudek et al., *Centrum władzy*, 152.

5. Adam Ważyk, "Poemat dla dorosłych," in *Poeta pamięta: antologia poezji świadectwa i sprzeciwu 1944–1984*, ed. Stanisław Baranczak (London: Puls, 1984), 66–72; from *Nowa Kultura* 6:34 (21 August 1955): 1–2.

6. Adam Ważyk, "Krytyka Poematu dla dorosłych," in *Wiersze i poematy* (Warsaw: PIW, 1957), 153–156.

7. Paweł Hoffman quoted by Toeplitz, "Adam Ważyk—poeta i historia." See also Czeslaw Milosz, "Poland: Voices of Disillusion," *Problems of Communism* 5:3 (May–June 1956): 24–30.

8. Torańska, *Oni*, 126.

9. Leon Kruczkowski, "O ideowe oblicze naszej prasy literackiej," *Trybuna Ludu* 315 (13 November 1955): 1038, ML.

10. Aleksander Wat, *Dziennik bez samogłosek*, ed. Krzysztof Rutkowski (London: Polonia, 1986), 180–181.

11. Mieczysław Jastrun, *Dziennik: Wybór z lat 1955–1960* (London: PULS, 1990), 30.

12. Jan Kott, *Still Alive: An Autobiographical Essay*, trans. Jadwiga Kosicka (New Haven: Yale University Press, 1994), 235–236; Andrzej Stawar, "O Szołochowie," *Twórczość* 11:6 (June 1956): 145–153.

13. "Notatka o sytuacji w Związku Literatów Polskich," JI/29, ADH.

14. "Aby wzmóc udział twórców w kształtowaniu naszego życia," *Nowe Drogi* 10:1 (79) (January 1956): 3–8, 4.

15. Antoni Słonimski, "O przywrócenie swobód obywatelskich," *Przegląd Kulturalny* 5:14 (5–11 April 1956): 3.

16. Kott, *Still Alive*, 181.
17. See ibid., 205. On the influence of French existentialism among communist writers in Czechoslovakia, see Marci Shore, "Engineering in the Age of Innocence: A Genealogy of Discourse inside the Czechoslovak Writers' Union, 1949–1967," *East European Politics and Societies* 12:3 (fall 1998): 397–441.
18. "Protokół Nr 217 posiedzenia Biura Politycznego z dnia 19 stycznia 1959 r," in Dudek et al., *Centrum władzy*, 323; "Notatka o sytuacji w Związku Literatów Polskich," JI/29, ADH; Kott, *Still Alive*, 207–210; Jastrun, *Dziennik: Wybór z lat 1955–1960*, 67.
19. Bohdan Drozdowski, "Władysław Broniewski," *Życie Literackie* 19 (11 May 1958).
20. Jastrun, *Dziennik: Wybór z lat 1955–1960*, 123. Przyboś left the Party following the execution of Imre Nagy in Hungary. See Grzegorz Wołowiec, *Nowocześni w PRL: Przyboś i Sandauer* (Wrocław: Wrocławska Drukarnia Naukowa PAN, 1999), 269.
21. "Jakub Berman," 17 November 1982, Warsaw, 325/1, AAN; "Protokół Nr 91 posiedzenia Biura Politycznego w dniach 2, 3, 4 i 5 maja 1956 r." in Dudek et al., *Centrum władzy*, 160–161; Józef Stępień, "'Ustąpienie' Jakuba Bermana z Biura Politycznego w świetle protokołu BP KC PZPR z 2–5 V 1956 r.," *Teki archiwalne* 2:24 (1997): 195–222.
22. Stępień, "'Ustąpienie' Jakuba Bermana," 202–205. Marian Spychalski (1906–1980) was a member of the KPP from 1931 and co-founder of the Polska Partia Robotnicza (Polish Workers' Party) during the war. The communist Władysław Gomułka was arrested in 1948 on charges of nationalist deviation. Despite pressure from Stalin, there was no public trial and Gomułka was not executed, but rather sentenced to house arrest. General Stanisław Tatar and eight other interwar military officers were accused of fascist conspiracy and sentenced to life imprisonment.
23. Stępień, "'Ustąpienie' Jakuba Bermana," 202.
24. See also "VIII Plenum KC PZPR 19–21 X 1956," *Nowe Drogi* 10:10 (October 1956): 91–95.
25. Stefan Jędrychowski, rozmowa z Grzegorzem Sołtysiakiem, 17 February 1994, K. 143, W/R 5, ADH.
26. Irena Olecka, interview, Warsaw, December 1997.
27. Lucyna Tychowa, interview, Warsaw, 25 August 2003.
28. Rózański remained in prison until October 1964. See Zdzisław Uniszewski, "Józef Różański" and "Samokrytyka Różańskiego," *Karta* 31 (2000): 111–155 and 116–126.
29. Jakub Berman, Untitled, 325/1, AAN.
30. See Perry Anderson's preface to Isaac Deutscher, *Marxism, Wars and Revolutions: Essays from Four Decades*, ed. Tamara Deutscher (London: Verso, 1984), v.
31. Władysław Krajewski, personal interview, Warsaw, 28 July 2003.
32. Olga Stande to T. Daniszewski (Kierownik Wydziału Historii KC PZPR), Łódź, 6 March 1956, 9889, AAN.
33. T. Daniszewski to Olga Stande, 6 September 1956, 9889, AAN. See also

C. Budzyńska, "Stanisław Ryszard Stande: Poeta—działacz—komunista," 9889, AAN.

34. "Orzeczenie Prokuratora Wojskowego ZSRR do sprawy Brunona Jasieńskiego wydane 17 grudnia 1955 roku" in *BJSW*, 184–193.

35. "Svidetel'stvo o smerti," 1861/2/20, RGALI.

36. Piotr Mitzner, "Śmierć futurysty," *Karta* 11 (1993): 76.

37. A. Iasenskii to Nikita Sergeevich Khrushchev, [1961], 1861/2/26, RGALI.

38. Grażyna Pietruszewska-Kobiela, *Pejzaż dramatyczny Anatola Sterna* (Częstochowa: Wyższa Szkoła Pedagogiczna w Częstochowie, 1989), 8.

39. Anatol Stern, *Bruno Jasieński* (Warsaw: Wiedza Powszechna, 1969), 9–19. See also Danishevskii to Tsentral'nyi Komitet Kommunisticheskoi Partii Sovetskogo Soiuza Otdel Istorii Partii, 9328, AAN; T. Daniszewski to Tow. Lewikowski, 24 August 1956, 9328, AAN; Celina Budzyńska to Wydział Historii Partii przy KC PZPR (na ręce tow. Daniszewskiego), Warsaw, 11 June 1956, 9328, AAN.

40. Anatol Stern, "Do przyjaciela: Pamięci Brunona Jasieńskiego," *Wiersze zebrane*, vol. I, ed. Andrzej K. Waśkiewicz (Cracow: Wydawnictwo Literackie, 1986), 407; from *Nowa Kultura* 18 (1956).

41. Zarębińska to Broniewski, Horochów, 8 April 1939, *KWB*, vol. II, 347–350.

42. Paweł Merlend, relacja, 731, AAN.

43. Stefan Żółkiewski to Broniewski, 26 March 1956, MB.

44. Bohdan Drozdowski, "Władysław Broniewski," *Życie Literackie* 19 (11 May 1958).

45. See Anna Kowalska, "Idą nasi pisarzy," *Przegląd Kulturalny* 20 (17 May–23 May 1956): 1; Leon Kruczkowski, "Na 20-lecie Zjazdu Lwowskiego," 1046, ML.

46. Grzegorz Lasota, "Rozmowa z towarzyszem Broniewskim," *Nowe Drogi* 10:5 (May 1956): 56–59.

47. Władysław Broniewski, "[Autobiografia literacka]," in *Władysław Broniewski*, ed. Feliksa Lichodziejewska (Warsaw: Państwowe Zakłady Wydawnictw Szkolnych, 1966), 127.

48. Paweł Merlend, relacja, 731, AAN; Grzegorz Lasota, "Rozmowa z towarzyszem Broniewskim," *Nowe Drogi* 10:5 (May 1956): 56–59.

49. H. K., "Telefoniczna rozmowa z Władysławem Broniewskim," 26 November 1959, 731, AAN.

50. "Pisarze przy pracy. Mówi Władysław Broniewski," in Lichodziejewska, *Władysław Broniewski*, 128–129.

51. Wasilewska to Broniewska, 20 December [1958?]. Copy provided by Ewa Zawistowska.

52. Adolf Rudnicki, "Spóźnioną gałazkę bzu," *Nowa Kultura* 5:6 (7 February 1954): 5.

53. Wanda Wasilewska to *Nowa Kultura*, 1953, 73/1/283, TsDAMLM.

54. Wasilewska to Broniewska, 24 June [1950]. Copy provided by Ewa Zawistowska.

55. Wanda Wasilewska to Janina Broniewska, 31 August 1954. Copy provided by Ewa Zawistowska.

56. Bierut to Wasilewska, Warsaw, 21 January 1955; Jakub Berman to Wasilewska, 21 January 1955, 73/1/697, TsDAMLM.

57. "Peredmova to knigi Ia. Bronevs'koi 'Iz zapisok . . . ,'" 1955, 73/1/285, TsDAMLM.

58. Wasilewska to Broniewska, 2 September [?]. Copy provided by Ewa Zawistowska.

59. Wasilewska to Broniewska, Kiev, 22 December 1955. Helena Zatorska, ed., *Wanda Wasilewska* (Warsaw: Wydawnictwa Szkolne i Pedagogiczne, 1976), 186–187.

60. Zofia Aldona Woźnicka, "O mojej siostrze," *WWW*, 48; Jurij Smołycz, "Organiczny stop motywów," *WWW*, 207–209.

61. Wasilewska to Broniewska, 6–10 April [1957?]. Copy provided by Ewa Zawistowska.

62. Jastrun, *Dziennik: Wybór z lat 1955–1960*, 26.

63. Quoted by Władysław Bartoszewski, *WAS*, 19.

64. Kruczkowski to Słonimski, 12 December 1956, Warsaw, 1064, ML.

65. Antoni Słonimski, "Portret prezydenta" and "Pochód," *Poezje* (Warsaw: Czytelnik, 1955), 364, 360–361.

66. Jastrun, *Dziennik: Wybór z lat 1955–1960*.

67. See Artur Starewicz, relacja, part 5, W-R/26, ADH.

68. "Protokół Nr 217 posiedzenia Biura Politycznego z dnia 19 stycznia 1959 r," in Dudek et al. *Centrum władzy*, 321–325.

69. Artur Starewicz, relacja, part 5, W-R/26, ADH.

70. Aleksander Wat, *Mój wiek: Pamiętnik mówiony*, 2 vols. (Warsaw: Czytelnik, 1998), vol. I, 236–237.

71. Grydzewski to Iwaszkiewicz, 26 March 1956. Mieczysław Grydzewski and Jarosław Iwaszkiewicz, *Listy 1922–1967*, ed. Małgorzata Bojanowska (Warsaw: Czytelnik, 1979), 91.

72. Grydzewski to Iwaszkiewicz, 12 May 1956. Ibid., 97.

73. Wierzyński to Grydzewski, New York, 23 September 1957. Rafal Habielski, ed., *Z listów do Mieczysława Grydzewskiego 1946–1966* (London: Polonia, 1990), 83–84.

74. 10 January 1954 in *WAS*, 111.

75. 15 April 1956 in *WAS*, 111.

76. Wanda Nowakowska, "Lechoń i Tuwim—dzieje przyjaźni," *Prace Polonistyczne* 51 (1996): 244–245. Lechoń's poem to Tuwim appeared in Grydzewski's *Wiadomości* on 6 February 1955. Count di Cagliostro was an eighteenth-century Italian figure involved in alchemy and the occult. He established Egyptian Rite Masonic lodges and in general led a rather scandalous life, traveling around the world before he was arrested by the Inquisition and given life imprisonment in a castle.

77. Wierzyński to Grydzewski, 15 June 1956 and 16 June 1956, New York;

Zdzisław Czermański to Grydzewski, 14 June 1956, New York. Habielski, *Z listów do Mieczysława Grydzewskiego*, 75–78, 230–231.

78. Iwaszkiewicz to Grydzewski, Sandomierz, 10 June 1956. Grydzewski and Iwaszkiewicz, *Listy 1922–1967*, 98–99.

79. Iwaszkiewicz to Grydzewski, Rome, 29 November 1958. Ibid., 127.

80. Adolf Rudnicki to Adolf Berman, 20 February 1954, P-70/58, AABB.

81. Mirski was active as a both a Party member and a writer. His books published between 1952 and 1963 included *Problemy krytyki i literatury, Bez stopnia*, and *Biegem Marsz*, a memoir of his time in the Bereza Kartuska prison camp in the 1930s. Michał Mirski, "Ankieta uczestnika Rewolucji Październikowej i wojny domowej w ZSRR," 20 November 1967, 4027, AAN.

82. Adolf Berman to Michał Mirski, Tel Aviv, 10 June 1956, 330/35, ŻIH.

83. Aleksander Wat, *My Century: The Odyssey of a Polish Intellectual*, trans. Richard Lourie (New York: Norton, 1988), 70; Wat, *Dziennik bez samogłosek*, 105.

84. Ola Watowa, *Wszystko co najważniesjze* (Warsaw: Czytelnik, 1990), 147.

85. Iwaszkiewicz to Zarząd główny RSW, "Prasa," Warsaw, 12 September 1955, A-86, AWPB.

86. Following Wat's death the parts of the novel he had written were published under his intended title. Aleksander Wat, *Ucieczka Lotha*, ed. Włodzimierz Bolecki (Warsaw: Czytelnik, 1996).

87. Wat, *Dziennik bez samogłosek*, 10, 45.

88. Ibid., 46–47.

89. Wat, *Mój wiek*, vol. II, 336–338; Wat, *Dziennik bez samogłosek*, 22, 40, 27, 218.

90. Wat, *Dziennik bez samogłosek*, 25–47.

91. Ibid., 3–4. Wieniawa-Długoszowski himself committed suicide in New York in 1942.

92. Ellipsis points in original. Wat, Ibid., 3.

93. Ibid., 12.

94. Aleksander Wat, *Poezje*, ed. Anna Micińska and Jan Zieliński (Warsaw: Czytelnik, 1997), 168. Jagganath was an image of a Hindu deity believed to contain the bones of Krishna. During Krishna's festival, Jagganath was pulled on a temple cart through the streets of Puri, Orissa. Devoted ones would throw themselves beneath the wheels of the cart and be crushed to death.

95. Watowa to Iwaszkiewicz, 25 December 1957, A-85, AWPB.

96. Iwaszkiewicz to Watowa, Stawisko, 5 January 1958, A-86, AWPB.

97. Watowa to Iwaszkiewicz, 8 January 1958, A-85, AWPB.

98. Wat, "Zeszyt ostatni," 14, AWPB.

99. Wat to Miłosz, 5 September 1960, Nervi, C-218, AWPB; Bohdan Drozdowski, "Rozmowy z pisarzami: Julian Przyboś," *Życie Literackie* 8:15 (13 April 1958): 3, 7; Aleksander Wat, "Nad koleżką profesora Heisenberga—rozmyślanie," *Nowa Kultura* 9:16 (20 April 1958): 6.

100. Słonimski to Wat, 17 December 1957, A-5, AWPB.

101. Ellipsis points in original. Stanisław Baliński to Aleksander and Ola Wat, London, 16 January 1958, A-3, AWPB.

102. Stanisław Wygodzki, "Spotkanie z 'Miesięcznikiem Literackim,'" *Polityka* 2:38 (20 September 1958): 6.

103. Irena Wygodzka to Watowa, 7 April 1957, C-204, AWPB.

104. "'Twarzą zwrócony do śmierci . . .'" Listy Aleksandra Wata do Józefa Wittlina," *Znak* 43 (February 1991): 8.

105. Jastrun, *Dziennik: Wybór z lat 1955–1960*, 89–90.

106. Anatol Stern, "Słowo wstępne," in Włodzimierz Majakowski, *Poezje*, ed. Mieczysław Jastrun, Seweryn Pollak, Anatol Stern, and Adam Ważyk (Warsaw: Czytelnik, 1957), 8.

107. Wat, *Dziennik bez samogłosek*, 13.

108. Jastrun, *Dziennik: Wybór z lat 1955–1960*, 146.

109. Feliksa Lichodziejewska, *Broniewski bez cenzury: 1939–1945* (Warsaw: Wydawnictwo Społeczne KOS, 1992), 23.

110. Isaac Deutscher, "U źródeł tragedii KPP," 1957, K. 42 (S V/7), ADH.

CHAPTER 10. THE END OF THE AFFAIR

Epigraph: Aleksander Wat, *My Century: The Odyssey of a Polish Intellectual*, trans. Richard Lourie (New York: Norton, 1988), 12.

1. Mieczysław Jastrun, *Dziennik: Wybór z lat 1955–1960* (London: Puls, 1990), 120.

2. "Jakub Berman," 17 November 1982, Warsaw, 325/1, AAN; "Protokół Nr. 91 posiedzenia Biura Politycznego w dniach 2, 3, 4 i 5 maja 1956 r.," in *Centrum władzy: Protokoły posiedzeń kierownictwa PZPR wybór z lat 1949–1970*, ed. Antoni Dudek et al. (Warsaw: Instytut Studiów Politycznych PAN, 2000), 160–161.

3. Jakub Berman to Władysław Gomułka, Warsaw, 9 May 1960. Józef Stępień, ed., *Listy do Pierwszych Sekretarzy KC PZPR (1944–1970)* (Warsaw: Wydawnictwo FAKT, 1994), 208–209. Original (two drafts) in 325/1, AAN.

4. Aleksander Wat, *Mój wiek: Pamiętnik mówiony*, 2 vols. (Warsaw: Czytelnik, 1998), vol. I, 69–70; Aleksander Wat, "'. . . jak upiór staję między wami i pytam o źródło złego' . . . ," *Na Antenie* 4:43 (6 November 1966): 1.

5. Jan Kott, *Still Alive: An Autobiographical Essay*, trans. Jadwiga Kosicka (New Haven: Yale University Press, 1994), 230–231.

6. Stawar to Wat, 17 May 1961; Stawar to Wat, 24 May 1961; Stawar to Wat, 17 June 1961, Meandre; B-170, AWPB.

7. Stawar to Wat, 25 July 1961, B-170, AWPB.

8. Kott, *Still Alive*, 236–237; Jerzy Giedroyc, *Autobiografia na cztery ręce* (Warsaw: Czytelnik, 1994), 194; "Informacja," 15 September 1961; T. Daniłowicz, "Notatka dla Tow. Amb. P. Ogrodzińskiego dot. Okoliczności pobytu Andrzeja Stawara we Francji," 27 September 1961; "Notatka dot. Pobytu Stawara na terenie Francji," Warsaw, 11 November 1961, 01224/1426, IPN.

9. Wat, *Mój wiek*, vol. I, 69–70; Watowa, *Wszystko co najważniejsze* (Warsaw:

Czytelnik, 1990), 141. Stawar's papers remained in France, with Giedroyc. "Notatka dot. Pobytu Stawara na terenie Francji," Warsaw, 11 November 1961, 01224/1426, IPN.

10. Kott, *Still Alive*, 236–237.

11. Wat, "'. . . jak upiór staję między wami,'" 1.

12. Wat, *Mój wiek*, vol. I, 69–70.

13. See Stanisław Witold Balicki, ed., *To ja—dąb: Wspomnienia i eseje o Władysławie Broniewskim* (Warsaw: PIW, 1978), 286–287; Lucjan Marek, "O Władysławie Broniewskim," 14 March 1962, 731, AAN; Adam Ważyk, "Przeczytałem *Mój wiek*," *Puls* 34 (1987): 48–55.

14. Wat, *My Century*, 14.

15. See teczka Stawara, 01224/1426, IPN.

16. Broniewski to Tadeusz Galiński (Minister Kultury i Sztuki), 18 October 1961, MB.

17. Władysław Broniewski, *Moje przyjaźnie poetyckie* (Warsaw: PIW, 1960).

18. See "Anka," in Władysław Broniewski, *Władysław Broniewski: Poezje 1923–1961* (Warsaw: PIW, 1995), 477–499.

19. Grydzewski to Wat, 28 February 1962, London, A-58, AWPB.

20. Wat to Mieczysław [Grydzewski], La Messuguière, 2 March 1962, C-219, AWPB.

21. Wat, "'. . . jak upiór staję między wami,'" 1.

22. Jarosław Iwaszkiewicz, "Mazowsze," in *Władysław Broniewski*, ed. Feliksa Lichodziejewska (Warsaw: Państwowe Zakłady Wydawnictw Szkolnych, 1966), 288; from *Życie Warszawy* 27 (1965).

23. Kazimierz Wierzyński, "Na śmierć Broniewskiego," in Władysław Broniewski, *Wiersze* (Paris: Instytut Literacki, 1962), 7–8.

24. Janina Broniewska, *Dziesięć serc czerwiennych* (Warsaw: Iskry, 1964), 125.

25. Ewa Zawistowska, personal correspondence, Greece, 23 January 2001.

26. Janina Broniewska, *Tamten brzeg mych lat* (Warsaw: Książka i Wiedza, 1973), 191–194.

27. List Vasilevs'koi v TsK KPRS pro poizdku na Kubu i Meksiku, 73/2/1, TsDAMLM.

28. Wanda Wasilewska, "Dzieciństwo," in *Wanda Wasilewska*, ed. Helena Zatorska (Warsaw: Wydawnictwa Szkolne i Pedagogiczne, 1976); Janina Broniewska, "Wanda Wasilewska," in *Żoliborz: wczoraj, dziś, jutro* (Warsaw: Książka i Wiedza, 1970), 203–204; Vanda Vasilevskaia, "O moikh knigakh," *Vecherniaia Moskva* 41:222 (19 September 1964), copy in 73/1/321, TsDAMLM.

29. Wanda Wasilewska, "Dwadzieścia lat temu," *Głos Żołnierza* 15:57 (11–12 May 1963): 1–2. Copy in 73/1/257, TsDAMLM.

30. Wanda Wasilewska, "Wspomnienia Wandy Wasilewskiej (1939–1944)," *Archiwum Ruchu Robotniczego* 7 (1982): 427.

31. "Wanda Wasilewska nie żyje," *Trybuna Ludu* 17:209 (31 July 1964). Copy in 73/1/817, TsDAMLM.

32. The original obituary appeared in *Izvestiia* 48:181 (31 July 1964). Copy in 73/1/817, TsDAMLM.

33. Aleksander Wat, *Dziennik bez samogłosek*, ed. Krzysztof Rutkowski (London: Polonia, 1986), 96, 143–146, 159.

34. Ibid., 69.

35. Ibid., 69–70, 79.

36. Wat to Jerzy Giedroyc, Nervi, 1960, C-219, AWPB.

37. Wat to Giedroyc, unsent letter ("list niewysłany [na skutek pojednawczego listu] G."), A-48, AWPB.

38. Aleksander Wat, "La mort d'un vieux bolchévik: Souvenirs sur Stieklov," *Le Contrat Social* 7 (1963); Aleksander Wat, "Śmierć starego bolszewika," *Kultura* 1–2 (1964): 27–40.

39. Wiktor Woroszylski to Aleksander and Ola Wat, 12 February 1963, Warsaw, C-202, AWPB.

40. *Szmalcownicy* refers to Poles who blackmailed Jews during the Nazi occupation. Wat to Miłosz, undated; Wat to Miłosz, 5 September 1960, Nervi, C-218, AWPB; Wat, *Dziennik bez samogłosek*, 201, 218–219.

41. Wat to Józef Czapski, C-219, AWPB.

42. Wat, *Dziennik bez samogłosek*, 79–83, 209, 217.

43. Wat, *My Century*, 261–262; Wat to Miłosz, 8 December 1965, C-218, AWPB.

44. Wat to Józef Czapski, 6 May 1967, C-222, AWPB; Wat, "Zeszyt ostatni," 14, AWPB; Wat, *Dziennik bez samogłosek*, 65, 186–188, 197, 216; Wat, "'. . . jak upiór staję między wami,'" 1.

45. Wat, *Dziennik bez samogłosek*, 170.

46. Ibid., 222–223; Wat, *Mój wiek*, vol. I, 63.

47. "Ewokacja," La Messuguière, February 1963, in Aleksander Wat, *Poezje*, ed. Anna Micińska and Jan Zieliński (Warsaw: Czytelnik, 1997), 24–27.

48. Wat, *Dziennik bez samogłosek*, 62.

49. Wat to Wittlin, 26 June 1965, [Berkeley], in "'Twarzą zwrócony do śmierci . . .': Listy Aleksandra Wata do Józefa Wittlina," *Znak* 43 (February 1991): 16; Wat, *Dziennik bez samogłosek*, 61–65, 158; Wat, *My Century*, 230, 293–294; Wat, *Mój wiek*, vol. II, 218.

50. Wat, *Dziennik bez samogłosek*, 148.

51. Ibid., 67–189; Wat, *My Century*, 287.

52. Wat, *Dziennik bez samogłosek*, 112–113.

53. Wat to Miłosz, Berkeley, [1964], C-222, AWPB.

54. Wat, *Dziennik bez samogłosek*, 79.

55. Miłosz to Wat, Berkeley, B-127, AWPB.

56. Miłosz to Wat, Berkeley, B-127, AWPB.

57. Wat, *Dziennik bez samogłosek*, 67, 93.

58. Wat to Miłosz, Berkeley, [1964], C-222, AWPB; Wat to Jerzy [Giedroyc], C-219, AWPB.

59. Wat, *Dziennik bez samogłosek*, 103–135.

60. Ibid., 130.

61. Wat to Jerzy [Giedroyć?], [c. 1965], C-219, AWPB.

62. Wat to Miłosz, Berkeley, [1964], C-222, AWPB.

63. Wat, *Dziennik bez samogłosek*, 206; Wat, *My Century*, 11–12, 96, 115–116; Wat to Wittlin, 26 June 1965, [Berkeley], in "Twarzą zwrócony do śmierci," 15.

64. Wat, *My Century*, 13.

65. Wat, *Mój wiek*, vol. I, 174.

66. Wat, *My Century*, 96.

67. Jerzy Giedroyc rejected publishing Wat's memoirs in their original form due to what he perceived to be errors in Wat's memory and some harshly critical remarks. Wat and Miłosz both refused to agree to Giedroyc's changes. Giedroyc, *Autobiografia na cztery ręce*, 196.

68. Adolf Rudnicki to Wat, B-153, AWPB.

69. Stanislaw Baranczak, "Skamander after Skamander: The Postwar Path of the Prewar Polish Pleiade," *Cross Currents* 9 (1990): 349.

70. From Antoni Słonimski, "Sąd nad Don Kichotem," excerpt translated in Baranczak, "Skamander after Skamander," 349.

71. Grzegorz Sołtysiak, "Trockiści," *Karta* 7 (1992). See also Kott, *Still Alive*, 180–181.

72. Antoni Słonimski, *Kroniki tygodniowe 1927–1939*, ed. Władysław Kopaliński (Warsaw: PIW, 1956), 138–139.

73. "Przemówienie kol. Antoniego Słonimskiego," K. 103, S V/16, ADH.

74. Isaac Deutscher, "An Open Letter to Wladyslaw Gomulka and the Central Committee of the Polish Workers' Party," 24 April 1966, in *Marxism, Wars and Revolutions: Essays from Four Decades*, ed. Tamara Deutscher (London: Verso, 1984), 128–131.

75. "Odpis tajne wystąpienie profesora U.W. Leszka Kołakowskiego na zebraniu dyskusyjnym zorganizowanym w dniu 21. 10. 1966 w Instytucie Historycznym UW przez Zarząd ZMS Wydziału Historycznego UW na temat 'Kultura polska w ostatnim 10-leciu,'" 22 October 1966, Warsaw, K. 103, S V/16, ADH.

76. Leszek Kołakowski to Biura Politycznego KC PZPR, 23 November 1966 in Stępień, *Listy do Pierwszych Sekretarzy*, 253.

77. "Informacja w sprawie prof. Leszka Kołakowskiego," K. 103, S V/16, ADH. Also see Michał Mirski to Biuro Polityczne Komitetu Centralnego PZPR, 24 November 1966, Warsaw, K. 103, S V/16, ADH; "Ankieta uczestnika Rewolucji Październikowej i wojny domowej w ZSRR," 20 November 1967, 4027, AAN; "Protokół z przeprowadzonych indywidualnych rozmów z pisarzami, sygnatariuszami listu do Biura Politycznego KC PZPR w sprawie przywrócenia praw członka PZPR L. Kołakowskiemu," 25 November 1966, K. 103, S V/16, ADH; "Zapiski z zebrania POP przy oddziale warszawskim ZLP," 9 December 1966, K. 103, S V/16, ADH.

78. Artur Starewicz, "Załączenie oświadczeń skierowanych do egzekutywy POP przy ZLP w Warszawie," 24 January 1967, Warsaw, K. 103, S V/16, ADH.

79. Julian Stryjkowski, *Ocalony na wschodzie* (Montricher: Les Editions Noir sur Blanc, 1991), 262–264.

80. "Odpis stenogramu wystąpienia Leszka Kołakowskiego w dniu 4.XII.1965 r," 0236/128/t-6, IPN.

81. "Notatka informacyjna o przebiegu zebrania sprawozdawczo-wyborczego POP przy ZLP," 2 February 1967, K. 103, S V/16, ADH.

82. Anatol Stern, *Bruno Jasieński* (Warsaw: Wiedza Powszechna, 1969), 17.

83. Anatol Stern, "Bruno Jasieński w Paryżu, czyli trzy portrety pisarza," *Kamena* 2 (21 January 1968): 4.

84. In fact Stern was not entirely alone in his devotion to Jasieński's memory. At least one graduate student in the Soviet Union wrote rather hagiographically about Jasieński as well, in particular about Jasieński's love for Tadzhikistan and his contribution to socialist culture there. The graduate student and his co-author put this in the context of the Polish nation's contribution to the revolutionary tradition. See A. Ia. Vishnevskii (kandidat istoricheskikh nauk) and V. A. Rudnitskii, "Pod znamenem proletarskogo internatsionalizma i edinstva," 9328, AAN.

85. Stern to Wat, 9 June 1963, A-5, AWPB. The reference is to the leaflet titled *Tak* (Yes) that Wat and Stern published together in 1918. See Wat, *Poezje*, 337–471.

86. Anatol Stern, "O czystość obyczajów w literaturze," *Kultura* 45 (7 November 1965): 11.

87. Wat to Jan Śpiewak, 24 December 1965, Antony (letter unsent in this version, "zmieniony, złagodzony"), C-222, AWPB.

88. Wat to Jan Śpiewak, 24 December 1965, Antony (letter unsent in this version, "zmieniony, złagodzony"), C-222, AWPB. Ważyk's memoirs were published in *Twórczość* in 1966; they later appeared as the book *Kwestia gustu*. In 1963 Stefan Staszewski encouraged Ważyk to write memoirs of his engagement with communism, but Ważyk was not so inclined, saying he felt disgust towards all of that. Untitled report, teczka Ważyka, 0246/1031, IPN.

89. Wat to Miłosz, 18 January 1966, C-218, AWPB.

90. Wat, "Zeszyt ostatni," 14, AWPB; Ola Watowa to Seweryna Broniszówna, 20 August 1967, Toulon, C-237, AWPB; Watowa, *Wszystko co najważniejsze*, 176–177.

91. Iwaszkiewicz to Seweryna Broniszówna, 5 August 1967, Stawisko, C-234, AWPB. Czesław and Janka Miłosz to Watowa; Grydzewski to Watowa; Alicja and Anatol Stern to Watowa; Kazimierz and Halina Wierzyńscy to Watowa, 31 July 1967, C-237, AWPB.

92. Watowa to Kocik, 13 September 1967, C-237, AWPB.

93. Watowa to Seweryna Broniszówna, 20 August 1967, Toulon, C-237, AWPB.

94. Wat, "Zeszyt ostatni," 1967, 14, AWPB.

95. Wat, "Zeszyt ostatni," 1967, 14, AWPB.

96. Wat, *Dziennik bez samogłosek*, 206–208.

97. Emphasis in original. Wat, "Zeszyt ostatni," 1967, 14, AWPB. Gail Glickman translated this letter from the original French.

98. "Prochy Alfred Lampego powrócą do kraju," *Trybuna Ludu* 283 (12 October 1964). Copy in 250/1, AAN.

99. Adolf Berman to Michał Mirski, 4 April 1962, Tel Aviv, 330/35, ŻIH.

100. Adolf Berman to Michał Mirski, 14 June 1964, Tel Aviv, 330/35, ŻIH; Adolf Berman to Michał Mirski, 28 November 1964, Tel Aviv, 330/35, ŻIH.

101. "Notatka dot. nadzwyczajnego zebrania OW ZLP," 29 February 1968, Warsaw, 0236/128/t-3, IPN.

102. Ewa Zawistowska, personal correspondence, Greece, 24 June 2003.

103. A collection of these cartoons originally published in *Żołnierz Wolności* in 1968 and 1969 can be found in Simon Wiesenthal, *Judenhetze in Polen* (Bonn: Brandt, 1969).

104. Władysław Gomułka, "Przemówienie na spotkaniu z warszawskim aktywem partyjnym," 19 March 1968 in *Przemówienia 1968* (Warsaw: Książka i Wiedza, 1969), 74–75.

105. Interior Ministry Report, 0204/1203/t-2, IPN. On the "anti-Zionist" campaign of March 1968 see Dariusz Stola, *Kampania antysyjonistyczna 1967–1968* (Warsaw: Institut Studiów Politycznych PAN, 2000); Mieczysław Rakowski, *Dzienniki polityczne 1967–1968* (Warsaw: Iskry, 1999); Grzegorz Sołtysiak and Józef Stępień, eds., *Marzec '68: Między tragedią a podłością* (Warsaw: Profi, 1998); Stefan Jędrychowski, rozmowa z Grzegorzem Sołtysiakiem, 17 February 1994, K. 143, W/R 5, ADH; Artur Starewicz, relacja, cz. 7, W-R/26, ADH. In English see Michael Steinlauf, *Bondage to the Dead: Poland and the Memory of the Holocaust* (Syracuse: Syracuse University Press, 1997); and Dariusz Stola, "The Anti-Zionist Campaign in Poland 1967–1968," in *Jewish Studies at the Central European University*, ed. Andras Kovacs and E. Andor, vol. II (Budapest: Central European University Press, 2002).

106. See "Wyjątki z referatu Jakuba Bermana—wice premiera Rady Ministrów PRL (Rząd Jedności Narodowej), członka Biura Politycznego i Sekretarza KC PPR oraz Sekretarza Polacy Syjon [sic] wygłoszonego w kwietniu 1945 na posiedzeniu Egzekutywy Woj. Komitetu Żydowskiego (wyjątki z stenogramu)," 01208/1303, IPN. The forged transcript attributes to Jakub Berman both his own position as a member of the Politburo and his brother's position as secretary of Poalei Zion. The same file contains the security apparatus's surveillance reports on Jakub Berman during this period. The security apparatus's interest continued long after the 1968 events, as evidenced by this and other Ministry of Internal Affairs files. See for example "Notatka," 10 February 1974, Warsaw, 0204/397/t-1, IPN.

107. Michał Mirski to Egzekutywa POP PZPR przy Oddziale Warszawskim Związku Literatów Polskich, 1969, 330/33, ŻIH.

108. *WAS*, 24; Baranczak, "Skamander after Skamander," 346–347.

109. Antoni Słonimski, *Poezje zebrane* (Warsaw: PIW, 1964), 457.

110. *WAS*, 19–21.

111. Władysław Bartoszewski and Zofia Lewinówna, eds., *Ten jest z ojczyzny mojej: Polacy z pomocą Żydom, 1939–1945* (Cracow: Znak, 1969).

112. Władysław Bartoszewski to Adolf Berman, Salzburg, 1 October 1968, P-70/63, AABB.

113. Emphasis in original. Władysław Bartoszewski to Adolf Berman, London, 18 August 1969, P-70/59, AABB.

114. "S" [Aleksander Masiewicki] to Adolf Berman, New York, 2 October 1970, P-70/63, AABB. Deianeira's burning shirt is an allusion to the Greek myth told by Sophocles in *Women of Trachis*. In this story Deianeira received blood from a centaur whom her husband, Hercules, had mortally wounded with an arrow. The centaur told her that the blood was a love potion which she could use if her husband ever lost his love for her. When Hercules became enchanted with a young princess, Deianeira made a shirt, soaked it with the blood potion, and presented it to Hercules as a gift. But the centaur had tricked her, and when Hercules put on the shirt it began to burn him alive. The nineteenth-century Polish poet Juliusz Słowacki draws on this motif in his poem "Grób Agamemnona." The source of Masiewicki's allusion is most likely these lines from the poem: "Zrzuć do ostatka te płachty ohydne, / Tę—Dejaniry palącą koszulę: / A wstań jak wielkie posągi bezwstydne. . . ."

115. Aleksander Masiewicki to Adolf Berman, New York, 14 March 1971, P-70/64, AABB.

EPILOGUE

Epigraph: Quoted in Jan Kott, *Przyczynek do biografii* (Cracow: Wydawnictwo Literackie, 1995), 200.

1. Władysław Bartoszewski, interview, Warsaw, 22 December 1997.

2. Ludwik was Bartoszewski's underground name during the war. Władysław Bartoszewski, interview, Warsaw, 22 December 1997. Jakub Berman's Ministry of Internal Affairs file contains various mentions of Adolf Berman's visits to Poland. See, for example, "Notatka," Warsaw, 16 January 1965, 01208/1303, IPN.

3. Teresa Torańska, *Oni* (Warszawa: Agencja Omnipress, 1990), 142–144.

4. Lucyna Tychowa, personal interview, Warsaw, 25 August 2003; Teresa Torańska, personal correspondence, Warsaw, 7 June 2002.

5. Teresa Torańska, personal correspondence, Warsaw, 7 June 2002.

6. Torańska, *Oni*, 16.

7. Jakub Berman, Wspomnienia, 325/33, AAN.

8. Jakub Berman, "Wokół Kongresów Intelektualistów w Wrocławiu w obronie pokoju (25–28 sierpnia 1948 r)," Warsaw, June 1978, 325/32, AAN.

9. Inspektor Wydziału IV, Dep. III MSW, Ppłk J. Jakubik, "Notatka ze spotkania z kp. 'Tatra,'" Warsaw, 16 January 1970, 0204/1203/t-2, IPN.

10. Antoni Słonimski, *Jedna strona medalu: Niektóre felietony, artykuły, recenzje, utwory poważne i niepoważne publikowane w latach 1918–1968* (Warsaw: Czytelnik, 1971).

11. Słonimski, radio interview with the Dutch journalist Dirk Verkijk. On Słonimski's dissident activities and contacts in the last two decades of his life see 0204/1203, IPN.

12. According to his Ministry of Internal Affairs file, Ważyk signed the petition

opposing the projected changes to the constitution on 31 January 1976. See 0246/1031, IPN.

13. Antoni Słonimski, "L'Ordre règne à Varsovie," *Kultura* (Paris) 3 (1976): 26–27.

14. The interview appeared in *Les Nouvelles Littéraires* on 22 January 1976. Czesław Miłosz, "Do Antoniego Słonimskiego," *Kultura* (Paris) 3 (1976): 28. See also Tony Judt, *Past Imperfect: French Intellectuals, 1944–1956* (Berkeley: University of California Press, 1992), 275–292.

15. *WAS*, 22–23.

16. "Notatka dot. przebiegu pogrzebu Antoniego SŁONIMSKIEGO w dniu 8.07.1976," Warsaw, 8 July 1976, 0204/1203/t-4, IPN.

17. Antoni Słonimski, "Z 'Alfabetu wspomnień' (inedita)," *Więź* 25:4/5 (April–May 1982); *WAS*, 22–23.

18. See the chapter "Ostatni zarząd Iwaszkiewicza" in Jerzy Putrament, *Pół wieku: Sierpień* (Warsaw: Czytelnik, 1987), 114.

19. Jakub Berman to Adam Ważyk, [1979], 325/3, AAN.

20. Julian Stryjkowski, *Ocalony na wschodzie* (Montricher: Les Editions Noir sur Blanc, 1991), 103–104.

21. Watowa to Seweryna Broniszówna, 20 August 1967, Toulon, C-237, AWPB.

22. Watowa to Seweryna Broniszówna, 1972, C-229, AWPB; Watowa to Seweryna Broniszówna, 17 January 1973, Paris, C-222, AWPB.

23. Emphasis in original. *Panna z Wilka* and *Brzezina* are stories by Iwaszkiewicz. Watowa to Iwaszkiewicz, 10 May 1973, Paris, A-85, AWPB.

24. Ola Watowa, *Wszystko co najważniejsze* (Warsaw: Czytelnik, 1990), 9, 36–38.

CONCLUSION

Epigraph: Julian Tuwim, *Bal w Operze* (Cracow: Wydawnictwo Literackie, 1999), 65. This long poem by Tuwim was written in 1936 but published only after the war.

1. Boris Groys, *The Total Art of Stalinism*, trans. Charles Rougle (Princeton: Princeton University Press, 1992), 14–15, 36, respectively.

2. Ibid., 44, 34. According to Katerina Clark, by the time socialist realism was instituted, the happy marriage between the avant-garde and Soviet power had reached its end, together with the revolution itself, for the liminality inherent in revolution ultimately could not be sustained. See Katerina Clark, *Petersburg: Crucible of Cultural Revolution* (Cambridge: Harvard University Press, 1995), 296.

3. Emphasis in the original. Stefan Kordian Gacki to Wat, 22 June 1965, A-3, AWPB. Gacki (1901–1984) was the editor of the futurist *Almanach Nowej Sztuki* between 1924 and 1926. In 1952 he emigrated to the United States, where he worked for Radio Free Europe and the émigré newspaper *Nowy Dziennik* in New York. My thanks to Michał Głowiński for his assistance in identifying the author of this letter.

4. Robert Wohl, *The Generation of 1914* (Cambridge: Harvard University Press, 1979), 5.

5. Aleksander Wat, *My Century: The Odyssey of a Polish Intellectual*, trans. Richard Lourie (New York: Norton, 1988), 12.

6. Aleksander Wat, *Dziennik bez samogłosek*, ed. Krzysztof Rutkowski (London: Polonia, 1986), 178.

7. Abel Kainer [Stanislaw Krajewski], "Żydzi a komunizm," *Krytyka* 15 (1983): 229.

8. Wat, *My Century*, 54.

9. Hans Ulrich Gumbrecht, *In 1926: Living at the Edge of Time* (Cambridge: Harvard University Press, 1997), 255.

10. Ola Watowa, *Wszystko co najważniejsze* (Warsaw: Czytelnik, 1990), 20.

11. Emphasis added. Slavoj Žižek, *The Plague of Fantasies* (London: Verso, 1997), 58.

12. Theodor Adorno and Max Horkheimer, *Dialectic of Enlightenment*, trans. John Cumming (New York: Continuum, 1996).

13. Jakub Berman, "Znieczulica—rodowód jednego słowa," January 1980, Warsaw, 325/32, AAN.

14. Robespierre: Lynn Hunt, *Politics, Culture, and Class in the French Revolution* (London: Methuen, 1986), 73.

15. This might be understood as the Derridean *aporia* of self-criticism, the moment when language subverts itself and meaning is no longer possible. I am grateful to Dena Goodman for conversations on this topic.

16. Jan Tomasz Gross, *Revolution from Abroad: The Soviet Conquest of Poland's Western Ukraine and Western Belorussia* (Princeton: Princeton University Press, 1988), 67.

17. Ibid., 120, 231.

18. A collection of photographs of Wasilewska can be found in 73/1/2238, TsDAMLM.

19. Janina Broniewska, "O mojej przyjaciółce Wandzie Wasilewskiej," *Promełej* (March 1975): 6.

20. Ibid.

21. Wasilewska to Broniewska, 24 VII 1948, quoted in *Wanda Wasilewska*, ed. Helena Zatorska (Warsaw: Wydawnictwa Szkolne i Pedagogiczne, 1976), 181.

22. Caroll Smith-Rosenberg, "The Female World of Love and Ritual: Relations between Women in Nineteenth-Century America," *Signs: Journal of Women in Culture and Society* 1:1 (1975): 27.

23. On the question of "identity" versus "identification," see Luisa Passerini, "The Last Identification: Why Some of Us Would Like to Call Ourselves European and What We Mean by This," in *Europe and the Other and Europe as the Other* (Brussels: PIE-Lang, 2000), 45–65.

24. See Julian Stryjkowski, *Ocalony na wschodzie* (Montricher: Les Editions Noir sur Blanc, 1991), 27–44. Also see Jacek Trznadel's interview with Stryjkowski in *Hańba domowa* (Warsaw: Agencja Wydawnicza Morex, 1997), 172.

25. Stryjkowski, *Ocalony na wschodzie*, 235.

26. Wat to Miłosz, 5 September 1960, Nervi, C-218, AWPB.

27. Antoni Słonimski, "Elegia miasteczek żydowskich," in *Poezje zebrane* (Warsaw: PIW, 1964), 495.

28. Adam Ważyk, "Przeczytałem *Mój wiek*," *Puls* 34 (1987): 53.

29. Aleksander Wat, *Dziennik bez samogłosek*, 7.

30. Anatol Stern, *Bruno Jasieński* (Warsaw: Wiedza Powszechna, 1969), 167.

31. Quoted in Grażyna Pietruszewska-Kobiela, *Pejzaż dramatyczny Anatola Sterna* (Częstochowa: Wyższa Szkoła Pedagogiczna w Częstochowie, 1989), 8.

32. Wat, *My Century*, 53–54. Cf: Mary Gluck, *Georg Lukács and His Generation, 1900–1918* (Cambridge: Harvard University Press, 1985).

33. Ważyk, "Przeczytałem *Mój wiek*," 53.

34. Aleksander Wat, *Mój wiek: Pamiętnik mówiony*, 2 vols. (Warsaw: Czytelnik, 1998), vol. I, 61.

35. Wat, *My Century*, 54.

36. Wygodzki to Tadeusz Borowski, 31 December 1945, Gauting. Tadeusz Drewnowski, ed., *Niedyskrecje pocztowe: Korespondencje Tadeusza Borowskiego* (Warsaw: Prószyński i S-ka, 2001), 61.

37. Gumbrecht, *In 1926*, 352; Žižek, *Plague of Fantasies*, 158.

38. My thanks to Brian Porter for his help in formulating this idea.

39. See Leszek Kolakowski's *Main Currents of Marxism: The Founders, the Golden Age, the Breakdown* (New York: Norton, 2005).

40. St. Inspektor Departamentu III MSW Płk. St. Borowczak, "Notatka Służbów" (tajne), Warsaw, 22 November 1963 and Mł. Inspektor Wydziału III Roman Koryl, "Analiza," Warsaw, 21 April 1976, 0246/1031, IPN.

41. Watowa, *Wszsytko co najważniejsze*, 26–27.

INDEX